THE IMITATION
OF CHRIST

The First English Translation of the 'Imitatio Christi'

EDITED BY

B. J. H. BIGGS

D0002407

Published for
THE EARLY ENGLISH TEXT SOCIETY
by the
OXFORD UNIVERSITY PRESS
1997

Oxford University Press, Great Clarendon Street, Oxford OX2 6DP

Oxford New York

Athens Auckland Bangkok Bogota Bombay
Buenos Aires Calcutta Cape Town Dar es Salaam
Delhi Florence Hong Kong Istanbul Karachi
Kuala Lumpur Madras Madrid Melbourne
Mexico City Nairobi Paris Singapore
Taipei Tokyo Toronto Warsaw

and associated companies in
Berlin Ibadan

Oxford is a trade mark of Oxford University Press

Published in the United States
by Oxford University Press Inc., New York

British Library Cataloguing in Publication Data
Data available

Library of Congress Cataloging in Publication Data
Data applied for

ISBN 0-19-722312-5

1 3 5 7 9 10 8 6 4 2

Typeset by Joshua Associates Ltd., Oxford
Printed in Great Britain
on acid-free paper by
Ipswich Book Company Ltd.

FOR MY PARENTS

PREFACE

Three English translations of the *Imitatio Christi* were made in the fifteenth and early sixteenth centuries. The first translation, edited here, is an anonymous translation of Books I to III only (omitting Book IV), entitled in the manuscripts *Musica Ecclesiastica*; it survives in four manuscripts and was not printed until the nineteenth century.[1] A second translation, made by William Atkynson, fellow of Pembroke Hall, Cambridge, also included only Books I to III, and was first printed by Richard Pynson in 1503; Atkynson's translation was issued together with a translation of Book IV made from a French version of the *Imitatio* by Lady Margaret Beaufort and first printed by Pynson in 1504.[2] A third translation, containing all four books, was first published probably in 1531; it has often been attributed to Richard Whytford, Brigittine monk of Syon Abbey, Middlesex, although it is probably not Whytford's work. This third translation appears to have been the source of most subsequent English versions.[3]

No study of the first English translation was published until J. K. Ingram, librarian of Trinity College, Dublin, edited the text from Dublin, Trinity College, MS 678 (F. 5. 8) for the Early English Text Society in 1893 (Extra Series, 63). Ingram's edition incorporated variant

---

[1] On the title *Musica Ecclesiastica*, see below, n. 71, pp. xxxix–lx.

[2] Four editions survive of this translation, two by Pynson and two by Wynkyn de Worde; the fourth edition lacks Book IV (*STC* ii. 393). On Atkynson, see *DNB* i. 698. A critical edition of his translation was made by W. C. Creasy, '*Imitatio Christi* (William Atkinson and Lady Margaret Beaufort, trans., 1503): A Critical Edition Together with a Micro-Computer Editorial Procedure' (unpublished Ph.D. dissertation, University of California at Los Angeles, 1982): see *DAI* 43 (1982), 1141–A.

[3] *STC* ii. 394. There is a modern-spelling edition of this translation by E. J. Klein, *The Imitation of Christ from the First Edition of an English Translation Made c. 1530 by Richard Whitford* (New York, 1941). Klein prepared a critical edition for the EETS (see p. xi), but unfortunately this was never published. For the view that the translation is not by Whytford, see G. Williams, 'Two Neglected London–Welsh Clerics: Richard Whitford and Richard Gwent', *Transactions of the Honourable Society of Cymmrodorion* (London, 1961), pp. 23–44 (pp. 30–2). For discussion of the dependence of subsequent translations on this version, see J. Hogg, 'The Contribution of the Brigittine Order to Late Medieval English Spirituality', in *Spiritualität heute und gestern*, AC 35 (Salzburg, 1982–), iii. 153–74 (pp. 171–4); on later translations, see also D. Crane, 'English Translations of the *Imitatio Christi* in the Sixteenth and Seventeenth Centuries', *RH* 13 (1975), 79–100; Klein, *op. cit.*, pp. xlviii–lx; and W. A. Copinger, *On the English Translations of the 'Imitatio Christi'*, Bibliographiana, 3 (Manchester, 1900).

readings taken from Cambridge, University Library, MS Gg. i. 16, and also included the text of the Atkynson–Beaufort translation; his text of the first translation was the basis of the modern-spelling edition issued in Everyman's Library in 1910 and many times reprinted.[4]

Two further manuscripts of the first translation have since been discovered, and the present edition is based on a new collation of all four.[5] Its aim is to establish as closely as possible the text of the translation, its subsequent scribal history, and its linguistic and stylistic charactersitics. For reasons of space, the focus is on the translation itself, rather than on the sources or content of the Latin original, although biblical sources and some of the mystical language and imagery used are mentioned in the Notes and indexed.[6]

I should like to acknowledge here my gratitude to Professor Anne Hudson, the supervisor of the thesis on which the present edition is based, for suggesting the *Imitation of Christ* as a research topic and for her generous help and support to me. I am also grateful to Dr A. I. Doyle for his help in many ways, and in particular for reading through a draft of the edition; I am of course responsible for all the errors that remain. For help of various kinds I am grateful to Mrs Carla Boys-Stones, Professor Valentine Cunningham, Dr Roger Ellis, Professor Douglas Gray, Dr Michael Hawcroft, Dr Roger Lovatt, Fr Paul Mommaers, Professor M. B. Parkes, Professor Michael G. Sargent, Dr H. L. Spencer, and Dr Laura Wright. For financial support I am grateful to the British Academy and St Cross College, Oxford, where I began work on this edition as a graduate student, and to Keble College, Corpus Christi College, Christ Church, and Trinity College, Oxford, where I variously held college lecturerships while completing it.

I am grateful to the Syndics of the Cambridge University Library for permission to print their MS Gg. i. 16 as the base text for this edition and to reproduce a page from it as the frontispiece. For permission to reproduce the other plates I am grateful to the Master and Fellows of Magdalene College, Cambridge; the Board of Trinity College, Dublin;

---

[4] In his introduction to the Everyman edition (Thomas à Kempis, *The Imitation of Christ*, London, 1910), Sir Ernest Rhys commented that the first translation 'is the most beautiful if the most incorrect of all English versions' (p. x). A study of the translation was made by B. Rosenberg, *Die älteste mittelenglische Übersetzung der 'Imitatio Christi' des Thomas von Kempen und ihr Verhältnis zum Original* (Leipzig, 1905). A modernized edition of the text of the translation found in MS CUL Gg. i. 16 was published by P. B. M. Allan as *The Book Called the Imitation of Christ* (London, 1923).

[5] They were first listed by Lovatt, p. 121.

[6] The spirituality of the *Imitatio* seems not to have received much attention; there is a convenient account by B. Spaapen in *DS* vii. 2355–68.

and the Keeper of Special Collections, Glasgow University Library. For permission to study and quote from the manucripts in their care I am grateful to the following: the Chef de la Section des Manuscrits, Bibliothèque Royale Albert Ier, Brussels; the Syndics of the Cambridge University Library; the Master and Fellows of Emmanuel College, Cambridge; the Master and Fellows of Magdalene College, Cambridge; the Master and Fellows of St John's College, Cambridge; the Archivist, Historisches Archiv, Cologne; the Librarian of Downside Abbey; the Board of Trinity College, Dublin; the College Archivist, Eton College; the Keeper of Special Collections, Glasgow University Library; the Librarian, Department of Special Collections, Koninklijke Bibliotheek, The Hague; the Curator of Manuscripts, Houghton Library, Harvard University; His Grace the Archbishop of Canterbury and the Trustees of Lambeth Palace Library; the Dean and Chapter of Lincoln; the Manuscripts Librarian, British Library; the Librarian, Servicio de Manuscritos, Incunables y Raros, Biblioteca Nacional, Madrid; the Keeper of Western Manuscripts, Bodleian Library, Oxford; the President and Fellows of Magdalen College, Oxford; and the Prior of St Hugh's Charterhouse, Partridge Green, Sussex.[7]

B.J.H.B.

---

[7] Two recent works came to my attention while this edition was in proof. On Stephen Dodesham (see below, p. xxi, n. 3), see now also the study by A. I. Doyle, 'Stephen Dodesham of Witham and Sheen', in *Of the Making of Books: Medieval Manuscripts, their Scribes and Readers: Essays Presented to M. B. Parkes*, ed. P. R. Robinson and R. Zim (Aldershot, 1997), pp. 94–115, which includes facsimiles and a list of Dodesham's manuscripts. On Thomas à Kempis (see below, p. xxxv, n. 53), see also the study by P. J. J. van Geest, 'Thomas a Kempis (1379/80–1471), een studie van zijn mens- en godsbeeld: Analyse en tekstuitgave van de *Hortulus Rosarum* en de *Vallis Liliorum*' (doctoral dissertation, Catholic Theological University of Utrecht, 1996), which includes a full, up-to-date bibliography.

CONTENTS

LIST OF PLATES

The plates are reproduced at approximately three-quarters of actual size and are unpaginated.

ABBREVIATIONS AND CONVENTIONS

A. ABBREVIATIONS

The abbreviations used for the titles of periodicals, series, and frequently-cited works are listed below. All other works referred to are cited in full at the first reference, and in abbreviated form (usually the author's name alone) subsequently; full details may be found in the Bibliography.

AV	The Authorized Version of the Bible (1611)
AC	Analecta Cartusiana
ABB	*Archives et Bibliothèques de Belgique*
AGKKN	*Archief voor de geschiedenis van de katholieke kerk in Nederland*
Ampe, Imitation	A. Ampe, *'L'Imitation de Jésus-Christ' et son auteur: Réflexions critiques*, Sussidi Eruditi, 25 (Rome, 1973)
Ampe, 'Verspreiding'	'De Verspreiding der *Imitatio Christi* als *Liber internae consolationis qui vocatur musica ecclesiastica*', in *Bijdragen over Thomas a Kempis en de Moderne Devotie uitgegeven ter gelegenheid van de vijfhonderdste sterfdag van Thomas a Kempis*, *ABB*, numéro spécial 4 (Brussels, 1971), pp. 158–71
AASS	*Acta Sanctorum*, ed. J. Bollandus, G. Henschenius *et al.*, new edition revised by J. Carnandet *et al.* (Paris, [1863]–)
Blaiklock	*The Imitation of Christ*, trans. E. M. Blaiklock, Hodder and Stoughton Christian Classics (London, 1979)
Bonardi and Lupo	P. Bonardi and T. Lupo, *'L'Imitazione di Cristo' e il suo autore*, 2 vols (Turin, 1964)
CCSL	Corpus Christianorum, Series Latina
DAI	*Dissertation Abstracts International*
Delaissé	L. M. J. Delaissé (ed.), *Le Manuscrit autographe de Thomas a Kempis et 'L'Imitation de Jésus-Christ': Examen archéologique et édition diplomatique du Bruxellensis 5855–61*, Publications de *Scriptorium*, 2, 2 vols (Paris, 1956)
DNB	*Dictionary of National Biography*, ed. L. Stephen and S. Lee, 22 vols (Oxford, 1921–2)

DS	*Dictionnaire de spiritualité ascétique et mystique*, ed. M. Viller *et al.*, 16 vols (Paris, 1937–94), cited by volume and column
EETS, os	Early English Text Society, Original Series (not indicated from no. 160 onwards)
EETS, es	Early English Text Society, Extra Series
EP	*The Enclyclopedia of Philosophy*, ed. P. Edwards, 8 vols (New York, 1957)
Huijben and Debongnie	J. Huijben and P. Debongnie, *L'Auteur ou les auteurs de 'L'Imitation'*, Bibliothèque de la *Revue d'histoire ecclésiastique*, 30 (Louvain, 1957)
ICC	The International Critical Commentary
Ingram	J. K. Ingram (ed.), *The Earliest English Translation of the First Three Books of the 'De Imitatione Christi'*, EETS, es 63 (1893)
Jordan	R. Jordan, *Handbook of Middle English Grammar: Phonology*, trans. E. J. Crook, Janua Linguarum, Series Practica, 218 (The Hague, 1974), cited by paragraph number
Knott	*The Imitation of Christ*, trans. B. I. Knott (Glasgow, 1963)
LALME	A. McIntosh, M. L. Samuels and M. Benskin, *A Linguistic Atlas of Late Mediaeval English*, 4 vols (Aberdeen, 1986)
Lees	R. A. Lees, *The Negative Language of the Dionysian School of Mystical Theology: An Approach to 'The Cloud of Unknowing'*, AC 107, 2 vols (Salzburg, 1983)
Lovatt	R. Lovatt, 'The *Imitation of Christ* in Late Medieval England', *TRHS*, Fifth Series, 18 (1968), 97–121
LS	*Leeds Studies in English*
Lupo	T. Lupo (ed.), *De Imitatione Christi libri quatuor*, Storia e Attualità, 6 (Vatican City, 1982)
MBDS	*Mittelalterliche Bibliothekskataloge Deutschlands und der Schweiz*, ed. P. Lehmann *et al.*, 4 vols (Munich, 1918–79)
MED	*Middle English Dictionary*, ed. H. Kurath, S. M. Kuhn *et al.* (Ann Arbor, Michigan, 1954–)
MMBL	N. R. Ker and A. J. Piper, *Medieval Manuscripts in British Libraries*, 4 vols (Oxford, 1969–92)
NAK	*Nederlands Archief voor Kerkgeschiedenis*
NCE	*New Catholic Enclyclopedia*, 15 vols (New York, 1967)

N&Q	Notes and Queries
NS	New Series
OCT	Oxford Classical Texts
ODS	D. H. Farmer, *The Oxford Dictionary of Saints* (Oxford, 1978)
OED	*The Oxford English Dictionary*, ed. J. A. H. Murray *et al.*, second edition prepared by J. A. Simpson and E. S. C. Weiner, 20 vols (Oxford, 1989)
OGE	*Ons Geestelijk Erf*
OTL	Old Testament Library
Plomer	H. R. Plomer *et al.*, *A Dictionary of the Printers and Booksellers Who Were at Work in England, Scotland and Ireland from 1668 to 1725* (Oxford, 1922)
Pohl	Thomas à Kempis, *Opera Omnia*, ed. M. J. Pohl, 7 vols (Freiburg im Breisgau, 1902–22)
Puyol, *Paléographie*	P. E. Puyol, *Paléographie, classement, généalogie du livre 'De Imitatione Christi'* (Paris, 1898)
Riehle	W. Riehle, *The Middle English Mystics*, trans. B. Standring (London, 1981)
RSV	*The New Oxford Annotated Bible with the Apocrypha: Revised Standard Version*, ed. H. G. May and B. M. Metzger (New York, 1977)
RTAM	*Recherches de théologie ancienne et médiévale*
RH	*Recusant History*
Sherley-Price	*The Imitation of Christ*, trans. L. Sherley-Price, Penguin Classics (Harmondsworth, 1952)
SM	*Studi Medievali*
STC	*A Short-Title Catalogue of Books Printed in England, Scotland and Ireland and of English Books Printed Abroad 1475–1640*, ed. A. W. Pollard and G. R. Redgrave, second edition revised by W. A. Jackson *et al.*, 3 vols (London, 1976–91)
TRHS	*Transactions of the Royal Historical Society*
Visser	F. Th. Visser, *An Historical Syntax of the English Language*, 3 vols (Leiden, 1963–73), cited by paragraph number
Whiting	B. J. Whiting and H. W. Whiting, *Proverbs, Sentences, and Proverbial Phrases from English Writings Mainly before 1500* (Cambridge, Mass., 1968)
YULG	*The Yale University Library Gazette*
ZKT	*Zeitschrift für katholische Theologie*

B. CONVENTIONS

Generally the Latin *Imitatio Christi* is referred to as the *Imitatio*, and the English translation edited here as the *Imitation*. Where the translation is being compared with its source, quotations from the *Imitation* are printed in romans within inverted commas, and quotations from the *Imitatio* are printed in italics; quotations from other English and Latin texts are generally treated similarly.

In Part I of the Introduction quotations from manuscripts in English are reproduced with original capitalization and punctuation; other quotations generally have modernized capitalization and punctuation. Quotations from the Latin *Imitatio* are from Delaissé and the punctuation is that of the autograph manuscript. In Parts II and III of the Introduction Delaissé's conventions for indicating corrections in the autograph manuscript are replaced by those described in the following paragraph; in Part V, the corrections recorded by Delaissé are not reproduced.

Where corrections are described, caret marks ˋ. . .ˊ surround insertions either above the line or in the margin, and angled brackets ⟨. . .⟩ surround letters written over erasure; where the angled brackets surround dots, nothing has been written over the erasure and the number of dots indicates the approximate number of letters erased. Dots are used without brackets where part of a word or phrase is missing because of a blot or tear in the manuscript. Where variants are quoted, the following conventions are used:

canc.	cancelled
om.	omitted
con.	editorial conjecture
|	change of line
||	change of folio

References to the *Imitation* are given in the order book, chapter, verse, e.g. 1.2.3 denotes verse 3 of chapter 2 of Book I. The division of the text into verses in the manner of the Bible was first made in the nineteenth century by P. E. Puyol, and is marked in the text of this edition.[1] The verse numbers correspond to the numbers in brackets in the margin of Delaissé's edition of the Latin. The numbering of the chapters of Book III follows that found in the manuscripts of the first English translation,

---

[1] Puyol based his division into verses on the punctuation in Turin, Biblioteca Nazionale, MS. E. vi. 12, the *Codex Aronensis*, which he used as base text in his edition of the *Imitatio* (*De Imitatione Christi libri quatuor* (Paris, 1886), pp. xxi–ii); see also Puyol, *Paléographie*, pp. 67–9.

in which the five prayers are treated as separate chapters (in most Latin manuscripts each prayer is treated as part of the preceding chapter). The numbering of the verses in the prayers is adjusted accordingly, the first verse of each prayer being treated as verse 1. The standard numbering of the books is used (that usually known as Book III appears as Text IV in Delaissé). Zero is used in chapter position for the list of chapters at the beginning of each book, and in verse position for the title of each chapter: thus 1.0.4 refers to the title of chapter 4 of Book I as it appears in the list of chapters at the beginning of Book I, and 1.4.0 refers to the title of the same chapter as it appears at the head of the chapter. 1.0.0 refers to the *incipit* of Book I. Where two numbers alone are used (as in the running head to the text), they refer to book and chapter, e.g. 3.6 refers to chapter 6 of Book III.

The following table enables references to the chapters of Book III of the translation to be converted to the numbering of the chapters of Book III in the Latin (Text IV in Delaissé). Where no figure is given opposite the English chapter number, the chapter in question is a prayer which in the Latin is treated as part of the previous chapter.

LATIN AND ENGLISH CHAPTER NUMBERING

Latin	English	Latin	English	Latin	English	Latin	English
1	1	–	17	28	33	44	49
2	2	16	18	29	34	45	50
3	3	17	19	30	35	46	51
–	4	18	20	31	36	47	52
4	5	19	21	32	37	48	53
5	6	20	22	33	38	49	54
6	7	21	23	34	39	50	55
7	8	22	24	35	40	51	56
8	9	23	25	36	41	52	57
9	10	–	26	37	42	53	58
10	11	–	27	38	43	54	59
11	12	24	28	39	44	55	60
12	13	25	29	40	45	56	61
13	14	26	30	41	46	57	62
14	15	27	31	42	47	58	63
15	16	–	32	43	48	59	64

STEMMA

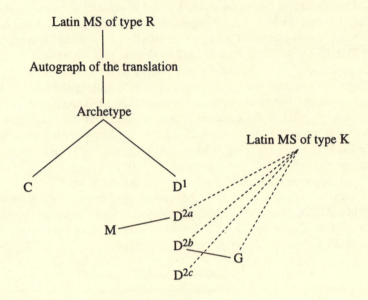

SIGLA

Manuscripts of the Latin source
K   Brussels, Bibliothèque Royale, MS 5855–61, as printed by Delaissé
R   London, British Library, MS Royal 7 B. VIII

Manuscripts of the first English translation
C   Cambridge, University Library, MS Gg. i. 16, s. $xv^{3/4}$
D^1 Dublin, Trinity College, MS 678 (formerly F. 5. 8), s. xv^2 (written
    by Stephen Dodesham, who died in 1482): original hand
D^2 Dublin, Trinity College, MS 678: corrector. The letters *a*, *b*, and *c*
    are used to distinguish different stages of correction
G   Glasgow, University Library, MS Hunter T. 6. 18 (written by
    William Darker and dated 1502)
M   Cambridge, Magdalene College, MS F. 4. 19, s. $xv^{ex.}/xv^{in.}$

INTRODUCTION

I. MANUSCRIPTS

A. DESCRIPTION OF THE MANUSCRIPTS

Since all four manuscripts contain only Books I–III of the *Imitation* and
nothing else, only in the case of C is a formal description of the contents
given. The other manuscripts have only minor variants in the wording
of the incipits and explicits of the three books: these are given in the
critical apparatus.

C. Cambridge, University Library, MS Gg. i. 16   s. xv$^{3/4}$
174 parchment leaves, size 225 mm by 150 mm, written space 150 mm
by 90 mm. Collation: two modern paper flyleaves, one medieval
parchment flyleaf, i–viii^8, ix^8 wants 1 (f. 65) and 8 (f. 72), x–xiv^8,
xv^8 wants 1–8 (ff. 113–20), xvi–xxii^8, xxiii^8 wants 8 (after f. 183), two
modern paper flyleaves. Medieval leaf signatures, where cropped
replaced by modern signatures in pencil; also modern quire numbering
in pencil; catchwords remain. Two sets of modern foliation: an older one
in ink, incorrect because various leaves are uncounted, and a more
recent one in pencil, correct and including in the numeration the leaves
which are now missing (ff. 1–183, flyleaves unfoliated). This foliation
has been used here. Written in single column, 20 lines per page; ruled in
black ink, pricking sometimes visible on outer edges of leaves. Chapter
headings and running heads (number of book) in red; initials (two-line)
in blue with red decoration; paragraph symbols in blue and red; text in
black ink, bastard anglicana, same hand throughout. Rebound in 1956.
Secundo folio *study be*. See frontispiece.[1]

---

[1] The following manuscripts also appear to have been written by the scribe of C (all in
bastard anglicana): Cambridge, Fitzwilliam Museum, MS McClean 129 (*Life of St
Katherine*); Princeton, University Library, MS Garrett 144 (Elements of Religion); and
Yale, University Library, MS Beinecke 281 (Lydgate, *Life of Our Lady*). There are
facsimiles of the Fitzwilliam and Yale manuscripts in M. R. James, *A Descriptive Catalogue
of the McClean Collection of Manuscripts in the Fitzwilliam Museum* (Cambridge, 1912), pl.
LXXXIII, and B. A. Shailor, *Catalogue of Medieval and Renaissance Manuscripts in the
Beinecke Rare Book and Manuscript Library, Yale University*, Medieval and Renaissance
Texts and Studies (Binghamton, NY, 1984–), ii, pl. 26.

1. ff. 1ʳ–43ᵛ: Book I of the *Imitation*. Begins: 'Ueni Domine Ihesu ¶ Here bigynneth the tretes called Musica ecclesiastica. [List of chapters of Book I follows.] Of the foloynge of cryste: and despysynge of alle vanytees worldely. Capitulum 1ᵐ. Oure lorde seith he that foloweth me goith not in darkenesse.' Ends: 'So muche þou shalte profite as þou putteste violence to thi selfe. ¶ Here endeþ the furste partie of Musica ecclesiastica.'

2. ff. 43ᵛ–69ʳ: Book II of the *Imitation*. Begins: '¶ And here bigynneþ the chapitres of the seconde boke. [List of chapters of Book II follows.] Here bigynneþ of the ammonycions drawynge gretely Inwarde. ¶ Of the Inwarde conuersacioun. ¶ Capitulum. primum. Oure lorde seithe that the Reawme of god is withe in: you.' Ends: 'þat by many tribulacions hit bihoveth vs to entree into the reaume of hevon. ¶ Here endeþ the ammonicions drawynge Inwarde.'

3. ff. 69ᵛ–183ᵛ: Book III of the *Imitation*. Begins: '¶ And here bygynneth the chapitres of the þridde boke of inwarde consolacion.' [List of chapters of Book III follows; the beginning of the text of Book III is missing because of the missing quire.] Ends: 'dresse him by the wey of pees to the cuntrey of euerlastynge clerenes. Amen. Amen. Amen. Here ende the boke of inwarde consolacion. Ueni Domine Ihesu.'

The name 'George Tylli' is written in a sixteenth-century hand on the verso of the flyleaf. C is listed in Bernard's catalogue of 1697 among the books of John Moore (1646–1714), then Bishop of Norwich but later translated to Ely; after Moore's death his collection of manuscripts and printed books was bought by George I and presented to the University of Cambridge.[2]

D. Dublin, Trinity College, MS 678 (formerly F. 5. 8)   s. xv²
121 parchment leaves, size 200 mm by 133 mm, written space 140 mm by 80 mm. Collation: three modern paper endleaves, i–viii⁸, ix⁸ wants 6 (before p. 138), x–xiv⁸, xv¹⁰, three modern paper endleaves. Half of the leaf containing pp. 142–3 is missing. There are medieval leaf signatures, the first quire denoted *a*. On the first leaf of some quires there is also another signature according to the alternative system whereby *a* denotes the second quire. Catchwords remain. The manuscript is paginated 1–241 in pencil in the bottom left-hand corner of each page; this was done

---

² [E. Bernard], *Catalogi librorum manuscriptorum Angliae et Hiberniae in unum collecti*, 2 vols (Oxford, 1697), vol. ii, part 1, pp. 368, 402. On Moore, see *DNB* xiii. 806–8, and C. Moore, *'The Father of Black-Letter Collectors': Memoir of the Right Reverend John Moore, D.D.* (London, 1885).

before what was originally f. 70 was cut out. The number 74 is repeated as 74a, so that all subsequent numbers are one short. Nevertheless this pagination has been used here. Written in single column, 24 or 25 lines per page; ruled in red ink, pricking visible in outer margins. Chapter headings in red; initials (two-line) blue and red; running head and text in black, sometimes faded to brown, anglicana, same hand throughout. Initial letters of sentences have yellow background. There are corrections to the text on almost every page, consisting of alterations by erasure, additions above the line, or additions in the margin: these are described in detail in section B below. The manuscript was rebound in 1892. Secundo folio *þ^u displesist*. See pl. 1 (*a*)–(*f*). Contents as for C; Book I begins on p. 1, Book II on p. 62, Book III on p. 96.

D is unsigned, but A. I. Doyle has identified its hand as that of Stephen Dodesham, a Carthusian monk who was also a prolific scribe. He appears to have started work before 1439; by 1462 he was a monk of the Charterhouse at Witham in Somerset; by 1471 he had moved to Sheen Charterhouse in Surrey, apparently because of a quarrel with the prior of Witham; he died in 1481/2. About twenty manuscripts have been identified as his work, and he may well have been a professional scribe before he joined the order.[3] On p. 1 of D appears the note 'Iohn Ramsey and Robert Allan merchantes in London', written in a sixteenth-century hand: as Lovatt has pointed out, since this note indicates that the manuscript was in London shortly after the Dissolution, the text may well have been written by Dodesham while he was at Sheen, i.e. between *c.* 1470 and 1482.[4]

There are several manuscript notes in various hands of seventeenth-century date in the margins of D, mainly biblical quotations or

---

[3] On Dodesham's career, see E. M. Thompson, *The Carthusian Order in England*, Church Historical Society, NS 3 (London, 1930), pp. 306–7; London, Lambeth Palace Library, MS 413, ff. 393ᵛ, 417ʳ; and London, British Library, MS Additional 17085, f. 124ʳ. On his work as a scribe, see A. I. Doyle, 'Book Production by the Monastic Orders in England (*c.* 1375–1530): Assessing the Evidence', in *Medieval Book Production: Assessing the Evidence*, ed. L. L. Brownrigg (Los Altos Hills, Calif., 1990), pp. 1–19 (pp. 14–15, 19, nn. 80–7), where references to published facsimiles of his work may be found, and A. S. G. Edwards, 'Beinecke MS 661 and Early Fifteenth-Century English Manuscript Production', *YULG* 66, supplement (1991), 181–96. Edwards lists fourteen of Dodesham's manuscripts; he also copied Cambridge, University Library, MS Kk. vi. 41 (*Speculum Peccatoris*); Cambridge, University Library, MS Additional 3042, ff. 116ʳ–25ʳ (*Directions for Praise and Prayer*); Cambridge, Trinity College, MS B. 14. 54 (*Of the Creed*, etc.); Downside Abbey, Somerset, MS 26542 (*Pricking of Love, Pore Caitif*, etc.); Karlsruhe, Landesbibliothek, MS St Georgen 12 (*Sanctilogium Salvatoris*), vol. i; and a supply leaf (f. 163) for London, British Library, MS Harley 630. See above, p. ix, n. 7.

[4] Lovatt, p. 121.

signatures, for example 'Charles Burdett' (p. 41), 'William Howe' (p. 110), and 'Hammand Warde' (p. 128). The name occurring most often among the signatures is that of Turney, for example 'Will Turney his book God give him Grace' (p. 37), 'Emor Turney' (four times on p. 78), '1655 William Turney His book' (p. 126), and 'William Turney of Seabrooke in the parish of Iveingho ye county of Bucks his Booke. Witnes hearvnto, Emor Turney' (p. 203).[5] The Turneys sold the manuscript in the second half of the seventeenth century, as is clear from a note found on p. 1 of D in a seventeenth-century hand: 'For Mr Henry Dodwell at Mr Tookes in St Pauls churchyard Bookseller'. Dodwell (1641–1711), fellow of Trinity College, Dublin, from 1662 to 1666 and Camden Professor of History at Oxford from 1688 to 1691, apparently made a transcript of the manuscript.[6] By 1697 it had passed to John Madden, President of the Irish College of Physicians, whose collection, as Ingram writes, 'was purchased after his death by Dr. John Stearne, Bishop of Clogher, who, dying in 1745, bequeathed his valuable collection of MSS., and amongst them, the English *Imitation*, to Trinity College, Dublin'.[7] D was used by Ingram as his base text for his edition of 1893 for the EETS.

G. Glasgow, University Library, MS Hunter T. 6. 18 (no. 136)   1502
125 parchment leaves, size 205 mm by 135 mm, written space 130 mm by 80 mm. Collation: four parchment flyleaves (the first of which may be a raised pastedown), i–xv[8], parchment flyleaf (which may also be a raised pastedown). The reasons for thinking that the first and last leaves may be raised pastedowns are that the manuscript has its original binding but no pastedowns, and that the first leaf, unlike the other three flyleaves which precede the first quire, is unfoliated. Medieval leaf

---

[5] There are several references to the Turneys in *The Victoria History of the County of Buckingham*, ed. W. Page, 4 vols and index (London, 1905–28), relating to their possession of a number of different manors over the sixteenth, seventeenth, and eighteenth centuries: see iii. 40, 339–40, 412–14, 418–19; iv. 87, 143, 472, 473 n., 493. Page makes no reference to them in connection with Seabrooke, a hamlet to the west of Ivinghoe, however.

[6] On Dodwell, see *DNB* v. 1084–6; Benjamin Tooke (c. 1642–1716) was a bookseller in St Paul's churchyard from 1670 and the king's printer in Dublin from 1669 to 1685: see Plomer, p. 293. Dodwell's transcript is mentioned in the preface to *The Christian Pattern; or, The Imitation of Jesus Christ, Being the Genuine Works of Thomas à Kempis*, second edition (London, 1710), pp. [lxi]–lxii (there is an error in the pagination at this point); the relevant passage is quoted by Ingram (p. xi).

[7] Ingram, p. xiii; Bernard, *Catalogi*, vol. ii, part 2, p. 59. On Stearne (or Sterne, 1660–1745), see *DNB* xviii. 1085–6.

signatures (two sets visible); catchwords remain. The first flyleaf is unfoliated; the second, third, and fourth are foliated i–iii in pencil; ff. 1–118 are so foliated in black ink in two hands, the older marking ff. 1–40 and every tenth folio thereafter, the more recent marking most of the rest; inaccuracies in foliation have been corrected in ink. This foliation has been used here. Text ends on f. 118ᵛ. Written in single column, 23 lines per page; ruled in black ink, pricking visible in outer margins. Chapter headings in red, initials (two-line) in red with blue decoration, red and blue paragraph signs; text in black, with yellow background to capital letters, fere-textura. On f. 1ʳ there is an illuminated two-line initial and a page-border of blue and red leaves decorated with gold dots. On f. 32ᵛ (the beginning of Book II) there is an illuminated two-line initial. The binding is medieval: it has seven thongs, of which only the middle five are now attached to the boards, the original bevelled oak boards, covered with faded red leather, and no decoration. Secundo folio *the trinite*. See pl. II. Contents as for C; Book I begins on f. 1ʳ, Book II on f. 32ʳ, Book III on f. 49ᵛ.

G was written in 1502 by William Darker, a monk of the Sheen Charterhouse, for Elizabeth Gibbs, fifth abbess of the Brigittine house at Syon, who died on 30 August 1518.[8] The following note is written on f. iʳ in the same hand as the main text:

O vos omnes sorores et fratres presentes et futuri orate queso pro venerabili matre nostra Elizabeth Gibbis huius almi monasterii abbatissa necnon pro deuoto ac religioso viro dompno Willielmo Darker in artibus magistro de domo Bethleem prope Shene ordinis cartuciensis qui pro eadem domina abbatissa hunc librum conscripsit anno dominice incarnacionis millesimo ccccc secundo.[9]

Darker may have studied at Oxford and been an usher at Eton College between 1469 and 1471; he died at Sheen in 1513.[10] Ten manuscripts have been identified as his work.[11]

---

[8] London, British Library, MS Additional 22285, ff. 2ʳ, 52ᵛ.

[9] An abbreviated form of the same note (omitting the reference to Darker) appears on the verso of the first flyleaf.

[10] The Eton Audit Rolls refer to a 'William Dacker or Darkar' who came from Oxford to be an usher: see Page, ii. 170–1; W. Sterry, *The Eton College Register 1441–1698* (Eton, 1943), p. xxxiii; and A. B. Emden, *A Biographical Register of the University of Oxford to A.D. 1500*, 3 vols (Oxford, 1957–9), i. 544. For Darker's obituary notice, see Partridge Green, Sussex, St Hugh's Charterhouse, MS B. 62, f. 171ᵛ, published by J. Clark, *The 'Chartae' of the Carthusian General Chapter: MS Parkminster B. 62 (1502–1513)*, AC 100:21, 2 vols (Salzburg, 1992), p. 244.

[11] On Darker as a scribe, see Doyle, 'Book Production', pp. 14, 19, n. 75, where

At the foot of f. 1ʳ of G is written 'William Vownynge', and on f. 68ᵛ 'Robart Smythe', both in secretary hands. On the verso of the first endleaf, above the Hunterian bookplate, on the right is written 'Thomas Martin' in a large humanist hand, and on the left, in a secretary hand, 'Donum amicissimi Thome Clarke de de [*sic*] Saxmundham generosi', and below this '2.2–', the price for which the book was sold. Thomas Martin (1697–1771), of Palgrave, Suffolk, was a noted eighteenth-century antiquary.[12] G was bought at a sale of Martin's books in 1770 by William Hunter (1718–83), whose collection, left on his death to three trustees for the use of his nephew Dr Matthew Baillie for twenty years, passed to the University of Glasgow in 1803.[13]

M. Cambridge, Magdalene College, MS F. 4. 19   s. xvᵉˣ·/xviⁱⁿ·

120 parchment leaves, size 200 mm by 130 mm, written space 135 mm by 90 mm. Collation: two modern paper flyleaves, i⁸–xv⁸, one modern paper flyleaf. Medieval leaf signatures are visible on some leaves; the second quire is denoted *a*. Catchwords survive, except on the last leaf of viii (f. 64ᵛ), where the bottom half of the page is left blank and some text is omitted, perhaps because the exemplar was defective. The first folio of each quire is numbered, correctly, in pencil (ff. 1–120). Written in single column, 23 lines per page; ruled in blue ink, pricking visible in some outside margins. Chapter headings and initials (two-line) in red; blue three-line initials at the beginnings of the three books (ff. 1ᵛ, 31ʳ,

references to published facsimiles of his work may be found. He copied the following manuscripts (all in fere-textura except Caligula, in a more current script, and Pembroke, in textura): Cambridge, University Library, MS Ff. vi. 33 (*Benjamin Minor*, etc.); Cambridge, Pembroke College, MS 221 (*Cloud of Unknowing*, in Latin, etc.); Lincoln, Cathedral Library, MS 64 (A. 6. 15; Carthusian Collectar), addition at foot of f. 3ᵛ (Collect for Christmas Eve); London, British Library, MS Additional 22121 (*Speculum Christiani*); London, British Library, MS Cotton Caligula A. ii, ff. 204ʳ–6ᵛ (Constitutions of the Carthusian General Chapter, 1491–1504); London, Lambeth Palace, MS 546, ff. 57ʳ–77ᵛ (Prayers before the Sacrament); Oxford, Bodleian Library, MS Lat. liturg. e. 21 (*Psalter*), f. 180ʳ⁻ᵛ (*Order of Lauds During the Week*); Oxford, Bodleian Library, MS Laud misc. 38 (*Dialogue of St Anselm and Our Lady*); Oxford, Bodleian Library, MS Laud misc. 517 (*Manner of Good Living*, etc.). I do not think that the other additions in the Lincoln manuscript attributed to Darker by R. M. Thomson, *Catalogue of the Manuscripts of Lincoln Cathedral Chapter Library* (Cambridge, 1989), p. 46, are his: see my article, 'The Language of the Scribes of the First English Translation of the *Imitatio Christi*', *LSE*, NS 26 (1995), 79–111 (n. 42, p. 109).

[12] *DNB* xii. 1182–3.

[13] *DNB* x. 302–5; see also N. R. Ker, *William Hunter as a Collector of Medieval Manuscripts: The First Edwards Lecture on Palaeography Delivered in the University of Glasgow* (Glasgow, [1983]), pp. 8–9, 20–1, 23.

50^r). Text written in black ink, sometimes faded to brown, textura, same hand throughout. The binding is post-medieval. Secundo folio *wyse but*. See pl. III. Contents as for C; Book I begins on f. 1^r, Book II on f. 30^v, Book III on f. 47^v.

M is unsigned, no other manuscripts written in the same hand have been identified, and there are no indications of the manuscript's medieval provenance. 'Edwarde ys my name' is written in a secretary hand in the margin of f. 18^v. In the top margin of f. 1^r is written in a humanist hand 'Liber Gilberti Bourne iuris utriusque doctoris et Noui Collegii socii perpetui'. Bourne matriculated at Oxford in 1572 aged 19 and died in 1595; as Lovatt notes, he 'had connexions with the English College at Douai and it is possible that he acquired the MS from this source'.[14] On f. 120^v a short poem is written in a similar humanist hand followed by the initials 'E.R.'. It is not known when Magdalene acquired the manuscript.

B. THE CORRECTIONS IN D

As was stated in the above description, D has a fairly substantial number of corrections, on average between five and ten per page: some are marginal, some are interlinear, and some have been made over erasure. Most of the corrections consist of the insertion or substitution of individual words, letters, or short phrases; there are also corrections to the capitalization and punctuation. The great majority of the corrections may be distinguished from the main text because they have been made using ink of a more brownish colour. This is an important factor in identifying short corrections which have been made over erasure, many of which cannot be identified from microfilm and would be difficult to identify from the manuscript itself, were it not for the difference in the colour of the ink. An example of this is the phrase *when ther ys lytell amendement* in pl. 1 (*a*), written over erasure and more clearly distinguishable as a correction in the manuscript than it is in monochrome reproduction.

Although the handwriting of the corrections varies to some extent, certain differences may be distinguished between the forms of the letters used in the corrections and those used by Dodesham. The corrections have a simpler form of *w* than that used by Dodesham, who in this

---

[14] Lovatt, p. 121; see also J. B. Wainewright, 'Gilbert Bourne', *N&Q*, Tenth Series, 6 (1906), 165, and J. Foster, *Alumni Oxonienses: The Members of the University of Oxford 1500–1714*, 4 vols (Oxford, 1891–2), i. 156.

manuscript consistently uses a more elaborate form (pl. I (*e*), margin, *knowe*; cf. *mowe* on the same line). In the corrections *d* usually has a simple curved back, whereas Dodesham's *d* has a looped back (pl. I (*b*), margin, *holde*; compare *vnder* on the same line; sometimes the corrector also has a looped form, however: pl. I (*d*), margin, *syde*). Long *s* and *f* in the corrections have a curved top, rather than a hooked top as in Dodesham's hand (pl. I (*b*), margin, *forgeueth*; compare *of* on the same line). In the corrections *g* sometimes has a curved stroke beginning on the upper right-hand side of the letter, absent in Dodesham's hand (pl. I (*c*), interlinear, *long*). The loop on the top of *h* sometimes, especially when preceded by *t*, forms a bulge to the left of the headstroke, absent in Dodesham's hand (pl. I (*f*), margin, *fallyth*).

The handwriting of the corrections is not entirely consistent, perhaps because they were made over a long period; compare *forgeueth* (pl. I (*b*), margin) with *to holde* just below. Nevertheless the palaeographical features just mentioned occur with reasonable consistency in the corrections written in brown ink, and this suggests that these corrections are not the work of Dodesham, but that of a second scribe. There is also a small number of corrections, not made in brown ink, which do not have these characteristics: these were no doubt made by Dodesham, either as he went along or shortly afterwards. Two strata may therefore be distinguished in the corrections: those made by Dodesham, in black ink (identified as D^1 in the apparatus of this edition); and those made by a different scribe, in brown ink (identified as D^2).

Comparison of the script of the D^2-corrections with the hand of William Darker, the scribe of G, reveals that Darker's hand has the paleographical characteristics identified above as being characteristic of the D^2-corrections: the simpler form of *w* (pl. II, l. 1, *woo, wol*); the *d* with the curved back (pl. II, l. 1, *declyne*); long *s* and *f* with a curved top (pl. II, l. 2, *suerte*; l. 3, *of*); the *g* with an upper loop curving to the right (pl. II, l. 4, *yong*); the *h* with a bulge to the right of the headstroke (pl. II, l. 2, *aperyth*). This palaeographical evidence suggests that at least some, if not all, of the corrections written in brown ink are the work of Darker.

An examination of the nature of the corrections themselves supports this view. As has been said, some of the corrections consist of the alteration of one or two letters in a word, and appear to have been made with the objective of correcting the spelling. Other corrections were made with the aim of making more substantial alterations to the text, and in the process use spellings which are more characteristic of Darker than they are of Dodesham.

(a) from p. 49

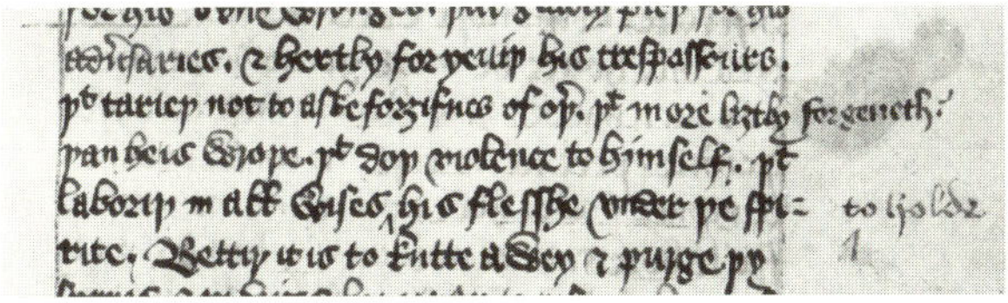

(b) from p. 53

(c) from p. 60

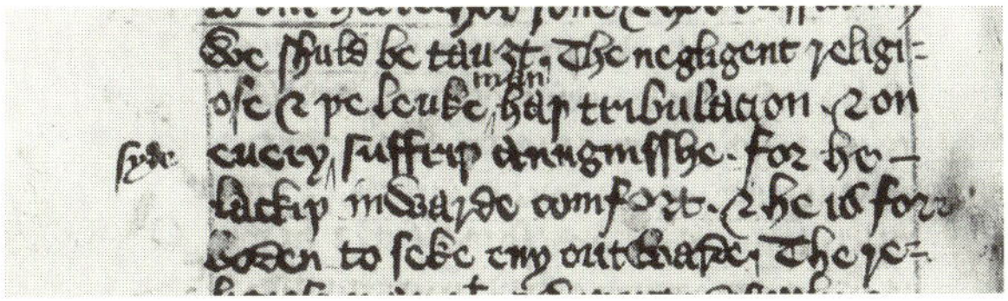

(d) from p. 60

(e) from p. 102

(f) from p. 140

Plate I
Dublin, Trinity College, MS 678 (D)
(Reproduced by permission of the Board of Trinity College, Dublin)

An example of a correction made with the aim of changing the form of a word, rather than the word itself, is the doubling of *o* when it represents a long vowel. This is found a large number of times in the case of the word *good*, in which Dodesham's usual spelling *gode* is frequently corrected to *g`o´ode*.[15] A few other words are treated similarly: *do`o´st* (3.9.10), *do`on´* (3.16.2), *go⟨o⟩* (1.19.30), *⟨oo⟩ne* (3.11.11), *o⟨only⟩* (3.2.17); *po⟨o⟩re* (1.18.12), *vng`o´odely* (1.8.9), *w`o´orde* (2.12.1, 3.39.3); *oo* spellings are also found in *`oone´* (2.12.28) and *`oonly´* (2.5.13). In G Darker consistently spells *good* with *oo* (for example, pl. II, l. 5, *goode*).

A second orthographical correction made by the corrector is the change made to some examples of verbs in the plural present indicative, where the ending *-in* or *-yn* has been written by the corrector over erasure. This has been done in the following instances:

abidi⟨n⟩ 3.18.8; *cess⟨in⟩* 1.24.16, *cess⟨yn⟩* 2.9.36; *et⟨in⟩* 1.25.34; *fortasti⟨n⟩* 3.18.8; *folowi⟨n⟩* 3.39.13, *fol⟨wyn⟩* 2.11.5, *folow⟨yn⟩* 2.11.6; *kep⟨yn⟩* 1.25.34; *labor⟨yn⟩* 1.25.34; *lyu⟨yn⟩* 3.6.33; *ow⟨yn⟩* 1.19.14; *praie⟨n⟩* 1.25.34; *presum⟨yn⟩*, dot of *i* and tail of *þ* visible under erasure 1.7.5; *red⟨yn⟩* 1.25.34; *remayne⟨n⟩* 3.58.18; *ris⟨yn⟩* 1.25.34; *set⟨tyn⟩* 3.12.4; *spek⟨yn⟩* 1.25.34; *striue⟨n⟩*, tail of *þ* visible under erasure 3.3.13; *wak⟨yn⟩* 1.25.34; *worship⟨yn⟩* 2.11.6.

In the cases of *presum⟨yn⟩* and *striue⟨n⟩* it is clear that an ending with *-þ* originally stood in the manuscript, and this was presumably true in the other cases as well: the corrector has preferred to substitute the midland form ending in *-n* for the southern form ending in *-þ*, although there are other instances of *-þ* endings which have not been corrected. All four manuscripts have present plural indicative forms ending in both *-þ* and *-n*; nevertheless it can be said that in G there are cases where Darker too has preferred an *-n* form to a *-þ* form (for example, *taken* at 3.1.3, where D has *takiþ*, uncorrected).

Four other general tendencies are discernible in the orthographic

---

[15] See the critical apparatus at 1.2.9, 1.3.17, 1.3.23, 1.4.7, 1.7.4, 1.7.10, 1.8.5, 1.9.10, 1.12.6, 1.14.7, 1.15.2, 1.19.1, 1.20.15, 1.21.6, 1.21.18, 1.22.37, 1.23.6, 1.24.29, 1.25.6, 1.25.11, 1.25.20, 2.3.4, 2.3.13, 2.4.4, 2.4.8, 2.6.1, 2.6.2, 2.6.3, 2.6.12, 2.8.12 (twice), 2.8.25, 2.9.26, 3.3.19, 3.5.8, 3.5.19, 3.7.10, 3.7.16, 3.8.19, 3.12.8, 3.16.7, 3.17.8, 3.18.8, 3.21.12, 3.23.28, 3.24.5, 3.28.7, 3.35.30, 3.36.21, 3.36.23, 3.39.14, 3.45.6, 3.56.4, 3.60.5, 3.60.7, 3.60.10, 3.60.27, 3.61.25, 3.62.23. Also found are the following: *go`o´d* 1.16.4, *go`o´de* 1.19.4, 1.19.27, 1.22.7, 2.10.13, 2.12.47, 3.10.13, 3.59.27, *g⟨oode⟩* 2.2.2, *goode*, second *o* added on line 2.8.12, *go⟨ode⟩* 3.4.5, *`goode´* 3.5.8, *`good´* 3.16.6, *g`o´odes* 1.22.8, 3.4.1, 3.11.17, 3.18.4, 3.18.8, 3.23.1, 3.24.4, 3.43.1 (twice), 3.64.16, *go`o´des* 3.9.11, 3.23.4, *g`o´odenes* 1.25.12, 2.4.7, 2.8.1, 3.24.9, 3.64.19.

corrections. Evidently the ending -*al* (corresponding to the Latin -*alis*) was preferred to -*el*, as in the following cases where the spelling of the vowel has been changed to *a*, presumably from *e*:

natur⟨a⟩ly 2.12.42, 3.24.5; *spiritu⟨a⟩l* 2.11.16, 3.59.31, 3.63.27; *spiritu⟨al⟩* 3.53.36; *supernatur⟨a⟩ly* 3.24.5; *supernatur⟨a⟩ll* 3.59.31.[16]

In each of these cases the spelling with *a* is found in G. Secondly, *s* is preferred to *c* by the corrector in *exercised* at 3.35.27, where the *s* has been altered from *c*; there is also the form *exerci⟨s⟩ed* at 3.54.14, where *c* is visible under the erasure. G spells *exercised* with an *s* in both these cases. Thirdly, the corrector uses *th* spellings more frequently than Dodesham, who usually has *þ*, as in the following cases:

be⟨fallith⟩ 1.18.21; `besemeth` 1.21.13; ⟨*chargith*⟩ 2.1.38; `drawith` 3.47.12; `fallyth` 3.21.12; ⟨*felyth*⟩ 3.8.16; `fyndeth` 2.8.12; `longit[h]` (cropped by binder) 3.39.3; *ned⟨ith⟩* 1.12.5; *ow⟨ith⟩* 1.11.17; `seith` 1.13.28, 2.12.32; `slydith` 2.9.13; ⟨*thynkyth*⟩ 3.8.16.

Fourthly, the corrector shows a preference in some cases for forms with final -*e*: in the forms *none* (3.58.11), *ware* (2.9.15), and *youe* (2.1.1), the final *e* has been added on the line by the corrector. Other spellings with final *e* in the corrections include `ande` (2.1.27) and ⟨*ande*⟩ (2.1.38, 3.11.9, 3.35.11, 3.45.13, 3.54.9): the spelling *ande* is not generally used by Dodesham. Spellings with *th* and final -*e* also occur frequently in G.[17]

The corrector has also made more substantial changes to the forms of certain words, which exhibit preferences for one form over another, or for one word over another similar word. The form *contrariou⟨snes⟩* is found five times with the ending so corrected; in each case C has *contrariouste* or its plural (*contrarioustes* or *contrarioustez*), which presumably originally stood in D, and G has *contrariousnes*.[18] Similarly, the

---

[16] At 3.53.31, however, an *e* has been written by the corrector in *natur⟨ely⟩*.

[17] Other changes to the orthography of the text include the following: *ch⟨ose⟩* 2.9.8; *cowches*, *w* altered from *u* 1.20.24; *ded⟨.⟩* ('dead'), *e* visible under erasure 3.49.1; *fl⟨y⟩eþ* 3.6.15, *fl⟨y⟩yng* 3.33.3; *fol⟨we⟩* 3.60.27; *ho⟨w⟩* 1.2.18, *howe*, *we* altered from *u* 1.13.30; ⟨*i*⟩*f*, *y* visible under erasure 3.8.22; *infirmite⟨es⟩* 3.45.19; ⟨*k*⟩*osse* 3.57.18; *l⟨a⟩mbe* 3.63.38; *le⟨e⟩ne* 1.14.11, 3.7.10; *ly⟨fe⟩* 1.22.29, 2.12.15; *l⟨y⟩fte* 3.48.9; *perpetu⟨all⟩* 3.7.31, *perpetu⟨e⟩ly* 3.55.11; *reioi⟨s⟩eþ*, *s* altered from *c* 3.59.23; *sor`o`ful* 1.20.35; *sotilte`e`s* 3.48.13; *swol⟨wyd⟩* 1.22.29; *þ⟨a⟩n* 1.2.8, 1.2.14, 1.2.19, 1.3.19, 1.3.20, 1.3.22, 1.3.24, 1.4.2, 1.4.6, 1.5.3, 3.36.4; *þyn* ⟨.⟩*eye*, *n* added on line 1.21.12, *þyn* ⟨.⟩*eye*, part of *n* visible under erasure 1.25.22; *vil⟨i⟩fie* 3.9.3; *whoule* ('howl'), *w* canc. 1.24.12; ⟨*y*⟩*euer* 2.10.25, ⟨*y*⟩*eue* 3.55.7, 3.57.7, 3.59.16, ⟨*y*⟩*euiþ* 3.59.15.

[18] At 3.7.3, 3.13.1, 3.13.4, 3.52.8, and 3.62.8.

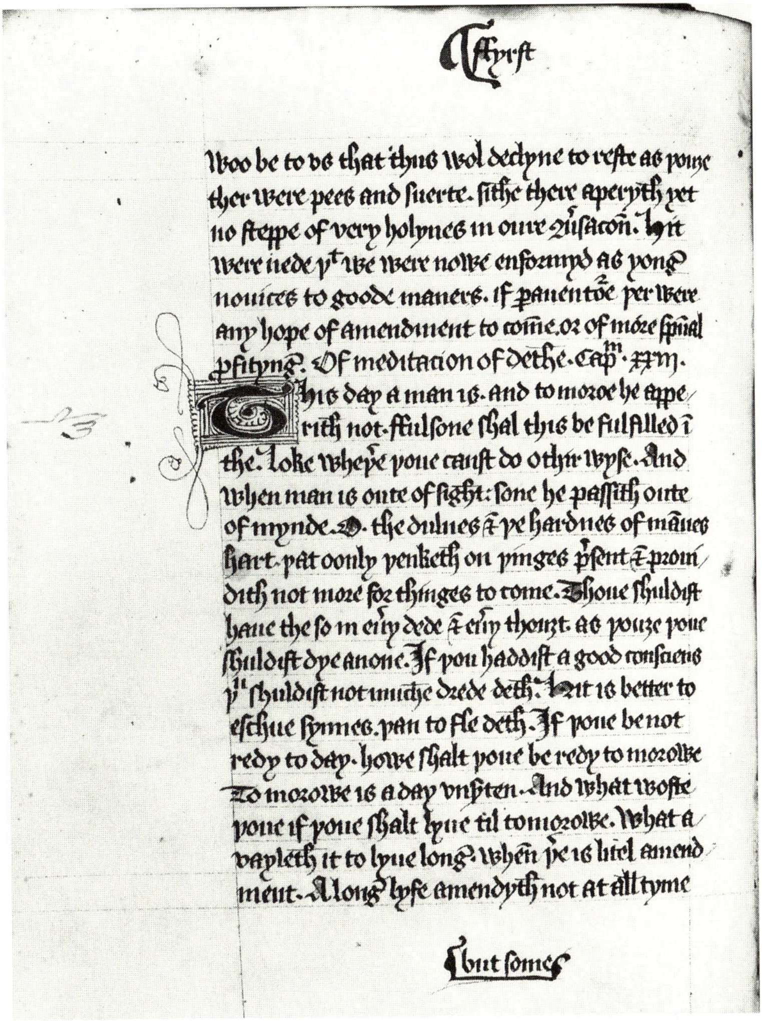

Woo be to þe þat þinє wol declyne to reste as þou3e
þer were pees and suerte. siþe þere aperyth yet
no steppe of very holynes in oure 2ufacon. Hit
were nede þt we were nowe enformyd as yong
nouices to good maners. if parauentre per were
any hope of amendment to come. or of more spiial
pfityng. Of meditacion of deþe. cap. xxm.

þis day a man is. And to morowe he appe
riþ not. ffulsone shal þis be fulfilled i
þe. loke where þou canst do oþir wyse. And
when man is oute of si3t: sone he passiþ oute
of mynde. ø. þe dulnes & þe hardnes of manes
hart. þat oonly þenkeþ on þinges present & proui
diþ not more for þinges to come. Þoue shuldist
haue þe so in eiry dede & eiry þou3t. as þou3e þou
shuldist dye anone. If þou haddist a good consciens
þu shuldist not muche drede deþ. Hit is better to
eschue synnes. þan to fle deþ. If þou be not
redy to day. howe shalt þou be redy to morowe
To morowe is a day vnstten. And what woste
þou if þou shalt lyue til tomorowe. What a
vayleth it to lyue long. when þe is litel amend
ment. Along lyfe amendyth not at all tyme

but some

Plate II
Glasgow, University Library, MS Hunter T. 6. 18, f. 24ᵛ (G)

noun *quiet* has ten times been corrected to a form of the type *quietnes*: the ending *-nes* or *-nesse* has been added by the corrector.[19] In each of these cases (except where C's text is lacking), C has *quiet* and G has *quietnes*. Thirdly, *slugged* and its derivatives *sluggedly* and *sluggednes* are ten times corrected over erasure to forms of the type *slugg⟨ush⟩* (once *slugg⟨usse⟩*), *slugg⟨usly⟩*, and *slugg⟨uss⟩ness*.[20] In each of these cases (except once where C's text is lacking) C has *slugged*, *sluggedly*, or *sluggednes* (which presumably originally stood in D), and G (except in two cases, where it has a different word altogether) has forms of the type *slugguse*, *sluggusly*, or *sluggusnes*, with or without *h*. In view of the possibility that G was copied from D, discussed in Part III below, these cases provide less good evidence that the corrections were made by Darker, because the occurrence of the corrected form in G could be as a result of copying from D and therefore not evidence for Darker's usual spelling. Nevertheless they are at least consistent with the possibility that the corrections are Darker's work.[21]

The palaeographical and orthographic characteristics of the corrections thus exhibit similarities with Darker's hand but do not provide conclusive evidence that they are his work. Given the variation possible within an individual scribe's spelling and handwriting in this period, however, one would not necessarily expect such evidence to be conclusive. What can be said is that many of the corrections which are written in brown ink have the same palaeographical characteristics as Darker's hand, and that there are certain orthographical similarities between the corrections and Darker's work. Moreover, although some of the brown corrections exhibit greater similarity to Darker's hand than others do, it does not seem possible to distinguish strata among them, partly because many of them are very short. In this edition, therefore, all of the brown corrections are assigned to the siglum D²; it is a reasonable assumption that the palaeographical and orthographic evidence suggests that some, if not all, of these corrections may be the work of Darker.

[19] At 1.9.4, 1.19.25, 1.20.28, 1.22.28, 2.6.4 (*vnquiete* G), 3.17.7, 3.25.7, 3.29.9, 3.31.10, and 3.56.5.

[20] At 1.18.17 (*slacke* G), 1.22.35, 1.25.6 (*slouthfull* G), 1.25.36, 3.3.9, 3.3.15; 3.21.8; 1.18.22, 1.18.23; and 3.30.1.

[21] Other examples of alterations in the form of words include the following: *accoun⟨tyd⟩*, *un* altered from *m* 1.2.15, *acco⟨wnte⟩* 1.2.17, *aco⟨un⟩te* 1.17.4, *acco⟨wnte⟩* 3.35.33; *afire*, *a* altered from *o* 3.2.17, *⟨a⟩ fyre* 3.15.13; *ali⟨enat⟩* 3.6.13, *⟨a⟩l⟨yenyd⟩* 3.58.7; *circuit⟨es⟩* 1.20.4; *cist⟨ercenses⟩* 1.25.35; *cl⟨ypp⟩ed* 2.9.22; *del⟨icates⟩* 1.24.24; *estym⟨att⟩* 2.11.26, *est⟨ymat⟩* 3.8.22; *ey`a´* 2.1.8; *me`n´* 3.3.12, 3.6.33, 3.21.17 (twice), 3.23.4, 3.35.26, 3.38.5; *mysch⟨aunces⟩* 3.22.14, 3.43.3; *nobl`n´esse* 3.9.11; *no`ne´* 1.13.8; *ref⟨uge⟩* 3.6.5, *refu⟨g⟩e* 3.64.13; *secre`te´* 1.13.8; *sh⟨uftyd⟩* 3.44.5; *suffi⟨r⟩|⟨.⟩aunce*, *s* visible under erasure 2.12.37.

II. SOURCE

A. AUTHORSHIP

This edition is not the place for a reappraisal of the various claims to the authorship of the *Imitatio*, which has been the subject of controversy since the early seventeenth century.[22] Nevertheless a brief account of the issue must be given, because the question of authorship is closely related to the equally controversial question of the relative priority of the various branches of the Latin textual tradition, and this has an important bearing on any attempt to discover what kind of Latin manuscript of the *Imitatio* was the immediate source of its first English translation.

The controversy over the authorship of the *Imitatio* has arisen because of the absence of a clear attribution in the manuscripts of the work.[23] The earliest dated manuscripts, many of which do not contain all four books of the text and do not bear the title *De Imitatione Christi*, do not mention the author's name;[24] later manuscripts attribute the work to a number of different authors, most commonly Thomas à Kempis (1379/80–1471), canon regular of the monastery of St Agnietenberg near Zwolle in the Netherlands,[25] and Jean Gerson (1363–1429), chancellor of the University of Paris.[26] Early printed editions are similarly divided, some attributing the work to Kempis, others to Gerson. Both these attributions have attracted considerable support over the centuries; that to Gerson, however, no longer enjoys

---

[22] On the controversy, see the article by A. Ampe, *DS* vii. 2338–55, which includes a bibliography to 1971. A fuller bibliography of the earlier stages of the controversy may be found in A. de Backer, *Essai bibliographique sur le livre 'De Imitatione Christi'* (Liège, 1864). For studies published since 1971, see the annual bibliographies in *OGE, ABB, AGKKN,* and *Kerktijd: Contactblad van de Vereniging voor Nederlandse Kerkgeschiedenis.*

[23] Huijben and Debongnie, pp. 75–88.

[24] Huijben and Debongnie provide a list of the earliest manuscripts (pp. 227–31): the earliest dated manuscript of Book I, Basle, University Library, MS A. xi. 67, is dated 1424; the earliest dated manuscript containing Books I–IV, Brussels, Bibliothèque Royale, MS 22084, is dated 1427. Thirty-eight manuscripts dated or datable between 1424 and 1439 are listed; none mentions the author's name.

[25] Huijben and Debongnie, p. 78: apart from the Kempis autograph, discussed below, the earliest dated manuscript attributing the *Imitatio* to Kempis is Munich, Bayerische Staatsbibliothek, MS lat. 4775, dated 1447: it is one of a group of early manuscripts of Bavarian origin (of which there are five datable before 1457) attributing the work to Kempis, or at least to a canon regular. On Kempis, see *DS* xv. 817–26.

[26] Huijben and Debongnie, pp. 84–6: the earliest dated manuscript attributing the *Imitatio* to Gerson is Paris, Bibliothèque Nationale, MS lat. 13597, dated 1460. On Gerson, see *DS* vi. 314–31.

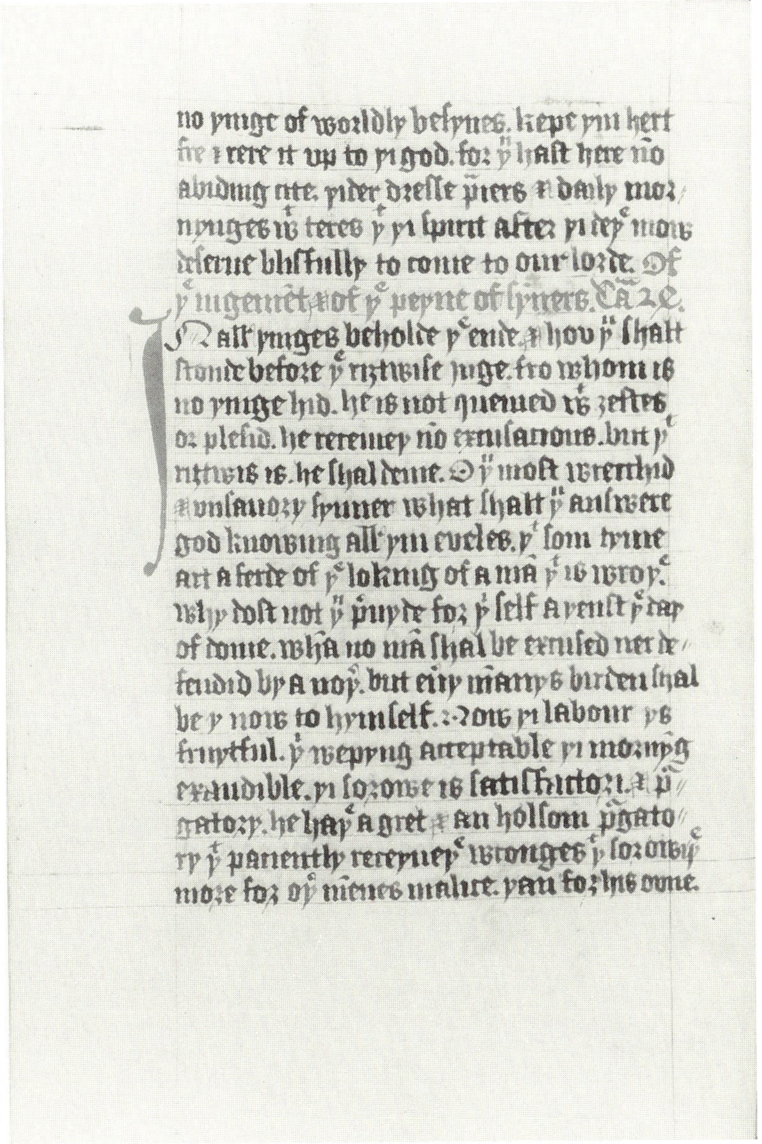
no þinge of worldly besynes. kepe þin hert
fre & rere it up to þi god. for þu hast here no
abiding cite. þider dresse þi pieres & daily mor
nynges wt teres þt þi spirit after þi deþe mow
deserve blisfully to come to our lorde. Of
þe iugement & of þe peyne of synners. Ca. 2e.
In all þinges beholde þe ende & hou þu shalt
stonde before þe riztwise iuge. fro whom is
no þinge hid. he is not quemed wt ziftes
or plesid. he receyveþ no excusaciouns. but þt
riztwis is. he shal deme. O þu most wretchid
& unsavory synner what shalt þu answere
god knowing all þin eueles. þt som tyme
art aferde of þe loking of a man þt is wroþe.
Why dost not þu purvey for þi self a yenst þe day
of dome. wha no man shal be excused ner de
fendid by a noþer. but euery mannys birden shal
be þi now to him self. Now þi labour ys
fruytful. þi wepyng acceptable þi mornyng
exaudible. þi sorowe is satisfactori & pur
gatory. he haþ a gret & an holsom purgato
ry þt paciently receyveþ wronges þe sorowiþ
more for oþer mennes malice. þan for his owne.

Plate III

Cambridge, Magdalene College, MS F. 4. 19, f. 25^{v} (M)

favour. As Jacques Huijben and Pierre Debongnie have shown, the *Imitatio* is not found in the early lists of Gerson's works and is different from them in style and tone, lacking Gerson's usual allusions to authorities and to his own works, his emphasis on system and method, and his precise terminology.[27] The attribution probably arose from the juxtaposition of the anonymous *Imitatio* and the works of Gerson in manuscript miscellanies;[28] it is rejected today by scholars both of Gerson (including his most recent editor) and of the *Imitatio*.[29]

It is probably fair to say that the attribution to Thomas à Kempis is that most favoured today. His case has been argued persuasively in 1957 in the most important post-war work on the authorship controversy, that by Huijben and Debongnie. The evidence in Kempis's favour is of various kinds; the most important piece of evidence, however, is the so-called 'autograph' manuscript, now Brussels, Bibliothèque Royale, MS 5855–61, which was the subject of an extensive study by L. M. J. Delaissé in 1956.[30] The condition of this manuscript has an important bearing on the Latin textual tradition in general. It was indisputably written by Thomas à Kempis and contains the four books of the *Imitatio* followed by nine other treatises, ending with the colophon: 'Finitus et completus anno domini M° CCCC° XLI° per manus fratris Thome Kempis in monte sancte Agnetis prope Zwollis.'[31] The manuscript shows signs of detailed and extensive correction, ranging from changes in punctuation to substitution of words and the erasure and addition of whole pages; the order in which the various works

[27] Huijben and Debongnie, pp. 331–49, esp. p. 337.

[28] See Huijben and Debongnie, p. 7 and n. 2; Bonardi and Lupo, i. 175, n. 1. In the catalogue of the library of Erfurt Charterhouse alone three manuscripts containing the *Imitatio* and a work by Gerson are mentioned (*MBDS* ii. 349, 353, 405); in particular, Gerson's *De Meditatione Cordis* is often associated with the *Imitatio*. It is possible that the *Imitatio* became associated with Gerson at the Council of Constance (1414–17), at which Gerson defended the Brethren of the Common Life against the criticisms of the Dominican Matthew Grabon: see C. M. D. Crowther, *Unity, Heresy and Reform, 1378–1460: The Conciliar Response to the Great Schism*, Documents of Medieval History, 3 (London, 1977), p. 19.

[29] J. Gerson, *Œuvres complètes*, ed. P. Glorieux, 10 vols (Paris, 1960–73), viii. vii; see also D. C. Brown, *Pastor and Laity in the Theology of Jean Gerson* (Cambridge, 1987), pp. 314–15, n. 92; Huijben and Debongnie, pp. 319–53; Bonardi and Lupo, i. 170–6; and Ampe, *Imitation*, pp. 56–63.

[30] A facsimile has been printed by C. Ruelens, *The Imitation of Christ: Being the Autograph Manuscript of Thomas à Kempis, 'De Imitatione Christi' Reproduced in Facsimile from the Original Preserved in the Royal Library at Brussels* (London, 1879).

[31] Delaissé, ii. 548.

occur in the manuscript, including that of the four books of the *Imitatio*, has also been altered.

Delaissé drew three conclusions from his study of the manuscript. First, that the manuscript was in preparation for a long period of time, at least twenty years, before it was assembled in its present form and the 1441 colophon written: this is shown by a gradual enlargement in the size of Kempis's handwriting, confirmed by comparison with other dated manuscripts which he copied.[32] This explains the existence of other manuscript copies of parts of the *Imitatio* dated as early as 1424. Secondly, changes to the titles of the four books, and the way in which they are listed on the contents page of the manuscript, indicate that Kempis originally conceived of them as independent treatises, rather than as component parts of a single work.[33] This explains why so many of the early manuscripts lack the title *De Imitatione Christi* and contain only Book I, or Books I to III. Thirdly, the appearance of the manuscript suggests that Kempis was the author, not merely the scribe of the text, for it is the author who would be most likely to have taken the trouble to make so many detailed corrections.[34]

Delaissé's conclusions were questioned in 1964 by Piergiovanni Bonardi and Tiburzio Lupo, who do not believe that Kempis was the author of the *Imitatio*. They interpret the phrase *finitus et completus* in the colophon as an indication that Thomas à Kempis was the scribe, rather than the author, and argue that the revisions are not those of an author, but those of a distracted copyist;[35] they also question Delaissé's view of the manuscript as a working copy for personal use, asking how it came to be copied as early as 1424 if it were kept in Kempis's cell.[36] While Bonardi and Lupo's work shows that the evidence of the autograph may be questioned, however, they have not succeeded in refuting Delaissé's view; in particular, they offer no evidence for supposing that the other nine treatises in the manuscript are not by Kempis (a point about which there is no serious doubt),[37] and so are

---

[32] Delaissé, i. 21–2.

[33] Delaissé, i. 50.

[34] Delaissé, i. 118.

[35] This point has also been made by B. Spaapen, 'Kanttekeningen bij de diplomatische uitgave van hs. Brussel 5855–61', *OGE* 32 (1958), 5–55, 128 (see e.g. p. 18).

[36] Bonardi and Lupo, i. 196–205.

[37] K. Hirsche, *Prolegomena zu einer neuen Ausgabe der 'Imitatio Christi' nach dem Autograph des Thomas von Kempen*, 3 vols (Berlin, 1873–94), ii. 1–88, quotes passages from each of them, and demonstrates their similarity to each other and to the *Imitatio* on grounds of style, particularly rhythm and rhyme, and content. The treatises are listed,

unable to prove that *finitus et completus* cannot introduce an authorial signature; moreover, they do not answer Delaissé's work on the corrections in the manuscript in any detail.

The historical evidence in Kempis's favour has been fully described by Huijben and Debongnie:[38] it includes the incipits and explicits of manuscripts of the *Imitatio*,[39] fifteenth-century chronicles and historical works,[40] library catalogues,[41] and notes in manuscripts of Kempis's other works,[42] all identifying him as the *Imitatio*'s author. Bonardi and Lupo have sought to cast doubt on this evidence, but their arguments are not generally convincing: they argue that there was a conspiracy in the Windesheim diocese to claim the work for Kempis, so that indications in manuscripts and texts from Windesheim are partisan and therefore not to be trusted.[43] They offer no evidence for such a conspiracy, however, and their view that the more precise a piece of evidence is, the more partisan and therefore the less reliable it must be, is not an adequate response to Huijben and Debongnie's work.[44]

Finally, it may be argued that the spirituality of the *Imitatio* is in keeping with the *devotio moderna* of the late fourteenth- and fifteenth-century

---

along with the four books of the *Imitatio*, in the first complete list of Kempis's works (The Hague, Koninklijke Bibliotheek, MS 75 G. 70, ff. 228ᵛ–31ʳ), dated 1488 (Huijben and Debongnie, pp. 134–6); it does not seem that they have ever been ascribed to anyone else.

[38] pp. 47–159.

[39] See above, p. xxx, n. 25; the oldest Dutch translation of Book I of the *Imitatio*, made by Godevard van den Briele in Eemstein in 1428, states that the work was originally written in Latin by a canon regular (Huijben and Debongnie, pp. 57–9).

[40] For example, Jan Busch's *Liber de viris illustribus ordinis canonicorum regularium monasterii in Windesheim*, in the second edition of which, dated 1464, Kempis is described as author of the *Imitatio*; Busch, who was one of the most active figures in the Windesheim diocese, would almost certainly have known him (Huijben and Debongnie, pp. 89–101). Hermann Ryd, in his *Descriptio monasteriorum congregationis Windesemensis*, relates a meeting he had with Kempis in 1454, and describes him as author of the *Imitatio* (Huijben and Debongnie, pp. 101–2).

[41] There are a number of these from the Windesheim diocese, dating from the late fifteenth and early sixteenth centuries (Huijben and Debongnie, pp. 127–59).

[42] For example, Cambrai, Bibliothèque de la Ville, MS 835, dated 1438, which contains a number of of Kempis's works; the incipit to his *Libellus Spiritualis Exercitii* states that it was published (*editus*) by brother Thomas, a canon regular in the Windesheim diocese, who also compiled (*composuit*) the four treatises of which the first begins *Qui sequitur me* (Huijben and Debongnie, pp. 69–74, esp. p. 70, n. 2). On other manuscripts containing biographical notes on Kempis describing him as author of the *Imitatio*, see Huijben and Debongnie, pp. 105–25.

[43] Bonardi and Lupo, i. 205–52.

[44] See, for example, Bonardi and Lupo, i. 220.

Netherlands. According to R. R. Post, the distinctive characteristic of this movement, inner devotion, was understood by its practitioners as

a deep consciousness of the personal relationship with God and a perpetual and intensive striving to direct all their work, prayer and spiritual exercises to God. This presupposes, however, the practice of the virtues of humility, obedience, purity, mutual love and mortification, out of love of God. . . . The imitation of Christ helps us to make progress along this road, hence the constant meditation on Christ's life and passion.[45]

This is consistent with the emphasis on the inner life in the *Imitatio*, and its stress on the importance of dependence on grace.

In rejecting the view that Kempis was the author of the *Imitatio*, Bonardi and Lupo argue that the attributions to Jean Gerson in some of the manuscripts of the text result from a tradition referring originally not to the chancellor of the University of Paris, but to one Giovanni Gersen, supposedly abbot of the Benedictine abbey of Santo Stefano at Vercelli between 1227 and 1243, and that Gersen was the author of the work.[46] The attribution to Gersen was first published by the Benedictine abbot Constantin Cajetan in the preface to his edition of the *Imitatio* of 1616, based on the *Codex Aronensis*,[47] which attributes the *Imitatio* to one Gersen or Gessen, *abbas*. Bonardi and Lupo argue that the *Aronensis* is datable on palaeographical grounds to the period 1330–60,[48] and that there are two other early manuscripts datable on palaeographical grounds to the fourteenth or even the thirteenth centuries: the *Bobbiensis* (1350–1410) and the *De Advocatis* (1280–1330).[49] Clearly, if any of these dates is correct, the *Imitatio* could not have been written by Kempis, who was born in 1379/80, but in fact the style of the script of these three manuscripts strongly suggests that they were written in the fifteenth century.[50] There is, indeed, no certain

---

[45] R. R. Post, *The Modern Devotion: Confrontation with Reformation and Humanism*, Studies in Medieval and Reformation Thought, 3 (Leiden, 1968), p. 679. On the *devotio moderna*, see also S. Axters, *The Spirituality of the Old Low Countries*, trans. D. Attwater (London, 1954), and A. Hyma, *The Christian Renaissance: A History of the 'Devotio Moderna'*, second edition (Hamden, Conn., 1965), although Hyma's theory of the origin of the *Imitatio* has not found general acceptance.

[46] Bonardi and Lupo, i. 253–87.

[47] Turin, Biblioteca Nazionale, MS E. vi. 12; Puyol also used this manuscript as the base text of his edition of the *Imitatio* (Paris, 1886).

[48] ii. 17–26.

[49] Respectively Paris, Bibliothèque Nationale, MS lat. 13598 (Bonardi and Lupo, ii. 26–8), and Vercelli, Archivio Capitolare Metropolitano, MS B (Bonardi and Lupo, ii. 7–14). Lupo used the *De Advocatis* as the base text in his edition of the *Imitatio* (Vatican City, 1982).

[50] 'Der Codex de Advocatis trägt alle Merkmale der schönen italienischen Hss. der 15.

evidence that Gersen even existed: no surviving medieval document refers to an abbot of Vercelli of that name.[51] It is most likely that the attribution to Gersen arose out of variation in the spelling of the name of Jean Gerson (the spelling *Gersen* is used in some of the early dated Italian manuscripts to denote the chancellor of Paris).[52]

Although the case for Kempis is not universally accepted, then, and it is possible that the author of the *Imitatio* was someone other than the three candidates discussed here, there is certainly a good deal more evidence for him than for anyone else; moreover, the hypothesis that the Kempis manuscript is the archetype of all other surviving copies helps to explain certain aspects of the textual tradition.[53]

B. TEXT

The *Imitatio* survives in over eight hundred manuscripts, and no full collation has been made.[54] The closest approximation to such a collation

Jhs. an sich' (H. Denifle, 'Kritische Bemerkungen zur Gersen–Kempisfrage', *ZKT* 6 (1882), 692–718 (p. 696); 7 (1883), 692–743, quoted by Ampe, *Imitation*, p. 107). In the *De Advocatis* manuscript, the end of the *Imitatio* is followed on the same folio by the beginning of the *De Meditatione Cordis* of Gerson, written in an italic humanist script; although the *Imitatio* is written in a display script, there are a number of similarities in the forms of certain letters, particularly the minuscule *g* and the ampersand (see Bonardi and Lupo, ii, tavola 6). I understand that Professor A. C. de la Mare dates all three manuscripts to the fifteenth century, detecting humanist influence on the forms of *d*, *g*, and ampersand in the text of the *Imitatio* in the *De Advocatis*; *a*, *d*, and *g* in the *Bobbiensis*; and long final *s* and *g* in the *Aronensis*; and that Professor Mirella Ferrari of the Università del Sacro Cuore, Milan, dates them after the Council of Constance (A. I. Doyle, private communication).

[51] Bonardi and Lupo, i. 273.

[52] See Ampe, *Imitation*, pp. 63–77, for an explanation of how this is likely to have occurred.

[53] In the 1940s J. van Ginneken argued, with very little evidence, that the *Imitatio* was originally written by Geert Groote and revised by Kempis; this argument has been refuted by Huijben and Debongnie (pp. 273–318). In 1973 Ampe suggested a theory, based on a note in certain manuscripts describing the text as *editus per quemdam Cartusiensis in Rheno*, that the *Imitatio* was written in a Rhineland charterhouse *c.* 1370 (Ampe, *Imitation*, pp. 113–24). He did not develop the argument at great length, however, and has now returned to the traditional view that Kempis is the author: see Thomas à Kempis, *De Navolging van Christus naar de Brusselse Autograaf vertaald door Gerard Wijdeveld, ingeleid en toegelicht door Bernard Spaapen en Albert Ampe: Inleiding tot de tweede uitgave* (Antwerp, 1985), pp. 28–42. A new critical edition of Kempis's *Opera Omnia* is in progress at the Titus Brandsma Instituut in Nijmegen as part of the *Opera Litteraria Devotionis Modernae* project: 'it is hoped that the process of editing the entire Kempis corpus, as well as the new techniques available for stylistic and literary analysis, may . . . assist in an eventual reconsideration of the vexed question of the genesis and authorship of the most famous of the treatises attributed to him' (*Thesaurus Thomae a Kempis curantibus Paul Chandler et CETEDOC*, Thesaurus Patrum Latinorum (Turnhout, 1994), p. vii). See above, p. ix, n. 7.

[54] S. G. Axters has identified 848 manuscripts: see his *De Imitatione Christi: Een*

is the work of P. E. Puyol, who collated sixty-seven selected manuscripts at the end of the nineteenth century.[55] Puyol held that Gersen was the author of the *Imitatio*, and based his edition on the *Codex Aronensis*, which he believed to be the earliest and best Italian manuscript; nevertheless many of his conclusions about the grouping of the manuscripts have been accepted by scholars of all parties. He divided the manuscripts which he collated into *classes*, *genres*, and *espèces*, according to key variants: there are two classes, A (Italian manuscripts) and B (transalpine manuscripts), which are divided into five genera, three in class A and two in class B; the genera are subdivided into twenty-one species. Many of the variants which separate the classes and genera from each other are slight (for example the inversion of two words, or the omission of a conjunction), but they are large in number and occur consistently. Puyol's system may be set out diagrammatically as follows:

Classes	A				B		
Genres	F	G	H	Hybrid	I	K	Hybrid
Espèces	a bc	de	fghi	l	mnopq	rsuv	xy

This diagram is a simplification, however, as the textual tradition is not the same for all four books of the *Imitatio*.[56]

Puyol's belief in the Italian origin of the *Imitatio* is reflected in his choice of sigla: he maintained that the Italian manuscripts (A) represented a better text than the transalpine manuscripts (B). His justification of the superiority of class A was rather sketchy, however, and it has been refuted by G. Udny Yule, who examined Puyol's 364 A–B variants from various aspects: assonance, symmetry, omission, dittography, style, sense, and grammar.[57] Yule judged that in 159 of these cases, one reading was superior to the other, and that in 139 cases (87% of those in which one reading was at fault), it was the A reading that was at fault. These results, which have been confirmed by a similar analysis by

handschrifteninventaris bij het vijfhondersdte verjaren van Thomas Hemerken van Kempen (Kempen, 1971), and 'Bijdrage tot de inventarizering van de *Imitatio*-handschriften: Addenda en dubia', *NAK* 56 (1975), 141–58.

[55] In addition to Puyol, *Paléographie*, see also his *Descriptions bibliographiques des manuscrits et des principales éditions du livre 'De Imitatione Christi'* (Paris, 1898) and *Variantes du livre 'De Imitatione Christi'* (Paris, 1898).

[56] Lupo's critical edition of the *Imitatio* is based on a modification of Puyol's system by R. Pitigliani (see Lupo's edition, pp. xiii–xiv).

[57] 'Puyol's Classes A and B of Texts of the *De Imitatione Christi*: A Critical Examination of his Evidence and Conclusions', *RTAM* 14 (1947), 65–88 (pp. 85, 87).

Huijben and Debongnie, constitute a strong argument for the priority of class B.[58] Bonardi and Lupo, holding with Puyol that A is superior, have sought to question Yule's approach, arguing that some of his judgements based on symmetry and style are subjective; they have not succeeded in refuting the general trend in favour of B established by Yule, however, and offer neither a detailed rebuttal of his judgements nor an analysis of their own in favour of A.[59]

It is generally accepted that the detail of the stemma is different for the different books of the *Imitatio*, because the four books were not always circulated together. Only in the case of Books II and III are the manuscripts divided into classes A and B as in the above diagram: in the case of Book I (which was often circulated independently) manuscripts of genera F and I are grouped together against those of genera G, H, and K.[60] In the case of Books II and III, Huijben and Debongnie have applied Yule's method to the 89 variants separating genus I from genus K: of the 46 of these variants where one reading is superior to the other, in all but one instance it is the K reading that is superior. A similar conclusion was reached in the case of Book I: Huijben and Debongnie follow van Ginneken in referring to genera F and I as class P, and genera G, H, and K as class Q, and applying Yule's method to the 39 variants separating P from Q, they find that Q is always superior.[61] The archetype, therefore, belongs to genus K, and this supports the attribution to Kempis, since the K manuscripts are mostly either from the Low Countries or Carthusian, and include the autograph (s2 in Puyol's notation).[62]

Huijben and Debongnie's conclusions about the priority of class B for Books II and III and class Q for Book I are supported by the way in which these classes are represented in the earliest dated manuscripts:[63] the first manuscript to contain all four books, dated 1427, contains a text

---

[58] Huijben and Debongnie, pp. 202–9.

[59] Bonardi and Lupo, i. 128–31; see the review of Lupo's edition by E. Menestò, *SM*, serie terza, 26 (1985), 841–3.

[60] The different stemmata of the different books of the *Imitatio* are comparable to the textual complications of books copied by the *pecia* system: as R. H. and M. A. Rouse have shown, 'the unit one must deal with, in establishing the text of a university book, is the *pecia*, rather than the codex' (*Preachers, Florilegia and Sermons: Studies on the 'Manipulus Florum' of Thomas of Ireland*, Pontifical Institute of Mediaeval Studies, Studies and Texts, 47 (Toronto, 1979), p. 177).

[61] Huijben and Debongnie, pp. 211–25.

[62] It is impractical to take the analysis further by applying Yule's method to the four species of genus K, *r*, *s*, *u*, and *v*, since there are too few variants separating them.

[63] Huijben and Debongnie, pp. 227–31.

of Book I of class Q and a text of Books II to IV of class B;[64] the first
dated manuscript to contain a text of class A, dated 1436, however, is the
twenty-eighth manuscript listed.[65]

A final important question in connection with the Latin textual
tradition concerns the revisions and corrections found in the autograph
manuscript. Since the earliest dated manuscript of the complete text is
dated 1427 and the autograph's colophon is dated 1441, it might be
expected that the early manuscripts would represent the autograph text
before it was corrected. Delaissé believed that any manuscript dated
before 1441 would present a different text from that now found in the
autograph because Kempis continued to work on his text up to that date,
and he showed from a palaeographical analysis of the autograph five
different stages in the evolution of the title of Book I: some of the earlier
versions are also found in other manuscripts.[66] Huijben and Debongnie,
however, found no correspondence between the distinctive variants of any
of the other classes and genera and the corrections in the autograph.[67]

If this conclusion is accepted, it would appear that Kempis had
substantially finished work on the *Imitatio* by 1427, and that the *finitus et
completus* of the 1441 colophon in the autograph manuscript refers to the
final assembly of the quires containing the four books of the *Imitatio*
with those containing other treatises to form the complete volume.
Kempis had meanwhile given the quires containing the *Imitatio* to copy,
but they were not bound together or marked with his name: this
explains why the early manuscripts are anonymous, and why different
selections of books are found. By 1441 he had regained his quires, and
bound them together with others he had written in the meantime to
form a complete volume, which he signed and dated.

C. THE ENGLISH RECENSION

There survive twenty Latin manuscripts of English origin, here referred
to as insular manuscripts so as to avoid confusion the with manuscripts

---

[64] Brussels, Bibliothèque Royale, MS 22084.

[65] Milan, Biblioteca Ambrosiana, MS 36. This is also the first dated manuscript to
number the four books as *liber primus*, etc., a characteristic of the Italian manuscripts,
rather than presenting them as separate treatises, as in the earlier transalpine manuscripts.

[66] Delaissé, i. 75.

[67] With reference to Book I, they write: 'Dans les corrections de l'autographe, il n'en est
aucune qui soit en rapport avec le texte P; aucune variante P ne s'y retrouve, aucune n'y
laisse un vestige quelconque, sous forme de rature ou de surcharge': in general, 'sauf rares
exceptions, les variantes du texte s'expliquent par l'évolution naturelle des copies' (pp. 224,
235).

of the first English translation.[68] The earliest dated insular manuscript
is Oxford, Magdalen College, MS 93, largely written by John Dygon of
the reclusory at Sheen: at the end of Book I there is a colophon to the
effect that Dygon finished copying that book in 1438. Roger Lovatt has
described the remainder of the text as follows:

After a blank folio Book II begins on a new quire in a different hand, but this
second hand has left various gaps in the text which have been filled in by
Dygoun. Another blank folio precedes Book III which follows the same pattern
as Book II until the middle of Chapter 30, with Dygoun filling in the passages
left blank by the second scribe. Then, from the middle of Chapter 30, Dygoun's
hand completes Book III. Unfortunately the last folio of Book III has
subsequently been removed from the manuscript and hence any colophon that
might have indicated the date of its completion is now missing.[69]

It may be concluded that Dygon first obtained access to a copy of Book
I, which he copied in 1438, and then acquired a text of Books II and III,
which he corrected and completed at some point between then and
1450, the approximate date of his death.[70] There survive four insular
manuscripts containing Book I alone (of which one, Cambridge, Trinity
College, MS 365, contains only chapters 1–13), one containing Books
III and IV, and fifteen containing Books I to III. Most of these
manuscripts bear the title *Musica Ecclesiastica*,[71] and all but two of

---

[68] Seventeen of them are described by Lovatt (pp. 117–20; see also pp. 100–6). To these
should be added three manuscripts identified by Ampe, 'Verspreiding', p. 167: Brussels,
Bibliothèque Royale, MS IV. 135; Cologne, Stadtarchiv, MS GB f° 27; and Madrid,
Biblioteca Nacional, MS 4311 (*olim* P. 133), all either of English origin or copied from
English exemplars. See below, p. xlvi.

[69] Lovatt, p. 102. On the Magdalen manuscript, see also W. A. B. Coolidge, 'The
Magdalen MS of the *Imitation*, 1438', *N&Q*, Sixth Series, 3 (1881), 181–2, 202–4, 222–4,
and A. G. Watson, *Catalogue of Dated and Datable Manuscripts c. 435–1600 in Oxford
Libraries*, 2 vols (Oxford, 1984), i. 138 (no. 827), ii, pl. 386 (an illustration of Dygon's hand
earlier in the manuscript).

[70] At least part of the *Imitatio* must have been known in England before 1438, as an
extract from it (Book I, chapter 5) is found in the *Donatus Devotionis* (2.3.2); this
compilation was made in 1430, so that 'this must be the earliest *datable* evidence of the
Imitatio in England' (A. I. Doyle, 'The European Circulation of Three Latin Spiritual
Texts', in *Latin and Vernacular: Studies in Late-Medieval Texts and Manuscripts*, ed. A. J.
Minnis, York Manuscripts Conferences: Proceedings Series, 1 (Cambridge, 1989), pp. 129–
46 (p. 138 and nn. 57–8); Doyle also notes that there is a copy of Book I of the *Donatus* in
Oxford, Magdalen College, MS 141, which belonged to Dygon). Two extracts from Book
II of the *Imitatio* (chapters 12 and 11) are also found in Dublin, Trinity College, MS. 321
(C. 4. 9), ff. 113ᵛ–15ʳ, copied in England in the mid-fifteenth century (M. L. Colker,
*Trinity College Library, Dublin: Descriptive Catalogue of the Medieval and Renaissance Latin
Manuscripts*, 2 vols (Aldershot, 1991), i. 321).

[71] The origin of the *Musica Ecclesiastica* title (which was also adopted in three English

the manuscripts containing Books I to III number the five prayers in
Book III as separate chapters, giving sixty-four chapters rather than the
usual fifty-nine; both these characteristics are distinctive of the insular
recension of the text. In order to ascertain where the insular manuscripts
stand in relation to the Latin textual tradition as a whole, Oxford,
Bodleian Library, MSS Laud misc. 215 (L) and Selden supra 93 (S)
were taken as a sample. The conclusions were as follows.

1. *The insular manuscripts belong to class B*

In 93 of the 115 variants listed by Puyol as distinguishing class A from
class B in Book II (80%), the two insular manuscripts collated have the
B reading, as in the following examples:

2.3.2 magis prodest] BLS, plus prodest A   2.4.5 libertate perfrueris] BLS
libertate frueris A   2.6.15 requirit gloriam] BLS, quaerit gloriam A
2.6.24 signum est] BLS, indicium est A   2.8.20 bene vivere] BLS, diu
vivere A   2.10.27 pro gratia data] BLS, pro gratia dei data A
2.12.25 extra converte te intra] BS, extra conuerte te iuxta L, extra et intra A
2.12.40 ut se sine] BLS, ut se non sine A   2.12.52 gloriam promerendam]
BLS, gloriam quae revelabitur in nobis promerendam A   2.12.59 quanta
quoque] BLS, quanta aedificatio esset A.[72]

translations of the *Imitatio* published in the late nineteenth and early twentieth centuries:
see Bibliography) is obscure. The theory discussed by Bonardi and Lupo (ii. 272) that it
arose out of the illustration in London, British Library, MS Royal 7 B. VIII (described
below, p. xlviii), is impossible because the Royal manuscript is later than the Magdalen
manuscript, which identifies the *Imitatio* as *Musica Ecclesiastica*, and in the Royal
manuscript the title clearly applies to the text rather than the illustration; no doubt the
illustration was chosen to fit the title of the text. Delaissé's suggestion (i. 90), that the title
was first used in the Bruges Charterhouse and thence passed to England, rests on the
incorrect assumption that Brussels, Bibliothèque Royale, MS 15138 is of Belgian
provenance; in fact it is insular (see below, p. xlvi, n. 88). A more likely theory is proposed
by Ampe, who has observed that Heinrich Kalkar's *Cantuagium* is listed in the catalogue of
the library at Erfurt Charterhouse as *Cantuagium, id est musica ecclesiastica* (*MBDS* ii. 341).
Ampe suggests that this title could have been transferred to the *Imitatio* as a result of the
juxtaposition of the *Imitatio* and the *Cantuagium*, bearing the *Musica Ecclesiastica* title, in
the same manuscript miscellany ('Verspreiding', pp. 170–1). This is possible, as there are
several manuscripts which contain the *Imitatio* together with Kalkar's works, for example,
Brussels, Bibliothèque Royale, MS 14069–88 (Huijben and Debongnie, pp. 62–3), and four
manuscripts listed in the Erfurt catalogue (*MBDS*, ii. 342–3, 352, 356, 405); indeed, a
work often attributed to Kalkar, the *Exercitatorium Monachale* (also known as the *Tractatus
de cottidiano holocausto spiritualis exercitii* or the *Speculum Peccatorum*), appears in some
manuscripts as Book II of the *Imitatio*: see Huijben and Debongnie, pp. 7 (and n. 2), 41; H.
Rüthing, *Der Kartäuser Heinrich Egher von Kalkar, 1328–1408*, Veröffentlichungen des
Max-Planck-Instituts für Geschichte, 18, Studien zur Germania Sacra, 8 (Göttingen,
1967), pp. 150–4; *DS* vii. 188–91. For a further indication of a possible connection between
the English recension and Erfurt Charterhouse, see below, pp. xliv–xlv.

[72] The lemmata are quoted from Puyol, *Paléographie*, pp. 80–9.

The reverse situation, with L and S agreeing with A against B, occurs only once; in the remaining 21 cases L and S are divided, but usually one of them has the B reading.

The first English translation was also made from a Latin text of class B. Out of 43 cases in Book II where it was discernible whether the translator was following a text containing an A or a B reading, and there were no variants among the manuscripts of the translation to affect the issue, in 37 cases (86%) the translation was closer to B, as in the following examples (for the sigla used for the manuscripts of the translation, see above, p. xviii):

2.8.20 bene vivere] B, diu vivere A, *English* welle lyffe CDMG   2.8.21 confidis aut laetaris] B, confidis et laetaris A, *English* truste or be gladde CDMG   2.8.30 deum gerere] B, jesum gerere A, *English* bere to god CDMG   2.9.23 in fervore et interdum in frigiditate] B, in frigiditate et interdum in fervore A, *English* in feruoure and sumtyme in coldenesse CDMG   2.10.27 pro gratia data] B, pro gratia dei data A, *English* for the grace yivon CDMG   2.11.10 ipsum in omni tribulatione] B, ipsum in tribulatione A, *English* him in every tribulacion CDMG   2.11.29 tunc vere] B, tunc vero A, *English* when he begynneþ verily CDMG   2.12.12 ut et tu tuam] B, ut tu etiam A, *English* þat þou shuldest bere thi CDMG   2.12.52 gloriam promerendam] B, gloriam quae revelabitur in nobis promerendam A, *English* the glory þat is to come CDMG.[73]

In the case of Book I, the main division is between classes P and Q. Huijben and Debongnie list 38 variants which distinguish between these two classes, and these too were collated with the two sample insular manuscripts L and S, together with two sample insular manuscripts containing Book I alone, Oxford, Bodleian Library, MSS Bodley 632 (Ω) and Digby 37 (Δ). In 23 cases (60%) the four sample manuscripts agree with P against Q, as in the following examples:

1.6.5 indignatur] Q, dedignatur PLSΩΔ   1.12.5 multas humanas consolationes] Q, multas consolationes PLSΩΔ   1.13.28 quatenus nos in omni tribulatione dignetur] Q, quatenus dignetur in omni tribulatione nos PLSΩΔ   1.13.28 dictum pauli] Q, dictum sancti pauli PLSΩΔ   1.18.19 regula magistri in omnibus effloruit] Q, regula in omnibus effloruit PLSΩΔ   1.24.34 placebit] Q, valebit PLSΔ, valebunt Ω   1.24.36 quid possis postea] Q, quid possis pati postea PLSΩΔ.[74]

---

[73] The lemmata are quoted from Puyol, *Paléographie*, pp. 80–9.
[74] The lemmata are quoted from Huijben and Debongnie, p. 212.

The reverse situation, with all the manuscripts agreeing with Q against P, occurs only once; in the remaining 14 cases, while not all of the insular manuscripts agree with P, they are generally closer to it than to Q; in some of these instances not all of the insular manuscripts provide a legible text. Since some of the variants are so slight that they could easily occur accidentally, it is reasonable to conclude that these four insular manuscripts are to be placed in class P rather than class Q.

The first English translation was also compared with the P and Q readings in each of the above 38 cases. There were 12 cases where the reading which the author of the translation is likely to have had in his exemplar was discernible (and no variants in the Middle English were in question); of these, in 9 cases (75% of those discernible), the translation agrees with the P reading:

1.2.0 sentire] Q, scire P, *English* knowynge CDMG   1.2.18 si videris alium] Q, si videris aliquem P, *English* if þou see any man CDMG 1.6.5 indignatur] Q, dedignatur P, *English* haþe disdeigne CDMG 1.11.17 profectus quotidie] Q, profectus noster quotidie P, *English* oure profit-inge . . . daily CDMG   1.13.10 bonum felicitatis nostrae perdidimus] Q, bonum felicitatis perdidimus P, *English* we loste þe gode of felycite CDMG   1.18.19 regula magistri in omnibus effloruit] Q, regula in omnibus effloruit P, *English* vnder rewle floured in hem alle CDMG 1.23.22 fiduciam feliciter moriendi] Q, fiduciam moriendi P, *English* truste to dye CDMG   1.24.34 placebit] Q, valebit P, *English* avayle CDMG   1.24.36 quid possis postea] Q, quid possis pati postea P, *English* what thou mowe suffre aftirwarde CDMG.[75]

It is reasonable to conclude that the translation too, like the four sample insular Latin manuscripts, is to be placed in class P rather than class Q.

2. The insular manuscripts belong to genus I

Since the *Musica Ecclesiastica* recension has a text of class B for Book II and class P for Book I, it is likely to belong to genus I, since that is the only genus common to both B and P. An analysis both of the sample insular manuscripts and of the translation confirms that this is the case. The following key variants distinguish between I and K:

2.8.14 pauperrimus est qui vivit sine iesu et ditissimus qui bene est cum iesu] AK, *om.* I   3.35.35 horum memento fili mi verborum] AK, *om.* I 3.62.3 si amplius fuisset commoveri non debuisses] AK, *om.* I.[76]

---

[75] The lemmata are quoted from Huijben and Debongnie, p. 212.
[76] Huijben and Debongnie, p. 210.

Each of these three verses is omitted in manuscripts of class I; they are also omitted in the fifteen insular manuscripts which contain Books I to III and in the first English translation. That the *Musica Ecclesiastica* recension belongs to genus I is confirmed by a more detailed examination of the 27 variants listed by Puyol as characteristic of the separation between I and K in Book II. In 17 of these cases (60%) the two sample insular manuscripts, L and S, agree with I against K, as in the following examples:

2.3.1 tene te] K, pone te IALS   2.3.4 ad bonum convertit] KA, ad bonum trahit ILS   2.5.1 non possumus] KA, non debemus ILS   2.6.27 cum deo intus nec] KA, cum deo nec ILS   2.12.36 graviores cruces] KA, altiores cruces ILS.[77]

In 5 cases both insular manuscripts share the K reading, and in 5 they have different readings which, however, are generally closer to I than to K.

There are 17 of these variants in which the reading of the translator's exemplar is discernible (and there are no variants in the English which affect the issue): of these, in 14 cases (80% of those discernible) the translation agrees with the I reading, as in the following examples:

2.3.1 tene te] K, pone te IA, *English* sette thiselfe CDMG   2.3.4 ad bonum convertit] KA, ad bonum trahit I, *English* draweþ . . . to gode CDMG   2.5.1 non possumus] KA, non debemus I, *English* we oweþ not CDMG   2.6.11 comitatur tristitia] KA, sequitur tristitia I, *English* sorowe foloweth CDMG   2.6.17 et pacatus] KA, et placatus I, *English* and plesed CDMG   2.12.36 graviores cruces] KA, altiores cruces I, *English* þe higher crosse C, þe heyer crosses DMG.[78]

In two cases the translation agrees with the K reading, and in one case the Latin manuscripts do not split along I/K lines.

From an examination of the text of Books I and II, then, it may be concluded that the insular manuscripts and the Middle English translation reproduce a text of class B, genus I. Two further attempts were made to ascertain more precisely the antecedents of the *Musica Ecclesiastica* recension. First, an attempt was made to locate the *Musica Ecclesiastica* recension among the four species of genus I: *m*, *n*, *o*, *p*, *q*, and *r*. This proved fruitless: it evidently belongs to none of the species identified by Puyol. Secondly, the translation was compared with

[77] The lemmata are quoted from Puyol, *Paléographie*, pp. 130–4.
[78] The lemmata are quoted from Puyol, *Paléographie*, pp. 130–4.

the Latin text in Lupo's edition and any discrepancies collated with the variant readings given in the critical apparatus. The discrepancies were also checked against a sample insular manuscript, Oxford, Bodleian Library, MS Selden supra 93 (S). The result of this investigation was that S is by far the closest to the English translation; it shares 40% more of the variant readings found in the Middle English than its nearest continental rival. There were no continental manuscripts that were consistently similar to the translation.[79]

It may be concluded, then, that the continental antecedents of the *Musica Ecclesiastica* recension and the first English translation are to be found among manuscripts having a text of class B, genus I (class P in the case of Book I). Lovatt's view that the *Musica Ecclesiastica* recension is of a 'pre-autograph' type should therefore be modified, since genus I is a derivative of genus K, which contains the autograph.[80] Most of the continental manuscripts of this genus come from Germany and Austria.[81] This means that the *Imitatio* may not have been brought to England from the Low Countries,[82] as the Dutch manuscripts are mainly of genus K.[83] So too are most of the Carthusian manuscripts, but it is nevertheless possible that the English text is of Carthusian origin, as there are at least three Carthusian manuscripts of genus I: Downside Abbey, Somerset, MS 48246 (dated 1428 and from the Erfurt Charterhouse),[84] Vienna, Staatsbibliothek, MS 4064, from the Charterhouse at Gemnitz (1439), and Downside Abbey, MS 48247, also from

---

[79] The closest are San Marino, Huntington Library, MS 901, from northern Germany, and St Paul im Lavanttal, Austria, Archiv des Benediktinerstiftes, MS 14, from Austria.

[80] Lovatt (p. 101) took this view because the date of the Magdalen manuscript (1438) is earlier than that of the colophon of the autograph (1441): he followed Delaissé in believing that any manuscript copied before 1441 would represent one of the 'premier états' of the text. As noted above, p. xxxviii, however, Huijben and Debongnie found few readings in other manuscripts derived from the autograph before it had been corrected.

[81] P. Künzle suggests that English copies of Heinrich Suso's *Horologium Sapientiae*, another text popular among Carthusians, may similarly derive from German exemplars: see his edition of the *Horologium*, Spicilegium Friburgense, 23 (Freiburg in der Schweiz, 1977), pp. 320–5.

[82] This was the view of Lovatt (pp. 106–10) and Delaissé (i. 90).

[83] On the importance of the Carthusians generally as agents in the circulation of devotional material, see M. G. Sargent, 'The Transmission by the English Carthusians of some Late Medieval Spiritual Writings', *JEH* 27 (1976), 225–40.

[84] It is listed by Huijben and Debongnie as MS Clifton 1; see *MMBL* ii. 464–6. Both this manuscript and Downside Abbey, MS 48247 'are Erfurt manuscripts identifiable in the Bülow sale in 1836', and therefore did not reach England until the nineteenth century (*MMBL* ii. 454). On the possible connection between the English recension and Erfurt Charterhouse, see above, p. xl, n. 71.

the Erfurt Charterhouse.[85] It is well known that the Carthusians disseminated texts over long distances between houses, and so it is possible that it was a text from a German or Austrian Charterhouse which came to England, rather than a text representative of the type more usually found in the Low Countries.[86] Given the large number of uncollated continental manuscripts, however, no certainty on this point is possible.

D. THE MIDDLE ENGLISH TRANSLATION

The search among the insular manuscripts for the immediate antecedents of the Middle English translation achieved clearer results. A comparison of the Middle English text with Delaissé's diplomatic edition of the autograph manuscript was made and the discrepancies noted; these discrepancies were then collated with the fifteen extant insular manuscripts which contain Books I to III. The result of this collation was that two manuscripts, Cologne, Stadtarchiv, MS GB fᵒ 27, and London, British Library, MS Royal 7 B. VIII, contained significantly more readings in common with the translation than the others. The following sigla are used:

E   Cambridge, Emmanuel College, MS 54
J   Cambridge, St John's College, MS 56
K   Brussels, Bibliothèque Royale, MS 5855–61 (the Kempis autograph)
L   Oxford, Bodleian Library, MS Laud misc. 215
N   Oxford, Magdalen College, MS 93
O   London, Lambeth Palace, MS 475
R   London, British Library, MS Royal 7 B. VIII

---

[85] *MMBL* ii. 466–8.
[86] This would fit in with Ampe's theory about the origin of the title *Musica Ecclesiastica*, discussed above, p. xl, n. 71. In his article 'Carthusian Participation in the Movement of Works of Richard Rolle between England and Other Parts of Europe in the 14th and 15th Centuries', in *Kartäusermystik und -mystiker*, AC 55, 5 vols (Salzburg, 1981–2), ii. 109–20, A. I. Doyle suggests further links between England and southern Germany and Switzerland, demonstrating the importance of the Trier and Basel Charterhouses in the circulation of Rolle's *Emendatio Vitae*: 'the Council of Basel as an entrepôt or carrefour of texts is a commonplace' (p. 114). P. Lehmann, 'Konstanz und Basel als Büchermärkte während der grossen Kirchenversammlungen', in his *Erforschung des Mittelalters: Ausgewählte Abhandlungen und Aufsätze*, 5 vols (Leipzig, 1941–62), i. 253–80, presents evidence for this, including two manuscripts of the *Imitatio* copied at Basel during the Council: Tübingen, Wilhelmsstiftsbibliothek, MS Gb. 687, copied for the Benedictine monastery at Wiblingen in 1433, and a manuscript which was copied for the Benedictines at Augsburg in 1437 (p. 274; cf. *MBDS* i. 422, 425, 428, 435).

S Oxford, Bodleian Library, MS Selden supra 93
T The Hague, Koninklijke Bibliotheek, MS 128 G. 17[87]
U Cambridge, University Library, MS Additional 6855
V Harvard, University Library, MS Lat. 241
W Brussels, Bibliothèque Royale, MS 15138[88]
X London, Lambeth Palace, MS 536
Y Brussels, Bibliothèque Royale, MS IV. 135[89]
Z Cologne, Stadtarchiv, MS GB f° 27[90]
Δ Oxford, Bodleian Library, MS Digby 37 (Book I only)
Θ Madrid, Biblioteca Nacional, MS 4311[91]
Λ London, British Library, MS Royal 8 C. VII (Book I only)
Φ Cambridge, Emmanuel College, MS 94 (Books III–IV only)
Ω Oxford, Bodleian Library, MS Bodley 632 (Book I only)

The other insular manuscripts had between 35 and 45 readings in common with the translation; R and Z each had over 60, of which the following 18 were found in both but in no other insular manuscript (except at 1.24.11 and 3.55.11):

1.21.15 cordis] ΚΟΧSLEJUTNVWYΘΩΔΛ, *om*. RZ, *English om*. CDMG 1.22.24 et tribularis] KOXSEUTNVWYΘΩΔΛ, et tribulares L, J *wanting, om*. RZ, *English om*. CDMG 1.22.24 tunc] KXSLETNV WYΘΩΔΛ, J *wanting*, quere deum nunc O, nunc U, dic nunc RZ, *English* þen seye nowe CDMG 1.23.25 nec] KOXSLEJUTNVWYΘΩΔΛ, ut RZ, *English*

---

[87] According to Lovatt, this manuscript is 'almost certainly of English origin', despite its present location; 'the MS. was acquired by Sir Thomas Phillipps in 1836 from the bookseller Thorpe, and sold to the Koninklijke Bibliotheek in 1898' (p. 118).

[88] This manuscript 'belonged to the Bruges Charterhouse by *c*. 1600 (fo. 1), but contains English annotations dating from the latter part of the fifteenth century. [It was] probably brought to Bruges by the exiled English Carthusians in 1546–47' (Lovatt, p. 117). Its English origin was doubted by F. Hendrickx, 'De handschriften van de kartuis Genadendal bij Brugge (1318–1580): I', *OGE* 47 (1973), 3–63 (pp. 20–31), but confirmed by J. P. Gumbert, 'Een Engels *Imitatio*-handschrift bij de Brugse kartuizers', *OGE* 48 (1974), 287–9 (cf. also F. Hendrickx, 'Reflecties over Brux., Cod. 15138', *OGE* 48 (1974), 290–4).

[89] Not listed by Lovatt, this manuscript contains Books I–III under the title *Musica Ecclesiastica*. Its English origin is shown by the signature 'Tho. Barker' on f. 46ʳ and the note 'Bought from Dr Pegge's library, 1798' on f. 96ʳ. See Librarie Halbart, *Catalogue des beaux livres, anciens et modernes, qui seront dispersés en vente publique le 29 avril 1961* (Liège, 1961), no. 108.

[90] Not listed by Lovatt, this manuscript contains Books I–III under the title *Musica Ecclesiastica*. See below, p. xlviii, and J. Vennebusch, *Die Theologischen Handschriften des Stadtarchivs Köln*, Mitteilungen des Stadtarchiv von Köln, 5 vols (Cologne, 1976–89), i. 29–31.

[91] Not listed by Lovatt, this manuscript contains Books I–III under the title *Musica Ecclesiastica*. It has recipes written in English in a secretary hand on f. 91ᵛ.

om. CDMG   1.24.11 perurgentur] KXLJNWYΩ, purgabuntur OSE, purgentur UTVΘ, pungentur RZΔΔ, *English* shul be prykked CDMG 1.25.3 in breui] KOXSLEJUTNVWYΘΩΔΔ, *om.* RZ, *English om.* CDMG 1.25.28 ihesus crucifixus] KXSLEJUTNVWΘΩΔ, ihesus christus crucifixus O, YΛ *wanting,* ihesus christus RZ, *English* ihesu criste CDMG   2.1.27–8] KOXSLEJUTNVWYΘ, *second halves of verses transposed* RZ, *English second halves of verses transposed* CDMG   2.8.6 ihesus vocat] KOXSLEJUNV WYΘ, ihesus T, ihesus venit et vocat RZ, *English* ihesus comeþ he calleþ CDMG   2.11.28–9 tunc vere (vero T) pauper et nudus spiritu esse poterit et cum propheta dicere quia vnicus et pauper sum ego] KOXSLJTNVWY, tunc vere pauper et nudus spiritu qui esse poterit et cum propheta dicere quia vnicus et pauper sum ego E, tunc vero pauper spiritus et nudus esse poterit et cum propheta dicere quia vnicus et pauper sum ego Θ, tunc vere pauper et nudus spiritu esse poterit et cum propheta dicere U, quia vnicus et pauper sum ego dicere poterit cum propheta cum vere pauper et nudus spiritu esse ceperit RZ, *English* for suche one may seie with þe prophete þat I am soole and pouer when he bigynneþ verily to be bare and pouer in spirite CDMG   3.0.3 et quod multi ea non ponderat] KOXSLJUTVWYΘΦ, EN *wanting, om.* RZ, *English om.* CDMG   3.0.57 ⟨sed magis verberibus reum⟩] KXLJUTVWYΘΦ, sed verberibus reum OS, EN *wanting, om.* RZ, *English om.* CDMG   3.2.8 cor non] KOXSLEJUTNVWYΘΦ, non RZ, *English* noþinge CDMG   3.6.32–3 est amor . . . in cunctis sensibus custoditus est amor subiectus (subiectus deo U) et obediens prelatis sibi vilis et despectus (suspectus OSE) deo deuotus et gratificus] KOXSLEJUTNV WYΘΦ, est amor . . . in cunctis sensibus custoditus deo deuotus et gratificus est amor subiectus et obediens prelatis sibi vilis et despectus RZ, *English* love is . . . kepte in alle wittes deuoute to god and kynde loue is subiecte and obediente to prelates vile and despecte CM, loue is . . . kepte in alle wittes deuoute to god and kinde loue is subiecte and obediente to prelates vile and despecte 'to hymself' D²G   3.22.20 virtutis] KOXSLEJUNV WYΘΦ, *om.* T, mentis RZ, *English* of soule CMD, of þe soule G   3.34.2 sed necesse habeo ad te confugere (effugere L)] KOXSLEJUTNV WYΘΦ, precor RZ, *English* I preie þee CDMG   3.55.11 venit hora] KOXSLEJUTNVWYΦ, *om.* RZΘ, *English om.* CDMG.[92]

R and Z are textually and palaeographically very similar, and although they contain a text of the *Musica Ecclesiastica* recension (including the distinctively English numbering of the five prayers in Book III as separate chapters), they were probably written in the Low Countries. R was bound at Bruges about 1480:[93] on the flyleaf is written 'Johannes

[92] The lemmata are quoted from Delaissé. Minor differences in word order between the Latin manuscripts are ignored.

[93] Lovatt, p. 105. On f. 3ᵛ it bears the arms Azure a Cock argent, which have not been identified.

Guillebert me ligavit', referring to a former binding.[94] It is quite a lavish book: the text is written in an elegant bastard secretary, and it has gold initials to each chapter and illuminations in the Flemish style; on f. 3^v there is a full-page miniature showing a pope playing the organ, a cardinal blowing the bellows, and two bishops singing from a book. Lovatt writes that 'during the second half of the fifteenth century several Englishmen, including Edward IV, are known to have patronized Flemish scribes and it seems most likely that the Royal MS was also produced under such circumstances': that is, an exemplar would have been sent from England to the Low Countries for a Flemish scribe to copy.[95] The manuscript was certainly part of the Royal Library by 1542, as it is listed in the Westminster Inventory of that year.[96] An equally fine book, Z was almost certainly written by the same scribe from the same exemplar, for an unknown client (the coat of arms on f. 6^r has not been identified).

R and Z were presumably written c. 1480; they are therefore a little late for either to have been the manuscript from which the translation was made (given that Dodesham died in 1481/2); moreover, they have some readings which are incompatible with the translation.[97] Nevertheless, their generally close resemblance to the text of the translation makes them the most important witness available to the text used by the translator, and the translation has therefore been compared with R where it appears to differ from K.

III. STEMMA

The attempt to establish the relationship between the four surviving manuscripts of the translation edited here is facilitated by the fact that

[94] John Guilebert, *alias* Messe, was apprenticed to John de Clerc in Bruges in 1465, made free of the guild in 1469, and had died by 1490; there are records of bindings made by him in the 1480s (W. H. J. Weale, *Bookbindings and Rubbings in the National Art Library, South Kensington Museum*, 2 vols (London, 1894–8), i. liv–lv).

[95] Lovatt, p. 105 and n. 5; C. L. Scofield, *The Life and Reign of Edward the Fourth*, 2 vols (London, 1923, repr. 1976), ii. 451–5. Manuscripts with similar Flemish illumination are listed in O. Pächt and J. J. G. Alexander, *Illuminated Manuscripts in the Bodleian Library, Oxford*, 3 vols (Oxford, 1966–73), i. 25–9; among these are a number which were either written in England or made for England.

[96] London, British Library, MS Additional 25469, f. 15^r. R's old pressmark, given on f. 2^r, was 534.

[97] See the Notes for 1.3.23, 1.5.3, 1.13.21, 1.15.1, 2.12.40, 3.37.13, and 3.57.15.

the translation is a close one: the translator has made no attempt to edit or rework the material, and the English follows the Latin syntax and vocabulary carefully, generally proceeding clause by clause.[98] Even where there is only a small difference between variants, therefore, it is possible to be reasonably confident in saying that the reading which is closer to the Latin is probably original.

There are also, however, two factors which complicate the task of establishing the stemma. The first is the presence of the D^2-corrections. Many of these corrections correspond to variants in the other manuscripts of the translation, and some appear to have been made with reference to the Latin text. Secondly, there is a small number of cases where variants in the English text correspond to variants among the Latin manuscripts, and this suggests that the corrector made reference to a Latin text which was different from that originally used by the translator.[99] In this analysis of the textual tradition, therefore, the outline of the stemma is first established without reference to passages where D has been corrected; secondly, the various groupings of manuscripts which result from the corrections in D are examined; and thirdly, variants corresponding to variants among the Latin manuscripts are discussed.

The stemma drawn is the simplest possible that is compatible with the evidence: possible intermediate stages are disregarded where they do not affect the essential genetic relationship in question.

A. THE STEMMA

1. *The archetype*

It is unnecessary to demonstrate that all four manuscripts are descended from the same translation: this is self-evident from the small size of the critical apparatus. But it is unlikely that the four manuscripts were copied from the translator's autograph, as there are two cases where all four agree in error:

Verum est quod vnusquisque libenter agit pro sensu suo: et inclinatur ad eos magis qui secum senciunt.

---

[98] For an analysis of the translator's method, see Part V below, pp. lxxiv–lxxix; divergences between the translation and the Latin are mentioned in the Notes.

[99] Similar corrections are found in two of the manuscripts of *The Pilgrimage of the Lyfe of the Manhode*, ed. A. Henry, EETS 288, 292, 2 vols (1985–8): see i. l–lxxxiii), and 'nexus corrections' (similar corrections in more than one manuscript) in manuscripts of the Wycliffite sermon cycle are described by Anne Hudson in *English Wycliffite Sermons*, ed. A. Hudson and P. Gradon, 5 vols (Oxford, 1983–96), i. 146–51.

Trewe hit is þat euery man [gladly doþe] aftir his owne witte, and is inclyned
moste to hem þat feleþ as he doþe. (1.9.6)
gladly doþe] *con.*, *om.* CDMG, *Latin* libenter agit KR.

Procul et de vltimis finibus, pretium eius. (cf. Proverbs 31.10)
His price is [farre] and fro þe vtmast costes. (2.11.18)
farre and fro þe vtmast costes] *con.*, and fro þe vtmast costes C, and fro þe
vttermest chost M, ⟨. .⟩ fro þe vt⟨termost coost⟩ D², from the vttermost cooste
G, *Latin* procul et de vltimis finibus KR.

These two errors, common to all four manuscripts, must be derived
from their common ancestor or archetype. If the archetype contained
these errors, it was probably a copy of the autograph manuscript of the
translation rather than the translator's autograph itself.[100]

2. *The two branches of the stemma: C and DMG*

The stemma has two branches descended from the archetype: C and
DMG. That C cannot be derived from D, M, or G is demonstrated by
the fact that they share over 150 errors at points where C has the correct
reading, including the following:

1.5.8 accepcion] C, excepcion DMG, *Latin* accepcione KR   1.9.12 matier]
C, maner DMG, *Latin* causa KR   1.11.7 lewke] C, leude DMG, *Latin*
tepidi KR   1.14.1 yen] C, eren DMG, *Latin* o⟨cu⟩los K, oculos R
1.14.4 pure] C, true DMG, *Latin* pura KR   1.20.19 overgrete] C, owne
DMG, *Latin* `nimiam´ K, nimiam R   1.23.17 byhiete] C, be here DMG,
Latin polliceri KR   1.24.32 talynge] C, talkyng DMG, *Latin* fabulacione
KR   2.8.15 grete¹] C, *om.* DMG, *Latin* magna KR
2.8.31 alone] C, *om.* DMG, *Latin* solus cum solo KR   2.9.6 hymselfe] C,
himself or þe worlde DMG, *Latin* seipso KR   2.9.14 consolacion] C,
exercitacion DMG, *Latin* consolacio KR   2.10.25 or of vile pryce for hit
may not be litel] C, *om.* DMG, aut nimis vile videbitur non enim paruum est
KR   2.12.3 hereþ] C, feliþ DMG, *Latin* audiunt KR   3.0.37 cupid-
ite] C, curiosite DMG, *Latin* cupiditatis KR   3.21.12 lucre] C, hyre DMG,
Latin lucrum KR   3.22.4 lyght] C, litel DMG, *Latin* leui KR
3.23.22 teres] C, dedes DMG, *Latin* lacrime KR   3.35.34 but to grete
peynes not to worshippes] C, *om.* DMG, *Latin* sed ad magna certamina non ad
honores KR   3.41.14 brawlinge] C, braggyng DMG, *Latin* querulosis
KR   3.64.20 clerenes] C, clennes DMG, *Latin* claritatis KR.[101]

---

[100] There are further cases where there may have been errors in the archetype at 1.0.25,
1.22.37, 1.23.43, 2.6.15, 2.12.2, 3.2.0, 3.29.2, 3.36.11, 3.51.25, and 3.51.30; these errors
may have arisen in the archetype, in the original translation itself, or in the Latin
manuscript from which the translation was made.

[101] There are further examples at 1.3.4, 1.3.34, 1.6.5, 1.6.7, 1.8.4, 1.8.6, 1.9.7, 1.10.5,

Conversely, there are over 120 isolative errors in C at points where D, M, and G have the correct reading, including the following (throughout this part of the Introduction lemmata are quoted from the text of this edition, i.e. in the spelling of C):

1.3.9 withouten] DMG, with C, *Latin* sine KR   1.22.34 vnneþe] DMG, how neþe C, *Latin* vix KR   1.23.7 hit is better to eschue synnes þen to flee dethe] DMG, *om.* C, *Latin* melius esset peccata cauere quam mortem fugere KR   1.23.44 now] DMG, new C, *Latin* nunc KR   1.24.2 god] DMG, *om.* C, *Latin* deo KR   1.24.40 alle] DMG, *om.* C, *Latin* totum KR 2.8.34 evon] DMG, *om.* C, *Latin* noctem KR   2.12.36 crosses] DMG, crosse C, *Latin* cruces KR   2.12.43 prosperite] DMG, profite C, *Latin* prosperitatis KR   3.2.4 of israel] DMG, *om.* C, *Latin* filii israel KR 3.7.4 standeþ] DMG, *om.* C, *Latin* stat KR   3.25.3 raþer] DMG, *om.* C, *Latin* pocius KR   3.37.7 not] DMG, *om.* C, *Latin* non KR 3.48.9 x yere] DMG, *om.* C, *Latin* decem annis KR   3.60.7 þi] DMG, þe C, *Latin* tuum KR   3.60.12 grace] DMG, *om.* C, *Latin* gracia KR 3.61.2 ioyneþ] DMG, ioyeþ C, *Latin* coniungit KR.[102]

3. *Relations within the group DMG*

M has over a hundred isolative errors, indicating that D and G cannot be derived from it, including the following:

1.10.11, 1.11.2, 1.11.7, 1.12.6, 1.13.0, 1.13.15, 1.13.28, 1.14.8, 1.15.1, 1.15.8, 1.18.6, 1.18.15, 1.19.3, 1.20.8 (twice), 1.20.29, 1.21.5, 1.22.9, 1.22.23, 1.22.33, 1.23.26, 1.23.46, 1.24.3, 1.24.10, 1.24.24, 1.25.15, 2.1.28, 2.1.35, 2.2.11, 2.3.14, 2.4.3, 2.4.13, 2.5.9, 2.5.10, 2.5.16, 2.6.15 (twice), 2.8.15, 2.8.28, 2.9.1, 2.9.2, 2.10.3, 2.12.35, 3.0.38, 3.1.3, 3.1.5, 3.2.15, 3.3.2, 3.3.23 (twice), 3.4.2, 3.4.4, 3.4.5, 3.4.6, 3.4.10, 3.5.7, 3.5.14, 3.5.16, 3.5.17, 3.5.19, 3.6.19, 3.7.5, 3.7.10, 3.8.0, 3.8.7, 3.8.19, 3.9.3, 3.9.11, 3.9.12, 3.10.13, 3.11.4, 3.11.16, 3.11.24 (twice), 3.13.0, 3.13.10, 3.15.16, 3.15.23, 3.16.0, 3.16.4, 3.16.9, 3.17.2, 3.21.11, 3.21.12, 3.22.4, 3.22.21, 3.23.6, 3.23.10, 3.23.17, 3.24.2–3, 3.24.9, 3.25.6, 3.26.0, 3.35.22, 3.37.7, 3.38.9, 3.39.20, 3.39.22, 3.45.6, 3.45.19, 3.46.0, 3.47.5, 3.48.2, 3.48.7, 3.48.10, 3.49.3, 3.50.1, 3.50.4, 3.50.28, 3.51.26, 3.54.7, 3.54.36, 3.57.1, 3.57.6, 3.57.10, 3.58.2, 3.58.18, 3.59.3, 3.61.7, 3.61.9, 3.62.6, and 3.63.10.

[102] There are further examples at 1.0.11, 1.3.34, 1.5.9, 1.9.4, 1.12.1, 1.12.2, 1.12.6, 1.13.3, 1.13.7, 1.13.16, 1.13.17, 1.13.27, 1.16.7, 1.18.6, 1.20.25, 1.21.1, 1.22.0, 1.24.2, 1.24.3, 1.24.12, 1.24.20, 1.25.4, 1.25.6, 1.25.25, 1.25.37, 2.1.6, 2.1.9, 2.1.14, 2.1.30, 2.1.41, 2.2.7, 2.2.12 (twice), 2.6.7, 2.6.15, 2.8.15, 2.9.26, 2.10.4, 2.10.16, 2.11.27, 2.12.52, 3.2.4, 3.2.6, 3.2.15, 3.3.2, 3.3.10, 3.4.2, 3.5.19, 3.5.22, 3.6.20, 3.7.14, 3.8.2, 3.8.16, 3.9.10, 3.10.6, 3.11.12, 3.11.24, 3.18.0, 3.23.11, 3.24.11, 3.25.10, 3.36.22, 3.37.7, 3.39.10, 3.42.6, 3.44.4, 3.47.10, 3.48.5, 3.48.8 (twice), 3.49.6, 3.50.2, 3.50.3, 3.50.21, 3.50.23, 3.52.14, 3.53.2, 3.53.15, 3.54.3, 3.54.5, 3.54.8, 3.54.9, 3.54.29, 3.54.33, 3.55.8, 3.55.11, 3.55.31, 3.56.1, 3.56.6, 3.57.8, 3.57.10, 3.59.8, 3.59.20, 3.60.9, 3.60.16 (twice), 3.60.27, 3.61.22, 3.62.14, 3.63.21, 3.63.22, 3.63.31, 3.63.40, 3.63.45, and 3.64.7; the case at 3.22.6 is probably similar.

1.2.12 if hit semeþ the þat thou canste many þinges and] CDG, `and´ M, *Latin* si tibi videtur quod multa scis et KR   1.12.7 prayeþ] CDG, prateþ M, *Latin* orat KR   1.16.9 large] CDG, *om.* M, *Latin* larga KR   1.22.3–4 in yerthe there is no man] CDG, *om.* M, *Latin* super terram nemo est KR   2.1.24 highe] CDG, *om.* M, *Latin* alta KR   2.5.12 reonnen] CDG, comen M, *Latin* percurristi KR   3.0.15 prive] CDG, peyne M, *Latin* occultis KR   3.3.16 vanite] CDG, vnyte M, *Latin* vanitatem KR   3.5.6 lovinge] CDG, leving M, *Latin* dilectione KR 3.11.10 siþe euery creature is bonde to serve the] CDG, *om.* M, *Latin* cum omnis creatura tibi seruire tenetur R, cui omnis creatura seruire tenetur K   3.18.8 trewe] CDG, *om.* M, *Latin* fideles KR   3.19.9 blessed^2] CDG, plesid M, *Latin* benedictus KR   3.23.10 darkeþ] CDG, drawiþe M, *Latin* obnubilant KR   3.49.7 floweth] CDG, folowiþ M, *Latin* defluit KR   3.50.31 fraile] CDG, present M, *Latin* fragili KR   3.55.26 ner hit is no nede þat man teche þee ner amonyshe þee of þoo þinges þat ar done] CDG, *om.* M, *Latin* et non opus est tibi ut quis te doceat aut ammoneat de hiis que geruntur K, et non opus est tibi ut quis te doceat aut moneat de hiis que geruntur R   3.58.3 confabulaciouns] CDG, consolacions M, *Latin* confabulacionem KR   3.60.24 þen alle þe wyse] CDG, *om.* M, *Latin* sapiencior vniuersis sapientibus KR.[103]

G has over sixty isolative errors, indicating that D and M cannot be derived from it, including the following:

1.3.15 exquisicion] CDM, execucion G, *Latin* esquisicione KR   1.9.9 to here] CDM, *om.* G, *Latin* audire KR   2.1.8 eya] M, ey`a´ D², ey C, haue doo G, *Latin* eya KR   2.1.25 for if þou flee deuoutly to the woundes] CDM, *om.* G, *Latin* si enim ad vvlnera . . . deuote confugis KR 2.6.14 glorie] CDM, ioy G, *Latin* gloriam KR   3.8.6 and as muche as he wolle and to whome he wolle] CDM, and to whome he woll and as muche as he woll G, *Latin* et quantum vult et cui vvlt KR   3.22.6 haue merci on me oute of the cleye þat I (*om.* C) styk not þerynne ner abide deiecte in eueri side] CDM, *om.* G, *Latin* miserere et eripe me de luto ut non infigar ne (neque R) permaneam deiectus usquequaque KR   3.30.5 lete not þe worlde deceyve me] DM, *om.* G (C *wanting*), *Latin* non me decipiat mundus KR

---

[103] There are further examples at 1.2.1, 1.2.17, 1.3.8, 1.3.23, 1.4.0, 1.8.3, 1.11.20, 1.16.13, 1.17.4, 1.18.15, 1.18.21 (twice), 1.20.3, 1.20.47, 1.21.21, 1.23.2, 1.23.15, 1.23.38, 1.23.40, 1.24.0, 1.24.1, 1.25.8, 1.25.17, 1.25.38, 1.25.41, 1.25.46, 2.1.24, 2.2.4, 2.2.8, 2.6.9, 2.6.23, 2.8.4, 2.9.31, 2.9.36, 2.10.6, 2.11.14, 2.11.17, 2.11.30, 2.12.27, 2.12.49, 2.12.54, 3.0.64, 3.3.11, 3.5.4, 3.6.2, 3.6.18, 3.6.20, 3.7.4, 3.7.7, 3.8.21, 3.9.2, 3.11.7, 3.11.17, 3.12.9, 3.13.15 (twice), 3.18.2, 3.20.4, 3.20.7, 3.21.12, 3.22.7, 3.23.17, 3.26.1, 3.27.3, 3.29.11, 3.32.3, 3.32.5, 3.37.4, 3.39.24, 3.40.6, 3.46.6, 3.47.4, 3.50.11, 3.51.6, 3.51.9, 3.55.12, 3.55.15, 3.56.4, 3.59.15, 3.61.19, 3.62.4, 3.62.14, 3.63.24, 3.63.31, 3.63.32, 3.63.35, and 3.63.46.

3.40.14 hevynesses] CDM, hevynes G, *Latin* grauitates KR   3.58.5 vaca-
cion] CDM, attendance G, *Latin* vacacionem KR   3.64.5 I chese raþer to
be a pilgryme with þe in yerþe þen to haue hevon withoute þe] CDM, *om.* G,
Latin eligo pocius tecum in terra peregrinari quam sine te celum possidere
KR.[104]

In contrast with M and G, D has only two possible isolative errors,
both of which could have been corrected by subsequent copyists:

1.23.20 sorowe] MG, sowe D, *om.* C, *Latin* dolebis KR   3.55.17 face]
CMG, fate D, *Latin* faciem KR.

At 1.23.20 M and G could both have changed 'sowe' to 'sorowe'
independently because it seemed appropriate in the context, and at
3.55.17 'fate' could similarly have been corrected to 'face'; t and c are
similar in D's hand. It is probable, therefore, that either M or G or both
are derived from D. This is more likely than the alternative supposition,
that all three are derived from a common ancestor and the scribe of D
made only these two mistakes.

Were both M and G copied from D, or only one of them? If only one
were copied from D, we should expect to find a number of cases where
D and that manuscript shared errors exclusively. These would be errors
introduced by the scribe of D and copied in the manuscript derived
from it. There are no errors shared exclusively by D and G. There are,
however, seven cases in which D and M agree in error and C and G
have the correct reading:

1.19.16 thi maners] CG, þe maner DM, *Latin* mores tuos KR
2.4.12 yvel] CG, idel DM, *Latin* mala KR   3.21.14 fightynge] CG,
victory DM, *Latin* certamine KR   3.51.17 my] CG, *om.* DM, *Latin* me
permittente KR   3.53.29 am^3] CG, was DM, *Latin* feror KR
3.59.29 newe^2] CG, nowe DM, nouum KR   3.63.8 þe whiche] C, þe
DM, whiche G, *Latin* ⟨que⟩ pax K, que pax R.

There is also the following case, at 3.14.7–3.15.1, where D and M share
an omission and C and G have alternative, equally correct, translations
of the Latin:

[104] There are further examples at 1.9.10, 1.11.7, 1.13.24, 1.13.27, 1.13.32, 1.15.3, 1.18.7,
1.20.44, 1.21.15, 1.22.19, 1.23.25, 1.24.12, 1.25.40, 1.25.46, 2.1.9, 2.2.9, 2.3.15, 2.9.13,
2.11.1, 2.12.70, 3.5.1, 3.5.12–13, 3.5.21, 3.6.5, 3.11.4, 3.11.9, 3.16.10, 3.17.4, 3.17.5,
3.19.14, 3.20.1, 3.27.2, 3.27.7, 3.29.10, 3.29.11, 3.29.12, 3.30.3, 3.31.10, 3.35.17, 3.35.21,
3.37.10, 3.39.9, 3.39.15, 3.40.4, 3.40.15, 3.42.7, 3.51.19, 3.55.19, 3.55.22, 3.55.23, 3.57.21,
3.60.7, 3.61.6, 3.63.24, and 3.64.13.

C

7 But forasmuche as þou lovest inordinatly thiselfe, þerfore þou dredeste to resigne thiselfe fully to þe wille of oþer. 8 But what grete þinge is þat, if þou, þat arte but asshon and nought, subdue þiselfe to man for God, sithe I, almyghty and highest, þat made alle þinges of nought, mekely made me sugget to man for þee, 9 and was made mekest of alle and lowest, for þou shuldest overcome thi pride with my mekenesse? 10 Lerne to obeye, þou duste! Lerne to meke thiselfe, þou yerthe and cleye, and to bowe thyselfe vnder the feete of alle! 11 Lerne to breke þine owne willes, and to yive þe vnder subieccion of alle. 12 Be wrothe ayenis thiselfe, and suffre no [b]ol[n]ynge pride to lyve in the, but shewe þe `so´ sugget and so litel þat al men mowe goo over þee and [t]rede vppon the as vppon myre of the streete. 13 What haste þou, veyne man, to compleyne? 14 Thou foule synnar, what haste þou to answer þi reprevars, þat so oftetymes haste offended thi God, and so oftetymes deserved helle? 15 But myne yen hathe spared þee, for thi soule was preciouse in my sight, for þou shuldeste know my love and be ever kynde to my benefaytes, and þat þou shuldeste yive thiselfe continuly to very subieccion by mekenes, and bere paciently þine owne despisinge. Of the pryve iugementes of God, leste we [be] lyfte vppe into pryde for goode þinges. Capitulum 15m. 1 Lorde, þou þondrest over me thi iugementes and alle toshakest alle my bones for drede and tremulynge, and my soule is gretely affrayed.

G

7 But forasmuche as þoue louest inordinately thiself, therfore þoue dredyst to resigne thyself fully to the wylle of other. 8 But what gret þinge is it to the, þat arte but duste and nouȝte, if þoue for God subdue the to man, when Y, almyȝty and moste hyȝe, þat haue create all þinges of nouȝte, mekely for the haue subdued me to man? 9 I was made mekist and lowest of all, þat þrowhe my mekenes þoue shuldist ouercome thy pryde. 10 Lerne, þoue duste, to obey. Lerne, þoue erth and slyme, to meke the, and to bowe the vndyr þe fete of all. 11 Lerne to breke thyne owne wyll, and to geue the to the subieccion of all other. 12 Stryve ayenst þiself, and suffyr no elacion to lyve in the, but shewe the so subiecte and litel þat all may walke vpon the, and trede the as the fenn of the hyȝeway. 13 What hast þou, vayn man, to complayne? 14 What mayst þoue, filthy synner, ayensay thy reprevers, which so ofte hast offendid God, and so ofte hast deserued hell? 15 But my mercifull eye hath sparyd þe, for thy soule was preciouse in my sight, þat þoue shuldist knowe my loue and euere for my benefites to be to me kynde, and contynually to geue the to true subieccion and mekenes, and paciently to suffyr thyne owne contempte. Of hydde domys to be consideryde. Capitulum xv. 1 Lorde, þoue soundyst thy domy`s´ vpon me and shakyst all my bones for drede and tremlyng, and my soule is gretely afrayde.

D

[7] But forasmoche as þou louest inordinatly þiself, þerfore þou dredist to
resigne þiself fully to þe will ˈof
otherˈ. [*Large caret and words not now
legible written in margin.*] ⟨Of hyd
domys to be consyderyd. Capitulum
xv. [1] Lorde, þou sowndyst thi domes
upon me and shakyst all⟩ ˈmyˈ bones
for drede and tremlyng, and my soule
is gretly affraied.

M

[7] But forasmuche as þou louest inordinatly þiself, þerfore þou dredist to
resigne þiself. [*Remainder of page left
blank.*] [1] Lorde, þou sowndist þi
domys vpon me and shakist al my
bonys for drede and tremelinge, and
my soule is gretly affraied.

K

[7] Quia adhuc nimis inordinate te diligis: ideo plene te resignare aliorum
voluntati trepidas. [8] Sed quid magnum, si tu qui puluis es et nichil, propter
deum te homini subdis; quando ego omnipotens et altissimus qui cuncta creaui
ex nichilo me homini propter te humiliter sub⟨ieci⟩? [9] Factus sum omnium
humilimus et infimus: ut tuam superbiam mea humilitate vinceres. [10] Disce
obtemperare puluis; disce te humiliare terra et limus: et sub omnium pedibus
incuruare. [11] Disce voluntates tuas frangere: et ad omnem subiectionem te dare.
[12] Exardesce contra te, nec paciaris tumorem in te viuere; sed ita subiectum et
paruulum te exhibe: ut omnes super te ambulare possint, et sicut lutum
platearum conculcare. [13] Quid ⟨habes⟩ homo inanis ⟨conqueri: [14] quid sordide
peccator potes⟩ contradicere exprobrantibus tibi; qui tociens deum offendisti, et
infernum multociens meruisti? [15] Sed pepercit tibi oculus meus; quia preciosa
fuit anima tua in conspectu meo: ut cognosceres dilectionem meam et gratus
semper beneficiis meis exsisteres; et ut ad ueram subiectionem et humilitatem
te iugiter dares: pacienterque proprium contemptum ferres. De ⟨occultis dei
ˈiudiciisˈ considerandis ne extollamur in bonis. Capitulum xiiii.⟩ [1] Intonas super
me iudicia tua domine; et timore ac tremore concutis omnia ossa mea: et
expauescit anima mea valde.[105]

The shared omission in D and M might at first suggest that only M, and
not G, was derived from D. But G's text here—exceptionally—is so
different from that of C that it must be an independent translation, the
result of conflation with the Latin. We may conclude that G is derived
from a manuscript with a lacuna at this point: the scribe of G perceived
that his exemplar was deficient, consulted a Latin manuscript, and filled
the gap himself. If G had independent recourse to a Latin manuscript

---

[105] There are the following variants in R: 7 plene te] K, te plene R   10 pedibus] K,
pedibus te R   12 tumorem] K, timorem R   viuere] K, vincere R   subiectum et
paruulum] K, paruulum et subiectum R   14 multociens] K, tociens R.

here, then, it is likely that the other seven apparently exclusively shared errors of D and M listed above (p. liii) also result from G's reference to the Latin.[106] Moreover, G also appears to have had recourse to the Latin in the following cases:

1.15.1 þogh] C, *om.* DM, but G, *Latin* sed KR   3.15.14 mekely and howe] C, and DM, mekely and G, *Latin* quam humiliter et abiecte KR 3.60.6 holenesse] C, holynes DM, helthe G, *Latin* sanitate KR.[107]

There is also a small group of ten cases of errors shared between C, D, and M. These would at first appear to conflict with the group DMG. But given that the group DMG is attested by over 150 shared errors, and that it is clear that G has had recourse to a Latin text in at least one instance, the cases of shared errors between C, D, and M probably also result from conflation from the Latin by G. In the cases discussed above, G was correcting errors that arose in D or D's exemplar. In the following cases, G was correcting errors which were present in the archetype:

1.13.28 temptacion] G, tribulacion CDM, *Latin* temptacione KR 1.22.11 to him] G, *om.* CDM, *Latin* ⟨ei⟩ K, ei R   2.1.3 of god] G, *om.* CDM, *Latin* ⟨dei⟩ K, dei R   3.0.48 science] G, conscience CDM, *Latin* scienciam KR   3.6.7 holy disciplines] G, disciplines of kunnynge CDM, *Latin* disciplinis sanctis KR   3.10.9 grete] G, *om.* CDM, *Latin* magna KR   3.25.2 to²] G, *om.* CDM, *Latin* audire KR 3.37.2 there be fetred] G, *om.* CDM, *Latin* compediti sunt KR   3.48.15 swetly] G, surely CD, sueerly M, *Latin* dulcit⟨er⟩ K, dulciter R   3.56.4 of me newe] con., of þe newe CDM, efte of me G, *Latin* iterum a me visiteris KR.

That G is correcting errors in the archetype here is significant. G's reading in the seven cases like that at 1.19.16 could conceivably have come from a missing exemplar. We could suppose that D and G were copied from this missing manuscript, and that M was copied from D. This would explain why D and M had an error, but G did not. But that interpretation will not work for the ten cases like that at 1.13.28, just cited, because in these cases G is correcting errors in the archetype. G cannot come from a branch of the stemma superior to the archetype, however, because it shares over 150 errors with D and

[106] For further evidence that G had independent recourse to a Latin text, see 1.15.14, 1.20.17, 1.25.19, 1.25.29, and 3.37.3: in these cases (discussed below, pp. lxvi–lxvii), CDM's reading corresponds to the Latin text found in R, and G's reading to that found in K.
[107] The case at 3.20.6, where D has a leaf missing, may be similar.

M, and so is undoubtedly a member of the DMG group. The ten cases
like that at 1.13.28 must result from conflation, then, and it is
therefore likely that the cases like that at 1.19.16 are also the result
of conflation. Thus the cases of errors shared exclusively between D
and M do not necessarily prove that M alone was copied from D and
that G was not. Indeed, the simplest explanation of the data is that
both M and G were copied from D, and that the scribe of G also
consulted a Latin text.[108]

If this conclusion—that M and G are both descended from D—is
accepted, one further question remains. Were they copied from D
directly, or were there one or more manuscripts intervening? If M
and G were both descended from D via one or more intervening
manuscripts, then we should expect to find some cases in which M and
G shared common errors against D. In fact, there are only three such
cases:

2.1.13 wyghtly] CD, liȝtly MG, *Latin* velociter KR   2.12.67 swetnesses]
CD, swettnesse MG, *Latin* suauitatibus KR   3.64.11 þousandes] CD,
þousand MG, *Latin* mille KR.

The common error at 3.64.11 may have arisen because in D the -*es*
abbreviation is not very clear. It is more likely that this error and those
at 2.1.13 and 2.12.67 arose independently in M and G than that there
was an intervening manuscript whose scribe copied D and made only
these three errors in the whole text.[109]

B. CORRECTIONS

With the outline of the stemma established, it is necessary to consider
those passages where D has been corrected by D^2. Three questions
arise here. First, were M and G copied from D before or after it was
corrected? Secondly, what is the nature of the corrections: do they
correct errors originally present in D^1, or do they create errors? And
thirdly, if they correct errors, what is the source of the correction?

When the corrections are compared with the readings of the other
manuscripts, a complex picture emerges. Some of the corrections are the
same as the readings found in M and G; in other cases the corrected

---

[108] It is not possible to prove that M and G are both derived from D; this is, however,
the simplest explanation, and it is in principle difficult to prove indisputably the descent of
two manuscripts from a common exemplar.

[109] There is also one other anomalous grouping, a case of shared error between C and M
which probably arose independently in the two manuscripts: 3.7.29 welle] DG, *om.* CM,
Latin multum precaue KR.

reading is found in G, but the original reading in M; in other cases again the correction does not correspond to a reading found in any other manuscript. It may be concluded, then, that the corrector worked over a period, and three stages of correction may be distinguished. Some corrections were made before either M or G were copied. Others were made after M was copied but before G was copied. Others still were made after both M and G had been copied. These stages are identified respectively as D^{2a}, D^{2b}, and D^{2c} on the stemma.

The nature of the corrections is also varied, and in this respect too the corrections may be divided into three classes. Some of the corrections result in errors. Others, by contrast, correct errors which had been introduced in D^1. Others again correct errors which are shared by D^1 and C, and which appear to have been introduced in the archetype.[110] These three types of correction are all found in each of the three stages, to give a total of nine classes altogether; the corrections belonging to each of these classes are described below.

1. *Corrections in D made before M and G were copied*

Corrections belonging to the first stage were made before M and G were copied, for in these cases the corrected reading agrees with that found in M and G.

(a) *Corrections introducing errors in D^2*

A number of D^2-corrections were made before M and G were copied and introduced errors, including the following; they gave rise to errors shared between D^2, M, and G:

1.7.12 one] C, o⟨þir⟩ D^2, oþer MG, *Latin* vni KR   1.9.6 witte and] C, 'witte' ⟨.⟩, *ampersand visible under erasure* D^2, witte MG, *Latin* pro sensu suo et KR   1.18.21 he takeþ] C, be⟨fallith⟩, b *altered from* h D^2, befalliþe MG, *Latin* accepit KR   1.19.8 or purposeþ] C, ⟨. . . . .⟩, purp *visible under erasure* D, *om.* MG, *Latin* quidquid arripiunt KR   1.24.12 there] C, þere, re *canc.* D, þe MG, *Latin* ibi KR   2.1.8 þis] C, þi⟨.⟩ D, þi MG, *Latin* huic KR   2.1.34 estemed] C, ⟨trowede⟩ D^2, trowed MG, *Latin* estimantur KR   2.9.22 butte whereyn] C, but wherin *canc.* D, *om.* MG, *Latin* sed in quo KR   3.5.2 assailinges] C, ass⟨em⟩linges D^2, assemlinges MG, *Latin* incursibus KR   3.6.28 iubilynge] C, ⟨ioynge⟩ D^2, ioynge MG,

---

[110] It should be noted that in cases where D^2 is correcting errors present in the archetype, it is the more correct readings that are 'readings of secondary origin': the manuscripts which are not derived from D in its corrected state, although agreeing in error, nevertheless derive those errors from the archetype (see M. L. West, *Textual Criticism and Editorial Technique* (Stuttgart, 1973), p. 32, n. 3).

Latin iubilans KR   3.9.4 whither I became þat] C, ⟨and fro whens I⟩
come ⟨for⟩ D², and fro whens I come for MG, *Latin* et quo deueni KR
3.35.11 abide²] C, ⟨ande⟩, abide *visible under erasure* D², and MG, *Latin* expecta
me expecta KR   3.41.5 light] C, ⟨s⟩ight D², siȝt MG, *Latin* die
KR   3.45.7 vii tymes] C, ⟨alway tymes⟩ D², alway tymes MG, *Latin*
septem tempora KR   3.48.9 mo] C, m⟨y⟩ D², my MG, *Latin* plures
KR.¹¹¹

In the following cases D² has retranslated the Latin. The example at
3.54.9 lends support to the supposition that D²'s corrections were made
in more than one stage: 'it' is a correction to a correction, since it is
inserted above the line in the middle of a passage which is itself written
over erasure. Only G also has 'it'; M does not. This suggests that 'it' was
added after M copied D²'s original correction, and before G was copied:

3.53.23 sende thin arowes and trou[b]led and shende mote be alle maner
contrariouse fantasies] C, sende oute þyn ⟨arwys⟩ and ⟨þou shalt trob`yll´ hem
and all þe fantasyes of þe enemye shall⟩ `be bore down´ D², sende oute þyn
arowis and þou shalt trobille hem and alle þe fantasyes of þe enemye shal be bore
dovn M, sende oute thi arowes and all the fantasies of þe enemy be troublede G,
Latin emitte sagittas tuas et ⟨conturbentur⟩ omnes fantas⟨ie inimici⟩ K, emitte
sagittas tuas et conturbentur omnis fantasie inimici R   3.54.9 þou oweste
putte myne ordinance bifore thi desire and alle by þe desired and folowe hit]
con., þou oweste `to folowe´ myne ordinance bifore thi desire and alle by þe
desired and folowe hit C, þou owist putte myn ordinaunce before þy desire and
⟨preferre ande folwe `it´ afore all⟩ `thynge´ D², þou owist putte myn ordinaunce
before þi desire and preferre and folow afore alle þinge M, þou owist putte myn
ordinaunce befor thy desire and preferre and folowe it afore all thyng G, *Latin*
meam ordinacionem tuo desiderio et omni desiderato preferre debes ac sequi
KR.

The following case appears to be similar. It appears that D², considering
'hydels' to be obscure, added the marginal gloss, which was copied by
M. Then D² changed the reading in the text to 'h⟨ernys⟩' and erased the
gloss; this revised reading was copied by G:

3.48.8 hydels] C, h⟨ernys⟩, *faintly in margin*: or hernings D², hideles or hernys
M, hernys G, *Latin* abscondita tenebrarum KR.

---

¹¹¹ There are further examples at 1.5.7, 1.14.5, 1.16.3, 1.16.4, 1.18.19, 1.19.22, 1.22.26,
1.25.15, 2.5.10, 2.5.17, 2.7.13, 2.8.31, 2.8.34, 2.10.28, 2.11.15, 2.11.16, 2.11.23, 2.12.6,
2.12.14, 2.12.32, 2.12.42, 2.12.44, 3.2.19, 3.5.8, 3.6.2, 3.6.29, 3.7.15, 3.8.4, 3.8.16, 3.8.17,
3.9.4, 3.9.5, 3.9.10, 3.12.1, 3.13.23, 3.48.9, 3.52.10, 3.54.6, 3.54.24, 3.54.26, 3.55.24,
3.59.24, 3.63.10, and 3.63.22–3.

In the following cases there are further developments in G. At 2.11.13 D² attempts to take the translation closer to the Latin, but omits the necessary negative, which is supplied by G; at 2.12.70 there is a further error in G, perhaps arising out of a misreading of *perlectis*; at 3.5.12 G omits the erroneous reading found in D²:

1.25.30 religiouse and the lewke] C, religiose and þe leuke 'man' D², religiose man and þe leuke M, and leuke religiouse man G, *Latin* religiosus negligens et tepidus KR   2.11.13 not to be seide] G, ⟨to be seyd⟩ D², to be seid M, not very C, *Latin* nonne omnes mercennarii sunt dicendi KR   2.12.70 þerfore over-radde] C, þer | ⟨ouer redd⟩ D², þer ouer red M, perfitly ouere redde G, *Latin* ergo perlectis KR   3.5.12 highe] C, heie 'here', heie *canc.* D², here M, *om.* G, *Latin* altum KR   3.11.9 þei renonce] C, ⟨ande⟩ ren⟨ouncyd⟩ D², and renounce M, and renouncyng G, *Latin* seculo renuncient KR.

(b) Corrections removing errors introduced in D¹

The following corrections were made before M and G were copied, and removed errors introduced in D¹; at 1.24.5 and 2.9.13 it is possible that D² has had recourse to the Latin, because its translation at this point is different from that in C, though equivalent in meaning to it:

1.7.6 not] CMG, 'not' D², *Latin* ne KR   1.10.4 withoute] CMG, wiþ'oute' D², *Latin* sine KR   1.24.5 to subdue] C, 'to holde' D², to holde MG, *Latin* subiugare KR   2.9.13 but the veri lover of criste and þe studiouse folowar of vertue falleþ not vppon consolacions] C, 'but þe very trewe louere of crist and studious folwer of vertu slydith ne not upon consolacyones', ne *canc.* D², but þe very trew louer of crist and studyous foloweþ of vertu he slydiþ neuer vpon consolacions M, but the verye true louer of cryst and studious folower of vertu slidyþ not vpon consolacions G, *Latin* sed verus amator christi et studiosus sectator virtutum non cadit super consolaciones KR 3.15.24 oure] CMG, 'oure' D², *Latin* domini KR   3.53.10 bee withoute] MG, 'be' wiþoute D², bee with C, *Latin* ero sine KR.

(c) Corrections removing errors present in the archetype

A number of D²-corrections were made before M and G were copied, and removed errors found in D¹ and C, including the following; because these errors occur in both branches of the stemma, they must have been present in the archetype:

2.8.12 ihesu fyndeþ] MG, 'ihesu fyndeth' D², *om.* C, *Latin* ihesum inuenit KR   2.11.19 yette] MG, 'ʒit' D², *om.* C, *Latin* adhuc KR 3.23.8 but þee onely] MG, 'but þe only' D², *om.* C, *Latin* sed te solum KR   3.39.3 but] MG, ⟨but⟩ D², ⟨. . .⟩ C, *Latin* sed KR   3.39.3 not þe worlde ner þat þat longeþ to him] G, 'not þe wor'l'de ne þat þat longit[h] to hym', longit[h] *cropped by binder* D², not þe worde ne þat þat longiþe to hym M, *om.* C, *Latin* sed amanti ⟨uerbum⟩ non mundum nec ea que in mundo sunt K, sed amanti verbum non mundum nec ea que in mundo sunt R 3.47.12 and draweþ into wikkednes] M, `and drawith into wikkydnes' D², . . rawith into vices G (*tear*), *om.* C, *Latin* et viciat KR          3.52.2 and alle mesure] MG, `and all mesure' D², *om.* C, *Latin* et mensuram KR 3.54.27 þerfore hit semeþ þee harde] MG, `þerfore it semiþ the harde' D², *om.* C, *Latin* ideo durum tibi videtur K, ideo tibi durum videtur R.[112]

The following cases are probably similar. In these instances D²'s correction is made on erasure. It is therefore not possible to prove that D¹ and C shared the same error, but the fact that in each case the erasure corresponds exactly with the variant makes this likely:

3.7.23 alle] MG, ⟨all⟩ D², any C, *Latin* omnem KR   3.11.25 shul] MG, s⟨hull⟩ D², shulde C, *Latin* consequentur KR   3.38.4 inconcussed] MG, ⟨inconcussyd⟩ D², vnmeved C, *Latin* inconcussus R, inconcussusque K 3.41.1 drede] MG, d⟨rede⟩ D², deme C, *Latin* metuas KR   3.53.12 shalt þou be to me] MG, ⟨shalt þou be⟩ `to me' D², þou shalt ‖ be C, *Latin* quando eris michi KR          3.55.25 and singuler] MG, `and' ⟨syngulere⟩ D², and everyþinge C, *Latin* et singula KR.

The following cases may result from checking against the Latin, as the errors in C and D¹ appear to result from mistranslation (*curat* as 'loveþ' at 2.1.38, and *ut* as 'þat' at 3.9.8):

2.1.38 he þat is welle-disposed withinforþe and ordinate he chargeþ not þe nyce and þe wondirfulle havynges and berynges of men] *con.*, he þat is ⟨wele disposyd ande ordeynyd inforth he chargith not þe wykkyd and wondyrfull hauyngys and be⟩ringes of men, *second* y *in* hauyngys *canc.* D², he þat is wel disposed and ordeynyd infurþe he chargiþe not þe wykkyd and wondirful hauyngys and beringes of men M, he þat is wel disposid and wel ordred withinfurth chargyth not the froward and wonderfull behavours of men G, he þat is not welle-disposed withinforþe and ordinate he loveþ þe nyce and þe wondirfulle havynges and berynges of men C, *Latin* qui ⟨intus⟩ b⟨ene⟩ dispositus est et ordinatus non curat mirabiles et peruersos hominum gestus K, qui intus bene dispositus est et ordinatus non curat peruersos et mirabiles hominum gestus R   3.9.8 as] MG, ⟨as⟩ D², þat C, *Latin* ut KR.

In the following cases D²'s attempts to remove errors in the archetype were less successful. At 2.9.3 D² seems to have removed 'þogh' by

---

[112] There are further examples at 1.15.1, 1.16.14, 2.1.12, 2.12.54, 3.3.13, 3.6.21, 3.20.10, and 3.35.14.

erasure; at 2.9.30 'worthi' was omitted in the archetype and D^2's added 'yn' is an attempt to make sense of the resulting text:

2.9.3 is it if] G, ⟨ys it⟩ D^2, is it M, þogh C, *Latin* est si KR   2.9.30 worthi highe] *con.*, highe C, hye 'yn' D^2, hye in M, hye in þe G, *Latin* non enim dignus est alta dei contemplacione KR.

2. *Corrections in D made after M was copied but before G was copied*

Corrections belonging to the second stage were not made until after M had been copied, for in these cases the corrected reading agrees with the reading found in G, but M has the original reading.

(*a*) *Corrections introducing errors in D^2*

A number of D^2-corrections were made after M was copied but before G was copied, and introduced errors, including the following; they gave rise to errors shared by D^2 and G:

2.11.26 alle þat may be estemed] M, alle þat may estemed C, allþ⟨o⟩ 'he' may be estym⟨att⟩ D^2, alþouȝe he may be estymate G, *Latin* quod grande estimari posset KR   3.15.18 hydels] CM, 'lurkynge' hidels, hidels *canc.* D^2, lurkyng G, *Latin* latebra KR   3.18.8 fortasteþ amonge] CM, fortasti⟨n⟩ amonge, amonge *canc.* D^2, fortasten G, *Latin* pregustant interdum KR   3.34.16 chaunge] CM, chaunge 'is' D^2, chaunge is G, *Latin* quanto michi difficilius tanto tibi facilior est hec mutacio dextere excelsi KR   3.43.3 myschieves] CM, mysch⟨aunces⟩ D^2, myschaunces G, *Latin* improbitatibus KR   3.50.24 counseile] CM, 'kepe' counseile D, kepe counseile G, *Latin* silere KR   counceyled] 'kepte' counseile D^2, kepte counseile G, *Latin* silendum KR   3.59.21 but] CM, ⟨and⟩ D^2, and G, *Latin* sed KR.[113]

In the following cases there are further complications. At 1.21.13 there is a further variant in M. 'Sat' accurately translates the imperfect tense of the Latin *deceret*, but it seems to have been thought obscure: M compensated by glossing; D^2, after M had been copied, substituted 'besemeth', which was copied by G. At 3.6.1 the error in D^2 arose out of an attempt to correct an original error in D^1. Presumably 'haste' dropped out in D^1, as is shown by M's reading; D^2's change to the present tense is an attempt to compensate for this. At 3.42.7 D^2 appears to have inserted the word 'not' and then cancelled it again:

1.21.13 sat] C, sat or behouyd M, ⟨. . .⟩'besemeth' D^2, besemethe G, *Latin* deceret KR   3.6.1 haste fouched save] C, vouchid saaf M, vouch⟨ist⟩ saaf

---

[113] There are further examples at 3.45.9, 3.45.10, 3.52.8, 3.60.25, and 3.61.4.

D², vouchist saue G, *Latin* dignatus es KR   3.42.7 maiste] CM, maiste
'not', not *canc.* D², mayst not G.

(b) Corrections removing errors introduced in D¹
A number of D²-corrections were made after M was copied but before
G was copied, including the following; they removed errors introduced
in D¹:

1.13.32 preserved] CG, pre⟨serued⟩ D², preferred M, *Latin* custodiuntur
KR   1.22.8 godes] CG, goodes, s *added on line* D², good M, *Latin*
bona KR   2.7.4 ihesu] CG, 'ihesu' D², *om.* M, *Latin* ihesum KR
2.10.24 special] CG, sp⟨ecial⟩ D², spirituel M, *Latin* speciali KR
3.6.24 of god] CG, *om.* M, 'of god' D², *Latin* dei KR   3.60.13 me] CG,
⟨me⟩ D², by M, *Latin* confortante me gracia KR   3.60.21 not] CG, ⟨not⟩
D², þat M, *Latin* ceteris non obtentis KR   3.63.32 þen þei] CG, 'þan
they' D², *om.* M, *Latin* quam is K, quam hii R.[114]

In the following cases there are further complications. At 1.22.16 D¹
omitted 'þoghe', and this error was transmitted to M. D² added 'þouȝe',
and changed the later 'þat' to 'yet'. At 3.8.22—where the translation is
extremely literal—it is hard to say whether 'estiemed' or 'estymat' was
in the archetype:

1.22.16 þoghe] *con.*, þat þoghe CG, þat 'þouȝe' D², þat M, *Latin* licet
KR   þat²] CM, ⟨yet⟩ D², yet G, *Latin* ut KR   3.8.22 estiemed
of þat if] *con.*, est⟨ymat⟩ of þat 'yf' D², estymate of þat if G, estiemed of þat
CM, *Latin* ex hoc existimanda si quis KR.

In the following cases it is possible that D² has referred to the Latin,
because the translations here are different from, though equivalent in
meaning to, those given in C:

1.23.10 if we amende but litel] C, but if we amende M, ⟨when ther ys lytell
amendement⟩ D², whenn þere is litel amendment G, *Latin* quando tam parum
emendamur K, quando parum emendamur R   1.24.5 haþ mercie] C, *om.*
M, 'forgeueth' D², forgeueth G, *Latin* miseretur KR   2.9.29 þat later or
raþer were not] C, þat later or raþer was M, 'but' þat later or raþer was D²,
'but' that latter or rather was G, *Latin* qui prius uel postea non fuerit temptatus
K, qui prius vel postea non temptatus fuerit R.

(c) Corrections removing errors present in the archetype
A number of D²-corrections were made after M was copied but before

---

[114] There are further examples at 1.11.6, 1.19.22, 2.8.8, 2.8.19, 2.9.26, 3.2.17, 3.6.12,
3.31.10, and 3.50.24; the cases at 3.32.5 and 3.33.6 (where C is wanting) may be similar.

G was copied, including the following; they removed errors found in D¹ and C which must have been present in the archetype:

1.2.11 but] G, ⟨but⟩ D², for CM, *Latin* sed KR   1.11.16 purer] G, pure`r´ D², pure CM, *Latin* puriores KR       1.16.15 frayle] G, `frayle´ D², *om.* CM, *Latin* fragilem KR   3.6.2 refreysshest] G, refressh⟨ist⟩ D², refreysshed CM, *Latin* recreas KR   3.21.12 falleþ to him] G, `fallyth to hym´ D², *om.* CM, *Latin* ei aliquid aduersi acciderit KR       3.36.4 more] G, mo⟨. .⟩, st *visible under erasure* D, moste CM, *Latin* quiecius KR       3.38.5 pure] G, `pure´ D², *om.* CM, *Latin* purior KR   3.46.4 I] G, ⟨y⟩ D², þou CM, *Latin* si recte me inspicio KR.¹¹⁵

In the following cases there are further complications. At 1.22.6 and 2.9.19 correction in D² attempts to compensate for a lacuna in the archetype, with a further alteration in G at 2.9.19. At 3.29.8, because C's text is lacking, it is not possible to tell whether the error originated in D¹ or the archetype; at 3.34.2 C too has attempted to remedy the deficiency in the archetype:

1.22.6 nowe] CDG, *om.* M   and seeke þat seithe] *con.*, and seeke C, now and seke M, ⟨that seyne⟩ D², þat seyne G, *Latin* dicunt multi imbecilles et infirmi K, dicunt nunc multi inbecilles et infirmi R   2.9.19 thi face fro me] *con.*, `þi face´ D², fro me G, *om.* CM, *Latin* auertisti faciem tuam a me KR       3.9.3 þi lyght nyghe] *con.*, `þi lyȝte nye´, þi lyȝte *canc.* D², þi lyght C, liȝt MG, *Latin* vicina cordi meo lux tua KR   3.29.8 and hit shal be trouble to þee] G, and it shal be trouble `to þe´ D², *om.* M, *Latin* et poterit fieri ut parum uel raro turberis KR (*C wanting*)       3.34.2 hit to] G, `it to´ D², `hit´ C, *om.* M, *Latin* in bonum mihi ipsam conuertas R, in bonum michi conuertas K.

All the corrections considered in this section are reflected in G but not in M. This indicates that M was copied before G, and that these corrections were made after M was copied but before G was copied; the corrector must have worked over the text several times. There is, however, a small number of corrections which result in cases of error shared exclusively between D² and M: in other words, the correction was carried over into M but not into G. These must be considered here, as taken by themselves they might suggest that G was copied first:

1.18.3 god hath served] CG, god ⟨which haue⟩ `seruyd´, h *visible under erasure under* w, which *canc.* D², god whiche haue serued M, *Latin* sancti et amici christi

---

¹¹⁵ There are further examples at 2.1.14, 3.6.33, 3.21.10, 3.39.10, 3.39.16, 3.42.8, 3.47.2, 3.47.5, 3.50.15, 3.50.24, 3.51.24, 3.60.16, and 3.60.19.

domino seruierunt KR   1.22.17 lithe so deepe] C, ly⟨ue⟩ so depe`ly´ D², lyue so depely M, lyene so depely G, *Latin* tam profunde in terrenis iacent KR   3.24.5 commendeþ] C, commend⟨id⟩ D², commendid M, commenden G, *Latin* commendant KR.

At 1.18.3, it appears that 'which' was added, erroneously, by D², copied by M, cancelled later by D², and the cancelled version copied by G. At 1.22.17 and 3.24.5, it appears that the erroneous corrections were copied in M but corrected again in G back to the original, correct, reading; given that the process of correction occurred in various stages over a period, it would not be impossible for the same passage to be corrected twice. It is simpler to suppose such an hypothesis in these two cases than to account for all the corrections listed above which are reflected in M but not in G.

3. *Corrections in D made after M and G were copied*

Corrections belonging to the third stage were made after both M and G had been copied, for in these cases the corrected reading is found in no other manuscript.

(a) *Corrections introducing errors in D²*

The following D²-corrections were made after M and G were copied, and gave rise to error in D²; they were not carried over into any other manuscript:

1.11.17 owed] CMG, ow⟨ith⟩ D², *Latin* deberet KR   1.12.4 wyttenes] CMG, witnes `of´ D², *Latin* interiorem testem deum KR      1.12.5 owed] CMG, owe⟨þ⟩ D², *Latin* deberet KR      1.12.5 neded] CMG, ned⟨ith⟩ D², *Latin* esset ei necesse KR      1.13.31 þere is hope] C, þere is hope in MG, þere`yn´ is hope ⟨. .⟩ D², *Latin* spes magni profectus erit KR   2.10.16 dewe] CMG, due `thy payne´ D², *Latin* deberi KR      3.21.9 putteþ] CMG, putti⟨d⟩ D², *Latin* improperat KR      3.23.4 me] CMG, me`n´ D², *Latin* michi KR   3.58.15 to⁵] CMG, *canc.* D, *Latin* ad omne . . . bonum KR.

In the following cases there are further complications. At 2.10.10 there is a further error in C; at 3.23.10 the correction attempts to compensate for an error in D¹; at 3.59.13 the situation is unclear:

2.10.10 refounde not alle ayein to] *con.*, refunde not ayen all to G, refounde not ayen ale M, refounde alle ayein to C, ⟨refunde⟩ not ayen all `or ȝotyn ow[t] ayen all´ to, ow[t] *cropped by binder* D², *Latin* nec totum refundimus KR

3.23.10 troubleþ me makeþ me sorye] C, troubliþe me sory M, troublen and
sorye me G, troubliþ me sor⟨e⟩ D², *Latin* conturbant contristant KR
3.59.13 stired] C, meved G, mevid red M, ⟨meu⟩'yd' ⟨sone⟩ D², *Latin* irritatur
leui iniurie uerbo KR.

(b) Corrections removing errors introduced in D¹

The following D²-corrections were made after M and G were copied,
and removed errors introduced in D¹:

2.5.13 alle] C, *om.* MG, 'all' D², *Latin* totum KR   3.2.8 the not spekynge
þei] C, þe spekynge þei M, þere spekyng G, ⟨the not⟩ spekyng þei D², *Latin* te
tacente cor non accendunt K, te tacente non accedunt R.

(c) Corrections removing errors present in the archetype

The following D²-corrections were made after M and G were copied,
and removed errors found in D¹ and C, which were present in the
archetype; at 1.19.24 it is again likely that the corrector has referred to
the Latin:

1.3.1–2 as hit is oure] ⟨as it ys oure⟩, ' *visible under erasure* D², þus hit is þat oure
CMG, *Latin* sicuti se habet nostra KR   1.19.24 of tyme] 'of tyme' D², *om.*
CMG, *Latin* temporis KR   3.36.14 desirers] desire⟨res⟩ D², desires C,
desiren M, þat desyren G, *Latin* plures reperiuntur contemplacionem desiderare
KR   3.54.26 þi] 'þi' D², *om.* CMG, *Latin* voluntati tue KR.

C. VARIANTS IN THE LATIN

It was shown in Part II that the translation was made from a Latin text
similar to that found in R, a text some stages removed from the
autograph manuscript, K. In this part it has been shown that conflation
with a Latin manuscript is evident both in G and in the corrections to
D. In the following cases it is clear that the Latin manuscript used by G
for conflation was closer to K than that used for the original translation:[116]

1.15.14 a sparkel] G, þat kunnynge CM, þat kunnyg M, *Latin* sintillam K,
scienciam illam R   1.20.17 þer] G, *om.* CDM, *Latin* sui 'ipsius' K, sui
R   1.25.19 oftely] G, feruently CDM, *Latin* frequencius K, feruencius
R   1.25.29 the feruent religiouse man bereþ alle þinges welle and takeþ
alle þat be commaunded him] G, *om.* CDM, *Latin* religiosus feruidus omnia

---

[116] If G's readings in these cases are derived from a Latin manuscript, then arguably the
text should not be emended. Since the K reading is clearly superior, however, it has
generally been adopted.

bene portat et capit que illi iubentur K, *om*. R ⁣ 3.37.2 puttinge] C, ⟨shapynge⟩ D², shapyng MG, *Latin* opponentes R, componentes K 3.37.3 alle þinge shal perisshe þat hath not his bigynnynge of god] G, *om*. CDM, *Latin* peribit enim totum quod non est ex deo ortum K, *om*. R.

The following cases make it clear that the D²-corrections were also made from a manuscript closer to K; these corrections are reflected in M and G:

3.45.8 my herte] MG, ʽmyn herteʼ D², *om*. C, *Latin* sed in te vno cor meum conuertatur K, sed in te vno conuertatur R ⁣ 3.46.8 be meked ner be fully oned to] C, ⟨be illumynyd ner⟩ fully ⟨onyd to⟩ D², be illumynid ner fully onyd to MG, *Latin* humiliari neque plene tibi vniri R, illuminari neque plene tibi vniri K.

The following cases are similar, but here the D²-corrections are reflected in G only. They were therefore made after M was copied:

1.25.1 seruice] G, ⟨seruyse⟩ D², iugemente CM, *Latin* seruicio K, iudicio R 3.40.4 my] CM, ⟨fre⟩ D², fre G, *Latin* mea R, mera K ⁣ 3.51.23 vnrightwise] CM, vnriȝtwi⟨sly⟩ D², vnriȝtwosly G, *Latin* iniustum R, iniuste K.

In the following cases the correspondence between the English and the Latin variants may be coincidental, because the potential for misreading is the same in either language, either where the English translation simply borrows the Latin as a loan word, or through homoeoteleuton:

1.4.0 prouidence] C, prudence DMG, *Latin* prouidencia K, prudencia R 1.20.47 turbacion] CDG, tribulacion M, *Latin* turbacionem K, tribulacionem R ⁣ 2.12.25 þiselfe byneþe turne thiselfe] C, þiʽself bynethe turne þiʼself D², þiself MG, *Latin* te infra conuerte te K, te R ⁣ 2.12.37 sufferuance] MG, suffi⟨r⟩|⟨.⟩aunce, s *visible under erasure* D², suffisaunce C, *Latin* ⟨sufferencia⟩ K, sufficiencia R.

In the following cases C's reading agrees with R, and DMG's with K:

3.0.4 a preyer to gete grace of deuocion capitulum quartum] C, *om*. DMG, *Latin* oracio ad implorandum deuocionis graciam iiii R, *om*. K ⁣ 3.37.1 perfitely] C, parfit DMG, *Latin* perfecte R, perfectam K ⁣ 3.57.13 þes not] C, not þis DMG, *Latin* hec R, hoc K ⁣ 3.58.5 to] C, of DMG, *Latin* deo vacacionem R, dei vacacionem K.

These cases are harder to account for; they too may be the result of coincidence, and at 3.58.5 it is possible that D's 'of' may have been written over erasure. There are also three cases of the opposite situation:

where C's reading is closer to K—although it only actually agrees with K at 3.35.23—and the other manuscripts are closer to R:

2.12.52 suffre alle alone] C, al allone suffre alle temptacions M, ⟨. .⟩ allone ⟨suf⟩'fyr al temptaciouns', al *visible under first erasure* D², allone suffyr all temptacions G, *Latin* eciam si solus omnes posses ⟨sustinere⟩ K, eciam si solus omnes passiones posses tunc sustinere R   3.35.23 not alle þenne] C, þan all DMG, *Latin* non est tunc totum perditum R, non est totum perditum K   3.54.10 for I] MG, ⟨for I⟩ D², I C, *Latin* nam desiderium tuum et frequentes gemitus audiui R, noui desiderium tuum et frequentes gemitus audiui K.

Finally, there is one case where CDG's reading agrees with R, and M's with K:

1.22.6 nowe] CDG, *om.* M, *Latin* nunc R, *om.* K.

D. CONCLUSIONS

On the basis of the above analysis the stemma on p. xviii above is suggested, and the manuscript used for the base text in the present edition is C. M and G are unsuitable because they are derived from D. D was printed by Ingram in his EETS edition of 1893; its corrected state means that it does not present a consistent text linguistically. C, on the other hand, has ten leaves missing. Although it has a large number of isolative errors, C has fewer errors than those of the DMG group. Apart from its missing leaves, therefore, C is the manuscript which requires the least emendation.

In all three aspects of the relationship between the manuscripts—the stemma, corrections, and variants in the Latin—a common phenomenon was evident: conflation with a Latin manuscript. It is evident from the variants used to establish the stemma that the scribe of G had had recourse to a Latin text; an examination of the corrections suggests strongly that the same was true of D²; and in the case of the variants in the Latin, both G and D² can be shown to have referred to a Latin manuscript similar to R. The characteristics of the corrections in D and the alterations in G are similar, and support the view advanced on palaeographical and orthographical grounds in Part I that Darker, who copied G, was also responsible for the D²-corrections.

It may be appropriate to conclude this section with a brief assessment of Darker's work as a corrector. It is evident he worked over the text several times, and compared it with a Latin manuscript. As described in Part I, he also made other kinds of correction—changes to the punctuation and capitalization, orthography, and morphology; he was evidently concerned for linguistic correctness and consistency, as well as with the text and its meaning. It is not surprising that the first English translation of the *Imitatio Christi* should have received this kind of treatment at the hands of an English Carthusian: as Michael Sargent has shown, the Carthusians were much concerned with textual purity, and the Carthusian Oswald de Corda's manual for correctors, *Opus Pacis*, gives advice on points of orthography, morphology, syntax, and punctuation—some of the points with which Darker was concerned.[117]

In particular, Darker's work may be compared with that of his contemporary at Sheen, James Grenehalgh, previously *magister scholarum* at Wells, who made a total of some 1800 annotations to twelve manuscripts and two printed books.[118] Grenehalgh's corrections include orthographical and textual corrections to a manuscript of *The Cloud of Unknowing*[119] (showing evidence of collation with another manuscript), and corrections to a copy of Wynkyn de Worde's *Scale of Perfection*[120] resulting from a comparison of it with Fishlake's Latin translation. Darker's career as schoolmaster and Carthusian was similar to Grenehalgh's, and so was his work as a corrector, although it was on a smaller scale. Both were concerned with orthography and usage; both were concerned with textual correctness; both were interested in comparing English and Latin versions of the same text. Sargent suggests that Grenehalgh's work should not be considered textual criticism in the modern sense, because he did not identify his sources or aim at publication.[121] In these respects Darker's work is a little different, perhaps slightly closer to modern textual criticism. The Latin text that Darker used for comparison was not derivative, like Fishlake's Latin translation of Hilton, but closer to the source—closer to the Kempis manuscript—than that available to the original translator of the *Imitation*. Moreover, he used his corrections to produce a fair copy when he wrote G for Elizabeth Gibbs of Syon.

---

[117] M. G. Sargent, *James Grenehalgh as Textual Critic*, AC 85, 2 vols (Salzburg, 1984), i. 19–21.

[118] Ibid. i. 76–8, 110–11, 213; see also the same author's 'James Grenehalgh: The Biographical Record', in *Kartäusermystik und -mystiker*, AC 55, 5 vols (Salzburg, 1981–2), iv. 20–54.

[119] Oxford, Bodleian Library, MS Douce 262 (Sargent, *James Grenehalgh as Textual Critic*, i. 240–7).

[120] Philadelphia, Rosenbach Museum and Library, H491 (ibid. ii. 330–472).

[121] Ibid. ii. 358–9.

IV. LANGUAGE

I have set out elsewhere a fuller analysis of the language of the four manuscripts of the *Imitation* and of the other manuscripts copied by the same scribes;[122] here, therefore, only a summary analysis, using the questionnaire and maps in *LALME*, is given.[123]

A. THE LANGUAGE OF THE MANUSCRIPTS

1. *The language of C*

C may be localized to the Surrey/Middlesex area as follows. The north, east midlands and East Anglia are eliminated by the forms *hem*, *her* for the third person pronoun, *muche*, *wolle/wol* for WILL, *worche* for WORK (verb), and *beeþ/beþ/beþe/bethe* for ARE (dot maps 40, 52, 164, 315, 128). The west midlands are eliminated by the forms *ayenis* for AGAINST, *many*, *þoghe*, and *whither/whiþer* (dot maps 225, 90, 202, 579). Much of the central midlands is eliminated by the form *furste* for FIRST (dot map 417). The south west, central south, and south east are eliminated by the forms *ouþer* for EITHER, *ar* for ARE, and *ner* for NOR; *ner* also eliminates the southern midlands and Essex (dot maps 404, 118, 487). The locality remaining contains south-west London, southern Middlesex, the extreme south of Buckinghamshire, the extreme east of Berkshire, and northern Surrey. Southern Middlesex is in the centre of this area.[124]

2. *The language of D*

The language of the other manuscripts is similar. D has been localized by *LALME* to a point in the south of Buckinghamshire.[125] The main

---

[122] See my article, 'The Language of the Scribes of the First English Translation of the *Imitatio Christi*', *LSE*, NS 26 (1995), 79–111.

[123] The dot maps are in numerical sequence in *LALME* i. 305–551.

[124] Other notable features of C's spelling include the following: long *z* has been misinterpreted in the spelling *hele* for 'zele' (1.0.11, 1.11.0, 1.18.6, 1.18.19, 2.3.8 (twice), 3.12.7 (*yeledeste* for 'zeldeste'); *zele* is spelt correctly at 2.5.4 and 3.63.9); *hode* for 'wode' (1.24.12); *wolde* for 'olde' (3.22.11); forms of *fouchesave* spelt with initial *f-* (1.16.3, 3.6.1, 3.11.6, 3.11.11, 3.57.5); *yerthe* and *yerthely* sometimes so spelt with initial *y-* (1.12.1, 1.13.2, 1.15.14, 1.17.4, etc.), and once with initial *h-* (*herþe* 3.23.11); syncope in *sette* (2.4.15) and *ende* (3.64.21), both pr. 3 sg.; use of medial *v* in e.g. *love* (1.2.15, 1.5.5, 1.7.2, etc.); *he* and *the* for 'ye' (2.11.27, 2.12.2). *Wolde* and *yerthe* are predominantly south-western spellings (Jordan, §283); *fouchesave* may be a reverse spelling indicating voicing of initial *f-*, a southern feature (Jordan, §215); *herthe* may also be a reverse spelling indicating loss of initial *h-* (Jordan, §293); *hode* could perhaps result from a combination of loss of *w* before *ō* (Jordan, §§162, 278) and a reverse spelling arising out of loss of inital *h-*.

[125] Grid 486 191 (*LALME* iii. 20).

differences between the language of D and C in respect of the points used to localize C above are that D has *biþ* in addition to *are* and *beþ*, *ayenst/aȝenst*, *þouȝ*, *first*, and *eiþer*; it also has *eny* for C's *any*. Similar areas of the country may be eliminated, however: the central and east midlands and Essex are eliminated by *biþ* (dot map 130), and the south east and south west are eliminated by *eiþer* and D's form *besy* (dot maps 402, 371). D also has the form *ovne/oune*, not found in northern Middlesex or London (dot map 498). The remaining area contains the extreme south of Middlesex, southern Buckinghamshire, the extreme east of Berkshire, and northern Surrey. *LALME*'s localization of D, in southern Buckinghamshire, is in the extreme west of this area: its more westerly location may be due to its forms *biþ* and *ovne*, neither of which is found in London or Middlesex.[126] It is less clear, however, why the extreme north of Surrey should have been eliminated as a possible location for D: it may have been because *biþ*-type forms are found in only two Surrey manuscripts.[127] D's profile is very similar to that of the other Dodesham manuscript profiled in *LALME*, which is localized in Middlesex,[128] and it is therefore probable that D too should have a more easterly location.

3. *The language of M*

The language of M is broadly similar to that of D: the main differences, as regards the points used for localization, are that it has the forms *owne/own* and *frist* for FIRST; *frist* eliminates parts of the central midlands and central southern England, including eastern Berkshire, southern Buckinghamshire, and southern Middlesex (dot map 418). M may therefore be located in northern Surrey, where there are three linguistic profiles containing the form *frist*, all of which are similar to M, although none is exactly the same.[129]

---

[126] Except that *bith* is found in another Dodesham manuscript, London, British Library, MS Additional 11305 (LP 6440), localized in Middlesex (*LALME* iii. 302): see the item maps for ARE (*LALME* ii. 86) and OWN (*LALME* ii. 320).

[127] See the item map for ARE (*LALME* ii. 86). The two manuscripts are Cambridge, University Library, MS Gg. i. 6, main hand (a Sheen manuscript containing *A Mirror to Devout People*), which has *byth* as a minority form (Grid 518 172, LP 5760, *LALME* iii. 496-7); and Oxford, Bodleian Library, MS Lyell 34 (*Davies's Chronicle*), which has *bith* and *bythe* (Grid 532 160, LP 5800, *LALME* iii. 499).

[128] See above, n. 126.

[129] LPs 5630, 5641, and 5770 (*LALME* iii. 493, 494, 497); for their location, see the item map for FIRST (*LALME* ii. 277-8).

4. *The language of G*

The language of G is also similar to that of D: the main difference is that it has *be* rather than *beþ/biþ*, and *owne/own*. Forms of the *be* type are not found in much of south-west England and the south-west midlands (dot map 123). G is therefore, like C and D, to be located within an area containing south London, southern Middlesex, the extreme south of Buckinghamshire, a small part of the extreme east of Oxfordshire, the extreme east of Berkshire, and northern Surrey, with the point at which Middlesex, Surrey, and Buckinghamshire meet at its approximate centre. This is consistent with the location in south-east Middlesex given in *LALME* to another manuscript copied by Darker, whose language is similar to that of G.[130]

5. *The language of the D²-corrections*

The language of the corrections in D is similar to that of G: the main difference is that it has the form *wyll* (it is of course rather a small sample). This supports the attribution of the corrections to Darker. *Hem, much, be/bee*, and *ner* are as in G (except that *mych* also occurs); of the other items found, *þan/than* and *thynk* may be used to eliminate the west midlands (dot maps 188, 297), and *but* and ⟨*euy*⟩*ll* eliminate parts of the south east and central southern England (dot maps 376, 982). The area remaining contains south London, southern Middlesex, a small part of southern Buckinghamshire, the extreme east of Berkshire, northern Surrey, and a small part of western Kent. A point on the Thames about half way between the Middlesex–London and Middlesex–Buckinghamshire borders is approximately in the centre of this area. Like that of G, the profile of the corrections is similar to the Darker manuscript analysed in *LALME*, which is localized in south-east Middlesex.[131]

6. *Conclusions*

It may be concluded, therefore, that the linguistic analysis of D and G supports the palaeographical evidence that they were written at the

---

[130] Cambridge, University Library, MS Ff. vi. 33, *A Ladder of Foure Ronges by the Which Men Mowe Wele Clyme to Heven* (LP 6460, Grid 515 177, *LALME* iii. 303); see also key map 6 (*LALME* ii. 388). This portion of the manuscript has been printed by P. Hodgson, *Deonise Hid Diuinite*, EETS 231 (1955, repr. with corr. 1958), pp. 100–17. The main differences between the language of this manuscript and that of G are that MS Ff. vi. 33 has *ne* for NOR (but G's form *ner* may well be archetypal, as discussed below, p. lxxiii), *werke* for WORK (verb), and *myche, mych* for MUCH.

[131] See previous note.

Charterhouse at Sheen in Surrey, and a similar analysis of the corrections in D supports the palaeographical and textual evidence that they are the work of Darker. The linguistic analysis of M suggests that it was copied by a scribe who learnt to write in northern Surrey, and that of C suggests a provenance of northern Surrey, Middlesex, or London. If C and M were not, like D and G, copied at Sheen, therefore, it is probable that they were written nearby; from the evidence of the surviving manuscripts the text does not appear to have been disseminated over a wide area.

B. THE LANGUAGE OF THE ARCHETYPE

An attempt was also made to localize the language of the archetype, on the basis of forms common to C and D, but not found in the other manuscripts copied by their scribes. The form *ner* comes into this category, and also the rather unusual mixture of *are* and *beþ/biþ* forms: Dodesham and the C-scribe prefer *ben* in their other manuscripts, and in over 90% of the instances of ARE, C and D have the same form, if *beþ* and *biþ* are treated as equivalents with a common origin in a *bVþ*-type form in the archetpye. The forms *muche* and *wolle/wol*, although also found in other manuscripts copied by Dodesham, are without parallel in the manuscripts of the C-scribe, whose orthography is more variable and hence more likely to reflect some of the characteristics of the exemplars used. In combination these forms eliminate the north, the east and west midlands, and much of the south. The area remaining contains Middlesex, southern Hertfordshire, southern Buckinghamshire, eastern Bedforshire, northern Surrey, and London. Southern Middlesex forms the centre of this area. Within this region, there are four linguistic profiles which contain the form most distinctive of the archetype, *ner*.[132] The points at which these four manuscripts have been localized enclose a parallelogram, at the centre of which is the part of northern Surrey which forms a peninsula enclosed by the Thames.[133] Although this localization cannot be regarded as definitive, it is certainly compatible with the other evidence connecting the translation with Sheen Charterhouse.[134]

---

[132] LPs 5630, 5800, 6390, and 6470 (*LALME* iii. 493, 499, 298, 304); LP 6470 is of London, Public Record Office, SC 1/51/46A–46C inclusive, letter from the confessor of Syon to Henry VI (Grid 512 179, Middlesex). See also the item map for NOR (*LALME* ii. 205–6).

[133] See key maps 5 and 6 (*LALME* ii. 387–8).

[134] It is notable that four of the six Sheen manuscripts which have been localized in

V. STYLE

Within the fourfold scheme of kinds of late Middle English translation
set out by Roger Ellis, literal, close, free, and erroneous, the *Imitation*
should be classed as a close translation.[135] It makes only very minor
modifications to the content of the Latin original, and follows closely
the sentence structure of the Latin. S. K. Workman has grouped it with
translations of the most usual kind in the period, in which the relationship between clauses is generally the same as in the Latin, but
constructions are modified as appropriate within the clause.[136] This
fidelity is made easier by the simplicity of the syntax of the Latin
Imitatio, which, as Betty Knott has pointed out, is

composed largely of short pithy sentences . . . [containing] carefully balanced
phrases in which the number of words is kept approximately equal and the
antithesis pointed by the use of alliteration and especially of rhyme. Another
frequently used stylistic device is the emphatic repetition of a group of words or
a similar construction in a number of succeeding sentences.[137]

The translator's faithful approach, although it sometimes results in a
slightly unidiomatic word order and idiom, is generally appropriate for
the *Imitatio*; it enables not only the content but also many of the
rhetorical characteristics of the original to be reproduced in the
translation.

I have set out elsewhere a detailed analysis of the style of the
translation.[138] The translator steers a middle course between rigidity
and freedom in his handling of the vocabulary, syntax, and rhetoric of his
source. In his choice of vocabulary, sometimes a Latin-derived word is
preferred, and in a few cases a Latin-derived word is used for the first
time (see the Appendix to the Introduction for a complete list of such

LALME have been placed within this area: see LPs 5750, 5760, 6440, and 6460 (*LALME*
iii. 496–7, 302–3). The points at which these four manuscripts have been localized are
adjacent to each other and form a small square straddling the eastern part of the border
between Middlesex and Surrey: see key map 6 (*LALME* ii. 388).

[135] 'The Choices of the Translator in the Late Middle English Period', in *The Medieval
Mystical Tradition in England: Papers Read at Dartington Hall, July 1982*, ed. M. Glasscoe,
Exeter Medieval English Texts and Studies (Exeter, 1982), pp. 18–46 (p. 33).

[136] *Fifteenth Century Translation as an Influence on English Prose*, Princeton Studies in
English, 18 (Princeton, 1940), p. 120.

[137] Knott, pp. 34–5.

[138] See my article, 'The Style of the First English Translation of the *Imitatio Christi*', in
The Medieval Translator 5, ed. R. Ellis and R. Tixier (Turnhout, 1996), pp. 187–211.

words); the overall impression of the style, however, is not markedly latinate in diction, because over 95% of the Latin-derived words used were well-established in the English of the period, and in about a quarter of the instances where a choice appeared to be possible an available Latin-derived word was rejected. On the level of syntax, while constructions within the clause are freely modified, constructions such as the accusative and infinitive and ablative absolute are sometimes reproduced in the translation, for by the later fifteenth century they had become acceptable in idomatic English. Thirdly, many of the rhetorical figures of balance and repetition characteristic of the *Imitatio* are also found in the translation, and although the frequent use of rhyme could not usually be reproduced, the translator has made some effort to compensate for this by shaping the prose of the translation with an eye to its rhetorical effect.

Some of these characteristics may be illustrated from the following typical passage:

[1] Habet Ihesus nunc multos amatores regni sui celestis: sed paucos baiulatores sue crucis. [2] Multos habet desideratores consolacionis: sed paucos tribulacionis. [3] Plures inuenit socios mense: sed paucos abstinencie. [4] Omnes cupiunt cum eo gaudere: pauci volunt pro eo aliquid sustinere. [5] Multi Ihesum sequuntur usque ad fractionem panis: sed pauci usque ad bibendum calicem passionis. [6] Multi miracula eius venerantur: pauci ignominiam crucis sequuntur. [7] Multi Ihesum diligunt: quamdiu aduersa non contingunt. [8] Multi illum laudant et benedicunt: quamdiu consolaciones aliquas ab ipso percipiunt. [9] Si autem Ihesus se absconderit et modicum eos reliquerit: aut in querimoniam vel in deiectionem nimiam cadunt.

[1] Ihesus hath many lovers of þe reaume of hevon, but fewe berars of his crosse. [2] He haþe many desirars of consolacions, and fewe of tribulacions. [3] He fyndeþ many felawse of þe table, and fewe of abstinence. [4] Alle desireþ to ioye with him, but fewe wol suffre any peyne for him. [5] Many foloweþ Ihesu vnto the brekynge of brede, but fewe vnto the drinkynge of þe cuppe of the passion. [6] Many worshippeth his miracles, but fewe foloweþ the repreve of the crosse. [7] Many lovethe Ihesu when none aduersite falleþ. [8] Many preyseþ him and blesseþ him whiles þei take any consolacions of him. [9] But if Ihesus hide him and a litel forsake hem, þei falle into a compleynynge or into over-grete deieccion.

(2.11.1–9)

The alterations made in the translation here are few. *Nunc* and *sui* are omitted from v. 1.[139] The singulars *consolacionis* and *tribulacionis* of v. 2 become the plurals 'of consolacions' and 'of tribulacions'. 'But' is

---

[139] R reads *non* for *nunc*, and some other manuscripts omit *nunc*; at least one also omits *sui* (Lupo, p. 117).

supplied between the two halves of the *antitheses* in vv. 4 and 6;[140] in v. 4 also *aliquid sustinere* is rendered 'suffre any peyne'. Otherwise, however, the meaning of the Latin is generally followed very closely.

In its treatment of vocabulary, the translation sometimes uses the anglicized equivalent of the word in the source (*consolacionis* 'consolacions', *tribulacionis* 'tribulacions', *abstinencie* 'abstinence', *miracula* 'miracles', *deiectionem* 'deieccion'),[141] sometimes a native equivalent (*sustinere* 'suffre', *fractionem* 'brekynge', *venerantur* 'worshippeth', *ignominiam* 'repreve', *laudant* 'preyseþ', *percipiunt* 'take', *absconderit* 'hide', *reliquerit* 'forsake').[142] Although it contains some latinate words ('abstinence', 'deieccion'), its diction as a whole is not overwhelmingly latinate.

In its syntax the translation follows the Latin clause by clause; this causes few difficulties here as the syntax is largely co-ordinate in the Latin. In this extract there is no significant difference between the syntax of the original and the translation, apart from the translation of the adjective *celestis* by the noun phrase 'of hevon' (v. 1).[143]

The Latin displays some of the typical features of the style of the *Imitatio*: the whole passage is built around *antithesis*, made more effective by frequent *homoeoteleuton*, either with a full rhyme or a half rhyme (*celestis . . . crucis*; *consolacionis . . . tribulacionis*; *mense . . . abstinencie*; etc.), and *anaphora* (*multi . . . multi . . . multi . . . multi*).[144] There is also the combined use of *isocolon*, *parison*, and *antithesis* in v. 6: *Multi miracula eius venerantur: pauci ignominiam crucis sequuntur*. The fact that the translator follows the Latin clause by clause means that the *antithesis* and *anaphora* are automatically reproduced in the translation. *Homoeoteleuton* is more difficult to achieve in an uninflected language, but it occurs in 'consolacions . . . tribulacions' (v. 2), where Latin loanwords are used, and also in 'with him . . . for him' (v. 4), where it is facilitated by the difference between Latin and English word order. In v. 8 the lack of *homoeoteleuton* is compensated for by the fact that in

---

[140] *Sed* is found in both these verses in some manuscripts (Lupo, p. 117).

[141] Of these words, 'consolation', 'tribulation', and 'abstinence' were well established in the English of the period; 'dejection' was rare.

[142] Of the anglicized equivalents of these Latin words, here rejected by the translator, 'sustain' and 'perceive' were well established; 'fraction', 'ignominy', 'laud', and 'relinquish' were rare; and 'abscond' and 'venerate' had yet to appear.

[143] The rendering of the gerundive *ad bibendum calicem passionis* by 'vnto the drinkynge of þe cuppe of the passion' avoids both the Early Version of the Wycliffite Bible's unidiomatic use of the passive infinitive and the Later Version's use of the active infinitive; it reflects the increased use of the verbal noun in late Middle English (Visser, §1036).

[144] The names and definitions of rhetorical figures are used here as in B. Vickers, *In Defence of Rhetoric* (Oxford, 1988, repr. with corr. 1989), pp. 491–8.

English *illum* and *ipso* are both automatically rendered 'him', thus creating *ploche*, and the translator may have deliberately intensified this effect by repeating 'him' in the phrase 'preyseþ him and blesseþ him' (*illum laudant et benedicunt*); this also creates a link with the final sentence, where *se* is rendered 'him'.[145]

The presence of *ploche* instead of *homoeoteleuton* in v. 8 here is typical of the effect of close translation on the rhetoric of the *Imitatio* which results from the simplicity of English inflexional morphology. Whereas the linking of different words used successively in similar syntactic positions through the similarity of their inflexional endings generally disappears in the translation, there is a compensating gain where the same word is used successively in different syntactical functions, for the inflexional simplicity of English means that it is exactly the same word, rather than an inflexional variant of it, that is repeated. This is an essentially automatic effect of translation into English, but there are also places where the translator's deliberate stylistic choice can be detected. This is so in the following passage, where the syntax of the Latin is a little more complex than that in the example just analysed:

[29] Esto purus et liber ab intus: sine alicuius creature implicamento. [30] Oportet te esse nudum et purum cor ad deum gerere: si vis vacare et videre quam suauis sit dominus. [31] Et reuera ad hoc non pervenies nisi gracia eius fueris preuentus et intractus; ut omnibus euacuatis et licenciatis: solus cum solo vniaris. [32] Quando enim gracia dei uenit ad hominem: tunc potens fit ad omnia. [33] Et quando recedit, tunc pauper et infirmus erit: et quasi tantum ad flagella relictus. [34] In hiis non debet deici nec desperare, sed ad voluntatem dei equanimiter stare: et cuncta superueniencia sibi ad laudem Ihesu Christi perpeti; quia post hyemem sequitur

[29] Be pure and free withinforthe, withoute implicamente or encombrance of any creature. [30] þou moste be bare, and bere to God a pure herte, if þou wolte taste and see howe swete God is. [31] And verily, þerto shalt þou neuer come, but yf þou be prevente and noryshed with his grace, þat, alle þinges voyded and conged, þou alleone be oned with him alone. [32] For whenne þe grace of God comeþ to a man, þen is he myghty to alle þinges. [33] And whenne hit goeþ aweye, þen shal he be pouer and vnmyghty and as a man onely lafte to scourgynges and peynes. [34] In thes þinges be not þrowen downe ner despeire not, but stande evonly at

---

[145] In the sentence 'For if þou be dede with him, þou shalt also lyffe with him', rendering *Quia si commortuus fueris: eciam cum illo pariter viues* (2.12.15), an effective *epistrophe* is naturally produced, intensifying the rhetorical effect of the sentence, by the difference in English word order and the absence of a single-word English equivalent of *commortuus*.

estas: post noctem redit dies, et post tempestatem magna serenitas.

the wille of God, and suffre alle þinges þat comeþ to þee to þe preysinge 'of' oure Lorde Ihesu Criste. For after wynter comeþ somer, and after [evon] comeþ day, and after tempeste comeþ clerenes.

(2.8.29–34)

Again the content of the original is hardly altered in the translation.[146] Two doublets are introduced, 'implicamente or encombrance' for *implicamento* and 'scourgynges and peynes' for *flagella*. (This procedure, although common in a number of fifteenth- and sixteenth-century texts, is rare in the *Imitation*: there are only eight other examples in Book II.) In v. 30 *vacare* is rendered 'taste', by confusion of Psalm 45.11 and Psalm 33.9.[147] In v. 34 the second person is used instead of the third, and in the last sentence *magna* is omitted in the translation. The vocabulary again is a mixture of native and latinate words (e.g. *nudum* 'bare', *infirmus* 'vnmyghty'; *preuentus* 'prevente', *tempestatem* 'tempeste'). The syntax again reproduces exactly the structure of the Latin, even in the more complex v. 31, where the ablative absolute is reproduced, *omnibus euacuatis et licenciatis* being rendered 'alle þinges voyded and conged'. The antithesis of vv. 32–3 has been enhanced by the *polyptoton* introduced in rendering *potens . . . infirmus* as 'myghty . . . vnmyghty', and the rhetorical effect of the translation is also evident in the last sentence. Its threefold structure is emphasized, first by the translation of both *sequitur* and *redit* as 'comeþ', and secondly by the addition of 'comeþ' to the third clause, where it has no parallel (although the variation in the Latin introduced by *magna* is lost). The translator has enhanced the rhetorical effect of this sentence by introducing *ploche*, producing a sentence as effective and idiomatic in English as its counterpart is in the Latin.[148]

It would be inappropriate to exaggerate the merits of this translation; nevertheless, it is fair to say that it is a generally effective close translation whose effectiveness is largely derived from its closeness.

[146] In v. 35, 'evon', omitted in C, has been supplied from DMG.

[147] See Note *ad loc.*

[148] Typical examples of rhetorical heightening involving other figures include the substitution of *isocolon* and *parison* for *epistrophe* in 'He be thi drede, he be thi love', rendering *Sit ipse timor tuus et amor tuus* (2.1.16), and the introduction of a *chiasmus* in 'Lorde, to þee shalle I crie, and I shalle preie to my God', rendering *Ad te domine clamabo: et ad deum meum deprecabor* (2.9.20).

With its innovative but not slavishly latinate vocabulary, generally idiomatic syntax, and conscious use of rhetoric, it succeeds in communicating much of the force of the original in the English vernacular.[149]

VI. CONCLUSIONS

Can anything be deduced about the translation's origin and purpose? It is datable to the mid-fifteenth century, and the archetype of the surviving manuscripts, if not the autograph of the translation itself, was written in London, Middlesex, or Surrey; two of the four surviving manuscripts, D and G, were copied at Sheen Charterhouse, as was the earliest dated manuscript of the Latin copied in England. The translation may therefore have been the work of a Carthusian monk of Sheen.[150] The fact that the text has not been edited or adapted, as so many vernacular translations were, and the presence of Latin loanwords which would be difficult to understand for a reader who did not know Latin, both suggest that the translator had a well-educated readership in mind. It is possible that the translation was made as a private devotional exercise; alternatively it could have been made for the nuns at Syon (this was at least true of one of its copies, G).[151] Whatever the translator's intention, with only four manuscripts surviving, closely related both textually and linguistically, the translation does not appear to have reached an extensive audience.[152] To reach the wide vernacular readership that it deserved, the *Imitatio Christi* had to await the publication of subsequent translations in the sixteenth century.

[149] This is less true of the second English translation (Atkynson's), which employs an aureate style with a tendency to expand on the original, resulting in rather a diffuse rendering: see Ingram, pp. xxiv–xxvii.

[150] On the English Carthusians' interest in the *devotio moderna*, see J. Hogg, 'The English Charterhouses and the Devotio Moderna', in *Historia et spiritualitas cartusiensis: colloquii quarti internationalis acta*, ed. J. de Grauwe (Destelbergen, Belgium, 1983), pp. 257–68.

[151] Translations made for the benefit of the Syon nuns include *The Orcherd of Syon*, ed. P. Hodgson and G. M. Liegey, EETS 258 (1966: see pp. vii, 1–2), and *The Myroure of Oure Ladye*, ed. J. H. Blunt, EETS, ES 19 (1873: see pp. 2–3, 70–1).

[152] Lovatt attributes the lack of widespread interest in the *Imitatio* to 'the rigid stratification, the lack of receptivity, the profound conservatism of late medieval English spirituality' (p. 117).

APPENDIX

NEW WORDS USED IN THE 'IMITATION'

The following words are apparently used for the first time in the *Imitation*, and are still current in English (i.e. not marked as obsolete in *OED*); those instances marked with an asterisk are not listed in *MED* (not in *OED* in the case of words in the range T–Z):

abiectely (3.15.14), **acceptably* (3.21.12), **anxiete* (3.8.4, 3.40.10 plural, 3.52.13, 3.56.4 plural), *cenobyes* (1.3.25), *circumfounded* (3.53.7, 3.60.6), *concupiscently* (3.58.19), *confabulacions* (3.57.6, 3.58.3), *contenciouse* (3.49.3), *contingently* (3.35.14), *diffinite* (3.24.11), *evagacions* (3.27.2), *fortasteþ* (3.13.8), *friuoles* (3.27.9), *imperturbable* (3.53.11), *impurete* (3.53.26), *indurable* (3.27.8), *inspiroure* (3.2.6), *over-casuely* (3.19.5), *penaly* (3.30.3), **recolleccion* (3.36.17), *subiective* (1.14.11), *supernaturely* (3.24.5), *taciturnite* (3.41.8), *trustyngly* (3.8.16), *vnferme* (3.64.13), *vnfruytfully* (1.10.7), *vnmortified* (1.3.16), *vnplesed* (3.25.11), *vnprovided* (3.50.15), *vnrested* (1.6.1), *vilyfie* (3.9.3), *vituperable* (1.19.11), *wylynes* (1.7.5).

The following words are apparently used for the first time in the *Imitation* and are now obsolete (i.e. so marked in *OED*):

doctrice (3.60.25), *enstreyted* (1.24.14), *indisciplynate* (2.3.14), *iubilynge* (3.6.28), *opinate* (3.51.29).

The following words were apparently used only in the *Imitation* and nowhere else:

*desiderantly (3.54.6: C has *desirantly*, apparently used only here), *distractely* (3.53.28), *exercitate* (2.9.30, 3.21.4), *exquisicion* (1.3.15, 3.38.7), *exute* (2.4.13), *eya* (2.1.8, 3.6.4, 3.21.27), *fruybly* (2.1.33), *freuyshe* (3.18.7, 3.23.10, 3.29.15, 3.42.13, 3.53.17, 3.56.5), *fruyshyngly* (3.63.23), *implicamente* (2.8.29), *indisciplinacion* (3.12.9), *iubilose* (3.39.17), *perseverable* (2.7.3), *temerarily* (3.29.8: G has *temer. .ily* with two letters scratched out), **vndefouleable* (3.61.6: DM have *vndefoulid*, G *vndefoyled*), *vnmortificate* (3.53.18), *vnpesed* (3.47.11), **vntransnatable* (3.15.17: DMG have *intransnatable*, apparently used only here).

BIBLIOGRAPHY

The bibliography is divided into two main sections: (A) Primary Sources and (B) Secondary Sources. Section A is subdivided into two subsections: (1) texts of the *Imitatio* and (2) other primary sources; the texts of the *Imitatio* are listed by language (Latin, English, Dutch). In section A subsection 1 editions of the *Imitatio* are listed alphabetically by editor's name within each language. In section A subsection 2 editions of anonymous medieval texts are listed under their titles. Editions of Kempis's works other than separate editions of the *Imitatio* are listed under THOMAS À KEMPIS; in titles of secondary works his name is spelt as it is in the work in question (continental scholars generally omit the grave accent). Where a work has more than one place of publication, only the first is given. Works cited in the list of abbreviations are not listed again here.

A. PRIMARY SOURCES

1. *Editions of the 'Imitatio'*

(a) *Latin*

HIRSCHE, K. (ed.), *Thomae Kempensis de Imitatione Christi libri quatuor*, second edition (Berlin, 1891)

KNOX-LITTLE, W. J. (ed.), *The Imitation of Christ . . . Facsimile Reproduction of the First Edition Printed at Augsburg in 1471–2* (London, 1893)

N[EWDIGATE], B. H. (ed.), *Thomae a Kempis de Imitatione Christi quae dicitur libri IV* (London, 1933) [Latin and English texts in parallel]

PUYOL, P. E. (ed.), *De Imitatione Christi libri quatuor* (Paris, 1886)

RUELENS, C. (ed.), *The Imitation of Christ: Being the Autograph Manuscript of Thomas à Kempis, 'De Imitatione Christi' Reproduced in Facsimile from the Original Preserved in the Royal Library at Brussels* (London, 1879)

[ZAINER, G. (ed.)], *Libellus Consolatorius . . . de Imitacione Christi* (Augsburg, [1471–2])

(b) *English*

ALLAN, P. B. M. (ed.), *The Book Called the Imitation of Christ* (London, 1923)

ATKYNSON, W., and M. BEAUFORT (trans.), *A Full Deuout and Gostely Treatyse of the Imytacion and Folowynge the Blessed Lyfe of our Moste Mercyfull Sauyoure Criste* (London, 1503–[4])

BIGG, C. (trans.), *The Imitation of Christ, Called Also the Ecclesiastical Music* (London, 1901)

CREASY, W. C. (ed.), '*Imitatio Christi* (William Atkinson and Lady Margaret

Beaufort, trans., 1503): A Critical Edition Together with a Micro-Computer Editorial Procedure' (unpublished Ph.D. dissertation, University of California at Los Angeles, 1982)

KLEIN, E. J. (ed.), *The Imitation of Christ from the First Edition of an English Translation Made c. 1530 by Richard Whitford* (New York, 1941)

KNOX, R., and M. OAKLEY (trans.), *The Imitation of Christ* (London, 1959)

LIDDON, H. P. (trans.), *Musica Ecclesiastica: The Imitation of Christ by Thomas Kempis* (London, 1889)

RHYS, E. (ed.), *The Imitation of Christ*, Everyman's Library, 484 (London, 1910)

STRAWLEY, J. H. (trans.), *The Imitation of Christ; or, The Ecclesiastical Music by Thomas à Kempis* (Cambridge, 1908)

WESLEY, J. (trans.), *The Christian's Pattern; or, A Treatise of the Imitation of Christ* (London, 1735)

[WHITFORD, R.] (trans.), *A Boke Newely Translated out of Laten into Englysshe Called 'The Folowynge of Cryste'* ([London, 1531?])

(c) *Dutch*

WIJDEVELD, G., *De navolging van Christus naar de Brusselse Autograaf*, second edition (Antwerp, 1985)

2. *Other primary sources*

AMBROSE, *De Officiis Ministrorum*, ed. M. Testard, 2 vols (Paris, 1984–92)

ARISTOTLE, *Metaphysica*, ed. W. Jaeger, OCT (Oxford, 1957)

—— *Complete Works: The Revised Oxford Translation*, ed. J. Barnes, 2 vols (Princeton, NJ, 1984)

AUGUSTINE, *De Trinitate*, ed. W. J. Mountain, CCSL 50, 2 vols (Turnhout, 1968)

—— *Confessiones*, ed. L. Verheijen, CCSL 27 (Turnhout, 1981)

BERNARD OF CLAIRVAUX, *Opera Omnia*, ed. J. Leclercq and others, 8 vols (Rome, 1957–77)

Biblia sacra juxta vulgatae exemplaria et correctoria romana denuo edidit divisionibus logicis analysique continua sensum illustrantibus ornavit Aloisius Claudius Fillion, ninth edition (Paris, 1925)

BONAVENTURE, *Opera omnia edita studio et cura pp. collegii*, 10 vols (Quaracchi, 1882–1902)

CATO, Dionysius, *Disticha*, ed. M. Boas (Amsterdam, 1952)

CICERO, *Epistulae*, ed. W. S. Watt and D. R. Shackleton Bailey, OCT, 3 vols (Oxford, 1958–82)

The 'Chartae' of the Carthusian General Chapter: MS Parkminster B. 62 (1504–1513), ed. J. Clark, AC 100:21, 2 vols (Salzburg, 1992)

'The Cloud of Unknowing' and 'The Book of Privy Counselling', ed. P. Hodgson, EETS 218 (1944)

'Deonise Hid Diuinite' and other Treatises on Contemplative Prayer Related to 'The Cloud of Unknowing', ed. P. Hodgson, EETS 231 (1955, repr. with corr. 1958)

English Wycliffite Sermons, ed. A. Hudson and P. Gradon, 5 vols (Oxford, 1983–96)

GERSON, J., *Œuvres complètes*, ed. P. Glorieux, 10 vols (Paris, 1960–73)

HORACE, *Opera*, ed. E. C. Wickham, rev. H. W. Garrod, OCT (Oxford, 1901, repr. 1947)

LUCAN, *De Bello Civili*, ed. D. R. Shackleton Bailey, Teubner Library of Greek and Latin Writers (Stuttgart, 1988)

Missale Romanum ex decreto ss. concilii Tridentini restitutum (Rome, 1909)

The Myroure of Oure Ladye, ed. J. H. Blunt, EETS, ES 19 (1873)

The Orcherd of Syon, ed. P. Hodgson and G. M. Liegey, EETS 258 (1966)

OVID, *Amores, Medicamina Faciei Femineae, Ars Amatoria, Remedia Amoris*, ed. E. J. Kenney, second edition, OCT (Oxford, 1994)

The Pilgrimage of the Lyfe of the Manhode, ed. A. Henry, EETS 288, 292, 2 vols (1985–8)

The Sarum Missal Edited from Three Early Manuscripts, ed. J. W. Legg (Oxford, 1916)

SENECA, *Ad Lucilium Epistulae Morales*, ed. L. D. Reynolds, OCT, 2 vols (Oxford, 1965)

SUSO, H., *Horologium Sapientiae*, ed. P. Künzle, Spicilegium Friburgense, 23 (Freiburg in der Schweiz, 1977)

THOMAS À KEMPIS, *Opera et Libri Vite*, ed. P. Danhausser and H. Rosweyden (Nuremberg, 1494)

——*Opera Omnia*, ed. H. Sommalius, second edition (Antwerp, 1607)

——*The Christian Pattern; or, The Imitation of Jesus Christ, Being the Genuine Works of Thomas à Kempis*, second edition (London, 1710) [contains a selection of Kempis's works, not including the *Imitation*]

——*Prayers and Meditations on the Life of Christ*, trans. W. Duthoit (London, 1904)

——*The Founders of the New Devotion*, trans. J. P. Arthur (London, 1905)

——*The Chronicle of the Canons Regular of Mount St Agnes*, trans. J. P. Arthur (London, 1906)

——*Sermons to the Novices Regular*, trans. V. Scully (London, 1907)

——*Meditations and Sermons on the Incarnation, Life, and Passion of Our Lord*, trans. V. Scully (London, 1907)

VIRGIL, *Opera*, ed. R. A. B. Mynors, OCT (Oxford, 1969, repr. with corr. 1972)

Wycliffite Sermons see *English Wycliffite Sermons*.

B. SECONDARY SOURCES

AXTERS, S., *The Spirituality of the Old Low Countries*, trans. D. Attwater (London, 1954)

——*De Imitatione Christi: Een handschrifteninventaris bij het vijfhonderdste verjaren van Thomas Hemerken van Kempen* (Kempen, 1971)

—— 'Bijdrage tot de inventarizering van de *Imitatio*-handschriften: Addenda en dubia', *NAK* 56 (1975), 141–58

BALL, C. J., *The Book of Job: A Revised Text and Version* (Oxford, 1922)

BARRON, D. G., *Jean Charlier de Gerson: The Author of the 'De Imitatione Christi'* (London, 1936)

[BERNARD, E.], *Catalogi librorum manuscriptorum Angliae et Hiberniae in unum collecti*, 2 vols (Oxford, 1697)

[BIBLIOTHÈQUE ROYALE ALBERT Iᵉʳ], *Thomas a Kempis et la dévotion moderne: Catalogue d'exposition organisée à l'occasion du cinq-centième anniversaire de la mort de Thomas a Kempis* (Brussels, 1971)

BIGGS, B. J. H., 'A Critical Edition of the First English Translation of the *Imitatio Christi*' (unpublished D.Phil. thesis, University of Oxford, 1992)

—— 'The Language of the Scribes of the First English Translation of the *Imitatio Christi*', *LSE*, NS 26 (1995), 79–111

—— 'The Style of the First English Translation of the *Imitatio Christi*', in *The Medieval Translator 5*, ed. R. Ellis and R. Tixier (Turnhout, 1996), pp. 187–211

BROWN, D. C., *Pastor and Laity in the Theology of Jean Gerson* (Cambridge, 1987)

BUTLER, D., *Thomas a Kempis: A Religious Study* (Edinburgh, 1908)

CHANDLER, P., *Thesaurus Thomae a Kempis curantibus Paul Chandler et CETE-DOC*, Thesaurus Patrum Latinorum (Turnhout, 1994)

COLKER, M. L., *Trinity College Library, Dublin: Descriptive Catalogue of the Medieval and Renaissance Latin Manuscripts*, 2 vols (Aldershot, 1991)

CONSTABLE, G. 'The Ideal of the Imitation of Christ', in his *Three Studies in Medieval Religious and Social Thought* (Cambridge, 1995), pp. 143–248.

COOLIDGE, W. A. B., 'The Magdalen MS. of the *Imitation*, 1438', *N&Q*, Sixth Series, 3 (1881), 181–2, 202–4, 222–4

COPINGER, W. A., *On the English Translations of the 'Imitatio Christi'*, Bibliographiana, 3 (Manchester, 1900)

CRANE, D., 'English Translations of the *Imitatio Christi* in the Sixteenth and Seventeenth Centuries', *RH* 13 (1975), 79–100

CROWTHER, C. M. D., *Unity, Heresy and Reform, 1378–1460: The Conciliar Response to the Great Schism*, Documents of Medieval History, 3 (London, 1977)

CRUISE, F. R., *Thomas à Kempis: Notes of a Visit to the Scenes in Which his Life Was Spent* (London, 1887)

DE BACKER, A., *Essai bibliographique sur le livre 'De Imitatione Christi'* (Liège, 1864)

DE MONTMORENCY, J. E. G., *Thomas à Kempis: His Age and Book* (London, 1906)

DENIFLE, H., 'Kritische Bemerkungen zur Gersen–Kempisfrage', *ZKT* 6 (1882), 692–718; 7 (1883), 692–743

DOYLE, A. I., 'Carthusian Participation in the Movement of Works of Richard

Rolle between England and Other Parts of Europe in the 14th and 15th Centuries', in *Kartäusermystik und -mystiker*, AC 55, 5 vols (Salzburg, 1981–2), ii. 109–20

—— 'The European Circulation of Three Latin Spiritual Texts', in *Latin and Vernacular: Studies in Late-Medieval Texts and Manuscripts*, ed. A. J. Minnis, York Manuscripts Conferences: Proceedings Series, 1 (Cambridge, 1989), pp. 129–46

—— 'Book Production by the Monastic Orders in England (*c.* 1375–1530): Assessing the Evidence', in *Medieval Book Production: Assessing the Evidence*, ed. L. L. Brownrigg (Los Altos Hills, Calif., 1990), pp. 1–19

EDWARDS, A. S. G., 'Beinecke MS. 661 and Early Fifteenth-Century English Manuscript Production', *YULG* 66, supplement (1991), 181–96.

ELLIS, R., 'The Choices of the Translator in the Late Middle English Period', in *The Medieval Mystical Tradition in England: Papers Read at Dartington Hall, July 1982*, ed. M. Glasscoe (Exeter, 1982), pp. 18–46

EMDEN, A. B., *A Biographical Register of the University of Oxford to A.D. 1500*, 3 vols (Oxford, 1957–9)

FOSTER, J., *Alumni Oxonienses: The Members of the University of Oxford 1500–1714*, 4 vols (Oxford, 1891–2)

GUMBERT, J. P., 'Een Engels *Imitatio*-handschrift bij de Brugse kartuizers', *OGE* 48 (1974), 287–9

HALBART, LIBRARIE, *Catalogue des beaux livres, anciens et modernes, qui seront dispersés en vente publique le 29 avril 1961* (Liège, 1961)

HENDRICKX, F., 'De handschriften van de kartuis Genadendal bij Brugge (1318–1580): I', *OGE* 47 (1973), 3–63

—— 'Reflecties over Brux., Cod. 15138', *OGE* 48 (1974), 290–4

HIRSCHE, K., *Prolegomena zu einer neuen Ausgabe der 'Imitatio Christi' nach dem Autograph des Thomas von Kempen*, 3 vols (Berlin, 1873–94)

HOGG, J., 'The Contribution of the Brigittine Order to Late Medieval English Spirituality', in *Spiritualität heute und gestern*, AC 35 (Salzburg, 1982–), iii. 153–74

—— 'The English Charterhouses and the Devotio Moderna', in *Historia et spiritualitas cartusiensis: colloquii quarti internationalis acta*, ed. J. de Grauwe (Destelbergen, Belgium, 1983), pp. 257–68

HYMA, A., *The Christian Renaissance: A History of the 'Devotio Moderna'*, second edition (Hamden, Conn., 1965)

ISERLOH, E., *Thomas von Kempen und die Kirchenreform im Spätmittelalter* (Kempen, 1971)

JAMES, M. R., *A Descriptive Catalogue of the McClean Collection of Manuscripts in the Fitzwilliam Museum* (Cambridge, 1912)

KER, N. R., *William Hunter as a Collector of Medieval Manuscripts: The First Edwards Lecture on Palaeography Delivered in the University of Glasgow* (Glasgow, [1983])

KAISER, O., *Isaiah 13–39: A Commentary*, OTL (London, 1974)

KETTLEWELL, S., *The Authorship of the 'Imitatio Christi'* (London, 1877)

—— *Thomas à Kempis and the Brothers of the Common Life*, 2 vols (London, 1882)

KISSANE, E. J., *The Book of Isaiah Translated from a Critically Revised Hebrew Text with Commentary* (Dublin, 1960)

LEHMANN, P., 'Konstanz und Basel als Büchermärkte während der grossen Kirchenversammlungen', in his *Erforschung des Mittelalters: Ausgewählte Abhandlungen und Aufsätze*, 5 vols (Leipzig, 1941–62), i. 253–80

MENESTÒ, E., review of Lupo's edition of the *Imitatio*, SM, serie terza, 26 (1985), 841–3

MOORE, C., *'The Father of Black-Letter Collectors': Memoir of the Right Reverend John Moore, D.D.* (London, 1885)

PÄCHT, O., and J. J. G. ALEXANDER, *Illuminated Manuscripts in the Bodleian Library, Oxford*, 3 vols (Oxford, 1966–73)

PAGE, W. (ed.), *The Victoria History of the County of Buckingham*, 4 vols and index (London, 1905–28)

POST, R. R., *The Modern Devotion: Confrontation with Reformation and Humanism*, Studies in Medieval and Reformation Thought, 3 (Leiden, 1968)

PUYOL, P. E., *Descriptions bibliographiques des manuscrits et des principales éditions du livre 'De Imitatione Christi'* (Paris, 1898)

—— *Variantes du livre 'De Imitatione Christi'* (Paris, 1898)

REISS, M., 'Die Zitate antiker Autoren in der *Imitatio* des Thomas von Kempen', in *Thomas von Kempen: Beiträge zum 500. Todesjahr . . . herausgegeben von der Stadt Kempen* (Kempen, 1971), pp. 63–77

ROSENBERG, B., *Die älteste mittelenglische Übersetzung der 'Imitatio Christi' des Thomas von Kempen und ihr Verhältnis zum Original* (Leipzig, 1905)

ROUSE, R. H. and M. A., *Preachers, Florilegia and Sermons: Studies on the 'Manipulus Florum' of Thomas of Ireland*, Pontifical Institute of Mediaeval Studies, Studies and Texts, 47 (Toronto, 1979)

SARGENT, M. G., 'The Transmission by the English Carthusians of some Late Medieval Spiritual Writings', JEH 27 (1976), 225–40

—— 'James Grenehalgh: The Biographical Record', in *Kartäusermystik und -mystiker*, AC 55, 5 vols (Salzburg, 1981–2), iv. 20–54

—— *James Grenehalgh as Textual Critic*, AC 85, 2 vols (Salzburg, 1984)

SCOFIELD, C. L., *The Life and Reign of Edward the Fourth*, 2 vols (London, 1923, repr. 1967)

SCULLY, V., *Life of the Venerable Thomas à Kempis* (London, 1901)

SHAILOR, B. A., *Catalogue of Medieval and Renaissance Manuscripts in the Beinecke Rare Book and Manuscript Library, Yale University*, Medieval and Renaissance Texts and Studies (Binghamton, New York, 1984–)

SPAAPEN, B., 'Kanttekeningen bij de diplomatische uitgave van hs. Brussel 5855–61', OGE 32 (1958), 5–55, 128

STERRY, W., *The Eton College Register 1414–1698* (Eton, 1943)

STORR, R., *Concordance to the Latin Original of the Four Books Known as 'De Imitatione Christi'* (London, 1910)

THOMPSON, E. M., *The Carthusian Order in England*, Church Historical Society, NS 3 (London, 1930)

THOMSON, R. M., *Catalogue of the Manuscripts of Lincoln Cathedral Chapter Library* (Cambridge, 1989)

TOY, C. H., *A Critical and Exegetical Commentary on the Book of Proverbs*, ICC (Edinburgh, 1899)

VENNEBUSCH, J., *Die Theologischen Handschriften des Stadtarchivs Köln*, Mitteilungen aus dem Stadtarchiv von Köln, 5 vols (Cologne, 1976–89)

VICKERS, B., *In Defence of Rhetoric* (Oxford, 1988, repr. with corr., 1989)

WATSON, A. G., *Catalogue of Dated and Datable Manuscripts c. 435–1600 in Oxford Libraries*, 2 vols (Oxford, 1984)

WAINEWRIGHT, J. B., 'Gilbert Bourne', *N&Q*, Tenth Series, 6 (1906), 165

WEALE, W. H. J., *Bookbindings and Rubbings in the National Art Library, South Kensington Museum*, 2 vols (London, 1894–8)

WEST, M. L., *Textual Criticism and Editorial Technique* (Stuttgart, 1973)

WHEATLEY, L. A., *The Story of the 'Imitatio Christi'* (London, 1891)

WILLIAMS, G., 'Two Neglected London–Welsh Clerics: Richard Whitford and Richard Gwent', *Transactions of the Honourable Society of Cymmrodorion* (London, 1961), pp. 23–44

WORKMAN, S. K., *Fifteenth Century Translation as an Influence on English Prose*, Princeton Studies in English, 18 (Princeton, 1940), p. 120

YULE, G. U., 'Puyol's Classes A and B of Texts of the *De Imitatione Christi*: A Critical Examination of his Evidence and Conclusions', *RTAM* 14 (1947), 65–88

EDITORIAL PRACTICE

The base manuscript is C, except in three passages as indicated below; emendations are introduced only where they can be justified by reference to the Latin, in view of the generally close nature of the translation. Where a manuscript other than the base text has a reading closer to the Latin than that of the base text, the text is therefore emended. It is arguable that no emendation should be introduced in cases where it is likely that the superior reading is the result of a correction made from a Latin manuscript (see above, pp. lxvi–lxviii); but since it is not always possible to distinguish such cases from cases where a manuscript preserves a better reading deriving from the archetype, it has seemed best to follow a consistent policy by preferring the reading closest to the Latin in all cases. The Latin is cited in the critical apparatus where the text has been emended, or where it shows the base text to have a superior reading to those in the other manuscripts.

Punctuation, capitalization, word-division, and the division into paragraphs are editorial. A system of numbered paragraphs was introduced by the seventeenth-century editor Henricus Sommalius and is followed in many editions and translations (the Kempis manuscript itself contains few paragraph divisions), but since Sommalius's division of the text does not always accord well with the sense, the division into paragraphs adopted here does not follow it consistently. Sommalius's paragraph numbers, however, are given in parentheses in the inner margins. The text has been divided into verses according to Puyol's system; the beginning of a new verse is indicated by a superscript number. Where a verse appears to be missing, this is because it is found in the Latin but not in the translation; the Latin is given in the Notes. The beginning of a new folio is indicated by a vertical line in the text; the new folio number is given in the outer margin. Book and chapter numbers are given on the running heads of each page.

Marginal or interlinear additions in C are enclosed within caret marks `. . .`; all appear to be the work of the main scribe. Emendations are enclosed within square brackets [. . .]. Abbreviations in both text and variants are expanded silently in accordance with the spelling of the manuscript. The expansion of the ending -tion when abbreviated in C has caused difficulties: -cōn has been expanded to -cion in e.g.

supportacion (1.0.16), because *-cion* is the scribe's usual form. *-cioñ* (where the last letter could be *n* or *u*, although in some cases it looks rather more like *n*) has been expanded to *-cioun* in e.g. *affecciouns* (1.0.6), although with some reluctance, as the form *-cioun* does not occur in full in the manuscript. *Yeñ* (1.23.15) presents a similar problem; it has been expanded to *yenn*.

There are three passages (2.12.19–30, 3.0.52–3.1.3 and 3.26.1–3.34.2) which are lacking in C owing to the loss of leaves; here, D has been used as the base text, and in order to ensure consistency of orthography, D's text (emended from M or G where necessary) is given in the spelling of C. As in the remainder of the text, marginal or interlinear additions in the base manuscript are indicated in the text by being enclosed within caret marks; where D is the base text such additions are also given in the apparatus, so that the apparatus contains a complete record of all the corrections in D in the scribe's orthography. Corrections made over erasure in D are indicated only in the apparatus and not in the text.

The critical apparatus aims to include all material variation from the base text, and all corrections (except those to punctuation and capitalization) in the manuscripts. In each case the lemma is cited from the edited text; where no siglum follows it is to be assumed that the lemma is found in the base text and such of the other three manuscripts as are not cited among the following variants and are not lacking text at that point. The sigla following a variant are given in the order CDMG; the variant is given in the spelling of the first manuscript cited. Where a lemma has more than one variant, the variants are, where possible, given in sequence from that closest to the lemma to the most distant. The Latin is given where it has been helpful in deciding whether or not to emend, preceded by the word *Latin*; K's text is generally given first, followed by R's if it is different; if R's reading is closer to the translation, however, it is given first instead. Delaissé's conventions for indicating corrections in K have been replaced by the simpler conventions adopted here and explained above, p. xvi. Linguistic variants (orthographic, phonological, and morphological) among the four manuscripts of the translation are not recorded; a separate entry in *MED* (in *OED* in the range T–Z) has generally been used as the criterion for material variation. Changes of line and folio are indicated where they help to explain how the variant in question arose.

[THE IMITATION OF CHRIST]

[BOOK I]

Here bigynneth the tretes called Musica Ecclesiastica.

1.0.0 here] DMG, ueni domine ihesu here C   1 the] *om.* DMG   2 2ᵐ] ii MG, 2 ʽiiʼ D²   3 the] *om.* DMG   3ᵐ] iii G, 3 ʽiiiʼ D²   4 prudence] (prudence) D¹   4ᵐ] iv G, 4 ʽivʼ D²   5 5ᵐ] v G, 5 ʽvʼ D²   6 6ᵐ] vi G, 6 ʽviʼ D²   7 7ᵐ] vii G, 7 ʽviiʼ D²   8 8ᵐ] viii G, 8 ʽviiiʼ D²   9 9ᵐ] ix G, 9 ʽixʼ D²   10 10ᵐ] x MG, 10 ʽxʼ D²   11 zele] DMG, hele C, *Latin* zelo KR   11ᵐ] ix G, 11 ʽxiʼ D²   12 12ᵐ] xii G, 12 ʽxiiʼ D²   13 13ᵐ] xiii MG, 13 ʽxiiiʼ D²   14 14ᵐ] xiv MG, 14 ʽxivʼ D²   15 15ᵐ] xv MG, 15 ʽxvʼ D²   16 capitulum 16ᵐ] capitulum xvi G, capitulum 16 ʽxviʼ D², *om.* M   17 17ᵐ] xvii MG, 17 ʽxviiʼ D²   18 of²] o M   18ᵐ] xviii MG, 18 ʽxviiiʼ D²   19 þe] *om.* M   exercices] DMG, exercites C, *Latin* exerciciis K, excerciis R (*cf. 1.19.0*)   19ᵐ] xix MG, 19 ʽxixʼ D²   20 and] and of DMG   20ᵐ] xx MG, 20 ʽxxʼ D²   21 21ᵐ] xxi MG, 21 ʽxxiʼ D²   22 22ᵐ] xxii MG, 22 ʽxxiiʼ D²

Of meditacyoun of dethe   *Capitulum* 23^m
Of the iugemente and of the paynes of synnars   *Capitulum* 24^m
[Of the fervente amendemente of alle mannes lyve   *Capitulum* 25^m]

Of the foloynge of Cryste and despysynge of alle vanytees worldely *Capitulum* 1^m

[1] Oure Lorde seith, 'He that foloweth me goith not in darkenesse.' (1)
[2] Thes ar þe wordes of Criste, in þe whiche we ar amonyshed to folowe his lyve and his maners, if we wol be verily illumyned and be delyuered fro alle maner blyndenes of herte. [3] Wherefore lette oure souerayne |

f. 2^r study be in the lyve of Ihesu Criste.

[4] The doctryne of Criste passeth the doctryne of alle seintes and holy (2) menne, and who þat had þ[e] spirite of Criste sholde fynde þere hidde manna. [5] But hit happeth þat many feleth but litel desire, of ofte hyringe of þe gospel, for þei haue not þe spirite of Criste. [6] For whoeuer wolle vndirstande the ʻwordes ofʹ Criste ple[nar]ly and s[a]uourly, he muste study to confourme alle his lyve to his lyue.

[7] What avayleth hit þe to dispute highe þinges of þe Trinite, if þou (3) lakke mekenes, whereby þou displese þe Trinite? [8] For high wordes makeþ not a man holy and rightwyse, but vertuouse lyue hit is þat makeþ a man dere to God. [9] I desire more to knowe compunccioun þen his diffinicion. [10] If þou coudeste al þe Bible withoute þe boke, and þe seyinges of alle þe philosophers, what shulde þat avayle þe withoute |

f. 2^v charite and grace?

[11] Alle other þinges in þe worlde, save onely to loue God and serve him alone, ar vanite of vanitez and alle vanite. [12] This is souerayne wysdame, bi despisinge of þe worlde a man to drawe hym to þe reaume of heuyn. [13] But a man to seke peryshinge rechesses and to truste in hem (4)

23 of^1] ʻxxiiiʹ of D^2 23^m] 23 D^2, xxiii MG   24 of^1] ʻxxiiiiʹ of D^2 24^m] 24 D^2, xxiiii MG   25 of^1 . . . 25^m] con., om. CDMG, Latin de feruenti emendacione tocius vite nostre KR (cf. 1.25.0)
     1.0 the] om. DG   vanytees worldely] worldly vanitez DG, worldly vanite M   1^m] 1 D   3 oure] ʻoureʹ D^2 4 þe] DMG, þo C, Latin et qui spiritum haberet KR   6 plenarly] con., pleynly CDMG, Latin plene KR   sauourly] DMG, souourly C, Latin sapide KR   confourme] ⟨con⟩fourʻmeʹ|me, second me canc. D^2 7 hit] om. DMG   displese] displ⟨esist⟩ D^2, displesist G   8 for] om. M   10 seyinges] sciences M, se⟨nt⟩en⟨ces⟩ D^2, sentences G, Latin dicta KR   philosophers] philophers D   grace] grae M   12 is] is a M   reaume] kyngdom G   13 peryshinge rechesses and] p⟨erisshyng ryches and⟩ D^2

is vanite, [14] and vanite hit is also to desire worshippes and a man to lyfte hymselfe on highe, [15] and vanite hit is to folowe þe desires of þe fleysshe and to desire þat þinge wherefore man muste aftirwarde grevously be punyshed. [16] Uany[te] hit is to desire a longe lyve and to take none hede of a goode lyve. [17] Uanyte hit is a man to take heede onely to þis presente lyve, and not to see bifore þoo þinges þat ar to come. [18] Vanite hit is to loue þat þinge þat passeþ awey with alle maner of swyftenesse, and not to haste | thider where ioyes abyden euerlastynge.   f. 3ʳ

(5)   [19] Haue mynde oftetymes of þat prouerbe þat þe ye is not fulfilled with sight, ner þe ere with herynge. [20] Study þerfore to withdrawe thi herte fro þe loue of þinges visible, and translate hem to þinges invisible. [21] For þei þat foloweþ her sensualite spotteþ her conscience and leseth the grace of God.

Of meeke knowynge of a mannes selfe
Capitulum secundum

(1)   [1] Eurie man naturely desireth to haue kunnynge. But kunnynge withoute þe grace and þe drede of God, what availeth hit? [2] Certeynly the meke ploweman þat serveþ God is muche better þen þe prowde philozopher þat, takinge none heede of his owne lyvinge, considereþ the course of hevon. [3] He þat knoweth hymself welle is vyle in his owne sight, and hath no delyte in mannes praysinges. | [4] If I knewe al þinges that ar in þe   f. 3ᵛ worlde, and be not in charite, what shulde þat helpe me byfore God, þat shal deme me aftir my dedes?

(2)   [5] Cesse fro ouer-grete desyre of kunnynge, for þereinne shal be founde grete distraccion and deceyte. [6] Thei þat ar kunnynge wolle gladdely be seene and holden wise, [7] and many þinges þer beþe whos knowleche avayleþ þe soule litelle or nought. [8] And fulle vnwise is he þat more entendeþ to oþer þinges þen to þe helthe of his soule. [9] Many wordes fulfylleþ not the soule, but goode lyve refreyssheþ þe mynde, and a pure conscience yeveþ a grete confidence to God.

14 on] an DMG   15 and¹] *om.* DMG   aftirwarde] astyrwarde M, *Latin* postmodum KR   16 uanyte] DMG, uany| C   none] noo G   19 ofte-tymes of þat prouerbe] of þat prouerbe oftetymes M   sight] þe siȝt DMG 20 hem] hym G, *Latin* te K, *om.* R

2.0 secundum] ii G, 2 'ii' D²   1 kunnynge but] knowynge M, *Latin* scire desiderat sed KR   þe²] *om.* DMG   2 none] noo G   4 aftir] astir M, *Latin* ex facto KR   8 þen to þe] þ(a)n to 'þe' D²   9 goode] 'a' g'o'ode D²

[10] The more and þe better þat þou canste, þe more grevously þou (3) shalte be deemed, but if þou lyue þe more holyly. [11] Be not lyfte vppe þerfore for any crafte or any kunnynge, [but] raþer drede for þe

f. 4[r] knowleche þat is | yiven the. [12] If hit semeþ the þat thou canste many þinges and arte vndirstandynge inowe, yeette ar þer many moo þinges þat þou knowest not. [13] Fele not highe of thiselfe, but raþer knoweleche þine ignorance. [14] Whereto wolte þou preferre þiselfe bifore any oþer, sithe many oþer ar founden better lerned and more wise in þe lawe of God þen þou? [15] If þou wolte lerne and can anyþinge profitably, love to not be knowen and to be acompted as nought.

[16] This is þe highest and moste profitable redinge, veri knowynge and (4) despisinge of a mannes selfe. [17] A man noþing to accompte of himselfe, but euermore to fele welle and highe of oþer folkes, [is] souerayne wysdame and perfeccioun. [18] If þou see any man synne openly or do grevouse synnes, thou owest not to deme þiselfe better, for þou woste

f. 4[v] neuer howe longe þou maiste | abide in goode. [19] Alle we be frayle, but þou shalte holde no man more frayle þenne thiselfe.

Of the doctryne of trowthe
Capitulum tercium

[1] B[l]isfulle is he whome trowthe hitselfe techeth, not by figures ner (1) voyces, but [as] hit is. [2] Oure opinyoun and oure felynge oftetymes deceyueþ vs and seeþ but lytel. [3] What availeþ grete enserchinge of hidde and darke þinges for þe whiche we shulle not be blamed in þe iugemente þoghe we knowe hem not? [4] A grete vnwysdame hit is þat we, settynge at noȝt profitable and necessary þinges, yive our vtmaste entendance to curiouse and harmefulle þinges. [5] We, havynge yen, seeþ not.

[6] And what charge to vs of general kyndes and special kyndes? [7] He to (2)

10 þe[1]] þe more M   holyly] holye G   11 but] G, ⟨but⟩ D[2], for CM, *Latin* sed KR   12 if . . . and] `and´ M, *Latin* si tibi videtur quod multa scis et KR 14 lawe] DMG, lawe of þen, of þen *canc.* C   þen] þ⟨a⟩n D[2]   15 acompted] accoun⟨tyd⟩, un *altered from* m D[2]   17 accompte] acco⟨wnte⟩ D[2]   of[1]] *om.* G highe] hyr M, *Latin* alte KR   is] DMG, *om.* C, *Latin* est KR   18 neuer] not DMG   howe] ho⟨w⟩ D[2]   19 þenne] þ⟨a⟩n D[2]

3.0 the] *om.* DMG   tercium] iii G, 3 `iii´ D[2]   1 blisfulle] DMG, bsysfulle C, *Latin* felix KR   hitselfe] hirself DMG   1–2 as hit is oure] ⟨as it ys oure⟩, ᵗ *visible under erasure* D[2], þus hit is þat oure CMG, *Latin* sicuti se habet nostra KR   3 what availeþ] what ⟨. . . . . . .⟩ auailiþ⟩, vailiþ *visible under erasure* D[1]   4 entendance] attendaunce DMG, *Latin* intendimus K, intendamus R   6 charge] charge `is´ D[2], charge is G, *Latin* quid cure nobis KR

whom þe Worde euerlastynge spekeþ is spedde and delyuered fro
multitude of opiniouns. [8]Of | one Worde comeþ al þinges, and one   f. 5ʳ
spekeþ al þinges, þat is þe bigynnynge þat spekeþ to vs. [9]No man
with[outen] hym vndirstandeþ ner demeþ rightwysly. [10]He to whome
alle þinges ar one, and draweþ alle þinges to one, and seeþ alle þinges in
one, may be stable in herte and pesibly abyde in God. [12]Oftetymes hit
werieþ me to here and rede many þinges: in þe, Lorde, is alle þat I wille
and desire. [13]Alle maner doctours holde þei her pees, and al maner
creatures kepe þei her silence in þi sight: speke þou to me alone.

(3)   [14]The more þat a man is inwardely oned alone to þee, þe mo þinges
and þe higher þinges he vnderstandeþ, for he takeþ his lyght of
vndirstandynge frome above. [15]A pure, simple, and a stable spirite is
not disparpled in many werkes, for he worcheþ al þinges to þe
worshippe of God, and laboureþ to | be ydel in him from al maner   f. 5ᵛ
exquisicion of propre witte.

[16]What letteþ the more and trowbleþ the more þen þi vnmortified
affeccion of herte? [17]A goode and a deuoute man furste disposeþ
withinforthe his werkes þe whiche he purposeþ to do outewarde,
[18]ner þoo werkes drawe not hym to desires of viciouse inclynacioun,
but raþer he boweþ hem to þe iugemente of right reson. [19]Who haþe a
strenger bataile þan he þat enforceþ to ouercome himselfe? [20]And þat
shulde be oure ocupacion: a man to overcome hymselfe, and euery daie
to be stronger þen hymselfe, and sumwhat profite into better.

(4)   [21]Alle maner perfeccion in þis worlde hath a maner of imperfeccion
annexid þerto, and oure speculacyon is not withoute darkenes on summe
side. [22]Meke knowinge of þiselfe is more acceptable to God þen depe |
inquisicion of kunnynge. [23]Kunnynge or bare and simple knowynge of   f. 6ʳ
þinges is not to be blamed, þe whiche in hitselfe considered is goode and
ordeyned of God; but goode conscience and vertuouse lyve is euer to be
preferred. [24]And forasmuche as many peple studieþ more to haue
kunnynge þen to lyue welle, þerfore oftetymes þei erreþ, and bringeþ
forþe litel fruyte or none.

7 fro] fro þe G   8 spekeþ¹] spekith to, to *canc.* G   al² . . . spekeþ²] *om.* M
9 withouten] DMG, with C, *Latin* sine KR   10 and³] *om.* M   14 þinges²]
om. DMG   his] *om.* M   15 disparpled] dispa⟨rcled⟩ D²   ydel] MG, yd ‖
ydel, *first* yd *canc.* D, ydel ydel C   exquisicion] execucion G, *Latin* esquisicione KR
17 goode] g`o´ode D²   18 to¹] to the G   inclynacioun] ⟨. .⟩ inclinacioun D
19 þan] þ⟨a⟩n D²   20 þen] þ⟨a⟩n D²   profite] to profite DMG   22 þen] þ⟨a⟩n
D²   23 kunnynge] *om.* M, *Latin* sciencia KR   þe] *om.* G   goode¹] g`o´ode D²
goode²] `a´ go`o´de D²   24 þen] þ⟨a⟩n D²

²⁵ O, if men wolde yiue so grete diligence to rote oute vices and to (5) plante vertues as þei do to meve questions, þer wolde not be so muche wykkednes in þe peple, ner so muche dissolucion in cenobyes and monasteryes. ²⁶ Certeynly at þe day of dome hit shal not be asked of vs what we haue redde, but what we haue done; ner what goode we haue saide, but howe religiously we haue lyved. ²⁷ Telle me nowe where ar

f. 6ᵛ þoo lordes and maistres | þat þou knewest sumtyme whiles þei lyved and floryshed in scoles? ²⁸ Nowe oþer men haue her prebendes, and I wote nere wheþer þei ones þenke vppon hem. ²⁹ In her lyves sumwhat þey appered, and nowe of hem spekeþ almoste no man. ³⁰ O Lorde, howe (6) sone passeþ þe glory of þis worlde! ³¹ Wolde God þat her lyve had been acordinge to her kunnynge, for þen had þey welle studyed and welle radde. ³² How many be þer þat perisheþ in þis worlde bi veyne kunnynge, þat lytel reccheþ of þe seruyce of God! ³³ And for þei chese raþer to be grete þen meke, þerfore þei vanyshe awey in her owne þoughtes.

³⁴ Uerily he is grete þat haþ grete charite. Uerily he is grete þat in hymself is lytel and meke, and sette at noght al heyght [of] worship. ³⁵ Uerily he is prudente þat demeþ al yerþely þinges as styngynge donge so þat he mowe wynne Criste, ³⁶ and he is verily welle lerned þat doþe þe wille of God and forsakeþ his owne. |

f. 7ᵣ

Of prouidence in mannes werkes
Capitulum 4ᵐ

¹ Hit is not to yif credence to euery worde ner to eueri styrynge, but (1) eueriþinge is to be peysed aftir God, warely and bi leyser. ² Alas, yvel of anoþer man is [sonner] bileved þen goode, and excused by infirmite; ³ but perfite [men] bileueþ not lyghtly al þinges þat men telleþ, for þei knoweþ mannes infirmite, redy to yvel and slydinge inowe in wordes.

⁵ Hereto hit longeþ also not to leue eueri mannes wordes ner þat þat (2) he hereþ or bilyeveþ lyghtly to telle oþer men. ⁶ Haue þi counseile with

---

28 nere] not DMG   34 uerily¹ . . . charite] *om.* DMG, *Latin* vere magnus est qui magnam habet caritatem KR   of] DMG, and C, *Latin* culmen honoris KR
35 uerily] verily he is grete þat haþ gret charite verily DMG, *Latin* vere KR
4.0 prouidence] prudence DMG, *Latin* prouidencia K, prudencia R   in] of M, *Latin* in KR   4ᵐ] iiii G, 4 'iv' D   2 sonner] *con.*, sundre C, raþer DMG, *Latin* facilius KR   þen] þ(a)n D²   3 perfite men] *con.*, perfite CM, 'þe' perfite D², the perfitte G, *Latin* perfecti viri KR   5 leue] beleue G

a wise man and a man of conscience, and seke raþer to be taght of þi bettir þen to folowe þine owne adinuencions.

[7] Goode lyue makeþ a man wise aftir God and experte in many þinges. [8] The more meke þat a man is, and þe more sugget to God, the more wise he shal be in alle þinges, and the more paciente.

Of redynge of scriptures
Capitulum 5[m]

(1) | [1] Trouþe is to be sought in holy wrytinges and not in eloquence. [2] Eueri   f. 7ᵛ holy writinge oweþ to be radde with þe same spirite wherewith hit was made. [3] We oweþ in scriptures raþer to seke profitablenes þen highenes of langage.

[4] We owe as gladly to rede symple and devoute bokes as highe bokes and profounde sentences. [5] Lete not þe auctorite of hym þat wryteþ, wheþer he be of grete lettur [o]r of lytel, chaunge þi conceyte, but lette þe love of pure trouþe drawe þe to þe love 'of God'. [6] Aske not who (2) seide þus, but take heede what is seide. [7] Menne passeþ, but þe trowþe of our Lorde abydeþ euerlastingly. [8] God spekeþ to vs in dyuerse wyses, withoute accepcion of persones.

[9] Oure curiouste oftetymes in redinge of scriptures [deceyueþ vs], in þat we serche curiouse sentence where hit is to be passed over symply and not curiously enquered. [10] If þou wolte drawe profite in redinge, rede mekely, simply, and truly, not desiringe to | haue a name of   f. 8ʳ kunnynge. [11] Aske gladly and here holdinge þi pees, and lete not þe parabolez of eldre men displese þee, for þei ar not brought forþe withouten cause.

6 a wise man] wise men MG, 'a' wise ⟨man⟩ D², *Latin* cum sapiente KR   þen] þ⟨a⟩n D²   7 goode] g'o'ode D²   man] *om.* M, *Latin* hominem KR

5.0 5ᵐ] v G, 5 'v' D²   3 þen] þ⟨a⟩n D²   5 or] DMG, er C, *Latin* uel KR   of³] *om.* DMG   þe to] *om.* M, *Latin* te trahat ad KR   6 þus] this G   7 menne passeþ] m⟨a⟩n passi⟨þ⟩ D², man passiþe MG, *Latin* homines transeunt KR   8 accepcion] excepcion DMG, *Latin* acceptione KR   9 deceyueþ vs] DMG, *om.* C, *Latin* nos impedit KR

Of inordinate affeccions
Capitulum 6ᵐ

[1] Wheneuer a man coveiteþ anyþinge inordinatly, anone he is vnrested in (1)
hymself. [2] The proude man and þe coveytouse man hath neuer reste; the
pore man and meke in spirite is delyted in multitude of pees.

[3] The man þat is not perfitely dede in himselfe is sone tempted and
sone ouercomen in smale þinges and of litel pryce. [4] He þat is feble in
spirite and yette in maner fleysly inclyned to þe sensible þinges may not
ly3tly withdrawe hym holy from erþely desires. [5] Wherfore oftetymes
when he withdraweþ him a litel he is sory, and haþe disdeigne when any
man withstandeþ his wille. [6] And if he opteyne þat he desireþ, anone he (2)

f. 8ᵛ   is greved in his conscience | þat he hathe folowed his owne passion, þe
whiche helpeþ noþinge to þe pees þat he haþ sought.

[7] Wherfore in withstandinge in passions stondeþ very pees of herte,
and not in servinge hem. [8] Wherfore þer is no pes in þe herte of þe
fleysly [man], ner in hym þat is al yiven to outwarde þinges, but in þe
feruent spirituel man.

Of fleynge of veyne hope and elacion
Capitulum 7ᵐ

He is veyne þat putteþ his hope in men or in creatures. [2] Be not (1)
ashamed to serve oþer men for þe love of Ihesu Criste and to be seene
pouer in þis worlde.

[3] Stande not vppon þiself, but sette þi truste in God. [4] Do þat in þe is,
and God shal be nyghe to þi goode wille. [5] Truste not in þine owne
kunnynge, ner in þe wylynes of any man lyving, but raþer in þe grace of
God, þat helpeþ meeke folke and makeþ lowe hem þat presumeþ of
hemselfe.

f. 9ʳ   [6] Reioyse þe not in rychesses, if | thou haue any, ner in frendes, if þei (2)
be myghtty, but in God þat yiveþ alle þinges and above al þinges desireþ

6.0 6ᵐ] vi G, 6 ʻviʼ D²   1 vnrested] vnrestfull G   2 þe] om. DMG
in²] in ʻþeʼ D², in the G   4 þe] om. DMG   desires] ⟨desires⟩ D¹   5 him]
om. DMG, Latin se subtrahit KR   7 in²] of DMG, Latin resistendo igitur
passionibus KR   8 þe¹] twice, first canc. D   þe fleysly man] DG, man þe
flesshely, man canc. M, þe fleysly herte C, Latin in corde hominis carnalis KR

7.0 7ᵐ] vii G, 7 ʻviiʼ D²   4 goode] gʻoʼode D²   5 presumeþ] presum⟨yn⟩,
dot of i and tail of þ visible under erasure D²   6 not] ʻnotʼ D², Latin ne KR

to yive hymselfe. [7]Lifte not vppe thiselfe of gretnes ner of beaute of body, þe whiche is corrupte and defowled with a lytel sikenes. [8]Plese not þiself of abilyte or of witte, leste þou displese God of whom comeþ al goode þat þou haste naturely.

(3)   [9]Accompte not þiselfe better þen oþer, leste perauenture þou be had as worse in þe sight of God, þat knoweþ what is in man. [10]Be not proude of goode werkes, for oþerweyes ar Goddes iugementez and oþerwyse mannes; for oftetymes þat pleseþ man displeseþ God. [11]Yf any goode þinges þou haue, bilyve better þinges of oþer, þat þou mowe kepe mekenes. [12]Hit shal not noye þe if þou sette þe vnder alle men; hit myght hynder muche if þou sette thiselfe afore one. [13]Continuel pees | is   f. 9ᵛ with the meke man, but in the herte of a proude man is ofte envye and indignacyon.

Of eschewinge of ouer-grete famyliarite
Capitulum 8ᵐ

(1)   [1]Shewe not thi herte to euerie man, but meve thi cause to him þat is wyse and dredeþ God. [2]Be rare amonge yonge puple and straunge folkes. [3]Blandyshe not riche men, and appiere not byfore grete men, [4]but acompeny þiself with meke and symple men, with deuoute and welle-manerde men, and trete of suche þinges as longeþ to edificacion. [5]Be not familiare to any womman, but generaly commende alle goode wymmen to God.

   [6]Desire to be famyliar onely with God and with his aungels, and (2)   eschewe knowleche of men. [7]Charite is to be had to alle men, but familiarite is not expediente. [8]Hit happeneþ sumtyme þat a persone vnknowen shyneþ bi bright fame, | whos presence offendeþ and makeþ   f. 10ʳ darke þe yen of þe biholdars. [9]We hope sumtyme to plese other of oure beynge and lyvynge togydres, and oftetymes we bygynne to displese thorowgh vngoodly maners founden in vs.

7 þe] om. G   9 as] canc. D, om. G   10 goode] g`o´ode D²      11 yf any goode þinges þou haue] yf þou haue eny good þinges M      goode] g`o´ode D² 12 myght] twice, first canc. C   hynder] hindre `þe´ D², hyndre þe G   one] o⟨þir⟩ D², oþer MG, Latin vni KR   13 a] þe DG
8.o ouer-grete] to grete DMG   8ᵐ] viii G, 8 `viii´ D²      3 and . . . men] om. M, Latin et coram magnatis non libenter appareas KR      4 þiself] þiself and appiete not before gret men but acompeny þiself M      with² . . . men²] om. DMG, Latin cum deuotis et morigeratis KR      5 goode] g`o´ode D²   6 onely] om. DMG, Latin soli KR   9 togydres] togedyre G   vngoodly] vng`o´odely D²

Of obedience and subieccioun
Capitulum 9ᵐ

¹Hit is right a grete þinge a man to stande vnder obedience and lyve (1)
vnder a prelate, and not be at his owne lyberte. ²Hit is muche more sure
to stande in subieccion þen in prelacye. ³Many ar vnder obedience more
of necessite þen of charite, and þei haue payne and sone and lightly
gruccheþ and shul neuer gete liberte of mynde tylle þei with alle her
herte subdue hemselfe for God. ⁴[R]enne here and þere, þou shalt neuer
fynde quiete but in meke subieccion vnder a prelate. ⁵Imaginacion and
f. 10ᵛ chaungynge of | places hath deceyved many one.

⁶Trewe hit is þat euery man [gladly doþe] aftir his owne witte, and is (2)
inclyned moste to hem þat feleþ as he doþe. ⁷But 'if' God be amonge vs
hit is nedefulle to vs sumtyme to forsake owre owne felynge for þe gode
of pees. ⁸Who is so wyse þat may fully knowe al þinges? ⁹Wherfore
truste not to muche in thyne owne felynge, but desire gladly to here
oþer mennes felynges. ¹⁰If þi felynge be gode, and þou for God leveste
þat and folowest anoþer mannes felynge, þou shalte profite more þerby.
¹¹I haue herde oftetymes þat hit is more sure to here and to take
counceyle þen to yive counseyle. ¹²Hit may welle be þat eueri man feele
welle, but a man nowyse to agree to oþer men when reson and þe matier
askeþ is token of pryde and of obstynacye.

f. 11ʳ ## Of eschewynge of superfluyte of | wordes
Capitulum 10ᵐ

¹Eschewe þe noyse and þe prese of men as muche as þou mayste, for (1)
tretynge and talkynge of seculer dedes, þough þei be brought forthe
with trewe and symple intencion, letteþ muche. ²For we bethe sone
defoyled and ladde into vanite. ³I haue willed me oftetymes to haue
holde my pees and not to haue bene amonge men.

9.0 9ᵐ] ix MG, 9 'ix' D²   1 be] to be M   3 and³] om. M   hemselfe]
hem DMG   4 renne] DMG, kenne C, *Latin* curre KR   fynde] DMG, fynde þou
shalt fynde C, *Latin* inuenies KR   quiete] quie'tnes' D², quietnes G   6 gladly
doþe] *con.*, om. CDMG, *Latin* libenter agit KR   witte and] 'witte' (.), *ampersand visible
under erasure* D², witte MG, *Latin* pro sensu suo et KR   7 if] *om.* DMG, *Latin* sed si
KR   9 to here] *om.* G, *Latin* audire KR   10 gode] g'o'ode D²   god]
DMG, gode C, *Latin* deum KR   þat] hit G, *Latin* hocipsum KR   profite more]
more profite DMG   12 matier] maner DMG, *Latin* causa KR   of²] *om.* DMG
          10.0 of³] DMG, of ‖ of C   10ᵐ] x M, 10 'x' D²   1 þe¹] þou DMG

⁴But whi speke we and talke we togydre so gladly, sithe we come but seldon home to silence withoute hurtynge of conscience? ⁵Therfore we talke so ofte togydres, for bi suche spekynges togydres we seke counforte euery of oþer, and to relieve þe herte þat is made wery with dyuerse þoughtes. ⁶And we speke muche of suche þinges as we love or desire, or
(2) suche þinges as ar contrary to vs. ⁷But alas, oftetymes veynly and vnfruytfully. | ⁸For suche outwarde counforte is a grete hynderar of f. 11ᵛ inwarde and heuonly consolacion.

⁹And þerfore we owe to wake and to praye þat oure tyme passe not ydely. ¹⁰If hit be leeffulle and expedient to speke, speke of suche þinges as longeþ to edificacioun. ¹¹Yvel vse and takynge none heede of oure gostely encrece and profitynge doþe muche to yvel kepinge of oure mowthes. ¹²Nerþelater, deuoute collacion of spirituel þinges, namely where men of one soule and one spirite ar felyshipped togydres yn God, helpeth gretely to spirituel profityng.

Of pees to be goten and [z]ele of profytynge
Capitulum 11ᵐ

(1) ¹We shulde haue muche pees if we were not occupyed with other mennes dedes and seyinges þat longeth not to oure cure. ²Howe may he longe abide in pees þat medeleþ him of oþer mennes | cures, þat seketh f. 12ʳ occasions outwarde, and seldon gedrith hym withinne hymselfe? ³Blisfulle ar the symple, for þei shul haue muche pees.
(2) ⁴Why were sum holy men sumtyme so perfite and so contemplatyve, ⁵but for þei studyed to mortifie hemselfe in alle wyses from erthely desires, and þerfore þei myght take heede to hemselfe and clyve to God with alle the inwarde of her hertes? ⁶But we ar occupyed with oure owne passions, and ar bysied ouermuche in transitorye þinges. ⁷Also seldon hit is þat we ouercome one vice perfitely, and we tende not euerie day to encrece; and þerfore we abide colde and lewke.

4 togydre] togidres DMG   withoute] wiþ'oute' D², *Latin* sine KR
5 togydres¹] togedre G   spekynges] spekyng DMG, *Latin* locuciones KR   togydres²]
togidre DMG   euery] eiþer DMG   6 or²] or of G   8 hynderar] hindring
DMG   11 none] no G   to yvel kepinge] to evel DM, to the evell G, *Latin* ad
incustodiam K, ad custodiam R   12 nerþelater] neuerþeles DMG   one¹] oo
DMG   soule] sowule, u *canc.* G   one²] oo DMG   togydres] togedre G
    11.0 zele] DMG, hele C, *Latin* zelo KR   11ᵐ] xi G, 11 'xi' D²   2 hym] *om.*
DMG, *Latin* se intrinsecus colligit KR   6 and] 'and' D², *om.* M, *Latin* et KR
ar²] *om.* G, *Latin* sollicitamur KR   7 one] eny DMG, *Latin* vnum KR   tende]
entend G, *Latin* accendimur K, tendimus R   lewke] leude DMG, *Latin* tepidi KR

[8] If we were perfitely dede to oureselfe and not intryked to muche (3) with outwarde þinges, þen myght we savoure godely þinges and sumwhat be experte of hevonly contemplacion. [9] The hole and the

f. 12ᵛ grettest impedimente is | for we ar not free fro passions and con- cupiscencez, ner we enforce not oureselfe to entre into þe wey of holy men and seyntes. [10] Also when þer commeþ a lytel aduersite, we beþ anone þrowen downe and turne vs to seke mannes counforte.

[11] If we wolde enforce vs to stande in bateyle as myghtty men, we (4) shulde see verily þe helpe of our Lorde come from heuon. [12] For he is redi to helpe alle hem þat fyghteþ for him and trusteþ in his grace, þat suffreþ vs to have occasions of fyghtynge þat we mowe haue þe victory.

[13] If we putte þe profitynge of relygion alleone in outwarde obser- uances, oure deuocion shal sone haue an ende. [14] But lete vs sette þe axe to þe rote þat we, purged of oure passions, mowe haue a pesible mynde.

[15] If eueri yere we destruyed groundely one vice, we sholde sone be (5)

f. 13ʳ perfite men. [16] But oftetymes we feele þe contrarye, | for we fynde oureselfe better and pure[r] in þe bigynnynge of oure conuersion þen after mani yeres of profession. [17] Oure feruoure and oure profitinge owed to encrece daily, but nowe hit semeþ a grete þinge if we mowe haue a parte of oure furste feruour.

[18] If we wolde in þe bigynnynge put 'to' a litel violence, we shulde mowe do alle þinges aftirwarde with esines and gladnes. [19] Hit is (6) greuouse to leve þinges acustumed, but hit is more grevouse a man to do ayenis his owne wille. [20] But if þou ouercome not smale þinges and light þinges, when shalt þou ouercome harder þinges? [21] Withstande þine inclynacioun and vnlerne yvel custume, leste lytel and litel hit bringe þee to gretter difficulte.

[22] O, if þou woldeste take heede howe muche pees þou sholdest gete to

f. 13ᵛ thiselfe, and howe muche gladnes þou shuldest cause to | other men in hauynge thiselfe welle, I suppose þat thou woldeste be more besie aboute spirytuelle profitynge.

---

12 is] 'is' D¹   occasions] occa occasions M   15 one] o DMG   16 ofte- tymes] oftetyme DMG   purer] G, pure'r' D², pure CM, *Latin* puriores KR   after] aster M, *Latin* post KR   of²] of our DMG   17 owed] ow⟨ith⟩ D², *Latin* deberet KR   18 shulde mowe] mouȝte G, *Latin* possemus KR   aftirwarde] asterwarde M, *Latin* postea KR   20 if] *om.* M, *Latin* sed si KR

Of the profite of aduersite
Capitulum 12ᵐ

(1) [1] Hit is goode to vs þat we haue sumtyme grevaunces and contrarietez,
for oftetymes þei calle a man into hymselfe, þat he mowe [knowe]
himselfe to be in an exyle, and þat he put not his truste in any yerthely
þinge. [2] Hit is goode þat sumtyme we suffre ayeinsayars and þat men
feele of vs yvel and unperfetly, yea þoghe we do welle and mene welle.
[3] Suche þinges helpeþ oftetymes to mekenes, and defendeþ vs fro
veyneglory. [4] For þen we seke better the inwarde wyttenes, God, when
we ar litel sette by outwarde of men, and litel credence is yiven to vs.

(2) [5] Therfore a man owed to ferme hymselfe in God, so þat hym neded not
to seke any | consolacions outewarde.   f. 14ʳ

[6] When a man welle-disposed [is] troubled or tempted or vexed with
yvel þoughtes, þen he vndirstandeþ God more necessary vnto hym,
withoute whom he perceyveþ that he may no gode þinge do. [7] Then he
morneþ, þen he wayleth, and þen he prayeþ for the miseries þat he
suffreþ. [8] Then also hit weryeþ hym to lyve any lenger; he desireth deþe,
þat he myght be dissolued and be with Criste. [9] Then also he perceyveþ
certeynly that perfite surete ner fulle pees may not be hadde in this
worlde.

Of the withstandynge of temptacions
Capitulum 13ᵐ

(1) [1] Alle the while þat we ar in þis worlde we mowe not be withoute
tribulacion and temptacion. [2] As hit is writen in Iob, 'Temtacion is
mannes lyve in yerthe.' [3] And þerfore euery man oweþ to be bysy aboute
his temptacions and wake in | praiers, þat þe enemy fynde no place [of   f. 14ᵛ
deceyvynge]; for he slepeþ never, but goþe aboute sekynge whom he

12.0 12ᵐ] 12 `xii´ D², xii G   1 calle] callei M   knowe] DMG, om. C, Latin
cognoscat KR   2 suffre] DMG, suffre sumtyme C, Latin paciamur KR   welle¹]
ev wel, ev canc. M, Latin bene KR   4 wyttenes] witnes `of´ D², Latin interiorem
testem deum KR   ar] ben DM, be G   5 owed] owe⟨þ⟩ D², Latin deberet KR
neded] ned⟨ith⟩ D², Latin esset ei necesse KR   6 is] DMG, om. C, Latin tribulatur
uel temptatur K, vel temptatur R   or¹] om. DMG, Latin uel KR   gode] g`o´ode
D²   7 prayeþ] prateþ M, Latin orat KR   8 desireth] desieþe M
13.0 the] om. DMG   temptacions] temptacioun DMG, Latin temptacionibus KR
13ᵐ] xiii MG, 13 `xiii´ D²   2 in²] on G   3 of deceyvynge] DMG, to deceyve
þe C, Latin locum inueniret decipiendi K, inueniret locum decipiendi R

may devoure. ⁴There is no man so perfite ner so holy but þat sumtyme hath temptacions, and we mowe not fully lakke hem.

⁵Nerthelater temptacions ar oftetymes right profitable to man, þogh (2) þei be heuy and grevouse; for in hem a man is meked, purged, and sharpely taught. ⁶Alle holy men haue gone and profited bi many tribulacions and temptacions, ⁷and þei þat myght not welle suffre temptacion were [made] men repreved and fayled in her weye. ⁸Ther is none ordre so holy ner no place so secrete but þer be temptacions or aduersitees. ⁹There is no man alle sure fro temptacions whiles he lyveþ, (3) for in owreselfe is whereof we be tempted, sithe we ar borne in f. 15ʳ concupiscence. ¹⁰When | one tribulacion or temptacion gothe, anoþer commeþ, and euer sumwhat shul we haue to suffre; for we loste þe gode of felycite.

¹¹Many men sekeþ to ouercome temptacions onely bi fleynge of hem, and falleþ more grevously into hem. ¹²By onely fleynge we mowe not overcome, but bi pacience and mekenes we shulle be strenger þen alle oure enemyes. ¹³He þat onely outwarde declyneþ fro temptacion, and (4) takeþ hit not vppe by the rote, shal litel profite, but rather temptaciouns shul come to hym ayeine, and he shal feele worse and worse. ¹⁴Thou shalt ouercome better litel and litel bi pacience and longanimite with the helpe of God þen with duresse and þine owne importunite. ¹⁵In temptacion oftetymes aske counseile. Be not harde to hym þat is f. 15ᵛ tempted, but yive hym counforte, as þou woldest wille | to be done to the.

¹⁶The bygynnynge of alle temptacions is [in]constance of herte and (5) litel truste in God; ¹⁷for as a shippe withowten gouernaunce is stired hiderwarde and thiderwarde with the wawes, so a man þat is remysse and holdeþ not stedfastely his purpose is dyuersely tempted. ¹⁸Fyre preveþ golde, and temptacion preveth þe rightwys man. ¹⁹Oftetymes we wote never what lythe in owre power to do, but temptacion openeþ what we bee. ²⁰Nerthelater, we owe to wake pryncipally aboute the bigyn- nynge; for þen is the enemy sonnest ouercomen if he be not suffred to

---

4 þat] at G   hath] he hath G   5 nerthelater] neuerþeles DMG   tempta-
cions] temptacious M   7 made] DMG, om. C, Latin facti sunt KR   8 ther]
neiþere DMG   none] no‵ne′ D²   secrete] sure ne secre M, sure ne secre‵te′ D², sure
ne sycure G, Latin secretus KR   be] biþ DM   11 more] muche more DMG,
Latin grauius KR   into] in DMG   13 hit] om. M   to] vpon DMG, Latin ad
KR   14 ouercome] ouercome hem DMG   15 woldest wille] wil‵te) D¹, wilte
MG, Latin optares fieri KR   16 inconstance] DMG, constance C, Latin incon-
stancia KR   17 so] DMG, so is C   19 never] not G   20 nerthelater]
neuerþeles DMG

entre into the durre of þe mynde, but anone as he knokketh lete meete hym at the entre. [22] Furste þer comeþ to mynde a symple thought, after þat a stronge imaginacion, and þen delectacion and a shrewde mevynge | and assentynge. [23] So the wykked enemy, whiles he is not withstanden in þe bigynnynge, entreth in litel and lytel tyl he be alle inne. [24] And the lenger þat a man taryeth in withstandynge, the more feble he waxeth continuly, and his enemye ayenst him more myghty. f. 16[r]

(6)   [25] Summe men haue moste grevouse temptacions in þe bygynnynge of her conuersion, summe in þe ende. [26] Summe by alle her lyve hathe none ese. [27] Many men ar tempted ful esily after þe wisdame and the equite of þe ordinance of God, þat peiseþ the states and `þe meritez of' men and ordeyneþ alle þinges to þe helthe of his chosen children.

(7)   [28] Wherefore we oweþ not to despeyre when we ar tempted, but þe more feruently praie God þat he vouchesaue to helpe vs in every tribulacion; for hee, as Seynt Poule seythe, shal make in t[empt]acion suche profitynge | þat we shul mowe suffre hit and abyde hit. f. 16[v]
[29] Wherfore lete vs meke oure sowles vnder þe myghty hande of God in euery tribulacion and temptacion; for hem þat ar meke in spirite he shal save and enhance.

(8)   [30] In temptacions and tribulacions is preved howe muche a man profiteþ, and þere is moste merite and vertue is beste shewed. [31] Hit is no grete þinge if a man be devoute and feruent if he feele none hevynesse; but if he suffre paciently in tyme of aduersite, þere is hope of grete profitynge.
[32] Summe men ar preserved fro grete temptacions and in smale ar dayly ouercomen, þat, so made meke, truste never in hemselfe in grete þinges, þat ar founden feble in so lytel þinges.

20 into] vnto DM   the[4]] `þe' D[2], om. M          23 withstanden] wiþstond⟨ed⟩ D[2]      24 he waxeth] om. G, Latin fit KR          26 none] no G      27 the[1]] om. DMG      peiseþ] DMG, preiseþ C, Latin pensat KR      þe[3]] om. DMG      helthe] hel⟨þ⟩e M, help G, Latin salutem KR      28 praie] to pray G      seythe] `seith' D[2]   temptacion] G, tribulacion CDM, Latin temptacione KR   mowe] om. DMG, Latin possimus KR   hit[1]] om. M   30 howe] howe, we altered from u D[2]
31 none] no G   þere is hope] þere is hope in MG, þere`yn' is hope ⟨. .⟩ D[2], Latin spes magni profectus erit KR   32 preserved] pre⟨serued⟩ D[2], preferred M, Latin custodiuntur KR   temptacions] temptacion G, Latin temptacionibus KR

Of fleynge of temerary iugement
Capitulum 14ᵐ

[1] Bowe þine yen to þiselfe, and be not a demar of oþer mennes dedes. [2] In (1)
f. 17ʳ | demynge other men a man laboureþ in veyne, oftetyme erreþ and
lyghtly synneth; but in demynge and discussinge a man selfe, euer he
laboureþ fructuously.

[3] As hit lyþe in oure herte, so for the moste parte we deme; and
lyghtly we lese trewe iugement for propre loue. [4] If God were euer þe
pure entencion of oure desire, we wolde not lightly be trowbled for
withstandynge of owre owne wytte, [5] but oftetymes sumwhat is hidde (2)
withinforþe or comeþ withouteforþe þat also draweþ vs.

[6] Many priuely sekeþ hemselfe in þinges þat þei done, and wote not
þerof. [7] Hit semeþ hem also to stande in her goode pees when alle þinges
fallen aftir her wille and her felynge; [8] and if hit falle oþerwise þen þei
desire, þey ar sone meued and ar sory.

[9] For dyuersite of opinions and of wittes oftetymes groweþ dissen-
f. 17ᵛ cions bitwene frendes and | neyghboures, bitwene relygiouse and
deuoute puple. [10] Olde custume is harde to breke, and almoste no man (3)
wol be ladde oþerweyes þen him semeþ hymselfe.

[11] If þou leyne more to þine owne reson þen to þe subiectiue vertue of
Ihesu Criste, hit wol be late or þou be a man illuminate; for God wol
haue vs perfitely sugget to hym, and by loue inflammate passe alle
maner mannes reson.

Capitulum 15ᵐ
Of werkes done of charyte

[1] Yuel is not to be done for noþinge in this worlde, ner for no mannes (1)
loue; þogh for þe profite of hym þat is nedy a gode werke [may]

14.0 capitulum 14ᵐ] om. M, capitulum 14 ʿxiiiiʾ D², capitulum xiiii G   1 yen]
eren DMG, Latin o⟨cu⟩los K, oculos R   2 oftetyme] oftetymes DMG   selfe]
ʿhymʾself D²   4 pure] true DMG, Latin pura KR   5 or] or ʿitʾ D², or it
MG   vs] vs ʿto inconuenyensʾ D², vs to inconuenyens MG, Latin quod nos eciam
pariter trahit K, quod eciam nos trahit R   7 goode] gʿoʾode D²   aftir] aster M,
Latin pro eorum velle KR   8 ar²] om. DMG, Latin cito mouentur et tristes fiunt
KR   10 oþerweyes] oþirwyse DMG   him] he G   11 leyne] le⟨e⟩ne D²
to²] om. M   passe] to passe G
15.0 capitulum 15ᵐ of werkes done of charyte] of workes done of charite capitulum 15ᵐ
M, of workes done of charite capitulum 15 ʿxvʾ D², of workes done of charite capitulum xv
G   1 no] om. DMG, Latin nullius KR   þogh] om. DM, but G, Latin sed KR

sumtyme [be] lafte, or elles chaunged for the better. ²For in this maner of wyse þe gode werke is not destruyed but chaunged.

³Withoute charite þe outwarde werke aveyleþ noght. ⁴But whatever be done of charite, be it never so symple ner | so litel, alle is fructuouse. ⁵For God peyseþ more of howe grete charite a man doþe a werke þen (2) howe grete a werke he dothe. ⁶He þat loueþ muche doþe muche. ⁷And he doþe much þat doþe a þinge welle. ⁸He doþe welle þat serueþ more þe comune weelle þen his owne wille. ⁹Oftetymes hit semeþ to be charite and hit is carnalyte, for carnal inclynacion, propre wille, hope of rewarde, affeccion of profite ar but seeldon oute of the weye, but euer redy.

(3)   ¹⁰He þat haþe very and perfite charite sekeþ hymselfe in noþinge, but onely desireth þe glory of God in alle þinges and above alle þinges. ¹¹Also he hath envie to no man, for he loueþ no propre ner private ioye, ¹²ner he wolle not ioye in hymselfe, but above alle þinges he desireþ to be made blisfulle in God. ¹³He ascryveþ to no man any goode þinge, but holy referreþ alle | þinges to God, of whom þei proceden originaly, in whom alle seintes resteþ fynaly. ¹⁴O, he that had verily [a sparkel] of charite, he shulde verily and trewly feele þat alle yerthely þinges ar fulle of vanite.

f. 18ʳ

f. 18ᵛ

Of beringe of other mennes infirmytees and defautes
Capitulum 16ᵐ

(1)   ¹Suche þinges as a man may not amende in hymselfe and in oþer he oweþ to suffre paciently til God ordeyne þe contrarie. ²Thenke peraventure þat hit is better to the to suffre suche contrarietez for thi prevynge and thi pacien[c]e, withowte þe whiche oure merites ar of lytel price. ³Nerthelater, þou oweste for suche impedimentes pray mekely (2) God þat he fouchesave to helpe the þat þou mowe bere benigly. ⁴Yf any suche be ones or twyes amonysshed, and wolle not agree ner be

1 may sumtyme be] MG, 'may' somtyme 'be' D², sumtyme C, *Latin* aliquando intermittendum est KR   2 of] *om.* G   gode] g'o'ode D²   3 noght] not G, *Latin* nichil KR   5 peyseþ] DMG, preyseþ C, *Latin* pensat KR   of] *om.* M   8 wille] wele DMG, *Latin* (volun)tati K, voluntati R   14 a sparkel] G, þat kunnynge CD, þat kunnyg M, *Latin* sintillam K, scienciam illam R   he²] *canc.* D verily and] *om.* DMG   alle] *twice* M

16.0 capitulum 16ᵐ] capitulum xvi G, capitulum 16 'xvi' D², *om.* M   1 and] ner G   ordeyne þe contrarie] oþerwyse ordeyneth G   2 pacience] DMG, paciente C, *Latin* paciencia KR   3 nerthelater] neuerþeles DMG   bere] (suffir) D², suffre M, suffre them G, *Latin* portare KR   4 suche] suche 'ther be þat' D², such þere be þat MG

f. 19ʳ counseyled, stryve not with hym, but | committe alle to God, þat his wille and his worshippe be done and had in alle his servandes, þat canne welle turne yvel into goode.

⁵ Studie to be paciente in suffrynge and beringe other mennes defautes and alle maner infirmytees, for þou haste many þinges þat muste be suffred of oþer men. ⁶ If þou mowe not make thyselfe suche as þou woldeste, howe mayste þou haue anoþer at þi plesance? ⁷ Gladdely we desire to haue oþer men p[er]fite, but we wol not amende oure owne defautes. ⁸ We wol þat oþer men be streytely correcte, `and we ourself (3) wol not be correcte´. ⁹ Oþer mennes large licence displeseþ vs, but we to oureselfe wol haue noþinge denyed þat we aske. ¹⁰ We wolle haue oþer restreyned bi statutes, and we wolle suffre vs in no wyse to be more restreyned. ¹¹ And þus hit appyereþ howe seeldon we peyse oure neyghboure as owreselfe. |

f. 19ᵛ   ¹² If alle men were perfite, what had we þan to suffre of oþer men for God? ¹³ Nowe þerfore God hath ordeyned þat we shulle lerne evyry to (4) bere oþers burdon, for þer is no man withowte defaute, no man withoute burdon, no man sufficient to hymselfe, no man wyse inowe to hymselfe; but we muste bere togydre, counforte togidre, helpe togydre, teche and ammonyshe togydre.

¹⁴ What eueri man verily is, beste [is] shewed bi occacion of aduersite. ¹⁵ For occasions make not a man [frayle], but þei sheweþ what þe man is.

Of religiouse lyve
Capitulum 17ᵐ

¹ Hit behoveþ that þou lerne to breke þiselfe in many þinges, if þou wolt (1) acorde and kepe pees with oþer. ² Hit is no litel þinge a man to dwelle in monasteries and congregacions and þere to lyve withoute querelle, and f. 20ʳ so trewly to | abide to his lyves ende. ³ Blysful is he þat þere lyveth welle and graciously endeth.

⁴ If þou wolte stande duely and profite, accompte þe as an exyle and a

4 goode] go`o´d D²      7 perfite] DMG, profite C, Latin perfectos K, profectus R      9 large] om. M, Latin larga KR      10 bi] by þe G      11 peyse] DMG, preyse C, Latin pensamus KR      13 evyry] euery `man´ D², euery man MG   no man wyse inowe to hymselfe] om. M, Latin nemo sibi satis sapiens KR   togydre¹] togidres DM   14 is²] MG, `is´ D², om. C, Latin patet KR      15 frayle] G, `frayle´ D², om. CM, Latin fragilem KR

17.0 17ᵐ] 17 MG, 17 `xvii´ D²   4 profite] parfite M, Latin proficere KR accompte] aco⟨un⟩te D²

pylgryme vppon yerthe. [5] Hit bihoveþ þee to be a fole for Criste if þou
(2) wolte lede a relygiouse lyve. [6] Habyte and tonsure lytel avaylen, but
chaungynge of maners and hoole mortificacion of þe passions maken a
very relygiouse man.

[7] He þat sekeþ oþer þen purely God and helthe of his sowle, he shal
not fynde but tribulacion and sorowe. [8] Ner he may not stande longe in
(3) pees, but if he enforce hymselfe to be leste and sugget to alle. [9] Thou
cameste to serve and not to governe. [10] Knowe weel þat þou arte called
to suffre and to laboure, not to be ydel and telle tales.

[11] Here ar men preved as golde in the fornayce. [12] Here may no man
stande, | but if he wolle meke himselfe with alle his herte for God.   f. 20ᵛ

Of the ensaumples of holy faders
Capitulum 18ᵐ

(1) [1] Biholde þe queke ensaumples of olde faders, in þe whiche shone
verey perfeccion, and þou shalt see howe litel hit is and allemoste
nought þat we doo. [2] Alas, what is oure lyve compared to hem? [3] Holy
men and þe frendes of God hath served oure Lorde in hunger and
thruste, in colde and nakednesse, in laboure and werynesse, in
wakynges and fastynges, in praiers and holy meditacions, in persecu-
cions and many repreves.

(2) [4] O, howe many and howe grevouse tribulacions suffred apostles,
martires, confessoures, virgynes, and alle religiouse þat wolde folowe the
steppes of Criste! [5] For they hated hir soules, þat is to seie her bod[ely]
lyves, þat þei myght kepe hem | into lyve euerlastynge. [6] O, howe streyte   f. 21ʳ
a lyve lyved holy faders in deserte! Howe longe and howe grevouse
temptacions suffred þei! Howe ofte were þei vexed of the enemy! Howe
continuel and howe fervent preiers offred þei to God! How sharpe
abstinences did þei! How grete [z]ele and fervoure had þei to spirituel
profitynge! Howe stronge bateyle kepte þei aboute destruccion of vices!
Howe pure and ryght intencion helde þei to God! [7] By þe daie þei

5 wolte] DMG, wolte if þou wolte C   6 þe] *om.* G   8 not stande longe]
'not' longe stonde D¹, not longe stonde MG   12 for] DMG, for for C
18.0 18ᵐ] xiii G, 18 'xviii' D²   1 shone] shewþe M, sh(yneþ) D², shyneth G,
Latin refulsit KR   3 god hath served] god ⟨which haue⟩ 'seruyd', h *visible under
erasure under* w, *which canc.* D², god whiche haue serued M, *Latin* sancti et amici christi
domino seruierunt KR   5 bodely] DMG, bodie C   6 zele] DMG, heele C,
Latin zelum KR   stronge] gret DMG, *Latin* forte KR   destruccion] DMG,
destruccions C, *Latin* edomacionem KR   7 by] in G, *Latin* per KR

laboured, and nyghtes þei yave hem to prayers, þoghe in labourynge þei cessed `not´ from inwarde preier. [8] Euerye tyme þei spended fructuously. (3) [9] Euery houre to take hede to God semed shorte, and for grete swetnesse of contemplacion sumtyme was foryeton þe necessite of bodely refeccion.

[10] Thei renounced al maner richesses, dignitees, worshippes, frendes | and kinne; þei kepte to haue noght of þe worlde. [11] Vnneþe þei toke þat was necessary to þe lyve, and sorowed to serve the bodi in his necessite. [12] Thei were pore of yerthely þinges, but right riche in grace and vertues. [13] Outewarde þei were nedy, but inwarde þei were refresshed with grace and gostely counforte. [14] To þe worlde þei were alienes, but (4) to God þei were familiar frendes. [15] To hemselfe þei semed as nought and despised of þe worlde, but in þe yen of God þei were preciouse and chosen. [16] Thei stode in very mekenes, þei lyved in symple obedience, þei walked in charite and pacience; and þerfore eueri day þei profited in spirite, and gate grete grace a[n]enste God. [17] Thei were yiven as in ensaumple to alle religiouse men, and þes oweþ to prouoke vs more to lyffe weelle and | profite þen the grete noumbre of slugged and lewke men to make vs remysse and laxe.

[18] O, how grete was þe feruoure of religion in the bigynnynge of his (5) institucion! [19] O, howe grete deuocion of preyer! Houe grete [z]ele of folowinge of vertue! Howe grete discipline þat tyme þrove! Howe grete reuerence and obedience vnder rewle floured in hem alle! [20] Witnesseth yette þe steppes þat ar lafte þat þei were verily holy men and perfite men, þat fightynge so doughtyly þrewe þe worlde vnder fote.

[21] Nowe is he acompted grete þat is not a brekar of þe rewle, þat can suffre paciently þat he takeþ. [22] O, þe sluggednes and þe necgligence of (6) oure tyme, [23] þat we so sone declyne fro oure raþer feruoure, and ar

---

7 nyghtes] `in´ þe niȝtes D², in þe niȝtes M, in the nyȝte G, *Latin* noctibus KR          not] *om.* M, `not´ D², *Latin* minime KR   8 fructuously] fruytfully DMG   9 euery] ⟨euery⟩ D²   houre] ⟨h⟩oure M   for] for `þe´ D, for the G   10 richesses] richesse DM, riches G, *Latin* diuiciis KR   12 pore] po⟨o⟩re D²   right] full G   14 familiar] familiare ⟨.⟩ D   15 of[1]] *om.* M, *Latin* huic mundo despecti KR   were] semed DMG, *Latin* erant KR   16 anenste] DM, an yenst G, ayenste C, *Latin* apud KR   17 lyffe weelle and profite] lyue and profite wel DMG   slugged] slugg⟨ussh⟩ D², slacke G   18 grete] gret deuocion of preier hov gret zele, *all except first* gret *canc.* M, *Latin* quantus KR   19 zele] DMG, hele C, *Latin* emulacio KR   þrove] proue`d´, p *altered from* þ D², proued MG, *Latin* viguit KR   20 yette] yit in M   þe[1]] ther G   verily] very G   men[2]] *om.* G   21 not] *om.* M, *Latin* non KR   can] cannot M, *Latin* potuerit KR   he takeþ] be⟨fallith⟩, b *altered from* h D², befalliþe MG, *Latin* accepit KR   22 sluggednes] slugg⟨uss⟩nes D², slugglysnes G   23 raþer] first G

wery to lyve for sluggednesse and werynes! [24]Wolde God þat þe profitynge of vertue slepe not vtterly in thee, þat haste | seene so f. 22ᵛ many ensaumples of devoute menne.

Of the exercices of a goode relygyouse man
Capitulum 19ᵐ

(1)   [1]The lyve of a goode relygiouse man oweþ to shyne in alle maner of vertue, þat he be suche inwarde as he appereþ outwarde to men. [2]And worthily hit oweþ to be muche more inwarde þan þat þat is seene outwarde, for God is oure byholdar, whom soveraynly we owe to worshippe whereeuer we be, and go clene in his sight as aungels.

[3]Every day we owe to renewe oure purpose and styrre oureselfe to fervoure, as þoghe we had þis day be furste converted, and seie, [4]'Helpe me, Lorde God, in my goode purpose, and in thi service, and graunte me this daie to bigynne perfitly; for noght hit is þat I haue done vnto þis tyme.'

(2)   [5]Aftir oure purpose, so is the | course of oure profitynge, and he þat f. 23ʳ wolle profite welle haþe nede of grete dilygence. [6]For if he þat purposeþ sadly fayleþ oftetymes, what shal falle of hym þat seldon or never purposeþ anyþinge sadly? [7]Nerthelater, in dyuerse maners hit happeneþ men to forsake her purpose; and þoghe þat appire lyght, yette hit is not withoute summe maner of hyndryng. [8]The purpose of rightwys men hangeþ rather in the grace of God þen in mannes owne wysedome, in whom þei truste euer in alle þinges þat þei doþe or purposeþ. [9]For man purposeth and God disposeth, ner mannes weye is not in man.

(3)   [10]If an acustumed exercice be sumtyme lafte bycause of pite or for profite of oure neyghboure, hit may sone be recovered ayeine. [11]But if hit be lyghtly forsaken, þorowgh hevynesse of soule or necglygence, hit is | vituperable and wol be founde noyouse. [12]Lette vs enforce vs as f. 23ᵛ muche as we canne, and yette shul we lyghtly fayle in many þinges.

23 sluggednesse] slugg⟨uss⟩nes D², sluggesnes G   24 seene] ⟨seen⟩ D²
19.0 exercices] exercise G, *Latin* exerciciis KR   19ᵐ] xix MG, 19 ˋxix' D²
1 goode] gˋoˊode D²   ofᵛ²] *om.* DMG   3 þis day] *om.* DMG, *Latin* hodie
KR   4 goode] goˋoˊde D²   5 ofᵛ²] to M   6 seldon] seldor M
7 nerthelater] neuerþeles DMG   þat appire] ⟨yt⟩ appere, *tail of þ visible under erasure*
D², it apere G, yt a propere M   8 whom] w⟨hich⟩ D², whiche M, þe whiche G,
Latin quo KR   þat] ⟨þat⟩ D²   or purposeþ] ⟨. . . . .⟩, purp *visible under
erasure* D, *om.* MG, *Latin* quidquid arripiunt KR   9 for man] ⟨for man⟩ D²
10 an] *canc.* D², *om.* G   sone be] be sone G   11 þorowgh] þo⟨ru⟩gh M

[13] But euermore sumwhat in certeyne is to be purposed, and namely ayenys þo þinges þat moste lette vs.

[14] Owre owtewarde and oure inwarde exercices bothe oweþ to be serched and kepte in ordre, for boþe ar expediente and helpinge to gostely profite. [15] If þou mow not continuly gedre thiselfe togedre, (4) namely sumtyme do hit, atte leste ones a day, þe mornyng or þe evontyde. [16] In the mornynge, purpose; [in] þe evontide, discusse thi maners, what þou haste bene þis day in worde, werke, and þought, for in þees peraventure þou haste ofte offended þi God and þi neyghboure.

[17] Gurde þe as a man ayenys þe fendes wykkednesse; refrayne |

f. 24ʳ gloteny, and þou shalte þe more esily restreyne alle þe inclynacion of þe fleisshe. [18] Be never alle ydelle, but ouþer be redinge or wrytinge or prayinge or þenkynge or sumwhat labouringe for þe commune profite. [19] Bodeli exercices ar to be done discretely, ner to be taken evonly and lyke of alle men.

[20] Tho þat ar not comune þinges ar not to be shewed outwarde, for (5) pryvate þinges ar more surely exerciced in secrete wyse. [21] Nerthelater, beware þat þou be not slowe to comune þinges and more redy to pryvate and singvler exercices. [22] But thoo þat ar due and enioyned treuly fulfilled, if þer be vacante tyme, yelde þe to thiselfe as þi deuocion desireþ.

[23] Alle mowe not haue one exercice, but one þis, anoþer þat, [as] is accordynge. [24] Also for congruence [of tyme], diuersite of exercices

f. 24ᵛ pleseþ; for summe ar more savory in festiual dayes, | and summe in feryal dayes. [25] Other we nedeþ in tyme of temptacion; oþer in tyme of pees and quiete. [26] Oþer we muste þenke when we ar sorie, and oþer when we be gladde in oure Lorde.

[27] In principalle festes, goode exercices oweþ to be renewed, and the (6) helpe of þe seintes more fervently to be sought. [28] Fro feste into feste we oweþ to purpose as þough we sholde þat tyme passe oute of þis worlde, and go to þe feste euerlastynge. [29] Therfore we owe to araye oureselfe

---

14 oweþ] ow⟨yn⟩ D²   15 atte] at DM, at the G   þe¹] ʼynʼ þe D², in the G
evontyde] evenyng DMG   16 in²] DMG, *om*. C   thi maners] þe maner DM,
Latin mores tuos KR   17 ayenys] ayent M   inclynacion] DMG, inclynacions C,
Latin inclinacionem KR   18 ouþer] eiþer DMG   19 ner] not DMG, *Latin*
nec KR   21 nerthelater] neuerþeles DMG   22 and] ⟨and⟩ D², *om*. M, *Latin*
et KR   fulfilled] fulfille⟨.⟩ D², fulfille MG, *Latin* expletis KR   be] be a G
23 one¹] o maner DMG, *Latin* vnum KR   as is accordynge] MG, as ʼisʼ according ⟨. .⟩
D², is accordynge to C   24 of tyme] ʼof tymeʼ D², *om*. CMG, *Latin* temporis
KR   dayes²] *om*. DMG   25 quiete] quiet⟨nes⟩ D², quietnes G   27 goode]
goʼoʼde D²   þe] *canc*. D², *om*. G   28 into] to G

more bisily in deuoute werkes and lyve þe more deuoutely and kepe
euerie obseruance the more streytely, as we þat shulle in hast receyue þe
(7) rewarde for oure laboure. [30] And if hit be delayed, lette vs accompte
oureselfe as men not fully redy, and vnworthy to come to so grete a
glory, the whiche shal be reveled in vs in tyme | ordeyned; and lete vs   f. 25ʳ
study to make vs redy to goynge oute of the body.

[31] 'Blysfulle is þat servant,' seithe Luke, 'whom oure Lorde, when he
comeþ, fyndeþ wakynge, [32] for I seye you verily, he shal sette hym above
alle his goodes.'

Of love of silence and to be alone
Capitulum 20ᵐ

(1) [1] Seke þe a convenient tyme to take heede to þiselfe, and þenke
oftetymes of þe benefaytes of God. [2] Leve curiouse þinges, [3] and rede
suche matiers þat rather yiveþ compunccion þen ocupacioun. [4] If þou
withdrawe þiselfe fro voyde spekynges and ydel circuites, and fro
vanitees and herynge of tidinges, þou shalt fynde tyme sufficient and
covenable for to haue swete meditacions.

[5] The grete holy men, whereas þei myght, þei fledde mennes fely-
(2) sheppe, and chase to lyve to Gode in secrete places. [6] One seyde, 'As
oftetymes | as I was amonge men, I came a lasse man,' þat is to seie, lasse   f. 25ᵛ
holy. [7] This we fynde by experience when we talke any while. [8] Hit is
lyghter a man to be alle stylle þen to not excede in worde. [9] Hit is more
lyght a man to abyde pryvely at home þen to sufficiently kepe hymselfe,
beinge owte. [10] Wherfore whoeuer purpose to come to inwarde and to
spirituel þinges, hit byhoveþ him to declyne fro þe prees with Ihesu.

(3)   [11] No man appiereþ surely outewarde, but he þat gladly loveth to
abyde at home. [12] No man spekeþ surely, but he þat is gladde to holde
his pees. [13] No man is surely above, but he þat wolle gladdely be byneþe.
[14] No man surely commaundeþ, but he þat hath lerned to obeye. [15] No
man ioyeth surely, but if he haue wyttenes of gode conscience.

---

30 the¹] *om.* G   to goynge oute of the body] to go⟨o . . . ⟩ oute of ⟨þe worlde⟩ D², to
go oute of þis worlde MG, *Latin* ad exitum KR
20.0 20ᵐ] 20 MG, 20 ʻxx' D²   3 yiveþ] zeueþe M   4 circuites] circuit(es
. . ⟩ D², circuites MG, circuitryes C, *Latin* circuicionibus KR   6 þat is to seie lasse
holy] ⟨þat is to say⟩ ʻlesse' holy D²   8 is] ʻis' G   lyghter] liʒtlier DM
to be alle] ay to be DMG, *Latin* omnino KR   worde] wordes DMG, *Latin* verbo
KR   9 to sufficiently] ⟨. .⟩ sufficiently ʻto' D²   10 prees with] ⟨cumpany of⟩
ʻpeple with' D², cumpany of peple with MG, *Latin* turba KR   11 gladly loveth]
loueþ gladly DMG   12 he] ʻhe' G   15 haue] haþe M   gode] gʻo'ode D²

¹⁶Nerthelater, þe surete of holy men was never withoute drede of |
f. 26^r   God, ner þei were the lasse besy and meke in hemselfe, þogh þei had
grete vertues and grace. ¹⁷The surete of shrewes groweth of pride and
presumpcion, and in the ende hit turneth into [þer] deceyte. ¹⁸Promitte
neuer thiselfe surete in þis worlde, þogh þou seme a gode relygiouse or a
deuoute hermyte. ¹⁹Oftetymes þei þat ar beste in mannes estimacion (4)
fallen moste perilously for her overgrete truste. ²⁰Wherfore hit is not
profitable þat þei lakke vtterly temptacions, but oftetymes be impugned,
lest þei be to sure, lest þei be lyfte vp bi pride; ner lette hem not lyghtly
declyne to outwarde consolacions.

²¹O, who þat never sought transitory gladnesse, who þat never
ocupyed him in þe worlde, howe gode a conscience sholde he kepe!
²²O, he þat wolde kutte awey al maner of veyne bysinesse, and wolde
f. 26^v   þenke alle|only on gostely and godly þinges, and sette alle his hope in
God, howe grete pees and quiete sholde he have!

²³Ther is no man worthi hevonly counforte but he dylygently (5)
exercice hymselfe in holy compunccioun. ²⁴If þou hertely be compuncte, entre into þi pryve closet and exclude alle worldely noyce, as hit
is wryten, 'Be ye compuncte in youre prive cowches.' ²⁵Thou shalt
fynde [þer] þat withoute þou shalt oftentymes leese. ²⁶The celle welle
continued waxeth swete, and the celle yvel kepte engendreþ werynes.
²⁷If in þe bigynnyng of þi conversion þou kepe þi celle and dwelle wel
þereinne, hit shal be to þe afterwarde as a dere and welbeloved frende
and moste plesant solace.

²⁸In silence and quiete profiteþ the deuoute soule, and lerneth þe (6)
privytees of scriptures. ²⁹þere he fyndeþ þe flodes of teres, wherewith bi
f. 27^r   euery nyght | he mowe wasshe and clense hymselfe, þat he mowe be þe
more familyar to his maker, þat he withdraweþ him far frome alle
seculer noyce. ³⁰He þat withdraweþ himselfe fro frendes and knowen
men, God shal neyghe vnto him with his holye aungels. ³¹Better hit is a
man to be hydde and take cure of himselfe, þenne takynge none heede of

---

16 nerthelater] neuerþeles DMG   17 þer] G, om. CDM, Latin sui 'ipsius' K,
sui R   18 relygiouse] religious ⟨man⟩ D², religious man MG   19 þei] 'þei'
D²   overgrete] owne DMG, Latin 'nimiam' K, nimiam R   20 vtterly] ⟨vttirly⟩
D²   be¹] CD, om. M, þat they be G   sure] seure 'and' D², seure and MG   not²]
om. G   21 gode] g'o'ode D²   sholde] shal M, sh⟨uld⟩ D²   22 on] of G
quiete] quiete'nes' D², quienes M, quietnes G   23 worthi] worthy of G
24 cowches] cowches, w altered from u D²   25 þer] DMG, om. C, Latin in cella
KR   oftentymes] oftetymes DMG   27 þou] canc. D   28 quiete]
quiete'nesse' D², quienesse M, quietnes G   29 more familyar] familiar‖miliar G
alle] om. DMG, Latin omni KR   30 god] go'o'd, second o canc. D²   neyghe] be
nye MG, 'drawe' nye D², Latin approximabit K, appropinquabit R   31 none] no G

himselfe to worche wonders. [32] Hit is commendable a man of religion
seldon to go oute, to flee to be seen, and not wille to see men.

(7)   [33] Wherto wolte þou see þat þe is not lyefulle to have? þe worlde
passeþ and his concupiscence. [34] The desires of sensualite drawen to
walkynge aboute; but when þe houre is passed, what cometh þereof but
grucchynge of conscience and dispercioun of herte? [35] A gladde goynge
oute oftetyme bryngeþ forthe a soriful comynge home, and | a gladde   f. 27ᵛ
wakynge over evon bryngeþ forthe a sory mornynge. [36] So every fleisly
ioye entreþ in plesantly, but in þe ende he byteþ and sleeþ. [37] What
maiste þou see elleswhere þat þou seest not here? [38] Loo here hevon,

(8) yerthe and alle elementes, and of þees alle þinges ar made. [39] What
mayste þou see elleswhere þat may longe abide vnder þe sonne?
[40] Peraventure þou waytest to be filled, but þou shalt never come
þerto. [41] If þou sawest alle þinges þat ar present, what wer þat but a
veyne sight?

[42] Lyfte vppe þine yen to God on high, and pray God for þi synnes
and thi necglygences. [43] Leve veyne to the veyne, and take þou hede to
tho þinges þat God commaundeþ þee. [44] Shitte thi durre vppon the and
calle to þee Ihesu thi love. [45] Dwelle with him in thi celle, for þou shalt
not fynde | elleswhere so grete pees. [46] If þou haddest not gone oute, ner   f. 28ʳ
herde no tidinges, þou sholdest þe bettir abyden in pees. [47] And sithe hit
deliteþ otherwhiles to here newe þinges, hit bihoveth folowyngly to
suffre turbacion of herte.

Of compunccioun of herte
Capitulum 21ᵐ

(1)   [1] Yf þou wolte any[wise] profite, kepe þee in the drede of God, and be
not in to grete lyberte, but refreyne þi wittes vnder disciplyne, and yive
not þiselfe to vncovenable gladnesse. [2] Yive the to compunccion of herte,
and þou shalte fynde deuocioun. [3] Compunccion openeþ many þinges,
þe whiche dissolucioun sone leseth.

33 þe is not lyefulle] is not lefull the G   35 oftetyme] oftetymes DMG   soriful]
sorˈoˈful D²   37 seest not] maist not se DMG, *Latin* non vides KR   43 the] *om.*
G   44 þee] *om.* G, *Latin* ad te KR   45 celle] ⟨celle⟩ D¹   46 ner] nor
DM   47 deliteþ] deliteþ þe DMG   þinges] tidynges DMG, *Latin* noua KR
bihoveth] bih(o)ueþe M   folowyngly] flouyngly M, *Latin* exinde KR   turbacion]
tribulacion M, *Latin* turbacionem K, tribulacionem R
    21.0 21ᵐ] 21 MG, 21 ˈxxiˈ D²   1 anywise] DMG, any C, *Latin* aliquid proficere
KR   the] *om.* M   3 leseth] leftþ D, lestþ M, *Latin* perdere KR

[4] Wonder hit is þat a man may at any tyme be glad, þat considereþ his exile and so many periles of his soule. [5] For lyghtenes of þe herte and (2) f. 28ᵛ necglygence of oure defautes we | feele not þe sorowes and the harmes of our soule, and oftetymes we lawgh veynely, when we shulde raþer by reson wepe. [6] Ther is no very liberte ner gode myrþe, but in þe drede of God with a gode conscience.

[7] Blisful is he þat may put awey euery lettynge distraccion and brynge himselfe to the onhed of holy compunccion. [8] Blisful is he þat voydeþ from hym alle þat may defoyle or greve his conscience. [9] Fyght manly: custume is overcome with custume. [10] If þou canste leve men, þei shulle wel leve and suffre the to do þine owne dedes.

[11] Drawe not to thee þe matiers of other men, and implye not thiselfe (3) in causes of grete men. [12] Haue thin ye furste vppon thiselfe, and ammonyshe thyselfe spiritually byfore alle other þat þou lovest beste. f. 29ʳ [13] If þou haue not the favoure of men, | be not sorye therfore, but lete þis be grevouse to thee, þat þou haste not þiselfe welle and circumspectily, as hit sat þe servant of God and a deuoute religiouse man to lyve.

[14] Oftetymes hit is more profitable and more sure þat a man have not many counfortes in þis lyve, aftir the fleysshe namely. [15] And þat we have not or þat we seldon feele godly consolacions, hit is oure owne defaute, for we seke not compunccion, ner we put not vttirly awey veyne and outewarde counfortes. [16] Knowleche þe not worthi godly consola- (4) cion but raþer worthy muche tribulacion.

[17] When a man is `perfitli´ compuncte, þen is alle the worlde grevouse and bitter to him. [18] A goode man fyndeþ sufficiant matier of sorowinge and wepynge. [19] Whether he considre of hymselfe or þenke on his f. 29ᵛ neyghboure, he | shal knowe þat no man lyveþ here withoute tribulacion. [20] And þe more streytely þat he considereþ himselfe, so muche more he soroweþ. [21] Matiers of rightwyse sorowe and of inwarde compunccion ar oure synnes and oure vices, whereinne we lye wrapped, so þat we mowe but seldon byholde hevonly þinges.

[22] If þou þoughtest ofter of dethe þen þou doeste of longe lyve, no (5) doute but þou woldeste more feruently amende thyselfe. [23] Or elles, if

5 soule] soules DMG, *Latin* anime nostre dolores KR   raþer by reson] by reson raþer DMG   6 gode¹] g`o´ode D²      8 defoyle] defoule DMG      11 causes] þe causes G      12 thin ye] þyn ⟨.⟩eye, n *added on line* D²      13 sat] sat or behouyd M, ⟨. . .⟩`besemeth´ D², besemethe G, *Latin* deceret KR   15 compunccion] compunccions G, *Latin* compunctionem KR   ner] nor G   18 goode] g`o´ode D²   19 of] ⟨. .⟩, of *visible under erasure* D, *om.* G   21 lye] be M, *Latin* iacemus KR   mowe] mowe not G   22 of¹] on DG   of²] on M

þou woldeste hertely biholde the peynes of helle and [purgatory], I
byleve þat þou woldeste gladdely suffree peyne, laboure, and sorowe,
dredynge no maner of rygoure. ²⁴But for þees gothe not to the herte and
yeette we love blandyshynges, therfore we remayne colde and slowe.

(6)　　　²⁵Oftetymes hit is nede of spirite wherof | þe wrecched body so　f. 30ʳ
lyghtly compleyneþ. ²⁶Praie þerfore mekely to oure Lorde, þat he yive
þee the spirite of compunccion, and seye with the prophete, 'Feede me,
Lorde, with the brede of teres, and yive [me] drynke in teres in mesure.'

Of the consideracioun of mannes miser[y]
Capitulum 22ᵐ

(1)　　¹Wrecched þou arte, whereever þou be, and whithereuer þou turne the
but if þou turne þe to God. ²What arte þou troubled þat alle þinge
commeþ not to thee as þou willest or desireste? ³Who is þat þat hath
alle þinge at his owne wille? Neþer I, ner þou, ner no man in yerthe.
⁴There is no man in þis worlde withoute summe manere of tribulacion
or angwysshe, þoghe he be kynge or [pope]. ⁵Then who is in beste case?
Forsothe, he þat may suffre anyþinge for Goddes sake.

(2)　　⁶Lorde, nowe | þer ar many weyke folke and seeke [þat seithe], ⁷'O,　f. 30ᵛ
howe goode a lyve þat man hath! Howe grete, howe riche, howe myghty,
howe highe he is!' ⁸But byholde hevonly godes, and þou shalt see þat
alle þees temporalle goodes beeþ as none, but þei beeþ fulle vncerteyne
and more grevynge þen esynge, for þei ar never had withoute bysines
and drede. ⁹Hyt is not mannes felycite to haue temporal goodes in
haboundaunce, but mediocrite sufficeþ hym.
¹⁰Uerely, hit is a misery to lyve vppon yerthe. ¹¹The more spirituel
þat a man wol be, the more þis present lyve appiereth [to him] bitter; for
he feleþ better and seeþ more clerely the defautes of mannes corrupcion.

---

23 and purgatory] DMG, and ⟨. . . . .⟩, and canc. C, Latin siue purgatorii KR
of²] of þinge of M　　　　25 nede] nede'nes' D², nedynes G　　　　26 yive¹] zeue M,
Latin det KR　　　me²] MG, ⟨me⟩ D², vs C, Latin michi KR
　　22.0 the] om. DMG　　　misery] DMG, miseries C, Latin de consideracione humane
miserie KR　　　22ᵐ] 22 MG, 22 'xxii' D²　　　1 withereuer] wiþer'so'euer D²,
whiþersoeuere G　　　3 þat¹] he G　　　3–4 in yerthe there is no man] om. M, Latin
super terram nemo est KR　　　4 pope] DMG ⟨. . . .⟩ C, Latin papa KR　　　6 nowe]
om. M　　　and seeke þat seithe] con., and seeke C, now and seke M, ⟨that seyne⟩ D², þat
seyne G, Latin dicunt multi imbecilles et infirmi K, dicunt nunc multi inbecilles et infirmi
R　　　7 goode] go'o'de D²　　　8 godes] goodes, s added on line D², good M, Latin
bona KR　　　goodes] g'o'odes D²　　　9 not] om. DMG, Latin non KR　　　11 to
him] G, om. CDM, Latin ⟨ei⟩ K, ei R

[12] For to ete, to drynke, to wake, to slepe, to reste, to laboure, and to be sugget to the necessitees of kynde is very mysery and an afflyccion to a

f. 31ʳ devoute | man, þat wolde fayne be lose and free fro synne. [13] The (3) inwarde man is fulle sore greved with bodely necessitees in þis worlde. [14] Wherefore the prophete prayeth devoutely þat he mowe be free fro hem, seyinge, 'Lord, delyver me fro my necessitees.'

[15] But woo to hem þat knowe not her miserie; but more woo to hem þat loveþ þis misery and þis corruptible lyve. [16] For þer beeþ summe þat so hertely clyppeth þis wrecched lyve, þoghe þei mowe vnneþe haue her necessaries with labourynge, yea and begginge, þat if they myght lyffe here ever, þei wolde take none heede of þe rewme of hevon. [17] O, the (4) mad men and oute of trewe bileve, that lithe so deepe in yerthely þinges þat thei savoure none hevonly þinges. [18] But þees wrecches yeet in the

f. 31ᵛ ende shulle grevously feele howe noght hit was and howe vile þat | þei haue loved.

[19] But the seintes of God and alle deuoute men and frendes of Criste have not take heede to þat that plesethe the fleysshe, ner to hem þat have floured in this worlde, but alle her hope and alle her intencion hath been to þinges everlastynge. [20] Alle her desire was borne vppe to þinges invisible and abidynge, lest by love of þinges uisible þei were drawen to þees loweste þinges.

[21] Brother, lese not þi confidence of profitynge to spirituel þinges. Yeet hast þou tyme and houre. [22] Whi wol þou tary thi purpose tille (5) tomorowe? [23] Arise and bygynne anone, and seie, 'Nowe is tyme of doinge; nowe hit is tyme of purgynge; nowe is tyme of amendynge.' [24] When þou arte yvel at ese, þen seye, 'Nowe is tyme of merite.' [25] Thou

f. 32ʳ muste go bi fire and water or [þou] come to refresshinge. [26] But yf | þou do force to thiselfe, þou shalt never overcome vice. [27] Alle the while þat we bere þis frayle body, we cannot be withoute synne, ner lyve withoute hevinesse and sorowe. [28] We wolde gladdely haue quiete from alle miserie, but forasmuche as bi synne we loste innocence, we loste also very blysfulnes. [29] And þerfore we muste kepe pacience and abide the

---

12 wake] wake ⟨.⟩ D   an] *canc.* D, *om.* G   a] a⟨.⟩ D   14 þat] þa M
16 þoghe] *con.*, þat þoghe CG, þat `þouȝe´ D², þat M, *Latin* licet KR   þat²] ⟨yet⟩ D²,
yet G, *Latin* ut KR   none] noo G   17 lithe so deepe] ly⟨ue⟩ so depe`ly´ D², lyue
so depely M, lyene so depely G, *Latin* tam profunde in terrenis iacent KR   19 but¹]
om. G, *Latin* autem KR   23 nowe is tyme of doinge nowe hit] now DMG, *Latin*
nunc tempus est faciendi nunc KR   24 merite] *canc.* C   25 bi fire and]
⟨þroghe fyre⟩ `and´ D², thorogh fyre and G   þou] DMG, to C   26 do force to]
do force to, *all except* force *canc.* D, force MG, *Latin* tibi vim feceris KR   28 quiete]
quiet`nes´ D², quietenes G   29 and¹] *canc.* D², *om.* G

mercie of God, til þis wikkednes go aweye and þis mortalite be swoloed
vppe of lyve.

(6)   [30] O, howe grete is mannes frayelte, þat is prone and redy to vices!
[31] þis daye þou arte shryven of thi synnes, and tomorowe þou doste lyke
synnes ayeine. [32] Nowe þou purposeste to be ware, and withinne ii
houres þou doste as þogh þou haddeste never taken suche purpose.
[33] Wherefore we haue grete cause to meeke oureselfe, and never to feele
any grete | thinge of oureselfe, for we beeþ so frayle and so vnstable. f. 32ᵛ
[34] Also hit may sone be loste bi necgligence, þat is [vn]neþe goten in
grete tyme bi grace.

(7)   [35] What shal falle of vs in þe ende, þat ar slugged so erly? [36] Woo be to
vs, þat þus wolle declyne to reste as þoghe þere were pees and surete,
sithe þere appiereþ yeet no steppe of veri holynesse in oure conuersacion. [37] Hit were nede þat we were newe enfourmed as yonge novices to
goode maners, if peraventure þere were hope of any amendement to
come, or of more spirituel prophitinge.

Of the meditacion of deþe
Capitulum 23ᵐ

(1)   [1] This daie a man is, and tomorowe he appiereþ not. [2] Ful sone shal þis
be fulfilled in þee: loke wheþer þou canste doo oþerwyse. [3] And when
man is oute of sight, sone he passeth oute of mynde. [4] O, the dulnesse
and the hardenesse of | mannes herte, þat onely þenkeþ on þinges f. 33ʳ
presente, and provideþ not more for þinges to come! [5] Thou shuldest
haue þee so in eueri dede and eueri þought as þoghe þou shuldeste dye
anone. [6] If þou haddest a goode conscience, þou shuldest not muche
drede dethe. [7] [Hit is better to eschue synnes þen to flee dethe.] [8] If þou
be not redy today, howe shalte þou be redy tomorowe? [9] Tomorowe is a
day vncerteyne, and what woste þou if þou shalte lyve [tille] tomorowe?

29 swoloed] swol⟨wyd⟩ D²   lyve] ly⟨fe⟩ D²   33 and . . . oureselfe²] om. DMG,
Latin nec vmquam aliquid magni de nobis sentire KR   beeþ] be MG   so²] ʻsoʼ
G   34 vnneþe] DMG, how neþe C, Latin vix KR   35 slugged] slug⟨gussh⟩,
D², slugguse G   37 newe] nowe DMG, Latin adhuc iterum K, adhuc ʻiterumʼ
R   goode] gʻoʼode D²   were hope of any] con., were any hope of any C, wer eny
hope of DMG, Latin si forte spes esset de aliqua futura emendacione KR
    23.0 the] om. DMG   23ᵐ] 23 MG, 23 ʻxxiiiʼ D²   2 wheþer] where M, Latin
quomodo KR   6 goode] gʻoʼode D²   dethe] þe M   7 hit . . . dethe] DMG,
om. C, Latin melius esset peccata cauere quam mortem fugere KR   9 tomorowe¹] tho
morwe, tho altered from the D², tho morow M   tille] MG, ʻtilʼ D, om. C

[10] What avayleþ hit to lyve longe, if we amende but litel? [11] And longe (2)
lyve amendeþ not at alle tymes, but sumtyme encreceþ synne. [12] Wolde
God þat we lyved weel in þis worlde one daie! [13] Many men accompteth
þe yeres of her conversion, but oftetyme litel is þe fruyte of amendemente. [14] If hit be dredfulle to dye, perauenture hit is more perilouse to
lyve longe.

f. 33ᵛ   [15] Blisfulle is he þat hath | þe houre of his deþe ever afore his yenn,
and þat eueri day disposeth himselfe to dye. [16] If þou haue seen any man
dye, þenke þat þou shalt goo the same weye. [17] When hit is mornynge, (3)
weene þiselfe þat þou shalt not come to þe evon; and when evon comeþ,
be not bolde to byhiete thiselfe þe mornynge. [18] Wherefore be euer redy,
and lyve so þat deþe fynde þee neuer vnredye. [19] Many men dyeþ
sodeynly and vnavysed; for what houre we weene not þe sonne of man
shal come. [20] When þat laste houre comeþ, þou shalt bigynne to feele
alle oþerwyse of thy lyve þat is passed, and þou shalt gretly [sorowe] þat
þou haste been so remysse and so necglygente.

[21] O, howe blessid is he þat laboureþ to be suche in his lyve as he (4)
desireþ to be founde in his deþe! [22] Thes shulle yive grete truste to dye:
f. 34ʳ   perfite | contempte of the worlde, fervente desire of profitynge in
vertues, love of disciplyne, laboure of penaunce, promptitude of
obedience, denyinge of hymself, berynge of alle maner aduersite for
the love of Criste. [23] Whiles þou arte hole, þou maiste do muche goode;
but when þou arte seeke, I wote not what þou maiste doo. [24] Fewe þer
beeþ þat ar amended bi seekenes, as þei þat goþe muche on pilgrymage
ar but seeldon þe holyer.

[25] Delaye not þe helthe of thi soule for truste of frendes and of (5)
neyghboures, for men wolle foryete þee sonner þen þou weneste. [26] Hit
is better nowe to make provision bytyme and sende byfore summe goode
þen [to] truste in oþer mennes helpe. [27] If þou be not bysie for thyselfe
nowe, who shal be besie for þee in tyme to comynge? [28] Nowe tyme is |
f. 34ᵛ   right preciouse, but alas þat þou spendest hit no more profitably,

10 if we amende but litel] but if we amende M, ⟨when ther ys lytell amendement⟩ D²,
whenn þere is litel amendment G, *Latin* quando tam parum emendamur K, quando parum
emendamur R   11 and] ⟨a⟩ D², a G, *Latin* ach K, ac R   at alle tymes] at all tyme
DG, alle tyme M   encreceþ] encrescit D   12 one] o DM   13 þe¹] þere
G   oftetyme] oftetymes DMG   15 afore] before DMG   disposeth] þenke and
disposiþe M, *Latin* disponit KR   17 evon¹] eventyde G   byhiete] be here DMG,
Latin polliceri KR   þe²] 'in' þe D², in the G   20 sorowe] MG, sowe D, *om.* C,
Latin dolebis KR   21 desireþ] desriþe M   22 promptitude] redy promptitude
M, redynes G   23 whiles] while DMG   24 on] a DMG   25 helthe]
helpe G, *Latin* salutem KR   26 byfore] tofore DM   to²] DMG, *om.* C
helpe] helþe DMG, *Latin* auxilio KR   27 to] *om.* DMG   28 no] not MG

whereinne þou mayste deserve wherof everlastingly to lyve! [29] Tyme shal
come þat þou shalt desire [o] daye or an houre for þine amendemente,
and thou wottest ner whether þou shalt gete hit.

(6)   [30] O, my dere frende, of howe grete peryle mayste þou make þee free,
and of howe grete drede delyver thiselfe, if þou be nowe evermore
dredfulle and suspecte of dethe! [31] Studye to lyffe so nowe, þat þou
mowe in the houre of dethe raþer ioye þen drede. [32] Lerne nowe to dye
to the worlde, þat þen þou mowe bygynne to lyffe with Criste. [33] Lerne
nowe to despice alle þinges, þat þou mowe þen goo freely to Criste.
[34] Chastyse nowe thi bodie by penaunce, þat þou mowe þen haue
certeyne confidence.

(7)   [35] And, þou fole, where|to þenkeste þou thiselfe to lyve longe, sithe   f. 35ʳ
þou arte sure of no day? [36] Howe many ar deceyved and ayenis al hope
drawen oute of the body! [37] How ofte haste þou herde men seie, 'þat
man was slayne with a swerde; he drowned; he, fallynge from highe,
brake his necke; he in etynge sodeynly waxed styffe; he in pleyinge toke
an ende; another with fire; anoþer with yron; anoþer with pestilence;
anoþer slayne amonge þiffes.' [38] And so þe ende of alle is deþe, and
mannes lyve passeþ awey sodeynly as a shadowe.

(8)   [39] Who shalle haue mynde of þe aftir deþe, and who shal praye for
the? [40] Do, my dere broþer, nowe, what þou mayste do, for thow woste
not when þou shalte dye, [41] and þou wotteste not what shal come to þee
aftir thi dethe. [42] Whiles þou haste tyme, | geder ryches immortalez.   f. 35ᵛ
[43] þenke noþinge but thi soule helthe. Charge onely þo þinges þat
longeþ to [God]. [44] Make þe n[o]w frendes, worshyppinge holy seyntes
and foloynge her werkes, þat when þou fayleste in þis lyve, þei receyve
(9) þee into euerlastynge tabernacles. [45] Kepe thiselfe as a pilgryme and a
geste vppon yerþe, to whom longeth noþinge of worldely bisinesse.
[46] Kepe thi herte free and rered vppe to þi God, for þou hast here none
abydynge cite. [47] Thider dresse preyers and dayly moorninges with teres,
þat þi spirite after thi dethe mowe deserve blysfully to come to oure
Lorde.

29 desire o] M, ⟨. . . desire oo⟩ D¹, desyre oon G, desire a C, *Latin* vnum . . . desiderabis
KR   ner] not DMG   30 delyver] ⟨. . . .⟩delyuere D   34 certeyne] cert⟨yn⟩
D²   38 ende] *om.* M, *Latin* finis KR   39 of] on DMG   deþe] þi deþe
DMG   40 not] *om.* M, *Latin* nescis KR   42 immortalez] immortale
DG   43 but] but of G   god] *con.*, þi soule DMG, *om.* C, *Latin* dei
KR   44 now] DMG, new C, *Latin* nunc KR   þei] they may G
45 yerþe] þe erþe DMG   46 rered] rere it DMG, *Latin* sursum erectum KR
none] no G   47 dresse] ⟨directe⟩ D²

Of the iugement and of the peynes of synners
Capitulum 24 [m]

[1] In alle þinges biholde the ende and howe þou shalte stande byfore the | (1)
f. 36ᵛ rightwyse iuge, from whom is noþinge hidde. He is not quemed with
yiftes; he receyveþ none excusacionz, but þat rightwyse is he shal deme.
[2] O þou moste wrecched and vnsavory synner, what shalt þou answere
[God], knowinge alle þine yvels, þat sumtyme arte aferde of the
loo[k]ynge of a man þat is wrothe? [3] Whi doste [þou] not previde for
thiselfe ayenste the daie of dome, when no man shal mow be excused ner
defended by another, but euerie mannes burdon shal be inowe to
himselfe? [4] Nowe thi laboure is fruytefulle, thi wepynge acceptable,
thy moornynge exaudible, thi sorowe is satisfactory and purgatory.

[5] He hath a grete and an holsome purgatorie þat paciently receyveþ (2)
f. 36ᵛ wronges, þat soroweth more for oþer mennes malyce þen | for his owne
wronges, þat gladdely preieth for his aduersaries and hertily foryeveþ
his trespassours, þat tarieþ not to aske foryevenesse of oþer, þat more
lyghtly haþ mercie þen he is wrothe, þat doþe violence to himselfe, þat
laboureþ in alle wyses to subdue his fleysshe vnder the spirite. [6] Bettir
hit is to kutte awey and purge thi synnes and thi vices here þen to
reserve hem to be purged in tyme commynge. [7] Uerily we deceyve
oureselfe bi inordinate love of oure fleisshe.

[8] What oþer þinge shal þat fire deuoure but onely thy synnes? [9] The (3)
more þat þou spareste þiselfe nowe and foloest þi fleysshe, þe lenger
þou shalte be punyshed and þe more matier of brennynge þou
reserveste. [10] In what þinges a man hath synned, in tho þinges a man
f. 37ʳ shal be | punyshed. [11] There slowe men shul be prykked with brennynge
prykkes, and glotenouse men shul be tormented with grete honger and
grete thurste. [12] There lecherouse men and lovers of her lustes shul be
poured one with brennynge pycche and stynkynge brymstone, and
envyouse shulle whowle for sorowe as [w]ode houndes. [13] And þere (4)

24.0 peynes] peyne M, *Latin* penis KR   24ᵐ] *con.*, 24 CMG, 24 'xxiiii' D²
1 yiftes] ȝeftes or plesid M, *Latin* placatur KR   none] noo G   2 god] DMG, *om.*
C, *Latin* deo KR   lookynge] DMG, loolynge C, *Latin* vultum KR   3 þou not]
DG, not þou M, not C   mow] *om.* DMG, *Latin* 'poterit' K, poterit R   another]
DMG, any other C, *Latin* alium KR   5 malyce] mali(ce) D¹   haþ mercie] *om.* M,
'forgeueth' D², forgeueth G, *Latin* miseretur KR   to subdue] 'to holde' D², to holde
MG, *Latin* subiugare KR   his⁴] the G   6 in] DMG, into C
10 þinges¹] þinge DMG, *Latin* quibus KR   11 slowe] slowful G   12 there]
þere, re *canc.* D, þe MG, *Latin* ibi KR   men] man G, *Latin* luxuriosi KR   envyouse]
þe enviouse M, þe envyouse 'men' D, the envious man G, *Latin* inuidiosi KR   whowle]
whoule, w *canc.* D (*in margin:* howle D²)   wode] DMG, hode C, *Latin* furiosi KR

shal no vice bee but þat he shal haue his owne propre torment. [14] There
proude men shul be fulfilled with alle maner shame and confusioun, and
coveytouse men shul be enstreyted with moste wrecched neede. [15] There
shal one houre be more grevouse in peyne þen an hundred yere here in
moste laborouse penance. [16] þere is no reste, no consolacioun to
dampned folke; here sumtyme men cesseþ fro laboures and ar solaced
by her frendes. |

[17] Be nowe besye and sorowynge for thy synnes, þat þou mowe stande   f. 37ᵛ
sure in þe day of iugement with blysful men. [18] Then shulle ryghtwyse
men stande in grete constance ayenst hem þat have angwysshed hem
and oppressed hem. [19] Then shal he sitte to deme þat nowe subdueþ
hym mekely to þe iugementes of men. [20] Then shal the pouer and the
meke haue grete truste, and the prowde m[a]n shal drede on every side.

(5) [21] Then hit shal appiere þat he was wyse in this worde þat lerned for
Criste to be a fole and despysed. [22] þen shal plese every tribulacion
suffred paciently for Criste and alle wykkednes shalle stoppe his
mowthe. [23] Then shal every devoute man ioye and euery vnrelygiouse
man sorowe. [24] Then shal the fleysshe þat hath been in afflyccioun | ioye   f. 38ʳ
muche more þen she þat hathe been noryshed in delyces. [25] þen shal þe
vyle habyte shyne bryght, and the sotylle clothe shal be darke. [26] Then
shal be more preysed a pouer cote þen a golden paleys. [27] Then shal
helpe more constante pacience þen alle the worldes myght. [28] þen shal
(6) be hygher exalted meke obedyence þen alle wordely wysdome. [29] Then
shal more glade a man a pure and a gode conscience þa[n] grete
philosophy. [30] Then shal peyse more contempte of riches þen alle tresore
of the yerthe. [31] Then shalte þou more be counforted of deuoute preyer
þen of delycate etynge. [32] Then thou shalte rather ioy of weel kepte
silence þen of longe talynge. [33] Then shulle more avayle holy werkes þen
many fayre wordes. [34] Then shal more avayle streyte lyve and harde |
penance þen alle yerthely delectacyoun.   f. 38ᵛ

[35] Lerne nowe to suffre in a lytel, þat þen thou mowe be delyuered fro
more grevouse paynes. [36] Preve here furste what thou mowe suffre
aftirwarde. [37] If thou mowe not suffre here so lytel þinges, howe shalte
þou mowe suffre everlastynge tormentes? [38] If nowe so litel a passion

13 þat he] it G   15 laborouse] laboriouse G   16 cesseþ] cess⟨in⟩ D²
20 meke] meke man G   man] DMG, men C, *Latin* superbus KR   24 she] he
DMG, *Latin* nutrita   delyces] delites M, del⟨icates⟩ D², delicatys G, *Latin* deliciis
KR   27 more] 'more' *twice, above line and in margin* D²   28 hygher] h⟨.⟩ier
D   29 gode] g'o'ode D²   þan] DMG, þat C, *Latin* quam KR   30 alle] all
þe DG, ⟨.⟩lle þe M   31 of¹] DMG, of þe C   32 talynge] talkyng DMG, *Latin*
fabulacione KR

makeþ þee impaciente, what shal helle do þenne? [39] Loo, verily thou maiste not haue ii ioyes, to be delyted in this worlde and aftirwarde to regne with Criste. [40] If þou haddeste lyved vnto nowe in worshippes and (7) lustes of the worlde, what myght [alle] þat avayle þee if hit happened þee to dye in this moment?

[41] Alle þinges þerfore ar vanite, save to love God and to serve him
f. 39ʳ alleone. [42] For he þat loveth God with alle his herte | dredeþ neyther dethe ner tormente, ner iugement ner helle, for perfite loue shal make to God a redye weye and a sure commynge. [43] He þat yeet delyteþ to synne, hit is no wonder þoghe he drede deþe and the iugement. [44] Nerþelater, hit is goode þat if love cannenot revoke þe fro synne, atte leste lete drede do hit. [45] For he that putteþ bihynde the drede of God may not longe stande in gode, but he shalle sone renne into the fendes gnares.

Of the fervente amendemente of alle mannes lyve
Capitulum 25 [m]

[1] Be wakynge and dilygente in the [seruice] of God, and þenke oftetymes (1) whereto þou cameste and forsokest the worlde. [2] Was hit not for þou woldeste lyve to God and be `a´ spiritual man? [3] Wherefore be feruente
f. 39ᵛ to profi|tynge, for þou shalte receyve meede for thi laboures and þen shal no more be drede ner sorowe in thi costes.

[4] Thou shalte laboure [nowe] a lytel, and thou shalte fynde grete reste and euerlastynge gladnesse. [5] And if þou abyde trewe and fervente in worchynge, withouten doute God shal be trewe and riche in rewardynge. [6] Thou oweste to kepe a goode hope þat þou shalte come to the victorie, (2) but hit is [not] bihofulle to make þe sure, leste þou waxe slugged or proude.

[7] There was a man in grete heuynesse, oftetymes doutynge bitwene drede and hope; and on a tyme encombred with grete sorowe, he felle downe prostrate in his preiers byfore an awter in the chirche. This he
f. 40ʳ þought in his mynde, 'Wolde God I wyste þat I shulde perseuere!' [8] And þen he herde within hymse[lf]e an answere | fro God, 'What and thou

40 alle] DMG, om. C, Latin totum KR   42 herte] DMG, herte withe ‖ alle his herte C   44 nerþelater] neuerþeles DMG   atte leste] at lest DM, at þe leste G   25.0 alle] al a D, a M, om. G   capitulum 25ᵐ] con., capitulum 25 CMG, `xxv´ capitulum 25 D²        1 seruice] G, ⟨seruyse⟩ D², iugemente CM, Latin seruicio K, iudicio R        4 nowe] DMG, om. C, Latin nunc KR        6 goode] g`o´ode D² not] DMG, om. C, Latin non KR   slugged] slugg⟨ussh⟩ D², slouthfull G   or] ⟨or⟩ D²   7 encombred] acombrede G   8 within hymselfe] DG, within hym serve C, om. M, Latin intus KR

wiste, what woldeste þou doo? [9] Doo nowe as þou woldest do þen, and þou shalte be sure inowe.' [10] And anone he was counforted and commytted himselfe to the wille of God, and the doutefulle fluctuacion cessed. [11] And he wolde no more serche curiously of þinges þat were to come, but rather studied to enquere whiche was the wylle of God welle-plesinge and perfite, to bigynne euerie goode werke and to perfourme

(3)   hit. [12] 'Truste in oure Lorde and do goodnesse,' seithe the prophete, 'and dwelle vppon þe yerþe, and þou shalte be fedde in þe ryches þerof.'

[13] One þinge þer is þat letteþ many men fro profitynge and fervente amendynge: horroure of difficulte and laboure of strivinge or of fight-tyynge. [14] Thei above alle oþer profiteþ in vertues þat enforceþ hemselfe | moste manly to overcome tho þinges þat ar moste grevouse and moste   f. 40ᵛ contrarye to hem. [15] For þere man moste profiteþ and moste ample grace deserveþ, where he moste overcometh himselfe and mortifieþ in spirite.

(4)   [16] But alle haue not lyche moche to overcome and mortifie. [17] Nerthe-later a diligent [zelator] shal be more myghty to profite, þogh he haue moo passions, þan he þat is welle-manerde, beynge lasse feruente to vertues. [18] And ii þinges specially helpen to grete amendynge: þat is a man to withdrawe hym with violence fro suche þinge as nature is viciously inclyned to, and to feruently laboure for the gode þat he moste nedeþ.

[19] Also studie moste to eschue and ouercome þoo þinges þat moste

(5)   [oftely] displese þee in oþer men. [20] Take þi profitynge | in everie place,   f. 41ʳ þat if þou here or see a goode ensample, be feruent to folowe hit. [21] If þou consider anyþinge þat is to be blamed, beware þat þou do hit not; and if þou doo hit at any tyme, study sone to amende hit. [22] As thin yghe considereþ oþer folke, so oþer men noteþ þee. [23] Howe swete hit is, howe mirye hit is to see feruent and deuoute breþeren and welle-manerde and vndir disciplyne! And howe sorowfulle and hevye hit is to see breþer goynge inordinatly, þat exercise not þoo þinges as þei ar called to! [24] Howe noyouse is hit a man to take none heede of the purpose of his callynge, and to bowe his witte to suche þinges as ar not committed to him!

---

8 woldeste þou] wo⟨ldest þou⟩ Dᴵ   11 goode] g`o´ode D²     12 goodnesse] g`o´odenes D²   ryches] richesse D   15 ample] *om.* MG, ⟨. . . . .⟩ D, *Latin* ampliorem KR   moste³] *om.* DMG, *Latin* magis KR   17 nerthelater] neuerþelater DM, neuertheles G   zelator] *con.*, yelar C, ⟨louer⟩, *tail of* y *visible under* l D², louer MG, *Latin* emulator KR   moo] muche M, *Latin* plures KR   19 oftely] G, feruently CDM, *Latin* frequencius K, feruencius R   20 goode] g`o´ode D² 22 thin yghe] þyn ⟨.⟩eye, *part of* n *visible under erasure* D²   24 none] noo G

[25] Haue mynde on þe purpose þat þou haste taken, and euer putte (6)
f. 41ᵛ bifore þee [þe] image of þe crucifixe. | [26] Thou maiste welle be ashamed,
biholdinge the lyve of oure Lorde Ihesu Criste, þat þou haste no more
studyed to confourme þee þerto, þoghe þou haue long been in þe weye
of God. [27] The religiouse man, þat intentively and deuoutely exerciceþ
himselfe in the moste holy lyve and passion of oure Lorde, he shal fynde
haboundantly alle þinges þat ar needfulle and profitable to him, ner he
shal haue no nede to seke any better þinge withoute Ihesu. [28] O, if Ihesu
Criste came into oure herte, howe sone and howe sufficiently we shulde
be taught!

[29] [The feruent religiouse man bereþ alle þinges welle, and takeþ alle (7)
þat be commaunded him.] [30] The necgligente religiouse and the lewke
hath tribulacion and on euery side suffreþ angwysshe, for he lakkeþ
inwarde counforte, and he is forbeden to seke any outwarde. [31] The
f. 42ʳ relygiouse man þat is withoute disciplyne | is open to a grevouse falle.
[32] He þat euermore sekeþ tho þinges þat ar moste laxe and moste
remisse shal euer be in anguysshe, for one þinge or oþer shal euermore
displese.

[33] Howe doþe many religiouse men þat ar streyted vnder claustralle (8)
disciplyne? [34] Lyven abstractely, eteþ poerly, ar clothed boystesly,
laboureþ gretely, spekeþ lytel, wakeþ longe, ryseth erly, preyeþ longe,
oftetyme redeþ and kepeþ hem in alle maner disciplyne. [35] Take heede of
the Cartusiensez, þe Sistewx, and monkes and monchynes of diuerse
religiouse, howe þei rise vppe euery nyȝt to singe to oure Lorde.
[36] Therfore hit is foule þat þou shuldest be slugged in so holy a
werke, where so grete multitude of relygiouse folke bygynneþ to ioye
to God. [37] Wolde God þat noght elles we hadde to do, but onely to (9)
f. 42ᵛ preyse oure | Lorde Ihesu Criste with [alle] oure herte! [38] Wolde God
þou neded never to ete, ner to drynke, ner slepe, but euer preise God
and take heede to spiritual studies! [39] þen þou shuldest be more blysfulle

25 þe²] DMG, om. C   26 welle be] be wel DMG   long been] ben ʾlong' D²,
be long G, ben M, Latin diu KR   27 intentively] intently G   29 the . . . him]
G, om. CDM, Latin religiosus feruidus omnia bene portat et capit que illi iubentur K, om.
R   30 religiouse and the lewke] religiouse and þe leuke ʾman' D², religiose man and
þe leuke M, and leuke religiouse man G, Latin religiosus negligens et tepidus KR   side]
ʾsyde' D²   32 one] o DM   displese] displese hym G   34 eteþ] et⟨in⟩
D²   laboureþ] labor⟨yn⟩ D²   spekeþ] spek⟨yn⟩ D²   wakeþ] wak⟨yn⟩ D²
ryseth] ris⟨yn⟩ D²   preyeþ] praie⟨n⟩ D²   oftetyme] oftetymes DMG   redeþ]
red⟨yn⟩ D²   kepeþ] kep⟨yn⟩ D²   35 cartusiensez] cartusiens G   sistewx]
cist⟨ercenses⟩ D, cisternens G   36 slugged] slugg⟨usse⟩ D², sluggyssh G
37 alle] DMG, om. C, Latin toto KR   38 to²] om. DMG   and] and to DMG
studies] þinges and studies M, Latin studiis KR   39 þou shuldest] shuldist þoue
G   more] þe more M

þen nowe, when thou serveste the fleisshe for any maner neede. [40] Wolde God þees necessitez were not, but onely spiritualle refeccions of þe soule, þe whiche we, alas, tasteþ fulle seldon!

(10)   [41] When a man is comen þerto þat he sekeþ his counforte of no creature, þen atte furste bigynneþ God to savoure him perfitly. [42] Then also he is welle contente of eueri chaunce; þen he wol not be gladde for no grete þinge, ner sorye for no lytel þinge, but putteþ hymselfe holy and trustely in God, þat is to hym alle þinges in alle þinges, to whom noþinge perisheþ ner dyethe, but alle þinges lyveþ to hym and ser | veþ   f. 43ʳ him at his bekenynge.

(11)   [43] Haue mynde ever of the ende, and þat tyme lost never comeþ ayeine. [44] Withoute besines and dilygence shalte þou never gete vertues. [45] If þou bigynne to be lewke, þou bygynneste to be yvel at ese. [46] But and þou yive thiselfe to feruoure, þou shalt fynde grete pees, and þou shalte feele lyghter laboure, for þe grace of God and love of vertue. [47] A feruent man and a dilygente is redy to alle þinges.

[48] Hit is more laboure in withstandynge vices and passions þen to suete in bodely laboures. [49] He þat escheweth not smale defautes litel and lytel shal slyde to gretter. [50] Thou shalte ever ioye at evon, if þou spende þe daie fruytefully. [51] Wake vppon thiselfe, stirre thiselfe, ammonyshe thiselfe, and howeeuer hit be of oþer, foryete not thiselfe. [52] So muche þou shalte profite, as þou | putteste violence to thiselfe.   f. 43ᵛ

Here endeþ the furste partie of Musica Ecclesiastica.

40 god] god þat DMG   fulle] but G, *Latin* satis KR   41 perfitly] hartly and parfitly M, *Latin* perfecte KR   42 bekenynge] beckyng G   43 of] on DMG   44 shalte þou] þou shalt G   46 feele] finde M, *Latin* sencies KR   for] throgh G, *Latin* propter KR   of²] o M   49 to] into DMG, *Latin* ad KR   53 partie] parte M

[BOOK II]

And here bigynneþ the chapitres of the seconde boke.

Here bigynneþ of the ammonycions drawynge gretely inwarde.

Of the inwarde conuersacioun
Capitulum primum

[1] Oure Lorde seithe that the reawme of God is withein you. [2] Turne (1) thiselfe to God with alle thi herte and forsake þis wrecched worlde, and thi soule shal fynde reste. [3] Lerne to despise outwarde þinges and to converte þee to inwarde þinges, and þou shalt see þe reaume [of God] come into thee. [4] For the reawme of God is pees and ioye in the Holy Goste, the whiche is not yiven to wykked menne. [5] Criste shal come to þee shewynge the his consolacion, if þou make to hym withinforthe a f. 44^v worthi dwellynge place. | [6] Alle his glorye and his worshippe is

2.0.0 here bigynneþ] now folowen DMG   boke] parte M, partie DG   1 1^m] i
DG   2 2^m] ii DG   3 a^2] *om.* DMG   3^m] iii DG   4 quartum] iiii
DG   5 5^m] v DG   6 6^m] vi DG   7 septimum] vii DMG   8 oure
lorde] *om.* DMG   octauum] viii DMG   9 9^m] ix DMG   10 10^m] x
DMG   11 11^m] xi DMG   12 12^m] xii DG   13 of] *om.* G
      1.0 the] *om.* DMG   1 you] youe, e *added on line* D^2 3 to^2] *om.* G   of
god] G, *om.* CDM, *Latin* ⟨regnum dei⟩ K, regnum dei R   4 the^3] *om.* G
6 his^2] *om.* DMG

withinforþe, and þere is [his] plesaunce. [7] His visitacion is comune and ofte withinne an inwarde man: with him is his swete talkynge, graciouse consolacion, muche wondirfulle familiarite.

(2)　[8] Ey[a], þou trewe soule, araye thi soule to þis spouse, þat he vouchesaue to come to þee and to dwelle in þee. [9] For þ[u]s he seithe, 'Whoso loveþ me shal kepe my worde, and to him we shul come and in him make oure dwellynge place.' [10] Wherfore yiffe Criste place, and as to alle oþer, holde hem oute. [11] When þou haste Criste, þou arte riche þen and hit sufficeth þe. [12] He shal be thi provisoure [and] þi trewe procutoure in alle þinges, so þat hit shal not nede þee truste in man. [13] Men ar sone chaunged and faylen wyghtly; Criste abideþ for ever and |

(3)　standeþ stedfastly vnto the ende. [14] Grete truste is not to be putte in a　f. 45ʳ [mortal] and a frayle man, þoghe he be profitable and welle biloued, ner grete sorowe to be taken, þoghe sumtyme he ayeinsaye and be contrary. [15] Thei þat ar þis day with the, tomorowe þei may be contrarie, and in contrari wyse they beþe oftetymes turned as þe wynde.

[16] Putte alle thi truste in God: he be thi drede, he be thi love. [17] He shal answere for þe, and do welle and as beste is. [18] Thou haste here no dwellynge citee, and whereeuer þou be þou arte an estraunger and a pilgryme. Here geteste þou no reste, but yf þou be inwardely oned to

(4)　Criste. [19] What lokeste þou aboute here, sithe þis is not the place of thi restynge? [20] In hevonly þinges oweþ to be þine habitacioun, | and alle　f. 45ᵛ yerthely ar to be considered as yn a maner of passinge. [21] For alle þinges passen, and þou alleso with hem. [22] Loke þat þou clyve not to hem, leste þou be take with hem and perisshe. [23] Lete thi þenkynge be to highe God, and þi preier be lyfte vppe vn[to] Criste withoute intermission. [24] If þou cannenot byholde highe celestial þinges, reste in þe passion of Criste and dwelle gladly in his holy woundes. [25] For if þou flee

6 his³] DMG, om. C, Latin et ibi complacet sibi KR　　　7 withinne] with DMG　　　8 eya] M, ey`a´ D², ey C, haue doo G, Latin eya KR　　　þis] þi(.) D, þi MG, Latin huic KR　　　9 þus] DMG, þis C, Latin sic KR　　　worde] wordys G, Latin sermonem KR　　　11 þen] om. DMG　　　12 and þi trewe procutoure] `and´ þy true procutour D², and thy true proctoure G, þi trewe procutoure C, and þi protectour M, Latin et fidelis procurator KR　　　truste] `to´ truste D², to truste MG　　　13 wyghtly] liȝtly MG, Latin velociter KR　　　14 mortal] G, ⟨mortall⟩ D², softe CM, Latin mortali KR　　　a²] om. DMG　　　ayeinsaye] ayensaiþ M　　　and³] DMG, and to C 16 he be¹] be he, b altered from h, h altered from b D², be he G he be²] b altered from h, h altered from b D², be he G　　　17 as] a⟨s⟩ D¹　　　18 an estraunger] a⟨s a straun⟩gere D², a straunger G, Latin extraneus `es´ K, extraneus es R　　　20 yerthely] erþely `þinges´ D², erthly thynges G　　　23 to] to þe DMG be²] om. G　　　vppe vnto] D, vp to G, vppe vnder C, vpon to M, Latin ad KR 24 highe] om. M, Latin alta KR　　　þinges] thynges and, and canc. G　　　25 for if þou flee deuoutly to the woundes] om. G, Latin si enim ad vvlnera . . . deuote confugis KR

deuoutly to the woundes and the preciouse prentes of Criste, thou shalt fynde grete counforte in tribulacion, ner þou shalt not gretly charge mannes despisinges, and þou shalt lyghtly bere bakbitynge wordes. [26] For Criste was despised of men in þis worlde, and in his grettest nede (5)

f. 46ʳ amonge repreves forsaken of his frendes and of his know|en men. [27] Criste wolde suffre and be despised, and þou wolte haue alle menne frendes and benefactours? [28] Criste had aduersaries and suffred shrewde spekars, and þou darste compleyne on anybody? [29] Whereof shal þi pacience be crouned, if þere come none aduersite? [30] Yf þou wolte suffre [no] contrarie, howe shalte þou be the frende of Criste? [31] Suffre for Criste and with Criste, yf þou wolte regne with Criste.

[32] If þou haddest ones perfitly entred into the inwardes of Ihesu and (6) haddeste savoured a litel of his brennynge love, þenne woldeste þou sette nought by þine owne profite ner harme, but raþer þou woldest ioye of repreve done to þee, for þe love of Ihesu makeþ a man to sette noght by hymselfe. [33] A lover of Ihesu and a very inwarde man and free fro

f. 46ᵛ inordinate | affeccions may freely turne hymselfe to God and lyfte hymselfe aboue hymselfe in spirite and þer reste fruybly.

[34] To whom alle þinges savoren as þei been, not as thei ar seide or (7) estemed, he is very wyse and taght more of God þen of men. [35] He þat can goo withinforþe and peyse lytel þinges withouteforthe, he sekeþ no places ner abideþ no tymes to haue deuoute exercices. [36] The inwarde man sone gedreþ himselfe togidre, for he never poureþ himselfe holy to outwarde þinges. [37] Outwarde laboure letteþ not hym, ner nedefulle occupacion for þe tyme, but so as þinges comen, so he yiveþ him to hem. [38] He þat is welle-disposed withinforþe and ordinate, he [chargeþ

---

25 criste] cryst in the whiche G   ner þou shalt not gretly] ⟨nor þou s⟩halt not ⟨gretly⟩ Dᴵ, nor þou shalt not gretly M, and þou shalt not gretely G   27–8 and benefactours criste] 'ande' | ⟨.⟩nd benefact⟨ours crist⟩, nd canc. D²   28 anybody] euerybody DMG, Latin aliquo KR   30 no] MG, noon D, om. C, Latin nichil KR   32 þenne woldeste þou] þov woldist þan DMG   þou woldest] twice, first canc. D   to²] om. DM   33 turne hymselfe] twice, first canc. D   34 alle þinges savoren] sauoure all thyngys G   estemed] ⟨trowede⟩ D², trowed MG, Latin estimantur KR   35 he¹] canc. D, om. MG   peyse] preise DM, preyse a G, Latin ponderare KR   38 he¹ . . . men] con., he þat is ⟨wele disposyd ande ordeynyd inforth he chargith not þe wykkyd and wondyrfull hauyngys and be⟩ringes of men, second y in hauyngys canc. D², he þat is wel disposed and ordeynyd infurþe he chargiþe not þe wykkyd and wondirful hauyngys and beringes of men M, he þat is wel disposid and wel ordred withinfurth chargyth not the froward and wonderfull behavours of men G, he þat is not welle disposed withinforþe and ordinate he loveþ þe nyce and þe wondirfulle havynges and berynges of men C, Latin qui ⟨intus⟩ b⟨ene⟩ dispositus est et ordinatus non curat mirabiles et peruersos hominum gestus K, qui intus bene dispositus est et ordinatus non curat peruersos et mirabiles hominum gestus R

not] þe nyce and þe wondirfulle havynges and berynges of men. | ³⁹ So f. 47ʳ
muche is a man lette and distracte, as þinges ar drawen to him.

(8)   ⁴⁰ Yf hit were welle with þee and þou were wel purged, alle þinges
shulde turne the to goode and to profite. ⁴¹ Many þinges as yette trouble
the and displese thee, for þou arte [not] yette dede to thiselfe ner
departed fro alle yerthely þinges. ⁴² Noþinge so defoileþ and intrikeþ
mannes herte as vnpure love in creatures. ⁴³ Yf þou forsake outwarde
counforte, thou shalt mowe biholde heuonly þinges and oftetymes haue
iubilacion withinforthe.

Of meke submission
Capitulum secundum

(1) ¹ Sette not muche þerby whoso be ayenis þee or with þee, but do so and
charge þat, þat God be with þee in eueriþinge þat þou doste. ² Haue a
gode conscience, and God shal defende þee. | ³ For him þat he wolle f. 47ᵛ
helpe, no mannes overthwartnes shal mowe noye. ⁴ Yf þou can be stille
and suffre, þou shalt see withoute any doute þe helpe of oure Lorde.
⁵ He knoweþ þe tyme and þe maner of helpinge þee, and þerfore þou
owest to reserve thiselfe to him. ⁶ To God hit longeþ to helpe and to
delyuer from alle confucion.

        ⁷ Oftetymes hit avayleþ to þe kepinge o[f] gretter meekenes þat oþer
(2) menne knowe oure defautes and repreve hem. ⁸ When a man mekeþ
himselfe for his defautes, þen he peseþ oþer lyghtly and esely makeþ
satisfaccion to hem þat were displesed.

        ⁹ The meke man God defendeþ and delyuereþ; þe meke man he loveþ
and counforteþ; to þe meke man he boweþ himselfe; to þe meke man he
graunteþ grete grace and aftir | his mekinge lyfteþ him to glory. ¹⁰ To þe f. 48ʳ
meke man he sheweþ his secretes and draweþ him and calleþ him swetly.
¹¹ The meke man, receyvinge reprevinges or wronges or confucion, is in
pees wel inowe, for he standeþ in God and not in the worlde.

    39 distracte] distraite DMG   40 þinges] om. DMG   41 not] DMG, om. C,
Latin non KR   42 defoileþ] defouliþ DMG   vnpure] impure DMG
    2.0 secundum] 2 `ii´ D², ii G   1 charge] char(ge) D¹   2 a] om. M
goode] g(oode) D²   þee] `þe´ G   4 see] be seen M, Latin videbis KR
5 þe²] om. DMG   thiselfe] DMG, þi thiselfe C   7 oftetymes] oftetyme M
of] DMG, or C, Latin ad maiorem humilitatem seruandam K, ad maiorem humilitatem
`seruandam´ R   8 peseþ] plesiþ M, Latin placat KR   9 man²] men G, Latin
homini KR   to³] in DM, into G, Latin ad KR   11 receyvinge reprevinges]
receiuyn(g repre)vinges D¹   wronges] wronge DMG, Latin contumelia R, om. K

[12] Accompte thiselfe ner to haue profite[d], tille þou feele þee lower þenne [alle] other.

Of a goode pesible manne
Capitulum tercium

[1] Sette thiselfe furste in pees, and þen shalt þou mowe pese oþer. [2] A (1) pesible man avayleþ more þen a grete lerned man. [3] A passionate man turneþ goode into yvelle, and sone leveþ yvel. [4] A gode pesible man draweþ alle þinges to gode. [5] He þat is welle in pese hathe suspecion to no man; he þat cannot be contente but is meved, he is shaken with many f. 48ᵛ suspecions, and neiþer he | canne be in reste, ner suffre oþer to be in reste. [6] Oftetymes he seithe þat he shulde not seie, and leveþ þat þat were more expedient to doo. [7] He considereþ what oþer men oweþ to doo, and takeþ none heede to his owne charge.

[8] Haue þerfore furste [z]ele to thiselfe, and þen mayste þou haue [z]ele to þi neyghboure. [9] þou canste welle excuse and coloure þine owne (2) dedes, but oþer mennes excusacions þou wolte not receyve. [10] Hit were more rightwyse furste to accuse þiselfe and excuse þi broþer. [11] Yf þou wolte be borne, bere þou anoþer.

[12] See howe farre þou arte yeette fro veri charite and mekenes, þe whiche cannenot be wrothe ner haue indignacion of no man, but only of hymselfe. [13] Hit is not grete a man to be conuersante with gode men and f. 49ʳ mylde men, for þat | pleseþ alle men naturely, and euerye man gladly haþe pees with hem þat feleþ as he doþe and suche he loveth. [14] But a man to lyve pesibly with harde and overthwarte men, and indisciplynate and contrariouse, is a grete grace and a commendable and a manly dede.

[15] Ther ar summe þat kepeþ hemselfe in pees and haþe pees with oþer (3) also. [16] And þer beeþ þat nouþer haþe pees to hemselfe, ner suffreþ not oþer to haue pees. To oþer þei be grevouse, but moste grevouse to hemselfe. [17] And þer beeþ þat holdeþ pees in hemselfe and studyeþ to

12 ner] neuer DMG   profited] DMG, profite C, *Latin* profecisse KR   þee] `þe´ G   alle] DMG, *om.* C, *Latin* omnibus KR
3.0 a] the G   tercium] iii MG, 3 `iii´ D²      3 leveþ] bileuiþ DMG 4 gode¹] g`o´ode D²   5 and] *om.* DMG   6 more] most M   7 consid-ereþ] DMG, considesidereþ C   none] no G   8 zele¹] DMG, hele C, *Latin* zelum KR   zele²] DMG, hele C, *Latin* zelare KR   10 and] and to DMG   12 þe] *om.* G   13 gode] g`o´ode D²      men¹] *om.* G      14 and²] *om.* DMG, *Latin* aut K, et R      15 hemselfe] hem G      oþer] all oþer G, *Latin* aliis KR      16 beeþ] biþ somme also DMG      nouþer] neiþer DMG      to¹] *om.* MG, `in´ D   not] *om.* DMG   17 beeþ] biþ `somme´ D², biþe summe MG   pees¹] her pes DMG

reduce oþer men to pees. [18] Nerthelater alle oure pees in þis wrecched lyve is rather to be sette in meke suffrynge þen in not felynge contraritees. [19] He þat canne welle suffre shal fynde moste pees: he is an overcomer | of himselfe [and] lorde of the worlde, þe frende of Criste f. 49ᵛ and the heire of heuon.

Of pure and symple intencioun
Capitulum quartum

(1) [1] A man is lyfte vppe fro yerthely þinges with ii wynges, þat ar simplycite and purete. [2] Simplicite oweþ to be in intencion, purete in affeccion. [3] Simplicite intendeþ God, purete takeþ him and tasteþ him. [4] There shal no gode dede lette þe yf þou be free withinforthe fro inordinate affeccion. [5] If þou intende ner seke noþinge elles but the plesinge of God and þe profite of thi neyghboure, þou shalte haue inwarde liberte.

[6] Yf þi herte were right, þen euery creature shulde be to þee a myrrour of lyve and a boke of holy doctrine. [7] Ther is no creature so (2) lytel ner so vile, but hit represente þe godenesse | of God. [8] If þou were f. 50ʳ inwarde goode and pure, þen shuldest þou see alle þinges withoute impediment and conceyve hem. [9] A pure herte perceþ hevon and helle. [10] Suche as eueri man is inwarde, so he demeþ outwarde. [11] If þere be any ioye in þis worlde, þe man of pure herte haþe hit. [12] And yf þer be in any place tribulacion and angwyshe, þat knoweþ beste an yvel conscience.

[13] Lyke as yron putte in the fire leseþ his ruste and is alle made bryght, so a man convertynge himselfe holy to God is exute and taken (3) fro þe body and chaunged into a newe man. [14] When a man bigynneþ to waxe lewke, þenne he dredeþ a litel laboure and receyveth gladdely outwarde consolacion. [15] But when he bigynneþ perfitly to overcome himselfe and to goo manly in þe weye | of God, þenne he sette litel bi f. 50ᵛ tho þinges þat bifore semed to hym ryght grevouse.

18 nerthelater] neuerþeles DMG   19 and¹] G, om. CDM, Latin sui et KR
4.0 quartum] iiii MG, 4 'iiii' D²   3 and tasteþ him] om. DMG, Latin et gustat
KR   4 gode] g'o'ode D²   7 represente] representith G   godenesse]
g'o'odenes D²   8 goode] g'o'ode D²   12 yvel] idel DM, Latin mala
KR   13 is alle] shal be DMG, Latin totum candens efficitur KR   himselfe]
him DMG

Of propre consideracion
Capitulum quintum

[1] We oweþ not to lyeve oureself ouermuche, for oftetymes grace lakkeþ (1)
and witte. [2] Litel lyght is in vs, and yette oftetymes we lese þat by
necglygence. [3] And also oftetymes we perceyve not howe blynde we ar
withinforthe. [4] Oftetymes yvel we doo, and worse, we excuse hit;
oftetymes we be meved and weneþ þat hit be a zele. [5] We repreve
smale þinges in other, and passeþ over owre owne þat ar gretter. [6] We
feele and peyse sone inowe what we suffre of oþer, but howe muche oþer
suffre of vs we take none heede. [7] He þat wolde pondre welle and trewly
f. 51ʳ   his owne defautes, | he shulde fynde noght to deme in oþer grevously.

[8] An inwarde man bifore al oþer cures takeþ cure of himselfe. [9] And he (2)
þat dilygently takeþ heede of himselfe holdeþ his pees lightly of oþer.
[10] Thou shalte never be inwarde and [a] deuoute man but yf þou kepe
silence of oþer men and specially biholde thyselfe. [11] If þou take heede
alleonely to God and to thiselfe, hit shalle litel meve the þat þou
perceyveste withoutforthe. [12] Where arte þou when þou arte not
presente to thiselfe? And when þou haste reonnen over alle þinges,
takynge none heede of þiselfe, what haste þou profited? [13] If þou wolte
haue pees and very onehede, þou muste sette alle aside and onely haue
thiselfe bifore þine yen. [14] And þenne þou shalte profite muche, if þou (3)
f. 51ᵛ   kepe halyday and | reste fro every temporal cure.

[15] þou shalte gretely faile yf þou sette by any temporal þinge. [16] Lete
noþinge be grete or highe or acceptable to þee, but purely God, or elles
þat is of God. [17] Alle þinge deme as veyne, þat is to seie, any counforte
þat comeþ of any creature. [18] The soule þat loveþ God, lete hir despise
alle þinges vnder God. [19] God alone, everlastinge and grete withoute any
mesure, fulfillynge alle þinges, he is the solace of mannes soule and verie
gladnesse of herte.

5.0 quintum] v G, 5 'v' D²   1 lyeve] b⟨eleue⟩, b *altered from* 1 D², beleue G, *Latin*
credere KR   lakkeþ] lacketh vs G   6 none] noo G   9 and . . . himselfe]
om. DMG, *Latin* et qui sibiipsi diligenter intendit K, et qui sibi diligenter intendit
R   10 and¹] *om.* DMG, *Latin* et KR   a] DMG, *om.* C   biholde] beholde ⟨and
se⟩ D², beholde and se MG, *Latin* respexeris KR   12 reonnen] comen M, *Latin*
percurristi KR   none] no G   13 alle] *om.* MG, 'all' D², *Latin* totum KR
onely] 'oonly'|nely, nely *written after hole and canc.* D²   16 or elles þat is of god] *om.*
DMG, *Latin* aut de deo sit KR   17 þat is to seie any] ⟨. .⟩ | ⟨. . .⟩, eny *visible under*
second erasure D, *om.* MG, *Latin* quidquid KR   19 any] *om.* G

Of the gladdenesse of a gode conscience
Capitulum 6^m

(1)   [1] The ioye of a gode man is þe wyttenesse of a gode conscience. [2] Haue a gode conscience and þou shalt ever haue gladnesse. [3] A gode conscience may bere right many þinges, and is right gladde `among´ aduersitez. [4] An yvel conscience | is euer dredful and oute of quiete. [5] Thou shalte   f. 52^r reste swetly, if thi herte reprehende þe not.

[6] Be not gladde, but when þou haste do welle. [7] Yvel men hath neuer very gladnesse, ner never feleþ inwarde pees, for as oure Lorde seithe, þer is no pees to wikke[d] men. [8] And if þei seie, 'We ar in pees; þer shal none yvels come vppon vs,' bilyeve hem not, for the wraþe of God shal rise sodeynly, and her dedes shul be brought into nought, and her þoughtes shul perisshe.

(2)   [9] A man to ioye in tribulacion is not grevouse to the lover, for so to ioye is to ioye in the crosse of Criste. [10] Shorte is þe glorie þat is yiven and taken of men, [11] and sorowe foloweth euer þe glorie of the worde. [12] þe glorie of gode men is in her conscience, and not in the mowthes of men. [13] þe gladnes | of rightwys men is of God and in God, and her ioye   f. 52^v is of trowþe. [14] He þat desireþ euerlastynge and veri glorie setteþ no cure of þat is temporalle. [15] And [he] þat sekeþ temporal glory, and despiseþ hit [not] of herte, he muste nedes [lasse] loue heuonly glory.

[16] He haþe grete tranquillite of herte þat setteþ noþer by preysinges (3)   ner blamynges. [17] Whos conscience is clene, he wolle sone be contente and plesed. [18] Thou arte not þe holyer þogh þou be preysed, ner þe more vile þogh þou be dispreysed. [19] What ar[t] þou, þat þou arte; þat God knoweþ þee to be, and þou maiste be seide no more. [20] If þou take hiede what þou arte withinforthe, þou shalte not recche what men seie of the. [21] Man seeþ in þe visage, and God in þe herte. [22] Man considereþ | þe dedes, and God peyseþ þe þoughtes.   f. 53^r

---

6.0 the] *om.* DMG   6^m] vi G, 6 `vi´ D²    1 gode[1]] g`o´ode D²   gode[2]] g`o´ode D²    2 gode] g`o´ode D²   3 gode] g`o´ode D²    4 oute of quiete] oute of quiete`nes´ D², vnquiete G   7 wikked] DMG, wikken C   8 none] no G   rise] arise DMG   9 is to ioye] *om.* M, *Latin* ⟨est⟩ gloriari K, est gloriari R   12 gode] g`o´ode D²   14 glorie] ioy G, *Latin* gloriam KR   15 he] DMG, *om.* C   sekeþ] sekiþ not DMG, *Latin* requirit KR   and[2]] but DMG, *Latin* aut KR   not] *con., om.* CDMG, *Latin* non KR   lasse] *con., om.* CDMG, *Latin* minus KR   16 noþer] neiþer DMG   17 sone be] be sone G   18 not] DMG, note C, *Latin* non KR   dispreysed] blamed or dispreised DMG   19 art þou] DM, ar þou C, þou art G   20 hiede] `hede´ D²

²³ A man euer to do welle, and holde litel of himselfe, is token of a
meeke soule. ²⁴ A man not to wille to be counforted of any creature is a
token of grete purete and of inwarde truste. ²⁵ He þat sekeþ none (4)
outwarde wittenesse for himselfe, hit appiereþ openly þat he hath
commytted himselfe alle holy to God. ²⁶ For he þat commendeþ
himselfe is not preved, as the apostle seithe, but whom God commendeþ. ²⁷ The state of þe inwarde man is to go with God, and to be
holden with no outwarde affeccioun.

Of the love of Ihesu above alle þinges
Capitulum septimum

¹ Blisfulle is he þat vnderstandeth what hit is to love Ihesu and to (1)
despice hymselfe for Ihesu. ² Hit bihoveþ þe lover to forsake alle þinges
for þe | loved, for Ihesus wol be byloved alone aboue alle þinges. ³ The
loue of a creature is failinge and vnstable; the loue of Ihesu is trewe and
perseverable. ⁴ He þat clyveth to a creature shal falle withe the slydynge
creature; he þat clippeþ Ihesu shal be made stedefaste for euer. ⁵ Love
him and holde hym faste as a frende þat, [alle] oþer goynge aweye, shal
not forsake þee, ner shal not suffre the to perisshe in þe ende. ⁶ Fro alle
þou muste be departe sumtyme, wheþer thou wolte or no. ⁷ Holde þe (2)
with Ihesu, lyvinge and dyinge, and committe the to his truste, þat, alle
oþer failynge, alone may helpe þe.

⁸ Thi biloved is of suche nature þat he wol admitte no straunger, but
he alone wol haue thi herte and þer sitte as a kinge in his propre trone.
⁹ If þou | coudeste welle voyde the frome euerie creature, Ihesus wolde
dwelle gladly with þee.

¹⁰ Thou shalte fynde almoste alle loste whateuer þou setteste in
creatures. ¹¹ Truste not ner leyne not vppon a wyndy reede, for eueri
fleshe is grasse, and alle his glory shal falle as þe floure of grasse. (3)
¹² Thou shalte sone be deceyved yf þou biholde onely to the vtter
apparence of men. ¹³ If þou seke þi solace and þi lucre in oþer, þou
shalte oftetymes fynde þi solace hyndrynge. ¹⁴ If þou seke Ihesu in alle

f. 53ᵛ

f. 54ʳ

23 meeke] me M, *Latin* humilis KR   25 none] no G, not M, *Latin* nullum KR
7.0 septimum] vii MG, 7 `vii´ D²   2 wol be byloved] wolde be loued DMG, *Latin*
vvlt . . . amari KR   4 ihesu] `ihesu´ D², *om.* M, *Latin* ihesum KR   5 þat alle
oþer] *con.*, þat oþer C, ⟨which all⟩ D², whiche alle MG, *Latin* qui omnibus KR   not²]
om. G   6 no] nat MG, not, t *added on line* D²   8 as] lyke G   9 dwelle
gladly] gladly dwelle DMG   13 fynde þi solace] ⟨fynde þyn⟩ D², finde þin MG,
Latin senties sepe solacium detrimentum R, sencies sepius detrimentum K

þinges, þou shalte fynde Ihesu. [15] And if þou seke thyselfe, þou shalt
fynde thiselfe, but to þine owne harme. [16] A man noyeþ himselfe more,
yf he sekeþ not Ihesu, þen al the worlde and alle his aduersaries.

Of the familiar frensheppe of Ihesu
Capitulum octauum

(1) | [1] Whenne Ihesus is nyghe, alle gode is nyghe, and noþinge semeþ   f. 54ᵛ
harde. [2] But whenne Ihesus is not nygh, alle þinge is harde. [3] Whenne
Ihesus speketh not withinne þee, counforte is but of lytel price. [4] But if
Ihesus speke one worde, þere is founden grete counforte. [5] Dyde not
Mary Maudeleyne rise oute of hir place, whereynne she wepped, anone
as Martha seide, 'Oure maister is nyghe and calleþ thee'? [6] Blisfulle is
þat man whom, when Ihesus comeþ, he calleþ fro teres to the ioye of
spirite.

[7] Howe drye and howe harde þou arte withoute Ihesu! Howe vnsavory,
howe veyne, yf þou coveyte anythinge withoute Ihesu! [8] Wheþer is not
(2)   more harme þen þoghe þou loste alle þe worlde? [9] What may the worlde
availe þee withoute Ihesu? [10] To be withoute Ihesu is a | grevouse helle;   f. 55ʳ
and to be with Ihesu is a swete paradice. [11] If Ihesus be with þee, þer
may none enemy noye þee. [12] He þat fyndeþ [Ihesu fyndeþ] a gode
tresore, yea gode above alle gode. [13] And he þat lesethe Ihesu leseth
overmuche, and more þen if he loste alle the worlde.
(3)   [15] Hyt is a grete crafte [a] man to can be conuersante with Ihesu, and
to can holde Ihesu is a grete prudence. [16] Be meke and pesible, and
Ihesus shal be with thee. [17] Be deuoute and restful, and Ihesus shal abide
with thee.
[18] Thou maiste sone chase oute Ihesu and lese his grace, yf þou wolte
declyne to outwarde þinges. [19] And if þou chace oute Ihesu and lese him,
to whom shalte þou flee, and what frende shalt þou seke? [20] Withoute a
frende þou maiste not welle lyffe, and but Ihesu be thi frende bifore alle |

16 sekeþ] seke G
8.0 octauum] viii G, 8 ˋviiiˊ D²   1 gode] gˋoˊodenes D², goodnes MG, *Latin*
bonum KR   2 þinge is] þinges are DMG   3 but] but harde, harde *canc.*
D   4 if] *om.* M, *Latin* si autem KR   one] o DM   6 of] of ˋþeˊ D², of the
G   8 not] it M, it ˋnotˊ D², *Latin* nonne KR   12 ihesu fyndeþ] MG, ˋihesu
fyndethˊ D², *om.* C, *Latin* ihesum inuenit KR   gode¹] goode, *second* o *added on line*
D²   gode²] gˋoˊode D²   gode³] gˋoˊode D²   13 leseth] ⟨he lesiþ⟩ D², he lesiþe
MG   15 grete¹] *om.* DMG, *Latin* magna KR   a²] DMG, *om.* C   can¹] *om.*
DMG, *Latin* ⟨scire . . . conuersari⟩ K, scire . . . conuersari R   19 him] his grace and
him M, his grace ⟨him⟩, his grace *canc.* D²

f. 55ᵛ oþer, þou shalte be over-sory and over-desolate. ²¹ Wherfore þou doste
folyly, if þou truste or be gladde in any oþer. ²² Hit is more eligible a man
to haue alle þe worlde contrary to him þen Ihesu offended. ²³ Amonge alle (4)
þerfore þat ar dere to þee, lete Ihesu be soule þi derlynge and thi special.

²⁴ Be alle men loved for Ihesu, and Ihesus for himselfe. ²⁵ Onely Ihesu
Criste is singulerly to be loved, þat onely is founden gode and trewe
bifore alle oþer frendes. ²⁶ For him and in him lete boþe frendes and
enemyes be dere to þee, and for alle þees he is to be preyed, that thei
mowe knowe him and love him. ²⁷ Desire never to be singlerly preysed
or loved, for þat longeþ to God alone, þat hath none lyke him. ²⁸ Ner
f. 56ʳ desire not þat any man be occupied in his | mynde aboute thi love, ᷉ner
be þou ocupied aboute none oþers love᷉.

²⁹ Be pure and free withinforthe, withoute implicamente or encom- (5)
brance of any creature. ³⁰ þou moste be bare, and bere to God a pure
herte, if þou wolte taste and see howe swete God is. ³¹ And verily, þerto
shalt þou neuer come, but yf þou be prevente and noryshed with his
grace, þat, alle þinges voyded and conged, þou alleone be oned with him
alone. ³² For whenne þe grace of God comeþ to a man, þen is he myghty
to alle þinges. ³³ And whenne hit goeþ aweye, þen shal he be pouer and
vnmyghty and as a man onely lafte to scourgynges and peynes. ³⁴ In thes
þinges be not þrowen downe ner despeire not, but stande evonly at the
wille of God, and suffre alle þinges þat comeþ to þee to þe preysinge
f. 56ᵛ ᷉of᷉ oure Lorde Ihesu Criste. For after | wynter comeþ somer, and after
[evon] comeþ day, and after tempeste comeþ clerenes.

Of lakkynge of alle manere solace
Capitulum 9ᵐ

¹ Hit is not grevouse a man to sette no pryce of mannes solace, whenne (1)
Goddes is nyghe. ² But hit is grete and right grete a man to mow lakke
boþe Goddes solace and mannes, and for þe worshippe of God gladly to

25 singulerly] singlerly DMG   gode] gᷓoᷓode D²   28 be²] be not
DMG   oþers] oþir DMG, Latin alicuius occuperis amore KR   29 implicamente
or] canc. G   31 conged] chonged M, ⟨changed⟩ D², changid G, Latin licenciatis
KR   alone] om. DMG, Latin solus cum solo KR   33 peynes] betinges or peynes
DMG   34 be] be ᷉þouᷓ D, be þou MG   to þe preysinge ᷉of᷉] preisyng ⟨. .⟩, of
visible under erasure D², preisyng MG, Latin ad laudem ihesu christi KR   evon] DMG,
om. C, Latin noctem KR   tempeste] tepest M
9.0 9ᵐ] ix MG, 9 ᷉ix᷉ D²   1 goddes] god DMG, Latin diuinum KR
2 mow] om. DMG, Latin posse carere K, carere R

suffre exile of herte, ner in noþinge seke himselfe, ner byholde to his
owne merite. ³ What grete þinge [is it if], grace comynge, þou be gladde
and deuoute? For þat houre is desirable to alle men. ⁴ He rideþ esily and
myrily, whom þe grace of God berithe. ⁵ And what wonder þoghe he
feele no burdon, þat is borne of þe Almyghty and ladde of the soverayne
ledar?

(2)   ⁶ Gladly | we take sumwhat for solac[e], and harde hit is a man to be   f. 57ʳ
drawen oute of hymselfe. ⁷ Seynt Laurence overcame the worlde with
his preste, for he despised alle þinge delectable in þe worlde, and
suffred benignely þat high preste Sixte, þat he moste loued, for þe love
of God to be take aweie from him. ⁸ þe love þerfore of þe creatoure
overcame þe love of man, and he chace þe welwillynge of God bifore
mannes solace. ⁹ So lerne þou to forsake for þe love of God sum dere
frende þat is necessary to þee; ¹⁰ ner bere hit not hevily when þou arte
forsaken of thi frende, knowynge þat atte laste we muste alle departe
everi from other.

(3)   ¹¹ Hit bihoveþ a man longe tyme and myghtily to strive with himselfe,
or a man shal canne perfitly overcome himselfe | and drawe alle his   f. 57ᵛ
affeccion into God. ¹² When a man standeþ vppon himselfe, he slydeþ
lyghtly to mannes consolacions, ¹³ but the veri lover of Criste and þe
studiouse folowar of vertue falleþ not vppon consolacions, ner he sekeþ
not suche sensible swetenesses, but raþer to suffre for Criste myghty
exercitacions and harde laboures.

(4)   ¹⁴ Wherefore when spiritual consolacion is yiven of God, receyve hit
with grete þankynges, and vnderstande hit þe yifte of God, and not thi
merite. Be not proude, ¹⁵ ner reioyce not to muche, ner presume not
veynly, but be þe more meke for þe yifte, and the more ware and the
more dredfulle in alle thi dedes, for þat houre shalle passe and
temptacion shalle folowe. ¹⁶ And when þe consolacion is taken aweye,

---

2 to³] om. M   3 is it if] G, ⟨ys it⟩ D², is it M, þogh C, Latin est si KR
comynge] comyng 'þoughe' D²   desirable] desiderable DMG   4 esily] ful esyly
G   5 þe] 'þe' G   6 solace] DMG, solaci C   hymselfe] himself or þe
worlde DMG, Latin seipso KR   7 seynt] seynt, sey blotted G   þat¹] þ⟨e⟩ D², the
G   8 chace] ch⟨ose⟩ D²   9 so] so, s blotted G   10 not] om.
DMG   11 to] om. DMG   a man²] he G   12 standeþ] stndiþ
M   13 but . . . consolacions] 'but þe very trewe louere of crist and studious
folwer of vertu slydith ne not upon consolacyones', ne canc. D², but þe very trew louer of
crist and studyous foloweþ of vertu he slydiþ neuer vpon consolacions M, but the verye
true louer of cryst and studious folower of vertu slydiþ not vpon consolacions G
swetenesses] swetnes G, Latin dulcedines KR   14 consolacion] exercitacion DMG,
Latin consolacio KR   hit²] it is, is added on line D², it is MG   15 ware] ware, e
added on line D²

f. 58ʳ despeire not anone, | but with mekenes and pacience abide þe hevonly visitacion, for God is of power to yive the gretter consolacion.

¹⁷ This is no newe ner no straunge þinge to hem þat ar experte in the weie of God, for oftetymes in grete seintes and holy prophetes haþe bene þis maner of alternacion. ¹⁸ Whereof one, grace beynge presente, (5) seide, 'I seide in myne haboundance, I shal never be meved.' ¹⁹ And when grace was absente, what he felte he reherced, seyinge, 'þou haste turned aweye [thi face fro me], and I was troubled.' ²⁰ Nerthelater, amonge þees he despeireþ not, but preieþ God more hertely, seyinge, 'Lorde, to þee shalle I crie, and I shalle preie to my God.' ²¹ And þen he reporteþ the fruyte of his preier, and witness[eth] hymselfe to be herde f. 58ᵛ of God, se[yinge], 'Oure Lorde hath herde and rueþ | on me, and is made my helpar.' ²² Butte whereyn? 'Thou haste,' he seithe, 'turned my sorowe into ioye, and clothed me alle aboute with gladnesse.' ²³ If hit were done þus with grete seintes, we feble and pouer oweþ not to despeire if sumtyme we be in feruoure and sumtyme in coldenesse. ²⁴ For þe Holy Spirite goþe and comeþ aftir the welplesinge of his wille. Wherefore seithe Iob, 'Thou visitest him bytyme, or in þe twylyght, and sodeynly þou prevest him.'

²⁵ Uppon what þerfore shal I hope or in whom shal I truste, but in þe (6) grete merci of God and onely in hope of heuonly grace? ²⁶ Wheþer þer be nyghe gode men or deuoute bretheren or trew frendes or holy bokes or feire tretes or swete songe and melodiouse ympnes, alle þees helpe f. 59ʳ but litel [and savoureþ but litel] when I | am forsaken of grace and lafte in my pouerte. ²⁷ Then is þer no better remedie þen pacience and denyinge of myselfe in the wille of God.

²⁸ I founde never man so religiouse ner deuoute þat feleþ not amonge (7) withdrawinge of grace or feleþ not sumtyme diminucion of feruoure. ²⁹ Ther was neuer seinte so highe ravished ner illumyned þat later or raþer were not tempted. ³⁰ For he is not [worthi] highe contemplacion of

17 no²] om. DMG   bene] ben in, in canc. G   18 one] i DM   19 thi face fro me] con., 'þi face' D², fro me G, om. CM, Latin auertisti faciem tuam a me KR   20 nerthelater] neuerthelater G   21 witnesseth] G, witnes⟨sith⟩ D², witnessinge CM   seyinge] s⟨aying⟩ D², and seyth G, seiþe CM, Latin testatur dicens KR   22 butte whereyn] but wherin canc. D, om. MG, Latin sed in quo KR   clothed] cl⟨ypp⟩ed D², clipped G, Latin circumdedisti KR   24 twylyght] twynliȝte G, Latin diluculo KR   26 þer] þei M, þei canc. D², om. G   gode] g'o'ode D²   and savoureþ but litel] MG, 'and' sauoriþ but litel D², om. C, Latin modicum sapiunt KR   29 þat later or raþer were not] þat later or raþer was M, 'but' þat later or raþer was D², 'but' that latter or rather was G, Latin qui prius uel postea non fuerit temptatus K, qui prius vel postea non temptatus fuerit R   30 worthi highe] con., highe C, hye 'yn' D², hye in M, hye in þe G, Latin non enim dignus est alta dei contemplacione KR

God þat is not exercitate for God in sum tribulacion. [31] And tribulacion going bifore is wonte to be a token of consolacion folowynge, for to hem þat ar preved in temptacions is promitted heuonly counforte. [32] 'He þat ouercomeþ,' seiþe oure Lorde, 'I shalle yif him to ete of the tree of lyve.'

(8) | [33] Heuonly counforte is yiven þat a man shulde be strenger to susteyne f. 59ᵛ aduersitees. [34] Temptacion also foloweþ, leste man be proude of the yifte. [35] The devel slepeth not, and þe fleysshe is not dede. [36] Wherefore cesse not to araye the to bataile, for bothe on þe right hande and on the lyfte hande ar ennemyes that never cesseth.

Of the kyndenes for þe grace of God
Capitulum 10[m]

(1) [1] Why sekeste þou reste, sithe þou arte borne to laboure? [2] Putte þe to pacience more þen to consolacions, and to bere þe crosse more þen to gladnesse. [3] What seculer man is þer þat wolde not gladly haue spiritual consolacion and gladnes, yf he myght haue hit euer? [4] For spirituel consolacions [passeþ] alle þe delyces of the worlde and alle fleisshely voluptes. [5] For al þe delicez | of þe worlde, ouþer they ar veyne or foule. f. 60ʳ [6] But spiritual delyces ar iocunde and honeste, engendred of the gentile vertues and infused into pure myndes by God. [7] But no man may vse þes diuine consolacions at his owne wille, for þe tyme of temptacion cesseþ not longe.

(2) [8] Fals liberte and propre truste ar muche 'contrary' to hevonly visitacion. [9] God doþe welle in yivinge grace of consolacion, but man doþe yvel, not yivinge alle to God with þankynges. [10] And þe yiftes of God mowe not flowe in vs, for we beþe vnkynde to þe yiver, and we refounde [not] alle ayein to the originalle welle. [11] Grace is euer dewe to him þat þankeþ worthily; and þat shal be take aweye fro þe proude man þat is wonte to be yivon to meke men.

31 and tribulacion] *om.* M, *Latin* temptacio KR   33 strenger] streng'ere', *first* e *altered from* o D², *Latin* forcior KR   35 not¹] neuere DMG   36 not] *om.* M, *Latin* non KR   on¹] in M   cesseth] cess⟨yn⟩ D²

10.0 the] *om.* DMG   10ᵐ] M, 10 CG, 10 'x' D²   3 seculer] secul⟨ar⟩ Dᴵ consolacion] consolacions DMG, *Latin* consolacionem KR   4 passeþ] DMG, *om.* C, *Latin* excedunt KR   delyces] delites M   5 delicez] delites M   ouþer] eiþer DMG   6 delyces] delites M   engendred] engendre M, *Latin* progenite KR the] *om.* DMG   7 diuine] godly G   10 refounde not alle ayein to] *con.*, refunde not ayen all to G, refounde not ayen ale M, refounde alle ayein to C, ⟨refunde⟩ not ayen all 'or ʒotyn ow[t] ayen all' to, ow[t] *cropped by binder* D², *Latin* nec totum refundimus KR   11 þankeþ] þankiþ, a *altered from* o D²

f. 60ᵛ [12] I wolle not of þat consolacion | þat shal take awey fro me (3)
compunccioun, ner I desire þat contemplacion þat shalle brynge me
into elacioun. [13] For not eueri highe þinge is holy, ner eueri swete þinge
goode, ner euery desire pure, ner euery dere þinge acceptable to God.
[14] I receyve gladly that grace whereof I am founde þe more meke, the
more dredfulle, and þe more redy to forsake myselfe.

[15] He þat is taught with the yifte of grace and lerned with the betynge
of subtraccion dar noþinge as[c]ryve to himselfe, but raþer wolle
knowleche himselfe pore and naked. [16] Yiffe to God þat is his, and
as[c]ryve to þee þat is þine. Yif God þankynges for his grace, and to
thiselfe gilte and peyne for þi gylte knowe to be dewe.

f. 61ʳ [17] Putte the euer at the lowest, and þe highest | shal be yiven to thee. (4)
[18] For the higheste may not stande withoute þe lowest. [19] The highest
seintes afore God ar lowest a[n]enste hemselfe; [20] and þe more gloriouse
þat þei be, the more meke þei ar in hemselfe. [21] Thei þat ar ful of
trouthe and heuonly glorye ar not desirouse of veineglorye; thei þat ar
grounded and confermed in God ar not proude. [22] And þei þat as[c]ryve
al to God, whatever gode þei receyve, thei seke not glorye euerie of oþer,
but þei wol þe glorie þat is only of God, and þei desire God to be
preised in himselfe and in his seintes above alle þinges, and into þat
euermore þei tendethe.

[23] Be kynde þerfore for a lytel þinge, and þou shalte be worthi to (5)
take gretter. [24] Lete also þe leste þinge be to þee as þe gretteste, and
f. 61ᵛ leste of price as a | special yifte. [25] If þe dignite of þe yivar be
considered, þere shal no yifte appere litel or of vile pryce, for hit
may not be litel þat is yiven of highe God. [26] Yea, yf he yiffe peynes
and betynges, hit oweþ to be taken in gree, for alle is done for oure
helthe, whateuer he suffre to come to vs. [27] He þat desireþ to kepe the
grace of God, lete hym be kynde for the grace yivon, and paciente
when hit is taken aweye. [28] Lete him preye þat hit come ayeine, and be
ware and meke þat he lese hit not.

13 goode] go`o´de D² 15 subtraccion] subtraccion `þerof´ D² ascryve]
DMG, astryve C 16 ascryve] DMG, astryve C dewe] due `thy payne´ D²,
Latin deberi KR 19 anenste] DM, ayenste C, an|yenst G, *Latin* apud KR
22 ascryve] DMG, astryve C into] to G 23 worthi] worþ M 24 special]
sp⟨ecial⟩ D², spirituel M, *Latin* speciali KR 25 yivar] (y)euer D² or of vile
pryce for hit may not be litel] *om.* DMG, *Latin* aut nimis vile videbitur non enim paruum
est KR of³] of þe DMG 26 in gree] ⟨gladly⟩ `in pacience´ D², full lese G, *Latin*
⟨gratum esse debet⟩ K, gratum esse debet R 27 aweye] awey `and´ D², awey and
MG 28 meke] meke `hym´ D², meke hym MG, *Latin* cautus sit et humilis KR

Of the fewnesse of lovers of the crosse of Criste
Capitulum 11 ͫ

(1) [1] Ihesus hath many lovers of þe reaume of hevon, but fewe berars of his crosse. [2] He haþe many desirars of consolacions, and fewe of tribulacions. [3] He fyndeþ many felawse of þe | table, and fewe of abstinence. f. 62ʳ [4] Alle desireþ to ioye with him, but fewe wol suffre any peyne for him. [5] Many foloweþ Ihesu vnto the brekynge of brede, but fewe vnto the drinkynge of þe cuppe of the passion. [6] Many worshippeth his miracles, but fewe foloweþ the repreve of the crosse. [7] Many lovethe Ihesu when none aduersite falleþ. [8] Many preyseþ him and blesseþ him whiles þei take any consolacions of him. [9] But if Ihesus hide him and a litel forsake hem, þei falle into a compleynynge or into over-grete deieccion.

(2) [10] But þeie þat love Ihesu for Ihesu, and not for any consolacions, þei blesse him in every tribulacion and angwysshe of herte, as in highest consolacion. [11] And þoghe he wolde never yiffe hem consolacion, yette

(3) wolde þei ever preise him and | ever þanke him. [12] O, howe myghty is þe f. 62ᵛ pure love of Ihesu, when hit is medled with no propre love ner propre profite! [13] Wheþer alle þei þat sekeþ euer consolacions ar not [to be seide] mercenaries and hired men? [14] Whether ar þei not preved lovers of hemselfe and not of Criste þat ever þenkeþ vppon her owne lucre and

(4) profite? [15] Where shal þer be founde one þat wolle serue God frely? [16] Seldon shal þer be founde any man so spirituel þat be naked fro alle þinges. [17] And who shal fynde a man very pouer in spirite and bare from every creature? [18] His price is [farre] and fro þe vtmast costes.

[19] Yif a man yive alle his substance, [yette] hit is as nought. [20] And if he do grete penance, yette hit is but lytel. [21] And yf he apprehende alle

---

11.0 lovers] þe louers DMG   11ͫ] xi G, ii ʼxiʼ D²   1 ihesus] ihesu G, *Latin* ihesus KR   his] þe DMG   2 tribulacions] tribulacion M   5 foloweþ] fol⟨wyn⟩ D²   6 worshippeth] worship⟨yn⟩ D²   foloweþ] folow⟨yn⟩ D² 7 none] no G   9 and a] ⟨ande a⟩ D²   13 not to be seide] G, ⟨to be seyde⟩ D², to be seid M, not very C, *Latin* nonne omnes mercennarii sunt dicendi KR   men] m⟨en⟩ D²   14 not¹] *om.* M, *Latin* nonne KR   15 where shal þer be founde] ⟨where is þere⟩ founde D², where is þere founde MG, *Latin* vbi inuenietur KR 16 founde any man so spirituel þat be naked fro alle þinges] eny man founde so spiritu⟨a⟩l þat ⟨wyll be nakyd from all. .⟩ ʼworldly þingesʼ D², eny man founde so spirituel þat will be nakid from alle worldly þingis MG, *Latin* inuenietur tam spiritualis aliquis qui omnibus sit nudatus R, ʼinueniturʼ tam spiritʼuʼalis aliquis qui omnibus sit nudatus K   17 every] eny M, *Latin* omni KR   18 farre and fro þe vtmast costes] *con.*, and fro þe vtmast costes C, and fro þe vttermest chost M, ⟨. .⟩ fro þe vt⟨termost coost⟩ D², from the vttermost cooste G, *Latin* procul et de vltimis finibus KR   19 yette] MG, ʼȝitʼ D², *om.* C, *Latin* adhuc KR

f. 63ʳ maner sci|ence, yeet is he farre. [22] And if he haue grete vertue and right feruente deuocion, yeet him lakkeþ muche; [23] þat is to seie, one þat is soueraynly necessarie to him. [24] What is þat? That, alle þinges forsaken, he forsake himselfe and go holy oute of himselfe and reteygne noþinge of propre love. [25] When he hath done alle þinges þat he knoweþ to doo, lete him fele himselfe to haue doo nought. [26] Lete him not pondre grete (5) alle þat may [be] estemed grete, but lete him in trouthe pronounce himselfe an vnprofitable servante. [27] As trouthe seithe, 'When [y]e haue done al þinges þat ar commaunded to youe, seithe þat we beþe vnprofitable servantes.' [28] For suche one may seie with þe prophete

f. 63ᵛ þat 'I am soole and pouer' [29] when he bigynneþ verily to be bare | and pouer in spirite. [30] Nerthelater, no man is rycher, no man is myghttier, no man more free þen he þat canne forsake himselfe and alle þinges and putte himselfe atte the loweste.

Of the kynges higheweie of the crosse
Capitulum 12ᵐ

[1] This worde, 'Denye þiselfe and take thi crosse and folowe me,' semeþ (1) an harde worde to many men. [2] But muche harder hit shal be to here [þis laste] worde, 'Goþe fro me, [y]e cursed puple, into the fire euerlastynge.' [3] Thei þat gladly hereþ and foloweþ the worde of þe crosse shal not drede of the worde of euerlastynge dampnacion. [4] This signe of the crosse shal be in hevon, when oure Lorde shal come to þe

f. 64ʳ iugemente. [5] Then alle þe servantes of the crosse þat haue confour|med hem to Criste in her lyve shul nyghe vnto Criste þe iuge with grete truste.

[6] Whi dredest þou þerfore to take þe crosse, wherby me goþe to the (2) reaume? [7] In the crosse is helthe; in the crosse is lyve; in the crosse is

23 þat is to seie one þat] ⟨but oo þynge⟩ D², but oo þinge M, but oon þinge G, *Latin* scilicet vnum quod KR   25 doo¹] ⟨be⟩ do D², be done G   26 alle þat may be estemed] M, alle þat may estemed C, allþ⟨o⟩ 'he' may be estym⟨att⟩ D², alþou3e he may be estymate G, *Latin* quod grande estimari posset KR   27 ye] DMG, he C, *Latin* feceritis KR   to] *om.* G   seithe²] sa⟨ye⟩ D², sey ye G   beþe] 'be' G   30 nerthelater] neuerlater DM, neuerthelater G   more] is more G   putte] *om.* M, *Latin* ponere KR   the] *om.* DM
12.0 12ᵐ] xii MG, 12 'xii' D²   1 worde¹] w'o'orde D²   thi] þi⟨.⟩ D
2 muche] muche more G   þis laste] con., þis DMG, *om.* C, *Latin* illud extremum KR   goþe] go⟨o⟩ D²   ye] DMG, the C   3 hereþ] feliþ DMG, *Latin* audiunt KR   euerlastynge] þe euerlastyng G   4 þe] *om.* DMG   5 shul] M, shul 'be' D², shull be G, shulde C, *Latin* accedent KR   6 me] men MG   reaume] reume 'of heuyn' D², reume of heuyn M, kyngdom of heuen G, *Latin* regnum KR

proteccion frome enemyes; [8] in the crosse is infusion of hevonly swettenesse; in þe crosse is strengthe of mynde; in þe crosse is ioye of spirite; [9] in the crosse is summe of vertue; in the crosse is perfeccion of holynesse. [10] Ther is none helthe of soule, ner hope of euerlastynge lyve, but in the crosse. [11] Take thi crosse, þerfore, and folowe Ihesu, and þou shalte go into þe lyve euerlastinge. [12] He þat bare his owne crosse is gone bifore and dyed for þee in the crosse, þat þou shuldest bere thi crosse and desire to dye in the crosse. [14] And if þou be felawe in peyne, | þou shalte be felawe in glorie.

f. 64ᵛ

(3)   [15] Loo, in þe crosse standeþ alle þinge, and in dyinge lythe alle, and þer is none oþer weye to lyve and to veri inwarde pees, but þe weie of þe holy crosse and of cotidiane mortifiynge, for if þou be dede with him, þou shalt also lyffe with him. [16] Walke þerfore wher þou wolte, seke whereuer hit pleseþ þee, and þou shalt fynde none higher weye above ner surer wey bineþeforthe þen the weye of the crosse. [17] Dispose and ordeigne alle þinges aftir þi wille and þi semynge, and þou shalte not fynde but a duete to suffre sumwhat ouþer wilfully or ayenis þi wille, and thou shalte euer fynde þe crosse. [18] Thou shalte ouþer suffre sorowe

(4)   in thi body, or tribulacion of spirite in þe sowle. [19] Ouþerwhiles þou | [shalte be forsaken of God, and sumtyme þou shalt be stired of thi neyghboure, and, þat more is, sumtyme þou shalte be grevouse to thiselfe. [20] And yette hit shal not lye in þi power to be esed ner delyuered with no remedy, ner no solace, but whiles God wolle þou muste nedes suffre and bere. [21] God wolle þat þou shalt lerne to suffre tribulacion withoute counforte, for þou shuldest subdue alle to him and be þe meker for tribulacion. [22] No man so hertely feleþ the passion of Criste as he þat suffreþ lyke þinges.

D, p. 90

[23] The crosse þerfore is ever redy, and oueralle hit abideþ þee. [24] þou maiste not flee hit: whereeuer þou renne and whereuer þou come þou berest thiselfe with þee, and euer þou shalte fynde thiselfe. [25] Turne þiselfe above, turne þi`selfe byneþe, turne thi'selfe outwarde, turne thiselfe inwarde, and in alle thes shalte þou fynde þe crosse, and oueralle

9 summe] þe summe DMG   10 none] no G   11 þe] om. DMG
12 in¹] ⟨on⟩ D², on G   in²] ⟨on⟩ D²   14 felawe¹] folower, r added on line D²,
folower MG, Latin socius KR   felawe²] felower, r added on line D², folower
MG   15 dyinge] ⟨dyeng⟩ D²   lyve] ly⟨fe⟩ D²   16 none higher] non
liȝter D, no liȝter MG, Latin non inuenies alciorem KR   17 aftir] aster M, Latin
secundum KR   ouþer] eiþer DMG   thou] so þou MG, `so' þou D²
18 ouþer] ⟨. . . eiþer .⟩ D¹, eiþer MG   þe] thy G   19 ouþerwhiles] oþerwhiles
DMG   19–30 shalte¹ . . . tribulacion] DMG, om. C (f. 65 missing)   25 þiselfe
byneþe turne thiselfe] þi`self bynethe turne þi'self D², þiself MG, Latin te infra conuerte
te K, te R   shalte þou] þou shalt M

hit is nedefulle to þee to kepe pacience, if þou wolte haue inwarde pes

D, p. 91 and deserve | a crowne everlastinge.

²⁶ If thou bere þe crosse gladly, hit shal bere þee and lede þee to a (5) desiderable ende whereas an ende shal be of suffrynge, þoghe hit be not here. ²⁷ Yf þou bere hit ayenis thi wille, þou makeste þiselfe an hevy burdon and grevest thiselfe more, and yette muste þou nedes susteyne hit. ²⁸ If þou putte aweye ʻoneʼ crosse, doutelesse þou shalt fynde anoþer, and peraventure more grevouse.

²⁹ Weneste þou ʻtoʼ skape þat never mortal man myght passe? (6) ³⁰ What seinte in þis worlde was withoute crosse and tribulacion?] |

C, f. 66ʳ ³¹ Not oure Lorde Ihesu Criste was withoute sorowe of passion one houre in alle his lyve. ³² He seithe, 'Hit bihove[d] Criste to suffre and to rise fro dethe, and so to entree into his glory.' ³³ And how sekeste þou another weye þen the kynges higheweye, þe crosse weye? ³⁴ Alle Cristes lyve was a crosse and a martirdame, and þou sekeste to thiselfe reste and ioye?

³⁵ Thou erreste, þou goeste oute of the weie, if þou seke oþer to þee (7) þenne tribulacions, for alle þis mortalle lyve is fulle of myseries, and marked alle aboute with crosses. ³⁶ And þe higher þat a man profiteþ in spirite, þe higher crosse[s] oftetyme he fyndeth, for þe peyne of his exyle groweþ more þorowe love. ³⁷ Nertheletar, þis man þus peyned is

f. 66ᵛ not withoute sum maner of counforte, for he feleþ grete fruyte | growe to him þorowe the suff[er]aunce of his crosse. ³⁸ For whiles he gladly (8) subdueþ him þerto, alle burdon of tribulacion is turned into truste of diuine consolacion. ³⁹ And the more þat þe fleisshe is þrowen downe bi affliccion, þe more þe spirite is strengthed bi inwarde grace. ⁴⁰ And oftetymes he is so gretely counforted and strengthed þat for desire of tribulacion and aduersite, for love of conformite to the crosse of Criste, he wolde not be withoute sorowe and tribulacion; ⁴¹ for the more acceptable he accompteþ him to God, the moo and the gretter peynes þat he mowe suffre for God.

26 an] ande M   27 yf] yt M, *Latin* si KR   28 one] ⟨.⟩ ʻoone' D², oon G, þe M   29 to] G, ʻto' D², *om.* M   30 crosse] þe crosse G   32 he seithe hit bihoved criste] *con.*, he seithe hit bihovethe criste C, it bihoued crist þe euaungeliste seiþe M, ⟨the euaungelist⟩ ʻseith'|ʻþe euaungeliste seyth' it bihoued crist D², hit behoued cryst seyth þe euaungelist G, *Latin* oportebat ait christum KR   rise] aryse G   33 þe] whiche is þe G   35 tribulacions] tribulacion DMG, *Latin* tribulaciones KR   36 crosses] DMG, crosse C, *Latin* cruces KR   oftetyme] oftetymes DMG   37 nertheletar] neuerþeles DG   sufferaunce] MG, suffi⟨r⟩|⟨.⟩aunce, s *visible under erasure* D², suffisaunce C, *Latin* ⟨sufferencia⟩ K, sufficiencia R   38 alle] al þe G   40 strengthed] streng`r´h|thed G   to] of DMG

⁴²This is not mannes myght, but the grace of Criste, þat may doo and dothe so grete þinges in freyle fleysshe, þat þorowe feruoure of spirite he take vppon him and love | þat þinge þat þe fleysshe euer naturelly f. 67ʳ
(9) fleeþ and abhorreþ. ⁴³Hit is not aftir þe man to bere þe crosse, to love þe crosse, to chastise þe body and brynge hit in þraldame, to flee worshippes, gladly to susteyne repreves and wronges, to despice himselfe and to wille to be despised, to suffre alle maner aduersitees with harmes, and to desire no maner pro[sper]ite in þis worlde. ⁴⁴Yf þou loke to thiselfe, þou maiste no suche þinge of thiselfe. ⁴⁵But if thowe truste in oure Lorde, strengeþ shal be yiven þe from heuon, and þe worlde and the flesshe shul be made sugget to þi commaundemente. ⁴⁶Ner þou shalte not drede thi enemy the devel, yf þou be armed with feithe and marked with the crosse.

(10)   ⁴⁷Putte þee þerfore, as a goode and a trewe servant of Criste, to bere manly | þe crosse of thi Lorde, crucified for þee þorowe love. ⁴⁸Make f. 67ᵛ
the redy to suffree many contrary þinges and diuerse incomoditees in þis wrecched lyve, for so he shal be with þee whereeuer þou be, and so thou shalte fynde him whereeuer þou be hidde. ⁴⁹Hit muste be so, and þer is no remedy of skapinge fro tribulacion of yvel men and sorowe, but þat þou suffre. ⁵⁰Drynke the chalyce of oure Lorde affectuously if þou desire to be his frende and to haue parte withe him. ⁵¹Consolacions committe to God: doo he þerwith as hit pleseþ him. ⁵²Put þou thiselfe to suffre tribulacions, and acompte hem as grettest consolacions, for þer a[r] no passions of þis tyme worthy to deserve the glory þat is to come, yea, þoghe þou myghtest suffre alle alone.

(11)   ⁵³When þou commest þerto þat | tribulacion is swete to thee and is f. 68ʳ
savory to þee for Criste, then deme hit welle with þee, for þou haste founde paradise in yerthe. ⁵⁴As longe as hit is grevouse to þee to suffre and þou sekest to flee hit, so longe hit shal be [yvel with þee], and

---

42 þat may doo and dothe so] ⟨that man . .⟩ doþe ⟨so⟩ D², þat man doþe so MG, *Latin* que tanta potest et agit KR   of²] of þe G   love þat] loueþ þat⟩ D², loueþ þat M   naturelly] natur⟨a⟩ly D²   43 and¹] ⟨to⟩ D², to MG, *Latin et* KR   maner¹]
manere of G   prosperite] DMG, profite C, *Latin* prosperitatis KR   44 þinge]
þinge 'doo' D², þinge do MG, *Latin* nichil huiusmodi ex te poteris KR   45 yiven]
yeue to D, youe to M, yeven to G   47 goode] go'o'de D²   a²] *om.* DMG
of²] ⟨. of⟩, *tail of* f *visible under* o D²   49 and¹] ⟨for⟩ D², for MG, *Latin et* KR
fro] for M, *Latin* a tribulacione KR   52 þou¹] *om.* M   ar] DMG, as C, *Latin*
sunt KR   suffre alle alone] al allone suffre alle temptacions M, ⟨. .⟩ allone ⟨suf⟩'fyr al
temptacions', al *visible under first erasure* D², allone suffyr all temptacions G, *Latin* eciam si
solus omnes posses ⟨sustinere⟩ K, eciam si solus omnes passiones posses tunc sustinere
R   54 hit shal be yvel with þee and] *con.*, shal it be ⟨euy⟩'ll with þe and' D², shal it
be euyll with þe and MG, hit shal be and C, *Latin* male habebis et KR

fleynge of tribulacion shal folowe þee oueralle. [55] If þou putte þe as þou (12)
owest to doo, to suffre and to dye, hit shal sone be better, and þou shalte
fynde pees.

[56] Yea, yf þou be ravyshed vnto the þridde hevon with Poule, þou arte
not yeet siker to suffre no contrary þinge. [57] For Ihesus seide, 'I shal
shewe him howe grete þinges he muste suffre for my name.' [58] To suffre,
þerfore, remayneþ to þee, yf þou wolte love and euer plese him.
[59] Wolde God þat þou were worthi to suffre anyþinge for þe name of (13)
f. 68ᵛ Ihesu! Howe grete glorye | shulde be to þee! Howe grete exultacion to
alle þe seintes of heuon! Howe grete edificacion of thi neighboure! [60] For
al men commendeþ pacience, þoghe fewe wolle suffre. [61] þou shuldest
gladly suffre for Criste, sithe men suffre muche more grevouse þinges
for the worlde.

[62] Knowe for certeyne þat þou muste lede a dyinge lyve. [63] And þe (14)
more þat a man dyeþ to himselfe, þe more he bigynneþ to lyve to God.
[64] Ther is no man apte to take heuonly þinges but he submytteþ
himselfe to bere aduersitees for Criste. [65] Ther is noþinge more
acceptable to God, noþinge more holsome to þee in þis worlde, þenne
gladly to suffre for Criste. [66] And if hit laye in þi choyce, þou shuldeste
raþer desire to suffre contrarye þinges for Criste, þenne to be refresshed
f. 69ʳ with many consolacions, for þou shuldest | be more lyke vnto Criste and
þe more confourmed to alle seintes. [67] For oure merite and the profitynge of oure estate standeþ not in swetnesses and consolacions, but
raþer in suffringe of grevouse þinges and tribulacions. [68] For if þer had (15)
been anyþinge more better or more profitable to man þenne to suffre,
Criste wolde verily haue shewed hit by worde and ensaumple. [69] But he
exhorted alle his disciples and alle hem þat desired to folowe him openly
to bere þe crosse, seiynge, 'Who þat wolle come aftir me, lete him denye
hymselfe and take his crosse and folowe me.' [70] Alle þinges þerfore over-
radde and serched, be þis þe final conclusion: þat by many tribulacions
hit bihoveth vs to entree into the reaume of hevon.

Here endeþ the ammonicions drawynge inwarde.

---

54 of] of it, it *canc.* D   folowe] *om.* M, *Latin* sequetur KR   55 putte] puttist
DMG   59 wolde] wol`de´|de, *second* de *canc.* D²   64 submytteþ] submitte
DMG   67 for oure] for oure | for oure, *first* for oure *canc.* D   swetnesses]
swettnesse MG, *Latin* suauitatibus KR   68 for] for and M   better] gretter and
better M   70 þerfore over-radde] þer | ⟨ouer redd⟩ D², þer ouer red M, perfitly
ouere redde G, *Latin* ergo perlectis KR   reaume] kyngdome G

[BOOK III]

3.0.0 bygynneth] folowen DMG   boke] boke that is DMG   1 capitulum
primum] *om.* DMG   to] vnto DMG   sowle] soule capitulum primum MG, soule
capitulum i D   2 2ᵐ] ii DG   3 that] of DM   3ᵐ] iii DMG   4 a . . .
quartum] *om.* DMG, *Latin* oracio ad implorandum deuocionis graciam iiii R, *om.*
K   5 capitulum 5ᵐ] capitulum iiii a praier to gete grace of deuocion capitulum v
DG, capitulum iiiiᵐ a preier to gete grace of deuocion capitulum vᵐ M, *Latin* v R, iii
K   6 6ᵐ] vi DG, *Latin* vi R, v K   7 7ᵐ] vii DG, *Latin* vii R, vi K
8 8ᵐ] viii DG, *Latin* viii R, vii K   9 9ᵐ] ix DG, *Latin* ix R, viii K   10 10ᵐ] x
DG, *Latin* x R, ix K   11 to] for to DM   11ᵐ] xi G, 11 ʽxiʼ D², *Latin* xi R, x
K   12 12ᵐ] xii G, 12 ʽxiiʼ D², *Latin* xii R, xi K   13 ayeine] ayenst DMG
13ᵐ] xiii G, 13 ʽxiiiʼ D², *Latin* xiii R, xii K   14 14ᵐ] xiiii MG, 14 ʽxiiiiʼ D², *Latin*
xiiii R, xiii K   15 prive] peyne M, *Latin* occultis KR   ayeine] aȝenst DMG
15ᵐ] xv G, 15 ʽxvʼ D², *Latin* xv R, xiiii K

---

16 desirable] desiderable DMG   16^m] xvi MG, 16 ʼxviʼ D², *Latin* xvi R, xv K
17 17^m] xvii MG, 17 ʼxviiʼ D², *Latin* xvii R, *whole verse om.* K   18 18^m] xviii MG, 18
ʼxviiiʼ D², *Latin* xviii R, xvi K   19 be] *om.* G   19^m] 19 MG, 19 ʼxixʼ D², *Latin* xix R,
xvii K   20 20^m] 20 MG, 20 ʼxxʼ D², *Latin* xx R, xviii K   21 21^m] 21 MG, 21 ʼxxiʼ
D², *Latin* xxi R, xix K   22 22^m] 22 MG, 22 ʼxxiiʼ D², *Latin* xxii R, xx K   23 23^m]
23 MG, 23 ʼxxiiiʼ D², *Latin* xxiii R, xxi K   24 24^m] 24 MG, 24 ʼxxivʼ D², *Latin* xxiiii R,
xxii K   25 25^m] 25 MG, 25 ʼxxvʼ D², *Latin* xxv R, xxiii K   26 26^m] 26 MG, 26
ʼxxviʼ D², *Latin* xxvi R, *whole verse om.* K   27 a . . . 27^m] *written after 3.0.29 in C, but*
correct position marked   27^m] 27 MG, 27 ʼxxviiʼ D², *Latin* xxvii R, *whole verse om.* K
28 28^m] 28 MG, 28 ʼxxviiiʼ D², *Latin* xxviii R, xxiiii K   29 29^m] 29 MG, 29 ʼxxixʼ
D², *Latin* xxix R, xxv K   30 howe] who M   30^m] 30 MG, 30 ʼxxxʼ D², *Latin* xxx
R, xxvi K   31 31^m] 31 MG, 31 ʼxxxiʼ D², *Latin* xxxi R, xxvii K   32 32^m] 32
MG, 32 ʼxxxiiʼ D², *Latin* xxxii R, *whole verse om.* K   33 33^m] 33 MG, 33 ʼxxxiiiʼ D²,
Latin xxxiii R, xxviii K   34 34^m] 34 MG, 34 ʼxxxiiiiʼ D², *Latin* xxxiiii R, xxix
K   35 35^m] 35 MG, 35 ʼxxxvʼ D², *Latin* xxxv R, xxx K

f. 71ᵛ

D, p. 99

36 36^m] 36 MG, 36 ʽxxxvi' D², *Latin* xxxvi R, xxxi K   37 cupidite] curiosite DMG, *Latin* cupiditatis KR   37^m] 37 MG, 37 ʽxxxvii' D², *Latin* xxxvii R, xxxii K   38 final] smal DMG, *Latin* finali KR   capitulum] *om.* G   38^m] 38 MG, 38 ʽxxxviii' D², xxxviii R, xxxiii K   39 that] ʽxxxix' that D²   39^m] 39 DMG, *Latin* xxxix R, xxxiiii K   40 that] ʽxl' that D²   40^m] 40 DMG, *Latin* xl R, xxxv K   41 ayeine] aȝent M, ayenste G, ʽxli' aȝenst D²   41^m] 41 DMG, *Latin* xli R, xxxvi K   42 of] ʽxlii' of D²   42^m] 42 DMG, *Latin* xlii R, xxxvii K   43 of] ʽxliii' of D²   43^m] 43 DMG, *Latin* xliii R, xxxviii K   44 that] ʽxliiii' that D²   44^m] 44 DMG, *Latin* xliiii R, xxxix K   45 that] ʽxlv' that D²   45^m] 45 DMG, *Latin* xlv R, xl K   46 of¹] ʽxlvi' of D²   contempte] con. . . . .e *blotted* D   worldely worshippes] temporall worship DG, tempal worship M   46^m] 46 DMG, *Latin* xlvi R, xli K   47 that] ʽxlvii' that D²   47^m] 47 DMG, *Latin* xlvii R, xlii K   48 ayenys] ʽxlviii' ayenst D²   science] G, conscience CDM, *Latin* scienciam KR   48^m] 48 DMG, *Latin* xlviii R, xliii K   49 owtewarde] ʽxlix' outwarde D²   49^m] 49 DMG, *Latin* xlix R, xliii K   50 that] ʽl' that D²   hit] *om.* M   50^m] 50 DMG, *Latin* l R, xlv K   51 of¹] ʽli' of D²   ayenis] ayenst þe DG, ayʽe'nst the M   51^m] 51 DMG, *Latin* li R, xlvi K   52–1.3 that . . . of¹] DMG, *om.* C (*f. 72 misssing*)   52 that] MG, ʽlii' that D²   52^m] *con.*, 52 DMG, *Latin* lii R, xlvii K

D, p. 101 | *Here bigynneþ þe þridde parte of inwarde con[sol]acion.*

Of þe inwarde spekynge of Criste vnto a soule
Capitulum primum

[1]'I shal here what oure Lorde God spekeþ in me. [2]Blisfulle is þat soule   (1)
þat hereþ oure Lorde spekynge in him and takeþ of his mouthe 'þe'
C, f. 73ʳ   worde of consolacion. [3]Blessed be þoo eres þat receyveþ of] | Goddes

53 53ᵐ] *con.*, 53 MG, 53 'liii' D², *Latin* liii R, xlviii K   54 54ᵐ] *con.*, 54 MG, 54
'liiii' D², *Latin* liiii R, xlix K   55 55ᵐ] *con.*, 55 MG, 'lv' D², *Latin* lx R, l K
56 56ᵐ] *con.*, 56 M, 56 'lvi' D², lvi | capitulum lvi G, *Latin* lvi R, li K   57 57ᵐ]
con., 57 MG, 57 'lvii' D², *Latin* lvii R, lii K   58 58ᵐ] *con.*, 58 MG, 58 'lviii' D²,
Latin lviii R, liii K   59 59ᵐ] *con.*, 59 MG, 59 'lix' D², *Latin* lix R, liiii K
60 of . . . 60ᵐ] *om.* G   60ᵐ] *con.*, 60 M, 60 'lx' D², *Latin* lx R, lv K   61 61ᵐ]
con., 61 M, 61 'lxi' D², lx G, *Latin* lxi R, lvi K   62 defautes] fauȝtes G   62ᵐ]
con., 62 M, 62 'lxii' D², lxi G, *Latin* lxii R, lvii K   63 63ᵐ] *con.*, 63 M, 63 'lxiii' D²,
lxii G, *Latin* lxiii R, lviii K   64 is] is not M   64ᵐ] *con.*, 64 M, 64 'lxiiii' D², lxiii
G, *Latin* lxiiii R, lix K   65 bigynneþ] . . . . . . eþe *blotted* M   consolacion] *con.*,
conuersacyon DG, conuersa. . . . *blotted* M, *Latin* consolacionis K, *om.* R
     1.0 of þe inwarde] . . . . warde *blotted* M   1 I] . *blotted* M   2 þe] 'þe'
D², the G, *om.* M

rownynge, and takeþ none hede of the rownynges of þis worlde. [4]Pleynly thoo eres ar blessed þat takeþ none hiede to the voyce sownynge outewarde, but alle inwarde þe techinge trouthe. [5]Blisfulle be þo yen þat ar closed to outwarde þinges, and intente to the inwarde þinges. [6]Blysfulle ar þei þat perseþ inwarde þinges and studyeþ to make hemselfe redy bi daily exercices more and more to take hevonly privitez. [7]Blisfulle ar þei þat desireþ to take hiede to God and casteþ hemselfe oute fro alle impedimentes of the worlde.

(2)   [8]'Take hiede herto, my soule, and close vppe þe durres of thi sensualite, þat þou mowe here what thi Lorde God spekeþ in þee. [9]Thus seithe þi biloved, "Thi helthe am I, þi pees, | and thi lyve.   f. 73ᵛ [10]Kepe the with me, and þou shalte fynde pees. [11]Leve alle transitorye þinges, and seke euerlasting. [12]What ar alle temporalle þinges but deceyvours? [13]And what helpeþ alle creatures, if þou be forsaken of þi creatour?" [14]Al oþer þinges þerfore sette aside, yelde thiselfe plesant and trewe to thi creatoure, þat þou mowe take very felycite.'

[*That trouthe spekeþ withinne withoute noyse of wordes*]
Capitulum secundum

(1)   [1]'Speke, Lorde, for thi servante hereþ. [2]I am thi servant: yive me vnderstandinge, þat I mowe know þi testimonies. [3]Bowe my herte into þe wordes of thi mouþe; flowe thy speche as swete dewe. [4]The children [of Israel] seide sumtyme to Moyses, "Speke þou to vs, and we shulle here þee; lette | not oure Lorde [speke], leste we dye." [5]Lorde, not soo, I   f. 74ʳ preie not so, but raþer with Samuel þe prophete mekely and affectuously I byseche thee, "Speke þou, Lorde, for thi seruante hereþ." [6]Speke þer[fore] not to me Moyses ner none of the prophetes, but speke [þou] raþer, Lorde God, inspiroure and illuminoure of prophetes, for þou alone withoute hem maiste teche me perfitely, [7]but þei withoute þee shulle noþinge profite.

3 none] no G   rownynges] rovnyng DMG, *Latin* susurracionibus KR   4 none] no G   5 blisfulle] blessed DMG   intente] intende DMG, *Latin* sunt intenti K, sunt attenti R   6 blysfulle] blessed DMG   7 alle] alle maner of M 11 alle] aster M   13 creatures DMG, creatoures C

2.0 that . . . wordes] *con.*, that the wordes of god ar to be herde withe mekenesse CDMG, *Latin* quod veritas intus loquitur sine strepitu uerborum KR (*cf. 3.0.2*)   secundum] 2 M, 2 'ii' D²   2 know] 'knowe' D²   3 swete] s(wete) D²   4 of israel] DMG, *om.* C, *Latin* filii israel KR   speke²] DMG, *om.* C, *Latin* loquatur KR   5 lorde] lorde lorde DMG, *Latin* domine KR   6 þerfore] DMG, þer C   þou¹] DMG, *om.* C, *Latin* tu pocius loquere KR

⁸'þei mowe welle sowne wordes, but þei yiffe no spirite. þei seie (2) passingly faire, but, the not spekynge, þei sette noþinge ofire. ⁹Thei bitake vs þe lettre, but þou openeste þe witte. ¹⁰Thei bringe forthe misteries, but þou makeste open þe vndirstandinge of the privytees. ¹¹þei telle oute commaundementes, but þou helpest to perfourme hem.

f. 74ᵛ ¹²Thei shewe þe weye, but þou makeste | stronge to go. ¹³þei worche alle withouteforþe, but þou techest and illuminest þe hertes. ¹⁴þei water withouteforþe, but þou yivest fecundite. ¹⁵The[i] crie with wordes, but to the heringe þou graunteste vndirstandynge.

¹⁶'Speke not þerfore Moyses to me, but þou, my Lorde God, (3) euerlastynge trowthe, ¹⁷leste I dye and be made vnfructuose, if I be onely amonyshed outwarde, and not sette afire inwarde. Therfore, leste the worde herde and not done be to me iugemente, or the worde knowen and not loved, or þe worde byleved and not kepte, ¹⁸speke þou, Lorde, for thi servant herethe. Thou haste wordes of lyve euerlastinge: ¹⁹speke to me to summe maner of counforte of my soule and to þe amendemente

f. 75ʳ of my lyve, and to | þee, Lorde, to preysinge, glory, and everlastynge worshippe.'

That þe wordes of Godde ar to be herde with mekenesse
Capitulum tercium

¹'Sone, here my wordes moste swete, and passinge þe konnynge of alle (1) the philosophers and alle þe wyse men of þis worlde. ²My wordes ar spirite and l[y]ve, [and] þei ar not to be peysed with mannes witte. ³Thei beþe not to be drawen to veyne plesance, but to be herde in silence and to be taken with mekenes and grete desire.'

⁴And I seide, 'Blysfulle is he whom þou haste lerned and hast taught him of thi lawe, þat þou mowe make him mitigacion from yvel daies, þat the yerþe be not desolate.'

8 the not spekynge þei] þe spekynge þei M, þere spekyng G, ⟨the not⟩ spekyng þei D², *Latin* te tacente cor non accendunt K, te tacente non accedunt R   ofire] ⟨a⟩ fire D²   15 thei] DMG, the C, *Latin* illi clamant KR   graunteste] ʒeuist DMG, *Latin* tribuis KR   17 vnfructuose] infructuose G   if I be onely] if I be onys M, ⟨lest⟩ I be o⟨only⟩ D², leste y be oonly G, *Latin* si fuero tantum KR   afire] a fire, a *altered from* o D²   19 þe] *om.* DM   lorde] *twice, first canc.* D   to⁵] ⟨be⟩ D², be MG, tibi autem ad laudem KR

3.0 wordes] wor⟨d⟩es D¹   tercium] 3 MG, 3 'iii' D²   1 konnynge] knouyng M   2 lyve and] G, lif DM, love C, *Latin* vita sunt nec KR   witte] wittes DMG, *Latin* sensu KR

(2)   [5] 'I,' sei[th]e oure Lorde, 'haue taught þe prophetes fro the bigyn-
nynge, and | vnto nowe I cesse not to speke to alle. But many beeþ harde   f. 75ᵛ
and defe at my voyce. [6] Many more gladly hereþ þe worlde þenne God.
[7] Thei sue more lyghtly the appetite of her fleysshe then the welle-
plesinge of God.

[8] 'The worlde promitteþ temporalle þinges and litel þinges, and he is
served with grete gredynesse. [9] I promitte moste highe þinges and
everlastynge, and dedely mennes hertes waxe slugged. [10] Who serveth
and obeyeþ me in alle þinges as men serveþ the worlde and h[is] lordes?
[11] The sea seide, "Be ashamed, Sydon," and yf þou aske þe cause, here
whye. [12] For a litel prebende, me renneth a longe weye; but for
euerlastinge lyve, vnneþe þe fote is ones lyfte vppe fro the yerþe. [13] A
þinge of lytel | price is bisily sought; oþerwhiles men stryveþ for [o]   f. 76ʳ
peny right shamefully; menne drede not to wery hemselfe nyght and
daie for a veyne þinge [or] for a litel promysse.

(3)   [14] 'But alas, for gode incommutable, for meede inestimable, for
souerayne worshippe, for endeles glorye, men wolle not suffre the
leste werynesse. [15] Be ashamed, þerfore, þou slugged and compleynynge
servante, þat þei ar more redy to perdicion þen þou to lyve. [16] Thei ioye
more at vanite þen þou at trouthe. [17] And loo, oftetymes þey ar
defrauded of her hope; but my promesse deceyveþ no man, ner leveþ
voyde no man þat trusteþ me. [18] That I haue promysed I shal yive; þat I
haue seide I shal fulfille, so þat a man abyde trewe in my love | vnto þe   f. 76ᵛ
ende. [19] I am þe rewardour of alle goode men, and a myghty prevar of
alle deuoute men.

(4)   [20] 'Wryte my wordes in thi herte, and trete hem dylygently; for in
tyme of tribulacion þei shul be ful necessary. [21] That þat þou knowest
not when þou redest, þou shalt trewly knowe in tyme of visitacion. [22] I
am wonte in ii maners to visite my chosen children, that is to seye with
temptacion and consolacion. [23] And every daie I rede hem to lessons, one
in blamynge her vices, anoþer in exhortynge hem to þe encrecinge of

---

5 seithe] DMG, seie C, *Latin* inquit KR   7 sue] folowe G   welleplesinge] wel
plesaunce DMG   8 gredynesse] gredynesse and DMG   9 slugged] slug-
g⟨ussh⟩ D², slugguse G   10 his] DMG, her C, *Latin* eius KR   11 sea
seide] seide see M, *Latin* ait mare KR   12 me] me'n' D², men MG
13 stryveþ] striue⟨n⟩, *tail of þ visible under erasure* D²   o] DMG, a *blotted* C, *Latin* vno
KR   drede] deden M   not to] ⟨not to⟩ D²   or] MG, 'or' D², *om.* C, *Latin* et
KR   15 þou] *om.* M   slugged] slugg⟨ussh⟩ D², slugguse G   16 vanite]
vnyte M, *Latin* vanitatem KR   17 trusteþ] trustyth in G   19 þe] *om.* DM
goode] g'o'ode D²   22 that is to seye] ⟨. . .⟩ 'that is to say' D²
23 in²] *om.* DMG, *Latin* exhortando KR   þe encrecinge of] euerlastyng ⟨. .⟩ D,
euerlastynge MG, *Latin* virtut⟨um incrementa⟩ K, virtutum incrementa R

vertues. [24]He þat hereth my wordes and despiceth hem hath þat shalle deme him in the laste daye.'

A preyer to aske grace of devocyon
Capitulum 4[m]

f. 77[r] | [1]'Mi Lorde God, alle my godes thou arte. [2]A[nd] who am I, þat I dar (5) speke to þee? [3]I am thi moste pouer seruant and an abiecte worme, muche porer and more contemptible þen I can seie or dar seie. [4]Nerthelater, haue mynde þat I am noght, þat I haue noght, þat I am noght worthe. [5]Thou alone arte gode, ryghtwise, and holy. þou maiste alle þinges, þou yivest alle þinges, þou fillest alle þinges, levinge voyde alone þe synner. [6]Bringe to mynde þi miseracions, and fulfille my herte with thi grace, for þou wolte not þat thi werkes shulde be voyde. [7]Howe (6) maie I suffre myselfe in þis wrecched lyve, but yf þou counforte me with thi mercie and thi grace? [8]Lorde, turne not awey thi face fro me,

f. 77[v] prolonge | not thi visitacion, withdrawe not thi consolacion, leste my soule be as yerthe withoute water to þee. [9]Lorde, teche me to do thi wille. Teche me to lyffe worthily and mekely for þee, [10]for þou arte my wysdame, þat knowest me trewly and knewest me or the worlde were made, and or I were borne in the worlde.'

That a man oweþ to be conuersant byfore God
in trouthe and in mekenesse
Capitulum 5[m]

[1]'Sone, go bifore me in trouthe, and in symplicite of herte seke me euer. (1) [2]He þat goþe bifore me in trouthe shal be made sure fro yvel assailinges, and trouthe shal delyuer him fro deceyvours and fro detraccions of

f. 78[r] wykked menne. [3]If trouthe delyuer þee, þou shalte be | veryly free, and þou shalt not recche of mennes veyne wordes.'

4.0 4[m]] 4 M, 4 'iiii' D[2], *Latin* iiii R, *om.* K   I godes] g'o'odes D[2]
2 and] DMG, a C, *Latin* et KR   I[2]] *om.* DMG, *Latin* ut audeam KR
4 nerthelater] neuerþeles DMG   þat I am noght þat I haue noght] *om.* DMG, *Latin*
quia nichil sum nichil habe(o) nichilque valeo K, quia nichil sum nichil habeo nichilque
valeo R   5 gode] go(ode) D[2], god M, *Latin* bonus KR   voyde] *om.* DMG, *Latin*
inanem KR   6 werkes] worke DMG, *Latin* opera KR   10 þat] þou DMG,
Latin qui KR
5.0 5[m]] 5 MG, 5 'v' D[2], *Latin* v R, (iiii) K   I in[2]] *om.* G, *Latin* et in KR
2 assailinges] ass(em)linges D[2], assemlinges MG, *Latin* incursibus KR   fro[3]] *om.*
M   3 veryly] very G, *Latin* vere KR

⁴'Lorde, hit is trewe þat þou seiste, and as þou saiste, so, I beseche þee, mote hit be with me. ⁵Lete thi trouthe teche me, thi trouthe kepe me, and bring me to an helefulle ende. ⁶Lete hir delyver me frome alle yvel affeccion and inordinate lovinge, and I shal goo with thee in grete liberte of herte.'

(2)   ⁷Trouthe seithe, 'I shalle teche þee þoo þinges þat ar right and plesant bifore me. ⁸þenke on þi synnes with grete displesance and moornynge, and neuer accompte þiselfe anyþinge for any goode werkes. ⁹Ueryly, a synnar þou arte, and encombred and wrapped in many passions. ¹⁰Of thiselfe euer þou drawest to noght; sone þou slydest, | sone þou arte overcomen, sone þou arte dissolued.   f. 78ᵛ

(3)   ¹¹'þou hast noþinge wherof þou mayste reioyce þee, but many þinges þou haste whereof þou owest to sette litel bi thiselfe, for þou ʽarteʼ more seke þen þou maiste conceyve. ¹²Wherfore lete noþinge seme grete to þee of alle þinges þat þou doste, noþinge preciouse, noþinge wonderfulle. Lete noþinge appiere to þe worthi any reputacion, for verily, þer is none oþer þinge highe, laudable, ner desirable, but þat is euerlastynge. ¹³And above al þinges euerlastynge, lete trouthe plese þee. ¹⁴Lete euer displese þee þi grettest vilenes and vnworthynesse. ¹⁵Drede noþinge so muche, blame ner flee noþinge so muche, as thi vices and þi synnes, þe whiche oweþ to displese | þee more þenne any worldely harme.   f. 79ʳ

¹⁶'Summe go not clerely bifore me, but þei beþe ladde with a maner of curioste and arrogance, willinge to knowe my secretes and to vnderstande þe highe þinges of God, takynge none heede of hemselfe and of her soule helthe. ¹⁷Thes folke, me beynge displesed, oftetymes fallen into grete temptacions and grete synnes for her pride and her

(4)   curiosite. ¹⁸Drede þe iugementes of God; be agaste of þe wraþe of him þat is almyghty. ¹⁹Discusse not the werkes of þe highest God, but serche thi wikkednesses, in howe many þinges þou haste trespassed and howe many gode dedes þou haste [negligently] lafte.

---

4 and as þou saiste] om. M, Latin sicut dicis KR   5 helefulle] helʽthʼful D², helthfull G   6 lovinge] leving M, Latin dilectione KR   7 bifore] to DMG, Latin coram KR   8 anyþinge] enyþinge ʽgoodeʼ D², enyþinge good MG, Latin aliquid KR   goode] gʽoʼode D²   12 oþer] ʽoʼþere M   highe] heie ʽhereʼ, heie canc. D², here M, om. G, Latin altum KR   desirable] desiderable DMG   þat] that þat G   12–13 euerlastynge and] om. G, Latin eternum KR   14 grettest] gret DMG, Latin maxima KR   vilenes] vilones M   15 þe] om. G   16 beþe] be(e) D², be M   a] all DMG, Latin quadam KR   ofˡ] DMG, of | of C   none] no G   17 and grete synnes] om. DMG, Latin magnas temptaciones et peccata KR   19 wikkednesses] wickednes DMG, Latin iniquitates KR   gode] gʽoʼode D²   negligently] DMG, om. C, Latin neglexisti KR

²⁰ 'Summe bereþ her deuocion alone in her bokes, summe in ymages, |
f. 79^v summe in outwarde signes and figures. ²¹ Summe hath me in mouþe,
but lytel is in the herte. ²² Ther beþe oþer þat, beynge illumyned in þe
vnderstand[ing]e and purged in affeccion, desiren laborously þinges
euerlastynge; greving hem to here of yerthely þinges, þei serveþ the
necessitees of nature with grete sorowe; ²³ and þees felethe what the
spirite of trouthe spekeþ in hem. ²⁴ For she techeþ hem to despice
yerþely þinges, to love hevonly þinges, to sette no price bi þe worlde,
and daie and nyght to desire hevon.'

Of the wonderfulle effecte of the love of God
Capitulum 6^m

¹ 'I blesse þee, hevonly Fader, þe Fader of my Lorde Ihesu Criste, for (1)
þou haste fouched save to haue mynde of me most pore. ² O Fader of
f. 80^r mercies and | God of alle consolacion, I þanke þee, þat refreysshe[st]
with thi consolacions me þat am vnworthi alle maner counforte. ³ I
blesse þee euer and glorifie þee with þine onely-bigoten Sone and þe
Holy Goste þe Counfortoure into worldes of worldes.

⁴ 'Eya, Lorde God, my holy lover, when þou shalt come into my herte,
alle myne inwardes shal ioye. ⁵ Thou arte my glory and þe exultacion of
my herte; þou arte my hope and my refute in þe day of my tribulacion.

⁶ 'But for I am feble in love and imperfite in vertue, þerfore I haue (2)
neede to be counforted of þee. ⁷ Wherefore visite me, Lorde, oftetymes,
and enfourme with [holy] disciplines. ⁸ Delyuer me frome yvel passions;
hele my herte fro alle inordinate affeccions, þat I, heled inwardely and |
f. 80^v welle purged, mowe be apte to love, myghty to suffre, stable to
perseuere.

⁹ 'Love is a grete þinge, a grete gode in every wise, þat alone maketh (3)
lyght euery hevy þinge and bereþ evonly euery vnevon þinge. ¹⁰ For hit
bereþ burdon withoute burdon, and euery bitter þinge hit makeþ swete

21 mouþe] þere mouth G   is] *om.* G, *Latin* est KR   22 vnderstandinge]
DMG, vnderstande C, *Latin* intellectu KR   24 she] he DMG
    6.0 6^m] vi DMG, *Latin* vi R, ⟨quin⟩tum K   1 haste fouched save] vouchid saaf M,
vouch⟨ist⟩ saaf D², vouchist saue G, *Latin* dignatus es KR   of²] on DMG
2 mercies] meries M, *Latin* misericordiarum KR   þat¹] þat ʻþou' D², þat þou MG,
Latin qui KR   refreysshest] G, refressh⟨ist⟩ D², refreysshed CM, *Latin* recreas KR
3 þe²] *om.* G   4 lorde] my lorde DMG, *Latin* domine KR   5 my refute] my
ref⟨uge⟩ D², succoure G, *Latin* refugium meum KR   7 holy disciplines] G,
disciplines of kunnynge CDM, *Latin* disciplinis sanctis KR   8 frome] fro myn
DMG

and savorye. [11] The noble love of Ihesu stireþ to do grete þinges and euer entiseþ to desire more perfite þinges. [12] Love wol be above, and not reteyned with any lowe þinges. [13] Love wol be free and alyene from alle worldely affeccion, leste his inwarde byholdinge be lette, leste he be wrapped inne and encombred by any temporal comodite, or falle vnder by any incomodite. [14] Ther is noþinge swetter þen love, noþinge | strenger, noþinge higher, noþinge bradder, noþinge more iocunde, noþinge fuller, noþinge better, in hevon ner in yerthe; for love is bore of God, ner hit may not reste but in God above alle creatures.

  f. 81ʳ

(4)   [15] 'The lover flyeþ, renneþ, and is gladde; h[e] is free and h[e] is not holden. [16] [Love] yiveþ alle þinges [for alle þinges] and hit hath alle þinges in alle þinges, for hit resteþ above al þinges in one sovereyne gode, of whome alle gode floweþ and procedeþ. [17] Hit lokeþ not to the yiftes, but converteþ him to the yiver above alle godes.

[18] 'Love oftetymes canne no mesure, but is feruent aboue alle mesure. [19] Love feleþ no burdone, hit acompteþ no laboures, hit desireth more þen hit may atteygne, [20] hit pleyneþ never of impossibilite, for | hit demeþ hi[t]selfe myghty to alle þinges, and alle þinges to be lyefulle to hit. [21] Hit is vailante þerfore to alle þinges, [and] hit fulfilleþ manye þinges and bryngeþ hem to effecte, [22] where he þat loveþ not faileþ and

  f. 81ᵛ

(5) lythe stille. Love wakeþ, and sleping hit slepeth not, love weryed is not wery, and love arted is not coarted, hit fered is not troubled, but as a queke flaume and a brennynge bronde he barsteþ vpwarde and passeþ surely. [23] He þat loveþ knoweþ what þis voice crieþ: [24] a grete crye in the eres of God is þat brennynge affeccion of the soule þat seithe, "My God, my love, þou arte alle myne and I þine!"

(6)   [25] 'Dilate me in love, þat I mowe lerne to taste with þe inwarde mouthe of my herte howe swete | hit is to love, and in love to melte and to swymme. [26] Be I holden with love, goynge above myselfe for excellent

  f. 82ʳ

---

12 and not reteyned] and receiued M, ⟨not⟩ receiued D², not receyved G, *Latin* nec . . . retineri KR   13 alyene] ali⟨enat⟩ D², alienate G   14 bore] bor⟨n⟩ D² 15 flyeþ] fl⟨y⟩eþ D², fleeth G   he¹] ⟨he⟩ D², hit CM, *om.* G   he²] ⟨he⟩ D², hit CM, *om.* G   not] 'not' D²   16 love] ⟨loue⟩ D², loue G, hit CM   for alle þinges] G, in all þinges DM, *om.* C, *Latin* pro omnibus KR   hit¹] *om.* G   above] *twice, first canc.* D   þinges⁵] þinges for it restiþe M   18 canne no] cannot M, *Latin* modum sepe nescit KR   19 burdone] ⟨bur⟩doon D²   laboures] labour DMG, *Latin* labores KR   20 hitselfe] DMG, himselfe C   and alle þinges] *om.* M, *Latin* quia cuncta sibi posse et licere arbitratur KR   21 and¹] MG, 'and' D², *om.* C, *Latin* et KR   effecte] affecte DM   22 arted] arced M   coarted] coarced M   is³ not] it no M   flaume] flame‖me, *second* me *canc.* D   barsteþ] beistiþe M, *Latin* erumpit KR   24 of god] *om.* M, 'of god' D², *Latin* dei KR   the²] *om.* DG

feruoure and asto[n]yinge. [27] Synge I a songe of love; folowe I the, my love, into heyghte, [28] and lete my soule faile in thi preisinge, iubilynge for love. [29] Motte I love þe more þen myselfe, and not myselfe but for þee, and alle in þee þat verily love þee, as þe lawe of love commaundeþ, shynynge oute of þee.

[30] 'Love is swyfte, pure, holy, iocunde, myry, stronge, paciente, trewe, (7) prudente, longe-abidynge, manly, and never sekinge himself. [31] Where-as any man sekeþ himselfe, þere anone he falleþ fro love. [32] Love is circumspecte, meke, and ryght, not softe, not lyght, not intendinge to

f. 82ᵛ   veyne þinges, sobre, chaste, stable, restefulle, | kepte in alle wittes, deuoute to God and kynde. [33] Loue is subiecte and obediente to prelates, vile and despecte [to himselfe], trustinge and hopinge euer in God, yea when God savoreþ him not, for withoute sorowe me lyveþ not in loue. [34] He þat is not redye to suffre alle þinges and to stande at (8) þe wille of his loved is not worthy to be called a lover. [35] Hit bihoveth þe lover gladly to clyppe to him alle maner harde þinges and bitter þinges for the loved, and not to bowe fro him for any contrary þinges þat happen to falle.'

Of previnge of verie love
Capitulum 7ᵐ

[1] 'Sone, yette arte þou no prudente and myghti lover.'   (1)
   [2] 'Whi, Lorde?'

f. 83ʳ   [3] 'Forasmuche as for litel contrariouste þou failest in | þinges taken and over-gredely sekest consolacion. [4] A stronge lover [standeþ] in temptacions, ner he wol not bylyeve the wyly persuasionz of the enemy. [5] As þou plesest him in prosperyte, so þou displesest him not in aduersite.

   [6] 'A prudent lover considereþ not so muche þe yifte of the louer as þe (2) love of þe yiver. [7] He peyseth more þe affeccion þenne þe value, and

---

26 asto[n]yinge] DMG, astoyinge C, *Latin* stupore KR   28 iubilynge] ⟨ioynge⟩ D², ioynge MG, *Latin* iubilans KR   29 motte I] ⟨lete me⟩ D², lete me G   þat] þat 'I' D², þat I MG, *Latin* qui uere amant KR   33 to himselfe] G, 'to hymself' D², *om.* CM, *Latin* sibi KR   yea] yea and DG, *Latin* eciam K, et R   me lyveþ] me'n' lyu⟨yn⟩ D², men lyuyn MG   34 þe] *om.* DM   35 maner] manere of G the] ⟨his⟩ D², his MG

7.0 7ᵐ] 7 MG, 7 'vii' D², *Latin* vii R, ⟨sex⟩tum K   1 no prudente and myghti] not a miȝty and a prudent DMG   3 litel contrariouste] a litel contrariouste M, a litel contrariou⟨snes⟩ D², a lytell contrariousnes G   4 standeþ] DMG, *om.* C, *Latin* stat KR   wyly] whly M, *Latin* callidis KR   5 plesest] displesist, dis *canc.* G   not] *om.* DMG, *Latin* nec KR   7 peyseth] plesiþe M, *Latin* attendit KR

setteþ alle yiftes farre binethe þe loved. [8] The noble lover resteþ not in the yifte, but in me above alle yiftes.

[9] 'Hit is not þerfore alle loste, þogh sumtyme þou feele not so welle of me and of my seintes as þou woldeste. [10] That gode and swete affeccion, þat þou perceyvest amonge, hit is an effecte of grace presente and a maner of fortaste | of þe hevonly countrey, uppon whom hit is not to   f. 83ᵛ leyne overmuche, for hit goþe and comeþ. [11] A man to fight ayeine þe yvel mevinges of þe soule and to despice þe suggestions of the devel is a token of vertu and of grete merite.

(3)   [12] 'Therfore lete no straunge fantasies brought inne of any matier trouble thee. [13] Kepe a myghti purpose and a right intencion to God. [14] Hit is none illusion þat sumtyme þou arte sodeynly ravysshed in an excesse, and turnest anone ayeine to þe wonte iapes of thi herte. [15] For þoo þou suffreste raþer þen doste, and as longe as þei displese þee and þou wrastelest ayeine, hit is merite and no perdicion.

(4)   [16] 'Knowe welle þat þee enemy laboureþ in | alle wyses to lette þi   f. 84ʳ desire in goode and to make þee voyde fro alle goode exercices, fro worshippinge of seintes, fro mynde of my holy passion, fro profitable þenkynge of thi synnes, fro kepinge of thi herte, and froo sadde purpose of profitinge in vertue. [17] He putteþ inne many yvelle þoughtes, þat he mowe cause in þee werynesse and horroure, and revoke þee fro preyer and holy redynge. [18] Meke confession displeseth him, and if he mowe, he wolle make þee to cesse from Holy Comunion. [19] Bylieve him not, ner take none heede of him, þoghe he oftetymes tende to þee grynnes of deceyte, [20] and impute hit to himselfe whenne he soweþ yvel þinges and vnclene. [21] And seie to him, "Be ashamed, þou vnclene spirite, and goo aweye, wrecche; | þou arte fulle vnclene þat bryngest suche þinges to   f. 84ᵛ myne eres! [22] Goo hennes, þou wikked deceyvoure, þou shalte haue no parte in me; but Ihesus shal be with me as a myghty fyghtter, and þou shalte stande confused! [23] I had lever dye and suffre a[lle] peyne þen consente to þee. [24] Holde þi pees and be stille! I wolle no more here þee, þoghe þou laboure to moleste me never so ofte. [25] God is myne illumynacion and my helthe: whome shal I drede? [26] If batailes be

7 alle] all þe DMG   10 gode] gᐟoᐟode D²   presente] om. DMG, Latin presentis KR   ofᵃ] of a G   leyne] le⟨e⟩ne D²   11 token of vertu] toke . . . . tu blotted D   14 none] noo G   þat] DMG, þat þou arte þat C, Latin quod KR   15 þoo] them G   ayeine] ayen 'hem' D², aȝen hem MG, Latin reniteris KR   16 goode²] gᐟoᐟode D²   18 to] om. G   19 none] noo G   to þee] þe G, Latin tibi KR   20 and¹] ⟨.⟩ D, om. MG   himselfe whenne] himse. . . . han blotted D   21 and¹] ⟨.⟩ D, om. MG   22 hennes] hen⟨s⟩ D²   23 alle] MG, ⟨all⟩ D², any C, Latin omnem KR

ayenis me, my herte shal not be aferde. ²⁷Oure Lorde is my helpar and my redemptoure.''

²⁸'Fight as a goode knyȝht, ²⁹and þoghe sumtyme þou falle þorowe (5) fraylete of fleysshe, resume strengthes more myghty þen þe rather,

f. 85ʳ trustynge on my more large grace, | and be [welle] ware of veyne complacence and pryde, ³⁰for þerby many men be ladde into erroure, and sumtyme þei slyde into a blyndenesse incurable. ³¹Lete hit be to þee into a perpetuel warenesse and mekenesse, þe fallynge of prowde menne presumynge of hemselfe.'

Of grace to be hidde vnder þe warde of mekenesse
Capitulum 8ᵐ

¹'Sone, hit is more profitable and more sure to þee to hyde the grace of (1) deuocion, and not to lyfte þiselfe vppe an highe, not muche speke þerof, ner muche to peyse hit, but raþer to dispise thiselfe and drede leste hit be yiven to þe vnworthy. ²Hit is [not] to clyffe over-towghly to þis affeccion, þat may so sone be turned into the contrary. ³Thenke in grace

f. 85ᵛ howe wrecched and nedye þou were | wonte to be withoute grace.

⁴'Ner þer is not þerin onely spirituel profiting when þou felest grace of consolacioun, but also when þou berest mekely and paciently þe withdrawynge þerof when hit is denyed, so þat þenne þou be not slowe fro study of preyer, ner þat þou lete not slyde aweye vtterly oþer werkes þat þou were wonte to doo, but as þou maiste beste, aftir þine vnderstandinge, gladly do þat in the is, and for no drynesse ner anxiete of mynde be not alle necglygente of thiselfe.

⁵'For þer beþe many to whom, when hit comeþ not as þei wolde, (2) anone þei beþe vnpaciente or slowe. ⁶Mannes wey is not evermore in his owne power, but to God hit is to yive and to counforte when he wolle, |

f. 86ʳ and as muche as he wolle, and to whome he wolle, as hit pleseth hym

27 redemptoure] redemere G   29 þorowe] þough M   þen] þan were G
welle] DG, om. CM, Latin multum precaue KR   31 perpetuel] perpetu⟨all⟩ D²

8.0 hidde] had DMG, Latin occultanda K, occulta R   8ᵐ] 8 MG, 8 'viii' D², Latin
viii R, vii, second i added on line K   1 vppe an] vpon DMG   2 not] DMG, om.
C, Latin non KR   4 þe] þee, second e canc. C   not²] 'not' D¹   were] 'art' D²,
art MG   but²] om. M   maiste beste] ⟨mayste⟩ D², Latin melius potueris KR
alle] ⟨. . .⟩ D, om. MG, Latin totaliter KR   5 vnpaciente] impacient DMG
6 evermore] euer DMG   and as muche as he wolle and to whome he wolle] and to
whome he woll and as muche as he woll G, Latin et quantum vult et cui vvlt KR

and no more. [7] Summe vndiscretly for grace of deuocion haue destruyed
hemselfe, for þei wolde do more þen þei myght, peysinge not þe mesure
of her lytelnesse, but folowinge more þe affeccion of the herte þenne þe
iugemente of reson. [8] And for they presumed gretter þinges þen God
was plesed withe, þerfore þei loste sone grace. [9] Thei were made nedye
and lafte as vile þat had sette her neste in hevon, þat þei, so meked and
made pouer, mowe lerne not to flye in her wynges, but to hope and to
truste vnder my feders.

[10] 'Thei þat as yette beþe newe and vnexperte in þe weye of God, but
if þei be gouerned bi þe counseile of discrete | men, þei mowe sone be
(3) deceyved and hurte. [11] And if þei wolle folowe her owne felynge more
þen bilyeve oþer þat ar exercised, þe ende wol be perylouse, namely if
þei wolle not be withdrawen fro her owne conceyte. [12] Thei þat semeþ
wise to hemselfe suffreþ but seldon to be governed by oþer. [13] Bettir hit
is to savoure but a litelle with mekenes and litel vnderstandinge þenne
grete tresoures of kunnynge with veyne complacence. [14] Bettir hit is þe
to haue litel þenne muche, whereof þou mowe be proude.

[15] 'He doþe not discretely inowe þat yiveþ him alle to gladnesse,
foryetinge his raþer pouerte and þe chaste drede of God, þat dredeþ to
leese grace þat is offred; [16] ner he savoureþ not vertuously inowe, þat in
tyme of | aduersite and any heuynesse hath [him] ouer-desperatly, and
(4) lasse trustyngly on me þenkeþ and feeleþ þen hit bihoveþ. [17] He þat in
tyme of pees wol be over-sure oftetymes in tyme of bataile is founden
deiecte and ferefulle. [18] If þou coudest at alle tymes abide meke and lytel
in thiselfe, and mesure and rewle thi spirite, þoue shuldest not falle so
sone into perile and into offence.

[19] 'Hit is gode counseile þat, the feruoure of spirite conceyved, þou
þenke what is to come, þe lyght goinge aweye; [20] the whiche when hit
happeneþ to falle, þenke ayeinwarde þat þe lyght may come ayeine, the
whiche I haue withdrawen for a tyme to thi warenesse and my glorie.
(5) [21] Suche a prevynge is oftetymes more profitable þen if þou | haddest
plesante þinges at þine owne wille. [22] For merites ar not to be estiemed

f. 86[v]

f. 87[r]

f. 87[v]

---

7 vndiscretly] indiscretly DMG   wolde] om. DMG, Latin voluerunt KR
8 gretter] gr`etter´ D²   9 to³] om. DMG   10 as yette beþe] biþe ȝit DMG
vnexperte] inexperte DMG   þe¹] they G   16 and¹] ⟨or⟩ D², or MG, Latin et
KR   him] DMG, om. C, Latin se gerit KR   ouer-desperatly] ouer dispatly M   on
. . . bihoveþ] ⟨thynkyth or felyth of me þan `it´⟩ behoueþ D², thinkþ or feliþe of me þan it
behoueþe MG   17 he þat in] ⟨for he þat in⟩ D², for he þat in MG, qui tempore
KR   19 gode counseile] g`o´ode D², gode MG, Latin concilium bonum est K, bonum
est consilium R   21 if] om. M, Latin si KR   22 estiemed of þat if] con.,
est⟨ymat⟩ of þat `yf´ D², estymate of þat if G, estiemed of þat CM, Latin ex hoc existimanda
si quis KR

of þat [if] a man hath many visions and consolacions, or elles he be wyse in scriptures or sette in highe degree; but if he be grounded in very mekenes and fulfilled with diuine charite, if he seke in alle þinges purely and holy the worshippe of God, yf he accompte himselfe as nought and despise himselfe in trouthe and ioye more to be despised and made lowe of oþer þenne to be worshipped, þere is merite and matier of hope.'

Of vile estimacion of himselfe in the sight of God
Capitulum 9ᵐ

[1] 'I shalle speke to my Lorde, þoghe I be duste and ashon. [2] If I acompte (1) myselfe more, loo, þou standest ayeine me, and my wikkednesses bereþ
f. 88ʳ wit|tenesse ayenis me, and I may not seie naye. [3] But and I vilyfie myselfe and bringe me to noght and fayle fro alle maner propre reputacion, and make meselfe duste, as I am, thy grace shal be merciful to me, and þi lyght [nyghe] to my herte; and alle maner estimacion, be hit never so litel, shal be drowned in the valey of my noghttynesse and shal perisshe for ever. [4] There þou shewest me myselfe, what I am, what I was, whither I bicame, þat I am noght and knewe not þereof. [5] If I be lafte to myselfe, loo, I am noght and alle infirmite. [6] If þou biholde me sodeynly, anone I am made stronge and am fulfilled with a newe ioye. [7] And a wonder þinge þat I am so sodeynly lyfte vppe and so be[ni]gly
f. 88ᵛ clypped of þee, þat with myne owne | weyght am euer borne downe lowe.

[8] 'This doþe thi love, freely goinge byfore me and helpinge me in so (2) many nedes and kepinge me fro grevouse periles and delyueringe me, [as] I may trewly seie, from yvels oute of noumbre. [9] I in myslyving loste

22 in²] in a G   yf] ⟨i⟩f, y visible under erasure D²
9.0 9ᵐ] 9 MG, 9 'ix' D², Latin ix R, viii, last i added on line K   2 ayeine] ayenst
DMG   and my wikkednesses bereþ wittenesse ayenis me and] om. M, Latin et dicunt
testimonium verum iniquitates mee KR   wikkednesses] wickednesse DG   and²] om.
DG, Latin nec KR   3 but] om. DMG, Latin si autem KR   vilyfie] vil⟨i⟩fie D²
meselfe] me DMG   þi lyght nyghe] con., 'þi lyȝte nye', þi lyȝte canc. D², þi lyght C, liȝt
MG, Latin vicina cordi meo lux tua KR   4 what¹] what þat M   whither I
became þat] ⟨and fro whens I⟩ come ⟨for⟩ D², and fro whens I come for MG, Latin et quo
deueni KR   knewe not þereof] knewe ⟨not myself⟩ D², knowe not myself M, knewe not
myself G, Latin nesciui KR   5 loo] lo 'ȝit' D², lo ȝit MG   alle] al 'in' D², al in
M, Latin tota infirmitas KR   7 benigly] DMG, beingly C, Latin benigne KR
8 as] MG, ⟨as⟩ D², þat C, Latin ut KR   9 I in myslyving] in mysliuyng M, I n⟨.⟩
mysliuyng 'I', n altered from in D², in myslyvyng y G, Latin me siquidem male viuendo R,
me siquidem male amando K

bothe þee and me, and in sekinge þee alon and in purely lovynge þee, I
founde boþe þee and me, and þorowe love I brought myselfe more
depely to nought. ¹⁰For þou, m[o]ste swete, doste with me above alle
maner merite and above þat þat I dare hope or preye.

¹¹'Blessed be þou, my God! For þoghe I be vnworthi alle godes, yette
þi noblesse and infinite godenesse cesseth not yea to do welle to þe
(3) vnkynde and farre turned aweye | fro thee. ¹²Conuerte vs, Lorde, to þee,   f. 89ʳ
þat we mowe be meke, kynde, and deuoute; for thou arte oure helthe,
oure vertue, and oure strengthe.'

That alle þinges are to be referred to God as to the laste ende
Capitulum 10ᵐ

(1) ¹'Sone, I owe to be thi laste and þi souerayne ende, if þou desire verily
to be blisfulle. ²Of and þorowe þis intencion shal be purged þine
affeccion, þat is oftetymes yvel bowed adowne to hitselfe and to
creatures. ³For if þou seke thiselfe in anyþinge, anone þou failest in
thiselfe and waxest drie. ⁴Wherfore to me referre alle þinges principally,
for I hit am þat haue yiven alle þinges. ⁵Considere alle þinges as
wellynge of þe higheste and moste souereyne gode; and | þerfore [þei] ar   f. 89ᵛ
to be reduced to me as to here original bigynnynge.

(2) ⁶'Of me litel [and] grete, pouer and riche draweþ queke water as of
the welle of lyve; and þei þat serueþ me willyngly and gladdely shul
receyve grace for grace. ⁷But he þat haue glory withoute me or be
delited in any private gode shal neuer be stabilysshed in veri ioy ner
delited in herte, butte shal be lette in many wises and angwysshed.
⁸Therfore þou oweste to as[c]ryve to thiselfe no maner of gode, ner
arette not thi vertue to any man, but al to God, withoute whome man
hath nought.

⁹'I yaue alle, and I wol haue alle ayeine, 'and with [grete] districcion I

9 sekinge] seging M   I²] and M   10 moste] DMG, muste C, *Latin* dulcissime
KR   doste] do'o'st D²   merite] merites, -es *abbreviation added on line* D², meritis
MG, *Latin* meritum KR   11 godes] go'o'des D²   noblesse] nobl'n'esse D²,
nobilnes G   þe] *con.*, þee C, me DMG, *Latin* benefacere eciam ingratis et longe a te
auersis KR   12 helthe] helpe DMG, *Latin* salus KR
10.0 10ᵐ] 10 MG, 10 'x' D², *Latin* x R, i(x)iii, *first* i *added on line*, iii *canc.* K
1 thi] þe M, þ(y) D²   2 of] *om.* DMG   adowne] dovn DMG   hitselfe] hirself
DMG, *Latin* affectus tuus . . . ad se ipsum . . . incuruatus KR   3 in thiselfe] *om.*
G   4 hit am] am he G   5 þei] DMG, *om.* C   6 and¹] DMG, *om.* C,
Latin et KR   8 ascryve] DMG, astryve C   arette] erette G   9 grete] G, *om.*
CDM, *Latin* magna KR

require þankynges'. ¹⁰This is trouþe, wherby is chaced awey þe vanite (3)
of glorie. ¹¹And if hevonly grace and verie charite entree inne, þere shal |
f. 90ʳ be none envye ner contraccion of herte, ner private love shal not ocupye
hit. ¹²For diuine charite overcomeþ alle þinges and dilateþ alle myghttes
of the soule. ¹³If þou savoure aright, þou shalte ioye alone in me, `þou
shalt trust alone in me', for þer is no man gode but God alone, þat is to
be preysed above alle þinges and to be blessed in alle þinges.'

That the worlde despysed hit is myry and swete to serue God
Capitulum 11ᵐ

¹'Nowe, Lorde, I shal speke ayeine, and kepe no silence. I shal seie in (1)
the eres of my God, my Lorde, my Kynge þat is on highe, "O Lorde,
howe grete is the multitude of thi swettennesse to hem þat drede þee!"
f. 90ᵛ ²But what arte þou to þi lovers? What to hem þat serve þee | with alle
her hertes? ³Verily the swettennesse of thi contemplacion þat þou
graunteste to thi lovers is vnspekable. ⁴Hereinne þou shewdest moste
þe swetnesse of thi charite, þat when I was not, þou madest me, and
whenne I erred fro þee, þou laddest me ayeine, for I shulde serve þee,
and þou commaundest me to love þee.

⁵'O þou welle of euerlastynge love, what shal I seie of þee? ⁶Howe (2)
may I foryete þee, þat fouchest save to haue mynde on me, yea, aftir þat
I failed and perisshed? ⁷Thou haste done mercie with thi seruant above
alle hope, and hast shewed grace and frenshippe above alle merite.
⁸What shal I yelde þee ayeine for þis grace? ⁹Hit is not yiven to alle þat,
f. 91ʳ alle þinges forsaken, þei renonce þe worlde and take a re||ligiouse lyve.
¹⁰Wheþer is þat a grete þinge þat I serue þee, `siþe euery creature is
bonde to serve the'? ¹¹Hit oweþ not to seme me a grete þinge to serve
þee, but rather þis appiereþ to me grete and wonderfulle, þat þou

---

11 none] noo G   12 alle²] all þe DMG   13 þou shalt trust alone in me] om.
DMG, Latin in me solo ⟨sper⟩abis K, in me solo sperabis R   gode] go`o´de D²
11.0 capitulum 11ᵐ] capitulum 11 M, capitulum 11 `xi´ D², xi G, Latin xi R, capitulum
ix, i canc. K   1 my²] ⟨m⟩y D²   4 hereinne] theryn G, Latin in hoc
KR   shewdest] shewist DMG, Latin ⟨ostendisti⟩ K, ostendisti R   for] ⟨þat⟩
D²   7 thou] ⟨t⟩hou D²   above] and boue M, Latin ultra KR   8 what
shal I yelde þee ayeine] ⟨. . . .⟩ what ȝelde I þe ayen D, what ȝelde I þe ayen M, what shall y
yelde ayen to the G   9 þei renonce] ⟨ande⟩ ren⟨ouncyd⟩ D², and renounce M, and
renouncyng G, Latin seculo renunicent KR   and] to G, Latin et KR   10 siþe
euery creature is bonde to serve the] om. M, Latin cum omnis creatura tibi seruire tenetur
R, cui omnis creatura seruire tenetur K   11 me¹] to me G

fouchest save to receyve ˋtoˊ thi servant me so pouer and so vnworthi,
and to one me to thi welbiloved seruantes.

(3)   ¹²ʻLoo, alle þinges þat I haue and with þe whiche I serue [þee] ar
þine. ¹³Nerthelater, in contrarie wise þou serueste me raþer þenne I
thee. ¹⁴Loo, heuon and yerþe, þat þou haste made vnto mannes seruice,
ar redy, and euerie daye dothe þat þou commaundest hem. ¹⁵And þat is
litelle, but over þat þou haste ordeined also aungels into mannes
ministerie. ¹⁶But hit passeþ alle þees, þat þou thiselfe vouchest save
to serue manne, and madest promysse | to yive þiselfe to him.   f. 91ᵛ

(4)   ¹⁷ʻWhat shal I yive þee for alle þees þousandes of goodes? ¹⁸Wolde
God I myght serve þee alle [þe] daies of my lyve! ¹⁹Wolde God at þe
leste I myght suffice to do þe worþi seruice one daie! ²⁰Verily þou arte
worthi alle maner seruice, alle worshippe, and euerlastynge preysinge.
²¹Uerily þou arte my Lorde, and I thi pouer seruante, þat am bounden
with alle my myght to serue þee, and never be wery of thi preysinges.
²²Thus I wolle and þus I desire, and what lakkeþ me, vouche þou save to
fulfille. ²³Hit is a grete worshippe and a grete glory to serve þee and to
sette alle þinges at no price for þee. ²⁴For þei þat willyngly subdueþ
hemselfe to thi moste holy seruice shul haue grace, and they þat for thy |
love putteþ aweye fleysshely delectacion shul finde þe consolacion of þe f. 92ʳ
Holy Goste. ²⁵Thei shul gete liberte of mynde [þat] entreþ into streyte
lyve and takeþ none hiede of no worldely cure.

(5)   ²⁶ʻO, the acceptable and the iocunde seruice of God, whereby a man
is verily made free and holye! ²⁷O, the holy state of religiouse servage,
þat makeþ man evon to aungels, plesante to God, fereful to fendes, and
commendable to alle Cristen menne! ²⁸O, the seruice to be clypped and
euer to be desired, whereby the highest and the souereyne gode is
deserved and ioye goten, þat shal dwelle withoute ende!ʼ

11 fouchest save] vouche saf DM   one] ⟨oo⟩ne D²   12 þe] DMG, þee C
þee] DMG, om. C, Latin vnde tibi seruio KR   13 nerthelater] neuerþeles
DMG   15 over] ⟨ouere⟩ D²   also] om. M   16 þees] om. DMG, Latin
hec KR   17 þousandes] þousand M, Latin milibus KR   goodes] gˋoˊodes
D²   18 þe] DMG, om. C   19 þe¹] om. DMG   one] o DMG
24 moste holy] om. DMG, Latin sanctissime seruituti KR   love] most holy loue DMG,
Latin amore KR   shul²] DMG, shulde C, Latin inuenient KR   25 shul] MG,
s⟨hull⟩ D², shulde C, Latin consequentur KR   þat] MG, caret mark D², om. C, Latin
qui KR   none] no G   27 fendes] sendes M, Latin demonibus KR
28 the³] om. DMG

That þe desires of þe herte must be examyned and modered
Capitulum 12ᵐ

f. 92ᵛ ¹'Sone, yette þou muste lerne muche þinge, þe whiche þou | haste not (1) welle lerned as yette.'

²'Lorde, what ar thoo?'

³'That þou putte thi desire holy aftir my wel-willynge and þat þou be not a lover of thyself, but a desirouse folowar of my wille. ⁴Desires oftetymes setteþ þee on fire and hugely styren þee, but considere wheþer þou be meved more for my worshippe or for þine owne profite. ⁵If I be in cause, þou wolte be welle contente whateuer I ordeyne. ⁶And if þer be anyþinge of þine owne sekinge þat is hidde privyly, þat hit is þat letteþ and greveþ. ⁷Beware, þerfore, þat þou leyne not to muche (2) vppon any desire bifore conceyved, me not counseyled, leste þee repente aftirwarde, and þat displese þat furste plesed and þat þou [z]eldeste for f. 93ʳ the bettir. ⁸For not | euery affeccion þat semeþ gode is to be folowed anone, ner contrarie affeccion to be fledde atte furste.

⁹'Hyt is expedient amonge to vse refrenacion, yea in gode studies and desires, leste bi importunite þou falle into distraccion of mynde, leste þou engendre sclaunder in oþer þorowe indisciplinacion, or elles leste þou be sodeynly troubled and falle by withstandinge of oþer. ¹¹And thi (3) fleysshe oweþ so longe to be chastised and constreyned to be sugget in servage, tille hit lerne to be redy to alle þinges, and to be contente with fewe and to delite in symple þinges, and not grucche ayeine suche þinge as is not conveniente therto.'

Of informacion of pacience and fyghtinge ayen concupissencez
Capitulum 13ᵐ

f. 93ᵛ |¹'Lorde, as I see, pacience is right needfulle to me; for manye (1) contrarioustez fallen in þis worlde. ²For howeever I ordeyne for my pees, my lyve may not be withoute bataile and sorowe.'

12.0 12ᵐ] 12 MG, 12 ˋxii' D², xii R, xi, i added on line K   1 lerne] ler`ne'||ne D²
þe] om. G   not welle] ⟨not⟩ D², not MG, Latin necdum bene KR   4 setteþ þee]
set⟨tyn þe⟩ D²   7 counseyled] ⟨councelde⟩ D²   þee] þoue D, Latin peniteat
KR   þat²] þat ˋþat' D², þat þat MG   þat þou²] om. G   zeldeste] con., yeledeste
C, heldist DMG, Latin zelasti KR   8 gode] g`o´ode D²   9 refrenacion]
refrenacion of mynde M, Latin refrenacione KR   gode] g`o´ode D²   importunite]
im⟨portunyte⟩ D²   11 þinge] om. DMG

13.0 ayen] ayenst DMG   concupissencez] concupiscence DMG, Latin concupiscen-
cias KR   13ᵐ] xiii MG, 13 ˋxiii' D², xiii R, xii, second i altered from . K
1 contrarioustez] contrariou⟨snes⟩ D², contrariousnes G

[3] 'So hit is, son, [4] but I wolde not þat þou se[ke su]che pees as lakkeþ temptacions and feleth no contrariouste; but þenne deme þee to haue founde pees, when þou arte haunted in diuerse temptacions and preved
(2) in many contrarioustez. [5] If þou seie þat þou maiste not suffree many þinges, howe wolte þou þenne suffre þe fire of purgatorye? [6] Of ii yvels þe lasse is ever to be chosen. [7] Wherfore þat þou mowe escape tormentes þat ar to come, studie to suffre evonly for God presente yvels.

[8] 'What trouest þou þat men | of þis worlde suffre nought or litel? f. 94ʳ [9] Naye, þou shalte not fynde þat, þoghe þou seke moste delicate menne. [10] "But þei haue," þou saiste, "many delectacions and they folowe her owne delectacions, and þerfore þei peise litel her tribulacions." [11] Be hit so, so þat þeie haue what þei wolle. But howe longe hopeste þou hit
(3) shalle endure? [12] Loo, þei þat ar haboundante in þis worlde shulle faile as the smoke, and þere shal be no remembrance of þe ioyes passed. [13] And yette whiles þei lyve, þei reste not in hem withoute bitternesse, werynesse and drede. [14] For oftetymes of þe same þinge whereof þei conceyve delectacion þei receyve payne and sorowe. [15] Hit falleth to hem rightwisly þat for þei inordinatly sekeþ delectacions and folowe | hem, f. 94ᵛ
(4) þat þei withoute confusion fulfille hem not. [16] O, howe shorte, howe inordinate, howe false, howe fowle þei alle be! [17] Nerthelater, for drunkenesse and blyndenesse þeye vndirstande not, but as dumme bestes renneþ into dethe of soule for a litel delectacion of corruptible lyve.

[18] 'Wherfore þou, sone, go not aftir þi concupiscences, but turne awey fro þine owne wille. Delite þee in God, and he shalle yive þee þe
(5) peticions of þi herte. [19] Loo, yf þou wolte verily be delyted and more haboundantly be counforted of me, loo in contempte of alle worldely þinges and in kuttynge aweye of alle lower delectacions shal be thi blessinge, and plentuouse consolacion shal be yeldon to thee. [20] And the more þat þou with|drawest þee fro consolacion of alle creatures, þe f. 95ʳ swetter and þe myghtier counfortes þou shalte fynde in me.

[21] 'But furste þou shalt not come to þees withoute tristesse and

4 wolde] wol DMG   seke . . . lakkeþ] *con.*, seche pees as lakkeþ C, seche pes and lacke DMG, *Latin* talem querere pacem que temptacionibus careat KR   feleth] fele DMG, *Latin* aut contraria non senciat KR   contrariouste] contrariou(snes) D², contrariousnes G   contrarioustez] contrariousnes G   5 þat] *om.* M   10 but] ⟨. .b⟩ut D², but þat M   and they folowe her owne delectacions] *om.* DMG, *Latin* et proprias delectaciones sequuntur R, ⟨et proprias⟩ sequuntur voluntates K   12 worlde] worlde here DMG   15 þat for þei] for þei þat M, *Latin* ut quia KR   and] and so M, *Latin* et KR   17 nerthelater] neuerþeles DMG   as] 'as' D² 19 þinges] *om.* DM   21 tristesse] sorow MG, ⟨sorwe⟩ D²

laboure of stryvinge. ²²The olde vsed custume wol withstande, but hit shal be overcomen bi a better custume. ²³The fleisshe wolle grucche ayein, but hit shal be refreyned with the feruoure of spirite. ²⁴The olde serpente wol stirre þe and bringe þee to bitternesse, but with preier he shal be dryven awey and with profitable laboure his comyng inne shal be stopped.'

Of obedience of a meke suggette by ensample of Ihesu Capitulum 14ᵐ

¹'Sone, he þat laboureþ to withdrawe him fro obedience, he withdraweþ (1) himselfe fro grace, and | he þat sekeþ to haue private þinges leseþ the comune þinges. ²He þat 'frely and' gladly subdueþ not himselfe to his souereyne, hit is a token þat his fleysshe obeyeþ not him perfitely yette, but oftetymes kykeþ ayein and gruccheth. ³Lerne þerfore to obeye þi souereyne swyftely, yf þou wille þat þi fleyssshe shal obeye þee. ⁴For þe vtter enemye is sonner overcome if the inner be destruyed. ⁵Ther is not a more grevouse ner a worse enemy of þe soule þen þou thiselfe not welle acording to the spirite. ⁶Hit bihoveþ þee in alle wise to take vppon the very despysinge of thiselfe, yf þou wolte prevayle ayein fleysshe and blode.

⁷'But forasmuche as þou lovest inordinatly thiselfe, þerfore þou (2) dredeste to resigne thiselfe fully to þe wille | of oþer. ⁸But what grete þinge is þat, if þou, þat arte but asshon and nought, subdue þiselfe to

f. 95ᵛ (left margin, opposite second paragraph)

f. 96ʳ (left margin, opposite last paragraph)

23 ayein] *canc.* D, *om.* MG, *Latin* remurmurabit KR   24 inne] *om.* DMG

14.0 ihesu] our lord ihesu DMG, *Latin* (ihesu christi) K, ihesu christi R   14ᵐ] xiiii MG, 14 'xiiii' D², *Latin* xiiii R, (xiii) K   1 withdrawe him] wiþdrawe himself DMG withdraweþ] dwithdrawiþe *sic* M   þat²] 'þat' D²   2 yette] 2 is not] nys M, (.)ys 'not' D²   6 the] the þe G   fleysshe] 'þi' flesshe D², þi flesshe MG 7–15 fully... despisinge] *om.* M, fully to þe will 'of other' D², fully to the wylle of other. ⁸But what gret þinge is it to the, þat arte but duste and nouȝte, if þoue for God subdue the to man, when Y, almyȝty and moste hyȝe, þat haue create all þinges of nouȝte, mekely for the haue subdued me to man? ⁹I was made mekist and lowest of all, þat þrowhe my mekenes þoue shuldist ouercome thy pryde. ¹⁰Lerne, þoue duste, to obey. Lerne, þoue erth and slyme, to meke the, and to bowe the vndyr þe fete of all. ¹¹Lerne to breke thyne own wyll, and to geue the to the subieccion of all other. ¹²Stryve ayenst þiself, and suffyr no elacion to lyve in the, but shewe the so subiecte and litel þat all may walke vpon the, and trede the as the fenn of the hyȝeway. ¹³What hast þou, vayn man, to complayne? ¹⁴What mayst þoue, filthy synner, ayensay thy reprevers, which so ofte hast offendid God, and so ofte hast deserued hell? ¹⁵But my mercifull eye hath sparyd þe, for thy soule was preciouse in my sight, þat þoue shuldist knowe my loue and euere for my benefites to be to me kynde, and contynually to geue the to true subieccion and mekenes, and paciently to suffyr thyne owne contempte G

man for God, sithe I, almyghty and highest, þat made alle þinges of nought, mekely made me sugget to man for þee, ⁹and was made mekest of alle and lowest, for þou shuldest overcome thi pride with my mekenesse? ¹⁰Lerne to obeye, þou duste! Lerne to meke thiselfe, þou yerthe and cleye, and to bowe thyselfe vnder the feete of alle! ¹¹Lerne to

(3)　breke þine owne willes, and to yive þe vnder subieccion of alle. ¹²Be wrothe ayeins thiselfe, and suffre no [b]ol[n]ynge pride to lyve in the, but shewe þe 'so' sugget and so litel þat al men mowe goo over þee and [t]rede vppon the as vppon myre of the streete.

¹³'What haste þou, veyne man, | to compleyne? ¹⁴Thou foule synnar,　f. 96ᵛ what haste þou to answer þi reprevars, þat so oftetymes haste offended thi God, and so oftetymes deserved helle? ¹⁵But myne yen hathe spared þee, for thi soule was preciouse in my sight, for þou shuldest know my love and be ever kynde to my benefaytes, and þat þou shuldeste yive thiselfe continuly to very subieccion by mekenes, and bere paciently þine owne despisinge.'

Of the pryve iugementes of God, leste we [be] lyfte vppe
into pryde for goode þinges
Capitulum 15ᵐ

(1)　¹'Lorde, þou þondrest over me thi iugementes and alle toshakest alle my bones for drede and tremulynge, and my soule is gretely affrayed. ²I stande astonyed and con|sider þat hevons ar not clene in thi biholdinge.　f. 97ʳ ³If þou foundest shrewdenes in aungels and sparedest hem not, what shal falle of me? ⁴Sterres felle fro hevon, and I, duste, what presume I? ⁵Whos werkes semed laudable felle to lowest þinges, and þei þat eete brede of aungels, I sawe hem delite hem in swynes draffe.

(2)　⁶'Therefore, Lorde, þer is no surete if þou withdrawe þine hande. ⁷There avayleþ no wisedame, if þou leve þe governance. ⁸There helpeþ no strengthe, if þou cesse to kepe. ⁹There is no chastite sure, if þou

12 bolnynge] con., volowynge C, Latin tumorem K, timorem R　　　trede] con., drede C, Latin conculcare

15.0 of . . . 15ᵐ] ⟨of hyd domys to be consyderyd capitulum xv⟩ D², of hydde domys to be consideryde capitulum xv G, om. M, Latin de occultis dei iudiciis considerandis ne extollamur in bonis xv R, de ⟨occultis dei 'iudiciis' considerandis ne extollamur in bonis capitulum xiiii⟩ K　　　be] con., om. C, Latin extollamur KR　　　1 lorde . . . my²] ⟨lorde þou sowndyst thi domes upon me and shakyst all⟩ 'my' D², lorde þou sowndist þi domys vpon me and shakist al my M, lorde þoue soundyst thy domy's' vpon me and shakyst all my G　　　5 lowest] the lowest G　　　brede of aungels] angels bred G hem²] om. DMG　　　7 þe] þi DMG defende hit not. [10]There avayleþ no kepinge, if thi holy wacchinge be not nyghe. [11]If we be forsaken, we be drowned and perysheþ. [12]And we

f. 97ᵛ be visited, we ar rered vppe and lyveþ. [13]We beeþ vnstable, | but by þe we be confermed. We waxe leuke, but by the we be sette afire.

[14]'O, houe mekely and howe abiectely hit sitteþ me to fele of myselfe! (3) [15]And howe noght to sette by is any gode þat I seme to haue! [16]O, howe depely I owe to submitte meselfe vnder thi depe groundelesse iugementes, Lorde, where I fynde meselfe to be noþinge elles but noght and noght! [17]O weyght vnmesurable, O sea vntransnatable, where I fynde noþinge of meselfe, but alle nought!

[18]'Where is the hydels of glory and worshippe? Where is þe truste conceyved of vertu? [19]Alle veyneglory is swoloed vp in þe depenes of þi iugementes vppon me. [20]What is every fleysshe in thi byholdynge? (4)

f. 98ʳ Wheþer shal cley reioyce hitselfe ayenis him þat makeþ hit? | [21]Howe may he be rered vppe in veyne speche, whos herte is sugget to God in trouthe? [22]Alle þe worlde shalle not rere vppe into pride whom trouthe hath made sugget to himselfe, ner he shalle not be meved bi the mowthes of alle his preysers þat stedefasteþ alle his hope in God. [23]For þei þat speketh in magnifiynge hemselfe, loo, alle ar noght, and þei shulle fayle with the sowne of her wordes. [24]But the trouthe of oure Lorde abydeþ for ever.'

Howe a man shalle stande and seie in everyþinge desirable
Capitulum 16ᵐ

[1]'Sone, seie þus at alle tymes, "Lorde, if hit please þee, be þis þus. (1) [2]Lorde, yf þis be thi worshippe, be þis done in thi name. [3]Lorde, if þou

f. 98ᵛ see hit be expedient and preve hit profitable | to me, graunte me to vse hit to thi worshippe. [4]But yf þou knowe þat hit be noyouse to me or not vaylable to [þe] helthe of my soule, take suche a desire fro me."

12 and¹] and 'if' D², if G   ar] are, a *altered from* b M   13 afire] (a) fyre D², on fire M   14 mekely and howe] and DM, mekely and G, *Latin* quam humiliter et abiecte KR   sitteþ] fittiþ D   16 meselfe¹] myself DMG   meselfe² to be] myself DMG, *Latin* me esse K, esse R   elles] elle(s) D²   17 vntransnatable] intransnatable DMG   meselfe] myself DMG   18 hydels] 'lurkynge' hidels, hidels *canc.* D², lurkyng G, *Latin* latebra KR   glory] ale glori M   19 in] *twice* M   23 alle] *om.* DMG, *Latin* omnes KR   24 oure] 'oure' D²

16.0 and seie] *om.* DMG, *Latin* ⟨ac dicendum⟩ K, ac dicendum R   desirable] desiderable DMG   16ᵐ] xvi MG, 16 'xvi' D², *Latin* xvi R, ⟨xv⟩ K   2 done in] do'on' ⟨in⟩ D²   4 yf] and G   þe helthe of] *con.*, helthe of C, helpe M, 'þe' helpe D², the help of G, *Latin* anime mee saluti KR

⁵ 'For not every desire commeþ of the Holy Goste, yea, þoghe hit seme to man ryght and goode. ⁶ Hit is harde ʽto' deme of trouthe wheþer a goode spirite or an yvel spirite stirre þee to desire þat or þat, or wheþer þou be meved of þine owne spirite. ⁷ Many in the ende ar deceyved þat in þe bygynnynge semed brought inne with a goode spirite.

(2)   ⁸ 'Wherfore with drede of God and mekenes of herte is to be desired and asked what desirable þinge þat comeþ to mynde; principally for with propre resignacion alle þinge is to be commytted to me, seiynge, ⁹ "Lorde, þou knowest howe hit | is beste: be hit þus or þus, as thou   f. 99ʳ wolte. ¹⁰ Yive what þou wolte, howe muche þou wolte, and when þou wolte. ¹¹ Do with me as þou wolte and as hit moste pleseth þee, and as is moste þi worshippe. ¹² Putte me where þou wolt, and do with me freely in alle þinges. ¹³ I am in thi handes: turne me and ayeine turne me rounde aboute. ¹⁴ Loo, I thi servante, redie to alle þinges, for I desire not to lyve to myselfe, but to þee; and þat, wolde God, myght be perfitely and worthely!"'

A preyer to doo the wille of God
Capitulum 17ᵐ

(3)   ¹ 'Moste benigne Ihesu, graunte me thi grace, þat hit mowe be with me and laboure with me, and abide with me to the ende. ² Graunte me ever to wille and desire þat is moste acceptable to þee and moste | derely   f. 99ᵛ pleseþ þee. ³ Thi wille be my wille, and motte my wille ever folowe þi wille and accorde to hit in alle wyse. ⁴ Be þer to me one willing and not willynge with þee, and lette me not wille ner not wille, but þat þou wolte or wolte not.

(4)   ⁵ 'Graunte me to die fro alle þinges þat ar in this worlde, and for þee to love to be despised and not knowen in þis worlde. ⁶ Graunte me above alle þinges desired to reste in þee and to pese my soule in þee. ⁷ Thou

5 seme] semyth G   6 a] the G   goode] ʽgood' D²   an] þe G   spirite²]
om. DMG   to²] om. G   7 goode] gʽoʼode D²   8 wherfore with] wher
. . . . . blotted D   desirable] desiderable DM, desyrefull G   9 wolte] wolt and
whan þou wolt DMG, Latin volueris KR   10 when þou wolte] om. G, Latin et
⟨quando⟩ vis K, et quando vis R   11 as³] as it DMG   13 me¹] om. M
17.0 17ᵐ] xvii MG, 17 ʽxvii' D², Latin xvii R, om. K   2 wille] do þy wille DMG,
Latin desiderare et velle K, desiderare R   3 motte my wille] my wyll mut G, mote
my w. . . blotted D   4 ner not wille] om. G, Latin nec aliud posse velle aut nolle
KR   5 love to] om. G, Latin amare contempni K, amari contempni R

arte very pees of herte; þou arte onely reste. Oute of þe alle þinges ar harde and oute of quiete. ⁸In þis pees þat is in þee, one souereyne, euerlastynge gode, motte I slepe and reste. Amen.'

That verie solace is to be sought in God alone
Capitulum 18ᵐ

f. 100ʳ | ¹'Whateuer I mowe þenke or desire to my solace, I abide hit not here, (1) but hereaftir, ²that if I alone had alle the solaces of þe worlde and myght vse alle þe delices, hit is certeyne þat þei mowe not longe endure. ³Wherfore, my soule, þou maiste not plenarly be counforted ner perfitely be refresshed, but in God, þe consolacion of pouer and þe vndertaker of meke men. ⁴Abide a litel while, my soule; abide Goddes promysse, and þou shalt haue haboundance of alle godes in hevon.

⁵'If þou coveite þees presente þinges over-inordinatly, þou shalte lese þoo everlastinge hevonly þinges. ⁶Lete temporal þinges be in vse, and everlastinge þinges in desire. ⁷Thou maiste be filled with no temporal f. 100ᵛ gode, for þou were not made | to freuyshe þoo. ⁸Yea, þoghe þou (2) haddeste alle godes þat ar made, þou maiste not be blysfulle. But in God, þat made alle þinges, shal be thi blysse and thi felicite, not suche as is sene and preysed of folyshe lovers of þis worlde, but suche as gode, trewe Cristen men abideþ, and spirituel men fortasteþ amonge, whos conversacion is in heven. ⁹Ueyne hit is and shorte alle mannes salace, ¹⁰but þat is blysfulle salace and trewe þat is perceyved withinforþe of trouthe.

¹¹'The deuoute man bereþ euer with him his counfortoure Ihesu and seithe to him, ¹²"Be nyghe to me, Lorde, in euerie place and everye tyme." ¹³Be þis my consolacion, gladly to wille to lakke alle mannes solace. ¹⁴And if thi consolacion lakke, þi wille and iuste probacion be to f. 101ʳ me as | a sovereyne solace. ¹⁵For þou shalt not perpetuelly be wrothe, ner þou shalt not þreten euerlastyngly.'

7 oute of quiete] oute of quietnes G, ⟨withowte⟩ quiete`nes´ D² 8 souereyne] souerayne `and´ D², souerayne and MG gode] g`o´ode D²

18.o verie] DMG, everie C, Latin verum KR 18ᵐ] xviii MG, 18 `xviii´ D², Latin xviii R, xvi, i added on line K 2 if] om. M, Latin si KR 4 godes] g`o´odes D² 6 þinges²] þinges be M 7 maiste] maist not DMG 8 godes] g`o´odes D² is¹] vs M of²] os M gode] g`o´ode D² trewe] om. M, Latin fideles KR abideþ] abidi(n) D² fortasteþ amonge] fortasti(n) amonge, amonge canc. D², fortasten G, Latin pregustant interdum KR 12 to me lorde] my lorde to me M

That alle maner bysines is to be sette in God
Capitulum 19ᵐ

(1) ¹'Mi sone, suffre me to do with þee what I wolle. I knowe what is moste
expediente to þee. ²þou þenkest as a man; þou felest in many þinges as
mannes affeccion studieþ.'

³'Lorde, hit is trewe þat þou seiste. ⁴þi bisinesse is more for me þen
any cure þat I canne bere for myselfe. ⁵He standeþ over-casuely and
lyke to falle þat casteþ not alle his bisynes into þee. ⁶So þat my wille
be right and abide stedefaste in þee, do of me what pleseþ þee. ⁷For
(2) hit may not be but gode, whateuer þou do of me. ⁸If þou wolte þat I
be in darkenes, | blessed mote þou be; and if þou wolte þat I be in   f. 101ᵛ
lyght, yeet blessed mote þou be. ⁹If þou vouchesave to counforte me,
blessed mote þou be; and if þou wolte þat I be troubled, be þou euer
ilyke blessed.'

¹⁰'Sone, so þou muste stande if þou desire to go with me. ¹¹þou
owest to be as redy to suffre as to ioye. ¹²As gladly þou owest to be nedy
and pouer as ful and riche.'

(3) ¹³'Lorde, I shal gladdely suffre for þee whateuer þou wolt come
vppon me. ¹⁴I wolle indifferently receyve of thi hande gode and yvel,
swete and soure, glad and sorowful, and for alle þinges þat falleþ to me
yif þee þankynges. ¹⁵Kepe me fro alle maner synne, and I shal not drede
deþe ner helle. ¹⁶Whiles þat þou þrowe me not awey for euer, | ner putte   f. 102ʳ
me not oute of þe boke of lyve, hit shal not noye me whateuer
tribulacion come to me.'

That temporal miseries bi ensaumple of Criste ar to be borne
Capitulum 20ᵐ

(1) ¹'Sone, I came downe from hevon for þi helthe. I toke vppon me thi
miseries, not of nede but for charite, for þou shuldest lerne by
pacience to suffre temporalle myseries not grucchingly. ²For fro þe
houre of my birþe into the daie of my goynge oute of þis worlde in

---

19.0 19ᵐ] 19 MG, 19 ʿxix' D², *Latin* xix R, xvii, *second* i *added on line* K   1 wolle]
wol⟨e⟩ D², wolde MG   9 me] ʿme' G   euer] *om.* G   ilyke] alike DMG
blessed²] plesid M, *Latin* benedictus KR   10 desire] desirest DMG   11–20.6
be . . . and²] *om.* D (*leaf missing between pp. 137 and 138*)   14 sorowful] sorowe G,
Latin triste KR

20.0 20ᵐ] 20 MG, *Latin* xx R, xviii, *last* i *altered from* . K   1 thi] the G, *Latin* tua
KR   of] for MG   2 into] vnto MG

þe crosse [me] lakke[d] never suffringe of sorowes. ³ I had grete lakke of temperal godes; I herde many compleyntes made of me; shames and repreves I susteyned benignely; for benefaites I receyved vnkyndenesse,

f. 102ᵛ for miracles blasfemyes, for | techinges reprehensions and blamynges.'

⁴ 'Lorde, for þou were paciente in thi lyve, þereinne fulfillynge þe (2) commaundemente of thi Fader, hit is worþi þat I, moste wrecched synnar, aftir þi wille susteyne myselfe paciently, and þat as longe as þou wolte, þat I bere þe burdon of þis corruptible lyve. ⁵ For if þis lyve be onerouse and hevy, yette bi thi grace hit is fulle meritory, and bi þine ensaumple and þe steppes of thi dedes to the feble and þe seke the more tolerable and the more clere, and muche more consolatory þen hit was sumtyme in the olde lawe, when þe yate of hevon was yette closed and also þe weye more darke, forasmuche as so fewe þat tyme toke any cure to seke the reaume of hevon. And nouþer [þei þat were iuste and to be

f. 103ʳ saved afore þi passion and þe] | dette of holy deþe myght þenne entre into the reaume of heuon.

⁶ 'O, howe grete þankynges am I bounden to yelde to þee, þat hast (3) vouched save to shewe to me and to alle Cristen men þe right weye and þe gode weye to þine everlastynge reaume! ⁷ Thi lyve is oure weie, and by thi holy pacience we go to þe, þat arte oure crowne. ⁸ But if þou haddeste gone afore and taught vs the weye, who wolde haue take any cure to haue folowed? ⁹ Alas, howe many wolde haue abiden alle afarre and byhynde, but if they had biholden þi clere ensaumples! ¹⁰ Loo, [yette] we waxe lewke, herynge of so many signes and [d]octrines. What wolde falle yf we had not so grete a lyght to folowe thee?'

---

2 me lakked] MG, þer lakkeþ me C, *Latin* defuit KR   3 repreves] MG, repreves and repreves C, *Latin* obprobia KR   4 fulfillynge] fulfillinge of M, *Latin* implendo preceptum KR   þe²] þi M   5 þe²] *om.* MG   þei . . . deþe] *con.*, þei þat were iuste and to be saued afore þi passion MG, gode menne þat payed her dette of holy deþe C, *Latin* neque qui 'tunc' iusti erant et saluandi ante passionem tuam et sacre mortis debitum K, neque tunc qui iusti erant saluandi ante passionem tuam et sacre mortis debitum R   reaume] blisse MG, *Latin* regnum KR   6 to yelde to] to geue G, to M, *Latin* teneor referre KR   7 thi¹] thiself and þi M, *Latin* tua KR   8 afore] tofore DMG   10 yette] MG, 'ȝette' D², *om.* C, *Latin* 〈adhuc〉 K, adhuc R   doctrines] DMG, toctrines C, *Latin* 〈doctrinis〉 K, doctrinis R   falle] 'a' falle D², haue fallen G, *Latin* 〈fieret〉 K, fieret R   a] 'a' D²

Of suffrynge of wronges, and | who is preved very pacient   f. 103ᵛ
Capitulum 21 ᵐ

(1) ¹'What is hit þat þou spekeste, sone? ²Cesse thi compleynynge, consideringe my passion and þe passion of oþer seintes. ³For þou haste not yette withstanden vnto shedinge of þi blode. ⁴Lytel hit is þat þou suffrest in comparison of hem þat suffred so grete þinges, so myghtily tempted, so grevously troubled, so manyfolde preved and exercitate. ⁵Hit bihoveþ þe þerfore to bringe to mynde oþeres grevous peynes, þat þou mowe the more myghtily and more esely bere thi smale peynes. ⁶And if þei seme not litel to þee, beware leste þi vnpacience cause þat. ⁷Nerthelater, wheþer þei be smale, wheþer þei be grete, studie to suffre alle paciently.

(2)   ⁸'The better þat þou disposest þee to suffre, the | more wisely þou   f. 104ʳ
doste and þe more þou deserueste and the eslyoure þou shalt bere hit, made redie þerto not sluggedly in herte and by vse. ⁹And seie not, "I may not suffre þis of suche a manne, ner I owe not to suffre suche þinges, for he didde me grete harme and putteþ thinges vppon me þat I nevere þought; but of anoþer I wolle suffre gladdely whatever I shal suffre." ¹⁰Suche a þought is ful folyshe, þe whiche considereþ not the vertue of pacience, ner of whom she is to be crowned, but take[þ] more

(3) hiede of þe persones and of þe offences done to him. ¹¹He is not very pacient þat wolle not suffre but as muche as he wolle and of whom he wolle. ¹²For þe very pacient takeþ none hiede wheþer he suffre of his prelate or of his piere or of his lower, | wheþer of a gode man and an   f. 104ᵛ
holy or he be exerciced of an overthwarte man and an vnworthi; but indifferentlye, whateuer aduersite and howe ofte bi any creature [falleþ to him], alle þat he takethe acceptably of þe hande of God and accompteþ þat as a grete lucre, for noþinge, be hit never so litel, so hit be suffred for God, shal passe withoute merite.

(4)   ¹³'Wherfore be þou spedde and redy to fightynge, if þou wolte haue

---

21.0 21ᵐ] 21 MG, 21 'xxi' D², *Latin* xxi R, ⟨xix⟩ K   1 cesse] cesse of
DMG   3 vnto] to the G   þi] my M   6 vnpacience] impacience
DMG   7 nerthelater] neuerþeles DMG   8 sluggedly] slugg⟨usly⟩ D², sluggusly G   9 putteþ] putti⟨d⟩ D², *Latin* improperat KR   10 takeþ] G, takeþ, þ
added on line D², take CM, *Latin* perpendit KR   done to him] to hym done G
11 and of whom he wolle] *om.* DMG, *Latin* et a quo sibi placuerit KR   12 none] no
G   gode] g'o'ode D²   whateuer] what DMG, *Latin* quantumcumque KR   falleþ
to him] G, 'fallyth to hym' D², *om.* CM, *Latin* ei aliquid aduersi acciderit KR   lucre]
hyre DMG, *Latin* lucrum KR   be³] be not M, *Latin* pro deo tamen passum KR

the victory. [14] Withoute fightynge maist þou not come to þe crowne of pacience. [15] If þou wolte not suffre, þou refusest to be crowned. [16] And if þou desire to be crowned, fight manly, suffre paciently. [17] Withoute laboure me commeþ not to reste, ner withoute fighttinge me comeþ not to victorie.'

f. 105ʳ　　[18] 'Lorde, make possible bi thi grace þat semeþ | me impossible by nature. [19] Thou knowest, Lorde, þat I may suffre litel, and þat I am sone þrowen downe with lytel aduersite. [20] Make, Lorde, þat every exercitacion of tribulacion be to me amiable and for thi name desirable. [21] For to suffre and to be vexed for þee is fulle holsome to my soule.'

Of confession of oure infirmite, and myseryes of þis lyve
Capitulum 22ᵐ

[1] 'I shalle knowleche ayenis myselfe myne vnrightwisnesse; I shalle (1) knowleche to þee myne infirmite. [2] Oftetymes a lytelle þinge þroweþ me downe and maketh me sory. [3] I purpose to doo myghtily, but when a litel temptacion comeþ, I am in grete angwysshe. [4] Otherwhiles of þinge of litel value risethe grevouse temptacion, and whiles I wene meselfe |

f. 105ᵛ　sumwhat sure, for I feele noþinge, I fynde meselfe oftetymes overcomen þorowe a lyght blaste.

[5] 'See þerfore, Lorde, my deieccion and my freylete, knowen to þee on (2) everie side. [6] Haue merci on me oute of the cleye, þat [I] styk not þerynne, ner abide deiecte in eueri side. [7] That hit is þat oftetymes rebukeþ me bifore þee and confoundeþ me, þat I am `so' slydynge and so weyke to withstande passions; [8] and þoghe I falle not fully to consente, yette her vexacion is grevouse and hevy to me, and hit weryeþ me so to lyve daily in stryfe. [9] And þerby is myne infirmite knowen to me, þat abhominable fantasies comeþ muche lightlyer þen þei go aweye.

[10] 'Wolde God, þou moste stronge God of Israel, lover of trewe soules, (3)

f. 106ʳ　þat þou | biholde þe laboure and þe sorowe of thi servante, and be

---

14 fightynge] victory DM, *Latin* certamine KR　　　　maist þou] þoue maist G
17 me¹] me`n′ D², men MG　　　me²] me`n′ D², men G　　　19 litel] a litell G
þrowen] ⟨þ⟩rowen D²　　　20 desirable] desiderable DMG
　　22.0 22ᵐ] 22 MG, 22 `xxii′ D², *Latin* xxii R, x⟨x⟩ K　　　4 of¹] of a G　　meselfe¹]
myself DMG　　meselfe²] myself DMG　　lyght] litel DMG, *Latin* leui KR
6 haue . . . side] *om.* G, *Latin* miserere et eripe me de luto ut non infigar ne⟨.⟩ permaneam
deiectus usquequaque K, miserere et eripe me de luto ut non infigar neque permaneam
deiectus vsquequaque R　　I] DM, *om.* C, *Latin* ut non infigar KR　　　7 þat¹] *om.*
M, *Latin* hoc est quod KR

assistente to him to whateuer þinge he goo. [11] Strengthe me with
heuonly myght, leste þe wolde man, þe wrecched fleisshe not yette
fully sugget to þe spirite, haue the better and þe lordeshipe, ayenis
whom hit bihoveþ to fyght alle the while me lyveþ in þis lyve most
wrecched.

[12] 'Alas, what lyve is þis, whereas lakkeþ never tribulacions and
miseries, where alle þinges ar fulle of grynnes and of enemyes! [13] For
one temptacion or tribulacion goynge awey, another comeþ; yea
sumtyme the furste conflicte yette durynge, oþer many comeþ vppon
vnwares.

(4)   [14] 'And howe may a lyve be loved, having so many bitternessez, sugget
to so many miseries and mischieves? [15] Howe also | is hit called a lyve,   f. 106ᵛ
þat engendreth so many deþes and pestilences? [16] And yette hit is loved
and sought of many to haue her delite þereinne. [17] The worlde is
oftetymes repreved þat hit is fals and veyne, and yette hit is not lyghtly
forsaken, for þe concupiscencez of the fleysshe haue to grete domina-
cion. [18] But summe þinges drawen to love, and summe to despite. [19] To
love þer draweþ desire of the fleisshe, desire of yen, and pride of lyve;
but peynes and miseries folowinge bringeþ forthe hate of þe worlde and
(5)   werynesse. [20] But alas, fals delectacion overcomeþ the mynde yiven to
the worlde, and so hit accompteþ delices to be vnder breres, for she hath
noþer sene ner tasted the swettenesse of God, ner þe inwarde mirthe of
soule.

[21] 'But þei þat despiseþ | perfitely þe worlde and studieþ to lyve to   f. 107ʳ
God vnder holy disciplyne, þe swettenes of God þat is promyssed to
trewe lovers is not vnknowen to hem; and thei see clerely howe
grevously the worlde erreþ and howe diuersly hit deceyveþ.'

---

14 be loved] 'be' beloued D², be beloued M, *Latin* potest amari KR   many] m D
(*tear*)   miseries] series D (*tear*)   mischieves] mysch⟨aunces⟩ D², myschaunses
G   15 also is hit called] *om.* D (*tear*)   many] m D (*tear*)   deþes and
pestilences] lences D (*tear*)   16 loved . . . many] lo D (*tear*)   16–17 þereinne
the worlde is] þer D (*tear*)   17 repreved . . . veyne] repre D (*tear*)   lyghtly . . .
þe] *om.* D (*tear*)   concupiscencez . . . dominacion] cupiscen D (*tear*)   con-
cupiscencez] concupiscence MG, *Latin* concupiscencie KR   18–19 summe[1] . . .
bringeþ] *om.* D (*tear*)   19 yen] the eyen G   20 soule] þe soule G   21 to
god] *om.* DMG, *Latin* deo KR

That a man oweþ to reste in God above alle his yiftes
Capitulum 23^m

[1] 'Above alle godes and in alle, my soule, þou shalt reste in oure Lorde (1) ever, for he is the everlastynge reste of seintes. [2] Graunte me, moste lovinge and moste swete Ihesu, above every creature, above alle helþe and alle beaute, above alle glorie and worshippe, above alle myght and dignyte, above alle kunnynge and subtilite, above alle riches and craftes, f. 107ᵛ above alle gladnes and exultacioun, | above alle fame and preysinge, above alle hope and promission, above al merite and desire, above alle yiftes þat þou maiste yiffe or infounde, above alle ioye and iubilacion þat mynde may take or feele, [3] farþermore above aungels and archangels, above alle the knyghthode of hevon, above alle þinges visible and inuisible, and aboue ʿalʾ þinges þat þou, my God, arte not.

[4] 'For þou, my God, arte beste above alle, þou alone arte highest, þou (2) alone moste myghty, þou alone moste sufficient and moste fulle, þou alone moste swete and moste solaciouse, þou alone moste feire and moste lovely, þou alone moste noble and moste gloriouse above alle f. 108ᵛ þinges, in whom alle godes ar togidres and perfitely and euer | haue be and shul be; and þerfore hit is litel and insufficient, whatever þou yiveste me biside thiselfe, or reueleste or promittest of thiselfe, þee not seyne ner fully goten. [5] For my herte may not verily reste ner be fully and al holy contente but hit reste in þee, and overpasse thi yiftes and eueri creature.

[6] 'O my moste swete spouse Ihesu Criste, moste pure lovar, Lorde of al (3) maner creature, who shal yive me feders of veri liberte, þat I mowe flye and reste in þee? [7] O when shal hit be yiven to me fully þat I mowe take hiede and see howe swete þou arte, my Lorde God? [8] When shal I atte fulle gedre meselfe in thee, þat for thi love I feele not myselfe [but þee onely], above alle felynge and alle maner in a maner not knowen to alle?

23.0 a] om. DMG   23ᵐ] 23 MG, 23 ʿxxiiiʾ D², Latin xxiii R, xxi, i altered from . K   1 above] boue D (tear)   godes] gʿoʾodes D²   in alle] om. D (tear)   oure lorde ever] our lorde god euer MG, om. D (tear), Latin domino semper KR   the] om. DMG   1–2 reste² . . . graunte] om. D (tear)   2 swete . . . creature] reature D (tear)   and alle beaute . . . glorie] lory D (tear)   above alle myght and dignyte above] abo D (tear)   and subtilite . . . riches and] om. D (tear)   above alle gladnes . . . preysinge above] om. D (tear)   hope . . . infounde above] om. D (tear)   promission] promys G   þat¹] MG, þat þat C, Latin que KR   4 godes] goʿoʾdes D²   me] meʿnʾ D², Latin michi KR   fully goten] goten fully DMG   5 thi] þi, i altered from e D²   6 creature] creatures DMG, Latin dominator vniuerse creature KR   8 atte] at ʿþeʾ D², at þe MG   but þee onely] MG, ʿbut þe onelyʾ D², om. C, Latin sed te solum KR

⁹ 'Nowe oftetymes I moorne and bere | myne infelicite with sorowe, f. 108ᵛ
¹⁰ for in þis valeye of teres þer comeþ many yvel þinges þat oftetymes
letteþ me, troubleþ me, makeþ me sorye, and darkeþ my mynde and
distracteþ me, and draweþ me and wrappeþ me inne, þat I may not haue
free commynge to þee and þat I may not fruyshe þo iocunde clyppinges
þat ar euer redi to holy spirites.

(4)   ¹¹ 'My sihynge and my manyfolde [sorowe] yn herþe mote hit meve
þee, ¹² O Ihesu, the bryghtnesse of euerlastinge glory, counforte of the
soule goynge in pilgrymage. At the is my mouþe withoute voyce, and
my silence spekeþ to thee. ¹³ Howe longe taryeþ my Lorde or he come?
¹⁴ Come he to me, his pover servant, þat he mowe make him gladde!
¹⁵ Putte he his hande and delyvere the wrecche from alle maner |
angwysshe. ¹⁶ Come, come, for withoute þee shal þer be no blisfulle f. 109ʳ
daie ner houre, for þou arte my gladnesse, and withoute þee my borde is
voyde. ¹⁷ I am a wrecche and in a maner emprysoned and grevously
fetred, tylle þou refreysshe me with the lyght of thi presence and make
(5) me free, and shewe me thi amiable visage. ¹⁸ Lete oþer men seke, for
þee, what oþer þinge hem lyketh; for me pleseth noþinge, ner shal plese,
but þou, my God, my hope and myne euerlastinge helthe. ¹⁹ I shal not
holde my pees ner I shal not cesse to prey, tille þi grace turne ayein to
me and þou speke withinforþe.'

²⁰ 'Loo, I am here! ²¹ Loo, I come to the, for þou calledeste me inwardely.
²² Thi teres, the desire of thi soule, thi humiliacion, þe contricion of thi
herte, þei haue bowed me and | brought me to thee.'   f. 109ᵛ

²³ And I seide, 'Lorde, I haue called on þee inwardly and desired to
haue my fruicion in þee; I am redy to forsake alle þinges for þe. ²⁴ Thou
verily stiredest me furste to seke þee. ²⁵ Wherfore, Lorde, be þou
blessed, þat haste done this godenesse with 'þi' servante, aftir þe
(6) multitude of þi mercye. ²⁶ What hath thi servante more to seie, Lorde,
bifore þee, but þat he meke himselfe gretely in thi sight, havinge euer in
mynde his owne wykkednesse and his vilete? ²⁷ For þer is none lyke þe
in alle þe innumerable þinges of hevon and yerthe. ²⁸ Thi werkes ar
ryght gode, thi iugementes trewe, and by thy providence alle þinges ar

---

10 troubleþ me makeþ me sorye] troubliþ me sory M, troublen and sorye me G,
troubliþ me sor(e) D², *Latin* conturbant contristant KR   darkeþ] drawiþe M, *Latin*
obnubilant KR   euer] *om.* DMG, *Latin* semper KR   11 sorowe] DMG, 'teres' C,
Latin desolacio KR   hit] *om.* DMG   17 a²] *om.* DMG   fetred] ferid DMG,
Latin grauatus K, pregrauat R   thi¹] my þi M, *Latin* tue RK   22 teres] dedes
DMG, *Latin* lacrime KR   and] DMG, and || and C   23 to¹] 'to' D²
26 hath] haue M   þat] *om.* M   27 innumerable] 'in'numerable G
28 gode] g'o'ode D²

governed. [29] Preysinge þerfore be to þee and glory, þou, the wysdame of
f. 110ʳ þe Fader! My mouthe, my soule, and al þinges | þat ar made, preyse þei
the and blesse the! Amen.'

Of the recordacion of the manyfolde benefaytes of Godde
Capitulum 24ᵐ

[1] 'Lorde, open my herte in þi lawe, and teche me to go in thi preceptes. (1)
[2] Graunte me to vnderstande þi wille, and with grete reverence and
diligente consideracion to remembre þi benefaites, boþe in general and
in special, þat I mowe þerfore worthily yelde þe þankes. [3] But I knowe
and knowleche þat I may not yelde due þankynges for the leste poynte.
[4] I am lasse þen alle thi godes yiven to me, and when I atten[d]e thi
noblesse, my spirite faileþ for the grettenesse þerof.

[5] 'Alle þat we haue in bodi and in soule, and alle þat we haue outwarde (2)
f. 110ᵛ or inwarde, naturely or superna|turely, alle ar thi benefaytes and
commendeþ [þee] as a benefactoure, holy and gode, of whom we
haue receyved al gode þinges. [6] And yf one haue taken moo, and
anoþer fewer, yette alle ar þine, and withoute þe may not the leste
þinge be hadde.

[7] 'He þat haþe received gretter may not reioyce him of his merite, ner
be lyfte vppe above oþer ner despise þe lasse; for he is more and better
þat lasse ascryveth to himselfe and in þankynge is more meke and more
deuoute. [8] And he þat weneþ himselfe to be more vile and demeþ
himselfe more vnworthy þenne alle oþer, he is more apte to receyve
gretter yiftes. [9] And he þat takeþ fewer oweþ not to be sorie, ner bere (3)
f. 111ʳ indignacion, ner envie to þe riccher, but raþer take | hiede to þee and
soueranly preyse thi godenes, þat so plentuously, so freely, so gladly
graunteste þi yiftes withoute accepcion of persones. [10] Alle þinges comeþ

24.0 24ᵐ] 24 MG, 24 `xxiiii´ D², Latin xxiiii R, xxi⟨i⟩ K   2 diligente] diligence
M   in²] om. DMG   2–3 yelde . . . due] ȝeue þe DMG, Latin ut digne tibi ex
hinc valeam gracias referre verum scio et confiteor nec pro minimo puncto ⟨me⟩ posse
debitas graciarum laudes persoluere K, ut digne tibi ex hinc valeam gracias referre verum
scio et confiteor nec pro minimo puncto me posse `debitas´ graciarum laudes persoluere
K   4 godes] g`o´odes D²   attende] DMG, attente C, Latin attendo KR
noblesse] nobl`n´esse D², nobylnes G   5 in²] om. G   naturely] natur⟨a⟩ly D²
supernaturely] supernatur⟨a⟩ly D²   commendeþ] commend⟨id⟩ D², commendid M,
commenden G, Latin commendant KR   þee as a benefactoure] con., as a benefactoure
CDM, the beneficiall G, Latin te beneficum KR   gode¹] g`o´ode D²
7 þankynge is] thankinges G   9 godenes] g`o´odenes D²   graunteste] grauntiþ
DM, Latin largiris K, largiaris R   accepcion] excepcion DMG, Latin accepcione KR

of þee, and þerfore þou arte to be preised in alle þinges. [11] Thou knowest what is expediente to be yiven to eueribodi, and whi þ[i]s hath more and þ[i]s lasse, hit is [not] to vs to discerne, but to þee, anenste whom alle merites ar diffinite.

(4)   [12] 'Wherfore, Lorde God, I accompte hit for a grete benefaite þat I haue not many þinges whereof preisinge and glory appiereþ outewarde and aftir man, [13] so þat a creature, þe poverte and the vilete of his persone considered, not onely conceyve not þerof hevynesse, sorowe, ner deieccion, but raþer consolacion and grete | gladdenes, for þou, God, chaseste   f. 111ᵛ in þis worlde pouer and meke and despised of the worlde into þi familyarez and householde men. [14] Wyttenesse hereof ar þine apostles, whom þou madeste princes above alle yerthe. [15] Thei were conuersante in þe worlde withoute compleynte, meke and symple withoute alle malyce and gile, insomuche þat þei ioyed to suffre rebukes and wronges for þi name, and þat þe worlde abhorreþ þei clypped to hem with grete wille.

(5)   [16] 'Wherfore noþinge oweþ soo to make gladde thi lover and the knower of þi benefaites as þi wille in him and the welplesinge of thi everlastinge disposicion, of þe whiche onely he oweþ to be contente and counforted, so þat as gladly he wolde be leste as | anoþer wol be moste,   f. 112ʳ and as welle pesed and contente in þe lowest place as in the furste, and as gladly despisable and abiecte and of no fame, as more worshipfulle and gretter in þe worlde þen oþer. [17] For þi wille and the love of þi worshippe oweþ to passe alle þinges, and more counforte him and more plese him þenne alle benefaites yiven hym or to be yiven hym.'

Of foure þinges þat bryng yn grete pees
Capitulum 25ᵐ

(1)   [1] 'Sone, nowe shalle I teche þee the weye of pees and of very liberte.'
       [2] 'Lorde, do þat þou saiste, for þat is greable to me [to] here.'
       [3] 'Study, sone, [raþer] to doo þe wille of anoþer þenne þine owne.
       [4] Chese euermore raþer to haue lasse þenne more. [5] Seke ever þe lower

11 þis . . . þis] DMG, þees . . . þees C, Latin iste . . . ille KR   not] DMG, om. C
diffinite] diffyned G   12 not] DMG, not | not C   13 þe] om. DMG   the]
om. MG, ⟨. .⟩ D   þi] þine DM   14 above alle] vpon all the G   15 gile]
DMG, gilte C, Latin dolo KR   16 wolde] wol DMG   and⁷] ⟨.⟩, ampersand visible
under erasure M   in þe worlde] DMG, twice C

25.0 þat bryng yn] bringing in to M, bringyng in DG   25ᵐ] 25 MG, 25 ʿxxvʾ D²,
Latin xxv R, xxiii, last i added on line K   2 þat] as G   greable] ful lese G   to²]
G, om. CDM, Latin audire KR   3 raþer] DMG, om. C, Latin pocius KR
4 euermore raþer] euer M

f. 112ᵛ place and to be vnder alle. | ⁶Desire euer and prey that þe wille of God be alle and holy done in þee. ⁷Loo, suche a man entreþ into þe costes of pees and quiete.'

⁸'Lorde, þis worde of þine is gretely shorte, but hit conteyneth in (2) hitselfe muche perfeccion. ⁹Hit is litel in seynge, but fulle of witte and plentuouse in fruyte. ¹⁰And if þis myght be trewly kepte of me, a lyght turbacion shulde [not] so sone springe in me. ¹¹And as oftetymes as I feele me vnplesed and greved, I fynde þat I haue gone fro þis doctrine. ¹²But þou maiste alle þinges, and euer loveste þe profitinge of mannes soule: encrece in me more grace, þat I mow fulfille þi worde and make perfite myne owne helthe.'

A preyer ayenste yvelle poughtes
Capitulum 26ᵐ

D, p. 151 ¹'My Lorde God, | [be not eloyned fro me; my God, biholde into my (3) helpe, for veyne þoughtes and grete dredes haue risen ayenst me, tormentynge my soule. ²Howe shal I escape vnhurte? Howe shal I breke hem?'

³'I shal go bifore þee,' he seithe, 'and I shal make lowe þe gloriouse of þe yerthe; I shal open þe yate of þe prisone, and I shal revele to þee þe inwarde of my secretes.'

⁴'Do, Lorde, as þou spekeste, and do flee fro þi visage alle wykked þoughtes. ⁵This is my hope and my soole consolacion, to flee to þee in euery tribulacion, to truste to þee and inwardely to calle vppon þee, and paciently to abide þi consolacion.'

A preier for illumynacion of mynde
Capitulum 27⁽ᵐ⁾

¹'Claryfie me, [gode Ihesu,] with þi clerenes of euerlastynge lyght and (4) bringe oute of þe habitacle of my herte alle maner of darkenes.

6 holy] hool DMG   in þee] om. DMG, *Latin* in te KR   7 quiete] quiete'nes' D², quyetnes G   9 in²] of DMG   10 not] DMG, om. C, *Latin* non KR
26.0 a preyer] om. DMG, *Latin* oracio KR   capitulum] om. G   26ᵐ] 26 MG, 26 'xxvi' D², *Latin* xxvi R, om. K   1–34.2 be . . . and] DMG, om. C (*ff. 112–20 missing*)   1 helpe] helþe M, *Latin* auxilium KR   3 gloriouse] gloriouse peple G   4 þou] om. M   do²] do, d *altered from* t D², make G   5 soole] oonly G
27.0 capitulum] om. G   27ᵐ] con., 27 MG, 27 'xxvii' D², *Latin* xxvii R, om. K
1 gode ihesu] G, om. DM, *Latin* ihesu bone KR   þi] the G

[2] Restreyne alle yvel evagacions and alle myghty temptacions. [3] Fight for me mightily, and bere oute þe wykked bestes, þe perilouse concupiscences I mene, þat pees be made in þi vertue and myght, and haboundance of þi preisinge sowne in þe holy halle, þat is, in | þe D, p. 152 pure conscience. [4] Commaunde wyndes and tempestes. Seie to þe sea, "Be in reste," and to þe norþen wynde, "Blowe not," and þere shal be grete tranquillite.

(5)   [5] 'Sende oute þi lyght and þi trouþe, þat þei mowe shyne vppon þe yerthe, for I am ydel yerthe and voyde, tille þou illumyne me. [6] Poure oute þi grace from above. Wasshe my soule with þat hevonly dewe. Minister waters of deuocion to water þe face of þe yerthe, to bringe forthe gode fruyte and of þe best. [7] Lyfte vppe þe mynde þat is pressed with þe hevy burdon of synne, and suspende alle my desire to hevonly þinges, þat, þe swetnesse of þe highe felicite ones tasted, hit lyke not to þenke on yerthely þinges.

(6)   [8] 'Ravishe me and delyuer fro alle indurable counforte of creatures, for noþinge create may fully quiete and counforte my appetite. [9] Ioyne me to þee with an vndepartable bonde of love, for þou alone sufficest to þe lover, and withouten þee alle þinges ar friuoles.'

Of eschuynge of curiouse inquisicion of oþer mennes lyvinge
Capitulum 28[m]

(1) | [1] 'Sone, be not curiouse, ne be besy. [2] What is þat or þat to þee? Folowe D, p. 153 þou me. [3] What is þat to þee, wheþer suche a man be suche or suche, or what þis man doþe or what he seithe? [4] þou haste no nede to answere for oþer, but for þiselfe þou muste yelde accountes. [5] Whereto wrappest þou and implyest þiselfe? [6] Loo, I knowe alle men, and see alle þinges þat ar done vnder hevon, and knowe howe it stondeþ with euery man, what he þenkeþ, what he wolle, and to what ende draweþ his intencion. [7] Wherefore to me alle þinges ar to be committed. Kepe þou þiselfe in goode pees, and lete þe stirer stirre as muche as he wolle. [8] Whateuer he do or seie shal falle vppon him, for he may not deceyve me.

2 alle²] om. G, Latin vniuersas R, om. K   3 myght] miȝti M, Latin uirtute KR þe³] thy G   þe⁴] om. G   4 norþen] northe G   5 ydel] vayne G illumyne] lyȝten G   7 lyke] lyketh G, Latin pigeat KR   8 delyuer] delyuere me G

28.0 28ᵐ] con., 28 MG, 28 'xxviii' D², Latin xxviii R, xxiiii K   5 þou] the G   7 goode] g'o'ode D²   pees] pepees M

⁹ 'Take none heede of the shadowe of a grete name, ner of þe (2)
familiarite of many, ner of private love of man. ¹⁰ For alle þees
engendreþ distraccions and grete darkenes in soule. ¹¹ I wolde gladly
speke my worde and shewe þe hidde þinges, if þou woldest diligently
D, p. 154 obserue my comynge and open to me þe durre of þi herte. ¹² Be | redy,
wake in preiers, and in alle þinges meke þiselfe.'

Whereinne standeþ pes of herte and very profitynge
Capitulum 29^[m]

¹ 'Sone, I seide, "I leve pes to you, I yive my pes to you; not as þe worlde (1)
yiveþ, so yive I."

² 'Alle men desireþ [pees], but alle men loveþ not þoo þinges þat
longeþ to very pees. ³ My pes is with meke men and mylde of herte. ⁴ þi
pes shal be in muche pacience. ⁵ If þou here me and folowe my voice,
þou shalte lyve in grete pes.'

⁶ 'What shal I do þerfore?'

⁷ 'In eueryþinge take heede what þou doste and what þou seiste, and
dresse alle þine entencion to plese me alone, and oute of me coveite
noþinge ner seke noþinge. ⁸ And also of oþer mennes dedes or seiynges
deme noþinge temerarily, ner medle not ner implye þee not with þinges
þat ar not committed to þee, and hit shal be trouble ‛to þee' litel or
seldon. ⁹ For a man never to fele trouble ner suffre none hevynesse in (2)
body ner in soule is not þe state of þis worlde, but þe state of
euerlastynge quiete. ¹⁰ Wherefore deme not þee to haue founde very
pes if þou fele no gref, ner þen alle to be welle if þou haue none
D, p. 155 adversarie, ner þee to be perfite | if alle þinges be aftir þi wille. ¹¹ Ner
þen accompte þee grete, ner specially biloved, if þou be in grete
delectacion, deuocion, or swetnesse, for hereinne is not knowen a very
lover of vertue, ner in þees standeþ not profitynge ner mannes
perfeccion.'

---

10 in] in þe G
29.0 29^m] con., 29 MG, 29 ‛xxix' D², *Latin* xxix R, xx(v) K   2 pees¹] con., om.
DMG, *Latin* pacem KR   8 temerarily] temer. .ily, *two letters scratched out* G
and hit shal be trouble to þee] and it shal be trouble ‛to þe' D², om. M, *Latin* et poterit fieri
ut parum uel raro turberis KR   9 quiete] M, quiete‛nes' D², quyetnes G
10 none adversarie] noo aduersite G, *Latin* si neminem pateris aduersarium K, si neminem
patiris aduersarium R   ner²] ner then G   aftir] aster M, *Latin* secundum
KR   11 biloved] to be loued G, *Latin* dilectum KR   if þou be] om. M, *Latin*
si . . . fueris KR

(3) 12 'Whereinne, þen, Lorde?'

13 'In offringe þiselfe with alle þine herte to þe wille of God, not sekinge þoo þinges þat ar þine, ner in litel ner in muche, ner in tyme ner in everlastingnes, so þat with one evon chier þou abide in yeldynge of þankynges bitwene plesant þinges and contrariouse, peysinge alle evonly. 14 Yf þou were so myghty and so longe of abidinge in hope þat, alle maner inwarde consolacion withdrawen, yette þou makeste redy þine herte to suffre gretter and moo, ner þou iustifiest not þiselfe as þoghe þou owedest not suffre so grete þinges, but iustifiest me in alle my disposicions, and preisest me as moste holy, þen goeste þou in þe very and right weye of pes, and þou maist hope certeynly to see my face ayeine in iubilacion. 15 And if þou mowe come to fulle contempte of þiselfe, knowe þat þou shalte þen fruyshe haboundance of pes aftir þe possibilite of þi dwellynge | place.'

D, p. 156

Of þe excellence of a free mynde, and howe hit is raþer goten by preier þen by redinge
Capitulum 30[m]

(1) 1 'Lorde, þis is þe werke of a perfite man, never to relesse þe soule fro intencion of hevonly þinges, and amonge many cures to goo in a maner withoute cure, not for slugg[ed]nes, but in a maner of a prerogative of a free mynde in clyvynge to no creature by inordinate affeccion.

(2) 2 'I biseche þee, my moste merciful God, preserve me fro þe cures of þis worlde, þat I be not to muche implyed; [fro] many necessitees of þe body, þat I be not taken with voluptes; fro alle obstacles of þe soule, þat I be not broken and þrowen downe with hevynesse. 3 I say not onely fro suche þinges as þe vanite of þe worlde coveiteþ with holė affeccion, but also fro þees miseries þat penaly greveþ þe soule of þi servant with þe commune course of mortalite and tarieþ hit þat hit may not entre into liberte of spirite as ofte as I wolde.

(3) 4 'O my God, ineffable swetnesse, turne into bitternesse alle fleysshely

---

12 lorde] good lorde G, *Latin* domine KR   13 chier] cheer, *first* e *altered from* i D²   14 of¹] *om.* G   consolacion] G, consolacion 'were' D², consolacion were M, *Latin* subtracta interiori consolacione KR   not¹] *om.* G   not²] ner M, *Latin* non deberes KR
30.0 capitulum] *om.* G   30ᵐ] *con.*, 30 MG, 30 'xxx' D², *Latin* xxx R, xxvi, i *altered from* . K   1 fro] fro the G   sluggednes] M, slug⟨gus⟩nes D², sluggusnes G   2 fro²] M, ⟨of⟩ D², of G   3 penaly] peynfully G, penaliter KR   I²]
⟨I⟩ D¹   4 ineffable] G, ineffabile DM

D, p. 157 counforte, þat draweþ me aweye | fro love of euerlastynge þinges, wikkedly drawynge me þerto vnder coloure of a presente delectable gode. ⁵My God, lete not fleysshe and blode overcome me; lete not þe worlde deceyve me and his shorte glory; lete not þe fende with his wyles supplante me. ⁶Yive me strengthe to withstande, pacience in suffrynge, constance in perseverynge. ⁷Yive for alle worldely consolacions þe moste swete vnccion of þi Holy Gost, and for fleysshely love, poure `in´to me þe love of þi name.

⁸'Loo, mete, drynke, clothe, and oþer þinges longynge to þe body ar (4) onerouse to a feruent spirite. ⁹Graunte me to vse suche noryshinges temperatly, and not to be wrapped to muche in desires. ¹⁰To caste alle þinges aweye is not lawefulle, for nature muste be susteyned. ¹¹But to seke superfluytes and suche þinges as moste delyteþ, holy lawe forbedeþ, ¹²for elles þe fleysshe wolde be wantowne ayenis þe spirite. ¹³Amonge þees I preie þat þy hande mowe governe me, and teche me what is to muche.'

That priuate love tarieþ a man moste fro þe highest goode
Capitulum 31 [ᵐ]

D, p. 158 ¹'Sone, hit bihoveþ þe to yive alle | `for alle´ and noþinge of þine to be (1) `to´ þiselfe. ²Knowe welle þat love of þiselfe noyeþ þee more þen anyþinge in þe worlde. ³Aftir þe love and affeccion þat þou berest, eueryþinge clyveþe to þee more or lasse. ⁴If þi love be pure, symple, and ordinate, þou shalte not be captive ner sugget to [þe] yerthely þinges.

⁵'Coveyte not þat þinge þat þou maiste not haue. ⁶Wille not to haue þat þinge þat may lette þee and pryve þee þine inwarde liberte. ⁷Hit is wonder þat þou committest not þiself to me of alle þe ground of þine herte with alle þinges þat þou maiste desire or haue.

⁸'Why arte þou consumed with veyne moornynge? What art þou (2) made wery with superfluouse cures? ⁹Stande at my wel-plesinge, and þou shalte suffre none hyndrynge. ¹⁰If þou seke þat or þat or wolde be þer or þer for þine owne profit and for þi more plesance, þou shalte

4 fro] fro the G   þinges] þinges and DMG   vnder] vnder þe G
5 fleysshe] þe flesshe G   lete² . . . me²] *om.* G, *Latin* non me decipiat mundus
KR   7 into] `in´to D²   9 to²] to þe body M   10 aweye] awey it M
31.0 31ᵐ] *con.*, 31 MG, 31 `xxxi´ D², *Latin* xxxi R, xxvii, i *added on line* K   1 for
alle] `for all´ D¹        noþinge of þine to be to] ⟨noþynge of þyn to be⟩ `to´ D²   2 þat]
þat þe G   4 þe] M, *canc.* D, *om.* G   6 þee²] þe of G   8 what] why
G   superfluouse] supflu M   9 none] no G

never be in quiete ner free fro bisynesse, for in eueryþinge shal be summe defaute and in euery place shal be þat þat is contrary.

(3)   [11] 'Therfore not eueryþinge goten and multiplied withouteforþe helpeþ, but raþer when hit is sette at | nought and kutte aweye by þe   D, p. 159 rote, [12] þe whiche is not onely vnderstonden of money and riches, but of ambicion of worshippe and desire of veyne preisinge, þe whiche alle passeþ with þe worlde. [13] þe place wardeþ but litel, if þer lacke a fervente spirite. [14] Ner þat pes shal longe stande þat is sought withouteforþe, if þe state of þe herte be vacant of a right fundement, þat is, but if þou stande in me, þou maiste welle chaunge, but not do better. [15] For an occasion growen and taken, þou shalte finde þat þou fleddest, and more þerto.'

A preier for purgacion of herte and hevonly wisdame
Capitulum 32[m]

(4)   [1] 'Conferme me, God, by þe grace of þe Holy Goste, [2] and yive vertue to be strengþed in þe inner man, and to make my herte voyde from alle vnprofitable bisynes, not to be drawen with diuerse desires of anyþinge vile or precious, but biholde alle þinges as þinges passinge, and me togydres [to passe] with hem, for þer is noþinge abidinge vnder sonne, where alle þinges ar vanite and affliccion of spirite. | [3] O, howe wise is he   D, p. 160 þat þus considereþ!

(5)   [4] 'Lorde, yive me hevonly wisdame, þat I mowe lerne to seke þee and finde `þee' above alle þinges, and above alle þinges to savoure þee and love þee, and aftir þe ordre of wisdame to vnderstande alle oþre þinges as þei be. [5] Graunte me prudently to declyne þe flaterer and paciently to suffre þe adversarie. [6] For þis is grete wisdame: not to be meved with euery wynde of wordes, ner to yive þe ere to yvel blandyshynge `of þe' marmayden. And þus men goþe surely in þe way bigonnen.'

10 quiete] M, quiete`nes' D², quyetnes G   free] om. G, Latin liber KR   shal be þat] G, ⟨shall be t⟩hat D², shalle se þat M, Latin erit quod aduersetur R, erit qui aduersetur K   12 þe¹] om. G   14 shal] shal ⟨. . .⟩ D   þou¹] it G
32.0 32ᵐ] con., 32 MG, 32 `xxxii' D², Latin xxxii R, om. K     2 to passe] G, om. DM, Latin transiturum KR     vnder] vnder þe G     3 considereþ] condriþ M, Latin considerat KR     4 þee²] `þe' D²G, om. M   5 prudently] prudenly M, Latin prudenter K, prudentem R   adversarie] G, aduersa⟨rie⟩ D², aduersite M, Latin aduersantem KR   6 of þe] `of þe' D²   marmayden] mermayde G

Ayenis þe tonges of detractours
Capitulum 33[m]

[1] 'Sone, bere not hevily if summe feele yvel of þee and seie þat þou (1)
woldest not gladly here. [2] þou owest to fele of þiselfe worse þinges and
bileve no man to be lower þen þiselfe. [3] If þou walke withinforþe, þou
shalte not peyse flyinge wordes. [4] Hit is no litel providence to kepe
silence in yvel tyme, and to turne inwarde to me, and not to be trowbled
with mannes iugemente.

[5] 'Lete not þi pes be in þe mowthes of men. [6] Whether þei seie welle, (2)
D, p. 161   whether þei seie yvel, þou arte 'not' therfore | anoþer man. [7] Where is
very pes and very glory? [8] Whether not in me? [9] And he þat coveiteþ not
to plese men, ner dredeþ not to displese men, he shal ioye in muche pes.
[10] Of inordinate love and veyne drede groweþ alle vnrestfulnesse of herte
and distraccion of wittes.'

That in tyme of tribulacion God is inwardly to be
called vppon and to be blessed
Capitulum 34[m]

[1] 'Lorde, be þi name blessed for ever, þat woldest þis temptacion to (1)
C, f. 121ʳ   come vppon me. [2] I may not flee it: I preie þee helpe me and] | turne
'hit' [to] me into gode.

[3] 'Lorde, nowe I am in tribulacion, and hit is not weel in my herte, but
I am gretely vexed with this presente passion. [4] And nowe, wel-biloved
Fader, what shal I seie? [5] "I am taken amonge angwyshes: [6] saue me in
þis houre"? [7] But þerfore I came into þis houre, þat þou shuldeste be
clarified when I shal be brou3t downe lowe and by þe delyuered. [8] Please
hit the, Lorde, to delyuere me, for I am pouer, and what may I doo and
whither shal I goo withoute þee? [9] Lorde, yive pes at this tyme. [10] Helpe
me, my Lorde God, and I shalle not drede howe muche ever I be
greved.

[11] 'And nowe amonge þees, what shal I seie? [12] Lorde, thi wille be (2)

33.0 33ᵐ] con., 33 MG, 33 'xxxiii' D², *Latin* xxxiii R, xxviii K   3 flyinge] fl⟨y⟩yng
D²   6 not] 'not' D²G, *om.* M, *Latin* non KR   9 men¹] men he shal ioy in
muche pes, *all except* men *canc.* D
     34.0 34ᵐ] con., 34 MG, 34 'xxxiiii' D², *Latin* xxxiiii R, xxix K   2 hit to] G, 'it to'
D², 'hit' C, *om.* M, *Latin* in bonum mihi ipsam conuertas R, in bonum michi conuertas
K   7 þe] þe be M

done, [13] and I haue welle deserved to | be troubled and greved. [14] Hit is   f. 121ᵛ
bihofulle also þat I suffre, and wolde God paciently, tille þis tempeste
passe and better be. [15] Thi almyghty hande is of power to take awey þis
temptacion fro me and to aswage his violence, þat I be not vtterly
overcomen, as þou haste done oftetymes with me, my God, my merci.
[16] And þe harder þat hit is to me, the lyghter hit is to the, þis chaunge of
þe right hande of the higheste.'

Of Goddes helpe to be asked, and truste of recoverynge of grace
Capitulum 35ᵐ

(1)   [1] 'Sone, I am the Lorde, counfortynge in the daie of tribulacion. [2] Come
to me whenne hit is not welle with the.

    [3] 'þis hit is þat moste letteþ hevonly counforte, for þou hast | so late   f. 122ʳ
recourse to preyer. [4] For bifore or þou preie me hertely, þou sekeste þe
menetyme many solaces, and refreysshest the in outwarde þinges. [5] And
þerþorowe hit comeþ þat alle avaylen but litel, tille þou take hiede þat I
am þat delyuer men trustinge in me, ner withoute me is none avaylynge
helpe, ner profitable counseile, ner durable remedye.

    [6] 'But now, takynge ayein spirite aftir tempest, waxe stronge in the
lyght of my miseracions, for I am nyghe, seithe scripture, to restore alle
(2)   þinges, not onely holy, but also haboundantly and over-heped. [7] Wheþer
is þer anyþinge harde to me, or shal I be lyke a man þat seithe and dothe
not? [8] Where is thi feithe? [9] Stande stedfastly and | perseuerantly. [10] Be of   f. 122ᵛ
longe hope and a stronge man. Consolacion shal come to the `in´ tyme.
[11] Abide me, abide: [12] I shal come and cure þee. [13] Hit is a temptacion þat
vexeþ the, and a veyne drede þat fereþ thee. [14] [What] bringeth bisy
caryinge of þinges þat ar contingently to come, but make the to haue
sorowe vppon sorowe? [15] Lete the malice of þe daie suffice to hit.
[16] Ueyne hit is and vnprofitable, a man to be troubled or reioyced of
þinges to come þat perauenture shal never falle.

16 chaunge] chaunge `is´ D², chaunge is G, *Latin* quanto michi difficilius tanto tibi
facilior est hec mutacio dextere excelsi KR
    35.0 35ᵐ] 35 MG, 35 `xxxv´ D², *Latin* xxxv R, ⟨xxx⟩ K   1 the²] þi M
3 moste letteþ] lettiþ most DMG   4 or] *om.* G   5 am] it am DM, am he
G   6 takynge ayein spirite] takin⟨.⟩ ayen spirite D, þe spirite taken ayen G
waxe] waxe þoue G   7 anyþinge] DMG, anyþinge any, any *canc.* C
11 abide²] ⟨ande⟩, abide *visible under erasure* D², and MG, *Latin* expecta me expecta
KR   14 what bringeth bisy] *con.*, butte bringeth bisy C, ⟨what⟩ bringiþ besy, b *visible
under* w D², what bringiþe yt besy M, what bryngyth in besy G, *Latin* quid importat
solicitudo KR   15 hit] it`self´ D², hitself G

[17] 'But hit is mannes condicion to be illuded with suche imagynacions, (3) and signe of a litel soule as yette to be drawen so lyghtly at þe suggestion

f. 123ʳ of the enemy. [18] For he takeþ none | hiede whether he illude and deceyve bi true or b[i] false, wheþer he þrowe downe by love of þinges presente or drede of þinges to come. [19] Lete not thi herte þerfore be troubled ner drede. [20] Bylyeve in me and haue truste in my mercye. [21] Whenne þou weneste oftetymes þat I am farre fro thee, þenne am I nexte. [22] When þou weneste thiselfe almoste loste, þenne oftetymes comeþ gretter lucre of merite. [23] Hit is 'not' alle þenne loste when the þinge falleth into the contrarie. [24] Thou owest not to deme aftir the presente felynge, ner so to clyve to any hevynesse whereof ever hit come, and take hit so as þoghe hope of skapinge were vtterly taken aweye.

f. 123ᵛ [25] 'Wene not thiselfe to be alle | forsaken, þoghe I sende þee summe (4) tribulacion for a tyme, or elles withdrawe desired consolacion, [26] for so me gothe to the reaume of hevon. [27] And þat withoute doute is more expedient to the and to the remenante of my servantes, þat ye be exerciced with contrarie þinges, þenne yf al þinges felle aftir youre lykinge. [28] Loo, I knowe hidde þoghtes, þat hit is gretely expedient for thi helthe þat þou be lafte amonge withoute savoure, leste þou be lyfte vppe in succedinge of thi desire and please thiselfe in þat þou arte not. [29] That I yave I may take awey, and restore hit ayeine when hit pleseth me. [30] Whenne I yive hit, hit is myne; when I withdrawe hit, I take not (5)

f. 124ʳ þine, | for myne is eueri gode þinge yiven, and eueri perfite yifte. [31] If I sende þe any hevines or any contrariouste, haue none indignacion þerof, ner let not thi herte falle, for lo, I may sone lyfte vppe ayeine, and chaunge eueri heuenesse into ioye. [32] Nerthelater, I am rightwyse and commendable whenne I do so with thee.

[33] 'If þou savoure aright and biholdeste treuly, þou owest never for aduersite sorowe so depely, but raþer ioye and yive þankynges, yea to accompte þis as for a singuler ioy, þat I, peynynge þe with sorowes,

17 and] and it is G   litel] weke G, *Latin* parui KR   þe] 'þe' D²   18 none] no G   and] or DMG   bi²] DMG, be C, *Latin* ueris an falsis K, per deum aut falsum R   or²] or by G   19 drede] drede suche DM   20 bylyeve] ⟨beleue⟩ D²   21 whenne . . . nexte] *om.* G, *Latin* quando tu putas te elongatum a me sepe sum propinquior KR   22 gretter] grettist DMG, *Latin* maius K, magis R   23 not alle þenne] þan all DMG, *Latin* non est tunc totum perditum R, non est totum perditum K   24 hit²] hir, r *altered from* t D², hir M   26 me] me'n' D², men MG   27 exerciced] exercised, s *altered from* c D², exercysed, y *altered from* u M   30 gode] g'o'ode D²   31 contrariouste] contrarious⟨nes⟩ D², contrariousnes G   none] no G   indignacion] ⟨ind⟩ignacion D²   eueri] eny, *abbreviation for* er *visible under erasure above* n D   32 nerthelater] neuerþeles DMG   33 accompte] acco⟨wnte⟩ D²

spare þe not. [34] "As the Fader loved me, so I love youe," seide I to my welle-biloved disciples, whom I sende not to temporal ioyes but to grete peynes, | not to worshippes but to despites, not to ydelnesse but to   f. 124ᵛ laboures, not to reste but to brynge forthe muche fruyte in pacience.'

Of recching never of alle creatures so the creatoure mowe be founde
Capitulum 36ᵐ

(1)   [1] 'Lorde, I nede yette more grace, if I shal come þider where no man ner oþer creature may lette me. [2] For as longe as anythynge withholdeth me, I may not flye frely to the. [3] He desired to flye frely þat seide, "Who shal yive me feders as a coluer, and I shal flye and reste?"

[4] 'What is mo[r]e resteful þen a symple ye? And what is more free þan he þatte desireþ noght in yerthe? [5] Hit bihoveþ therfore to overpasse everie creature, and to | forsake himselfe perfitely, and stande in excesse   f. 125ʳ of mynde, and to see þe creatoure of alle to haue noþinge lyke with his creatures. [6] And but yf a man be spedde fro alle creatures, he may never freely intende to godly þinges. [7] Therfore þer ar founden but fewe contemplative men, for fewe canne fully sequestre and departe hemselfe fro perishinge creatures.

(2)   [8] 'Therfore þerto is required grete grace þat mowe lyfte vp the soule and ravishe hir above hirselfe. [9] And but a man be lyfte vppe in spirite, and delyuered from alle creatures and alle holy oned to God, whateuer he canne, whatever he haue, hit is of lytel weyght. [10] He shal be longe litel, and shal lye bineþe, | þat accompteþ anyþinge grete but alonely one   f. 125ᵛ þat is withoute mesure and euerlastinge gode; [11] and alle þat [is not God] is noght and for noght to be accompted.

[12] 'There is a grete difference bitwene him þat is illumyned with wisdame and a deuoute man, and him þat is lettred and studiouse in science, called a clerke. [13] That doctrine is muche more noble þat welleþ from above of Goddes influence þen þat þat is laborously goten bi mannes witte.

34 but[1] . . . worshippes] *om.* DMG, *Latin* sed ad magna certamina non ad honores KR
36.0 so] so þat G   36ᵐ] 36 MG, 36 'xxxvi' D², *Latin* xxxvi R, xxxi, i *altered from* .
K   4 more] G, moᐸ. .ᐳ, st *visible under erasure* D, moste CM, *Latin* quiecius KR
þen] þ(a)n D²   5 and[2]] and to DMG   to[3]] *om.* DMG   7 hemselfe]
himself DM, hem G   8 hir] hirself D, hitself MG   hirselfe] hitself G, *Latin*
semetipsam K, seipsam R   9 but] but if M   11 þat is not God] *con.*, þat C,
saf þat DMG, *Latin* quidquid deus non est nichil est KR   13 laborously]
laboriously G

¹⁴'Ther ar many desire[r]s of contemplacion, but þei studieþ not to (3) exercice tho þinges þat ar required þerto. ¹⁵Hit is a grete lette þat menne abideþ in signes and sensible þinges, and takeþ litel cure of

f. 126ʳ perfite mortificacion. ¹⁶I not what hit is ner what | spirite we be ladde with, ner what we mene, we þat ar called spirituel men, þat we haue so muche laboure and so muche bisynesse aboute transitory þinges and vile þinges, but of our inwardes we þenke fulle seldon, gederynge oure wittes togedre.

¹⁷'Alas, anone aftir a litel recolleccion, we breke oute ner we weye not (4) oure werkes with a streyte examinacion. ¹⁸Where oure affeccions lythe, we takeþ none hyede, and howe vnpure al oure [werke]s ar, we vayle not. ¹⁹Euerie flesshe had corrupte his weye and þerfore folowed the grete flode. ²⁰Wherfore whenne oure inwarde affeccion is muche corrupte, hit muste nedes be þat the worchinge folowynge, shewar of lakkynge of

f. 126ᵛ inwarde strengthe, be cor|rupte.

²¹'Of pure herte procedeþ fruyte of gode lyve. ²²Menne askeþ howe (5) muche a man hathe, but [of] howe muche vertue he doþe, no man þenkeþ. ²³Hit is enquered if he be myghti, ryche, feyre, able, or a gode writer, a gode synger, a gode labourer; but howe pouer he be in spirite, howe pacient, howe mylde, howe deuoute, and how inwarde, many men speke not of. ²⁴Nature biholdeþ the outwarde þinges of man, but grace turneþ hymselfe alle inwarde. ²⁵Nature is oftetymes deceyved, but grace trusteþ in God þat she be not deceyved.'

Of denyinge of himselfe and forsakynge of alle cupidite
Capitulum 37ᵐ

f. 127ʳ ¹'Sone, þou maiste not haue perfitely lyberte but þou denye | thiselfe (1) vtterly. ²[There be fetred] alle proprietaries and lovers of hemselfe, coveytouse, curiose, wandrers aboute, sekinge euer softe þinges and not tho þat ar of Iesue Criste, but oftetymes feynynge and puttinge ayeine

14 desirers] desire⟨res⟩ D², desires C, desiren M, þat desyren G, *Latin* plures reperiuntur contemplacionem desiderare KR   15 perfite] 'perfite' G   16 not] wot not G   18 affeccions] affeccion G   none] no G   oure werkes] DMG, oures C, *Latin* omnia K, omnia nostra R   21 gode] g'o'ode D²   22 of] DMG, *om.* C, *Latin* ex quanta virtute ag⟨it⟩ K, ex quanta virtute agit R   23 gode¹] g'o'ode D²   gode²] g'o'ode D²   gode³] g'o'ode D²

37.0 37ᵐ] 37 MG, 37 'xxxvii' D², *Latin* xxxvii R, xxxii, *second* i *altered from* . K   1 perfitely] parfit DMG, *Latin* perfecte R, perfectam K   but] but if MG   2 there be fetred] G, *om.* CDM, *Latin* compediti sunt KR   curiose] cupiose M   puttinge] ⟨shapynge⟩ D², shapyng MG, *Latin* opponentes R, componentes K   ayeine] *om.* G þat þinge þat may not stande. ³[Alle þinge shal perisshe þat hath not his bigynnynge of God.]

⁴'Holde a shorte and a consummate worde: "Leve alle, and þou shalt fynde alle; forsake coveytinge, and þou shalte fynde reste." ⁵Entrete þis in thi mynde, and when thou haste fulfilled hit, þou shalt vnderstande alle þinges.'

(2)   ⁶'Lorde, þis is not one daies werke, ner children pleye, but, þat more is, in þis shorte worde is included alle perfeccion of religiouse folke.'

⁷'Sone, þou oweste [not] to be turned aweie ner anone to be alle þrowen downe [when] þou hereste the weye of perfite menne, | but raþer f. 127ᵛ to be provoked to higher þinges, and at the leste to suspire þerto by desire. ⁸Wolde God hit were so with thee, and þat þou were comen þerto, þat thowe were no lover of thiselfe, but stodest purely at the bekenynge of me and of him þat I haue putte above þee as fader; þen shuldest þou plese me gretely, and thi daies shulde passe with grete ioye and in grete pees. ⁹Thou haste many þinges yet to forsake, þe whiche but yf þou resigne holy to me, þou shalte not gete þat þou askest. ¹⁰Wherfore I make persuasion to þee to bye golde of me þat þou mowe be made riche, þat is hevonly wysdame, tredynge vnderfote alle þees lowe þinges. ¹¹Putte byhynde alle yerthely | wysdame, and alle propre complacence.   f. 128ʳ

(3)   ¹²'I haue seide to þee to bye vile þinges and of litel price for preciouse þinges in mannes reputacion. ¹³For very and heuonly wisdame semeþ litel and of no price and allemoste foryeten in þis worlde, not to fele highe of hemselfe, ner to seke to be magnified in yerthe. Many preche withe the mouthe, but in lyvinge þei discorde farre þerfroo. Nerthelater, hit is a preciouse margarite and hydde fro many.'

Of vnstablenes of herte and of intencion to be had to God
Capitulum 38ᵐ

(1)   ¹'Sone, bilyeve not þine owne affeccion þat nowe is, for hit shalle sone be chaunged into anoþer. ²As longe as þou lyveste, þou arte sugget to

---

3 alle . . . god] G, *om.* CDM, *Latin* peribit enim totum quod non est ex deo ortum K, *om.* R   4 fynde¹] haue M, *Latin* inuenies KR   coveytinge] covetyse G 6 one] o DM   7 not] DMG, *om.* C, *Latin* non KR   when] MG, ⟨. . .⟩ whan D, but C, *Latin* audita via perfectorum KR   the leste] last DMG, *Latin* ad minus KR   8 the] þe *added on line* D², *om.* M   bekenynge] beckyng G   9 þe] *om.* G   10 is] is with G, *Latin* id est celestem sapienciam KR   13 hemselfe] hymself M   nerthelater] neuerþeles DMG

38.0 to god] in gode G, *Latin* ad deum KR   38ᵐ] 38 MG, 38 'xxxviii' D², *Latin* xxxviii R, xxxiii, *last* i *altered from* . K   1 nowe is] is nowe G

f. 128ᵛ   mutabilite, yea, þoghe þou | wolte not, so þat thou shalte be founden
nowe gladde, nowe sorye; nowe plesed, nowe troubled; nowe devoute,
nowe indevoute; nowe studyouse, nowe slugged; nowe hevye, nowe
lyght.

³ 'But aboue þees chaunges standeþ the wyse man and welle taught in
spirite, takinge none hyede what he feele in himselfe, nor on wheþer side
þe wynde of vnstablenesse blowe, but þat alle þe intencion of his mynde
mowe profite to the dewe and moste best ende. ⁴For so he may abide (2)
one and the same [inconcussed], with the simple ye of intencion directed
to me withoute cessinge amonge so many dyverses chauncez.

f. 129ʳ   ⁵ 'For the more [pure] þat the ye of intencion is, þe more sted|fastly
me gothe amonge dyverse stormes. ⁶But in many þe ye of intencion is
darked, ⁷for anone þei biholden a delectable þinge þat appiereþ, and
seldon is any founde free froo the venome of propre exquisicion. ⁸Soo
the Iewes sumtyme came into Betanye to Martha and Marie, not for
Ihesu alone, but for þei wolde see Lazare. ⁹Wherfore the yee of
intencion muste be clensed, þat hit be simple and fortheryght, and
directe to me aboue alle variant þinges þat ar bitwene.'

That to him þat loveth, God savoureth above alle þinges
Capitulum 39ᵐ

¹ 'Lo, my God and alle þinges! ²What wolle I more, and what more (1)
f. 129ᵛ   blisful þinge may I desire? ³O, þe | savorye and the swete worde, [but] to
him þat loveþ the Worde of þe Fader, [not þe worlde ner þat þat longeþ
to him].

⁴ 'Loo, my God and alle þinges! ⁵To him þat vnderstandeþ þer is
seide inowe, and ofte to reherce is iocunde to the lover. ⁶Certeinly, the
beynge presente, alle þinges ar iocunde, and the beyng absente, alle

2 wolte] wol DMG   be] *om.* M   slugged] slugg⟨ussh⟩ D², sluggusshe G
3 none] no G   nor] ner DMG   on] DMG, one C, *Latin* qua parte KR   but²]
but alle M   moste] *om.* G   4 inconcussed] MG, ⟨inconcussyd⟩ D², vnmeved C,
Latin inconcussus R, inconcussusque K   dyverses] diuerse MG   5 pure] G,
'pure' D², *om.* CM, *Latin* purior KR   me] me'n' D², men M   9 me] me allone
DMG, *Latin* ad me dirigendus KR

39.0 39ᵐ] 39 MG, 39 'xxxix' D², *Latin* xxxix R, xxxiiii, *last* i *altered from* . K
2 wolle] wolde DMG   3 the¹] *om.* G   but] MG, ⟨but⟩ D², ⟨. . .⟩ C, *Latin* sed
KR   worde²] w'o'orde D²   not . . . him] G, 'not þe wor'l'de ne þat þat longit[h] to
hym', longit[h] *cropped by binder* D², not þe worde ne þat þat longiþe to hym M, *om.* C,
Latin sed amanti ⟨uerbum⟩ non mundum nec ea que in mundo sunt K, sed amanti verbum
non mundum nec ea que in mundo sunt R   5 reherce] reherse it G

þinges ar lothe and wery. ⁷Thou makeste in the herte tranquillite, grete
pees and solempne gladnesse. ⁸Thou makest to fele welle of alle, and in
alle þinges to preyse þee, ner þer may [noþinge] longe plese withoute
þee. ⁹But if hit shal be acceptable and savoure welle, hit bihoveþ thi
grace to be nyghe, and to make hit savorie with þe condimente of thi
wysdame.

(2)   ¹⁰'To whom þou savourest, what shal not savoure him | aryght? f. 130ʳ
¹¹And to whom þou savourest not, what þinge may turne hym to
myrthe? ¹²But the wordly wyse menne fayleþ in thi wysdame, and þey
þat savoure the flesshe, for þer is muche vanite, and here is founden
dethe. ¹³But þei þat bi despisinge of yerthely þinges and mortificacion
of the fleysshe foloweþ þee beþe knowen verily to be wise men, for thei
ar translate fro vanite to verite, and fro the fleysshe to the spirite. ¹⁴To
thes menne God savoureth, and whateuer of gode þei fynde in
creatures, alle þat þei refere to the preysinge of her maker.
¹⁵Unlyke, nerthelater, and muche vnlyke is the savoure of the creatoure
and þe creature, of everlastingnes and of tyme, of lyght increate and
lyght illuminate. |

(3)   ¹⁶'O thou lyght perpetuel, passinge alle lyghtes create, [caste] fro f. 130ᵛ
above [lyghtynyng, persinge] alle the inwardes of my herte. ¹⁷Purifye,
make gladde, claryfie, and quyken my spirite with his powers to clyve to
the in iubilose excessez. ¹⁸O, when shal þat blessed and desirable houre
come, þat þou fille me with þi presence and þou be alle þinges in alle
þinges? ¹⁹As longe as þis is not yiven, shal þer no fulle ioye be.

²⁰'Alas, yet lyveþ in me the olde man. He is not alle crucyfied; he nys
not perfitely dede. ²¹Yette he coveyteth ayenis þe spirite and meveth
inwarde bateiles, and suffreþ not the reaume of þe soule to be in quiete.
²²But þou þat haste lordeshippe over the power of þe sea | and swagest f. 131ʳ
þe mevinge of his flodes, aryse and helpe me. ²³Bringe to noght folkes
þat wolle haue bateiles. Knokke hem downe in thi myght, ²⁴and shewe

6 lothe] lothsome G   7 solempne] solempnite M   8 noþinge] G, ʼnoþingʼ
D², not M, om. C, Latin nec potest aliquid sine te diu placere KR   9 but] for G,
Latin sed KR   10 to] G, ⟨. . to⟩ D², and to CM, Latin cui KR   shal] DMG, shalt
C, Latin quid . . . sapiet KR   12 the¹] om. G   13 foloweþ þee beþe] folowi(n)
þe be⟨. .⟩ D²   14 gode] gˋoˊode þinge D², good þinge MG   15 nerthelater]
neuerþeles DMG   creatoure] creˋaˊtoure G   everlastingnes] euerelastyng thyngys
G, Latin eternitatis KR   of³] of⟨. .⟩ D, ofte M   16 caste . . . persinge] G, ⟨caste
þoue fro aboue lyȝtenyng pershyng⟩ D², shynynge and lyghtynynges perse fro above CM,
Latin fulgura choruscacionem de sublimi penetrantem KR   alle] .ll smudged G
18 desirable] desiderable DMG   20 nys not perfitely] is not parfitly all DMG, Latin
non est perfecte mortuus KR   21 quiete] quieteˋnesˊ D², quyetnes G
22 mevinge] mevinges DMG, Latin motum KR   flodes] flowynges G

thi gretnes, and be thi right hande glorified, for ther is to me none oþer
hope ner refute but in þee, my Lorde God.'

That in þis lyve þer is no surete fro temptacioun
Capitulum 40ᵐ

¹'Sone, þou arte never sure in þis lyve, but as longe as þou lyvest, ever (1)
spirituel armoure is necessary to þee. ²þou dwellest among enemyes;
þou arte impugned on þe right hande and on the lyfte hande. ³Where-
fore if þou vse not on everie side þe shilde of pacience, þou shalt not be
f. 131ᵛ longe withoute a wounde. | ⁴Farthermore, yf þou sette not þi herte fixe
and ferme in me with my wille to suffre for me, þou shalt not mowe
suffre þis brennynge ner come to þe victory of seintes. ⁵Hit bihoveþ the
þerfore to passe alle þinges manly, and to vse a myghty hande ayenis
þinges put ayenis þe. ⁶For [to] the victour is yiven manna, and to the
cowarde is lafte muche myserie.

⁷'If þou seke reste in þis worlde, howe shalt þou þenne come to reste (2)
everlastinge? ⁸Set not thiselfe to grete reste, but to muche pacience.
⁹Seke verie pees not in yerthe, but in hevon, not in menne ner in other
creatures, but in God alone. ¹⁰For the love of God þou owest to suffre
f. 132ʳ alle þinges, laboures and sorowes, temptacions, vexacions, | anxietez,
necessitees, infirmitez, wronges, oblocucions, reprehencions, humilia-
cions, confusiouns, correccions, and despites. ¹¹Thes þinges helpeth to
vertue; þees preven the knyght of Criste; þees maken the hevonly
crowne. ¹²I shal yelde everlastinge meede for a litelle laboure, and
infinite glorie for a transitorie shame.

¹³'Weneste þou to haue at alle tymes at thi wille spirituelle consola- (3)
cions? ¹⁴My seintes had not so, but many hevynesses, diuerse temptacions, and grete desolacions. ¹⁵But þei had hemselfe in alle þinges
paciently, and trusted more to God þenne to hemselfe, knowinge þat
passions of þis tyme ar not worthi to deserve the glorie þat is to come. |
f. 132ᵛ ¹⁶Wolte þou haue anone þat that many men cowde vnneþe gete aftir
many teres and grete laboures? ¹⁷Abide þe Lorde, do manly, and be

---

24 me] come M, *Latin* michi KR   refute] refuge DG
40.0 40ᵐ] 40 MG, 40 `xl´ D², *Latin* xl R, xxx⟨v⟩, iiii *visible under erasure* K   4 ferme]
stedfast G, *Latin* fixe KR   my] ⟨fre⟩ D², fre G, *Latin* mea R, mera K   6 to the
victour] DG, to þe victory M, the victour C, *Latin* vincenti KR   manna] manna þat is to
sey angels fode G   10 oblocucions] obloquyes G   12 laboure] labov. .re
laboure, labov. .re *written around hole in parchment and canc.* C   14 hevynesses]
hevynes G, *Latin* grauitates KR   15 glorie] ioye G, *Latin* gloriam KR

counforted; and mystruste not, ner goo not aweye, but constantly putte forthe bothe bodi and soule for þe glory of God, [18] and I shal yelde ayeine moste plenarly: I shal be with the in everie tribulacion.'

Ayenis veyne iugementes of menne
Capitulum 41[m]

(1) [1] 'Sone, caste thi herte into oure Lorde stedfastly, and d[red]e no mannes iugemente where þi conscience yeldeþ the pure and innocente. [2] Hit is gode and blisful a man so to suffre, ner þat shal not be grevouse to him þat is meke in herte, trustinge | to God more þen to himselfe. [3] Many   f. 133[r] menne spekeþ many þinges, and þerfore litel feithe is to be yiven. [4] And to plese alle menne is not possible. [5] For þou, Poule, studyed to plese alle menne in our Lorde, and was made alle þinges to alle menne; nerthelater he accompted as for a leste þinge to be demed by mannes light.

(2) [6] 'He dyd inowe for oþer mennes edificacion and helthe as muche as in him was or he myght do, but he myght not lette but þat sumtyme he sholde be demed and despised of other. [7] Therfore he comitted alle to God, þat knewe alle þinge, and defended himselfe with pacience and mekenesse ayenis the mouthes of wykked spekars and of hem þat | þenkeþ veyne þinges and lyes, makynge boste at her owne lykinge.   f. 133[v] [8] Nerthelater oþerwhiles he answered, leste by his taciturnite occasion of offendinge myght haue been yiven to the feble in feithe.

(3) [9] 'What arte þou, þat dredest so muche of a mortal man, [10] þat þis daie is, and tomorowe appiereþ not? [11] Drede God, and be not aferde of mannes dredes. [12] What may any man ayenist þe with wronges or with wordes? [13] He noyeþ more himselfe þen þee, whatever he be. [14] Haue þou God afore þine yen, and strive not with brawlinge wordes. [15] And if þou for the tyme semest to haue the worse, and to suffree shame þat þou hast not deserved, grucche not þerfore, ner lasse | not thi crowne by   f. 134[r] impacience, but raþer loke vppe to me into hevon, þat am myghti to delyuer fro alle confucion and wronge and to yelde to everie man aftir his werkes.'

41.0 41[m]] 41 MG, 41 `xli' D², Latin xli R, xxxvi, i altered from . K   1 drede] MG, d⟨rede⟩ D², deme C, Latin metuas KR   5 nerthelater] neuerþelater DMG   a] ⟨þe⟩ D², þe G   light] ⟨s⟩ight D², siȝt MG, Latin die KR   7 þenkeþ] þenk⟨yn⟩ D²   lyes] lyes at C, lyes and DMG   8 nerthelater] neuerþeles DMG 10 tomorowe] tomorowe he G   12 man] man do DMG   14 god] god euere DMG   afore] before DMG   brawlinge] braggyng DMG, Latin querulosis KR   15 lasse not] make not lesse G   delyuer] delyuere þe G

Of pure resignacion of a mannes selfe
Capitulum 42ᵐ

[1]'Sone, forsake thee, and þou shalt fynde me. [2]Stande withoute choyce (1) and withoute alle maner proprete, and þou shalt wynne euer. [3]For anone as þou haste resigned thiselfe and not take thiselfe ayein, þer shal be þrowen to þee more grace.'

[4]'Lorde, howe ofte shal I resigne meselfe, and whereinne shalle I forsake myselfe?'

[5]'Ever and in everie houre, as in lytel, so in grete. [6]I outetake f. 134ᵛ noþinge, but in | alle þinges I wolle fynde [þee] made bare. [7]Elles howe maiste þou be myne and I þine, but if þou be depreved inwarde and outwarde fro alle propre wille? [8]The more swyftely þat þou doste þis, the better [hit] shal be with the; and the more ple[nar]ly and clerely, the more þou shalt plese me and the more þou shalt wynne.

[9]'Summe resigneþ, but with summe excepcion, [10]for þei truste not (2) fully to God, wherfore þei laboure to provide for hemselfe. [11]Summe also furste offren alle, but aftirwarde þorowe litel temptacion þei gone ayeyne to her owne propre, and þerfore thei profiteþ not in vertue. f. 135ʳ [12]Thes folke cometh not to very liberte of herte, ner to þe grace of | my iocunde familiarite, but hole resignacion and daily offringe of h[e]mselfe furste made, withoute þe whiche onhed of fr[ui]cion standeth not ner shal not stande.

[13]'I haue seide to the ful ofte and yette I seie ayeine: forsake thiselfe, (3) resigne vppe þiselfe, and þou shalt fruyshe grete pees. [14]Yive alle for alle, seke noþinge, aske noþinge ayeine; stande purely and vndoutably in me, and thou shalte haue me. þou shalt be free in herte, and darkenesses shul not overgo thee. [15]To þat enforce þee, þat preie þou, þat desire þou, þat þou mowe be despoyled of alle maner proprete, and þou bare folowe bare Ihesu, and dye to thiselfe and lyve everlastingly to me. f. 135ᵛ [16]þen shul | ende alle veyne fantasies, wykked conturbacions, and superflue cures. [17]Thenne also shal go aweie inordinate drede, and inordinate love shal die.'

42.0 a] om. M   42ᵐ] 42 MG, 42 'xlii' D², Latin xlii R, xxxvii, second i added on line K   2 þou] þo G   4 meselfe] myself DMG   5 grete] mykyll G 6 þee] DMG, om. C, Latin te KR   7 howe] om. G, Latin quomodo KR   maiste] maist 'not', not canc. D² mayst not G   myne] DMG, my myne C   8 hit] G, 'it' D², om. CM   plenarly] con., pleynly CDM, fully G, Latin plenius KR   clerely] clerly it is don DMG   þou shalt¹] shalt þoue G   þou shalt²] shalt þoue G   11 litel] a litel M   12 hemselfe] DG, himselfe CM   þe²] om. G   fruicion] DMG, frincion C, Latin vnio fruitiua KR   16 superflue] superfluus DG

Of gode governaunce in outwarde þinges
Capitulum 43ᵐ

(1) ¹'Sone, þou owest diligently intende herto, þat in everie place, everie
accion or outwarde ocupacion, þou be inwarde free, and myghtie in
thiselfe, and alle þinges vnder þee and þou not vnder hem; þat þou be
lorde and governoure of thi dedes, not servaunt, but raþer exempte and
a very Hebrewe goynge into þe sorte and liberte of the sones of God, þat
standeth vppon þes presente godes and byholden everlastinge; þat
biholden þinges transitorye with | þe lyfte yie, and hevonly þinges   f. 136ʳ
with þe right yie; whom temporal þinges drawen not to clyve to hem,
but thei rather drawe suche godes to serve God weel with, as þei ar
ordeyned of God and institute of þe sovereyne werkeman, þat leveth
noþing inordinate in his creature.

(2) ²'Also yf þou in everie chaunce standest not in outwarde apparence,
ner with þe fleyshely yie turneste aboute to þinges seen or herde, but
anone in everie cause þou entreste with Moyses to aske counseile of oure
Lorde, þou shalt here oftetymes Goddes answere, and þou shalte come
ayein instructe in þinges presente and þat ar to come. ³Moyses at alle
tymes had recourse to þe tabernacle | for doutes and questions to be   f. 136ᵛ
assoyled, and fledde to the helpe of preier for relevinge of periles and of
myschieves of menne. ⁴So þou owest to flee into the secretari of þi
herte, bisechinge inwardely the helpe of God. ⁵For Iosue and the
children of Israelle, as hit is radde, were deceyved of Gabaonytes, for
þei asked no counseile furste of our Lorde, but yivinge to muche
credence to swete wordes were deluded with a false pitee.'

That manne be not importune in worldely bysinesse
Capitulum 44ᵐ

(1) ¹'Sone, at alle tymes committe to me thi cause, for I shal dispose hit
welle in covenable tyme. ²Abide myne ordnance, and þou shalte feele
þerof profitinge.'

43.0 43ᵐ] MG, 43 'xliii' D², *Latin* xliii R, 'xxxviii' K   1 thiselfe] self G (*tear*)
vnder²] nder G (*tear*)   dedes] dedy G (*tear*)   hebrewe] hebre G (*tear*)   þes] pes
canc. D², *om.* MG   godes¹] g'o'odes D²   and⁸] ⟨. ande⟩ D²   godes²] g'o'odes
D²   3 myschieves] mysch⟨aunces⟩ D², myschaunces G, *Latin* improbitatibus
KR   4 the¹] *om.* G (*tear*)   inwardely] ynward G (*tear*)   5 of²] of þe
G   but] bu G (*tear*)
44.0 44ᵐ] 44 MG, 44 'xliiii' D², *Latin* xliiii R, xxxix K   1 covenable] con. . . .nte
G (*tear*)   2 feele] le G (*tear*)

f. 137[r]   [3]'Lorde, | right gladly I committe to the alle þinges, for litel may my þenkinge profite. [4]Wolde God þat I clyved [not] overmuche to chaunces þat ar to come, þat I myght offre myselfe to thi welplesinge withoute taryinge!'

[5]'Sone, oftetymes a man is sore meved aboute a þinge þat he desireth, (2) but whenne he is comen þerto, he bigynneþ to fele oþerwise; for affeccions ar not abidinge aboute one þinge, but þei be shuffed from one to anoþer. [6]Hit is not þerfore a litel þinge, yea amonge leste þinges a man to forsake himselfe.

[7]'Uerie profitinge is denyinge of a mannes selfe, and a man so denyed (3) is fulle free and ful sure. [8]But þe olde enemye, adversarie to alle goode,

f. 137[v]   cesseth not froo | temptacion, but daie and nyght he lythe in awayte, if he myght bringe hedily the vnware man into the gnare of deceyte.

[9]'Wakeþ, therfore, and preieth,' seithe oure Lorde, 'þat ye entre not into temptacion.'

That man hathe no gode of himselfe whereof to reioyce
Capitulum 45[m]

[1]'Lorde, what is man, þat þou haste mynde on hym, or þe sone of man, (1) þat þou visitest him? [2]What deserved man, þat þou shuldest yive him thi grace? [3]Lorde, what may I compleyne if þou forsake me, or rightwisely pretende ayenis þee, if þou do not þat I aske? [4]Certeynly,

f. 138[r]   þis may I þenke in trowthe and seie, "Lorde, I am nought, I | may noght, I haue no gode of myselfe, but in alle þinges I feile and euer drawe to noght. [5]And but yf I be holpen of þee and inwardely enfourmed, I am made alle lewke and dissolute."

[6]'But þou, Lorde, arte ever one and abidest one everlastyngly, ever (2) gode, ryghtwyse, and holy, doynge alle þinges welle and holyly, and disposinge alle þinges bi wysdame. [7]But I, þat am more prone to

3 committe] com G (*tear*)   profite] *om.* G (*tear*)   4 not] DMG, *om.* C, *Latin* vtinam non KR   myselfe] self G (*tear*)   5 oftetymes] tetymes G (*tear*)   þinge[1]] th G (*tear*)   desireth] d⟨.⟩siriþ D   bigynneþ] nneth G (*tear*)   one[1]] o DM   shuffed] sh⟨uftyd⟩ D[2], shuftyd MG, *Latin* impellunt KR   7 selfe] elf G (*tear*) 9 wakeþ] wake ye G

45.0 man] a man DMG   45[m]] 45 MG, 45 `xlv´ D[2], *Latin* xlv R, x⟨l⟩ K   1 þat[1]] DMG, *twice* C   2 what] w.at G (*tear*)   thi grace] þ . . . . ace G (*tear*) 3 forsake] f. . .ake G (*tear*)   þat] as G   4 þenke] th G (*tear*)   noght[1]] no G (*tear*)   þinges] thyn G (*tear*)   5 yf I be holpen] y. . . . . .lþen G (*tear*)   yf] *om.* DM   6 gode] g`o´ode D[2]   welle . . . þinges] *om.* DMG, *Latin* ac sancte agens omnia et disponens cuncta R, ac sancte agens omnia et disponens K

faylinge þenne to profitynge, am not ever abidinge in the same estate, for vii tymes ar chaunged vppon me. ⁸Nerthelater, hit is sone amended, whenne hit pleseth þee to put ʻtoʻ an helpinge hande, for þou alone without mannes socoure maiste helpe and conferme me in suche wise | þat my chier be no more chaunged into diuerse, but þat in þe alone [my herte] be conuerted and reste.   f. 138ᵛ

(3)   ⁹ʻWherefore yf I cowde weel caste awey alle mannes consolacione, and for getinge of devocion or for necessite compellynge soght þee, for þer is no man þat canne counforte me, þen myght I worthily truste in thi grace, and ioye of yiftes of newe exultacion.

(4)   ¹⁰ʻþankynges be to the, wherof alle comeþ when hit is welle with me. ¹¹For I am vanite and noght bifore þee, a man inconstante and seke. ¹²Wherof þerfore may I reioyce me, or whi coveyte I to be had in reputacion? ¹³Wheþer not of noght? And þat is moste veyne þinge. ¹⁴Uerily, veyneglorie is an yvel pestilence | and gretteste vanite, for hit draweþ fro veri glorie and despoyleþ of hevonly grace. ¹⁵For whiles a man pleseth himselfe, he displeseth þee, and whiles he gapeþ aftir mannes preisinges, he is deprived very vertuz.   f. 139ʳ

(5)   ¹⁶ʻFor verie glory and holy exultacion is to reioyce in þee and not in himselfe, to ioye in thi name and not in mannes propre vertue, ner to delite in no creature, save for þee. ¹⁷Ipreysed be þerfore thi name, ʻnot myneʻ; magnified be thi werke, and not myne; blessed be thi holy name, but to me be noþinge yiven of mannes preysinges. ¹⁸Thou arte my glorie, þou arte þe exultacion of my herte. ¹⁹In the shal I reioyce, and ioye and ioye alle daie, for myselfe noght but in | myne infirmitez.   f. 139ᵛ

(6)   ²⁰ʻLete the Iewes seke glorie everie of oþer; I shalle seke þat þat is of God alone. ²¹For alle mannes glorie, alle temporal worshippe, alle worldely highnesse, compared to þine everlastinge glorie, is vanite and folye. ²²O my trouthe and my mercie, my God, blessid Trinite, to the

7 vii tymes] ⟨alway tymes⟩ D², alway tymes MG, Latin septem tempora KR   8 nerthelater] neuerþelater DMG   my herte] MG, ʻmyn hertʻ D², om. C, Latin sed in te vno cor meum conuertatur K, sed in te vno conuertatur R   9 and for] ⟨oþer for⟩ D², oþer for G   or] o⟨.⟩, r visible under erasure D   soght] ⟨to seke⟩ D², to seke G, Latin siue propter deuocionem adipiscendam siue propter necessitatem qua compellor te querere K, siue propter deuocionem adipiscendam siue propter necessitatem qua compellor te quererem R   10 when] ⟨as ofte⟩ ʻasʻ D², as ofte as G, Latin quociescumque KR   12 þerfore] r G (tear)   had] h. .de G (tear)   13 and þat is] ⟨ande that þat is⟩ D², and of þat þat is G, Latin et hoc vanissimum est KR   14 of] fro DMG   15 aftir] aster M, Latin dum inhiat laudibus K, dum laudibus inhiat R   deprived] depryued ʻofʻ D², depriuede of G   17 ipreysed] ⟨.⟩preised, y visible under erasure D²   19 and ioye²] om. DMG, Latin gloriabor et exsultabo KR   infirmitez] infirmite⟨es⟩ D²

alone be preisinge and worshippe, vertue and glorie, by worldes infinite. Amen.'

Of contempte of alle worldely worshippe
Capitulum 46ᵐ

[1] 'Sone, yf þou see oþer menne worshipped, drawe no suche þinge to   (1) thee, but raþer to be despised and made lowe. [2] Lyfte vppe thi herte to me into hevon, and mennes despisinge in yerthe shalle not | make the sorye.'

f. 140ʳ

[3] 'Lorde, we beeþ in blyndenesse, and sone ar deceyved of vanite. [4] Lorde, yf [I] biholde me aright, þer was never wronge done to me of no creature, [5] wherfore of ryght I haue noþinge to compleyne ayenis þee.   (2) [6] Forasmuche as I haue ofte and grevously offended þee, rightwisely is everie creature armed ayenis me. [7] To me þerfore is due confucion and despite, but to the preˋiˊsinge, worshippe, and glory. [8] And but if I make redie myselfe to þat, þat I wolle gladly be despised of eueri creature, and forsaken and vtterly seme nought, I may not be pesed inwardely and stabilyshed, ner spiritualy be meked, ner be fully oned to thee.'

That oure pees is not to be sette in menne |
Capitulum 47ᵐ

f. 140ᵛ

[1] 'Sone, if þou sette thi pees with any persone for þine owne felynge and   (1) lyvinge togydres, þou shalt be vnstable and vnpesed. [2] But and thou haue recourse to the trouþe [ever] lyvinge and abidinge, þe frende þat goþe fro the or dieþ fro the shalle not make the sorie. [3] In me oweth to stande the love of the frende, and whoever semeþ gode to the and dere in þis lyve is to be loved for me. [4] Withoute me frenshippe is not worþe ner may not endure, ner þe love is not very ner pure þat I couple not.

22 and²] an G (*tear*)   amen] men G (*tear*)
46.0 worldely] *om.* DMG, *Latin* temporalis KR   46ᵐ] xlvi G, 46 ˋxlviˊ D², 48 M, *Latin* xlvi R, xli, i *altered from* . K   4 I] G, ⟨y⟩ D², þou CM, *Latin* si recte me inspicio KR   6 forasmuche] for as ofte and as muche M   8 if] *om.* M wolle] wolde M   be meked ner be fully oned to] ⟨be illumynyd ner⟩ fully ⟨onyd to⟩ D², be illumynid ner fully onyd to MG, *Latin* humiliari neque plene tibi vniri R, illuminari neque plene tibi vniri K
47.0 47ᵐ] 47 MG, 47 ˋxlviiˊ D², *Latin* xlvii R, xl⟨ii⟩ K   2 trouþe] tr G (*tear*) ever] G, ˋeuerˊ D², *om.* CM, *Latin* semper KR   fro¹ the] he G (*tear*)   3 semeþ] seˋmeˊ|the, the *altered from* me M   loved] biloued DMG   4 me] my M, *Latin* sine me KR   very ner] ⟨very true and⟩ D², very and true and G

[5] 'Thou owest to be so dede fro suche affeccions of men byloved þat [as muche as] in the is, þou shuldest wille to be withoute alle mannes felyshippe. | [6] The farþer þat a man goeþ fro alle yerthely solace, þe more he neyheþ vnto God. [7] Also the more profoundely þat a man goþe downe into himself and waxeþ vile to himselfe, þe higher he stieþ vppe to God.

f. 141ʳ

(2)   [8] 'He þat ascryveþ any gode to himselfe, he letteþ the commynge of grace of God into him, for the grace of the Holy Gost sekeþ ever the meke herte. [9] If þou coudest perfitely noghty þiselfe, and voyde thiselfe fro alle love of creatures, þenne shulde I welle into þe with grete grace. [10] Whenne þou lokest to creatures, þine affeccion is withdrawen fro the creatoure. [11] Lerne in alle þinges to overcome thiselfe for thi creatour, and þen shalte þou mowe atteygne to the knowleche of God. [12] Howe litel | ever hit be that is biholden and loved inordinatly, hit tarieth fro the higheste love [and draweþ into wikkednes].'

f. 141ᵛ

Ayenis veyne and seculer science
Capitulum 48ᵐ

(1)   [1] 'Sone, let not þe feire and þe sotile seiinges of men meve þee, for þe reaume of God is not in worde, but in vertue. [2] Take hiede to my wordes, the whiche setteþ hertes afire and illumyneþ myndes, bryngeth in compunccion, and manyfolde consolacion. [3] Rede never noþinge to seme better taght or wiser; studie for mortificacion of synnes and vices, for þat shal avayle the more þen knowleche of many harde questions.

(2)   [4] 'When þou hast radde and knowen many þinges, hit bihoveth ever to have recourse to one principal: [5] I am he | þat techeth man kunnynge, and graunte to meke menne more clere vnderstandinge þa[n] may be taught of man. [6] To whom I speke shal sone be wise, for he shal profite

f. 142ʳ

5 dede] ded(.) D   as muche as] G, ⟨as⟩ 'muche as' D², þat C, om. M, Latin quantum ad te pertine⟨re⟩t K, quantum ad te pertinet R   alle] om. DMG, Latin omni KR   7 þe] þe | þe M   10 affeccion] DMG, affeccions C, Latin subtrahitur tibi aspectus creatoris KR   11 knowleche] kno G (tear)   12 and loved] ed G (tear)   and² . . . wikkednes] M, 'and drawith into wikkydnes' D², . . rawith into vices G (tear), om. C, Latin et viciat KR

48.0 48ᵐ] 48 MG, 48 'xlviii' D², Latin xlviii R, xliii, last i added on line K   1 þe feire and þe] ⟨þe fayr⟩ 'and' þe D², þe fayre and G   2 afire] ⟨a⟩ fire D² illumyneþ] enlumyneþe M   consolacion] consolacionys DMG, Latin consolacionem KR   3 to] to þe C, þe to DMG   þen] þan þe G   4 bihoveth] behoueth þe G   recourse] a recourse G   5 þan] DMG, þat C, Latin quam KR   6 profite gretely] grety profite DMG

gretely in spirite. ⁷Woo to hem þat enqueren manye curiouse þinges of men, and of þe weye to serve me chargeth but litel. ⁸Tyme shal come whenne þer shal appiere þe mayster of maistres, Criste Ihesus, to here the lesson of alle aungels, þat is, to [serche þe] conscience of alle men, and [þen] shal Ierusalem be serched in lanternes, and þen shul be open þe hydels of darkenesse, and þen shul argumentes of tonges be in pes.

⁹'I hit am þat in a poynte lyfte vppe þe meke soule, þat he shal take f. 142ᵛ mo resons of everlastinge trouthe þenne þoghe | he had studied [x yere] in scoles. ¹⁰Lo, I teche withoute noyce of wordes, withoute confusion of opinions, withoute desire of worshippe, withoute fighttinge of argumentes. ¹¹I hit am þat teche to despice yerthely þinges, to be wery of þinges presente, to seke hevonly þinges, to savoure þinges everlastinge, to flee worshippes, to suffre sclaunders, to put alle hole truste in me and coveyte noþinge oute of me, and above alle þinges to love me brennyngly.

¹²'A certein man in lovinge me entierly lerned godly þinges and spake (3) merveyles. ¹³He profited more in forsakynge alle þinges þenne in studyinge of soteltez. ¹⁴But to summe I speke comune þinges, to f. 143ʳ summe specialle; ¹⁵to summe | I appiere s[wet]ly in signes and figures, and to summe I revele misteries in grete lyght. ¹⁶Ther is one vois of þe bokes, but hit enfourmeþ not ilyke, for I am the doctoure of trowthe withinforthe, enserchoure of the herte, vnderstander of the þoughtes, promoter of the werkes, delynge to everie as I deme worthi.'

Of not drawinge outewarde þinges to a man
Capitulum 49ᵐ

¹'Sone, in many þinges esteme thiselfe as dede vppon þe yerþe, and to (1) whom alle þe worlde be crucified. ²And many þinges þou muste passe

7 and] þat DMG, *Latin* et KR   8 serche þe] DMG, *om.* C, *Latin* examinaturus KR   þen¹] DMG, *om.* C, *Latin* tunc KR   hydels] h⟨ernys⟩, *faintly in margin:* or hernings D², hideles or hernys M, hernys G, *Latin* abscondita tenebrarum KR   9 hit am] am it G   lyfte] l⟨y⟩fte D²   mo] m⟨y⟩ D², my MG, *Latin* plures KR   þenne] more þan MG, 'more' þan D²   x yere in scoles] MG, x yere in 'scolis' D¹, in scoles C, *Latin* decem annis studuisset in scholis KR   10 noyce] voice DMG, *Latin* strepitu KR   11 hit am] am it G   teche] techiþ MG, teche'th' D   12 merveyles] mervelouse þinges G   13 more] DMG, *twice* C   soteltez] sotilte'e's D²   15 swetly] G, surely CD, sueerly M, *Latin* dulcit⟨er⟩ K, dulciter R   16 one] o DM, ilyke] alike DMG   everie] eueryoone G
49.0 49ᵐ] 49 MG, 49 'xlix' D², *Latin* xlix R, xliv K   1 esteme] ⟨suppose⟩ D, suppose G   dede] ded(.), e *visible under erasure* D

over with a defe ere, and þenke raþer on tho þinges þat longeþ to thi pees. [3] Hit is more profitable to turne aweie þine yen fro þinges þat | displesen, and to leve everie man his owne felynge, þen to strive with contenciouse wordes. [4] If þou stande welle with God and biholde his iugemente, þou shalt bere hit the more esily if þou be overcomen.'   f. 143ᵛ

(2)   [5] 'O Lorde, whiþer ar we comen? [6] Loo, temporal harme is soroed: me laboureþ and renneþ for lytel getinge, and spirituel harme is foryeton, and [vn]neþe late comeþ to mynde ayeine. [7] That þat avayleth litel or nought is take hiede to, and þat is sovereynly necessarie is necglygently passed over, for man floweth alle oute to outewarde þinges, and but he turne sone ayeine, gladly he lythe and resteþ in outwarde þinges.'

That hit it is not to bylyeve alle menne, and of lyght lapse | of wordes   f. 144ʳ
Capitulum 50ᵐ

(1)   [1] 'Lorde, yive me helpe fro tribulacion, for mannes helthe is veyne. [2] Howe ofte haue I [not] founden feithe and truste where I wende to haue hadde hit? [3] Howe ofte also haue [I] founde hit where I leste presumed? [4] Veyne þerfore is truste of man, but þe helþe of rightwyse men is in þee, God. [5] Blessed be þou, Lorde my God, in alle þinges þat fallen to vs.

(2)   [6] 'We be seke and vnstable, sone deceyved and sone chaunged. [7] Who is þat þat so warely and so circumspectely may kepe himselfe in alle þinges, but þat sumtyme he shal come into summe deceyte and summe perplexite? [8] But he þat trusteþ in þee, Lorde, and seketh þee with a symple herte, slydeþ not so lyghtly. [9] And | if he falle into any   f. 144ᵛ tribulacion, or be wrapped in any perplexite, he shal sone be delyuered þerof bi þee or counforted by þee, for þou shalte not forsake hem þat trusteth in þee into þe ende.

(3)   [10] 'Seldon is founden a trusty frende þat is perseverante in alle the necessites of his frende. [11] So, Lorde, in alle þinges þou arte moste trusti, and amonge alle þer is not suche another. [12] O, howe welle savoured þat holy soule þat seide, "My mynde is sadded in God, and

---

3 yen] eye DMG, *Latin* oculos KR   leve] leve to G   6 vnneþe] DMG, howe neþe C, *Latin* uix KR   7 þat²] *twice* G   floweth] folowiþ M, *Latin* defluit KR   50.0 50ᵐ] 50 MG, 50 'l' D², *Latin* l R, xlv K   1 fro] ⟨of⟩ D², of G, *Latin* de KR   helthe] helpe DMG, *Latin* salus KR   2 not] DMG, *om.* C, *Latin* non KR   3 I¹] DMG, *om.* C   4 helþe] helpe DMG, *Latin* salus KR   6 sone¹ . . . chaunged] sone chaunged and sone deceyued DMG   11 so] sothly G   moste] *om.* M, *Latin* fidelissimus KR   not] non M

grounded in Criste." [13] If hit were so with me, mannes drede shulde not
so solicite me, ner þe dartes of wordes shulde not meve me.

[14] 'Who may bifore see and beware of alle þinges? [15] [If] þinges bifore (4)
sene oftetymes hurteþ, | what doo þenne þinges vnprovided but hurteþ
grevously? [16] But whi previded not I better to myselfe, wrecche þat I
am? Also whi byleved I so lightly oþer men? [17] But we ar men, and we ar
none oþer þenne frayle men, þoghe we be demed and called of oþer men
as aungels. [18] Whom shalle I leeve, Lorde? Whom but þee, [19] þat arte
trouthe, þat deceyvest not ner mayste not be deceyved? [20] And on þe
oþer side, everie man is a lyar, seke, vnstable, and slydinge, and specialy
in wordes, so þat vnneþe may be bilyeved anon þat þat sowneth weel
and rightwysely in a mannes ere.

[21] 'Howe prudently warnedeste þou to beware of men, and þat a (5)
mannes familiarez ar his enemyes, | and þat hit is [not] to bilyeve
whoever seie, "Loo þere" and "Loo here". [22] I am taght, and, wolde
God, to more warenes, and not to foly to me. [23] "Beware," seide one,
"beware: kepe a[n]enst thiselfe þat I seie." [24] And whiles I kepe silence
and wene hit be hydde, he myƷt not counseile þat he asked to be
counceyled; but anone discovered boþe me and him, and wente his
weye. [25] Fro suche fables and vnware men, Lorde, defende me, þat I falle
not into her handes, ner do no suche þinges. [26] Yive into my mouthe a
trewe worde and a stable, and a fals wyly tonge make farre fro me.

[28] 'O, howe gode and howe pesible hit is a man not to speke of oþer (6)
men, ner indefferently bilyeve alle þinges, ner | lyghtly speke hit forthe,
to revele himselfe to fewe, þee euermore to be sought as a biholder of
the herte, and not to be borne aboute with every wynde of wordes, but
to desire alle þinges inwarde and outwarde aftir the welplesinge of thi
wille! [29] Howe sure þinge hit is for conservacion of hevonly grace to flee
mannes apparence, ner desire suche þinges þat shulde yive matier of
wondringe outewarde, but with alle maner bisynesse to folowe þoo
þinges þat makeþ amendement of lyve and fervoure of spirite!

[30] O, to howe many hath noyed vertue knowen and preysed! [31] And (7)

15 if] G, ⟨if⟩ D², but if M, but C, *Latin* si KR   16 not I] I not DMG   I²] I | I
D   20 þe] þat DMG   vnneþe] vnneþe⟨th⟩ D², vnneþes M   21 þou] þou
men DMG   not] DMG, *om.* C, *Latin* nec K, non est R   23 anenst] DMG,
ayenst C, *Latin* apud KR   24 wene hit be hydde he] G, ⟨wene it be hydde .⟩ he D²,
wene hit be hydde and he C, whan I went it be hid and he M, *Latin* dum ego sileo et
absconditum credo nec ille silere potest KR   counseile] ʻkepe´ conseile D², kepe
counseile G, *Latin* silere KR   counceyled] ʻkepte´ counseile D², kepte counseile G,
Latin silendum KR   26 tonge] ʻtunge´ D²   28 þee] yea DMG, *Latin* te
KR   be²] ʻbe´ D²   to⁶] *om.* DMG

howe holsumly hath grace kepte vnder silence avayled in this fraile lyve,
| þat is alle temptacion and knyghthode.'   f. 146ᵛ

Of truste to be hadde in God ayenis yvelle wordes
Capitulum 51ᵐ

(1) ¹'Sone, stande stedfastly, and truste in me. ²For what ar wordes, but
wordes? ³þei flyeþ bi the eyer, but þei hurte not a stone. ⁴If þou be
gilty, þenke þat þou wolte gladly amende thiselfe. If þou knowe þiselfe
in noþinge giltie, þenke þat þou wolte suffre hem gladly for God. ⁵Hit
is lytel inowe þat þou amonge suffre wordes, þat mayste not yette suffre
stronge betinges. ⁶And whi takeste þou so smale þinges to herte, but for
þou arte fleysshely, and takest hiede more to man þenne bihoveþ? ⁷And
for þou dredeste to be despised, þou wolte not be repreved for þine |
excessez and sekest the shadoes of excusacions.   f. 147ʳ

(2) ⁸'But byholde thiselfe better, and þou shalt knowe þat yette þe worlde
lyveth in þee, and veyne love of plesinge of menne. ⁹But alle the while
þat þou fleest to be rebuked and confounded for thi defautes, hit
appiereþ verily þat þou arte not very meke, ner the worlde dede to þee,
ner þou crucified to the worlde. ¹⁰But here my worde, and þou shalte
not charge x þousande of wordes of menne. ¹¹Loo, yf alle þinges were
seide ayenis þee þat coude maliciously be feyned ayenis the, what shulde
þei noye þee, if þou woldest suffre hem vtterly to passe, and woldest no
more sette by hem þenne a strawe? ¹²Wheþer mowe þei take oute one

(3) here fro þe? ¹³But | he þat hathe none herte withinforþe ner hath not f. 147ᵛ
God bifore his yen is sone meved with a worde of blamynge. ¹⁴But he
þat trusteþ in me and coveiteþ not to stande to his owne iugemente shal
be withoute drede of man.

¹⁵'Lo, I am iuge and knowar of alle secretes. ¹⁶I knowe howe alle
þinge is done; I knowe þe wrongedoar and the suffrer. ¹⁷Oute fro me
wente þis worde, and by my suffrance þis hath fallen, þat þoughtes of
many hertes myght be shewed oute. ¹⁸I shal deme þe gylty and the

(4) innocente, but with a pryve iugement, for I wolde preve boþe. ¹⁹Mannes

---

31 fraile] present M, *Latin* fragili KR
51 51ᵐ] 51 MG, 51 'li' D², *Latin* li R, xlvi, i *added on line* K   5 not] 'not'
D²   6 for] þat M, *Latin* quia KR   bihoveþ] 'it' bihoueth D², it bihoueth
G   9 fleest] felest M, *Latin* refugis KR   10 of¹] *om.* DMG   12 oute
one here] oon heer oute DMG   13 not] no M   14 drede] the drede G
16 the] *om.* DMG   17 my] *om.* DM, *Latin* me permittente KR

f. 148ʳ wittenesse oftetymes fayleth and deceyveth, but my iugemente is trewe, wherfore hit shal stande and shal not be sub|verted. ²⁰Hit is hidde oftetymes and is open but to fewe as to alle þinges, but hit never erreþ, ner may not erre, þoghe to the yen of vnwise menne hit appiere not rightwyse.

²¹'Wherefore in everi iugement recourse oweþ to be hadde to me, and not leyne to propre abitremente. ²²For the rightwyse man shal not be sorye, whatever come to him fro God. ²³Yea, þoghe anyþinge vnrightwise be broght forþe ayenis hym, he shal not muche charge hit, ner he shal not ioye veynly, yf he be resonably excused bi oþer. ²⁴For [he] (5) þenkeþ þat I serche þe hertes and þe reynes, and þat I deme not after þe

f. 148ᵛ face and aftir mannes apparence. ²⁵For oftetymes in myne yen | hit is founden culpable þat to þe iugemente [of man] semeþ laudable.'

²⁶'Lorde God, rightwise iuge, myghti and pacient, þat knowest mannes fraylte and mannes shrewdenes, be my strenght and alle my truste. ²⁷For my conscience sufficeþ not to me. Thou knowest þat I knowe not, and þerfore I owed in everi blamynge and repreving to meke myselfe and suffre myldely. ²⁸Mercifulle Lorde, foryive me as ofte as I haue not done soo, and yive me grace of more large suffrance. ²⁹For thi copiouse mercie is better to me for getinge of indulgence þenne myne opinate rightwysnes for defendinge of my hidde conscience. ³⁰And

f. 149ʳ þoghe I fynde no gylte in my conscience, yette in þat may | not I iustifie myselfe, for in þi syght shal no man lyvinge be iustifyed.'

That alle grevouse þinges ar to be suffred for lyve to come
Capitulum 52ᵐ

¹'Sone, lete not tho laboures þat thou haste take vppon þee for me make (1) þe not wery, ner tribulacions þrowe þee alle downe, but lete my promyse in eueri aventure strengeþ þe and counforte þee. ²I am sufficiente to

19 wittenesse] wittes G, *Latin* testimonium KR   fayleth] fafailiþ M   21 not] not to DMG   23 vnrightwise] vnriȝtwi(sly) D², vnriȝtwosly G, *Latin* iniustum R, iniuste K   24 he þenkeþ] G, ⟨he þenketh⟩ D², they þenkeþ CM, *Latin* pensat KR   serche] enserche DMG   after] aster M, *Latin* secundum KR   25 of man] *con.*, of man it DMG, *om.* C, *Latin* hominum KR   26 þat] þou DMG, *Latin* qui . . . nosti KR   27 I owed in everi] in euery I owid M   29 copiouse] plentewose G   30 shal . . . be] *con.*, shal no man lyvinge can be C, no man liuyng can be DMG, *Latin* iustificabitur KR
52.0 for] for þe G   52ᵐ] 52 MG, 52 'lii' D², *Latin* lii R, xlvii, *second* i *added on line* K   1 not²] ⟨. . .⟩, not *visible under erasure* D², *om.* MG   þee²] þe not DMG

rewarde above alle maner [and alle mesure]. ³þou shalte not laboure long, ner þou shalte not ever be greved with sorowes. ⁴Abyde a litel while, and þou shalte see a swyfte ende of alle yvels. ⁵One houre shalle come when alle laboure shal cesse, and alle noyce. ⁶Litel hit is and shorte | alle þat passeþ with tyme.

f. 149ᵛ

(2)   ⁷'Do þat þou doste, laboure trewly in my vyneyarde: I shal be thi rewarde. ⁸Write, rede, synge, morne, kepe silence, preie, suffre manly contrarioustes, for everlastynge lyve is worþe alle þees, and muche more and muche gretter bateils. ⁹Pees shalle come in one daye knowen to oure Lorde, ¹⁰and of þat tyme shal be nouþer day ner nyght, but lyght perpetuelle, infinite bryghtnesse, sovereyne pees, and siker reste. ¹¹Thou shalte not seie þen, "Who shal delyvere me fro þe body of þis dethe?" ¹²Ner þou shalte not crie, "Wo me, for my dwellynge here is over-longe taryed!" ¹³For deþe shal be þrowen downe hedlynge, and helthe shal be with|oute favtinge; none anxiete, blysful iocundite, swete companyny and plesante to biholde.

f. 150ʳ

(3)   ¹⁴'O, yf þou haddeste sene þe perpetuel crownes of seintes in hevon, and in howe muche glorie þei ioye nowe, þat summetyme in þis worlde were demed contemptible and as folke vnworthi to lyffe, forsoþe anone þou woldest meke thiselfe vnto þe yerthe, and woldest raþer desire to be sugget vnder alle þen to be above one; ner þou woldest not desire þe myry dayes of this worlde, but raþer þou woldeste ioye to suffre tribulacion for God, and woldest take as for a grete lucre to be accompted for noght amonge men.

(4)   ¹⁵'O, yf þees þinges savoured þee, and entred | into thi herte, howe durste þou ones compleyne þee? ¹⁶Wheþer alle laboryouse þinges be not to be suffred for everlastinge lyve? ¹⁷Hit is no litel þinge to wynne or to lese þe reaume of God. ¹⁸Lifte vppe þerfore þi visage into hevone! Loo, I and alle my seintes with me, þei þat in þis worlde haue hadde grete bateile! Nowe þei ioyeth, nowe þei be counforted, nowe thei be sure, nowe þei reste, and withoute ende shul abide with me in the reaume of my Fader.'

f. 150ᵛ

2 and alle mesure] MG, 'and all mesure' D², *om.* C, *Latin* et mensuram KR
7 vyneyarde] vyneȝerde 'and' D², vyneȝerde and MG   8 contrarioustes] contrari-
ou(snes) D², contrariousnes G, *Latin* contraria KR   9 one] oo DMG   10 of]
after *altered from* of D², after MG, *Latin* huius scilicet temporis KR   be] þer be
DMG   perpetuelle] perpetuel, *last* e *altered from* a D²   11 seie þen] þen seie
marked for reversal C   12 wo me] wo 'to' me D², wo to me MG   13 be
þrowen] drawe M, 'be' || drawe D², be drawe G   favtinge] sautyng M, fayling G, *Latin*
indefectiua KR   14 sugget] DMG, sugget and C, *Latin* affectares pocius omnibus
subesse KR   16 laboryouse] laborose DM   18 þei þat] ⟨which þat⟩ D²,
whiche þat M, whiche G

Of the daie of eternite and þe angwysshes of þis lyve
Capitulum 53^m

[1]'O the moste blisful dwellynge-place of þat highe cite! [2]O the moste (1)
f. 151^r clere daie of everlastingnes, whome no [n]yght makeþ darke, | but
sovereyne trouthe ever byshyneþ hit, þe day ever gladde, ever sure, and
never chaungynge state into contrarie! [3]O, wolde God þat þat day had
ones shyned, and alle þees temporalle þinges had take an ende! [4]And þis
daie shyneth to seintes in a perpetuel bright clerenesse, but to pilgrymes
al afarre and by a mirroure.

[5]"The citezeins of hevon knoweþ howe ioyouse is þat daie; þe exiled (2)
sones of Eve waylon, so sorowfulle is þis daie. [6]The daies of þis tyme ar
litel and yvel, fulle of sorowes and angwysshes, [7]where man is defouled
with many synnes, is tyed with many passions, streyned with many
dredes, distente with many cures, distracte with many curiosites, |
f. 151^v wrapped in many vanitees, circumfounded with many errours, broken
with many laboures, greved with many temptacions, made softe and
weyke with delices, tormented with nede and poverte.

[8]'O, whenne shal þer be an ende of alle þees yvels? When shal I be (3)
delyvered fro the wrecched þraldame of vices? [9]When shal I, Lorde,
haue mynde of þee allone? When shal I at fulle be gladde in þee?
[10]Whenne shal I bee with[oute] ani impedimente in veri liberte, withoute grevaunce of soule or body? [11]Whenne shal þer be sadde pees, pees
i[m]perturbable, and sure pees withinne and withoute, pees ferme on
every side? [12]Goode Ihesu, when shal I stande to see þee? When shalle I
f. 152^r biholde þe glory of thi reaume? When [shalt þou] | be [to me] alle þinges
in alle þinges? [13]Whenne shal I be with þe in thi reaume þat þou haste
ordeyned to thi welbyloved fro everlastinge? [14]I am lafte pouer and an
exyle in the lande of enemyes, where ar daily bateiles and gretteste
infortunes.

[15]'Counforte myne exile, swage my sorowe, for to þe suspireþ alle my (4)
desire. [16]For alle þat þe worlde offreþ to me as solace is to me an hevy

53.0 53^m] 53 MG, 53 'liii' D², *Latin* liii R, xlviii, *last i added on line* K   2 no nyght]
G, non niȝt DM, no myght C, *Latin* ⟨quam nox non obscurat⟩ K, quam nox non obscurat
R   trouthe] trouth|þe, þe *canc.* D²   contrarie] þe contrarie DMG   5 ioyouse]
ioyfull G   7 defouled] defoyled G   is²] ⟨. .⟩ D², *om.* MG   with⁵] *om.* M
9 of] on DMG   10 bee withoute] MG, 'be' wiþoute D², bee with C, *Latin* ero sine
KR   11 pees²] per M   imperturbable] DMG, inperturbable C, *Latin* imperturbabilis KR   12 goode] go'o'de D²   shalt þou be to me] MG, ⟨shalt þou be⟩ 'to
me' D², þou shalt ‖ be C, *Latin* quando eris michi KR   13 reaume] ⟨regne⟩ D²,
regne MG   15 sorowe] DMG, sorowes C, *Latin* dolorem KR

burdon. [17] I desire to fruyshe þee inwardly, but I may not take þee. [18] I wille to clyve to hevonly þinges, but fleysshely þinges and vnmortificate passions depresseth me. [19] I wolle in my mynde be above alle þinges, but magre me I am constreyned to be byneþe. [20] So I, vnhappy man, fight with myselfe and am made grevouse | to myselfe, whiles the spirite sekeþ f. 152ᵛ þat is above and þe fleisshe þat is byneþe.

(5)   [21] 'O, what suffre I withinforþe, whiles I entrete hevonly þinges in my mynde, and þe compayny of fleisshely þinges comeþ ayenis me when I pray? [22] My God, be not farre fro me; declyne not fro thi servant in wrathe. [23] Lyghton oute thi shynynge and waste hem; sende thin arowes and trou[b]led and shende mote be alle maner contrariouse fantasies. [24] Gedre togydres alle my wittes to þee; make me to foryete alle worldely þinges, and graunte sone to caste aweye and despice alle fantasies of vices. [25] Thou trouthe eternal, succurre me, þat no vanite meve me. | [26] Come, hevonly swetnesse, and make flee fro thi visage alle maner f. 153ʳ impurete. [27] Foryive me also and mercifully forgete, as oftetymes as in my preier I þenke on any oþer þinge þen on þee. [28] I knowleche verily þat I am wonte to haue me þere fulle distractely. [29] And many tymes I am not þere where I stande or sytte bodely, but raþer I am þere where I am borne with my þoughtes. [30] Where my þoght is, þere am I, and whereas my þoght is oftetymes, þere I love. [31] That þinge cometh sone to mynde þat naturelly delyteþ or pleseþ þorowe vse.

(6)   [32] 'Wherefore þou, trowthe, seideste openly, "Whereas is thi tresore, þere is thi herte." [33] If I love hevon, I am gladde to þenke on hevonly þinges. | [34] If I love þe worlde, I ioye of þe worldes felicite, and sorowe of f. 153ᵛ the worldes adversite. [35] If I love þe fleysshe, I ymagine oftetymes on suche þinges as longen to the fleisshe. [36] If I love the spirite, I haue a delite to þenke on spirituel þinges. [37] Whatever þinges þat I love, of hem gladly I speke and here, and þe images of suche I bere to my house. [38] But blysfulle is þat man þat for þee, Lorde, yiveth alle creatures lycence to goo her weie, þat doþe violence to nature, þat crucifieþ the

18 wille] ⟨desire⟩ D², desire MG   20 whiles] while DMG   fleisshe] flesshe 'sekyth' D², flesshe sekiþ MG   21 and] (.) D², om. MG, Latin et KR 23 sende . . . fantasies] sende oute þyn ⟨arwys⟩ and ⟨þou shalt trob'yll' hem and all þe fantasyes of þe enemye shall⟩ 'be bore down' D², sende oute þyn arowis and þou shalt trobille hem and alle þe fantasyes of þe enemye shal be bore dovn M, sende oute thi arowes and all the fantasies of þe enemy be troublede G, Latin emitte sagittas tuas et ⟨contur-bentur⟩ omnes fantas⟨ie inimici⟩ K, emitte sagittas tuas et conturbentur omnis fantasie inimici R   troubled] con., trouvled C   24 alle²] DMG, alle alle C   29 am³] was DM, Latin feror KR   30 whereas] wher G   oftetymes] om. DMG, Latin frequenter KR   31 naturelly] natur⟨ely⟩ D²   32 is¹] om. M   36 spir-ituel] spiritu⟨al⟩ D²

concupiscences of the fleysshe with fervoure of þe spirite, þat with a clere conscience he mowe offer to the a pure preyer, and be worthi to be

f. 154ʳ presente to þe queres of aungels, alle yerthely | þinges excluded withinne and withoute.'

Of desire of everlastynge lyve, and howe grete þinges
ar promitted to fyghtars
Capitulum 54ᵐ

[1] 'Sone, when þou felest þe desire of everlastynge blysse to be infounded (1) into þe fro above, and þou desireste to goo oute of the tabernacle of the body, þat þou mowe byholde my clerenes withoute shadowe of chaungeablenes, dilate þi herte and receyve this holy inspiracion with alle maner desire. [2] Yelde to the sovereyne bounte moste large þankynges, þat dothe with the so worthely, visiteþ mercifully, exciteþ ardently, lyfteþ vppe myghtily, leste þou with thine owne weyght slyde downe to yerthely þinges. [3] For þou takeste | not þis with þine owne

f. 154ᵛ bought, ner þine owne enforcynge, but onely by dignacyon of the most highe grace and of godly biholdinge, þat þou mowe profite þe more in vertue[s] and gretter mekenes and make þe redy to bateiles þat ar to come and to clyve to me with alle þine affeccion, and þat þou study to 'serue' me with a fervente wille.

[4] 'Sone, oftetyme the fire brenneþ, but withoute flaume and smoke hit (2) styeth never vppe. [5] So the desires of summe men ar lyfte vppe to hevonly þinges, and nerthelater þei ar not free fro temptacion of fleisshely affeccion. [6] And þerfore þei do not in alle wises purely for þe worshippe of God þat þei aske so desi[de]rantly of God. [7] And suche

f. 155ʳ is ofte|tymes thi desire, þat þou haste seide shulde be so importune. [8] For þat is [not] pure and perfite þat is done for propre profite.

[9] 'Aske þat þinge þat is to the not delectable ner comodiouse, but þat (3) is to me acceptable and worshipfulle, for if þou deme rightwysely, þou

38 and[1]] and to DMG

54.0 54ᵐ] 54 MG, 54 'liiii' D², *Latin* liiii R, xl(ix) K   2 bounte] bonyte, y *altered from* u D², goodnes G   mercifully] so mercifully G   ardently] so ardently G myghtily] so myʒtlye G   3 þat[1]] þatf M   vertues] DMG, vertue C, *Latin* virtutibus KR   4 oftetyme] oftetymes DMG   withoute] (withowte) D² 5 nerthelater] neuerþeles DMG   temptacion] DMG, temptacions C, *Latin* temptacione KR   affeccion] neuerþeles DMG, *Latin* carnalis affectus KR   6 þat] 'in þat' þat D², in þat þat MG, *Latin* quod KR   desiderantly] DMG, desirantly C   7 thi] þe DMG, *Latin* tuum KR   8 not] DMG, *om.* C, *Latin* non KR   9 to the not] not to þe DMG

oweste [putte] myne ordinance bifore thi desire and alle by þe desired, and folowe hit. [10][For] I haue herde thy desire and thi manyfolde moornynges. [11]Nowe þou woldest be in þe lyberte of þe glory of the sones of God; now deliteþ þee þe house everlasting and the hevonly countrey fulle of ioye. But yeet is not þis houre comen: there is as yeet anoþer tyme, tyme of bateyle, tyme of laboure and of previnge. [12]þou desireste to be | fulfilled with the moste sovereyne gode, but þou mayste   f. 155ᵛ not execute þat nowe. [13]"I am," seithe oure Lorde; "abide me tille the reaume of God come."

(4)   [14]'As yette þou arte to be preved in yerþe and to be exerciced in many þinges. [15]Consolacion shal be yiven þe ever amonge, but copiouse fulfillynge is not graunted. [16]Be þou counforted, þerfore, and be stronge, as wel in doynge as in suffringe þinges contrary to nature. [17]Hit bihoveth þe to be cloþed in a newe man, and to be chaunged into anoþer. [18]Hit bihoveþ the to do oftetymes þat þou wolte not doo, and to forsake þat þou wolte do. [19]That þat pleseth oþer shal cause profitinge, but þat þat pleseth þiselfe shal not | profite. [20]That oþer men seie shalle be herde; þat   f. 156ʳ þou seyste shal be accompted as noght. [21]Oþer menne shulle aske and (5)   take; þou shalte aske and not gete. [22]Oþer shul be grete in mennes mouthes; of þe menne shulle holde her pees. [23]To oþer þis or þat shal be commytted; þou shalt be demed to noþinge profitable. [24]Wherfore kynde shal sumtime be sory and suffre grete bateile, if þou in silence bere þees þinges. [25]In thes and many oþer like þe trewe servant of God is wonte to be preved, howe he mowe denye and breke himselfe.

[26]'Ther is vnneþe any suche þinge in the whiche þou nedest to dye so muche as to see and suffre suche þinges as ar contrary to [þi] wille, | principally when þou arte commaunded to do suche þinges as semeþ to   f. 156ᵛ þe disconuenient and leste profitable. [27]And for þou darste not withstande þe higher power sette above þe vnder oure Lorde, [þerfore hit

9 putte] DMG, 'to folowe' C, *Latin* preferre KR   alle . . . hit] ⟨preferre ande folwe 'it' afore all⟩ 'thynge' D², preferre and folow afore alle þinge M, preferre and folowe it afore all thyng G, *Latin* meam ordinacionem tuo desiderio et omni desiderato preferre debes ac sequi KR   10 for I] MG, ⟨for I⟩ D², I C, *Latin* nam desiderium tuum et frequentes gemitus audiui R, noui desiderium tuum et frequentes gemitus audiui K 11 þee þe] þe 'the' D²   13 I am] ⟨I⟩ 'am' D², I am it G   14 exerciced] exercised, s *altered from* c D²   18 wolte¹] woldist DMG   þou wolte do] ⟨þou wol⟩'dist' do D², þou woldist do MG   20 that] that þat G   24 kynde] nature G   in silence bere] ⟨feyne to⟩ here D², feyne to here MG, *Latin* si silens portaueris hec R, si silens portaueris K   25 and¹] and in DMG   26 in . . . dye] ⟨which þou nedist 'to be'thynke þe in⟩ D², whiche þou nedist to beþinke þe in MG, *Latin* in quo tantumdem mori indiges KR   þi] 'þi' D², *om.* CMG, *Latin* voluntati tue KR 27 þerfore . . . harde] MG, 'þerfore it semiþ the harde' D², *om.* C, *Latin* ideo durum tibi videtur K, ideo tibi durum videtur R

semeþ þee harde] to go at anoþer mannes bekonynge and to leve alle þine owne felynge.

²⁸ 'But, sone, peyse the fruyte and þe swyfte ende of alle þees (6) laboures, and the meede grete withoute mesure, and þen shalte þou haue no grevance þerof, but a myghti counforte of pacience. ²⁹ For þis litel wille þat þou forsakest frely þou shalte [ever] haue þine owne wylle in hevon. ³⁰ There þou shalte fynde whatever þou wolte, and alle þat þou mayste desire. ³¹ þere shal be plente of alle gode withoute drede of |

f. 157ʳ lesinge or forgoinge. ³² Ther þi wille, ever beinge one with me, shal never coveite straunge þinge ner private. ³³ [Th]er shal no man withstande þe, ner shal no man compleyne on þe; no man shal lette þee, no man shal contrary þee, but alle þinges desired shul be presente togidre and shul refresshe alle þi desire and fulfille hit to the highest. ³⁴ There shal I yelde glorie and worshippe for shame and repreve, a palle of preisinge for mornynge, for the lowest place þe sete of þe reaume durynge into worldes. ³⁵ There shal appiere þe fruyte of obedience; þere þe laboure of penance and meke subieccion shul be crowned gloriously.

f. 157ᵛ ³⁶ 'Wherefore bowe þiselfe nowe mekely vnder þe handes of alle, | ner (7) take none heede who seide þis or commaunded þis, but charge þat sovereynely þat wheþer prelate or lasse þen þou or evon to þe aske anyeþinge of the or meeue anyþinge to þe, þat þou take alle to gode, and studie to fulfille hit with a pure wille. ³⁷ Lete [one] seke þat, anoþer þat; lete him reioyce him þerinne, and him hereinne; lete þees be preised in þis and in þousande þousandes; but ioye þou nouþer in þis ner in þat, but in contempte of þiselfe and in my welleplesinge and worshippe. ³⁸ This is ever to be desired of þe, þat boþe by lyve and by dethe God be ever glorified in thee.'

That the desolate manne oweþ to offre himselfe
into the handes of Godde
f. 158ʳ   *Ca|pitulum 55ᵐ*

¹ 'Lorde God, holy Fader, blessed mote þou be nowe and everlastingly, (1) for as þou wolte, so hit is done, and þat þou doste is gode. ² Gladde mote

29 ever] DMG, *om.* C, *Latin* semper KR   31 drede] DMG, dredre C, *Latin* timore KR   33 ther] DMG, ner C, *Latin* ibi KR   ner] C, þere DMG   be] DMG, be to C   36 none] no G   þat²] *om.* DMG, *Latin* hoc magnopere curato ut KR   37 one] DMG, anoþer C   nouþer] neiþer DMG
55.0 55ᵐ] 55 MG, 55 'lv' D², *Latin* lv R, ⟨l⟩ K   1 god] DMG, gode C, *Latin* deus KR

þi servant be in þee and not in himselfe, ner in none oþer þinge, for þou alleone arte verye gladnesse: þou arte my hope and my crowne, þou arte my ioye and my worshippe. ³What hath þi servant, but þat he hath taken of þe, and þat withoute his merites? ⁴Alle þinges ar þine, þat þou haste yiven and þat þou haste made.

(2)　⁵'I am pouer and in laboures fro my youthe, and my soule is oftetymes scrye vnto þe teres; and sumtyme hit is troubled towarde hitselfe for encombrance of | passions. ⁶I desire þe ioye of pees; þe pees　f. 158ᵛ of þi sones I aske, þat ar fedde of þe in þe lyght of consolacion. ⁷If þou yiffe pees, yf þou infounde holy ioye, þe soule of þi servante shal be fulle of modulacion and devoute in thi preisinge. ⁸But if þou withdrawe þee, as þou arte wonte to do fulle ofte, hit may not renne the weye of þi commaundementes, but raþer his knees ar bowed to knokke þe breste, for hit is not [with] him as hit was yesturday and þe oþer daye, whenne thi lanterne shyned vppon his hede, and he was defended vnder þe shadowe of þi wynges fro temptacions fallynge vppon him.

(3)　⁹'Rightwyse Fader and ever to be preysed, þe houre is comen þat þi servant be | preved. ¹⁰Lovely Fader, hit is worthy þat þis houre þi servante　f. 159ʳ suffre sumwhat for þee. ¹¹Fader perpetuelly to be worshipped, lete þi servant lyffe inwardely ever a[n]enst þee, whom þou kneweste fro þe bygynnynge so to be þat he shulde for a litel tyme falle as outewarde; ¹²for a litel tyme lete him be sette lytel by, meked, and fayle afore menne; lete him be broken with passions and languores, þat he may rise ayeine with þee in þe morowetide of a newe lyght and be claryfied in hevonly þinges.

(4)　¹³'Holy Fader, þou haste so ordeyned and willed, and þat is done þat þou haste commaunded. ¹⁴For þis is thi grace to þi frende in þis worlde, to suffre and to be troubled for þi love, howe | ofte and of whommeever　f. 159ᵛ þou suffrest hit to be done. ¹⁵Withoute þi counseyle and thy providence and withoute cause is noþinge done in yerthe. ¹⁶Gode hit is to me, Lorde, þat þou haste meked me, þat I mowe lerne þi iustificacionz and caste aweye al maner elacions of herte and presumpcions. ¹⁷Hit is profitable to me þat shame and confusion haþe covered my face, þat I mowe require þe to my counforte raþer þen men. ¹⁸I haue lerned herby to drede þine inscrutable iugemente, þat peynest þe rightwyse man with þe wykked, but not withoute rightwysnes and equite.

7 yiffe] ⟨y⟩eue D²　　　　　8 with] DMG, *om.* C, *Latin* non est illi KR
11 perpetuelly] perpetu⟨e⟩ly D²　　　anenst] DMG, ayenst C, *Latin* apud te KR
12 fayle] fayled M, *Latin* deficiat KR　　14 is] 'is' D²　　　15 providence]
prudence M, *Latin* prouidencia KR　　16 maner] *om.* DMG　　17 face] fate D,
Latin faciem KR　　　18 peynest] skorgyst G

¹⁹ 'Lorde, I þanke þe þat thou haste not spared myne yvels, but þat (5)
f. 160^r þou haste bryssed me with betinges, | puttinge into me sorowes and
sendynge into me angwysshes withinne and withoute. ²⁰ There is none
þat may counforte me of alle þat ar vnder hevon but þou, my Lorde
God, þe hevonly leche of soules, þat smyteste and heleste, þat ledest to
the lowest places and bringest fro þens ayeine. ²¹ Thi disciplyne is vppon
me, and thi rodde she shal teche me.

²² 'Lo, wel-biloved Fader, I am in thi handes, I incline me vnder þe (6)
rodde of thy correccion; smyte my bakke and my nekke, so þat I bowe to
þi wille my crokednesse. ²³ Make me a meke disciple, as þou arte wonte
to do, þat I mowe go entierly at þi bekenynge. ²⁴ To þee I committe me
f. 160^v and alle myne to correcte, for hit is better | to be correpte here þen in
tyme commyng.

²⁵ 'Thou knowest alle þinges and [singuler], and noþinge is hidde fro
þe in mannes conscience. ²⁶ Thou knowest þinges to come or þei be
done, ner hit is no nede þat man teche þee ner amonyshe þee of þoo
þinges þat ar done in yerthe. ²⁷ Thou knowest what is expedient to my
profitinge, and howe muche tribulacion deserveþ to purge þe ruste of
my vices. ²⁸ Do with me þi desired wel-willynge, and despice not my
synfulle lyve, to none better knowen ner clerer þen to þee alone.

²⁹ 'Graunte me, Lorde, to knowe þat is to be knowen, and to love þat (7)
is to be loved, and to preyse þat sovereynly pleseþ þee, to haue þat in
f. 161^r reputacioun þat | appiereth preciouse to the, and to blame þat is foule in
þine yen. ³⁰ Suffre not me to deme aftir the sighte of þe outwarde yen,
ner yive sentence aftir the herynge of eres of vnlerned men, but to
discerne in trewe iugemente bothe of þinges visible and spirituel, and
above alle þinges ever to enquere aftir þe wille of thy welplesinge.
³¹ Mennes wittes ar oftetymes deceyved in demynge; also lovers of þis (8)
worlde ar oftetymes [blended] yn lovinge onely þinges visible. ³² What is
a man þe better þerfore þat he is accompted þe gretter of man? ³³ The
deceyvable bigyleth þe deceyvable, þe veyne þe veyne, þe blynde þe
blynde, þe seke þe seke, whiles he lyfteþ him vppe and verily more

---

19 haste bryssed] C, brysed DM, brysist G, *Latin* attriuisti KR   22 vnder] to G,
Latin sub virga KR   23 go entierly] walke G, *Latin* ut ambulem ad omnem nutum
tuum KR   24 correpte] (chastysyd) D², chastised MG, *Latin* corripi KR
25 and singuler] MG, 'and' (syngulere) D², and everyþinge C, *Latin* et singula KR
26 thou] thouh M   ner¹ . . . done] *om*. M, *Latin* et non opus est tibi ut quis te doceat
aut ammoneat de hiis que geruntur K, et non opus est tibi ut quis te doceat aut moneat de
hiis que geruntur R   27 of] DMG, *twice* C   29 þat¹] þat þat G   be¹] *om*.
DM   30 not me] me not DM   to²] *om*. DMG   31 blended] DM, blynded
G, *om*. C, *Latin* falluntur KR   32 þe²] ⟨. .⟩, þe *visible under erasure* D², *om*. G

con|foundeþ him whiles he veynly preiseþ him. [34] For howe muche þat f. 161ᵛ
everye man is in þine yen, Lorde, so muche he is and no more, as seithe
meke Fraunceis.'

That manne muste yive him to lowe werkes when highe werkes faylen
Capitulum 56ᵐ

(1) [1] 'Sone, þou maiste not ever stande in þe moste fervente desire of
vertues, ner abide stedfastly in þe highest degree of contemplacion, but
þou haste nede amonge for the original corrupcion to descende to lower
þinges and bere [þe] burdon of þis corruptible lyve ayenis wille and
with werynesse. [2] As longe as þou bereste a dedly body, þou shalt fynde
hevynes and grevance of herte. [3] Hit bihoveth þerfore oftetymes in the |
fleysshe to wayle vnder þe burdones of þe fleisshe, inasmuche as þou f. 162ʳ
maiste not withoute cessinge clyffe to spirituel studyes and diuine
contemplacion.

(2) [4] 'Then hit is spedefulle to þe to drawe þe to meke and outwarde
werkes, and to take recreacion in gode active ocupacions, abidinge my
commynge and the highe visitacion with a stedfaste truste; and to suffre
paciently þine exile and drynes of soule, tille þou be visite of [m]e newe
and delyuered from alle anxietes. [5] For I shal make þe to foryete þi
laboure and fruysshe inwarde quiete. [6] I shal open bifore þee þe medowes
of scriptures, þat þou with a dilated herte mowe renne þe weye of [my]
commaundementes. [7] And þen þou shalte seye, | "þe passions of þis f. 162ᵛ
tyme ar not worthi to the glorye þat shal be reveled in vs."'

That man accompte himselfe worthi no consolacion
Capitulum 57ᵐ

(1) [1] 'Lorde, I am not worthi þi consolacion ner no spirituel visitacion, and
þerefore þou doste rightwysly with me when þou forsakest me nedy and
desolate. [2] For if I myght poure oute teres lyke þe sea, yette were not I

56.0 56ᵐ] 56 MG, 56 'lvi' D², Latin lvi R, li, i added on line K   1 þe³] DMG, om.
C   ayenis] ayenst 'þi' D², ayenst þi G   2 dedly] ded body dedly, ded body canc.
M   4 þe²] om. M, Latin consurgere R, confugere K   gode] g'o'ode D²   of me
newe] con., of þe newe CDM, efte of me G, Latin iterum a me visiteris KR
5 quiete] quiete'nes' D², quyetnes G   6 my] DMG, thi C, Latin mandatorum
meorum KR
57.0 worthi] worthy of G   57ᵐ] 57 MG, 57 'lvii' D², Latin lvii R, lii, second i added on
line K   1 þi] no DMG, Latin consolacione tua KR   no] om. M

worthi þi consolacion. ³ Wherfore I am noþinge more worthi þen to be
scourged and punyshed, for I haue oftetymes offended þee, and forsaken
þe gretely in many þinges. ⁴ Wherfore, very reson peysed, I am not
worthi þe leste consolacion.

f. 163ʳ   ⁵ 'But þou, graciouse and | merciful Lorde, þat wolte not þat thi
werkes shulde perisshe, to shewe þe richesses of thi godenes into þe
vessels of mercie over alle propre merite, fouchest save to counforte þi
servant above alle mannes mesure. ⁶ For thi consolacions ar not as
mannes talynges or confabulacions.

⁷ 'What have I done, Lorde, þat þou shuldest yive me any hevonly (2)
consolacion? ⁸ I haue no remembrance of any gode þat I haue done, but
þe very trowthe is þat I haue bene ever redy and pro[n]e to vices and
slowe to amendemente, ⁹ þe whiche I may not denye. ¹⁰ If I wolde seie
oþerwise, þou wolde stande ayenis me and þere wolde [no] man defende
me. ¹¹ What haue I deserved for my synnes but helle and everlastinge
f. 163ᵛ   fire? ¹² I know|leche in trowþe þat I am worthi alle maner of scornynge
and despite, ner hit sittiþ not me to be noumbred amonge þi devoute
servantes. ¹³ And þoghe I here þes not esily, nerthelater for trouþe I shal
ayenis myselfe repreve my synnes, þat I mowe þe lyghtlyer gete þi
mercie. ¹⁴ What shal I seie, a gilty man and fulle of alle confucion? ¹⁵ I (3)
haue no worde to speke, but onely þis worde, "I haue synned, Lorde, I
haue synned: haue mercie on me, foryive me!" ¹⁶ Suffre me a litel while
þat I may wayle my sorow or ever I go to þe darke lande, covered with
þe darkenes of dethe.

¹⁷ 'What requireste þou moste of þe gilty and the wrecched synnar,
f. 164ʳ   but þat he be converted and meke himselfe for his | synnes? ¹⁸ In veri
contricion and mekenesse of herte is broght forþe hope of foryivenesse:
þe troubled conscience is reconsiled, grace loste is repayred, man is
defended fro wraþe þat is to come, and God and þe meke soule meteþ in
an holy kosse.

¹⁹ 'Contricion of synnes is to þe, Lorde, an acceptable sacrifice, (4)
smellynge muche swetter þen any sote incence. ²⁰ This is also þat
acceptable oynement þat þou woldest shulde be poured vppon thi
moste holy feete, for þou haste never despised þe contrite and þe

5 richesses] ryches G   godenes] g'o'odenes D²   mercie] mercy 'ande' D², mercy
and MG   fouchest save] vouchesaf DM, vouchesauest G   6 talynges] talkinges
DMG, Latin confabulaciones KR   7 yive] ⟨y⟩eue D²   8 ever] euer⟨.⟩ D
prone] DMG, prove C, Latin pronum KR   10 stande] say DMG, Latin stares KR
no] DMG, om. C, Latin non esset qui defenderet KR   12 of] om. M   not] om.
DMG   13 þes not] not þis DMG, Latin hec R, hoc K   nerthelater] neuerþeles
DMG   18 kosse] cvsse M, ⟨k⟩osse D²   19 incence] en'cen'ce D²

meked herte. ²¹There is þe place of refute fro þe visage of þe wrathe of þe enemy. ²²þere is amended and wasshen aweye alle þat is contracte and defouled elleswhere.' |

That þe grace is not medled with hem þat savoureth yerthely thynges　f. 164ᵛ
Capitulum 58ᵐ

(1)　¹'Sone, my grace is preciouse, and suffreþ not hirselfe to be mengled with straunge þinges ner yerþely consolacions. ²Wherfore hit bihoveþ þe to caste awey alle impedimentes of grace, yf þou desire to receyve þe infusion þerof.

³'Aske to þiselfe a secrete place, love to dwelle alleone with þiselfe, seke confabulaciouns of none oþer, but raþer put oute to God a devoute preyer þat þou mowe have a devoute mynde and a pure conscience. ⁴Deme alle þe worlde as noght. ⁵Put vacacion to God bifore alle oþer þinges. ⁶For þou maiste not boþe take hiede to me and delyte þee in | þinges transitory. ⁷Hit bihoveþ to be eloyned fro knowen and dere f. 165ʳ frendes, and kepe þe mynde private fro alle temporal solace. ⁸So bischeþ the blessed apostle Petre, þat alle trewe Cristen men conteygne and holde hemselfe in þis worlde as straungers and pilgymes.

(2)　⁹'O, howe grete truste shal be to þe manne þat shal dye, whom affeccion of none yerthely þinge withholdeþ in þis worlde! ¹⁰But þus to haue þe herte departed from alle þinges a seke and a weyke soule cannenot take, ner þe bestly man knoweþ not þe liberte of þe inwarde man. ¹¹Nerthelater, who þat wolle be very spirituel, hit bihoveþ him to renounce boþe hem þat be farre and hem þat ar nyghe, and of none so | muche to beware as of hymselfe. ¹²If þou overcome thiselfe perfitly, þou f. 165ᵛ shalte þe more lyghtly put vnder fote alle oþer þinges. ¹³Hit is perfite victorie a man to overcome himselfe. ¹⁴Whoeuer kepe himselfe so vnder, þat sensualite obeye to reson and reson to me in alle þinges, he shal be a very victour of himselfe and lorde of þe worlde.

21 refute] refuge D, socoure G, *Latin* locus refugii KR　　22 elleswhere] DMG, elleswhere | elleswhere C
58.0 þe] *om.* G　　58ᵐ] 58 MG, 58 'lviii' D², *Latin* lviii R, lii(i) K　　1 hirselfe] itself DMG　　2 alle] *om.* DMG, *Latin* omnia KR　　3 confabulaciouns] consolacions M, *Latin* confabulacionem KR　　5 vacacion to] vacacion of M, 'þe' vacacion of D², þe attendance of G, *Latin* deo vacacionem R, dei vacacionem K　7 bihoveþ] behoveth the G　　eloyned] ⟨a⟩l⟨yenyd⟩ D², alyenyd MG, *Latin* elongari KR　　8 conteygne] conte⟨yne⟩ D²　　9 withholdeþ] wiþholdiþ ⟨. . . .⟩ D　11 nerthelater] neuerþeles DMG　　none] none, e *added on line* D², noon suche M　12 lyghtly] DMG, lyghtly þou shalte C　　14 þat] *om.* M　　to²] 'to' G

[15] 'If þou desire to styghe vppe to þe heyght of perfeccion, þou muste (3) bigynne manly and sette þe axe to þe roote, þat þou mowe rote vppe and destruye alle inordinate inclinacion to thiselfe, and to alle private and materialle gode. [16] Of þis vice þat a man loveþ himself to inordinately

f. 166ʳ   hengeþ almoste alle þinge þat is groundely to be overcomen, | [17] the whiche yvel overcomen and putte vnder, anone forþewith shal þer be grete pees and tranquillite. [18] But for fewe þer ar þat laboureþ perfitely to dye to hemselfe, ner plenarly streccheþ not hemselfe [withoute hemselfe], þerfore þei remayneþ implyed and encombred in hemselfe, þat þei mowe not be lyfte vppe in spirite above hemself. [19] Who þat desireþ frely to walke with me, hit bihoveþ nedes þat he mortifie alle his shrewde and inordinate affeccions, and þat he clyve to no creature concupiscently with no private love.'

Of diverse mevinges of nature and of grace
Capitulum 59ᵐ

[1] 'Sone, attende diligently þe mevinges of nature, for þei ar fulle (1)

f. 166ᵛ   contrary and sotilly meved, and þei | can vnneþe be perceyved, but if hit be of a spirituel man and a man inwardely illumined. [2] Alle folke desirethe þat is gode, and in her wordes and in her dedes þei pretendeþ summe maner of gode; wherefore muche [folke] ar deceyved vnder coloure of gode.

[3] 'Nature is wyly and draweþ many men and holdeþ hem as in a gnare, and deceyveþ hem and haþe hir ever as for an ende, sekynge none oþer. [4] But grace gothe symply, and declyneþ from alle þat semeþ yvel, pretendinge no falsnes ner deceytes, and doþe alle þinges purely for God, in whom finaly she resteþ.

[5] 'Nature dyeþ ayenis his wille; he wolle not be þrowen downe ner (2)

f. 167ʳ   overcomen, ner be vnder ner willingly come vnder yokke. | [6] But grace studyeþ and labourethe to mortificacion of himselfe; he withstandeþ

---

15 to⁵] canc. D, Latin ad omne . . . bonum KR   16 to inordinately] ⟨to in⟩ordinatly D²   almoste alle þinge] all þinge almost DG, alle þinges almost M overcomen] DMG, overcomen þat is growndely to be over|comen C   17 and¹] þe whiche and M   shal þer] þer shal DMG   18 for] om. DMG, Latin sed quia KR   plenarly] fully G   not¹] om. DMG   hemselfe withoute hemselfe] MG, hem'self withowt hem'self D², hemselfe C, Latin extra se tendunt KR   remayneþ] remayne(n) D²   implyed] implicate G
59.0 59ᵐ] 59 MG, 59 'lix' D², lix R, ⟨liiii⟩ K   2 folke²] DMG, om. C 3 for] om. DMG, Latin ⟨se semper⟩ pro fine habet K, se semper pro fine habet KR 4 þinges] þinge DMG   5 his] hir DMG   þrowen] drowen M   6 studyeþ and labourethe] laboriþ and studieþ DMG   to¹] to þe G   himselfe] itself DMG

sensualite; he sekeþ to be made sugget; he desireþ to be overcomen; he
wolle not vse his owne liberte, but he loveþ to be vnder disciplyne; he
coveiteþ to haue lordeshippe over nobodye, but to lyve, to stande and to
be onely vnder God, redie for God to be mekely enclined and bowed to
every creature þat man is.

⁷'Nature laboreþ for his owne profite, and takeþ hiede what lucre
may come to himselfe alone. ⁸But grace considereþ not what is
profitable and comodiouse [to one], but to many.

⁹'Nature receiveþ gladly worshippe and reverence, but grace yiveþ
alle worship and glorie frely to God.

(3)   ¹⁰'Nature dredeþ shame and | despite, but grace ioyeþ to suffre for þe   f. 167ᵛ
name of Ihesu.

¹¹'Nature loveþ ydelnes and bodely reste, but grace cannot be voyde
ner ydel, but gladly takeþ vppon him laboure and travaile.

¹²'Nature sekeþ to haue curiouse þinges and feire þinges, and loþeþ
alle vile þinges and grosse þinges. But grace delyteþ in simple þinges
and lowe þinges, and despiseþ none asperite, ner refuseþ not to be
cloþed in olde cloþes.

¹³'Nature biholdeþ temporal þinges and ioyeþ of yerþely wynnynges
and soroweþ for worldely harmes and is stired to wraþe with a litel
worde of wronge. ¹⁴But grace attendeþ everlastinge þinges, ner clyveþ
not to temporal þinges, ner is troubled with þe losse of hem, ner is not
angred with sharpe wordes, for he | setteþ alle his ioye and his tresoure   f. 168ʳ
in hevon, where noþinge perisheþ.

(4)   ¹⁵'Nature is coveitouse and more gladly takeþ þen yiveþ; he loveþ his
propre and his private godes. ¹⁶But grace is fulle of pite; she is comune,
she eschuethe singuler þinges and is contente with fewe, and demeþ
more blisfulle to yive þenne to take.

¹⁷'Nature enclynethe to creatures, to her owne flesshe, to vanitees, to
discourses and rennynge aboute. ¹⁸But grace draweþ to God and to
vertues, renounceþ creatures, fleeþ þe worlde, hateþ þe fleisshely
desires, restreyneþ wandrynges aboute, and is ashamed to appiere in
open places.

¹⁹'Nature gladlye receyveþ outewarde counfortes, whereinne hit maye

---

6 þat man is] ⟨of⟩ man⟨kynde⟩ D², of mankynde MG, *Latin* omni humane creature
KR   8 to one] DMG, *om.* C   12 not] *om.* DMG   13 stired] meved G,
mevid red M, ⟨meu⟩'yd' ⟨sone⟩ D², *Latin* irritatur leui iniurie uerbo KR   14 and]
and alle M   15 yiveþ] ⟨y⟩euiþ D²   his²] *om.* DMG   godes] goodnes M, *Latin*
propria et priuata KR   16 yive] ⟨y⟩eue D²   18 þe¹] *om.* M   19 whereinne . . . wittes] *om.* DMG, *Latin* in quo delectetur ad sensum KR

f. 168ᵛ   be delited as to þe outwarde | wittes. [20] But grace delyteþ in the soverayne gode above [alle] þinges visible.

[21] 'Nature doþe alle þinges for propre lucre and for his owne profite, (5) and can do noþinge freely; but if he do any benefaite, he wolle wayte to haue as gode or better or preisinge or favoure, and desireþ þat his dedes and his yiftes shulde be preised and muche sette by. [22] But grace sekeþ no temporal þinges, ner sekeþ none oþer mede but Godde, whom soole he desireþ for his rewarde, ner he desireþ no more of temporal þinges þen as mowe be helpinge to him to getinge of everlastinge þinges.

[23] 'Nature reioyceþ of many frendes and allyes, and ioyeþ of noble (6) f. 169ʳ   places and of grete | birþe, lawgheþ vppon myght and power, blan-dysheþ ryche folke, and haþe plesance in suche as ar lyke to himselfe. [24] But grace loveþ his enemyes; he is not provde of multitude of frendes, ner accompteþ neiþer place ner birþe, but if þer be þe more vertue þere; he fauoureþ more þe pover þen þe riche; he haþe more compassion on þe innocent þen on þe myghty; he ioyeþ with þe trewe man, not with þe false man; and ever exhorteþ to gode, to seke more grace, and to be lyke þe Son of God in vertues.

[25] 'Nature compleyneþ sone of fawtinge and of grevance. But grace stedefastly bereþ poverte and neede.

[26] 'Nature reflecteþ alle þinge to himselfe, and for himselfe he stryveth (7) f. 169ᵛ | and argueþ. [27] But grace reduceþ alle þinges to God, of whom þei welleþ oute groundely and originally; he ascryveþ noþinge þat gode is to himselfe, ner presumeþ noþinge proudely, ner stryveþ not ner preferreþ not his sentence bifore oþres, but in everi felynge and in everi vndirstanding submitteþ himselfe to þe everlastynge wisdame and to Goddes examinacion.

[28] 'Nature coveyteþ to knowe secretez and to here newe þinges; he wolle appiere outewarde and by felynge haue experience of many þinges; he desireþ to be knowen and to do suche þinges whereof preysinge and wondrynge myght aryse. [29] But grace takeþ none hiede to perceyve newe f. 170ʳ   þinges and curiouse, for alle | þis groweþ of corrupcion, sithe þer is noþinge newe and durable vppon yerþe.

20 alle] DMG, *om.* C, *Latin* super omnia visibilia KR   21 lucre] DMG, lucre and for his owne propre lucre C   noþinge] noþ.nge *blotted* G   but] ⟨and⟩ D², and G, *Latin* sed KR   to] *om.* M   22 ner¹] nor DM   23 reioyceþ] reioi(s)eþ, s *altered from* c D²   24 of¹] of the G   neiþer] *om.* DMG   þe¹] þere G þere] *canc.* D², *om.* MG, *Latin* ⟨nisi⟩ virtus maior ⟨ibi⟩ fuerit K, nisi virtus maior ibi fuerit R   27 gode] go'o'de D²   felynge] fe'lynge' D²   28–9 whereof . . . þinges] *om.* M, *Latin* vnde laus et ammiracio procedit sed gracia non curat noua nec curiosa percipere KR   29 none] no G   newe²] nowe DM, nouum KR   yerþe] þe erþe DMG

30 'Grace also techeþ to restreyne þe wittes, to eschue veyne plesaunce and ostentacion, suche þinges as ar commendable and wonderful mekely to hide, and of eueryþinge and euery science to seke oute þe fruyte of profite and Goddes preisinge and his worship. Grace desireþ ner him ner his werkes to be openly preched, but desireþ God to be blessed in his yiftes, þat graunteþ alle þinges of his pure largesse.

(8)   31 'This grace is a lyght supernaturelle and a special yifte of God, and þe propre signacle of þe chosen children of God and þe arneste of everlastinge helþe, for he lyfteþ vppe man frome yerthely þinges to love hevonly þinges, and of | him þat is fleysshely he makeþ spirituel.   f. 170ᵛ 32 Wherfore þe more þat nature is holde vnder and overcomen, the more grace is poured inne, and þe inwarde man is every day renewed aftir þe image of God with newe visitacions.'

Of corrupcion of nature and of the myghte of grace
Capitulum 60ᵐ

(1)   1 'Mi Lorde God, þat haste made me into þine image and lykenes, graunte me þis grace þat þou haste shewed to be so grete and so needeful to mannes helþe, þat I mowe overcome my moste wykked nature, þat draweþ me to synnes and into perdicion. 2 For I feele in my fleysshe þe lawe of synne contraryinge þe lawe of my mynde, and ledynge | me as a caytyfe to obeye þe sensualite in many þinges, ner I   f. 171ʳ may not withstande his passions, but if thy moste holy grace poured into my herte be assistente to me.

(2)   3 'Needefulle hit is to haue þi grace, yea, and þi grete grace, þat kynde mowe be overcomen, þat is ever redy to yvel of yonge age and adolescence. 4 For nature slyden and viciate bi þe furste man Adam þorowe synne, þe peyne of þat spotte hath comen downe into alle menne, so þat nature, þat was welle and evonly made by þee, is nowe sette for vice and infirmite of corrupte nature, inasmuche as his mevinge, lafte and relicte to himselfe, draweþ ever to yvel and to lowe þinges. 5 And þat litel goode | strengthe þat is lafte is as but a litel   f. 171ᵛ

30 him] him'self' D², himself MG   openly preched] prechid openly DMG 31 supernaturelle] supernatur⟨a⟩ll D²   þe¹] a DMG   arneste] enest ernest M, *Latin* pignus KR   spirituel] spiritu⟨a⟩l D²
60.0 60ᵐ] 60 MG, 60 'lx' D², *Latin* lx R, l⟨v⟩ K   1 into¹] to DMG   to²] to *twice, first canc.* D²   2 contraryinge] contrienge M   þe³] *om.* M   3 kynde] ⟨nature⟩ D², nature G   be overcomen] ouercome M   adolescence] adolescency G   4 downe] adovn DMG   5 goode] g'o'ode D²   as but a litel] but as a G

sparkel, hydde in asshen. ⁶This is naturel reson, circumfounded on everi
side with darkenesse, havinge yeet iugement of gode and yvel, and distance
of trewe and false, þoghe hit be vnmyghtye to fulfille þat hit appreveþ, ner
hit vseþ not nowe fulle lyght of trouþe, ner holenesse of affeccions.

⁷'Hereþorowe hit is, my God, þat aftir þe inwarde man I delite me in (3)
thy lawe, knowinge þ[i] commaundement to be gode and iuste and holy,
previnge also al synne and alle yvel to be fledde. ⁸But in my fleysshe I
serve þe lawe of synne, while þat I obey more sensualite þen reson.
⁹Hereþorowe hit [is] þat to wille gode comeþ to me, but to do hit in
f. 172ʳ   dede I fynde not in me. ¹⁰Wherfore ofte|tymes I purpose many gode
þinges, but for þi grace lakkeþ, þat shulde helpe myne infirmite,
þoroughe a light resistence I turne bakke and fayle. ¹¹Hereþoroughe
hit happeneþ þat þoghe I knowe þe weie of perfeccion, and þat I see
clerely what I owe to doo, yeet I am so pressed with þe weight of myne
owne corrupcion þat I may not aryse to more perfeccion.

¹²'O Lorde, how moste necessarie is [grace] to bigynne gode, to (4)
profite in gode, and to be perfite in gode. ¹³For withoute hir I may do
noþinge, but in þee I am myghti to alle þinges, strengthinge me grace.

¹⁴'O þat veri hevonly grace, withoute whome proprely þer ar no
merites ner none yiftes of nature to be peysed! ¹⁵Lorde, withoute grace,
f. 172ᵛ   as anenste þe, þei beeþ | of no value, neyther craftes ner rychesses ner
beaute nor strengeþ ner witte ner eloquence. ¹⁶For yiftes of nature ar
comune to gode and to yvel, but þe propre yifte of þe chosen childeron
is grace or charite, wherwith who þat be nobleyed [shal] be worþi
euerlasting[e] lyve. ¹⁷This grace is so eminent and so excellent þat
neiþer yifte of prophecie ner worchinge of miracles ner speculacion, be
hit never so highe, is of any estimacion withoute hir. ¹⁸Yea, neiþer feiþe,
ner hope, ner oþer vertues ar acceptable to þe withoute grace and
charite.

¹⁹'O þ[ou] moste blisfulle grace, þat þe pover in spirite makeste riche (5)

5 sparkel] sparke M, *Latin* tamquam scintilla KR   6 on] in DMG   holenesse]
holynes DM, helthe G, *Latin* sanitate KR   7 hereþorowe] ⟨therfore⟩ D², therfore
MG   þi] DMG, þe C, *Latin* mandatum tuum KR   gode] g'o'ode D²   and²] and
|| and *first canc.* D²   synne] synnes G, *Latin* peccatum KR   8 þat] *om.* DMG
more] more þe DMG   9 is] DMG, *om.* C, *Latin* hinc est quod KR   10 gode]
g'o'ode D²   12 grace] DMG, *om.* C, *Latin* gracia KR   13 hir] hit DG
me] ⟨me⟩ D², by M, *Latin* confortante me gracia KR   14 ner none] ne no DMG
16 ar] 'are' G   to¹] boþe to G   but] G, but þat, þat *canc.* D², but þat CM   be¹]
'be' G   shal] DMG, *om.* C, *Latin* digni habentur KR   euerlastinge] DMG,
euerlastingly C, *Latin* vita eterna KR   17 neiþer] neiþer 'þe' D², neyþere þe
G   19 þou] G, þ⟨ou⟩ D², þat CM, *Latin* o beatissima gracia KR

in vertue, and þe meke in herte makeste riche in many godes! [20] Come, descende vnto | me, fulfille me bityme with þy consolacion, leste my   f. 173[r]
soule fayle for werynesse and drynesse of mynde!

[21] 'Lorde, I biseche þe þat I mowe fynde grace in þine yen, for þi grace sufficeþ to me, oþer þinges not had þat nature desireþ. [22] If I be tempted and vexed with many tribulacions, I shal not drede whiles thi grace is with me. [23] She is my strengthe; she yiveþ me counseile and helpe. [24] She is more myȝtti þen alle enemyes; she is more wyser þen

(6)   alle þe wyse; [25] she is maistres of trowþe, doctrice of discipline, light of the herte, þe solace of pressure and þrowinge downe, dryver awei of sorowe, taker awei of drede, norisher of devocion, and bryngar forthe of teres. [26] What am I withoute | hir but a drie tree and an vnprofitable   f. 173[v]
stokke?

[27] 'Wherefore, Lorde, lete þi grace evermore goo afore me and folowe me and make me to be continuly and bysily yiven to gode werkes by oure Lorde Ihesu Criste, thi Sone. [Amen].'

That we owe to denye oureselfe and folowe Criste by the crosse
Capitulum 61[m]

(1)   [1] 'Sone, as muche as þou maiste go oute of thiselfe, so muche þou maiste go into me. [2] As a man to coveyte noþinge withouteforþe makeþ inwarde pees, so a man inwardely to forsake himselfe ioy[n]eþ and onethe to God. [3] I wolle þat þou lerne perfite abnegacion of thiselfe in my wille withoute contradiccion and compleynynge. [4] Folowe me: I am wey, trowthe, and lyve. Withoute wey | me goþe not; withoute trouthe me   f. 174[r]
knoweth not; withoute lyve me lyveþ not. [5] I am the weye þat þou shalte folowe; I am the trouthe þat þou shalt bilyeve; and the lyve þat þou shalte hope. [6] I am the weye vndefouleable, þe trouþe infallible, þe lyve

---

21 not] ⟨not⟩ D², þat M, *Latin* ceteris non obtentis KR   24 more²] *om.* DMG
þen . . . wyse] *om.* M, *Latin* sapiencior vniuersis sapientibus KR   25 and þrowinge
downe] and þrower dovn M, (.) þrower doon 'and' D², þrower downe and G, *Latin*
solamen pressure KR   27 folowe] fol⟨we⟩ D²   gode] g'o'ode D²   amen]
DMG, *om.* C, *Latin* amen KR
     61.0 61[m]] 61 MG, 61 'lxi' D², *Latin* lxi R, lvi, i *added on line* K   1 oute . . . me]
⟨out fro þe⟩ 'so mych mayste þou go into me' D², out fro þe so muche maist þou go into
me MG   2 ioyneþ] DMG, ioyeþ C, *Latin* coniungit KR   onethe] oneþ 'hym'
D²   4 wey¹] M, wey of C, 'þe' wey D², þe wey G, *Latin* ego sum via veritas et vita
KR   me . . . me . . . me] men . . . men . . . men DMG   5 lyve] lif ⟨. . . . . .⟩, þe
life *visible under erasure* D   þou³] *om.* M   6 vndefouleable] vndefoulid DM,
vndefoyled G, *Latin* inuiolabilis KR   infallible] vnfallible G

interminable. [7] I am þe most evon weye, moste sovereine trowþe, very lyve, lyve increate and lyve blisfulle.

[8] 'If þou dwelle in my weie, þou shalte knowe trouþe, and trowþe shal (2) delyver þe, and þou shalte take everlastinge lyve. [9] If þou wolte entre to lyve, kepe þe commaundementes. [10] If þou wolte knowe trowþe, byleve me. [11] If þou wolte be perfite, selle alle þinges. [12] If þou wolte be my disciple, denye þiselfe. [13] If þou wolte haue þe lyve þat is to come, despice | þis þat is presente. [14] Yf þou wolte be enhaunced in hevon, meke þiselfe in þe worlde. [15] If þou wolte regne with me, bere my crosse, [16] for onely þe servantez of þe crosse fynden þe weie of blisse and of everlastinge lyght.'

f. 174ᵛ

[17] 'Lorde Ihesu, for þi weie was streyte and despised of the worlde, (3) graunte me to folowe þee with þe worldes despisinge. [18] For þe servante is no gretter þenne his lorde, ner þe disciple above his maister. [19] Lete þi servante be exercised in thi lyve, for þer is my helthe and veri holynes. [20] Whatever I here or rede byside þat, hit refressheþ not ner delyteþ not plenarly.'

[21] 'Sone, for þou haste redde and knowest alle þes þinges, þou arte (4) blisfulle if þou do hem. [22] He þat hath my commaunde|mentes and kepeþ hem, he hit is þat loveþ me, and I shal love him and shewe myselfe to him, and shall make him [an heir] in þe reaume of my Fader.'

f. 175ʳ

[23] 'Lorde Ihesu, as þou haste seyne and promitted, so be hit to me, and so mote I deserve. [24] I haue taken of þi hande þe crosse, and so shal I bere hit to my dethe, as þou had leyde vppon me. [25] Uerily the crosse is þe lyve of a gode monke, and þe ledar to paradise. [26] Hit is bigonnen: hit is not lyefulle to go bakwarde, ner hit is not bihofulle to forsake hit.

[27] 'Eya, broþeren, go wee togydres; Ihesus shal be with vs. [28] For Ihesu (5) we haue taken þis crosse; for Ihesu persevere we in þe crosse. [29] He shal be oure helpe, þat is oure ledar and our predecessoure. [30] Loo, | oure kynge goþe bifore vs, þat shal fight for vs! [31] Lete vs folowe manlye! Lete no man drede terrours; be we redye to dye myghtily in bateile. Lete vs put no spotte in oure glory in fleynge fro þe crosse.'

f. 175ᵛ

---

7 lyve²] om. DMG, *Latin* vita vera vita increata vita beata R, vita vera ⟨vita beata vita increata⟩ K   9 entre to lyve] lyue DMG, *Latin* ingredi KR   13 haue] haue þiself M, *Latin* si vis beatam vitam possidere KR   18 disciple] disciple 'is' D²   19 is] 'is' G   holynes] om. M, *Latin* sanctitas KR   20 not²] om. G   22 an heir] DMG, om. C, *Latin* sedere mecum R, consedere mecum K   24 had leyde] had leide it M, ha⟨st⟩ leide it D², hast leyde it G, *Latin* imposuisti KR   25 gode] g'o'ode D²   27 eya] ⟨haue 'doo'⟩ D², haue doo MG, *Latin* eya KR

That a man be not þrowen downe to muche yf he falle in any defautes
Capitulum 62[m]

(1) [1]'Sone, pacience and mekenesse in aduersite pleseth me more þen muche iubilacion and deuocion in prosperite. [2]Whi doþe a lytel þinge saide or done ayenis þee make þe sory? [4]Hit is no newe þinge; hit is not þe furste, ner shal not be þe laste, yf þou lyve longe. [5]Þou arte manly inowe alle þe while no contrarie comeþ ayenste þe; [6]thou canste counseyle welle and laboure oþer menne | with wyse wordes. [7]But when a sodeyne tribulacion comeþ to þi yate, þou fayleste boþe in counseile and in strengthe. [8]Take hyede to þine fraylete, wherof þou haste experience in smale obiectes and contrarioustez.

f. 176ʳ

[9]'Nerthelater, þees alle ar done for þi helþe, and when þei and suche

(2) oþer fallen, [10]purpose as weel as þou canste in þi herte þat if þei touche þe þat þei þrowe þe not downe, ner longe encombre þee, [11]and atte leste suffree paciently, yf þou cannot suffre ioyngly. [12]And if þou cannot here hit gladly, and felest in þiselfe a loþinge, restreyne þiselfe and lette noþinge inordinate passe þi mouthe, þat myght be to þe smale and to þe feble occasion of fallynge. [13]The meving þat | wolde oute shal sone reste, and, grace turnynge ayein, þe inwarde sorowe shal sone be made swete. [14]"Yeet I lyffe," seithe oure Lorde, "redy to helpe þee, and [to] counforte þee more þen I am wonte, so þat þou truste in me and inwardely and devoutely preie to me."

f. 176ᵛ

(3) [15]'Be myghti in soule, and gurde þee and make þee redy to more sufferance. [16]Hit is not alle done in ydel, if þou perceyve þiselfe oftetymes troubled or grevously tempted. [17]Thou arte a man, and not God; þou arte flesshe, and none aungel. [18]Howe maiste þou abide ever in one state of vertue, sithe þat lakked þe furste aungel in hevon and þe furste man in paradise? [19]I hit am þat rere to helthe hem þat moorneþ, and bringe to my godhed hem | þat knoweþ her owne infirmite.'

f. 177ʳ

(4) [20]'Lorde, blessed be thi worde, swete to my mouthe above þe hony and þe honycombe. [21]What shulde I do in so grete tribulacions and in myne angwysshes, but if þou counfordedeste me with þi holy wordes?

62.0 a] *om.* M   62[m]] 62 MG, 62 'lxii' D², *Latin* lxii R, (lvii) K   4 shal not] DG, shalte not C, shal M   6 canste] must DMG, *Latin consulis* KR   8 in] in many DMG   contrarioustez] contrariou(snes) D², contrariousnes G   9 nerthelater] neuerþeles whan DMG   þees alle] alle þese M   10 as weel] DMG, *twice* C   14 seithe . . . and[1]] *om.* M, *Latin* dicit dominus iuuare te paratus KR   to[2]] DMG, þee C   15 in] in more suffraunce it is not alle doon, all except in *canc.* M   18 one] oo DMG   19 hit am] (am it) D², am it G   helthe] hel(th) D², hele M   21 in[2]] *om.* G   þou] *om.* M

[22] Whiles atte laste I mowe come to þe porte salutz, what rekkeþ me what þinges and howe grete þinges I suffre? [23] Graunte me a gode ende; graunte me a graciouse goynge oute of þis worlde. [24] Haue mynde of me, my God, and dresse me in the right weye to thi reaume. Amen.'

Of highe þinges and prive iugementes of God not to be serched
Capitulum 63ᵐ

f. 177ᵛ   [1] 'Sone, beware that thou dispute not of highe matiers and of þe | pryve (1) iugementes of God: why þees is forsaken, and anoþer is taken vppe to s[o] grete grace; whi þees is so gretely peyned, and he is so excellently lyfte vppe. [2] Thes þinges passeþ alle mannes faculte, ner þer is reson ne disputacion þat sufficeþ to serche Goddes iugemente.

[3] 'Wherfore, when þe enemy bryngeþ suche þinges to mynde, or elles curiouse men askeþ þee, answere and seie with Dauid, "Lorde, þou arte iuste, and þi iugement is rightwyse. [4] þe iugementes of God ar trewe and iustifyed in hemselfe." [5] My iugementes ar to be dradde and not to be serched, for þei beeþ incomprehensible to mannes vnderstandinge.

[6] 'Enquere noþer ner dispute not of þe merites of seintes, who is (2)
f. 178ʳ   holier þen anoþer, | or who is gretter in the reaume of hevon. [7] Suche þinges oftetymes engendreþ stryves and vnprofitable contencions and noryshen pryde and veyneglorie, wherof growen envyes and discencions, whiles þees is aboute proudely to preferre one seinte and anoþer anoþer. [8] A man to wille to enserche and to knowe suche þinges bringeþ forþe no fruyte, but raþer displeseþ seintes, for I am no God of discencion, but of pees, þe whiche pees standeþ more in very mekenes þenne in propre exaltacion.

[9] 'Summe with a maner zele of love ar drawen with more affeccion to (3) þees seintes or to þoo seyntes, but þat affeccion is more of þe man þen hit is godly. [10] I hit am þat made alle seintes; I graunted grace; I yave |
f. 178ᵛ   glory. [11] I knowe the merites of every; I preve[nt]ed hem in blessinges of

22 salutz] (of helth) D², of helth MG   23 gode] g'o'ode D²   24 dresse]
⟨directe⟩ D², directe G

63.0 63ᵐ] 63 MG, 63 'lxiii' D², *Latin* lxiii R, lviii, *last i added on line* K   1 so
grete] *con.*, so hye DMG, *see* grete C, *Latin* ad tantam graciam assumitur KR
6 noþer ner] neiþer DMG   of²] 'of' D   7 envyes] enviose G   one] o
DM   8 enserche] serche DMG   no²] not MG   þe whiche] þe DM, whiche
G, *Latin* ⟨que⟩ pax K, que pax R   10 hit am] am it G   I²] ⟨and⟩ D², and MG,
Latin ego KR   yave] haue DMG, *Latin* prestiti KR   11 every] euery man G
prevented] MG, preuen⟨tyd⟩ D², preveyned C, *Latin* preueni KR

swetnesse; [12] I predestinate hem bifore worldes. [13] I chase hem oute of þe worlde; þei chace not me bifore. [14] I called hem by grace; I drewe hem bi mercy. [15] I ladde hem bi diuerse temptacions; I poured into hem grete

(4) consolacions. [16] I yave perseverance; I crowned her pacience. [17] I know þe furste and þe laste; I clyppe hem alle with an inestimable love. [18] I am to be preysed in alle my seintes; I am to be blessed above alle þinges and to be worshipped in every of hem whom I haue so graciously magnified and predestinate, withoute any merites goynge bifore.

[19] 'He þerfore þat despiceþ one of my leste, worshippeþ not þe grete, for I made boþe þe grete and þe smale. | [20] And he þat doþe hyndringe f. 179ʳ to any of my seintes doþe derogacion to me and to alle oþer in þe reaume of seintes. [21] Alle ar one bi þe bonde of charite; þei feele þe same

(5) and alle one; þei wolle þe same, and alle [þei] love hem into one. [22] And yette, þat is moste highe of alle, þei love [me] more þen hemselfe and her merites. [23] For þei, ravished above hemselfe and drawen oute of her propre love, gone alle and hole into þe love of me, in whom þei reste fruyshyngly. [24] Ther is noþinge þat may turne hem awey or þrowe hem downe, as þei þat, beinge fulle of everlastinge trowþe, brennen in an vnquenchable fyre of charite.

[25] 'Wherfore lette fleysshely and bestely cesse to dispute of þe state of seintes, þat cannenot love but | propre and pryvate ioyes. [26] Thei putteþ f. 179ᵛ aweye and addeþ to aftir her owne inclinacion, not as hit pleseþ þe

(6) everlastinge trouthe; [27] in many þinges ignorantly, namely þei þat but lytel illumyned can seldon love anybodi with perfite spirituel love. [28] Thei be gretely drawen yeet with naturel affeccion and mannes frensheppe to þes and to them; and as þei haue hem in þes lower þinges, so þei imagine in hevonly thinges. [29] But þer is a distance incomparable bytwene þoo þinges þat imperfite man þenken, and þoo þat men illumyned by highe reuelacion biholden.

(7) [30] 'Beware, þerfore, sone, þat þou trete not curiously of suche þinges as passeþ þi konnynge, but raþer entende and laboure þerto þat þou mowe be founden, | þoghe hit be þe leste, in the reaume of hevon. f. 180ʳ [31] And if a man knewe whatte seinte were holyer o[r] gretter þenne

---

21 þei³] DMG, *om.* C, *Latin* et omnes in vn⟨u⟩m se diligunt, o *visible under erasure*, m *of* vnum *added on line* K, et omnes in vnum se diligunt KR 22 me] DMG, *om.* C, *Latin* plus me quam se KR 22–3 hemselfe . . . and¹] hemself and 'soo' D², hemself and soo MG, *Latin* quam se et sua merita diligunt nam supra se rapti KR 24 hem²] *om.* DMG as þei þat] for þei G, *Latin* quippe qui KR brennen] brennynge M, *Latin* (ardescunt) K, ardescunt R 25 bestely] bestly 'men' D², bestly men MG 27 spirituel] spiritu(a)l D² 29 þoo¹] þinges þo M 31 or] DMG, of C

anoþer in þe reaume of hevon, what shulde þat knowleche awayle, but yf a man bi þe same knowleche meked himselfe bifore me and arose into gretter preysinge of my name? [32] Thei ar muche more acceptable to God þat þenkeþ on þe gretnesse of her synnes and of [þe] litelnesse of her vertues, and howe farre þei beþe fro perfeccion of seintes, þen þei þat disputen of the gretnesse and of þe litelnesse of seintez. [33] Better hit is to preye seintes with devoute preyers and teres and to desire her gloriouse suffragiez with a meke soule, þen to serche her secretes with veine inquisicion.

f. 180ᵛ   [34] 'Thei be welle contente | and in þe beste maner, yf men cowde be (8) contente and restreyne her veine speches. [35] Thei reioyceþ not of her owne merites; þei ascryveþ to hemselfe no godenesse, but alle to me, for I yave hem alle þinges of myne infinite charite. [36] Thei ar fulfilled with so grete love of the Godhed and so overflowinge ioye, þat noþinge lakkeþ hem of glory, noþinge fayleþ hem of blisse. [37] Alle seintes, þe higher þat þei ar in glory, þe more meke þei beþe and þe nere to me. [38] Therfore hit is wryten þat þei leyde her crownes bifore God and felle downe prostrate bifore þe Lambe, and worshipped him into worldes of worldes.

[39] 'Many askeþ who is grettest in þe reaume of hevon þat knoweþ not f. 181ʳ   wheþer þei shul be worþi | to be accompted amonge the leste. [40] This is a (9) grete þinge, a man to be þe leste in hevon, where alle be grete and [alle] ar called þe sones of God, and so þei shulle be. [42] When þe disciples asked who was gretteste in þe reaume of hevon, þei hadde þis answere, "But if ye be converted and made as smale children, ye shul not entre into þe reaume of hevon." [43] Whoever þerfore meke him as þis litel childe, he is gretteste in þe reaume of hevon.

[44] 'Woo to hem þat haue dedignacion to meke hemselfe wilfully with (10) smale children, for þe lowe yate of þe reaume of hevon shal not admitte hem to entre inne. [45] Woo also to riche men þat haþe her consolacion[s] here, for, pouer entrynge into þe reaume of hevon, þei shul stande f. 181ᵛ   withoute, | waylinge. [46] Ioye ye, meke folkes, and beeþ gladde, ye pouer, for youres is þe reaume of God, so þat ye goo in trowthe.'

---

31 knowleche¹] knowing DMG   awayle] auaile þe M, *Latin* quid ei hec noticia prodesset KR   32 gretnesse¹] grenes M, *Latin* magnitudine KR   þe²] DMG, om. C   þen þei] `þan they´ D², *om.* M, *Latin* quam is K, quam hii R   of³ þe] *om.* G 35 of¹] in M, *Latin* non gloriantur de KR   38 lambe] l(a)mbe D²   40 þe¹] *om.* G   alle²] DMG, *om.* C, *Latin* omnes KR   42 converted] DMG, con| converted C   45 haþe] ha⟨ue⟩ D²   consolacions] DMG, consolacion C, *Latin* consolaciones KR   for] for þe G   46 folkes] folke DMG   of] of heuene M, *Latin* regnum dei KR

That alle hope and truste is to be fycched onely in Godde
Capitulum 64ᵐ

(1)   ¹ 'Lorde, what is þe truste þat I haue in þis lyve, or what is my grettest solace of alle þinges apperinge vnder hevon? ² Wheþer not þou, my Lorde, of whos merci is no noumbre? ³ Where was hit welle with me withoute þee, or when myght hit be yvel, þee beinge presente? ⁴ I hadde lever be pouer for þe þen riche withoute þee. ⁵ I chese raþer to be a pilgryme with þe in yerþe, þen to haue hevon withoute þe. ⁶ Where þou arte, þere is hevon, and where þou arte not, | þere is dethe and helle.   f. 182ʳ ⁷ Thou arte to me in desire, and þerfore aftir þe hit is needefulle to moorne, to crie, [and] to prey. ⁸ I may fully truste in none þat may helpe me in oportune necessitez, but alleone in þe, my God. ⁹ Thou arte my hope, þou arte my truste, þou my counforte and moste feiþefulle in alle þinges.

(2)   ¹⁰ 'Alle oþer askeþ and sekeþ her owne comoditez; þou pretendeste alone my helthe and my profitinge, and turneste alle þinges to me into goode. ¹¹ Yea, þoghe þou ley me oute to diuerse temptacions and aduersitees, alle þat þou ordeyneste to my profite, þat arte wonte to preve þi chosen children in þousandes of maners; ¹² in the whiche previnges þou oweste to be no lasse loved and preysed þenne if | þou   f. 182ᵛ fulfilledest me with hevonly consolacions.

(3)   ¹³ 'In þe, þerfore, my Lorde God, I putte alle my hope and alle my refute; in þe þerfore I sette alle my tribulacion and myne angwyshe, for I fynde alle vnferme and vnstable, whatever I biholde oute of þee. ¹⁴ For many frendes shul not avayle, ner many helpars shul not mowe, ner many wyse counseiloures yive profitable counseile, ner bokes of doctours yive counforte, ner no preciouse substance of gode deliuere, ner no secrete ner myry place make sure, if þou be not assistente, helpinge,

(4)   counfortinge, enfourmynge, and kepynge. ¹⁵ For alle þinges þat semeþ to be for pees and felycite to be goten, the beinge absente, ar not worþe ner in | trowthe yiveþ noþinge longynge to verie felicite. ¹⁶ Thou, þerfore,   f. 183ʳ arte þe ende of alle godes, þe highenesse of lyve, þe profundite of scriptures; and to hope in þe above is þe moste myghtti solace of thi servantes.

64.0 64ᵐ] 64 MG, 64 'lxiiii' D², *Latin* lxiiii R, l⟨ix⟩ K   5 I . . . þe²] *om.* G, *Latin* eligo pocius tecum in terra peregrinari quam sine te celum possidere KR   7 and²] DMG, *om.* C, *Latin* et KR   9 þou²] þoue art G, *blotted* D   11 þousandes] þousand of M, þousande 'of' G, *Latin* mille KR   12 to be no lasse] no lasse to be DMG   13 refute] refu⟨g⟩e D², refuge G   vnferme] vnstedfast G, *Latin* infirmum KR   16 godes] g'o'odes D²

[17] 'To the ar myne yen dressed, my God, Fader of mercies. [18] Blesse and sanctifie my soule with an hevonly blessinge, þat hit mowe be þi holy habitacion and þe sete of þine everlastinge glorye, and þat noþinge be founden in the temple of thi dignite þat mowe offende þe yen of thi mageste. [19] Byholde into me aftir þe grettenesse of þi goodenesse and þe multitude of þi miseracions, and here þe preier of þi pover seruante, beynge in exile alle afarre in þe region of þe shadowe of dethe. |

f. 183ᵛ [20] Defende and kepe the soule of þi litel servante amonge so many periles of þis corruptible lyve, and, thi grace goinge with, dresse him by the wey of pees to the cuntrey of euerlastynge clerenes. Amen.'

Here ende the boke of inwarde consolacion.

17 dressed] d⟨yrecte⟩ D², dyrected G   19 goodenesse] g⟨o⟩odenes D²
20 dresse] d⟨yrecte⟩ D², directe G   clerenes] clennes DMG, *Latin* claritatis KR
amen] DMG, amen amen amen C, *Latin* amen KR   21 here . . . consolacion] *om.*
M   consolacion] consolacion ueni domine ihesu C, consolacyoun deo gracias DG, *Latin*
consolacionis R, *om.* K

NOTES

The Notes have four aims: to indicate where the translation departs from its Latin source, to explain obscurities, to provide references to biblical and other sources, and to comment on the language of the translation where words are used innovatively or in a way that is significant in the Christian mystical tradition. Because a full treatment of the relationship between the manuscripts with all relevant examples is given in Part III of the Introduction, textual matters are not generally covered further in the Notes beyond the provision of cross-references to the discussion in the Introduction of the passages concerned. As was stated in the description of editorial practice (see above, p. lxxxviii), emendations have been introduced into the text only where they can be justified with reference to the Latin in the light of the generally close nature of the translation: since in all such cases the Latin is cited in the critical apparatus and may there easily be compared with the readings of the manuscripts of the translation, emendations are not generally discussed further in the Notes.

Divergences between the translation and the Latin were identified by a comparison between the translation and the Latin text as found in K (quoted from Delaissé) and are mentioned in the Notes. Where a divergence from K may be explained with reference to the Latin text found in R, R's reading is also given. Sometimes readings from other insular manuscripts are given where they may explain the translation; for the meaning of the sigla used for these manuscripts, see above, pp. xlv–xlvi. Occasionally it is noted where the translation follows K and is different from R, but a systematic comparison of the text with R was not made.

The Notes aim to provide some indication of the considerable extent to which the *Imitation* draws on the Bible and on the language of the Christian mystical tradition.[1] Biblical references are to the Vulgate text, with the AV verse numbering, where different, shown in brackets; the standard English names of the books of the Bible are used. 'Vulgate' in brackets after a biblical reference implies that here it is only the Vulgate and not AV that provides a parallel with the *Imitation*. Where mystical language and imagery is noted, reference is made to the standard treatment in Riehle, where further discussion and references may be found.[2] An attempt is also made to identify new uses of words as noted in *MED* and *OED*.

[1] On the use of classical sources in the *Imitatio*, see M. Reiss, 'Die Zitate antiker Autoren in der *Imitatio* des Thomas von Kempen', in *Thomas von Kempen: Beiträge zum 500. Todesjahr . . . herausgegeben von der Stadt Kempen* (Kempen, 1971), pp. 63–77.

[2] In a few instances the metaphorical language noted seems to have a significance in the *Imitation* that is slightly different from its significance in the texts discussed by Riehle. See also relevant articles in *DS* for further discussion of many of the elements in the *Imitation*'s spirituality.

Modern translations of the *Imitatio* are quoted where helpful in explaining difficult passages, but where obscure words or phrases are treated in the Glossary they are not generally noted again here.

BOOK I

1.0.0. R reads *Incipit tabula prime partis libri interne consolacionis qui vocatur musica ecclesiastica*, K simply ⟨*Incipiunt capittula*⟩. On R's rubric, see Ampe, 'Verspreiding', pp. 162–71: there are several manuscripts which apply the title *Liber interne consolacionis*, originally the title of Book III alone, to Books I–III as a whole, presumably because a scribe, seeing this title in the explicit of Book III in a manuscript which contained only Books I–III, took it as applying to the whole work. On the title *Musica Ecclesiastica*, see above, pp. xxxix–xl, n. 71.

1.0.1–24. The Roman numerals in D have been added by D² in the margin to the lists of chapters of all three books.

1.0.3. See 1.3.0 n.

1.0.4. 'In mannes werkes' renders *in agendis*.

1.0.11. On C's reading 'hele', see Introduction, p. lxx, n. 124.

1.0.17. 'Of lyuynge in monastery' renders *De monastica vita*.

1.0.18. The translation follows R in omitting *sanctorum*, which in K modifies *patrum* ('faders').

1.0.22. 'Of mannes misery' renders *humane miserie*.

1.0.25. The title of chapter 25, missing in all four manuscripts of the translation at this point, is supplied from 1.25.0; 'of alle mannes lyve' renders *tocius vite nostre*. The translation does not give the title of Book I; R reads *Incipit liber interne consolacionis qui vocatur musica ecclesiastica. Et diuiditur in tres partes principales. Prima pars continet xxv capitula.* K reads *Incipiunt ammoniciones ad spiritualem vitam vtiles.*

1.1.0–2. *Qvi sequitur me non ambulat in tenebris* (John 8.12). In v. 1. 'foloweth' renders *sequitur*, but in the title of the chapter 'of the foloynge' renders *de imitacione* and in v. 2 'to folowe' renders *imitemur*. 'Imitate' and 'imitation' are not used in this translation: according to *OED*, 'imitation' is first used in English in the title of Atkynson's translation of the *Imitatio* (1502), 'imitator' in Lord Berners's preface to his translation of Froissart (1523), and 'imitate' in More's *On the Passion* (1534); Atkynson uses 'follow' in his translation of vv. 1–2. On the distinction between following Christ and imitating him, and on the imitation of Christ generally, see G. Constable, 'The Ideal of the Imitation of Christ', in his *Three Studies in Medieval Religious and Social Thought* (Cambridge, 1995), pp. 143–248 (pp. 145–7). The idea of imitating Christ is derived from St Paul: see 1 Corinthians 4.16 and 11.1, Ephesians 5.1, Philippians 3.17,

I Thessalonians 1.6 and 2.14, and 2 Thessalonians 3.7,9; also Hebrews 6.12 and 13.7. In v. 1 'oure' has been added; in v. 2, as often in the translation, 'alle maner' renders *omni*. 'Blyndenes of herte' renders *cecitate cordis*: cf. Mark 3.5 (Vulgate) and Ephesians 4.18; also 1.3.5 and n., 2.5.3. The imagery of illumination and blindness in v. 2 picks up 'darkenesse' in v. 1. On the imagery of light in mystical texts, see Riehle, pp. 80–1, and cf. such passages as 1.3.14, 1.14.11, 3.2.6, 3.20.10, 3.39.16–17, 3.53.4, and 3.59.31.

1.1.3. The Latin is *Summum igitur studium nostrum sit: in vita Ihesu Christi meditari*; *meditari* has been omitted in the translation. Kempis saw meditation on the life of Christ as a central means of imitating him; his works include *Orationes et meditationes de vita Christi* (Pohl, v. 1–361), translated by W. Duthoit as *Prayers and Meditations on the Life of Christ* (London, 1904).

1.1.4. 'Seintes and holy menne' is a doublet rendering *sanctorum*. The second 'of Criste' has been added. Hidden manna was promised to everyone who conquers in the letter to the church at Pergamum (Revelation 2.17).

1.1.5. The first 'of' is not to be taken with 'desire': the Latin is *multi ex frequenti auditu euangelii paruum desiderium senciunt*, i.e. 'many, because they have heard the gospel so often, feel little desire, for they do not have the spirit of Christ' (cf. Romans 8.9).

1.1.6. Here and at 3.42.8 the MSS reading 'pleynly' corresponds to the Latin *plene*. Since at 3.18.3, 3.58.18, and 3.61.20 *plene* is rendered 'plenarly', and at 3.40.18 *plenissime* is rendered 'moste plenarly', it is probable that an abbreviated form of 'plenarly' has been misread here. Although *MED* glosses 's[a]uourly' (*sapide*) here as 'with spiritual understanding', it is more likely to mean 'with relish': on the idea, common in the mystical tradition, that spiritual knowledge is savoury, which reflects the etymological connection between *sapientia* and *sapere*, see Riehle, p. 109, and cf. 1.11.8 and n., 1.22.17, 1.25.41, and 3.39. 'Confourme' renders *conformare*: on the importance of the *conformitas Christi* in the mystical tradition, an idea ultimately derived from Romans 8.29, see Riehle, pp. 148–9, and cf. 1.25.26 and 2.12.5. 'To his lyue' renders *illi*, referring to Christ.

1.1.7. 'Displese' represents the subjunctive *displiceas*: D²'s correction to 'displ⟨esist⟩' suggests that he regarded this use of the subjunctive after 'whereby' as inappropriate. The theme of the uselessness of intellectual knowledge is developed in such passages as 1.2, 1.3, 1.5, 1.24.28–9, and 3.36.12–13. On anti-intellectualism in the mystical tradition, see Riehle, p. 14; on the importance of meekness, see Riehle, pp. 64–5, 111, and cf. such passages as 2.2, 3.3, 3.5, and 3.8.

1.1.8. 'For' corresponds to *vere*.

1.1.9. 'To knowe' renders R's *scire compunctionem quam scire eius diffinicionem* rather than K's *se⟨ntire⟩ compunctionem: quam scire eius diffinicionem*, which points the contrast between affective feeling and intellectual knowing more effectively.

1.1.10. The translation omits *totum*, the object of *prodesset* ('avayle'), and follows R in omitting *dei* from K's *sine caritate dei et gratia.*

1.1.11. The Latin is *Vanitas vanitatum et omnia vanitas: preter amare deum et illi soli seruire*: 'alle other þinges in þe worlde' has been added. The first clause is derived from Ecclesiastes 1.2, the second from Matthew 4.10 (itself a combination of Deuteronomy 6.5 and 6.13); cf. also 1.24.41.

1.1.12. 'Bi despisinge of þe worlde' renders *per contemptum mundi*; cf. 1.23.22. 'To drawe hym' renders *tendere*.

1.1.13. 'But' renders Latin *igitur*.

1.1.14. 'To lyfte hymselfe on highe' renders *in altum ˋstatumˊ se extollere.*

1.1.15. 'To folowe þe desires of þe fleysshe' renders *carnis desideria sequi* (cf. Galatians 5.16). 'þat þinge' renders *illud*, i.e. anything for which one will afterwards be punished, rather than a particular sin; so too in v. 18.

1.1.16. 'To take none hede' renders *parum curare.*

1.1.18. 'Where ioyes abyden euerlastynge' renders *vbi sempiternum gaudium manet.*

1.1.19. *Non saciatur oculus visu: nec auris impletur auditu* (Ecclesiastes 1.8); *impletur* has been omitted from the last clause.

1.1.20. *Stude ergo cor tuum ab amore visibilium abstrahere: et ad invisibilia te transferre*, i.e. '. . . and turn yourself to invisible things'; R omits *te*, and it was probably this omission in his Latin text that led the translator to supply 'hem' (presumably referring to 'þinges') as an object for 'translate'.

1.2.0. On the importance of self-knowledge as a prerequisite for spiritual growth, see Riehle, pp. 57–8, and cf. 2.5.0.

1.2.1. *Omnis homo naturaliter scire desiderat*—a rendering of the first sentence of Aristotle's *Metaphysics* (I. i. 980ᵃ).

1.2.2. *Melior est profecto humilis rusticus qui deo seruit: quam superbus philosophus qui se neglecto cursum celi considerat*: cf. Augustine, *Confessions* 5.4.7 and *De Trinitate* 4.1.

1.2.4. Both the syntax and the sentiment of this verse (though not the exact words) are reminiscent of 1 Corinthians 13.1–3; cf. 2.11.19–22.

1.2.8. 'þen to þe helthe of his soule' renders R's *quam hiis que saluti anime sue deseruiunt*; K omits *anime.*

1.2.13. *Noli altum sapere: sed ignoraciam tuam magis fatere*: with the first clause cf. Romans 11.20 and 12.16.

1.2.14. 'Of God' has been added.

1.2.15. The precept *ama nesciri et pro nichilo reputari* is also found in Kempis's *Alphabetum Monachi* I (Pohl, iii. 315). *Ama nesciri* was a guiding principle of the early brothers of the house at Mount St Agnes as they strove to do each other's work without gaining any recognition: see chapter 3 of Kempis's *Chronicon canonicorum regularium montis sancte Agnetis* (Pohl, vii. 348).

1.3.0. As is clear from 1.3.1, 'doctryne of trowthe' (*doctrina veritatis*) refers to a person's being taught by truth.

1.3.1. *Felix quem veritas per se docet, non per figuras et voces transeuntes: sed sicuti se habet. Transeuntes* has been omitted; only D²'s reading 'as' accurately translates the Latin. The verse recalls God's statement to Aaron and Miriam that he spoke to Moses *ore ... ad os ... et palam, et non per aenigmata et figuras* (Numbers 12.8).

1.3.4. 'Settynge at no3t' renders *neglectis*; 'yive our vtmaste entendance' renders *vltro intendimus*.

1.3.5. *Oculos habentes non videmus*: cf. what was said to Judah in Jeremiah 5.21; also Isaiah 6.9–10, Matthew 13.13–15, John 12.40, Acts 28.26–7, and Romans 11.8.

1.3.6. *Quid cure nobis de generibus et speciebus?* On *genera* and *species*, 'terms used in Aristotelian metaphysics to define the nature of reality and being' (Knott, *ad loc.*), see *NCE* vi. 339, viii. 554–5; *EP* v. 35, 60.

1.3.7. 'Spedde and delyuered' is a doublet rendering *expeditur*.

1.3.8. *Ex vno verbo omnia; et vnum loquuntur omnia: et hoc est principium, quod et loquitur nobis.* 'One speke þ al þinges' is a misleading translation of *vnum loquuntur omnia*, i.e. 'all things speak of one Word'. In response to the Pharisees' question, 'Who are you?', Jesus replied, *Principium, quia et loquor vobis* (John 8.25, Vulgate; AV, however, has 'Even the same that I said unto you from the beginning'); cf. also Revelation 1.8. With the beginning of the verse cf. John 1.1–3.

1.3.10. *Cui omnia vnum sunt, et omnia ad vnum trahit, et omnia in vno videt; potest stabilis corde esse: et in deo pacificus permanere.* For the use of 'one' here, cf. v. 11 and n.; the idea of abiding in God is derived from Jesus' exhortation in John 15.1–10.

1.3.11. This verse, *O veritas deus: fac me vnum tecum in caritate perpetua*, though present in both K and R, is omitted in the translation; the idea of being one in God is derived from Jesus' prayer for the disciples in John 17.21, that of everlasting love from the promise of the restoration of Israel in Jeremiah 31.3. On the central mystical idea of union with God, see Riehle, pp. 89–92, and cf. 1.3.14, 2.1.18, 2.8.31, 3.36.9, and 3.61.2.

1.3.12. 'Lorde' has been added.

1.3.13. 'Alone' (*solus*) is to be construed with 'þou'.

1.3.14. The sense of the first clause has been altered; the Latin is *Quanto aliquis magis sibi vnitus et interius simplificatus fuerit*; see 2.1.1 n. *Sine labore*, which modifies *intelligit* ('vnderstandeþ'), has been omitted.

1.3.15. 'Disparpled' renders *dissipatur*. The last clause renders *in se ociosus ab omni propria exquisicione esse nititur* (R has *occiose*), i.e. 'strives within himself to be free from all self-seeking'; the addition of 'witte' changes the meaning to 'all seeking of personal knowledge'. This and 3.38.7 are the only citations of 'exquisicion' (*exquisicione*) in *MED* and *OED*.

1.3.16. 'Vnmortified affeccion of herte' renders *immortificata affectio cordis*. This is the first citation of 'vnmortified' in *OED*.

1.3.18. On 'right reson' (*recte racionis*), see *NCE* xii. 118.

1.3.22. 'Is more acceptable to God' corresponds to *cercior via est ad deum* in K; R originally had *cercior est ad deum*; *uia* has been inserted in the margin, possibly in a different hand. 'Depe inquisicion of kunnynge' renders *profunda sciencie inquisicio*, i.e. 'deep searching after knowledge'.

1.3.23. 'Bare and simple' renders *quelibet simplex*; this is the only point in the *Imitatio* at which its otherwise unreservedly anti-intellectual position is qualified. 'Ordeyned of God' corresponds more closely to K's *a deo ordinata* than to R's *ab omnipotente deo ordinata*, an indication that the translation is unlikely to have been made from R itself, but from a manuscript related to it.

1.3.24. The mention of bringing forth fruit (*fructum ferunt*) is another reference to John 15: see vv. 4–8. 'Or none' is stronger than the Latin's *pene nullum*.

1.3.25. 'To rote oute vices' renders *ad extirpanda vicia*; it is the only citation of the phrase 'rote oute' in the sense 'to root out (vices), eradicate' in *MED*. 'To meve questions' renders *ad mouendas questiones*. 'Wykkednes' corresponds to *mala et scandala*. 'Cenobyes and monasteryes' is a doublet rendering *cenobiis*; this is the only citation of 'cenoby' in *MED*.

1.3.27. 'Nowe' should be taken with 'ar' (*dic michi vbi sunt modo*). 'Knewest' renders *bene nouisti*. 'Scoles' corresponds to *studiis*.

1.3.28. 'Ones' has been added.

1.3.29. 'Almoste' has been added.

1.3.30. *O quam cito transit gloria mundi*. This verse appears to be the origin of the proverb *Sic transit gloria mundi* (cf. 1 John 2.17 and 1.20.33). 'Lorde' has been added.

1.3.33. *Euanescunt in cogitacionibus suis* (Romans 1.21).

1.3.34. 'Lytel and meke' is a doublet rendering *paruus*.

1.3.35–6. The effective variation in word-order here ('Uerily he is prudente . . . he is verily welle lerned') has been introduced by the translator (the Latin is *Vere prudens est . . . et vere bene doctus est*; R has *hic* before *prudens*). In v. 35

'styngynge' has been added; cf. Paul's characterization of everything as *stercora* in comparison with Christ (Philippians 3.8).

1.4.0. The confusion in the manuscripts between 'prouidence' and 'prudence' may have arisen because in K itself the chapter title has *prudencia* in the list of chapters and *prouidencia* at the head of the chapter itself; R has *prudencia* in both cases. Since *prouidencia* here means 'forethought', the difference in meaning is not so very great.

1.4.1. The construction 'hit is not to yif credence' illustrates the use of the active infinitive to render the gerundive *non est credendum* ('credence is not to be given'); cf. Ecclesiasticus 19.16 (AV 19.15). 'Styrynge' renders *instinctui* (see Glossary); 'peysed' renders *ponderanda*.

1.4.2. 'Bileved' renders *creditur et dicitur*; 'and excused by infirmite' is an erroneous translation of *ita infirmi sumus*.

1.4.3. D²'s reading "þe' perfite' is the only citation of 'perfite' as a noun in the sense 'righteous or virtuous people' in *MED*. 'Al þinges þat men telleþ' corresponds to *omni enarranti* in K, *omnia enarranti* in R. 'Redy to yvel and slydinge inowe in wordes' renders *ad malum procliuam: et in verbis satis labilem*: the two phrases are derived from Genesis 8.21 and Ecclesiasticus 14.1 and 19.16.

1.4.4. This verse, *Magna sapiencia, non esse precipitem in agendis: nec pertinaciter in propriis stare sensibus*, though present in both K and R (which has *magna est sapiencia* and *sensibus stare*), has been omitted.

1.4.5. The omission of the previous verse means that 'hereto' (*ad hanc*) lacks a referent: it originally referred to *sapiencia*. 'Eueri mannes wordes' is a free rendering of *quibuslibet hominum verbis*. 'Telle oþer men' omits the metaphor in the Latin *aliorum aures effundere*.

1.4.6. *Cum sapiente et consciencioso viro concilium habe*: cf. Tobit's instruction to Tobias in Tobit 4.19 (AV 4.18).

1.4.7. With the phrase 'experte in many þinges' (*expertum in multis*) cf. Ecclesiasticus 34.9.

1.4.8. *In se*, which modifies *humilior* ('the more meke'), has been omitted.

1.5.0. *Sanctarum*, which modifies *scripturarum* ('scriptures'), has been omitted.

1.5.1. *Veritas est in scripturis sanctis querenda: non eloquencia*, i.e., 'Truth, not eloquence, is to be sought in the holy scriptures'. The translator has taken *eloquencia* as ablative rather than nominative singular.

1.5.3. This is the only citation of 'profitablenes' (*vtilitatem*) in the sense 'spiritual benefit' in *MED*. 'Highenes of langage' corresponds to K's *subtilitatem sermonis* and RZ's *vtilitatem sermonis*, another indication that the translation was not made from R or Z. Possibly the translator read *sublimitatem* (Lupo lists three manuscripts with this reading).

1.5.4. 'Sentences' has been added: the Latin is *sicut altos et profundos* (*sc. libros*).

1.5.5. 'Of grete lettur [o]r of lytel' renders *vtrum parue uel magne literature.* 'Chaunge þi conceyte' renders *te offendat.* 'To þe love `of God"* corresponds to *ad legendum* in both K and R (although R's text could also be expanded *legem domini*).

1.5.6. This point was made by Seneca when giving Lucilius advice in the form of a quotation from Epicurus rather than a maxim of his own: he was critical of those *qui in verba iurant nec quid dicatur aestimant, sed a quo (Epistulae Morales 12.11).*

1.5.7. Cf. the mention of human transience in Psalm 38.7 (AV 39.6) and of God's everlasting truth in Psalm 116.2 (AV 117.2).

1.5.8. The phrase 'accepcion of persones' was used in the Wycliffite Bible in its translation of Romans 2.11 (the text alluded to here), *non est enim personarum acceptio apud deum*, 'For there is no respect of persons with God' (AV), i.e. 'God shows no partiality' (RSV). See *OED s.v.* 'acception'.

1.5.9. 'In þat we serche curiouse sentence' corresponds to *cum volumus intelligere et discutere* in the Latin.

1.5.11. 'Here holdinge þi pees' renders *audi tacens verba sanctorum*; the last two words in the Latin have been omitted (cf. Ecclesiasticus 32.12–13, AV 32.8–9). For 'parabolez of eldre men' (*parabole seniorum*), see Glossary and Ecclesiasticus 8.9.

1.6.1. This is the first citation of 'vnrested' (*inquietus*) in *OED*.

1.6.2. With 'the pore man and meke in spirite' cf. Matthew 5.3 and Psalm 36.11 (AV 37.11).

1.6.3. 'Perfitely dede in himselfe' renders *perfecte in se mortuus*; see also 1.11.8.

1.6.4. 'Feble in spirite and yette in maner fleysly inclyned to þe sensible þinges' renders *infirmus in spiritu et quodammodo adhuc carnalis et ad sensibilia inclinatus.*

1.6.5. The translator has construed *leuiter* ('a litel') with *subtrahit* ('withdraweþ'); it should properly be construed with *dedignatur* (R's reading, followed by the translator; K has *indignatur*), 'haþe disdeigne', and be translated 'easily', i.e. 'he easily takes offence' (Knott). K has a colon separating *leuiter* from *subtrahit.* 'Withdraweþ' refers to his withdrawing from earthly desires (v. 4).

1.6.6. 'In his conscience' corresponds to *ex reatu consciencie.*

1.6.7. C's 'withstandinge in passions' is retained as the *lectio difficilior* and the reading which is marginally closer to the Latin, but possibly DMG's 'of' should be preferred.

1.7.0. The translator has omitted *fugienda* (rendered 'to be fledde' at 1.0.7) from the title, *De vana spe et elacione fugienda.*

1.7.5. The last clause renders *qui adiuuat humiles et de se presumentes humiliat*: cf.

Proverbs 3.34 (quoted in James 4.6 and 1 Peter 5.5), Judith 6.15 (Vulgate), and Luke 1.52. This is the first citation of 'wylynes' (*astucia*) in *OED*.

1.7.6. With the idea of rejoicing (*glorieris*) not in riches but in God, cf. Jeremiah 9.23–4, 1 Corinthians 1.31, and 2 Corinthians 10.17.

1.7.8. 'Of whom comeþ' renders *cuius est*.

1.7.9. With the idea that God 'knoweþ what is in man' cf. John 2.25.

1.7.11. 'Any goode þinges' is a slightly misleading translation of the Latin *aliquid boni*, meaning 'any good' in the moral sense.

1.7.12. Cf. Bernard, *Sermones in Cantica Canticorum* 37.4.7 (*Opera*, ed. J. Leclercq *et al.* (Rome, 1957–77), ii. 13). D²'s "þe" has no support in the Latin.

1.8.1. With 'shewe not thi herte to euerie man' cf. Ecclesiasticus 8.22. 'Meve thi cause' renders *age causam tuam*, i.e. 'discuss your business' (Knott) or 'ask counsel' (Sherley-Price). Cf. the advice to associate with those who are wise and fear God in Ecclesiasticus 9.21 and 37.15 (AV 9.14 and 37.12).

1.8.2. This is the only citation of 'rare' (*rarus*) meaning 'seldom found' in *MED*. 'Straunge folkes' renders *extraneis* (see Glossary).

1.8.3. *Cum diuitibus noli blandire: et coram magnatis non libenter appareas*. With the second clause cf. Proverbs 25.6; *libenter* has been omitted in the translation.

1.8.4. With *que edificacionis sunt* cf. Romans 14.19.

1.8.6. *Soli deo et angelis suis opta familiaris esse*: on the importance of *familiaritas cum deo* in the mystical tradition, see Riehle, pp. 97–101, and cf. 2.1.7, 2.8, 3.24.13, and 3.42.12. On 'knowleche' (*noticiam*), see Glossary.

1.8.8–9. The sense of these verses is that 'it sometimes happens that someone personally unkonwn to us enjoys a high reputation, but that when we meet him, we are not impressed. Similarly, we sometimes imagine that our company is pleasing, when in reality we offend others by our ill behaviour' (Sherley-Price). 'Beynge and lyvynge togydres' is a doublet rendering *coniunctione*. The translation adds 'oftetymes', but follows R in omitting K's *magis*, which modifies *displicere* ('to displese').

1.9.1. 'At his owne lyberte' renders *sui iuris*.

1.9.3. 'Sone and lightly' is a doublet rendering *leuiter*. On 'liberte of mynde', see 3.30.0 n.

1.9.4. 'Vnder a prelate' corresponds to *sub regimine prelati* in K, *sub prelati regimine* in R.

1.9.6. On the variants, see Introduction, pp. xlix–l. It is the presence of 'and' in C that makes it clear that this is an omission in the archetype rather than in the translator's autograph.

1.9.7. Here and in v. 10, 'felynge' renders *sentire*; in v. 9 it renders *sensus*. See Glossary.

1.9.9. *Eciam*, which modifies *velis* ('desire'), has been omitted.

1.9.10. Because C consistently distinguishes between 'gode' (or 'goode') meaning 'good', and 'god' (or 'godde') meaning 'God', 'gode' has been emended to 'God' here; cf. 3.4.5.

1.9.11. *Enim* has been omitted.

1.9.12. 'Eueri man feele welle' renders *bonum sit vniuscuiusque sentire* (R has *vnicuique*), meaning 'each man's opinion may be good'.

1.10.1. 'þe noyse and þe prese' is a doublet rendering *tumultum*; 'tretynge and talkynge' is a doublet rendering *tractatus*; 'trewe and symple' is a doublet rendering *simplici*.

1.10.4. 'Withoute hurtynge of conscience' renders *sine lesione consciencie*.

1.10.6. The Latin's second *multum*, which modifies *diligimus* ('we love'), has been omitted.

1.10.7. This is the first citation of 'vnfruytfully' (*frustra*) in *OED*.

1.10.9. 'We owe to wake and to praye' renders *vigilandum est et orandum* (cf. Matthew 26.41).

1.10.10. On speaking so as to edify, see Ephesians 4.29.

1.10.11. 'Yvel vse' renders *malus vsus*, i.e. 'bad habits' (Knott). 'Gostely encrece and profitynge' is an expansion of *profectus*. 'Doþe muche to yvel kepinge of oure mowthes' renders *multum facit ad incustodiam oris nostri*, i.e. 'make[s] us careless in guarding our lips' (Knott).

1.11.0. '[Z]ele of profytynge' renders *zelo proficiendi*, i.e. 'zeal for spiritual progress'.

1.11.2. 'þat sekeþ occasions outwarde' renders *qui occasiones forinsecus querit*, i.e. 'who seeks opportunities outside his sphere' (Blaiklock). 'Gedrith hym withinne hymselfe' renders *se intrinsecus colligit*: on 'the gathering of the soul into itself' as a preparation for mystical union, see Riehle, p. 57, and cf. 1.19.15, 2.1.36, 3.23.8, 3.36.16–17, and 3.53.24.

1.11.5. 'Mortifie hemselfe' (*seipsos mortificare*) is the only citation of 'mortifien' as a reflexive verb in *MED*: on spiritual mortification, see Riehle, pp. 137–8, and cf. Romans 8.13 and Colossians 3.5; also 2.12.15. The last two clauses render *et ideo totis medullis cordis deo inherere, atque libere sibi vacare potuerunt*: on cleaving to God, see Riehle, p. 129, and on 'take heede' as a translation of *vacare*, see Riehle, pp. 59–60; cf. also 3.1.7 and 3.23.7.

1.11.6. 'But' has been added. *Nimium*, which modifies *occupamur* ('we ar occupied'), has been omitted.

1.11.7. 'Tende' renders R's *tendimus* rather than K's *accendimur*.

1.11.8. 'Not intryked to muche with outwarde þinges' renders *exterius minime implicati*, the reading of insular manuscripts O and E (S has *exterius minime* *multiplicati*) rather than KR's *interius minime implicati* 'not too much inwardly entangled'. On savouring godly things, cf. Jesus' rebuke to Peter in Matthew 16.23.

1.11.9. 'Holy men and seyntes' is a doublet rendering *sanctorum*. *Perfectam* (which modifies *viam* ('wey') in K; R has *perfecte*) has been omitted.

1.11.10. *Nimis*, which modifies *cito* ('anone'), has been omitted.

1.11.11. Cf. Jehaziel's prophecy that Judah would see the Lord's help *super vos* when she was threatened by the Moabites, the Ammonites, and the Syrians by the ascent of Ziz (2 Chronicles 20.17).

1.11.12. 'Alle' has been added.

1.11.14. With 'sette þe axe to þe rote' cf. the words of John the Baptist in Matthew 3.10.

1.11.15. 'We destruyed groundely' renders *extirparemus*.

1.11.17. Cf. Bernard, *Sermones de Diversis* 27.5 (*Opera*, ed. Leclercq, vol. vi, part 1, p. 201).

1.11.18. 'Put 'to' a litel violence' renders *modicam violenciam faceremus*.

1.11.21. *In principio*, which modifies *resiste* ('withstande'), has been omitted.

1.11.22. 'In hauynge thiselfe welle' renders *teipsum bene habendo*, i.e. 'by your good behaviour'.

1.12.1. 'Grevaunces and contrarietez' renders *grauitates et contrarietates*, i.e. 'troubles and adversities'. 'þei calle a man into hymselfe' renders *hominem ad cor reuocant*.

1.12.2. 'Ayeinsayars' renders *contradictores*.

1.12.4. 'We seke better the inwarde wyttnenes, God' renders *melius interiorem testem deum querimus*, i.e. 'we more readily turn to God as our inward witness' (Sherley-Price), or 'we are more ready to listen to God's assuring voice within' (Knott).

1.12.5. 'A man owed to ferme hymselfe in God' renders *deberet se homo in deo taliter firmare*.

1.12.8. *Tunc tedet eum diucius viuere; et mortem optat venire: ut possit dissolui et cum Christo esse:* cf. Paul's response to hardship in 2 Corinthians 1.8 and Philippians 1.23.

1.13.2. The second clause renders *Temptacio est vita humana super terram*; the biblical verse reads *Militia est vita hominis super terram* (Job 7.1, Vulgate).

1.13.3. Cf. Peter's command *vigilate in orationibus* (1 Peter 4.7) and his warning about the devil (1 Peter 5.8).

1.13.5. 'Meked, purged, and sharpely taught' renders *humiliatur, purgatur et eruditur*.

1.13.7. 'Were [made] men repreved and fayled in her weye' renders *reprobi facti sunt et defecerunt*.

1.13.10. 'We lost þe gode of felycite' renders *bonum felicitatis nostre perdidimus*, i.e. 'man has lost the blessing of original happiness' (Sherley-Price).

1.13.11. 'Many men sekeþ to ouercome temptacions onely bi fleynge of hem' is an expansion of *multi querunt temptaciones fugere*.

1.13.12. *Veram*, which modifies *humilitatem* ('mekenes'), has been omitted.

1.13.14. DMG's 'hem' has no support in the Latin. 'Longanimite' renders *longanimitate*, used in the Vulgate rendering of such passages as Colossians 1.11, alluded to here; see *OED s.v.* 'With duresse and þine owne importunite' renders *cum duricia et importunitate propria*, i.e. 'by harshness and impatience' (Knott).

1.13.18. 'Golde' corresponds to *ferrum* (cf. 1.17.11 and n.): the verse is in effect a combination of Ecclesiasticus 31.31a and 27.6b (AV 31.26a and 27.5b).

1.13.19. The last clause renders *temptacio aperit quid sumus*, i.e. 'temptation reveals our true nature' (Sherley-Price).

1.13.20. 'The bigynnynge' corresponds to *inicium temptacionis*. The last clause renders *sed extra limen statim ut pulsauerit illi obuiatur*, i.e. 'he must be repulsed at the threshold, as soon as he knocks' (Sherley-Price).

1.13.21. This verse, *Vnde quidam dixit. Principiis obsta: sero medicina paratur* (Ovid, *Remedia Amoris* 91), present in both K and R, has been omitted. The omission could be due to *homoeoteleuton* (the previous sentence ends with the word *obuiatur*), although this would be unlikely if a manuscript similar to R were used by the translator, since R adds the following pentameter *cum mala per longas conualuere moras*, an addition which according to Lupo's apparatus is found in a number of manuscripts, especially the Italian ones. In its original context Ovid's advice concerned the necessity of beginning early one's resistance to love.

1.13.22. *Nam primo occurrit menti simplex cogitacio; deinde fortis ymaginacio: postea delectacio et motus prauus et assensio.*

1.13.24. 'Waxeth' is to be understood with 'his enemye' as well as with 'he'.

1.13.28. See 1 Corinthians 10.13. *Vtique*, which in the *Imitatio* modifies *faciet* ('make'), has been omitted. 'Suffre hit and abyde hit' is a doublet rendering *sustinere*.

1.13.29. With *humiliemus ergo animas nostras sub manu dei* cf. Judith 8.16 (Vulgate) and 1 Peter 5.6; with *quia humiles spiritu saluabit et exaltabit* cf. Psalm 33.19 (AV 34.18) and Luke 1.52.

1.13.30. The last two clauses render *et ibi maius meritum consistit: et virtus melius patescit*.

1.14.2. This is the only citation of 'discussinge' (*discutiendo*) in the sense 'examining' in *MED*.

1.14.3. The Latin here is *sicut nobis res cordi est, sic de ea frequenter iudicamus*, i.e. 'our feelings about anything often affect the way we judge it' (Knott); R reads *eo* for *ea*, and it may have been because his Latin text had this reading that the translator omitted *de ea*.

1.14.4. 'Entencion' renders *intencio*, 'the directing of the will to God in contemplative prayer' (P. Hodgson (ed.), *'The Cloud of Unknowing' and 'The Book of Privy Counselling'*, EETS 218 (1944), p. 185), on which see Riehle, pp. 62–3, and cf. 1.18.6, 1.22.19, 2.4, 3.10.2, 3.30.1, and 3.38. 'For with-standynge of owre owne wytte' renders *pro resistencia sensus ⟨nostri⟩*, i.e. 'when our opinions are contradicted' (Sherley-Price).

1.14.5. *Sed sepe aliquid ab intra latet, vel eciam abextra concurrit: quod nos eciam pariter trahit*, i.e. 'very often some inner impluse or outward circumstance draws us to follow it' (Sherley-Price).

1.14.7. The first clause renders *videnter eciam in bona pace stare*.

1.14.8. 'And' renders *autem*; 'but' would have been clearer. 'Meved' renders *mouentur* (see Glossary).

1.14.10. 'Almoste' has been added; *libenter*, which modifies *ducitur* ('wol be ladde'), has been omitted.

1.14.11. *Uel industrie*, which is parallel to *racioni tue* ('þine owne reson'), has been omitted. This is the only citation of 'subiective' in *MED*, which follows *OED* in glossing it as 'characteristic of someone who is submissive', but since it refers to the power of Christ (*virtuti subiectiue Ihesu Christi*) it must mean 'subduing' (cf. Philippians 3.21). 'Late' renders *raro et tarde*; 'alle maner mannes reson' renders *omnem racionem*. On imagery of fire in the mystical tradition, see Riehle, pp. 81–2, and cf. e.g. 3.2.8, 3.2.17, and 3.6.22; on love and reason, see Riehle, p. 93.

1.15.1. The translation follows R in omitting *libere*, which modifies *intermitten-dum est* ('[may] . . . [be] lafte') in K; the translation 'hym þat is nedy', however, follows K's *indigentis* rather than R's *diligentis*.

1.15.2. The translation misses part of the point of this sentence, that the good work is not only changed, but changed for the better: *in melius commutatur*.

1.15.3. Cf. Paul's teaching on the uselessness of works without charity in 1 Corinthians 13.1–3.

1.15.4. 'So symple ner so litel' corresponds to the Latin *paruum sit et despectum* without rendering the full force of *despectum*, 'despised'.

1.15.5. 'Of howe grete charite' is an expansion of *ex quanto*; 'howe grete a werke' renders R's *quantum* rather than K's *o⟨pus quod⟩*.

1.15.9. In the Latin the list of qualities is *naturalis inclinacio, propria voluntas, spes retribucionis, affectus commoditatis*. 'But euer redy' has been added.

1.15.10. Cf. Paul's teaching on charity's selflessness in 1 Corinthians 13.5. 'And above alle þinges' has been added.

1.15.11. 'No propre ner private' is an expansion of *nullum privatum.*

1.15.12. 'þinges' corresponds to *bona* in the Latin.

1.15.14. On the '[sparkel] of charite', cf. 3.60.5 and n.

1.16.0. 'Infirmytees and defautes' is a doublet rendering *defectuum.*

1.16.2. 'To the to suffre suche contrarietez' corresponds to *sic.*

1.16.4. 'Agree ner be counseyled' is an expansion of *acquiescit.* The antecedent of the second 'þat' is 'God': cf. Genesis 50.20 (Vulgate).

1.16.5. 'Suffrynge and beringe' is a doublet rendering *tolerando.*

1.16.13. The first 'togydre . . . togidre' renders *inuicem . . . inuicem*; the second 'togydre . . . togydre' renders *pariter.* With 'evyry to bere oþers burdon' cf. Galatians 6.2; with 'no man withoute burdon' cf. Galatians 6.5; with 'no man sufficient to hymselfe' cf. Ecclesiasticus 11.26 (AV 11.24); with 'no man wyse inowe to hymselfe' cf. Proverbs 3.7; with 'bere togydre' cf. Colossians 3.13; with 'counforte togidre' cf. 1 Thessalonians 5.11.

1.16.14. *Virtutis* has been omitted; the translator may have misread it as *veritatis,* as 'verily' does not correspond to anything in the Latin.

1.17.0. The Latin title is *De monastica vita.*

1.17.2. On being faithful to death, see Revelation 2.10.

1.17.4. The idea of being a pilgrim and an exile on the earth is derived from Hebrews 11.13; see also 1 Chronicles 29.15, Psalm 38.13 (AV 39.12), and 1 Peter 2.11; and cf. 1.23.45 and 2.1.18.

1.17.5. The idea of being a fool for Christ is derived from 1 Corinthians 4.10; cf. also 1.24.21. In contrast with the title of the chapter, 'relygiouse' here renders *religiosam* (so too in the next verse).

1.17.7. With 'fynde but tribulacion and sorrowe' cf. Psalm 114.3 (AV 116.3).

1.17.8. With 'be leste' cf. Luke 22.26; with 'sugget to alle' cf. 1 Peter 2.13.

1.17.10. 'To be ydel and telle tales' renders *ad ociandum vel fabulandum.*

1.17.11. The souls of the righteous are said to be proved as gold in the furnace in Wisdom 3.6.

1.18.0. 'Of holy faders' renders K's *sanctorum patrum* rather than R's *patrum.* On the desert fathers, see *NCE* iv. 793.

1.18.1. 'Olde faders' corresponds to *sanctorum 'patrum'* in the Latin. The translation follows R in omitting *et religio,* which is parallel to *perfectio* ('perfeccion').

1.18.3. Cf. Paul's accounts of his various sufferings in 1 Corinthians 4.11–13, 2 Corinthians 11.27 and 12.10, 1 Thessalonians 2.9, and 2 Thessalonians 3.8; cf. also Deuteronomy 28.48. 'Of God' renders *Christi.* On the variants, see Introduction, pp. lxiv–lxv.

1.18.5. 'þat is to seie her bod[ely] lyves' corresponds to *in hoc mundo* in the Latin. The idea of hating one's soul in order to keep it is derived from John 12.25.

1.18.6. *Et abdicatam*, which together with *strictam* modifies *vitam* ('lyve'), has been omitted. On 'intencion', see 1.14.4 n.

1.18.7. *Diutine*, which modifies *vacabant* ('yave hem'), has been omitted. The fathers fulfilled Paul's command to pray without ceasing (1 Thessalonians 5.17).

1.18.15. 'Chosen' renders R's *electi* rather than K's final reading *d'i'lecti*, in which *d* has been altered from *e*.

1.18.16. Cf. Paul's command to walk in love (Ephesians 5.2).

1.18.17. There are several doublets in this sentence: 'lyffe weelle and profite' renders *bene proficiendum*; 'slugged and lewke men' renders *tepidorum*; 'remysse and laxe' renders *relaxandum*.

1.18.18. 'Of religion' corresponds to *omnium religiosorum*; *sancte*, which modifies *institucionis* ('institucion'), has been omitted.

1.18.19. Presumably the strong preterite 'þrove' was misunderstood by D², who changed it to 'prove'd'', altering the original þ to p, and understanding 'þat' as introducing a relative clause with 'tyme' as its subject (the adverbial phrase 'þat tyme', meaning 'at that time', had been introduced by the translator). The translation follows R in omitting *magistri*, which follows *sub regula* ('vnder rewle').

1.18.23. 'Sluggednesse and werynes' renders *lassitudine et tepore*.

1.18.24. *Sepius*, which modifies *vidisti* ('haste seene'), has been omitted.

1.19.1. The metaphorical 'shyne' has been introduced by the translator: the Latin is *pollere*.

1.19.2. 'Byholdar' renders *inspector* (cf. Proverbs 24.12).

1.19.7. 'þoghe þat appire lyght, yette hit is not withoute summe maner of hyndryng' corresponds to *leuis omissio exerciciorum vix sine aliquo dispendio ⟨transit⟩* (R reads *amissio* for *omissio*).

1.19.8. The Latin is *Iustorum propositum in gracia dei pocius quam in propria sapiencia pendet: in quo et semper confidunt*. The antecedent of 'whom' is 'God'; in altering 'whom' to 'w⟨hich⟩' D² may have thought that 'wysedome' was being referred to. 'Doþe or purposeþ' is a doublet rendering *arripiunt*.

1.19.9. This verse appears to be the source of the proverb *Homo proponit, sed deus disponit* (cf. Proverbs 16.9). The last clause renders *nec est in homine via eius*, i.e. 'man's destiny is not in his own hands' (Sherley-Price); cf. Jeremiah 10.23.

1.19.10. 'Bycause of pite' renders *pietatis causa*, which could either mean 'because of piety', i.e. 'for some spiritual reason' (Knott) or 'because of pity', i.e. 'to perform some act of mercy' (Sherley-Price).

1.19.11. The second 'hit' here refers to the forsaking of the exercise, rather than the exercise itself. This is the first citation of 'vituperable' (*culpabile*) in *OED*.

1.19.15. On gathering oneself together, see 1.11.2 and n. The translation follows R in omitting *et*, which precedes *ad minus* 'atte leste'.

1.19.17. Cf. God's command to Job to gird up his loins like a man (Job 38.3).

1.19.19. 'Evonly and lyke' is a doublet rendering *equaliter*.

1.19.21. 'Pryvate and singvler' is a doublet rendering *singularia*.

1.19.22. *Integre*, which together with *fideliter* modifies *expletis* ('fulfilled'), has been omitted. 'Yelde þe to thiselfe' renders *redde te tibi*, i.e. 'give your attention to yourself' (Knott).

1.19.23. The Latin is *aliud isti aliud illi magis deseruit*.

1.19.29. The first 'more' has been added. *A deo*, which modifies *percepturi* ('receyue'), has been omitted.

1.19.30. 'To come' renders R's *adesse* rather than K's *adhuc*. With the mention of the glory to be revealed in us cf. Romans 8.18.

1.19.31–2. Cf. the parable of the servants whose lord had gone to a wedding (Luke 12.37,43–4). In v. 32 'for' has been added.

1.20.4. 'Voyde spekynges and ydel circuites' renders *superfluis locucionibus, et ociosis circuicionibus*, i.e. 'unnecessary talk and aimless visits' (Sherley-Price); C's reading 'circuitryes' is not found in *MED* or in *OED* except in the twentieth-century electrical sense. 'Vanitees and herynge of tidinges' corresponds to *nouitatibus ⟨et rumo⟩ribus audiendis*; perhaps the translator read *vanitatibus* for *nouitatibus*. 'Swete' renders *bonis*.

1.20.5. 'To lyve to' renders R's *viuere* rather than K's *seruire*. On secrecy in the mystical tradition, see Riehle, pp. 100–1, and cf. 3.58.3.

1.20.6. An allusion to Seneca's remarks on shunning a crowd: *Numquam mores quos extuli refero. . . . Quid me existimas dicere? avarior redeo, ambitiosior, luxuriosior? immo vero crudelior et inhumanior, quia inter homines fui* (*Epistulae Morales* 7.1–3). 'þat is to seie, lasse holy' has been added.

1.20.7. *Sepius*, which modifies *experrimur* ('we fynde by experience'), has been omitted.

1.20.8. DM's reading 'liȝtlier' is the only citation of the comparative of 'lightly' *adj.* (*facilius*) in *MED* or *OED*.

1.20.10. An allusion to Jesus' withdrawal from the crowd (*declinavit a turba*, Vulgate) after he had healed the lame man at the pool of Bethesda (John 5.13).

1.20.11. 'No man appiereþ surely' renders *nemo secure apparet*, i.e. 'no one can safely appear in public' (Blaiklock).

1.20.13. 'Is . . . above' and 'be byneþe' render *preest* and *subest* (see Glossary).

1.20.15. The idea that conscience is a witness is derived from 2 Corinthians 1.12; cf. 2.6.1.

1.20.17. 'Hit turneth into [þer] deceyte' renders *in decepcionem sui `ipsius' vertitur* (R omints *ipsius*), i.e. 'ends in self-deception' (Sherley-Price), or 'in the end it betrays them' (Knott).

1.20.19. 'Fallen most perilously for her overgrete truste' renders *grauius periclitati sunt propter suam `nimiam' confidenciam*, i.e. 'have often been in greatest danger, because they have become too self-confident' (Knott).

1.20.20. 'Ner' renders R's *nec* rather than K's *ne* ('lest').

1.20.22. 'Gostely' renders *salutaria*.

1.20.24. *In cubilibus vestris compungimini* (Psalm 4.5, AV 4.4). According to *OED* the word 'compunct' is derived from the Vulgate rendering of this verse (AV has 'commune with your own heart upon your bed').

1.20.27. 'Dere and welbeloved' is a doublet rendering *dilecta*.

1.20.28. On God's privity (*abscondita*), see Riehle, pp. 100–1, and cf. Ecclesiasticus 39.3 and 2.2.10.

1.20.29. On mystical tears, see Riehle, p. 44, and cf. Psalm 6.7 (AV 6.6) and 1.21.26 and n. The second 'þat' renders *quanto*: a clearer translation would have been 'the more he withdraws'.

1.20.33. 'þe worlde passeþ and his concupiscence' is a further allusion to 1 John 2.17 (cf. 1.3.30).

1.20.34. 'Dispercioun of herte' renders *cordis dispersionem*; this is the only citation of 'dispercioun' in the sense 'distraction, confusion' in *MED*.

1.20.36. Similar language is used of wine in Proverbs 23.31–2.

1.20.39. The idea of earthly things not abiding under the sun is derived from Ecclesiastes 2.11.

1.20.41. *Si cuncta videres presencia*, i.e. 'if you could see all things at once before you' (Blaiklock).

1.20.42. Cf. the command to lift up one's eyes on high in Isaiah 40.26 (also Psalm 122.1, AV 123.1) and the exhortation to pray for one's sins in Ecclesiasticus 3.4 (AV 3.3).

1.20.43. 'Leve veyne to the veyne' renders *dimitte vana vanis* (see Glossary); cf. the command to think on the things commanded by God in Ecclesiasticus 3.22.

1.20.44. Cf. the commands to shut one's door in Isaiah 26.20 and Matthew 6.6.

1.21.1. A similar attitude towards the fear of God is found in Proverbs 23.17. The latter part of the verse renders *noli esse nimis liber, sed sub disciplina cohibe omnes sensus tuos: nec inepte te tradas leticie*.

1.21.4. *Perfecte*, which modifies *letari* ('be glad'), has been omitted; 'considereþ' renders *considerat et pensat*.

1.21.5. 'þe sorowes and the harmes' is a doublet rendering *dolores*.

1.21.7. 'Brynge himselfe to the onhed of holy compunccion' renders *ad vnionem se recolligere sancte compunctionis*.

1.21.8. On 'voydeþ', see Riehle, pp. 59–64, and cf. e.g. 2.7.9, 2.8.31, 3.32.2, and 3.47.9.

1.21.12. 'Spiritually' renders R's *spiritualiter* rather than K's *specialiter*.

1.21.13. On the variants, see Introduction, p. lxii.

1.21.15. The translation follows R in omitting *cordis*, which follows *compunctionem* 'compunccion' in K.

1.21.23. 'Peyne, laboure, and sorowe' renders *laborem et dolorem*.

1.21.24. *Valde*, which modifies *pigri* ('slowe'), has been omitted.

1.21.26. *Ciba me domine pane lacrimarum: et potum da michi in lacrimis in mensura* (Psalm 79.6, AV 80.5): see 1.20.29 n.

1.22.6. On the variants, see Introduction, p. lxiv. Cf. Paul's mention of the weak and sick in 1 Corinthians 11.30.

1.22.8. 'þen esynge' has been added.

1.22.12. *Magna*, which along with *vere* modifies *miseria* ('mysery'), and *omni*, which modifies *peccato* 'synne', have been omitted.

1.22.14. *De necessitatibus meis erue me domine* (Psalm 24.17, AV 25.17).

1.22.15. The phrase *corruptibilis vite* is found in 2 Maccabees 6.25 (Vulgate).

1.22.16. 'þis wrecched lyve' is an expansion of *hanc*. On the variants, see Introduction, p. lxiii.

1.22.17. On the variants, see Introduction, pp. lxiv–lxv. 'Thei savoure none hevonly þinges' renders *nichil nisi carnalia sapiant*: cf. Romans 8.5 and see 1.1.6 n.

1.22.19. 'Hem þat have floured in this worlde' renders *que in hoc tempore floruerunt* and refers to things rather than people. On 'intencion', see 1.14.4 n.

1.22.21. *Noli frater amittere confidenciam proficiendi ad spiritualia*, i.e. 'do not lose hope of progess in the spiritual life' (Sherley-Price); cf. Hebrews 10.35.

1.22.23. 'Of purgynge' render's N's *purgandi* rather than K and R's *pugnandi*; 'nowe is tyme of amendynge' renders *nunc aptum tempus est emendandi*.

1.22.24. 'þen seye' renders R's *dic nunc* rather than K's *tunc*. The translation follows R in omitting K's *et tribularis*, which follows *male habes* ('þou arte yvel at ese').

1.22.25. The imagery here is derived from Psalm 65.12 (AV 66.12).

1.22.29. On patience, cf. Hebrews 10.36; on wickedness passing, cf. Psalm 56.2

(AV 57.1); on death being swallowed up, cf. 1 Corinthians 15.54. On the mystical idea of being swallowed up into God, see Riehle, pp. 139–40.

1.22.30. The idea of human nature's being *prona . . . ad vicia* is derived from Genesis 8.21.

1.22.34. *Multo labore*, which modifies *acquisitum est* ('is . . . goten'), has been omitted.

1.22.36. Cf. Paul's warning of the dangers of a false sense of peace and security in 1 Thessalonians 5.3. 'Steppe' renders *vestigium*, i.e. 'trace'.

1.22.37. The Latin is *Bene opus esset quod adhuc iterum instrueremur tamquam boni nouicii ad mores optimos* (*iterum* is added in the margin in R). It is difficult to say whether C's 'newe' or DMG's 'nowe' should be preferred here, as 'nowe' could render *adhuc* and 'newe' *iterum*. 'Yonge' corresponds to *boni*.

1.23.1–2. The order of these two verses has been reversed in the translation. With v. 1 cf. 1 Maccabees 2.63. The Latin of v. 2 is *Valde cito erit tecum hic factum: vide aliter quomodo te habeas*, i.e. 'Very soon all will be over with you in this life, so ask yourself how you will fare in the next' (Knott); the translator has misunderstood the contrast of *hic . . . aliter*, 'here . . . elsewhere'.

1.23.18–20. 'What houre' renders *hora qua*; the meaning is 'at an hour which we do not expect' (cf. Jesus' warning in Matthew 24.44). See Introduction, p. liii.

1.23.21. *Et prudens*, parallel to *felix* ('blessid'), has been omitted.

1.23.22. The translation follows R in omitting *feliciter*, which in K modifies *moriendi* ('to dye').

1.23.25. K's text reads *Noli confidere super amicos et proximos; nec in futurum tuam differas salutem*; for the second clause R reads *ut in futurum salutem tuam differas*, and it was presumably this reading in his Latin text that caused the translator to make the two clauses one.

1.23.28. The translation follows R and many Latin manuscripts in omitting the phrase `nunc sunt dies salutis: nunc tempus acceptabile` (2 Corinthians 6.2), which is added in the lower margin in K after *preciosum* ('precrouse'). The last part of the sentence renders *in quo promereri vales vnde eternaliter viuas*, i.e. 'in which it is in your power to win merit, whence you may live eternally' (Blaiklock).

1.23.32. *Disce nunc mori mundo: ut tunc incipias viuere cum Christo* (cf. Romans 6.8).

1.23.34. The idea of chastising the body is derived from 1 Corinthians 9.27.

1.23.38. With 'þe ende of alle' cf. Ecclesiastes 7.3 (AV 7.2); with man's life passing as a shadow cf. Psalm 143.4 (AV 144.4).

1.23.40. 'Do' corresponds to *age age*.

1.23.42. With 'whiles þou haste tyme' cf. Galatians 6.10; with 'ryches immortalez' cf. Luke 12.33.

1.23.44. This is a paraphrase of Jesus' instruction in Luke 16.9.

1.23.45. See 1.17.4 n.

1.23.46. *Non habes hic manentem ciuitatem* (Hebrews 13.14). Cf. 2.1.18.

1.23.47. 'Moorninges' renders *gemitus*: see Riehle, pp. 42–3, and cf. 3.54.10 and 3.62.19. The translation follows R in omitting *Amen* from the end of the chapter.

1.24.1. 'Rightwyse' renders *districtum*.

1.24.2. 'Knowinge alle þine yvels' modifies '[God]'. The question 'What shalt þou answere [God]?' recalls Job 31.14.

1.24.3. With 'euerie mannes burdon shal be inowe to himselfe' cf. Galatians 6.5.

1.24.5. The sense of the first part of this verse has been slightly changed from that in the Latin: *Habet magnum et salubre purgatorium paciens homo: qui suscipiens iniurias plus dolet de alterius malicia, quam de sua iniuria* (R reads *sui* for *sua*). 'Trespassours' corresponds to *culpas*; *frequenter*, which modifies *violenciam . . . facit* ('doþe violence'), is omitted. 'Hertily' renders *ex corde*. Cf. Matthew 5.44 and 18.35.

1.24.6. *Modo*, which modifies *purgare* and *resecare* ('kutte awey and purge'), has been omitted.

1.24.9. 'þe more matier of brennynge þou reserveste' renders *maiorem materiam comburendi reseruas*, i.e. 'the more fuel you keep for the fire' (Knott).

1.24.10. The appropriateness of punishment to sin is taught in Wisdom 11.17 (AV 11.16).

1.24.11. 'Shul be prykked' renders R's *pungentur* rather than K's *perurgentur*.

1.24.12. On C's form 'hode', see Introduction, p. lxx, n. 124.

1.24.14. This is the only citation of 'enstreyted' (*artabuntur*) in *MED*.

1.24.18. This reward of the just is promised in Wisdom 5.1.

1.24.19. 'Sitte to deme' corresponds to *stabit ad iudicandum*.

1.24.21. See 1.17.5 n.

1.24.22. *Omnis iniquitas oppilabit os suum* (Psalm 106.42, AV 107.42).

1.24.29. 'Grete' renders *docta*.

1.24.34. 'Avayle' renders R's *valebit* rather than K's *placebit*.

1.24.36. 'What thou mowe suffre aftirwarde' renders R's *quid possis pati postea*; K omits *pati*.

1.24.37. 'Mowe not' renders E's `*non*' *vales* or T's `*non*' *valeas* (*nec . . . valeas* Θ, *vix wales* XLW) rather than K's *vales* or R's *valeas*.

1.24.41. Almost a repetition of 1.1.11: see n. there.

1.24.42. 'Shal make to God a redye weye and a sure commynge' renders R's *securum ad deum iter faciet et accessum* rather than K's *securum ad deum accessum facit.*

1.24.44. *Gehennalis*, which modifies *timor* ('drede'), has been omitted.

1.24.45. Cf. Paul's warning against 'the fendes gnares' (*diaboli laqueos*) in 1 Timothy 6.9.

1.25.0. 'Mannes' is closer to E's *tocius vite* than to K's *tocius* ⟨*vite nostre*⟩ (R also has *tocius vite nostre*).

1.25.1. The command *esto vigilans* also occurs in Revelation 3.2.

1.25.3. 'Be feruente to profitynge' renders R's *ad profectum ferueas* rather than K's *ad profectum serueas*. The translation also follows R in omitting K's *in breui*, which modifies *recipies* ('þou shalte receyve'). The idea of 'meede' (*mercedem*) is derived from 1 Corinthians 3.8. 'In thi costes' renders *in finibus tuis*, which seems to mean 'with you'; similar phrases are used of Israel in such passages as Leviticus 26.6 (AV 'in the land').

1.25.4. Cf. the mention of great rest after a little labour in Ecclesiasticus 51.35 (AV 51.27).

1.25.10. 'Counforted' renders *consolatus et confortatus*.

1.25.11. With 'the wylle of God welle-plesinge and perfite' cf. Romans 12.2; with 'euerie goode werke' cf. 2 Timothy 3.17.

1.25.12. *Spera in domino et fac bonitatem ait propheta, et inhabita terram: et pasceris in diuiciis eius* (Psalm 36.3, AV 37.3).

1.25.13. 'Of strivinge or of fighttynge' is a doublet rendering *certaminis*.

1.25.14. 'Thei' renders R's *illi vero* rather than K's *enimuero illi*.

1.25.15. 'Himselfe' is to be understood as the object of 'mortifieþ' as well as of 'overcometh'.

1.25.17. 'Welle-manerde' renders *bene morigeratus*, here and at 1.25.23. It may be that C's 'yelar' resulted from a miscopying of an abbreviated form of 'zelator', rendering the Latin *emulator*. For the misreading of *z* as *y*, cf. M's occasional spellings *zeueþe* (1.20.3), *zeue* (1.21.26), and see Introduction, p. lxx, n. 124. 'Shal be more myghty to profite' renders *valencior erit ad proficiendum*, i.e. 'will be better fitted to make progress' (Knott).

1.25.18. Cf. Aristotle, *Ethics* 2.9.

1.25.23. With the phrase 'goynge inordinatly' (*inordinate ambulantes*) cf. 2 Thessalonians 3.6.

1.25.24. 'Bowe his witte' renders *sensum inclinare* (see Glossary).

1.25.26. On 'confourme', see 1.1.6 n.

1.25.27. The translation follows R in omitting K's *ibi*, which modifies *inueniet* ('he shal fynde'); pleonastic pronouns such as 'he' here are rare in this translation.

1.25.28. 'Criste' renders R's *Christus* rather than K's *crucifixus*.

1.25.30. 'Tribulacion' renders R's *tribulacionem* rather than K's *tribulacionem super tribulacionem*. 'Counforte' renders *consolacione*.

1.25.31. This is the only citation of 'open to' (*patet*) in the sense 'in danger of (sth.), liable to suffer (sth.)' in *MED*.

1.25.32. 'Moste laxe' renders *laxiora*; this is the only citation of 'laxe' in the sense 'of religious rules or practices: slack, undisciplined' in *MED*.

1.25.33. 'Ar streyted' renders *artati sunt*.

1.25.34. *Raro exeunt*, which comes at the beginning of the verse, has been omitted. This is the only citation of 'abstractely' (*abstracte*) with the meaning 'withdrawn from the world and worldly interests' in *MED*. The reversal of word order in the last two-word phrase ('oftetyme redeþ') is an effective rhetorical variation.

1.25.37. *Et ore*, which is parallel to *toto corde* ('with [alle] oure herte'), has been omitted.

1.25.40. On spiritual tasting (*degustamus*), see Riehle, pp. 108–9, and cf. e.g. 2.4.3, 3.6.25, and 3.22.20.

1.25.41. On 'savoure', see 1.1.6 n.

1.25.42. With the statement that God is *omnia et in omnibus* cf. Colossians 3.11. *Incunctanter*, which modifies *deseruiunt* ('serveþ') has been omitted.

1.25.43. The first clause renders *memento semper finis*.

1.25.52. The translation follows most of the insular manuscripts (though not R) in omitting *Amen* from the end of the chapter.

1.25.53. The translation of this verse is closer to R's *Explicit prima pars libri interne consolacionis qui vocatur musica ecclesiastica* than to K's *Expliciunt ammoniciones ad spiritualem vitam vtiles*.

BOOK II

2.0.0. K has *Incipiunt capitula*; R has *Incipit secunda pars eiusdem libri*.

2.0.8. 'Oure Lorde' has been added.

2.0.11. 'Criste' renders R's *Christi* rather than K's *Ihesu*.

2.0.13. This verse renders K's *Incipiunt ammoniciones ad interna trahentes* (with 'gretely' added); R has nothing at this point.

2.1.1. *Regnum dei intra vos est* (Luke 17.21). On inwardness, 'a fundamental prerequisite for the mystic', 'the gathering of the soul into itself', see Riehle, pp. 56–8, and cf. e.g. 1.3.14, 2.5.10, and 3.1.

2.1.2. 'Turne thiselfe' renders *conuerte te*: cf. Joel 2.12 and Jesus' promise of rest in Matthew 11.29.

2.1.3. 'To converte þee to inwarde þinges' renders *ad interiora te dare*.

2.1.4. Cf. Paul's description of the kingdom of God in Romans 14.17.

2.1.5. Cf. the description of the princess's glory as *ab intus* ('withinforthe') in Psalm 44.14 (AV 45.13).

2.1.7. 'Comune and ofte' is a doublet rendering *frequens*; 'with him is his' has been added; *multa pax*, which follows *grata consolacio* ('graciouse consolacion'), has been omitted. See 1.8.6 n.

2.1.8. Cf. Samuel's exhortation to the people of Israel to prepare their hearts to the Lord in 1 Kings (AV 1 Samuel) 7.3. On Christ as the soul's spouse, see Riehle, p. 37, and cf. 3.23.6; on God's dwelling in the soul, see Riehle, pp. 130–1. The only citation of 'eya' (*eya*) in *MED* or *OED* is from the *Imitation*.

2.1.9. *Si quis diligit me sermonem meum seruabit; et ad eum veniemus: et mansionem apud eum faciemus* (John 14.23).

2.1.12. This is the only citation of 'procutoure' (*procurator*) in the sense 'a spiritual guardian or protector' in *MED*.

2.1.13. On the variants, see Introduction, p. lvii. With 'Criste abideþ for ever' cf. John 12.34.

2.1.16. Evidently D² considered inverted word order to be more appropriate in this construction. Cf. the exhortation to trust God with one's whole heart in Proverbs 3.5.

2.1.18. On 'citee', see 1.17.4 n. and 1.23.46 n.; on 'oned', see 1.3.11 n.

2.1.20. Cf. Paul's longing for a heavenly habitation in 2 Corinthians 5.2.

2.1.23. 'Lete thi þenkynge be to highe God' is an adaptation of Wisdom 5.16 (Vulgate), interpreting *cogitatio* as being on the part of men rather than on the part of God; the idea of prayer being lifted up without ceasing is derived from Psalm 140.2 (AV 141.2) and 1 Thessalonians 5.17.

2.1.24–5. The motif of the soul's resting in Christ's wounds is Franciscan; see Riehle, pp. 118, 130, and cf. v. 32.

2.1.27–8. The translation follows R in exchanging the second clauses of these two verses from their position in K.

2.1.31. This is a reference to the faithful saying that if we suffer with Christ we shall also reign with him, quoted by Paul in 2 Timothy 2.12.

2.1.33. The translation follows R in omitting K's *et veritatis*, which follows *amator Ihesu* ('a lover of Ihesu'). 'Lyfte hymselfe aboue hymselfe in spirite' renders *eleuare supra seipsum in spiritu*, language suggestive of the 'ecstatic stepping of man out of himself' (Riehle, pp. 92–4). This is the only citation of 'fruybly' (*fruitiue*) in *MED* or *OED*.

2.1.34. Cf. Bernard, *Sermones de Diversis* 18.1 (*Opera*, ed. Leclercq, vol. vi, part 1, pp. 157–8). 'To whom alle þinges savoren as þei been' renders *cui sapiunt omnia prout sunt*, i.e. he who 'can value all things as they really are' (Knott); see 1.1.6 n. On being taught by God, cf. Isaiah 54.13.

2.1.35. *Qui ab intra scit ambulare, et modicum ab extra res ponderare; non requirit loca nec expectat tempora: ad habenda deuota exercicia*, i.e. 'The man who knows how to walk the road of the inward life and set little store by things outside himself, has no need of special places nor set times to perform his exercises of devotion' (Knott).

2.1.36. The verbs here are *se recolligit* and *se . . . effundit*; see 1.11.2 n. This is the only citation of 'poureþ' (*effundit*) in the sense 'to devote oneself to' in *MED* or *OED*.

2.1.38–9. For the Latin of v. 38, see apparatus. 'Havynges and berynges' is a doublet rendering *gestus*. The meaning is: 'The man whose inner life is well-ordered and disposed is not troubled by the strange and perverse ways of others; for a man is hindered and distracted by such things only so far as he allows himself to be concerned by them' (Sherley-Price). On the variants, see Introduction, p. lxi. DMG's reading 'distraite' (*distrahitur*) is the only citation of the word in *MED* in the sense 'distracted'.

2.1.40. 'Alle þinges shulde turne the to goode' renders *omnia tibi in bonum cederent* (cf. Romans 8.28).

2.1.42. On the defouling of the divine image in man, see Riehle, p. 148.

2.1.43. Cf. the psalmist's refusal to be comforted in Psalm 76.3 (AV 77.2). On the use of the word 'biholde' to express the *visio dei*, see Riehle, pp. 122–7.

2.2.0. On meeknes, see 1.1.7 n.

2.2.3. 'Overthwartnes' renders *peruersitas*.

2.2.4. On seeing the Lord's help, see 1.11.11 n.

2.2.5. 'þou owest to reserve thiselfe to him' renders *te debes illi resignare*.

2.2.6. Cf. the man of God's words to Amaziah in 2 Chronicles 25.8.

2.2.9. This is the only citation of 'mekinge' (*depressionem*) in the sense 'becoming humble' in *MED*. Cf. the description of God as comforting the meek in 2 Corinthians 7.6 and giving grace to the humble in 1 Peter 5.5 (also James 4.6 and Proverbs 3.34).

2.2.10. On God's secrets (*secreta*), see 1.20.28 n.; on being drawn by God, see Riehle, pp. 57, 74–5.

2.2.11. 'Reprevinges or wronges' is a doublet rendering R's *contumelia*, which is lacking in K.

2.3.3. This is the only citation of 'passionate' (*passionatus*) in the sense 'easily angered' in *MED*.

2.3.5. 'Meved' renders *commotus*, i.e. 'troubled'.

2.3.11. Cf. Paul's exhortation to mutual forbearance in Ephesians 4.2.

2.3.14. *Nobis*, which precedes *contrariantibus* ('contrariouse'), has been omitted. The second 'and' renders K's *aut* rather than R's *animo*. This is the only citation of 'indisciplynate' (*indisciplinatis*) in *MED*.

2.3.16. 'To hemselfe' has been added.

2.4.0. *Mente*, the noun which *pura* ('pure') modifies, has been omitted. On 'intencioun', see 1.14.4 n.

2.4.3. On tasting God, see 1.25.40 n.

2.4.6. 'To þee' has been added. The thought here is slightly different from the idea in the mystical tradition that the soul itself is a mirror of God (Riehle, p. 154).

2.4.9. On piercing in the mystical tradition, see Riehle, p. 94, and cf. 3.1.6 and 3.6.22.

2.4.13. This is the only citation of 'exute' (*exuitur*) in *MED* or *OED*. 'Fro þe body' renders R's *a corpore* rather than K's *a torpore*. See 3.7.14 n.

2.5.0. *De propria consideracione*, i.e. 'On knowing oneself' (Blaiklock); see 1.2.0 n.

2.5.1. 'Oweþ' renders R's *debemus* rather than K's *possumus*. *Nobis*, which modifies *deest* ('lakkeþ'), has been omitted.

2.5.3. On inner blindness, see 1.1.1 n and 1.3.5 n.

2.5.4. 'Oftetymes we be meved' renders *passione interdum mouemur*.

2.5.10. On inwardness, see 2.1.1 n.

2.5.12. 'When þou haste reonnen over alle þinges' renders *quando omnia percurristi*, i.e. 'when you have occupied yourself in countless affairs' (Sherley-Price).

2.5.13. 'Onehede' renders *vnionem*.

2.5.14. 'Kepe halyday and reste' renders *te ⟨feriatum⟩ . . . conserues*.

2.5.19. Cf. the statement that God fills heaven and earth in Jeremiah 23.24.

2.6.1. 'Ioye' renders *gloria*. On conscience as a witness, see 1.20.15 n.

2.6.4. This is the only citation of the phrase 'oute of quiete' (*inquieta*) in *MED*.

2.6.5. On the benefits of having a heart that does not condemn one, see 1 John 3.21.

2.6.7. *Non est pax impiis* (Isaiah 48.22).

2.6.8. The translation follows R in omitting *et qui⟨s⟩ nobis nocere audebit*, which follows *non venient super nos mala* ('þer shal none yvels come vppon vs'), said by the false prophets in Micah 3.5,11; on false peace cf. also 1 Thessalonians 5.3. On the idea of thoughts perishing, cf. Psalm 145.4 (AV 146.4).

2.6.9. On glorying in tribulations, cf. Romans 5.3; on glorying in the cross, cf. Galatians 6.14. 'Criste' renders *domini*.

2.6.13. On rejoicing in the truth, cf. 1 Corinthians 13.6.

2.6.15. C's text here results in an inconsistency between the first clause and the other two clauses ('[he] þat sekeþ temporal glory, and despiseþ hit', etc.); this suggests that the text has become corrupt and that DMG's reading ('he þat sekiþ not temporal glory, but despisiþ it', etc.), which is consistent but means the opposite of the Latin (*qui temporalem requirit gloriam aut non ex animo . . . contempnit*, etc.), is an attempt to remove the inconsistency. The first clause has therefore been left as in C, and the second and third clauses emended so as to be consistent with the first clause and with the Latin.

2.6.19. The second half of this verse represents a slight recasting of the Latin: *nec maior dici vales quam deo teste sis.*

2.6.21. With this distinction between human and divine perception cf. God's instruction to Samuel when he was choosing David among the sons of Jesse (1 Kings (AV 1 Samuel) 16.7).

2.6.26. 'The apostle' renders R's *apostolus* rather than K's *beatus Paulus*: cf. 2 Corinthians 10.18 (*non enim qui seipsum commendat ille probatus est . . . sed quem deus commendat*).

2.6.27. The translation follows R in omitting *intus*, which modifies *ambulare* ('to go'). On walking with God, see Genesis 5.22–4 and Micah 6.8.

2.7.2. The first 'alle þinges' renders R's *omnia*, which is lacking in K. It is difficult to tell whether C's 'wol be byloved' or DMG's 'wolde be loued' should be preferred.

2.7.3. This is the only citation of 'perseverable' (*perseuerabilis*) in *MED* or *OED*.

2.7.4. 'Clyveth' renders *adheret* (see 1.11.5 n.); 'clippeþ' renders *amplectitur*. On the mystical embrace, see Riehle, pp. 39–40, and cf. 3.9.7, 3.23.10, and 3.63.17.

2.7.5. On the idea of holding God, see Riehle, p. 129, and cf. 2.8.15.

2.7.8. On the image of God sitting in the soul, see Riehle, pp. 132–3.

2.7.11. The idea of the 'wyndy reede' is derived from Isaiah 36.6 and Matthew 11.7; the idea that 'eueri fleshe is grasse' is derived from Isaiah 40.6–7 and 1 Peter 1.24–5.

2.7.13. The second 'þi solace' renders R's *solacium*, which is lacking in K.

2.7.14. *Vtique*, which modifies *inuenies* ('þou shalte . . . fynde'), has been omitted.

2.8.0. On friendship with God, see Riehle, p. 22.

2.8.5. The translation follows R in omitting *illi*, which modifies *dixit* ('seide'). Martha called Mary to meet Jesus as he came to Bethany to raise Lazarus from the dead (John 11.28–9).

2.8.6. This translation of this verse renders V's *Felix homo quem Ihesus vocat de lacrimis ad gaudium spiritus* rather than R's *Felix homo quando Ihesus venit et vocat de lacrimis ad gaudium spiritus* or K's *Felix hora: quando Ihesus vocat de lacrimis ad gaudium spiritus*.

2.8.8. The sense of this verse has been slightly obscured by the translator's omission of *hoc*, the subject of *est* ('is').

2.8.12. Cf. the description of a faithful friend as treasure in Ecclesiasticus 6.14.

2.8.13. 'If he loste' has been added.

2.8.14. The translation follows R in omitting this verse, which appears thus in K: *Pauperrimus est qui viuit sine Ihesu: et ditissimus qui bene est cum Ihesu.*

2.8.15. On the idea of holding God, see 2.7.5 n.

2.8.19. Cf. Peter's words to Jesus in John 6.68–9.

2.8.23. 'þi derlynge and thi special' renders *dilectus specialis*. On the description of Jesus as darling, see Riehle, pp. 36–7.

2.8.27. The idea that God 'hath none lyke him' is derived from Jeremiah 10.6 and Micah 7.18.

2.8.28. 'Aboute thi love' corresponds to *tecum* in K, which is omitted in R. Perhaps the translator was following the Latin as given in R and inserted 'aboute thi love' to fill the lacuna. The end of this verse has been omitted in the translation, which appears in both K and R as *sed sit Ihesus in te et in omni bono homine*.

2.8.29. 'Implicamente or encombrance' is a doublet rendering *implicamento*. This is the only citation of 'implicamente' in *MED* or *OED*.

2.8.30. 'Taste' corresponds to *vacare*: in the Latin Psalm 45.11 (AV 46.10, *Vacate et videte quoniam ego sum deus*) has been conflated with Psalm 33.9 (AV 34.8, *Gustate et videte quoniam suavis est dominus*): cf. 3.23.7. On the laying bare of the soul, see Riehle, pp. 61–4, and cf. 2.11.17, 2.11.29, 3.42.6, and 3.42.15.

2.8.31. 'Alle þinges voyded and conged' renders *omnibus euacuatis et licenciatis*, i.e. 'once you have cast aside and forsaken all else' (Sherley-Price); Knott takes *omnibus* to refer to people, and translates 'enabling you to dismiss all others and send them right away'. On union with God, see 1.3.11 n.

2.8.32. On being 'myghty to alle þinges' (*potens . . . ad omnia*), cf. Philippians 4.13.

2.8.33. 'Scourgynges and peynes' is a doublet rendering *flagella*.

2.8.34. 'Oure Lorde' has been added; *magna*, which modifies *serenitas* ('clerenes'), has been omitted. On the calm that follows a storm, cf. Tobit 3.22 (Vulgate).

2.9.3. On the variants, see Introduction, pp. lxi–lxii.

2.9.5. On God as 'ledar' (*ductore*), cf. Deuteronomy 1.30.

2.9.7–8. St Laurence, one of the seven deacons at Rome who was closely associated with Pope Sixtus II, was martyred in AD 258 shortly after Sixtus had been killed in the persecution of Valerian. According to Ambrose, when Laurence saw Sixtus being led away to be beheaded, he lamented that he had to remain alive when Sixtus was to die, and asked to be his partner in martyrdom. Sixtus replied that it would be more fitting for him to remain, for if he waited he would have his own more glorious death later. Laurence obeyed his master, and after three days he was killed by being roasted on a gridiron (*De Officiis Ministrorum* 1.41.204–6; see also *ODS*, pp. 237–8, and *AASS Augusti* (1867–8), ii. 485–532, esp. p. 492). In v. 7, 'alle þinge delectable' renders *omne quod in mundo delectabile videbatur* (the last two words are reversed in R).

2.9.11. On spiritual affection, see Riehle, p. 98.

2.9.13. On the variants, see Introduction, p. lx.

2.9.14. 'Grete' has been added.

2.9.17. 'Holy' corresponds to *antiquis* in the Latin: presumably the translator read *sanctis*.

2.9.19. On the variants, see Introduciton, p. lxiv.

2.9.18–22. This passage is derived from Psalm 29.7–12 (AV 30.6–11); for a stylistic analysis, see Biggs, 'Style', pp. 188–9. In v. 20 'amonge þees' renders ⟨*inter*⟩ *hec*. In v. 21 it is difficult to tell whether C's or D²MG's readings should be preferred; D²MG's have been chosen as being closer to the Latin. 'Of God' has been added.

2.9.24. 'Holy' has been added. *Beatus*, which modifies *Iob*, has been omitted. The last sentence renders *Visitas eum diluculo: et subito probas illum* (Job 7.18): 'bytyme, or in þe twylyght' is a doublet.

2.9.25. The first *sola*, which modifies *magna misericordia* ('þe grete merci'), has been omitted; cf. Psalm 51.10 (AV 52.8) and 1 Peter 1.13.

2.9.26. 'Feire tretes' corresponds to the Latin plural *tractatus pulchri*. 'Melodiouse' has been added.

2.9.27. This is the only citation of the phrase 'denyinge of myselfe' (*abnegacio mei*) in *MED*.

2.9.29. 'Ravished' renders *raptus*: on the mystical *raptus*, see Riehle, pp. 94–6, and cf. 2.12.56 and n., 3.7.14, 3.27.8, 3.36.8, and 3.63.23.

2.9.30. This and the instance at 3.21.4 are the only citations of 'exercitate' (*exercitatus*) in *MED*. On the variants, see Introduction, p. lxii.

2.9.32. This promise was made in the letter to the church at Ephesus (Revelation 2.7).

2.10.1. The idea that man is born to labour is derived from Job 5.7.

2.10.6. 'Gentile' has been added; the Latin is *ex virtutibus progenite.*

2.10.7. On using (*frui*) the gifts of God, see Riehle, pp. 105–6.

2.10.10. On the variants, see Introduction, p. lxv. This is the only citation of 'refounde' (*refundimus*) in the sense 'to return (God's grace through thanksgiving)' in *MED.* For imagery of flowing and pouring in the mystical tradition, see Riehle, pp. 86–8, and cf. v. 6 and 3.2.3.

2.10.11. 'To meke men' corresponds to the Latin singular *humili.*

2.10.15. 'The betynge of subtraccion' (*subtractionis verbere*) refers to the withdrawal of grace. *Non . . . quidquam boni* has been rendered 'noþinge'.

2.10.16. *Hoc est,* which precedes *deo gracias pro gracia tribue* ('yif God þankynges for his grace'), has been omitted. Cf. Jesus' words to the Pharisees when they asked him about paying tribute to Caesar (Matthew 22.21).

2.10.21. Cf. Paul's exhortation against being desirous of vainglory in Galatians 5.26.

2.10.22. A reference to Jesus' rebuke to the Jewish leaders for seeking honour (*gloria*) from one another and not the honour that comes from God alone (John 5.44). 'Into þat euermore þei tendethe' renders *semper in idipsum tendunt,* i.e. 'they are always seeking this end' (Knott).

2.10.23. This and 3.14.15 are the only citations of 'kynde' (*gratus*) in the sense 'grateful' in *MED.*

2.11.0. 'Criste' renders R's *Christi* rather than K's ⟨*Ihesu*⟩.

2.11.1. The metaphor of bearing the cross is derived from Jesus' words to the multitude that whoever did not bear his cross and follow him could not be his disciple (Luke 14.27; cf. also his words to the disciples in Luke 9.23).

2.11.2. On this verse, see Introduction, p. lxxv.

2.11.3. Cf. the characterization of the false friend in Ecclesiasticus 6.10.

2.11.5. On the breaking of the bread, cf. Luke 24.35; on the drinking of the cup, cf. Matthew 20.22.

2.11.9. This and 3.22.5 are the only citations of 'deieccion' (*deiectionem*) in a non-astrological sense in *MED.*

2.11.10–13. In v. 10, the translation follows R in omitting *propriam,* which modifies *aliquam consolacionem* ('any consolacions'). On v. 13, see above, p. lx.

2.11.17. On being poor in spirit, cf. Matthew 5.3; on being bare, see 2.8.30 n.

2.11.18. The difficulty of this verse is derived from the obscurity of the Vulgate rendering of Proverbs 31.10 (*Procul et de vltimis finibus, pretium eius*), a misleading translation of the Hebrew whose meaning is uncertain: see C. H. Toy, *A Critical and Exegetical Commentary on the Book of Proverbs,* ICC (Edinburgh, 1899), pp. 543, 68. Most English translations of the Bible follow the Septuagint: AV has 'Her price is far above rubies' (in its original context the sentence refers to the rarity of a good wife). See Introduction, p. l.

2.11.19–22. The syntax here again recalls that of 1 Corinthians 13.1–3 (cf. 1.2.4). On giving all one's substance (v. 19), cf. 1 Corinthians 13.3 and Song of Songs 8.7; on understanding all knowledge (v. 21), cf. 1 Corinthians 13.2.

2.11.23. For the *vnum . . . necessarium*, see Luke 10.42.

2.11.24. 'Go holy oute of himselfe' renders *a se totaliter exeat*, i.e. 'leave self entirely behind' (Knott), although there may also be a hint of the mystical *excessus* (see 3.7.14 n.).

2.11.26. 'Alle þat' renders *quod*, referring presumably to the good works that the man may have done; 'what' would have been a clearer rendering. This is the only citation of 'pronounce' (*pronunciet*) in the sense 'confess' in *MED*.

2.11.27. Cf. Jesus' words to the disciples after the parable of the unprofitable servants in Luke 17.10.

2.11.28–9. The translation renders R's *Quia vnicus et pauper sum ego dicere poterit cum propheta: cum vere pauper et nudus spiritu esse ceperit* rather than K's *Tunc vere pauper et nudus spiritu esse poterit: et cum propheta dicere. Quia vnicus et pauper sum ego*. See Matthew 5.3 and Psalm 24.16 (AV 25.16), and 2.8.30 n.

2.12.0. *Sancte*, which modifies *crucis* ('crosse'), has been omitted.

2.12.1. *Abnega temetipsum: tolle crucem tuam, et sequere Ihesum* (cf. Matthew 16.24). 'Me' renders R's *me* rather than K's *Ihesum*.

2.12.2. A reference to Jesus' words *Discedite a me maledicti in ignem eternum* in the parable of the sheep and the goats (Matthew 25.41).

2.12.3. The phrase 'the worde of þe crosse' (*uerbum crucis*) is derived from 1 Corinthians 1.18.

2.12.4. Jesus spoke of the appearance of the sign of the son of man in heaven in Matthew 24.30.

2.12.5. On 'confourmed', see 1.1.6 n.

2.12.8. On 'hevonly swettenesse', see 3.3.1 n.

2.12.11. 'þou shalte go into þe lyve euerlastinge' is a further reference to the parable of the sheep and the goats (Matthew 25.46).

2.12.12. 'þat bare his owne crosse' renders *baiulans sibi crucem* (cf. John 19.17).

2.12.13. The translation follows R in transposing this verse, *Quia si commortuus fueris: eciam cum illo pariter viues* (Romans 6.8), to 2.12.15.

2.12.15. On spiritual mortification, see 1.11.5 n.

2.12.17. The first clause renders *Dispone et ordina omnia secundum tuum velle et videre*, i.e. 'even if you arrange everything to suit your own views and wishes' (Knott).

2.12.19. 'Stired' renders *exercitaberis*, 'troubled' (Sherley-Price). On being 'grevous' (*grauis*) to oneself, cf. Job 7.20 (Vulgate).

2.12.25. Ingram read D²'s correction as 'turne þiself nether', but 'by' is clearly visible before 'nethe' (although the space between the *y* and the *n* is very slightly wider than one would expect within a word). What Ingram took as the *r* at the end of 'nether' is in fact a full stop just below the beginning of the crossbar of the *t* of 'turne'.

2.12.32. *Oportebat . . . Christum pati, et resurgere a mortuis: et ita intrare in gloriam suam* (cf. Luke 24.46,26).

2.12.33. 'þe crosse weye' renders *via sancte crucis*. This is the only citation of 'crosse weye' in the sense 'way of the cross' in *MED* and *OED*.

2.12.35. 'Thou erreste, þou goeste oute of the weie' renders R's *erras erras* rather than K's *erras*; the translation also follows R in omitting *pati*, which in K is the verb governing *tribulaciones*. The point that 'alle þis mortalle lyve is fulle of myseries' echoes Job 14.1.

2.12.37. The translation omits *multipliciter*, which modifies *afflictus* ('peyned').

2.12.40. 'Counforted and strengthed' is a doublet rendering K's *confortatur* rather than R's *conuertitur*. On 'conformite', see 1.1.6 n.

2.12.43. Cf. Paul's remarks about chastising and subduing his body in 1 Corinthians 9.27.

2.12.46. *Christi*, which modifies *cruce* ('with the crosse'), has been omitted.

2.12.50. On drinking imagery in the mystical tradition, see Riehle, pp. 41–2.

2.12.52. Cf. Paul's comparison between present suffering and future glory in Romans 8.18; also Bernard, *Sermones in Annuntiatione Dominica* 1.2 (*Opera*, ed. Leclercq, v. 14).

2.12.56. On the mystical *raptus* (cf. 2 Corinthians 12.2–4), see 2.9.29 n.

2.12.57. This warning was conveyed to Paul by Ananias (Acts 9.16).

2.12.61. The translation alters the sense of this verse, by omitting *modicum*, the object of ⟨*pati pro*⟩ *Christo* ('suffre for Criste').

2.12.68. 'Man' corresponds to *saluti hominum* in the Latin (Y omits *saluti*).

2.12.69. 'Alle his disciples' corresponds to *sequent⟨es⟩ se discipul⟨os⟩*: see Matthew 16.24.

2.12.70. Cf. the words of Paul and Barnabas to the churches in Asia (Acts 14.21, AV 14.22). On the variants, see Introduction, p. lx.

2.12.71. This verse renders K's *Expliciunt ammoniciones ad interna trahentes* rather than R's *Explicit secunda pars libri interne consolacionis qui vocatur musica ecclesiastica*.

BOOK III

3.0.0. This verse appears as *Capitula libri sequentis* in K, and as *Incipit tercia pars eiusdem libri* in R.

3.0.3. The translation follows R in omitting the end of the verse: *et quod multi ea non ponderant*.

3.0.4. Together with the titles of the other prayers (3.0.17, 3.0.26, 3.0.27, and 3.0.32), this verse does not appear in the list of chapters in K, in which the chapters are accordingly numbered from 1 to 59 rather than from 1 to 64.

3.0.7. 'Love' renders R's *amoris* rather than K's *amatoris*.

3.0.14. *Christi* has been omitted from the end of this verse.

3.0.15. 'Ayeine pride' paraphrases *ne extollamur in bonis*.

3.0.16. See 3.16.0 n.

3.0.20. *Equanimiter*, which modifies *ferende* ('suffred'), has been omitted.

3.0.23. 'Alle þinges' renders *omnia bona et dona*.

3.0.29. The first 'very' corresponds to *firma*.

3.0.30. The Latin has been slightly recast: *De eminencia libere mentis quam supplex oracio magis meretur quam lectio* (R reads *qua* for *quam* and *frequens loquucio* for *lectio*).

3.0.38. *Habenda* has been omitted from the end of the verse.

3.0.39. *Et in omnibus* has been omitted from the end of the verse.

3.0.45. The Latin has been slightly recast: *Quod homo nichil boni ex se habet et de nullo gloriari potest*.

3.0.46. 'Worshippes' renders the Latin singular *honoris*.

3.0.51. 'Ayenis' paraphrases *quando insurgunt*.

3.0.54. 'Gostely' has been added.

3.0.57. The translation follows R in omitting ⟨*sed magis verberibus reum*⟩ from the end of the verse.

3.0.60. *Diuine*, which modifies *gracie* ('grace'), has been omitted, as in Θ.

3.0.64. *Solo*, which modifies *deo* ('God'), has been omitted.

3.0.65. This verse appears as *Incipit liber interne consolacionis* in K, and as *Sequitur tercia pars* in R.

3.1.0. *Fidelem*, which modifies *animam* ('soule'), has been omitted. On the idea, central to Book III, of dialogue between Christ and the soul, see Riehle, pp. 116–9.

3.1.1. *Audiam quid loquatur in me dominus deus* (Psalm 84.9, AV 85.8).

3.1.3. 'Of Goddes rownynge' corresponds to *venas diuini susurri* (R reads *susurii*), an idea derived from Job 4.12 (Vulgate); possibly a word rendering *venas* has dropped out. On the whispering of God to the soul, see Riehle, pp. 117–18.

3.1.4. 'Alle' has been added. See 2.1.1 n.

3.1.6. On inner seeing, see Riehle, p. 123; on piercing imagery, see 2.4.9 n; on God's privity, see Riehle, pp. 100–1, and cf. 3.2.10.

3.1.7. 'Take hiede' here renders *vacare* (see 1.11.5 n.); in v. 3 the phrase renders *aduertunt*, in v. 4 *auscultant*. 'Casteþ hemselfe oute fro' renders *se excuciunt*, i.e. 'shake themselves free from' (Blaiklock).

3.1.9. On the idea of God as the believer's 'helthe' (*salus*), cf. Psalm 34.3 (AV 35.3); on God as peace, see Riehle, pp. 135–6, and cf. Ephesians 2.14 and such passages as 3.17.7, 3.23, 3.29, and 3.52.10.

3.2.1. *Loquere domine: quia audit seruus tuus* was Samuel's reply to the call of God in the temple (1 Kings (AV 1 Samuel) 3.10).

3.2.2. The idea of knowing God's testimonies is derived from Psalm 118.125 (AV 119.125), of which this verse is a quotation.

3.2.3. The idea of the believer bowing (*inclina*) to God's words (or words inspired by him) is derived from Psalm 77.1 (AV 78.1); the image of inspired words flowing like dew is derived from Deuteronomy 32.2 (cf. 2.10.10 and n.). 'Swete' has been added.

3.2.4. The Israelites said this when they were afraid of the thunder, the smoke, and the sound of the trumpet when Moses received the Ten Commandments (Exodus 20.19).

3.2.6. This is the only citation of 'inspiroure' (*inspirator*) in *MED*. On God as 'illuminoure', see 1.1.0–2 n. The idea that the believer is best taught by God directly, rather than by human teachers, may be derived from 1 John 1.27.

3.2.8. 'Noþinge' suggests that the translator's source omitted *cor* from K's *cor non accendunt*; R omits *cor* but reads *non accedunt*. On fire imagery, cf. v. 16 and see 1.14.11 n.

3.2.9. 'þou openeste þe witte' renders *sensum aperis*, a phrase used of Jesus when he was teaching the disciples before the ascension (Luke 24.45); the distinction between letter and spirit made by Paul in 2 Corinthians 3.6 is also in mind.

3.2.10. On 'privytees' (*signatorum*), see 3.1.6 n.

3.2.13. On the idea that God illuminates the heart, cf. Ecclesiasticus 2.10 (Vulgate).

3.2.14. On the idea that God gives gives fecundity, cf. 1 Corinthians 3.7.

3.2.15. On the idea that God gives understanding, cf. Job 32.8.

3.2.17. 'Therfore' has been added; in the Latin v. 17 is all one sentence, and a new sentence begins at the beginning of v. 18. With 'the worde herde and not done' cf. Romans 2.13 and James 1.22.

3.2.18. *Enim*, which modifies *habes* ('thou haste'), has been omitted. 'Thou haste wordes of lyve euerlastinge' is a quotation of Peter's words to Jesus in John 6.69 (AV 6.68).

3.2.19. The collocation 'preysinge, glory, and . . . worshippe' is derived from 1 Peter 1.7.

3.3.0. The translation follows R in omitting the second half of this title, *et quod multi ea non ponderant*. On meekness, see 1.1.7 n.

3.3.1. The translation follows R in omitting the second *uerba* in K's *uerba mea uerba suauissima*. On the sweetness of God, see Riehle, pp. 108–9, and cf. 3.6.25 and 3.22.20.

3.3.2. Jesus said to the disciples that his words were spirit and life in John 6.64 (AV 6.63).

3.3.3. 'Thei beþe not to be drawen to veyne plesance' renders *non sunt ad vanam complacenciam trahenda*, i.e. 'they are not to be quoted for vain pleasure' (Sherley-Price), or 'you must not turn them to fit your empty complacency' (Knott).

3.3.4. The statement that the man who is instructed and taught by God is blessed and refreshed is derived from Psalm 93.12–13 (AV 94.12–13); the idea of desolation in the earth is derived from Isaiah 3.26, where Jerusalem is referred to figuratively as sitting desolate on the ground (*desolata in terra sedebit*), but the translation misrepresents the Latin *et non desoletur in terra* (*quem tu erudieris*—'he whom þou haste lerned'—being the subject): presumably the translator did not read *in*.

3.3.11. The sea speaks in Isaiah's oracle proclaiming judgement against the port of Tyre, though it is the prophet rather than the sea who tells Sidon to be ashamed (Isaiah 23.4).

3.3.12. *A multis*, which modifies *leuatur* ('is . . . lyfte vppe'), has been omitted.

3.3.13. 'Bisily' has been added.

3.3.14. 'Alas' renders R's *pro dolor* rather than K's *proch pudor*. On such negative vocabulary, see Lees, pp. 243–5.

3.3.20. The Israelites were commanded to have the words of God in their hearts (Deuteronomy 6.6–7).

3.3.22. The antithesis between temptation (or tribulation) and consolation (see *DS* ii. 1617–34) is a recurring theme of Book III.

3.3.24. 'Hereth' renders RJ's *audit* rather than KZ's *habet*. 'Hath þat' renders *habet qui*, i.e. 'has one who'. The verse is a paraphrase of Jesus' words in John 12.48.

3.4.2. Abraham acknowledged the incongruity of man's speaking to God in his intercession for Sodom (Genesis 18.27), from which there is a further quotation at 3.9.1.

3.4.4. *Domine* has been omitted. On being nothing, cf. 2 Corinthians 12.11, and see Riehle, pp. 64–6.

3.4.5. On the idea that God alone is good, cf. Jesus' words to the rich young ruler at Luke 18.19; on the idea that he alone is 'ryghtwise' (*iustus*), cf. Nehemiah's prayer at 2 Maccabees 1.25; on the idea that there is none holy like him, cf. 1 Kings (AV 1 Samuel) 2.2; on the idea that he can do all things, cf. Job 42.2; on the idea that he gives all things, cf. 1 Timothy 6.17; on the idea that he fills all things, cf. Jeremiah 23.24.

3.4.6. The psalmist prayed to God *reminiscere miseracionum tuarum* in Psalm 24.6 (AV 25.6); the point that God does not desire his works to be void is made in Wisdom 14.5.

3.4.8–9. The psalmist prayed to God not to turn his face from him, feared that his soul might be as earth without water, and asked God to teach him to do his will in Psalm 142.6–10 (AV 143.6–10). 'Prolonge' renders *prolongare*, i.e. 'delay'.

3.5.0. 'Be conuersant byfore God' renders *coram deo conuersandum*, i.e. 'have fellowship with God' (Blaiklock). On meekness, see 1.1.7 n.

3.5.1. *Ambula coram me in veritate* is an echo of David's charge to Solomon in 3 Kings (AV 1 Kings) 2.4. The command to seek God in simplicity of heart is an echo of Wisdom 1.1; *tui*, which modifies *cordis* ('herte'), has been omitted.

3.5.2–3. The idea of truth delivering (*liberabit*) is derived from Jesus' words in John 8.32; the idea of the person so delivered being 'veryly free' is derived from John 8.36.

3.5.4. 'þat þou seiste' has been added.

3.5.7. On the importance of doing what is pleasing to God, cf. 1 John 3.22.

3.5.12. The second sentence has been slightly recast: it probably renders R's *nil altum vere laudabile et desiderabile* rather than K's *nil altum nil vere laudabile et desiderabile*, but 'for' has been added. See Introduction, p. lx.

3.5.13. The translator has construed *eterna* ('euerlastynge') with *omnia* ('al þinges'), when it should probably be taken with *veritas* ('trouthe').

3.5.14. 'Vilenes and vnworthynesse' is a doublet rendering *vilitas*.

3.5.16. 'Clerely' renders *sincere*; ⟨*quidam*⟩ *non sincere* ⟨*coram me ambulant*⟩ echoes Tobit's prayer of repentance (Tobit 3.5).

3.5.17. 'Me beynge displesed' renders ⟨*me*⟩ *eis aduersante* (R reads *me in eis aduersante*).

3.5.18. Cf. the mention of fearing God's judgements in Psalm 118.120 (AV 119.120) and of the wrath of the Almighty in 2 Maccabees 7.38.

3.5.21. The contrast between mouth and heart is derived from Isaiah 29.13, quoted by Jesus with reference to the Pharisees in Matthew 15.8.

3.5.22. On the illumination of the understanding, see Riehle, pp. 123–4.

3.5.23. On the speaking of the Spirit of truth, see John 16.13; on the Spirit's speaking in the believer, see Matthew 10.20.

3.6.0. Some of the most intense language of mystical love is found in this chapter.

3.6.1. On the variants, see Introduction, pp. lxii–lxiii.

3.6.2. 'God of alle consolacion' renders *deus tocius consolacionis*, a phrase used by Paul in 2 Corinthians 1.3.

3.6.4. On God as the believer's lover, see Riehle, pp. 36–7, 88, and cf. 3.22.10 and 3.23.6. 'Alle myn inwardes shal ioye' renders *exultabunt omnia interiora mea*, possibly an echo of Proverbs 23.16 (*exultabunt renes mei*).

3.6.5. On God as the believer's glory, cf. Psalm 3.4 (AV 3.3); on God as his exultation of heart, cf. Psalm 118.111 (AV 119.111); on God as his hope, cf. Psalms 90.9 (Vulgate) and 141.6 (Vulgate); on God as his refuge in the day of tribulation, cf. Psalm 58.17 (AV 59.16) and Jeremiah 16.19.

3.6.6. 'Counforted' renders *confortari et consolari*.

3.6.7. 'Enfourme with [holy] disciplines' renders *instrue disciplinis sanctis*; perhaps CDM's reading arose from a Latin reading *disciplinis scientiae*. Cf. Elihu's words in Job 33.16.

3.6.9–10. Cf. Paul's statement that love bears all things (1 Corinthians 13.7).

3.6.13. 'Wrapped inne and encombred' renders *implicaciones sustineat*.

3.6.14. 'Love is bore of God' echoes the statement made in 1 John 4.7 that love is of God and he who loves is born of God.

3.6.15–17. The Latin is: *Amans volat currit et letatur: liber est et non tenetur. Dat omnia pro omnibus: et habet omnia in omnibus; quia in vno summo super omnia quiescit: ex quo omne bonum fluit et procedit. Non respicit ad dona: sed ad donantem ⟨se conuertit⟩ super omnia bona* (R reads *summo bono* for *summo*). In the Latin the subject is *amans* throughout; but the translator seems to have understood *amor* to have been the subject of most of the verbs. On the soul's soaring up to God in flight, see Riehle, pp. 72–3, and cf. 3.23.6 and 3.36.2–3; on the motif of the soul as a running lover, derived from such passages as Song of Songs 1.3 (AV 1.4), see Riehle, pp. 70–2; on the understanding of creation as flowing out of God, see Riehle, pp. 87–8. The first 'gode' in v. 16 renders R's *bono*, which is lacking in K. Cf. Paul's phrasing in 1 Corinthians 13.7.

3.6.22. 'Love wakeþ, and sleping hit slepeth not' may be an echo of *ego dormio, et cor meum vigilat* (Song of Songs 5.2). The image of the soul's leaping up towards God ('barsteþ' renders *erumpit*: see Riehle, pp. 71–2) is here powerfully combined with the images of fire and piercing ('passeþ' renders *pertransit*): see 1.14.11 n. and 2.4.9 n.

3.6.24. For the phrase *in auribus dei*, see Bernard, *Sermones in Psalmum Qui Habitat* 16.1 (*Opera*, ed. Leclercq, iv. 481).

3.6.25. 'Dilate me in love' renders *dilata me in amore*; on the *dilitatio cordis*, 'the idea of the heart being extended through its desire for God and through the working of divine grace', derived from Psalm 118.32 (AV 119.32), see Riehle, p. 94, and cf. 3.10.12 and 3.54.1. The occurrence of 'dilate' at 3.54.1 is one of two citations in *MED* in the sense 'to make the heart more responsive'; Riehle notes the use of 'dilate' in the *Imitation* here, and observes that the word is not used in a mystical sense in the ealier English mystical texts. On mystical tasting, see 1.25.40 n.; on sweetness, see 3.3.1 n.; on the idea of the soul's melting into God (cf. Song of Songs 5.6, Vulgate), see Riehle, p. 141.

3.6.27. The idea of singing a love song is found in Isaiah 5.1, where God is the singer, and of course in the Song of Songs; on mystical song, see Riehle, p. 121. On the idea of the soul's ascending to God, see Riehle, pp. 69–70, and cf. 3.9.7.

3.6.28. There are only two citations of 'iubilynge' (*iubilans*) in *OED* or *MED*.

3.6.30–2. This passage again echoes the phrasing of Paul's treatment of love in 1 Corinthians 13.4–7.

3.6.32. The translation's rendering 'deuoute to God and kynde' at this point follows R, which reads *deo deuotus et gratificus* here; in K these words appear in v. 33 after *sibi vilis et despectus.*

3.7.0. 'Love' renders R's *amoris* rather than K's *amatoris*.

3.7.3. 'þou failest in þinges taken' renders R's *defecis in acceptis* rather than K's *deficis a ceptis*, i.e. 'you abandon what you have begun' (Sherley-Price).

3.7.5. The sense of this verse has been changed: 'þou plesest' and 'þou displesest' correspond to *placeo* and *displiceo* in the Latin, with God as the subject.

3.7.11. 'Suggestions' renders R's *suggestiones* rather than K's *suggestionem*.

3.7.14. On the mystical *raptus*, see 2.9.29 n.; on the mystical *excessus*, which corresponds to the pseudo-Dionysian term *ekstasis*, 'an ecstatic stepping of man out of himself', see Riehle, pp. 92–4; Lees, pp. 214–5, 263–9; 3.36.5 and n.; and cf. 3.54.1.

3.7.15. *Inuite*, which modifies *pateris* ('þou suffreste'), has been omitted.

3.7.16. The translation follows R in omitting *antiquus*, which in K modifies *inimicus* ('enemy'). 'Holy' has been added; *pia*, which modifies *memoria* ('mynde') has been omitted.

3.7.21. The Latin is *Vade immunde ⟨spiritus⟩, erubesce miser*; cf. Jesus' words to the devil when he was tempted (Matthew 4.10) and to the unclean spirit in the Gerasene demoniac (Mark 5.8).

3.7.22. The idea that God will be with the believer who is persecuted as a mighty warrior, and that his enemy will stand confounded, echoes Jeremiah's assertion of God's defence of him (Jeremiah 20.11).

3.7.24. Cf. Jesus' words when he stilled the storm (Mark 4.39).

3.7.25–7. This passage is derived from Psalms 26.1,3 (AV 27.1,3) and 18.15 (AV 19.14).

3.7.28. *Certa tamquam miles bonus*; cf. Paul's command *labora sicut bonus miles* (2 Timothy 2.3).

3.7.31. *Stulte*, which modifies *presumencium* ('presumynge'), has been omitted.

3.8.1. The language of lifting here refers to pride rather than to a mystical experience.

3.8.4. 'Anxiete' (*anxietatem*) is not cited in *MED*, nor in *OED* before *c.* 1525 (cf. 3.40.10, 3.52.13, 3.56.4). *Quam sentis*, which modifies *anxietatem mentis*, has been omitted.

3.8.6. The idea that a man's way is not in himself is derived from Jeremiah 10.23.

3.8.9. Those who are proud enough to have their nest among the stars are rebuked in Obadiah 4; the idea of hoping under God's feathers is derived from Psalm 90.4 (AV 91.4).

3.8.12. The translation follows N in omitting *humiliter*, which in K and R modifies *paciuntur* ('suffreþ').

3.8.16. This is the first citation of 'trustyngly' (*fidenter*) in *OED*.

3.8.18. *Bene*, which modifies *moderare* ('mesure'), has been omitted.

3.8.22. On the variants, see Introduction, p. lxiii.

3.9.1. Cf. Abraham's words to God in his intercession for Sodom (Genesis 18.27).

3.9.2. The idea of God standing against one is derived from Balaam's comment on the angel standing in his way (Numbers 22.34).

3.9.3. On the variants, see Introduction, p. lxiv. This is the first citation of 'vilyfie' (*vilificauero*) in *OED*. On mystical annihilation, see 3.4.4 n.

3.9.4. 'Whither I bicame' renders *quo deueni*, i.e. 'what I have become' (Sherley-Price). The idea of being brought to nothing and not knowing is derived from Psalm 72.22 (Vulgate).

3.9.7. *Valde*, which modifies *mirum* ('a wonder þinge'), has been omitted. On ascending to God, see 3.6.27 n.; on the mystical embrace, see 2.7.4 n.

3.9.8. On the variants, see Introduction, p. lxi.

3.9.9. 'In myslyving' renders R's *male viuendo* rather than K's *male amando*; *me*, the object of the gerundive in each case, has been omitted; the first 'bothe þee and' has been added. The language of losing and finding here is derived from Jesus' words in John 12.25; cf. Matthew 10.39 and 16.25, Mark 8.35, and Luke 9.24 and 17.33.

3.9.11. There is a similar exclamation in Psalm 18.46 (AV 17.47).

3.9.12. 'Lorde' has been added; the prayer 'conuerte vs' is an echo of Psalm 79.20 (AV 80.19); on God as our 'helthe' (*salus*), cf. Isaiah 33.2; on God as our 'vertue' (*virtus*), cf. Psalm 45.2 (AV 46.1); on God as our 'strengthe' (*fortitudo*), cf. Psalms 30.4 and 42.2 (AV 31.3 and 43.2).

3.10.2. On intention, see 1.14.4 n.

3.10.6. See Jesus' promise to the woman at the well of living water, the spring of water welling up to eternal life in John 4.10–14 (cf. Revelation 21.6). On receiving grace for grace, cf. John 1.16.

3.10.7. 'Haue' is presumably subjunctive here. 'Delited' renders R's *delectabitur* rather than K's *dilatabitur*, which forms an antithesis with *angustiabitur* ('angwysshed': cf. Psalm 119.32 (AV 118.32) and 2 Corinthians 6.11–12).

3.10.8. The translation follows R in omitting *da*, which in K is the main verb of the clause *sed totum da deo* ('but al to God').

3.10.9. This is the first citation of 'districcion' (*districtione*) in the sense 'strictness, severity' in *MED*.

3.10.12. *Vincit enim omnia diuina caritas*; cf. Virgil's *Omnia vincit Amor: et nos cedamus Amori* (*Eclogues* 10.69, from Gallus' song on the impossibility of giving up his unrequited love for Lycoris). On 'dilateþ', see 3.6.25 n; on the powers of the soul (traditionally memory, intelligence, and will), see Riehle, pp. 142–5.

3.10.13. 'If þou savoure aright' renders *si recte sapis*, i.e. 'if you are truly wise'. Jesus told the rich young ruler that no-one is good except God alone (Luke 18.19).

3.11.1. *O quam ⟨magna multitudo dulcedinis tue domine: quam abscondisti timentibus te⟩* (Psalm 30.20, AV 31.19); *quam abscondisti* has been omitted.

3.11.4. `*Michi*', the indirect object of ⟨*ostendisti*⟩ ('þou shewdest'), which has been inserted in the margin of K and is lacking in R, has been omitted. *Longe*, which modifies *errarem* ('I erred'), has been omitted. The perfect *precepisti* has been rendered as the present tense 'þou commaundest'.

3.11.8. Cf. the psalmist's question in Psalm 115.12 (AV 116.12).

3.11.10. On the idea that all creatures serve God, cf. Judith 16.17 (AV 16.14).

3.11.12. *Omnia tua sunt* is an echo of David's prayer of thanks to God in 1 Chronicles 29.14.

3.11.14–15. The point that the heavens are made to serve humankind is made in

Deuteronomy 4.19 (Vulgate); a similar point about angels is made in Hebrews 1.14.

3.11.24. The translation follows R in omitting *suauissimam*, which modifies *consolacionem* ('consolacion'), and *omnem*, which modifies *carnalem . . . delectacionem* ('fleysshely delectacion').

3.11.25. *Magnam*, which modifies *libertatem* ('liberte'), has been omitted. 'Lyve' renders R's *vitam* rather than K's *viam*: in K the reference is to the narrow way leading to life mentioned by Jesus in Matthew 7.14.

3.11.28. 'The highest and the souereyne' is a doublet rendering *summum*.

3.12.3. This is the first citation of 'desirouse' (*cupidus*) in the sense 'devoted (person)' in *MED*.

3.12.8. The translation follows R in omitting *sed*, which precedes *neque* ('ner'), and the second *omnis*, which modifies *contraria affectio* ('contrarie affeccion').

3.12.9. This is the only citation of 'indisciplinacion' (*indisciplinacionem*) in *MED* or *OED*.

3.12.10. The translation follows R in omitting this verse: *Interdum uero oportet violencia uti et uiriliter appetitui sensitiuo contraire; nec aduertere quid uelit caro et quid non uelit: sed hoc magis satagere, ut subiecta sit eciam nolens spiritui.*

3.12.11. The translation follows R in rendering *caro* as 'fleysshe'; *caro* is omitted in K (it is understood from the previous verse). Cf. Paul's remarks about subduing his body in 1 Corinthians 9.27.

3.13.0. 'Of informacion of pacience' renders *de informacione paciencie*, i.e. 'on learning patience'.

3.13.1. The translation follows R in omitting *deus*, which follows *domine* ('Lorde') in K. The necessity of patience is stressed in Hebrews 10.36.

3.13.2. For the sorrow of life, cf. Psalm 30.11 (AV 31.10).

3.13.4. 'Contrariouste' corresponds to the plural *contraria*.

3.13.6. *De duobus malis minus est semper eligendum*; cf. the pseudo-Ciceronian *Epistula ad Octavianum* 8, where a similar point is made when it is argued that Antony's despotism would have been preferable to that of Octavian (Cicero, *Epistulae*, ed. W. S. Watt and D. R. Shackleton Bailey, OCT, 3 vols (Oxford, 1958–82), iii. 217). The phrase was proverbial: see Whiting, p. 165.

3.13.12. Those who are abundant in the world are mentioned in Psalm 72.12 (AV 73.12); the enemies of the Lord are said to vanish like smoke in Psalm 36.20 (AV 37.20).

3.13.18. The command not to follow one's desires but to turn away from one's own will is quoted from Ecclesiasticus 18.30; the command to delight in God who will fulfil the petitions of one's heart is quoted from Psalm 36.4 (AV 37.4).

3.13.19. In v. 19, 'consolacion' renders *consolacio*; in v. 20, 'consolacion' renders *solacio* and 'counfortes' renders *consolaciones*.

3.13.22. Cf. Augustine, *Confessions* 8.11.25.

3.13.24. The devil is referred to as *serpens antiquus* in Revelation 12.9. *Magnus*, which modifies *aditus* ('comynge inne'), has been omitted.

3.14.4. 'If the inner be destruyed' renders R's *si interior vere fuerit deuastatus*; K reads *si interior homo non fuerit deuastatus*.

3.14.5. On the idea of being an enemy of one's own soul, cf. Tobit 12.10.

3.14.8. On the idea of *creatio ex nihilo*, cf. 2 Maccabees 7.28.

3.14.7–3.15.1. On this passage, see Introduction, pp. liii–lvi.

3.14.10. On the idea that man is dust, cf. Genesis 3.19.

3.14.12. The form 'volowynge' presumably arose from a misreading of *b* as a looped *v* and of *n* as *u* in original 'bolnynge': see *OED* s.v. 'volowynge', and cf. 3.53.23 and n. The psalmist treats his enemies as if they were 'myre of the streete' in Psalm 17.43 (AV 18.42).

3.14.15. On the idea of God's eye sparing those who deserve judgement, cf. Ezekiel 20.17; on the idea of a soul being precious in someone's sight, cf. Saul's words after David had spared him on the hill of Hachilah in 1 Kings (AV 1 Samuel) 26.21. 'þine owne despisinge' renders *proprium contemptum*, from the context probably 'when you are treated with contempt' (Knott) rather than 'self-contempt' (Blaiklock).

3.15.2–3. Eliphaz states that the heavens are not clean in God's sight in Job 15.15 and mentions the angels' wickedness in Job 4.18; the point that God did not spare the angels is made in 2 Peter 2.4.

3.15.4. The fall of the stars is described in Revelation 6.13.

3.15.5. Manna is described as the bread of the angels in Psalm 77.25 (AV 78.25); the prodigal son was pleased to eat pigs' food after he had squandered his inheritance (Luke 15.16).

3.15.6. 'Surete' corresponds to *sanctitas* in K, *sanctitatis curacio* in R. Perhaps the translator read *securitas*.

3.15.10. The translation omits *propria*, which modifies *custodia* ('kepynge'). On the importance of God's watching, cf. Psalm 126.1 (AV 127.1).

3.15.11. Possibly an allusion to the disciples' request to Jesus to still the storm on the sea of Galilee: 'Lord, save us: we perish' (Matthew 8.25).

3.15.14. This is the only citation of 'abiectely' (*abiecte*) in *MED*.

3.15.16–17. On the deepness of God (cf. Psalm 35.7, AV 36.6), see Riehle, pp. 82–3, 140–1; on sea imagery in the mystical tradition, see Riehle, pp. 139–41; on mystical annihilation, see 3.4.4 n. This is the only citation of DMG's reading 'intransnatable' (*intransnatabile*) in *MED* or *OED*; 'vntransnatable' is not cited.

3.15.18. The meaning is, 'Where can there lurk any trace of pride, any confidence in my own goodness?' (Knott).

3.15.19. On being swallowed up into God, see 1.22.29 n.

3.15.20. The comparison of man's questioning God with the incongruity of clay's questioning the potter is derived from Isaiah 45.9, quoted by Paul in Romans 9.20.

3.15.22. 'Rere vppe into pride' is an expansion of *eriget*. This is the only citation of 'stedefasteþ' (*firmauit*) in the sense 'to fix (one's hope) firmly, hold resolutely' in *MED*.

3.15.23. 'In magnifiynge hemselfe' has been added.

3.15.24. *Veritas autem domini manet in eternum* (Psalm 116.2, AV 117.2).

3.16.0. The Latin is ⟨*Qualiter standum sit ac dicendum in omni re desiderabili*⟩, i.e. 'What you should feel and say when you meet something you would like' (Knott).

3.16.1. Cf. the instruction to submit one's plans to God's will in James 4.15.

3.16.11. 'Wolte' renders R's *vis* rather than K's *scis*; on the other hand, 'do with me' renders K's *fac mecum* rather than R's *fiat mecum*.

3.16.14. On the characterization of the believer as God's servant, cf. Psalm 118.125 (AV 119.125).

3.17.1. With 'þat hit mowe be with me and laboure with me' cf. the prayer for wisdom in Wisdom 9.10.

3.17.3–4. On the need to forsake one's own will, see Riehle, p. 66.

3.17.6. On resting in God, see Augustine, *Confessions* 5.1 and Riehle, pp. 135–6, and cf. 3.23.

3.17.8. *In idipsum*, which follows *in hac pace* ('in þis pees'), has been omitted. On sleeping and resting in peace, cf. Psalm 4.9 (AV 4.8); on mystical sleep, see Riehle, pp. 136–7.

3.18.7. The only citations of 'freuyshe' (*fruenda*) in *MED* or *OED* are from the *Imitation* (cf. 3.23.10, 3.29.15, 3.42.13, 3.53.17, 3.56.5).

3.18.8. 'Blysfulle' corresponds to *felix et beata*. 'Gode, trewe Cristen men' renders *boni Christi fideles*. *Ac mundicordes*, which follows *spirituales* ('spirituel men') in K (R has *et misericordes*), has been omitted. This is the only citation of 'fortasteþ' (*pregustant*) in *MED*. The idea that Christians' 'conuersacion', i.e. citizenship (*conuersacio*), is in heaven is derived from Philippians 3.20.

3.18.15. On the idea that God will not be angry for ever, cf. Psalm 102.9 (AV 103.9).

3.19.0. 'Bysines' renders *sollicitudo*, i.e. 'anxiety' (Knott).

3.19.2. 'Studieþ' renders R's *studet* rather than K's ⟨*suadet*⟩.

3.19.5. 'Over-casuely and lyke to falle' renders *nimis* . . . *casualiter*; this is the only citation of 'over-casuely' in *MED*. On casting one's anxieties on God, cf. 1 Peter 5.7.

3.19.6. The translation follows R in omitting *domine*, which stands at the beginning of the verse in K.

3.19.8-9. On receiving good and evil indifferently from the hand of God, cf. Job 2.10.

3.19.16. On God's not spurning the afflicted for ever, cf. Psalm 76.8 (AV 77.8); on the promise that he will not blot out of the book of life the name of him who conquers, cf. Revelation 3.5.

3.20.3. 'Reprehensions and blamynges' is a doublet rendering *reprehensiones*.

3.20.4. *Maxime*, which modifies *implendo* ('fulfillynge'), has been omitted; *pro salute mea*, which modifies *portem* ('bere'), has been omitted.

3.20.5. *Ad celum*, which modifies *via* ('weye'), has been omitted, as has `*tunc*`, modifying *erant* ('were'), inserted in the margin in K and present in R. The meaning of the last sentence is 'and even those who in former days were righteous and to be saved could not enter the kingdom of heaven until your passion and the atonement of your sacred death' (Sherley-Price).

3.20.10. *Tuis*, which modifies *tot signis* ('so many signes'), has been omitted. The connection between following Jesus and walking in light is derived from John 8.12: see 1.1.1 and n.

3.21.3. This point, which compares the Christian's struggle with that of Christ, is derived from Hebrews 12.4.

3.21.9. 'Whatever I shal suffre' changes the sense of the Latin, which is *et sicut pacienda videro*.

3.21.11. 'As muche as he wolle' renders *quantum sibi visum fuerit*.

3.21.12. *A quo homine*, which precedes *vtrum a prelato suo* ('wheþer . . . of his prelate'), has been omitted. *Apud deum*, which modifies *poterit sine merito transire* ('shall passe withoute merite'), has been omitted. 'Acceptably' (*gratanter*) is not cited in *MED*, nor in *OED* before 1535.

3.21.13. 'Spedde and redy' is a doublet rendering *expeditus*.

3.21.18. Cf. Jesus' words after his encounter with the rich young ruler, that what is impossible with men is possible with God (Luke 18.27).

3.22.1. The first clause is derived from Psalm 31.5 (AV 32.5); *domine*, which precedes *infirmitatem meam* ('myne infirmite'), has been omitted.

3.22.4. *Pene*, which modifies *deuictum* ('overcomen'), has been omitted.

3.22.5. The believer's request to God to see his 'deieccion and . . . freylete' is derived from Psalm 24.18 (AV 25.18).

3.22.6. The petition 'Haue merci on me oute of the cleye' is derived from the request of the psalmist (Psalm 68.2–3,15, AV 69.1–2,14).

3.22.9. *Semper*, which modifies *irruunt* ('comeþ'), has been omitted.

3.22.10. On God as the believer's lover, see 3.6.4 n.; on the promise of God's presence wherever one goes, cf. Joshua 1.9.

3.22.11. The exhortation not to give in to 'þe wolde man' is derived from Paul's teaching in Ephesians 4.22.

3.22.19. *Mund⟨i⟩*, which modifies `amorem' ('love'), has been omitted, as has *iuste*, which is lacking in R but in K modifies *sequentes ea* ('folowinge'). The lust of the flesh and the lust of the eyes and the pride of life are said to be not of the Father but of the world in 1 John 2.16.

3.22.20. 'Hit accompteþ delices to be vnder breres', i.e. 'counts it a delight to lie among the brambles' (Sherley-Price), is derived from the Vulgate text of Job's description of the social outcasts who scorn him, *qui . . . esse sub sentibus delicias computabant* (Job 30.7). *Delicias computabant* is a misleading translation of the Hebrew, whose meaning is obscure. C. J. Ball, *The Book of Job: A Revised Text and Version* (Oxford, 1922), rejects the Vulgate translation (pp. 348–9); RSV has 'under the nettles they huddle together'. 'þe inwarde mirthe of soule' renders R's *internam mentis amenitatem* rather than K's *internam virtutis amenitatem*. On spiritual tasting and sweetness, see 1.25.40 n. and 3.3.1 n.

3.22.21. 'Lovers' renders R's *amatoribus* rather than K's *abrenunciatoribus*.

3.23.1. 'Godes' renders R's *bona*, which is lacking in K.

3.23.2. The main point of the sentence—*in te . . . requiescere*, dependent on *da mihi* ('graunte me')—has been omitted. *Super omnem suauitatem et consolacionem*, which follows *super omnem famam et laudem* ('above alle fame and preysinge'), has also been omitted; 'promission' renders R's *promissionem* rather than K's *promissiones*; 'yiftes' renders *dona et munera*.

3.23.3. 'Alle the knyghthode of hevon' renders *omnem exercitum celi*, which Micaiah saw when Ahab was enticed to the battle with the king of Arama at Ramoth-gilead that was to result in his death (3 Kings (AV 1 Kings) 22.19).

3.23.4. The translation follows R in omitting *domine*, which in K precedes *deus meus* ('my God').

3.23.5. Cf. Augustine, *Confessions* 1.1.1.

3.23.6. On Christ as the soul's spouse, see 2.1.8 n.; on him as a lover, see 3.6.4 n.; on flying imagery, see 3.6.15 n., and cf. the psalmist's prayer in Psalm 54.7 (AV 55.6).

3.23.7. This verse again combines allusions to Psalm 45.11 (AV 46.10, *Vacate et videte quoniam ego sum deus*) and Psalm 33.9 (AV 34.8, *Gustate et videte quoniam suavis est dominus*): cf. 2.8.30. On the translation of *vacare* as 'take hiede', see 1.11.5 n.

3.23.8. On 'gedre' (*recolligam*), see 1.11.2 n.; on 'felynge' as a mystical term, see Riehle, pp. 110–13.

3.23.10. The translation follows R in rendering *sepius impediunt* as 'oftetymes letteþ' at the beginning of the list of verbs, though it does not follow R in repeating it in the same place as it comes in K, after *obnubilant* ('darkeþ my mynde'). On the mystical embrace, see 2.7.4 n. On the variants, see Introduction, pp. lxv–lxvi.

3.23.12. Jesus is said to be the brightness of God's glory in Hebrews 1.3.

3.23.15. Cf. the psalmist's prayer to God to stretch forth his hand and deliver him in Psalm 143.7 (AV Psalm 144.7).

3.23.17. On the presence of God in the mystical tradition, see Riehle, pp. 100–1.

3.23.18. The psalmist refers to God as his hope in Psalm 90.9 (Vulgate); everlasting salvation is mentioned in Isaiah 45.17.

3.23.19. The translation follows R's reading *donec gracia tua reuertatur mihi tuque intus loquaris* rather than K's *donec gracia tua reuertatur: michi⟨que tu⟩ intus loquaris*.

3.23.20. Cf. the promise in Isaiah 58.9: 'Then you shall call, and the Lord will answer; you shall cry, and he will say, Here I am.' There is a hint here of the *ludus amoris*, 'in which God plays, as it were, hide and seek with the questing soul': see Riehle, pp. 40–1.

3.23.23. On the *fruicio dei*, see Riehle, pp. 105–7, and cf. 3.53.17 and 3.63.23.

3.23.25. This verse combines allusions to Psalm 118.65 (AV 119.65, *Bonitatem fecisti cum servo tuo, domine, secundum verbum tuum*) and Psalm 105.45 (AV 106.45, *Penitunt eum secundum multitudinem misericordiae suae*).

3.23.27. On the idea that there is none like God, cf. Psalm 39.6 (Vulgate).

3.23.28. On the idea that the works of the Lord are very good, cf. Ecclesiasticus 39.21 (AV 39.16); on the idea that his judgements are true, cf. Psalm 18.10 (AV 19.9).

3.24.1. Cf. the prayer that God will open the heart of the Jews in Egypt to God's law in 2 Maccabees 1.4, and the command to walk in his commandments in Ezekiel 20.19.

3.24.2. Cf. Paul's command to understand the will of God in Ephesians 5.17.

3.24.5. This is the only citation of 'supernaturely' (*supernaturaliter*) in *MED*. CDM's reading here is slightly misleading, as it omits *te*: the Latin is *et te beneficum pium ac bonum commendant*, i.e. 'and commend you as a merciful and good benefactor'. On the variants, see Introduction, pp. lxiv–lxv.

3.24.9. On 'accepcion of persones' see 1.5.8 n.

3.24.11. This is the only citation of 'diffinite' (*diffinita*) in *MED*.

3.24.13. 'Familyarez and householde men' renders *familiares et domesticos*; see 1.8.6 n.

3.24.14. Cf. the psalmist's prophecy that the king will make his sons princes in all the earth in Psalm 44.17 (AV 45.16).

3.24.15. 'Conuersante in þe worlde withoute compleynte' renders *sine querela conuersati in mundo*; cf. Philippians 3.6. On being without malice and guile, cf. Peter's command in 1 Peter 2.1. The apostles rejoiced to be counted worthy to suffer dishonour for the name of Jesus when they were beaten by the council in Jerusalem (Acts 5.41).

3.24.16. The reference to the lowest and first places may be derived from the parable of the marriage feast (Luke 14.10).

3.25.1. Cf. Zecharaiah's prophecy in the Benedictus that Jesus would guide our feet into the way of peace (Luke 1.79).

3.25.6. Cf. the petition in the Lord's prayer *fiat voluntas tua* (Matthew 6.10).

3.25.11. This is the first citation of 'vnplesed' (*implacatum* R, *impacatum* K) in *OED*.

3.25.12. Cf. Job's affirmation of God's omnipotence in Job 42.2.

3.26.1. Cf. the psalmist's petition to God not to be far from him and to make haste to help him in Psalm 70.12 (AV 71.12).

3.26.3. Cf. the prophecy in the oracle that describes his call of Cyrus that God would make low the great ones of the earth, break the doors of bronze and bars of iron, and give hidden treasures (Isaiah 45.2–3).

3.27.2. This is the only citation of 'evagacions' (*euagaciones*) in *MED*.

3.27.4. An allusion to the great calm which followed Jesus' rebuking the winds and the sea during the storm on the Sea of Galilee (Mark 4.39).

3.27.5. Cf. the psalmist's petition to God to send out his light and his truth in Psalm 42.3 (AV 43.3), and the description of the earth as without form and void before God said, 'Let there be light' (Genesis 1.2).

3.27.6. Cf. the stream that watered the face of the earth at the creation (Genesis 2.6). On imagery of pouring and flowing in the mystical tradition, see Riehle, p. 87.

3.27.8. This is the only citation of 'indurable' (*indurabili*) in *MED*; on the mystical *raptus*, see 2.9.29 n.

3.27.9. On the use of the word 'join' for mystical union, see Riehle, pp. 91–2; on the idea of the bond of love, derived from Hosea 11.4, see Riehle, pp. 51–2. This is the only citation of 'friuoles' (*friuola*) in *MED*.

3.28.1. 'Ne be besy' renders R's *nec gerere solicitudines* rather than K's *nec vacuas gerere sollicitudines*.

3.28.2. Cf. Jesus' command to Peter to follow him after he had rebuked him for his curiosity concerning John (John 21.22).

3.28.4. Cf. Paul's teaching that each of us must give an account of himself to God (Romans 14.12).

3.28.9. The phrase *magni nominis vmbra* was used by Lucan of Pompey at the beginning of the civil war with Caesar (*De Bello Civili* 1.135).

3.28.11. On 'hidde þinges' (*abscondita*), see Lees, pp. 215–6, 254–5. With 'open to me þe durre of þi herte' cf. Jesus' request to the Laodiceans to open the door to him (Revelation 3.20).

3.28.12. Cf. Peter's command to watch in prayers (1 Peter 4.7), and the exhortation to humble oneself in all things in Ecclesiasticus 3.20 (Vulgate).

3.29.1. These were Jesus' words to the disciples in John 14.27.

3.29.8. This is the only citation of 'temerarily' (*temere*) in *MED* or *OED*. On the variants, see Introduction, p. lxiv.

3.29.11. 'In grete delectacion, deuocion, or swetnesse' renders R's *in magna fueris delectacione deuocione atque dulcedine*; K omits *delectacione*.

3.29.14. Cf. Elihu's assertion that the man who prays to God will see his face with joy (Job 33.26).

3.29.15. With 'haboundance of pes' cf. Psalm 71.7 (AV 72.7). This is the only citation of 'possibilite' (*possibilitatem*) in the sense 'facilities, conveniences' in *MED*; the meaning is that 'you will enjoy such abundance of peace as is possible where you dwell', i.e. on earth (Blaiklock).

3.30.0. See note on 3.0.30; here the translation does not follow R's reading *frequens loquucio*. On spiritual freedom, see Riehle, p. 66.

3.30.1. On intention, see 1.14.4 n.

3.30.3. This is the only citation of 'penaly' (*penaliter*) in *MED*.

3.30.5. The Latin has been abridged: *non me vincat deus meus non vincat caro et sanguis* (R repeats *me* before the second *vincat*).

3.30.12. Cf. Paul's teaching about the flesh and the spirit in Galatians 5.17.

3.30.13. 'And teche me what is to muche' corresponds to *et doceat: ne quid nimium fiat*: presumably the translator did not read *ne*.

3.31.1. 'And noþinge of þine to be 'to' þiselfe' renders *et nichil tui ipsius esse*, i.e. 'and be nothing of your own'.

3.31.4. ⟨Bene⟩, which modifies *ordinatus* ('ordinate'), has been omitted; 'þou shalte not be captive ner sugget to [þe] yerthely þinges' renders *eris sine captiuitate rerum*.

3.31.7. On the ground of the soul, see Riehle, pp. 152–6.

3.31.11. *Ex corde*, which modifies *decisa . . . radicitus* ('kutte aweye by þe rote'), has been omitted.

3.32.2. Cf. Paul's prayer for the Ephesians to be strengthened with might through the spirit in the inner man (Ephesians 3.16). The translation follows SEJYZ in omitting K's *et angore*, which follows *sollicitudine* 'bisynes'; R has *et sugestione* at this point. On the point that all things are vanity and affliction of spirit, cf. Ecclesiastes 1.14.

3.32.4. *Tue*, which modifies *sapiencie* (the second occurrence of 'wisdame'), has been omitted.

3.32.6. On not being carried about with every wind of doctrine, cf. Ephesians 4.14. The mention of the 'marmayden' may be a reference to the description of the desolation of Babylon in Isaiah 13.22: *Et respondebunt ibi ululae in aedibus ejus, et sirenes in delubris voluptatis.* *Sirenes* is a misleading rendering of the Hebrew, whose exact meaning is uncertain (E. J. Kissane, *The Book of Isaiah Translated from a Critically Revised Hebrew Text with Commentary* (Dublin, 1960), p. 156); RSV has 'Hyenas will cry in its towers, and jackals in the pleasant places'. O. Kaiser comments that the desert animals in this verse 'occupy a curious position between the world of animals and that of demons, and [their] presence helps to increase the uncanny nature of the ruins' (*Isaiah 13–39: A Commentary*, OTL (London, 1974), pp. 20–1).

3.33.4. 'Providence' corresponds to *prudencia*: presumably the translator read *prouidencia*; see 1.4.0 n.

3.34.1. Cf. the benedictions in Psalm 112.2 (AV 113.2) and Daniel 2.20. 'þis temptacion' renders R's *hanc temptacionem* rather than K's *hanc temptacionem et tribulacionem*.

3.34.2. 'I preie þee' renders R's *precor* rather than K's *sed necesse habeo ad te confugere*. On the variants, see Introduction, p. lxiv.

3.34.4–7. These verses paraphrase Jesus' meditation on his approaching death after his triumphal entry into Jerusalem (John 12.27). In v. 7, *valide*, which modifies *humiliatus* ('brouȝt downe lowe'), has been omitted.

3.34.8. Cf. the psalmist's prayer for deliverance in Psalm 39.14 (AV 40.13).

3.34.10. Cf. the psalmist's prayer in Psalm 108.26 (AV 109.26).

3.34.12. Cf. Jesus' words in Gethsemane (Matthew 26.42).

3.34.15. Cf. the mention of God's almighty hand in Wisdom 11.18 (AV 11.17), and the description of God as *misericordia mea* in Psalm 58.18 (AV 59.17).

3.34.16. Cf. the psalmist's mention of the change of God's right hand (in modern versions of the Bible understood as a temporary change for the worse) in Psalm 76.11 (AV 77.10).

3.35.1. Cf. the characterization of God as comforting in the day of tribulation in Nahum 1.7.

3.35.6. With 'the lyght of my miseracions' cf. Ecclesiasticus 36.1 (Vulgate); with the assurance that God is near cf. Psalm 118.151 (AV 119.151) and Philippians 4.5. 'Scripture' corresponds to *dominus*.

3.35.7. With the idea that nothing is too difficult for God cf. Jeremiah 32.27; with the assurance that he keeps his promises cf. Numbers 23.19.

3.35.12. Cf. Jesus' promise to the centurion whose servant was paralysed (Matthew 8.7).

3.35.14. 'þinges þat ar contingently to come' renders *futuris contingentibus*; this is the only citation of 'contingently' in *MED*.

3.35.15. Cf. Jesus' words in the Sermon on the Mount (Matthew 6.34).

3.35.19. Cf. Jesus' reassurance to the disciples in John 14.1,27.

3.35.21. The rendering 'þat I am farre fro thee' is slightly different from the Latin *te elongatum a me*.

3.35.28. On God's knowledge of hidden thoughts, cf. Psalm 43.22 (AV 44.21). This is the only citation of 'succedinge' (*successu*) in the sense 'successful outcome, fulfillment' in *MED*.

3.35.30. Cf. the teaching about gifts in James 1.17.

3.35.32. *Multum*, which modifies *recommendabilis* ('commendable'), has been omitted.

3.35.33. Cf. Job's expression of his desire for death (Job 6.10).

3.35.34. Cf. Jesus' affirmation of his love for the disciples in John 15.9, and his interpretation of the seed that fell on good soil as bringing forth fruit with patience in Luke 8.15.

3.35.35. The translation follows R and a number of other manuscripts in omitting this verse, *Horum memento fili mi verborum*.

3.36.3. The speaker was David, in Psalm 54.7 (AV 55.6): see 3.23.6 n.

3.36.4. For the *simplici oculo*, see Matthew 6.22.

3.36.5. For the mystical *excessus mentis*, see 3.7.14 n.; the phrase is used to describe Peter's vision in Acts 10.10 and 11.5, and in various senses in Psalms 30.23 (Vulgate) and 67.28 (Vulgate) and in 2 Corinthians 5.13. On the *visio dei*, see Riehle, pp. 122–7, and cf. 3.53.12.

3.36.8. On the mystical *raptus*, see 2.9.29 n.; on the use of 'above' here, see Lees, pp. 263–9, and cf. 3.63.23.

3.36.9. On union with God, see 1.3.11 n.

3.36.11. DMG's 'all saf þat' would represent the approximate sense of the Latin, but the fact that C omits 'saf' suggests that an originally closer rendering has been corrupted.

3.36.12. In the Latin, *Est magna differencia, sapiencia illuminati et deuoti viri: et* *sciencia literati atque studiosi clerici*, the contrast is between the devout man's wisdom and the scholar's knowledge rather than between the two men themselves. On anti-intellectualism, see 1.1.7 n.

3.36.13. This is the only citation of 'laborously' (*laboriose*) in the sense 'earnestly, strongly' in *MED*.

3.36.16–17. The second 'so muche' renders *ampliorem*; the translation follows R in omitting *plene*, which in K modifies *recollectis sensibus* ('gederynge oure wittes togedre'). On the notion of gathering, see 1.11.2 n. *Recollectionem* is rendered 'recolleccion' in v. 17; 'recolleccion' is not cited in *MED*, nor in *OED* before 1598.

3.36.19. Cf. God's displeasure on seeing the earth before the flood (Genesis 6.12).

3.36.21. Cf. Paul's teaching on the fruit of a pure heart (1 Timothy 1.5).

3.37.1. Cf. Jesus' exhortation to his followers to deny themselves (Matthew 16.24).

3.37.2. Cf. Paul's warnings against lovers of self (2 Timothy 3.2) and those who do not seek the things of Christ (Philippians 2.21).

3.37.4. This is the only citation of 'consummate' (*consummatum*) used as an adjective in *MED*.

3.37.6. Cf. the response of the Israelites to Ezra's request to them to make confession of their sins (Ezra 10.13).

3.37.8. 'Thi daies' renders *tota vita tua*.

3.37.10. *Ignitum*, which modifies *aurum* ('golde'), has been omitted; cf. the *aurum ignitum probatum* which the Laodiceans were advised to buy from Christ to make themselves rich (Revelation 3.18).

3.37.11. *Humanam*, which together with *propriam* modifies *complacenciam* ('complacence'), has been omitted.

3.37.12. 'Vile þinges and of litel price' is a doublet rendering *viliora*; *preciosis et altis in rebus humanis* is rendered 'preciouse þinges in mannes reputacion'.

3.37.13. Cf. Paul's warning against pride in Romans 12.16. 'For' renders K's *nam* rather than RZ's *non*; *valde*, which modifies *vilis et parua* ('litel and of no price'), has been omitted; 'allemoste foryeten in þis worlde' renders *pene obliuioni tradita*; *quam*, referring to *sapiencia* ('wisdame'), which is the object of *oretenus predicant* ('preche withe the mouthe'), has been omitted. With the idea that wisdom is 'a preciouse margarite' cf. the parable of the pearl of great price (Matthew 13.45–6); with the idea that it is 'hydde fro many' cf. the parable of the treasure hidden in a field (Matthew 13.44).

3.38.0. *Finali*, which modifies *intencione* 'intencion', has been omitted.

3.38.2. 'Plesed' renders R's *placatus* rather than K's *pacatus*.

3.38.4–6. On such expressions as the eye of the soul or the eye of reason, see Riehle, p. 123; on the simple eye, see 3.36.4 n.; on intention, see 1.14.4 n. In v. 6, *pure*, which modifies *intencionis* ('of intencion'), has been omitted.

3.38.7. *Totus*, which modifies *liber* ('free'), has been omitted.

3.38.8. The Jews came to see Lazarus because they had heard that Jesus had raised him from the dead (John 12.9).

3.39.0. On spiritual savouring, see 1.1.6 n. The translation follows S in omitting *et in omnibus*, which in K and R follows *super omnia* ('above alle þinges').

3.39.1. Cf. Paul's prediction that God will be all in all (1 Corinthians 15.28).

3.39.3. 'Of þe Fader' has been added; the second *him* refers to the world. The meaning is that the saying 'Behold my God and my all' is sweet only to those who love the Word (the incarnate Logos), not to those who love the world (cf. 1 John 2.15).

3.39.7. 'Thou makeste in the herte tranquillite' renders *tu facis cor tranquillum*.

3.39.8. The first 'alle' (*omnibus*) probably refers to all things.

3.39.12. On the connection between the flesh and death, cf. Romans 8.5–6.

3.39.16. Cf. the psalmist's prayer for God to send lightning on his enemies in Psalm 143.6 (AV 144.6), and see 1.1.0–2 n.

3.39.17. This is the only citation of 'iubilose' (*iubilosis*) in *MED* or *OED*. On cleaving to God, see 1.11.5 n; on 'excessez', see 3.7.14 n.

3.39.18. See 3.39.1 n.

3.39.20–1. Cf. Paul's teaching about the old man and the spirit and the flesh in Romans 6.6,10 and Galatians 5.17.

3.39.22–4. Cf. the psalmist's affirmation of God's power over the sea in Psalm 88.10 (AV 89.9); his petitions to God to arise and help him in Psalm 43.26 (AV 44.26), to bring those who desire battles to nought in Psalm 67.31 (AV 68.30), and to afflict his enemies by his power in Psalm 58.12 (AV 59.11); and the prayer that God's right hand will be glorified in Ecclesiasticus 36.7 (AV 36.6). In v. 24, ⟨*queso*⟩, which governs *ostende . . . magnalia tua* ('shewe þi gretnes'), has been omitted.

3.40.4. 'My' renders R's *mea* rather than K's *mera*.

3.40.6. Manna was promised to him who conquers in the letter to the church in Pergamum (Revelation 2.17).

3.40.15. The comparison between present sufferings and future glory is derived from Romans 8.18.

3.40.17–18. There are similar petitions in Psalm 26.14 (AV 27.14), and a similar promise of God's presence in Psalm 90.15 (AV 91.15). In v. 18, 'and' has been added.

3.41.3. *Multi multa loquuntur*: see Dionysius Cato, *Disticha* 1.13.

3.41.5. 'þou' is the translator's addition: *et si Paulus omnibus studuit in domino placere*. Paul wrote to the Corinthians that he tried to please all, that he had become all things to all men, and that he regarded himself as under God's judgement rather than man's (1 Corinthians 10.33, 9.22, and 4.3–4).

3.41.7. 'The mouthes of wykked spekars' is a paraphrase of *ora loquencium iniqua*, which the psalmist believed would be stopped by God (Psalm 62.12, AV 63.11). In the Latin those 'makynge boste at her owne lykinge' are a third group against whose mouths Paul defended himself (*atque pro libitu suo queque iactancium se defendit*), but DMG's 'and' does not fit in with the syntax of the rest of the sentence. Possibly something has dropped out of the text.

3.41.8. Perhaps Paul's defence of himself before Agrippa in Acts 26 is in mind here. 'To the feble in feithe' is an expansion of *infirmis*. This is the first citation of 'taciturnite' (*taciturnitate*) in *OED*.

3.41.9. Cf. the encouragement not to fear in Isaiah 51.12.

3.41.10. This was said of sinners by Mattathias in his dying speech (1 Maccabees 2.63).

3.41.13. *Nec poterit iudicium dei effugere*, which precedes *quicumque est ille* ('whatever he be'), has been omitted.

3.41.14. Cf. Paul's command to Timothy in 2 Timothy 2.14.

3.41.15. On judgement according to works, see Matthew 16.27 and Romans 2.6.

3.42.0. The translation follows O in omitting *et integra*, which along with *pura* ('pure') modifies *resignacione* ('resignacion'); *ad optinendam cordis libertatem*, which comes at the end of the verse, has also been omitted. The only citations of 'resignacion' (*resignacione*) in *MED* in the sense 'surrender to God, resignation of oneself to God' are from the *Imitation*.

3.42.6. On the laying bare of the soul, see 2.8.30 n.

3.42.7. On the variants, see Introduction, pp. lxii–lxiii.

3.42.8. On 'ple[nar]ly', see 1.1.6 n.

3.42.11. 'þorowe litel temptacion' corresponds to *temptacione pulsati*.

3.42.12. The translation follows R in omitting *puri*, which in K modifies *cordis* ('of herte').

3.42.14. Cf. the psalmist's affirmation that the darkness that covers him is not dark to God in Psalm 138.11 (AV 139.11).

3.43.0. The last part of the title, *et recursu ad deum in periculis*, has been omitted.

3.43.1. *Nec empticius*, which is parallel to *non seruus* ('not servaunt'), has been omitted; the second 'God' has been added. This is the only citation of 'Hebrewe' (*hebreus*) in *MED* in the sense 'a person following the precepts of the Old Testament'.

3.43.3. For Moses' dialogue with God in the tent of meeting, see Exodus 33.7–11.

3.43.4. On the soul's withdrawal into itself, see Riehle, pp. 58–8.

3.43.5. Fearing that the Israelites would kill them if they knew they lived locally, the Gibeonites pretended to have come from afar and made a treaty with them; the Israelites then had to keep them alive (Joshua 9). 'For þei asked no counseile furste of our Lorde' paraphrases *quia os domini prius non interrogauerunt* (Joshua 9.14).

3.44.4. 'þat I myght offre' renders *sed . . . offerrem*.

3.44.8. 'Lythe in awayte' paraphrases *graues molitur insidias*.

3.44.9. These were Jesus' words to the disciples when he returned to find them sleeping in Gethsemane (Matthew 26.41).

3.45.0. 'Whereof to reioyce' renders *et de nullo gloriari potest*.

3.45.1. This verse is a quotation from Psalm 8.5 (AV 8.4).

3.45.4. On being nothing, see 3.4.4 n.

3.45.6. On God's remaining the same, cf. Psalm 101.28,13 (AV 102.27,12).

3.45.7. Daniel said that seven times would pass over Nebuchadnezzar when interpreting the dream which predicted his madness (Daniel 4.22, AV 4.25).

3.45.8. Hannah's countenance was 'no more chaunged into diuerse' (*amplius in diuersa non mutetur*) when she had recovered her spirits after receiving Eli's blessing in 1 Kings (AV 1 Samuel) 1.18.

3.45.9. On casting away impediments to devotion, see Riehle, p. 63.

3.45.17. With the expressions of praise and blessing here cf. Psalms 112.1, 91.6, and 112.2 (AV 113.1, 92.5, and 113.2).

3.45.18–19. Cf. the psalmist's affirmation that God is his glory in Psalm 3.4 (AV 3.3), that his testimonies are the joy of his heart in Psalm 118.111 (AV 119.111), and that his people will rejoice in his name all day in Psalm 88.17 (AV 89.16); also Paul's boasting only in his weaknesses in 2 Corinthians 12.5.

3.45.20. Jesus accused the Jewish leaders of seeking glory from each other in John 5.44.

3.45.22. See 3.34.15 n. The translation follows R in including 'Amen', which is lacking in K. Cf. the doxologies in Revelation 5.13 and 1 Timothy 1.17.

3.46.1. *Et eleuari*, which is parallel to *honorari* ('worshipped'), has been omitted.

3.46.6. This point may be derived from the idea that God will arm creation to punish his enemies (Wisdom 5.18).

3.46.7. A similar antithesis is made in Daniel's prayer of confession (Daniel 9.7).

3.46.8. On union between man and God, see Riehle, pp. 89–92.

3.47.1. This is the only citation of 'vnpesed' (*implicatus*) in *OED*.

3.47.2. '[Ever] lyvinge and abidinge' echoes the description of Christ's priesthood in Hebrews 7.24–5.

3.47.3. *Multum*, which modifies *carus* ('dere'), has been omitted.

3.47.6–7. The two halves of each of these sentences have been reversed in the translation. The Latin is: *Tanto homo deo magis appropinquat: quanto ab omni solacio terreno longius recedit. Tanto eciam alcius ad deum ascendit: quanto profundius in se descendit et plus sibiipsi vilescit* (R has *tanto homo appropinquat deo* as the first clause). On the soul's ascent to God, see Riehle, pp. 69–70, and cf. 3.58.15.

3.47.8. *Autem* has been omitted from the beginning of the sentence.

3.47.10. 'þine affeccion is withdrawen fro the creatoure' corresponds to *subtrahitur tibi aspectus creatoris*; perhaps the translator read *affectus*.

3.47.12. '[And draweþ into wikkednes]' corresponds to *et viciat*.

3.48.1. This point was made by Paul in 1 Corinthians 4.20.

3.48.2. *Ingerunt*, which governs *consolacionem* ('consolacion'), has been omitted.

3.48.3. 'Synnes and vices' is a doublet rendering *viciorum*.

3.48.5. On God as teacher, cf. Psalm 93.10 (AV 94.10). 'Meke menne' corresponds to the *paruulis* to whom God is said to give understanding in Psalm 118.130 (AV 119.130).

3.48.6. 'For' renders *et*.

3.48.8. The Latin reads *Veniet tempus quando apparebit magister magistrorum Christus dominus angelorum, cunctorum auditurus lectiones*. *Angelorum* is to be construed with *dominus*; the translator did not read *dominus* and therefore wrongly construed *angelorum* with *cunctorum . . . lectiones*. There is a combined allusion to Zephaniah's warning that God will search Jerusalem with lamps for those who are to be punished (Zephaniah 1.12) and to Paul's warning that God will bring to light things now hidden in darkness (1 Corinthians 4.5). On the variants, see Introduction p. lix.

3.48.11. On burning in mystical texts, see Riehle, pp. 80, 110, and cf. 3.63.24.

3.48.14–16. *Omnes*, the object of *informat* ('enfourmeþ'), has been omitted. 'The doctoure of trowthe' renders R's *doctor veritatis* (the reading of almost all the Latin manuscripts) rather than K's *doctor veritas*. God is described as revealing mysteries in Daniel 2.28; as *scrutator cordis* in Wisdom 1.6, Jeremiah 17.10, Revelation 2.23, and 1 Chronicles 28.9; and as apportioning to each as he thinks worthy in 1 Corinthians 12.11.

3.49.1. The Latin is *In multis oportet te esse inscium, et estimare te tamquam mortuum super terram* (R repeats *esse* before *tamquam*): *te esse inscium et* has been omitted. On being ignorant, cf. Ecclesiasticus 32.12 (Vulgate); on being crucified to the world and *vice versa*, cf. Galatians 6.14.

3.49.3. This is the only citation of 'contenciouse' (*contentiosis*) in *MED*.

3.49.7. On the description of 'being distracted and diverted by the creatural world' as a 'flowing away' of the soul, see Riehle, p. 187. 'Lythe and resteþ' is a doublet rendering *iacet*.

3.50.1. This verse is a quotation of Psalm 59.13 (AV 60.11).

3.50.4. Cf. the psalmist's affirmation that the salvation of the righteous is in God in Psalm 36.39 (AV 37.39).

3.50.8. Cf. the commendation of those who trust in the Lord in Psalm 124.1 (AV 125.1), and of those who seek him in simplicity of heart in Wisdom 1.1.

3.50.9. 'Or be wrapped in any perplexite' corresponds to *quocumque modo fuerit etiam implicatus*; R omits *modo*. In following the text found in R the translator failed to perceive the relationship between this and the previous clause: the translation should be 'and if he falls into any temptation, however entangled he may be, he will soon be delivered by you'. Cf. Sarah's trust that God would deliver those in tribulation (Tobit 3.21, Vulgate), and Judith's trust that he would not forsake those who trust in him (Judith 13.17, Vulgate).

3.50.10. 'Necessites' renders R's *necessatibus* rather than K's *pressuris*.

3.50.11. *Solus*, which modifies *es fidelissimus* ('arte moste trusti'), has been omitted.

3.50.12. This was reputedly said by St Agatha, a saintly woman of Catania in Sicily, whose true date is uncertain but who is traditionally supposed to have been martyred in AD 251. She was seized by the consul Quintinian and handed over to be corrupted by the depraved Aphrodisia and her daughters; Agatha is said to have spoken these words in response to their temptations. See *ODS*, pp. 4–5, and *AASS Februarii*, 3 vols (1863–5), i. 599–662 (p. 621).

3.50.14. The translation of this verse is a paraphrase of the Latin: *Quis omnia preuidere, quis precauere futura mala sufficit?*

3.50.15. This is the first citation of 'vnprovided' (*improuisa*) in *OED*.

3.50.20. The statement that 'everie man is a lyar' is derived from Psalm 115.11 (AV 116.11); cf. Romans 3.4.

3.50.21. Cf. Jesus' instruction to the disciples to beware of men and of the members of their own household (Matthew 10.17,36), and his warning against against those who would proclaim false Christs (Matthew 24.23).

3.50.22. *Dampno meo* (R omits *meo*), which modifies *doctus sum* ('I am taght'), has been omitted.

3.50.24. It is possible that C's 'and', between 'hydde' and 'he myȝt not counseile', is original, as the Latin is *Et dum ego sileo et absconditum credo; nec ille silere potest* *quod silendum petiit.* 'And' could therefore render *nec*, but it produces misleading syntax in English, as 'he my3t not counseile' is clearly the main clause on which the preceding clause is dependent.

3.50.27. The translator has followed R in omitting this verse, which is given thus in K: *Quod pati nolo: omnimode cauere debeo.*

3.50.28. Cf. the description of God as *inspector cordis* in Proverbs 24.12, and Paul's warning against being swayed by false doctrine in Ephesians 4.14.

3.50.30. *Prepropere* (*prospere* in R), which modifies *laudata*, has been omitted.

3.50.31. On life as 'knyghthode' (*milicia*), cf. Job 7.1 (Vulgate). 'Is' renders *fertur*.

3.51.0. 'Ayenis yvelle wordes' is a paraphrase of *quando insurgunt uerborum iacula.*

3.51.4. 'Hem' renders R's *hec* (referring to *uerba*) rather than K's *hoc.*

3.51.6. *Adhuc*, which modifies *carnalis es* ('þou arte fleysshely'), has been omitted.

3.51.9. On being crucified to the world, see 3.49.1 n.

3.51.15. Cf. Susanna's prayer to God *qui absconditorum es cognitor* after she had been condemned to death for adultery on the false testimony of the elders (Daniel 13.42).

3.51.16. 'Alle' has been added.

3.51.17. Cf. Simeon's prediction of the far-reaching effects of Jesus' ministry to Mary when she brought him to the temple (Luke 2.35).

3.51.19. 'Fayleth and deceyveth' is a doublet rendering *fallit.*

3.51.22. Cf. the assurance that the just man will not be made sad in Proverbs 12.21 (Vulgate).

3.51.24. On God as *scrutans corda*, see 3.48.16 n.; on not judging by appearances, cf. John 7.24.

3.51.26. The same attributes are applied to God in Psalm 7.12 (Vulgate).

3.51.27. 'Blamynge and repreving' is a doublet rendering *reprehensione.*

3.51.28. *Iterum* (R has *igitur*), which modifies *dona* ('yive'), has been omitted.

3.51.29. This is the only citation of 'opinate' (*opinata*) in *MED* and the only citation of it in this sense ('supposed') in *OED*.

3.51.30. Cf. Paul's statement that he was not aware of anything against himself (1 Corinthians 4.4). *Remota misericordia tua*, an allusion to Augustine's *Confessions* (9.13.34), which modifies *non iustificabitur* ('be iustifyed'), has been omitted. The point that no-one living will be justified in God's sight is derived from Psalm 142.2 (AV 143.2).

3.52.0. 'Lyve to come' renders *eterna vita.*

3.52.7. Cf. Jesus' parables about labouring in a vineyard in Matthew 20.1–16 and 21.28–32, and God's promise that he would be Abraham's reward in Genesis 15.1.

3.52.8. 'Muche more and muche gretter' is a doublet rendering *maioribus*.

3.52.11. Cf. Paul's question in Romans 7.24.

3.52.12. Cf. the psalmist's cry in Psalm 119.5 (Vulgate).

3.52.13. The downfall of death is prophesied in Isaiah 25.8.

3.53.4. Cf. the description of light in Tobit's hymn of praise (Tobit 13.13, Vulgate). 'Al afarre' is a paraphrase of *non nisi a longe*; *in terra*, which modifies *peregrinantibus* ('pilgrymes') has been omitted (cf. the mention of pilgrims in Hebrews 11.13 and of seeing in a mirror in 1 Corinthians 13.12).

3.53.5. 'Sorowfulle' is a paraphrase of *amara et tediosa*.

3.53.6. Cf. Jacob's characterization of his sojourning (Vulgate *peregrinationis*) in Genesis 47.9, and the description of human labour in Ecclesiastes 2.23.

3.53.7. This and the occurrence at 3.60.6 are the only citations of 'circum-founded' (*circumfunditur*) in *MED*. The last 'many' has been added. 'Nede and poverte' is a doublet rendering *egestate*.

3.53.8. Cf. Paul's characterization of creation as awaiting liberty from bondage (Romans 8.21).

3.53.9. Cf. the psalmist's promise to have mind of God's justice alone in Psalm 70.16 (AV Psalm 71.16).

3.53.11. This is the only citation of 'i[m]perturbable' (*imperturbabilis*) in *MED*.

3.53.12. On Jesus being all in all, cf. 1 Corinthians 15.28 and Colossians 3.11; on the *visio dei*, see 3.36.5 n.

3.53.13. Cf. Jesus' description of the heavenly kingdom in Matthew 25.34.

3.53.17. On the *fruicio dei*, see 3.23.23 n.

3.53.18. This is the only citation of 'vnmortificate' (*immortificate*) in *OED*.

3.53.19. *Carne*, which modifies *subesse cogor* ('I am constreyned to be byneþe'), has been omitted; a more accurate translation of the Latin would be: 'by the flesh I am forced against my will to be beneath'.

3.53.20. Cf. Paul's description of himself as *infelix homo* (Romans 7.24) and Job's sense of being burdonsome to himself (Job 7.20, Vulgate).

3.53.21. *Mox*, which modifies *occurrit* ('comeþ ayenis me') has been omitted.

3.53.22. Cf. the psalmist's petitions to God not to be far from him in Psalm 70.12 (AV 71.12) and not to turn away from him in anger Psalm 26.9 (AV 27.9).

3.53.23. 'Trou[b]led and shende' is a doublet rendering ⟨*conturbentur*⟩ (for misreading of *b* as *v* see 3.14.12 n.); 'contrariouse fantasies' renders *fantas*⟨*ie* *inimici*). Cf. the psalmist's prayer for God to send lightning and arrows on his enemies in Psalm 143.6 (AV 144.6). D² has retranslated the Latin here.

3.53.24. On the notion of gathering, see 1.11.2 n.; on forgetting worldy things, see Riehle, p. 60.

3.53.26. This is the only citation of 'impurete' (*impuritas*) in *MED*.

3.53.28. This is the only citation of 'distractely' (*distracte*) in *MED* or *OED*.

3.53.32. These were Jesus' words in the Sermon on the Mount after his exhortation to store up treasure not on earth, but in heaven (Matthew 6.21).

3.53.38. Cf. Paul's teaching on crucifying the flesh in Galatians 5.24.

3.54.1. For the image of the body as a tabernacle or tent, see 2 Peter 1.13. 'Clerenes' renders *claritatem*; cf. Jesus' prayer for his followers in John 17.24, and the description of divine light in James 1.17. On the mystical *excessus*, see 3.7.14 n.; on dilating the heart, see 3.6.25 n.

3.54.3. This is one of three citations of 'dignacyon' (*dignacione*) in the sense 'the gracious act of God in treating man as worthy or in conferring favor on him' in *MED*. On cleaving to God, see 1.11.5 n.

3.54.4. 'But withoute flaume and smoke hit styeth never vppe' renders R's *sed sine fumo et flamma non ascendit*; K omits *et*, making *flamma* the subject of *ascendit*.

3.54.6. This is the first citation of 'desiderantly' (*desideranter*) in *MED*.

3.54.9. On the variants, see Introduction, p. lix.

3.54.10. On mourning, see 1.23.47 n.

3.54.11. 'þe lyberte of þe glory of the sones of God' is derived from Romans 8.21.

3.54.13. Cf. the command to wait for the Lord in Zephaniah 3.8, and Jesus' promise of the coming of God's kingdom in Luke 22.18.

3.54.16. Cf. God's words to Joshua after the death of Moses (Joshua 1.7).

3.54.17. Cf. Samuel's prediction that Saul would receive prophetic gifts in 1 Kings (AV 1 Samuel) 10.6 and Paul's teaching on the new man (Ephesians 4.24 and Colossians 3.10). On being clothed with Christ (cf. Romans 13.14), see Riehle, p. 63.

3.54.24. 'And suffre grete bateile, if þou in silence bere þees þinges' renders R's *et magnum certamen sustinebit si silens portaueris hec*; K reads *et magnum si silens portaueris*, i.e. 'it will be a great thing if you can bear it in silence'.

3.54.26. This is the only citation of 'disconuenient' (*disconueniencia*) in the sense 'inconvenient, disadvantageous' in *MED*.

3.54.31. 'Of lesinge or forgoinge' is a doublet rendering *amittendi*.

3.54.34. 'Glorie and worshippe for shame and repreve' is a paraphrase of *gloriam pro contumelia perpessa*. Cf. the promise in Isaiah 61.3.

3.54.37. 'In þis and' has been added; *solius*, which modifies *mei* ('my'), has been omitted.

3.54.38. Cf. Paul's trust that Christ would be magnified in his body, whether by his life or by his death (Philippians 1.20).

3.55.0. 'That' renders R's *quod* rather than K's *qualiter*.

3.55.2. *Domine*, which comes at the end of the sentence, has been omitted.

3.55.5. Cf. the psalmist's complaint in Psalm 87.16 (AV 88.15).

3.55.6. On being fed by God, see Riehle, p. 108.

3.55.7. On pouring imagery, see 3.27.6 n.

3.55.8. On the imagery in this verse, cf. Psalm 118.32 (AV 119.32), Genesis 31.2,5, 1 Maccabees 9.44, Job 29.3, and Psalm 16.8 (AV 17.8).

3.55.11. In K this sentence reads: *Pater perpetue venerande venit hora quam ab eterno presciebas affuturam; ut ad modicum tempus succumbat foris seruus tuus: viuat uero semper apud te intus.* It has been recast in the translation, probably because the translator's text, like R, omitted *venit hora*; the translation also follows R in omitting *uero*. (R also reads *passioni tue* for *perpetue* and *et* for *ut*.) John 17.1 may be in mind here; cf. the titles given to the Father in 3.55.9,13 with John 17.25,11.

3.55.13. Cf. Judith's affirmation that what God has planned has been done (Judith 9.4, Vulgate).

3.55.15. Cf. Eliphaz's statement that nothing is done without cause (Job 5.6, Vulgate).

3.55.16. This is an elaboration of the psalmist's sentiment in Psalm 118.71 (AV 119.71).

3.55.17. 'Shame and confusion' is a doublet rendering *confusio*: cf. Psalm 68.8 (AV 69.7). On the variants, see Introduction, p. liii.

3.55.18. On the idea that suffering afflicts both the righteous and the wicked, see Ecclesiastes 9.2.

3.55.20. Cf. the lament that Jerusalem has none to comfort her (Lamentations 1.2) and the assertion that God strikes and heals (Deuteronomy 32.39) and leads down and brings up again (Tobit 13.2). On God as the doctor of souls, see Riehle, pp. 79–80.

3.55.21. Cf. the psalmist's awareness of God's discipline (Psalm 17.36, Vulgate).

3.55.23. *Pium et*, which precedes *humilem discipulum* ('a meke disciple'), has been omitted, as has *bene*, which modifies *facere consueuisti* ('þou arte wonte to do').

3.55.25. Cf. the acknowledgement of divine omniscience by the disciples (John 16.30) and by Job (Job 42.2).

3.55.30. Cf. the characterization of the Messiah's judgement in Isaiah 11.3.

3.55.34. The translation follows R in omitting *sanctus*, which in K follows *humilis* ('meke'). See Bonaventure, *Legenda Sancti Francisci* 6.1 (*Opera Omnia edita studio et cura pp. collegii*, 10 vols (Quaracchi, 1882–1902), viii. 520).

3.56.6. Cf. the psalmist's promise to run in the way of God's commandments in Psalm 118.32 (AV 119.32).

3.56.7. See 3.40.15 n.

3.57.0. The translation follows R in omitting the remainder of the title, ⟨*sed magis verberibus reum*⟩.

3.57.2. On tears, see 1.20.29 n.

3.57.5. The imagery here is derived from Romans 9.23 (*ut ostenderet divitias gloriae suae in vasa misericordiae, quae praeparavit in gloriam*).

3.57.6. This is the only citation of 'confabulacions' (*confabulaciones*) in *MED* (cf. 3.58.3).

3.57.8–9. The translator has construed *verum est* ('þe very trowthe is') with the preceding sentence (*sed semper ad vicia pronum: et ad emendacionem pigrum fuisse*), rather than with what follows, *et negare non possum*, i.e. 'it is true and I cannot deny it'.

3.57.15. The first 'worde' renders *os* (R reads *habes* rather than KZ's *habeo*).

3.57.16. The imagery of 'þe darke lande, covered with þe darkenes of dethe' is derived from Job 10.20–1.

3.57.18. On the mystical kiss, see Riehle, pp. 38–9.

3.57.19. *Humilis*, which modifies *contricio* ('contricion'), has been omitted, as has *in conspectu tuo*, which modifies *odorans* ('smellynge'). 'Of synnes' renders K's *peccatorum* rather than R's *peccatoris*.

3.57.20. Cf. the account of Mary's pouring the ointment on Jesus' feet in John 12.3–8, and the assurance of God's acceptance of the contrite in Psalm 50.19 (AV 51.17).

3.58.0. *Dei*, which modifies *gracia* ('þe grace'), has been omitted.

3.58.3. 'Put oute' corresponds to *effunde*: perhaps the translator originally wrote 'pour out'. On secrecy, see 1.20.5 n.

3.58.5. This is the first citation of 'vacacion' (*vacacionem*) in the sense 'leisure for, or devoted to, some special purpose; hence, occupation, business' in *OED*.

3.58.8. See 1 Peter 2.11 (*obsecro vos tanquam advenas et peregrinos abstinere vos a carnalibus desideriis*). 'Alle' has been added.

3.58.10. On 'þe bestly man' (*animalis homo*), cf. 1 Corinthians 2.14.

3.58.15. 'To þe heyght of perfeccion' renders *ad hunc apicem*; see 3.47.7 n. Cf. John the Baptist's words on putting the axe to the root of the tree in Luke 3.9, and the imagery of uprooting in Jeremiah 1.10.

3.58.18. 'Implyed and encombred' renders *implicati*. On the soul's stretching out to God, see Riehle, p. 70.

3.58.19. This is the only citation of 'concupiscently' (*concupiscenter*) in *MED* or *OED*.

3.59.1. *Et gracie*, which follows *nature* ('nature'), has been omitted.

3.59.2. *Sub specie boni multi falluntur*. Horace remarked that most poets were deceived *specie recti*, by being over-ambitious, for example (*Ars Poetica* 25).

3.59.3. 'Sekynge none oþer' has been added.

3.59.4. 'Gothe symply' renders *simpliciter ambulat* (cf. Proverbs 10.9); on abstaining from evil, cf. 1 Thessalonians 5.22. 'Falsnes ner deceytes' is a doublet rendering *fallacias*.

3.59.6. Cf. the instruction to be subject to all in 1 Peter 2.13.

3.59.8. '[To one]' renders '*sibi*'. Cf. Paul's teaching on seeking what is profitable to many in 1 Corinthians 10.33.

3.59.9. Cf. the exhortations to give glory and honour to God in Psalms 28.2 and 95.7 (AV 29.2 and 96.7).

3.59.10. On suffering for Christ, see 3.24.15 n.

3.59.11. This is the first citation of 'voyde' (*vacua*) in the sense 'unmployed' in *OED*. 'Laboure and travaile' is a doublet rendering *laborem*.

3.59.14. Cf. Jesus' teaching on laying up treasure in heaven in Matthew 6.19–20.

3.59.16. 'Fulle of pite' renders *pia*. Cf. Paul's reminder to the Ephesian elders of Jesus' teaching that it is more blessed to give than to receive (Acts 20.35).

3.59.17. 'Discourses and rennynge aboute' is a doublet rendering *discursus*.

3.59.20. This verse has been abridged: the Latin is *sed gracia in solo deo querit consolari: et in summo bono super omnia visibilia delectari.*

3.59.23. 'Myght and power' is a doublet rendering R's *potencie* rather than K's *potentibus*, i.e. 'powerful men'.

3.59.24. Cf. Jesus' command to love one's enemies in the sermon on the mount (Matthew 5.44). 'þe pover þen þe riche' and 'þe innocent þen on þe myghty' render *pauperi quam diuiti* and *innocenti quam potenti*, which are singular and would have been more clearly rendered 'the poor man', etc. 'To gode' renders *bonos*, the object of ⟨exhort⟩*atur* (perhaps the translator originally wrote 'the good'); 'more grace' corresponds to *meliora carismata* (cf. 1 Corinthians 12.31).

3.59.25. This is one of three citations of 'fawtinge' (*defectu*) in *MED*, the only one in the sense 'want, scarcity'. 'Poverte and neede' is a doublet rendering *inopiam*.

3.59.27. 'Groundely and originally' is a doublet rendering *originaliter*.

3.59.29. 'Of corrupcion' corresponds to *de vetustate corrupcionis*: cf. Ecclestiastes 1.10 (AV 1.9).

3.59.30. 'Wonderful' renders *digne miranda*. 'Openly' has been added.

3.59.31. With 'signacle' (*signaculum*) cf. Romans 4.11; with 'arneste' (*pignus*) cf. Ephesians 1.14.

3.59.32. On the *imago dei* doctrine (cf. Genesis 1.26), see Riehle, pp. 142–5, and cf. 2 Corinthians 4.16, Colossians 3.10, and 3.60.1.

3.60.0. *Diuine*, which modifies *gracie* ('grace'), has been omitted.

3.60.2. This verse is derived from Paul's treatment of his inner struggle in Romans 7.23.

3.60.3. 'Of yonge age and adolescence' is a doublet rendering *ab adolescencia sua* (cf. God's words after the flood in Genesis 8.21).

3.60.4. 'Evonly' renders R's *recte* rather than K's *recta* (i.e. 'upright': cf. Ecclestiastes 7.30, AV 7.29). 'Ever' has been added.

3.60.5. 'Goode' has been added. On the divine spark, see Riehle, p. 155, and cf. 1.15.14.

3.60.6. *Magna*, which modifies *caligine* ('darkenesse'), has been omitted. Cf. the description of the mature as being able to distinguish good from evil in Hebrews 5.14.

3.60.7–9. Cf. Paul's account of the the paradox of simultaneously delighting in the law of God after the inward man and serving with the flesh the law of sin in Romans 7.12,18–25.

3.60.11. 'More perfeccion' renders *perfectiora*, literally 'more perfect things'.

3.60.12. *Tua*, which modifies *gracia* ('[grace]'), has been omitted.

3.60.13. Cf. the stress on the necessity of Christ in John 15.5 and Philippians 4.13.

3.60.16. '[Shal] be worþi euerlasting[e] lyve' renders *digni habentur vita eterna*, i.e. 'will be counted worthy of eternal life'.

3.60.21. Cf. Paul's assurance of the sufficiency of God's grace in 2 Corinthians 12.9.

3.60.22. *Mala*, the object of *non timebo* ('I shal not drede'), has been omitted (cf. Psalm 22.4, AV 23.4).

3.60.25. This is the first citation of 'doctrice' (*doctrix*) in *MED*: cf. Wisdom 8.4, where the phrase *doctrix discipline* is applied to wisdom. 'Of pressure and þrowinge downe' is a doublet rendering *pressure*.

3.60.26. With the 'drie tree' cf. Ecclesiasticus 6.3; with the 'vnprofitable stokke' cf. Isaiah 14.19; The translation follows R in omitting *ad eiciendum*, which in K follows *stips inutilis*.

3.60.27. This verse is a quotation from the collect for the seventeenth Sunday after Trinity in the Sarum Missal (ed. J. W. Legg (Oxford, 1916), p. 188), or the collect for the sixteenth Sunday after Pentecost in the Tridentine Missal.

3.61.2. 'Ioy[n]eþ and onethe' is a doublet rendering *coniungit*; on union with God, see 1.3.11 n.

3.61.3. This is the only citation of 'abnegacion' (*abnegacionem*) in the sense 'self-denial, renunciation' in *MED*.

3.61.4. With 'folowe me' cf. Jesus' command to Matthew (Matthew 9.9); 'I am wey, trowthe, and lyve' is a quotation from John 14.6.

3.61.6. 'Vndefouleable' (*inuiolabilis*) is not cited in *OED*.

3.61.8. Cf. Jesus promise of freedom to those who by continuing in his word know the truth in John 8.31–2, and Paul's promise of eternal life in 1 Timothy 6.12.

3.61.9–12. These verses recall Jesus' words to the rich young ruler in Matthew 19.17,21 and to the disciples in Matthew 16.24.

3.61.15. 'Bere my crosse' renders *porta crucem mecum*: perhaps the translator read *meam*. See 2.11.1 n.

3.61.17. 'Weie' renders R's *via* rather than K's *vita*; cf. Matthew 7.14.

3.61.18. Cf. Jesus' words that the disciple is not above his master nor the servant above his lord in Matthew 10.24.

3.61.21. This point is developed from Jesus' words in John 13.17.

3.61.22. 'Shall make him [an heir]' paraphrases *consedere mecum* (R reads *sedere mecum*). Cf. Jesus' promise to love and manifest himself to the person who keeps his commandments in John 14.21, and to grant him who conquers to sit with him on his throne in Revelation 3.21.

3.61.24. 'I haue taken' renders R's *suscepi* rather than K's *suscepi suscepi*; 'and so shal I bere' renders R's *et portabo* rather than K's *portabo et portabo*.

3.61.25. Cf. Thomas à Kempis, *Cantica* 5 (*Versus de Sancta Cruce*), line 1 (Pohl, iv. 249).

3.61.29. This is the only citation of 'predecessoure' (*precessor*) in a figurative sense in *MED*.

3.61.30. Cf. Nehemiah's assurance that God would fight for his people (Nehemiah 4.20).

3.61.31. Cf. Hezekiah's encouragement to the Israelites not to fear (2 Chronicles 32.7), and Judas Maccabeus' exhortations to them to be ready to die in battle (1

Maccabees 3.59) and to maintain their honour rather than flee (1 Maccabees 9.10).

3.62.3. The translation follows R in omitting this verse, given in K as *Si amplius fuisset: commoueri non debuisses.*

3.62.6. 'Thou canste counseyle welle and laboure oþer menne with wyse wordes' renders R's *Bene eciam consulis et alios nosti laborare verbis*; K reads *roborare* for *laborare.*

3.62.8. This is the only citation of 'obiectes' (*obiectis*) in the sense 'an obstacle, hindrance' in *MED*.

3.62.9. The rendering 'and' means that the translation is closer to R's *tunc hec et similia contingunt* than to K, which reads *cum* for *tunc*: in K the clause is subordinate to the previous one (the previous sentence in the English): *tamen pro salute tua ista fiunt.*

3.62.11. This is the only citation of 'ioyngly' (*gaudenter*) in the sense 'cheerfully' in *MED*.

3.62.12. 'In þiselfe' has been added; 'þat myght be to þe smale and to þe feble occasion of fallynge' paraphrases *vnde paruuli scandalizentur.*

3.62.14. With the assurance 'yeet I lyffe' cf. the promise in Isaiah 49.18. 'Inwardely and' has been added.

3.62.15. 'Be myghti in soule' renders K's *animequior esto* (cf. Baruch 4.30), rather than R's *an nequior est*; 'gurde þee and make þee redy' is a doublet rendering *accingere.*

3.62.18. The first 'furste' has been added.

3.62.19. On mourning, see 1.23.47 n., and cf. the promise of comfort in Job 5.11.

3.62.20. The comparison of the sweetness of God's word to honey and the honeycombe is derived from Psalms 18.11 and 118.103 (AV 19.10 and 119.103).

3.62.24. Cf. Nehemiah's prayer to God to remember him (Nehemiah 13.31).

3.63.3–4. 'Answere and seie with Dauid' expands *responde illud prophete*. Cf. the faith in God's justice expressed in Psalms 18.10 and 118.137 (AV 19.9 and 119.137).

3.63.5. Cf. Paul's characterization of God's judgements as incomprehensible and his ways as unsearchable (Romans 11.33).

3.63.7. Cf. Paul's warnings against contention in 2 Timothy 2.23 and Titus 3.9.

3.63.8. 'I am no God of discencion, but of pees' is derived from 1 Corinthians 14.33.

3.63.11. *Mee*, which modifies *dulcedinis* ('of swetnesse'), has been omitted. With 'prevented hem in blessinges of swetnesse' cf. Psalm 20.4 (AV 21.3).

3.63.12. With 'predestinate hem bifore worldes' cf. Romans 8.29.

3.63.13. Cf. Jesus' assertion that he chose the disciples in John 15.16,19.

3.63.14. With 'called . . . by grace' cf. Galatians 1.15; with 'drewe . . . bi mercy' cf. Jeremiah 31.3.

3.63.17. On the mystical embrace, see 2.7.4 n.

3.63.19. Cf. Jesus' command not to despise one of the little ones in Matthew 18.10, and the teaching that God made both the little and the great in Wisdom 6.8 (AV 6.7).

3.63.21. 'And alle one' has been added. 'And alle [þei] love hem into one' renders *et omnes in vn⟨u⟩m se diligunt* (the *m* of *vn⟨u⟩m* has been added on the line, and *o* is visible under the erasure under the ⟨*u*⟩), i.e. 'and they all love each other as one'. Cf. John 17.21.

3.63.23. 'Alle and hole' is a doublet rendering *toti*. This is the only citation of 'fruyshyngly' (*fruitiue*) in *MED* or *OED*; see 3.23.23 n. On 'ravished', see 2.9.29 n.; on 'above', see 3.36.8 n.

3.63.24. See 3.48.11 n.

3.63.25. 'Propre and pryvate' is a doublet rendering *priuata*.

3.63.27. 'In many þinges ignorantly' renders R's *in multis ignoranter* rather than K's *in multis est ignorancia*, i.e. 'in many it is ignorance'.

3.63.37. *Et dilectiores exsistunt* (R reads *doctiores* for *dilectiores*) has been omitted from the end of the verse.

3.63.38. In rendering *viuentem*, the object of *adorauerunt* ('worshipped') in K and R, as 'him', the translation is perhaps following a text such as that of U and T, which omit *viuentem*. The picture of worship here is derived from Revelation 4.9–10.

3.63.41. This verse, *Minimus erit in mille: et peccator centum annorum morietur* (cf. Isaiah 60.22 and 65.20), has been omitted.

3.63.42–3. See Matthew 18.1–4.

3.63.45. On the woe due to the rich, cf. Luke 6.24.

3.63.46. On the blessing due to the poor, cf. Luke 6.20; on walking in truth, cf. Isaiah 38.3, 2 John 4, and 3 John 3,4.

3.64.8. 'þat may helpe me in oportune necessitez' is an attempt to render R's *qui in necessitatibus auxilietur oportunis*; K has ⟨*oportunius*⟩ for *oportunis*, i.e. 'to give me timely help in my necessities'.

3.64.9. Cf. the psalmist's trust in God as his hope in Psalm 141.6 (Vulgate).

3.64.10. Paul criticized those who sought their own interest (Philippians 2.21), and affirmed that all things work together for good for those who love God (Romans 8.28).

3.64.11. On the variants, see Introduction, p. lvii.

3.64.13. This is the first citation of 'vnferme' (*infirmum*) in *OED*.

3.64.14. 'Ner many helpars shul not mowe' renders *neque fortes auxiliarii adiuuare poterunt*: presumably the translator did not read *adiuuare* and intended 'mowe' in the sense 'avail'. 'Of gode' has been added; 'counfortinge' renders *confortes consoleris*.

3.64.15. 'In trowthe' has been added.

3.64.16. 'Scriptures' renders *eloquiorum*. 'Above' corresponds to *super omnia*: perhaps 'all' has dropped out of the translation.

3.64.17. *In te confido* (cf. Psalm 24.2, AV 25.2), which follows *ad te ⟨sunt oculi mei⟩* ('to the ar myne yen dressed': cf. Psalm 140.8, AV 141.8), has been omitted. The title 'Fader of mercies' is derived from 2 Corinthians 1.3.

3.64.18. On 'sete', see 2.7.8 n.

3.64.19. Cf. the trust expressed in the multitude of God's mercies in Psalms 50.3 and 68.17 (AV 51.1 and 69.16); Daniel's request for his prayer of confession to be heard in Daniel 9.17; and the mention of the land of the shadow of death in Isaiah 9.2.

3.64.21. R has *Explicit tercia et vltima pars libri interne consolacionis: qui vocatur musica ecclesiastica*; K has an erased line.

GLOSSARY

The Glossary aims to record only those forms or senses which might cause difficulty to a modern reader. Words which have the same spelling and meaning as in Modern English are therefore not included; neither are words which have the same meaning as in Modern English but exhibit the following variations in spelling: *i/y, þ/th, u/v, u/w, a/au, e/ea, e/ee, ew/ue, o/oo, ou/ow, ai/ei/eie, ck/k, ld/d, ite/ight*; variation in syllables not bearing the main stress between *a/e/i/o/u, ee/ei, o/ou/u, er/re*; variation in final syllables between *s/es, s/z, i/ie, -cion/-tion/-sion*; doubling of consonants; addition or absence of final *-e* (at the end of a word or of the first element of a compound). Words which differ from Modern English only because of regular Middle English inflections (i.e. those found in Chaucer plus the ending *-eth* and variants for the present plural indicative) are also not included.

The spelling of the headword is usually that found most frequently; variations in spelling within the parameters listed above are only noted where the first instance of one of the senses cited exhibits such a variant. Generally only one reference is given for each form and sense cited. Where a word has one sense which remains in Modern English and another sense which does not, only the second is included; consequently not all inflections of a headword are necessarily listed. Where a word is included because its stem differs in form from Modern English, the first occurring example of each of its inflections is given. Generally definitions are given next to the form they gloss, except that in the entries for common verbs the various definitions are given at the beginning and the inflexions grouped together at the end; here the appropriate references are given for both definitions and forms. References to emended forms are preceded by an asterisk.

In the alphabetical arrangement *i* is treated as *i* when it represents a vowel and *j* when it represents a consonant; *v* is treated as *u* when it represents a vowel and *v* when it represents a consonant; *y* is treated as *i* when it represents a vowel and *y* when it represents a consonant; *þ* is treated as *th*. The standard EETS abbreviations are used.

abhominable *adj.* hateful 3.22.9

abide, abyde *v.* remain 1.2.18, 1.11.7, 2.1.13, 3.19.6, 3.20.9, 3.45.6; endure 1.13.28; await 1.22.29; expect 3.18.1; wait 3.18.4. **abidest** *pr. 2 sg.* 3.45.6; **abideþ** *pr. 3 sg.* 2.1.13; **abide** *pr. pl.* 1.11.7; *pr. subj. sg.* 3.19.6; *imp. sg.* 3.18.4; **abidinge, abidynge** *pr. p.* eternal 1.22.20; constant 3.44.5; **abiden** *pp.* 3.20.9.

abitremente *n.* opinion 3.51.21

abiecte *adj.* rejected 3.24.16

abiectely *adv.* lowlily 3.15.14

abnegacion *n.* ~ *of thiselfe* self-denial 3.61.3

aboute *prep.* at 1.13.20; ~ *destruccion of* in order to destroy 1.18.6; *is* ~ *to* seeks to 3.63.7; *be besie* ~ see besie.

above *adj. is* ~ rules 1.20.13

abstinences *n. pl.* fasts 1.18.6

abstractely *adv.* apart from the world 1.25.34

accepcion *n.* 1.5.8 *see n.*

acceptable *adj.* pleasing 3.11.26

acceptably *adv.* gladly 3.21.12

accompte *v.* consider 1.2.15, 1.7.9, 1.19.30, 3.0.57, 3.21.12; count up 1.23.13; take account of 3.6.19; believe 3.22.20; *noþing to* ~ *of himselfe* to consider himself as nothing 1.2.7. **accompteþ, acompteþ** *pr. 3 sg.* 1.23.13, 3.6.19, 3.21.12, 3.22.20; *accompteþ him refl.* considers himself to be 2.12.41; **accompteth** *pr. pl.* 1.23.13; **accompte** *pr. subj. sg.* 3.0.57; *imp. sg.* 1.7.9; ~ *þe as refl.* consider yourself to be 1.17.4; **accompted** *pa. t. sg.* considered it 3.41.5; **accompted, acompted** *pp.*

1.2.15; counted 3.63.39; *accompted for* considered as 3.36.11

accorde, acorde *v.* be in harmony 1.17.1; ~ *to* be in harmony with 3.17.3; **accordynge** *ppl. adj.* fitting 1.19.23

accountes *n. pl.* account 3.28.4

acompeny *imp. sg. refl.* ~ *þiself with* keep company with 1.8.4

acompted, acompteþ *see* accompte

acorde *see* accorde

acustumed *pp.* accustomed 1.11.19

addeþ *pr. pl.* ~ *to* add 3.63.26

adinuencions *n. pl.* fabrications 1.4.6

adowne *adv.* down 3.10.2

afarre *adv. alle* ~ far off 3.20.9

aferde *adj.* afraid 1.24.2

affeccion *n.* desire 1.3.16; feelings 3.5.22; **affeccions, affecciouns** *pl.* 1.0.6; feelings 3.60.6

affectuously *adv.* lovingly 2.12.50

affrayed *pp.* frightened 3.15.1

afire, ofire *adv.* on fire 3.2.8, 3.2.17

afore *prep.* before 1.7.12

aftir *prep.* according to 1.2.4; pertaining to 1.21.14; for 3.64.7; ~ *God* in accordance with the will of God 1.4.1; ~ *þe man* in accordance with man's natural inclination 2.12.43; ~ *þe inwarde man* in my inner self 3.60.7

aftirwarde *adv.* afterwards 1.1.15

agaste *adj. be* ~ *of* fear 3.5.18

agree *v.* comply 1.16.4; ~ *to* agree with 1.9.12

alyene *adj.* apart 3.6.13

alienes *n. pl.* strangers 1.18.14

alle *adj.* ~ *maner* every kind of 1.1.2; ~ *maner of* great 1.1.18; ~ *þinge* everything 1.22.2; *adv.* entirely 1.13.9; *n.* everything 2.12.15

alleone *adv.* only 1.11.13

alleonely, alleonly, alonely *adv.* only 1.20.22, 2.5.11, 3.36.10

alternacion *n.* change 2.9.17

amiable *adj.* pleasant 3.21.20; loving 3.23.17

ammonicions, ammonycions *n. pl.* counsels 2.12.71, 2.0.13

ammonyshe *v.* admonish 1.16.13; **amonyshe** *pr. subj. sg.* 3.55.26; **ammonyshe** *imp. sg.* 1.21.12; **amonyshed** *pp.* 1.1.2

amonge *prep.* sometimes 2.9.28; *prep.* ~ *þees* in all this 2.9.20

amonyshe, amonyshed *see* ammonyshe

an *prep.* on 3.8.1

and *conj.* if 1.25.46

anenst, anenste *prep.* from *1.18.16; ~ *hemselfe* in their own eyes *2.10.19; ~ *whom* in whose opinion 3.24.11; ~ *thiselfe* to yourself 3.50.23; ~ *þee* in your presence 3.55.11; *as* ~ *þe* in your sight 3.60.15

angred *pp.* angered 3.59.14

angwysshe *n.* distress 1.22.4; **angwysshes** *pl.* afflictions 3.0.53

angwysshed *pp.* distressed 1.24.18

anywise *adv.* at all *1.21.1

annexid *pp.* associated 1.3.21

anone *adv.* soon 1.6.1; at once 1.22.23; ~ *as* as soon as 1.13.20

apparence *n.* appearance 2.7.12; outward appearance 3.50.29

appiere, appere *v.* appear 1.24.21, 2.10.25; **appiere** *pr. 1 sg.* 3.48.15; **appereþ, appyereþ** *pr. 3 sg.* 1.16.11, 1.19.1; **appiereþ** *pr. pl.* 3.24.12; **appire, appiere** *pr. subj. sg.* 1.19.7, 3.51.20

apprehende *pr. subj. sg.* understand 2.11.21

appreveþ *pr. 3 sg.* approves 3.60.6

apte *adj.* fit 2.12.64

araye *v.* prepare 1.19.29

arette *v.* attribute 3.10.8

aryse *v.* progress 3.60.11; **arose** *pa. t. sg. arose into* rose to 3.63.31

arneste *n.* pledge 3.59.31

arose *see* aryse

arowes *n. pl.* arrowes 3.53.23

arted *pp.* confined 3.6.22

as *conj.* when 3.53.27; *rel. pr.* that 1.25.23

ascryve *v.* ascribe *2.10.15; *imp. sg.* *2.10.16; *pr. pl.* 2.10.22; **ascryveþ** *pr. 3 sg.* 1.15.13; *pr. pl.* 3.63.35

ashon *n. pl.* ashes 3.9.1

aske *v.* request 3.4.0; **askest** *pr. 2 sg.* ask for 3.37.9; **aske, askeþ** *pr. pl.* require it 1.9.12; ask for 1.16.9; **aske** *imp. sg.* 3.42.14; ~ *to* seek for 3.58.3; **asked** *pp.* requested 3.16.8

asperite *n.* roughness 3.59.12

assailinges *n. pl.* assaults, attacks 3.5.2

assistente *adj.* helpful 3.22.10; assisting 3.64.14

assoyled *pp.* resolved 3.43.3

astonyed *pp.* amazed 3.15.2

astonyinge *vbl. n.* wonderment *3.6.26

at *prep.* by 3.35.17; ~ *the* in your presence 3.23.12; ~ *fulle* to the full 3.53.9; *atte* at the 1.19.15

atteygne *v.* attain 3.6.19

attende *pr. 1 sg.* consider 3.24.4; *imp. sg.* observe 3.59.1; attendeþ *pr. 3 sg.* pays attention to 3.59.14

auctorite *n.* authority 1.5.5

aventure *n.* eventuality 3.52.1

awayle *v.* avail 3.63.31

awayte *n.* wait 3.44.8

awter *n.* altar 1.25.7

ayeine, ayein *adv.* again 1.13.13; back 2.10.10; in return 3.11.8; *see also* ayenis

ayenis, ayenst, ayeine, ayeins *prep.* against 1.11.19, 1.13.24, 3.0.13, 3.14.12; amid 3.0.51

ayeinsayars *n. pl.* antagonists 1.12.2

ayeinsaye *pr. subj. sg.* contradict 2.1.14

ayeinwarde *adv.* on the other hand 3.8.20

ayenst *see* ayenis

bakke *n.* back 3.55.22

bakke *adv.* back 3.60.10

bare *adj.* stripped 2.11.17; naked 2.11.29; *in alle þinges made* ~ naked of everything 3.42.6

barsteþ *pr. 3 sg.* leaps 3.6.22

bateyle *n.* battle 1.11.11; bateiles, batailes *pl.* armies 3.7.26; battles 3.39.21

be *v.* be 1.0.7; *howe grete truste shal* ~ *to þe manne* what great confidence shall that man have 3.58.9; ~ *for* make for 3.64.15. be, been, beeþ, beþe *pr. pl.* 1.2.7, 1.22.8, 2.1.34, 3.63.34; be *pr. subj. sg.* 1.13.23; *pr. subj. pl.* 3.61.31; wer *pa. t. subj. sg.* 1.20.41; beeþ *imp. pl.* 3.63.46; be, bene *pp.* 1.10.3, 1.19.3

been, beeþ, bene *see* be

benefaite *n.* favour 3.24.12; benefaytes *pl.* 1.20.1

benigly, benignely *adv.* good-naturedly, patiently 1.16.3, 2.9.7

benigne *adj.* kind 3.17.1

benignely *see* benigly

bere *v.* endure 1.16.3; have 3.19.4; berest *pr. 2 sg.* 3.31.3; bereþ *pr. pl.* 3.5.20; *imp. sg.* bear with 2.3.11; drive 3.27.3; beringe *vbl. n.* tolerating 1.16.0; borne *pp.* sustained 2.3.11

besie, besy, besye, bysie, bysy *adj.* busy 1.11.22; careful 1.20.16; solicitous

1.24.17; meddlesome 3.28.1; *be* ~ *aboute, be* ~ *for* be concerned about 1.13.3, 1.23.27

besines, bisinesse, bisynes, bisynesse, bysines, bysinesse, bysynesse solicitude 1.20.22; effort 1.22.8; business 1.23.45; effort 1.25.44; care 3.0.19; concerns 3.32.2; application 3.50.29

bestely, bestly *adj.* natural 3.58.10; natural men 3.63.25

Betanye *proper n.* Bethany 3.38.8

beþe *see* be

better *comp. adj.* ~ *be* better times come 3.34.14; 1.3.20 *see* profite

bi, by *prep.* for 1.13.26; with 1.20.20; by way of 3.0.61; through 3.51.3

bicame *pa. t. sg. whither I* ~ to what I have come 3.9.4

bye *v.* buy 3.37.10

bifore, byfore *adv.* ahead 1.23.26; in the sight of 3.0.5; *see* ~ look ahead to 1.1.17; ~ *see* foresee 3.50.14; ~ *sene* foreseen 3.50.15; 3.12.7 *see* conceyve

bigonnen *pp.* begun 3.32.6; *hit is* ~ we have begun 3.61.26

byhiete *v.* promise 1.23.17

bihofulle *adj.* fitting 1.25.6; necessary 3.34.14

biholde, byholde *v.* consider 1.21.23, 2.9.2; biholde *pr. subj. sg.* ~ *to* look at 2.7.12; biholdeste *pr. 2 sg.* perceive 3.35.33; biholde, byholde *imp. sg.* look to 1.24.1; ~ *into* look to 3.26.1; look on 3.64.19; biholdinge, byholdinge *vbl. n.* vision 3.6.13; sight 3.15.2; regard 3.54.3; biholden *pp.* seen 3.20.9; regarded 3.47.12

bileve *n. oute of trewe* ~ faithless 1.22.17

byneþe *adj.* under authority 1.20.13

bineþeforthe *adv.* beneath 2.12.16

byshyneþ *pr. 3 sg.* illumines 3.53.2

bysie, bysy *see* besie

bisinesse, bisynes, bisynesse, bysines, bysinesse, bysynesse *see* besines

bisily *adv.* busily 1.19.29

bitake *pr. pl.* convey to 3.2.9

bityme, bytyme *adv.* early 3.60.20; in time 1.23.26; early in the morning 2.9.24

blame *v.* censure 3.55.29; *imp. sg.* 3.5.15; blamynge *vbl. n.* accusation 3.51.13; blamynges *pl.* 2.6.16

blandyshynge *vbl. n.* seductive flattery

3.32.6; **blandyshynges** *pl.* things which delight and flatter us 1.21.24

blasfemyes *n. pl.* blasphemies 3.20.3

blended *pp.* deceived *3.55.31

blisfulle *adj.* happy *1.3.1

blysfully *adv.* happily 1.23.47

blysfulnes *n.* happiness 1.22.28

boystesly *adv.* poorly 1.25.34

bolnynge *ppl. adj.* swelling *3.14.12

bonde *pp.* bound 3.11.10

borde *n.* table 3.23.16

bore *pp.* born 3.6.14

borne *see* bere

boste 3.41.7 *see* makeste

bowe *v.* submit 1.3.18, *refl.* 3.14.10; turn 1.14.1; bow down *refl.* 2.2.9; ~ *into* incline to 3.2.3. **boweþ** *pr. 3 sg.* 1.3.18, 2.2.9; bowe *imp. sg.* 1.14.1; bowed *pp.* caused to submit 3.23.22; submitted 3.59.6; *bowed adowne* inclined 3.10.2

bradder *comp. adj.* broader 3.6.14

brake *see* breke

brawlinge *ppl. adj.* quarrelsome 3.41.14

breke *v.* overcome 3.26.2; *pr. pl.* ~ *oute* break off 3.36.17; brake *pa. t. sg.* broke 1.23.37

brenneþ *pr. 3 sg.* burns 3.54.4; brennen *pr. pl.* 3.63.24; brennynge *ppl. adj.* 1.24.11; *vbl. n.* 3.40.4; 1.24.9 *see* matier

brennyngly *adv.* ardently 3.48.11

breres *n. pl.* briars 3.22.20

breþer, breþeren, broþeren *n. pl.* brethren 1.25.23, 3.61.27

bringar *n.* ~ *forthe* producer 3.60.25

bryngeþ *pr. 3 sg.* ~ *forthe* results in 1.20.35; bryng, bringe *pr. pl.* bringe *forthe* set forth 3.2.10; bryng yn bring 3.25.0; bringe *imp. sg.* bringe *oute* remove 3.27.1; brought, broght *pp. brought forþe* told 1.5.11; discussed 1.10.1; produced 3.51.23; *brought inne of* arising from 3.7.12; *brought inne with* led by 3.16.7

bryssed *pp.* bruised 3.55.19

broght *see* bryngeþ

bronde *n.* torch 3.6.22

broþeren *see* breþer

brought *see* bryngeþ

but *conj.* unless 1.20.23; without 3.42.12; ~ *if* unless 1.2.10; ~ *for* except for the reason that 1.11.5; ~ *þat* who does not 1.13.4; that not 3.50.7

caytyfe *n.* captive 3.60.2

came *pa. t. sg.* came away 1.20.6

can *v.* know 1.1.10, 1.2.10, 1.2.15, 3.6.18, 3.36.9; know how to 2.8.15; can 2.7.9, 3.40.16, 3.45.9, 3.63.34. canste *pr. 2 sg.* 1.2.10; canne *pr. 3 sg.* 3.6.18; *pr. subj. sg.* 3.36.9; coudeste *pa. t. 2 sg.* 1.1.10, 2.7.9; cowde *pa. t. pl.* 3.40.16; *pa. t. subj. sg.* 3.45.9; *pa. t. subj. pl.* 3.63.34

caryinge *vbl. n.* ~ *of* worrying about 3.35.14

Cartusiensez *n. pl.* Carthusians 1.25.35

casteþ *pr. pl.* ~ *hemselfe oute fro* free themselves from 3.1.7; caste *imp. sg.* send *3.39.16; *caste into* commit to 3.41.1

case *n. in beste* ~ in the best situation 1.22.5

cause *n.* case 3.43.2; *if I be in* ~ if it is for my sake 3.12.5; 1.8.1 *see* meve; causes *pl.* affairs 1.21.11

cenobyes *n. pl.* religious houses 1.3.25

certeyne *adj. in* ~ definite 1.19.13

cesse *v.* cease 3.3.5; cesseþ, cesseth *pr. 3 sg.* 2.10.7, 3.44.8; *pr. pl.* 1.24.16, 2.9.36; cesse *imp. sg.* 1.2.5; *pr. subj. sg.* 3.15.8; cessed *pa. t. sg.* 1.25.10; *pa. t. pl.* 1.18.7; cessinge *pr. p.* 3.38.4

chace, chase *v.* drive 2.8.18, 2.8.19; chaced *pp. chaced awey* put to flight 3.10.10; *see also* chese

chapitres *n. pl.* chapters 2.0.0

charge *n.* responsibility 2.3.7; *what* ~ *to vs of* what concern do we have with 1.3.6

charge *v.* care about 2.1.25; chargeþ *pr. 3 sg.* *2.1.38; chargeth *pr. pl.* ~ *of* care about 3.48.7; charge *imp. sg.* pay attention to 1.23.43; take care about 2.2.1

chase *see* chace; chese

chaunce *n.* event 1.25.42; chaunces *pl.* 3.44.4

chaungeablenes *n.* changing 3.54.1

chaunged *pp.* are ~ *vppon* have changed over 3.45.7; *be* ~ *into diuerse* become sad 3.45.8

chese *pr. 1 sg.* choose 3.64.5; *pr. pl.* 1.3.33; *imp. sg.* 3.25.4; chace, chase *pr. pl.* 2.9.8, 3.63.13; chaseste *pa. t. 2 sg. chaseste pouer into þi familyarez* chose poor men to become your friends 3.24.13; chace, chase *pa. t. pl.* 1.20.5, 3.63.13

chier *n.* mood 3.29.13; face 3.45.8

childeron, children *n. pl.* children 3.60.16; ~ *pleye* child's play 3.37.6

chirche *n.* church 1.25.7

choyce *n.* preference 3.42.2

circuites *n. pl.* walking about 1.20.4

circumfounded *pp.* surrounded 3.53.7

circumspecte *adj.* careful 3.6.32

circumspectily *adv.* carefully 1.21.13

citezeins *n. pl.* citizens 3.53.5

claryfie *imp. sg.* enlighten 3.27.1; clarified *pp.* glorified 3.34.7

claustralle *adj.* monastic 1.25.33

cleye *n.* mire 3.22.6

clere *adj.* bright 3.53.2

clerely *adv.* straightforwardly 3.5.16

clerenes, clerenesse *n.* fair weather 2.8.35; brightness 3.27.1; splendour 3.53.4; light 3.64.20

clerke *n.* scholar 3.36.12

clyffe *see* clyve

clyppe *v.* embrace 3.6.35; clippeþ *pr. 3 sg.* 2.7.4; clyppeth *pr. pl.* 1.22.16; clyppinges *vbl. n.* embraces 3.23.10; clypped *pp.* 3.9.7

clyve, clyffe *v.* cling 2.1.22, 2.7.4, 3.8.2, 3.30.1; ~ *to* entangle 3.43.1; ~ *to* be concerned about 3.44.4. clyveth *pr. 3 sg.* 2.7.4; clyve *pr. subj. sg.* 2.1.22; clyved *pa. t. sg.* 3.44.4; clyvynge 3.30.1

closet *n.* room 1.20.24

clothe *n.* clothing 1.24.25

cloþed *pp. be ~ in* put on 3.54.17

coarted *pp.* constrained 3.6.22

collacion *n.* discussion 1.10.12

coloure *n. vnder ~ of* in the guise of 3.30.4

coloure *v.* put a good complexion on 2.3.9

coluer *n.* dove 3.36.3

comeþ *pr. pl. ~ vppon* come upon one 3.22.13; commynge, comynge *pr. p.* to come 1.24.6; *to comynge* to come 1.23.27; commynge *vbl. n.* access 1.24.42

commynge *see* comeþ

comodiouse *adj.* convenient 3.54.9

comodite *n.* good fortune 3.6.13; comoditez *pl.* interests 3.64.10

compayny *n.* company 3.52.13

compellynge *vbl. n. for necessite ~* because forced by necessity 3.45.9

complacence *n.* complacency 3.7.29; *propre ~* complacency with yourself 3.37.11

compuncte *adj.* repentant 1.20.24

comune *adj.* common 1.15.8; generous 3.59.16

conceyte *n.* opinion 1.5.5

conceyve *v.* understand 2.4.8; *pr. pl.* hope to receive 3.13.14; *pr. subj. sg.* receive 3.24.13; conceyved *pp.* 3.8.19; *bifore conceyved* preconceived 3.12.7; *conceyved of* produced by 3.15.18

condimente *n.* seasoning 3.39.9

confabulacions *n. pl.* conversations 3.57.6

conferme *v.* strengthen 3.45.8; *imp. sg.* 3.32.1; confermed *pp.* established 2.10.21, strengthened 3.15.13

confoundeþ *pr. 3 sg.* brings shame on 3.22.7; confounded *pp.* humiliated 3.51.9

confourmed *pp. ~ to* made like 2.12.66

confucion, confusion *n.* confusion 2.2.6; shame 3.13.15

confused *pp.* defeated 3.7.22

confusion *see* confucion

conged *pp.* sent away 2.8.31

congregacions *n. pl.* communities 1.17.2

congruence *n. for ~ of tyme* to suit the season *1.19.24

conservacion *n.* keeping 3.50.29

consideracion *n.* pondering 1.0.22; reflection 3.24.2

considereþ *pr. sg.* observes 1.2.2; consider *pr. subj. sg.* 1.25.21

constance *n.* firmness 1.24.18

constreyned *pp.* compelled 3.12.11

consummate *adj.* all-important 3.37.4

conteygne *pr. subj. pl.* keep 3.58.8

contingently *adv.* possibly 3.35.14

continued *pp. welle ~* continually used 1.20.26

contraccion *n.* narrowing 3.10.11

contracte *pp.* marked 3.57.22

contradiccion *n.* arguing 3.61.3

contrary, contrarie, contrari *adj.* against you 2.1.14; *in ~ wyse* in the opposite direction 2.1.15; on the other hand 3.11.13; *adv.* oppositely 3.59.1; *n. into the ~* against you 3.35.23; *into ~ to* the opposite 3.53.2

contrary *v.* oppose 3.54.33; contraryinge *pr. p.* contending with 3.60.2

contrarietez *n. pl.* adversities 1.12.1

contrariouse *adj.* contrary 2.3.14; adverse 3.29.13; hostile 3.53.23

contrariouste *n.* opposition 3.7.3; trouble 3.35.31; **contrarioustez** *pl.* 3.13.1

conturbacions *n. pl.* disturbances 3.42.16

conuersacion, conversacion *n.* manner of living 1.22.36; citizenship 3.18.8

conuersante, conuersant *adj.* be ~ with associate with 2.3.13; keep company with 2.8.15; *were* ~ *in* lived in 3.24.15; *be* ~ *byfore* have fellowship with 3.5.0

conversion *n.* life as a monk 1.20.27

conuerte, converte *v. refl.* turn 2.1.3; *imp. sg.* ~ *vs* make us turn 3.9.12; **converteþ** 3.6.17; **convertynge** *pr. p.* 2.4.13; **conuerted** *pp. in þe be conuerted* turned to you 3.45.8

copiouse *adj.* abundant 3.51.29

correccions *n. pl.* criticisms 3.40.10

correcte *pp.* corrected 1.16.8

correpte *pp.* reproved 3.55.24

corrupte *pp.* corrupted 1.7.7

costes *n. pl.* shores 2.11.18; *in thi* ~ within your boundaries 1.25.3

cote *n.* cottage 1.24.26

cotidiane *adj.* daily 2.12.15

coudeste *see* can

counforte *n.* comfort 1.10.5; **counfortes** *pl.* 1.21.14

counforte *v.* comfort 1.16.13; **counforteþ** *pr. 3 sg.* 2.2.9; **counforte** *pr. subj. sg.* 3.4.7; *imp. sg.* 3.53.15; **counfordedeste** *pa. t. 2 sg.* 3.62.21; **counfortynge** *pr. p.* **counforted** *pp.* 1.24.31

Counfortoure *n.* Comforter 3.6.3

counseile *v.* conceal 3.50.24; **counceyled** *pp.* 3.50.24; *see also* counseile n.

counseile *n. haue þi* ~ *with* consult 1.4.6

counseyled *pp.* counselled 1.16.4; consulted 3.12.7

couple *pr. 1 sg.* join 3.47.4

coveyte *v.* desire 3.45.12; **coveiteþ, coveyteth** *pr. 3 sg.* 3.33.9; *coveyteth ayenis* desires what is contrary to 3.39.21; **coveytinge** *vbl. n.* desire 3.37.4

covenable *adj.* suitable 1.20.4; due 3.44.1

cowches *n. pl.* beds 1.20.24

cowde *see* can

crafte *n.* skill 1.2.11; **craftes** *pl.* 3.23.2

create *pp.* created 3.27.8

creatoure *n.* creator 2.9.8

creature *n.* creation 3.43.1

credence *n.* good opinion 1.12.4

Cristen *adj.* Christian 3.11.27

crosse *n.* ~ *weye* way of the cross 2.12.33

cuntrey *n.* land 3.64.20

cure *n.* responsibility 1.11.1; care 2.5.14; *take* ~ *of* have regard to 1.20.31; take trouble about 3.36.15; *setteþ* ~ *of* 2.6.14 *see* **sette**; **cures** *pl.* business 1.11.2; worries 3.42.16

curiosites *see* curiouste

curiouse *adj.* difficult 1.5.9; recondite 1.20.2; intricate 3.59.12

curiously *adv.* in detail 1.5.9

curiouste *n.* curiosity 1.5.9; **curiosites** *n. pl.* unnecessary questions 3.53.7

custume *n. olde vsed* ~ old habit 3.13.22

darke *adj.* obscure 1.3.3; *makeþ* ~ displeases 1.8.8

darked *see* **darkeþ**

darkenes *n.* obscurity 1.3.21

darkeþ *pr. pl.* darken 3.23.10; **darked** *pp.* obscured 3.38.6

darste *pr. 2 sg.* dare 2.1.28

deceyte *n.* delusion 1.2.5; deception 3.7.19; **deceytes** *pl.* deceptions 3.59.4

deceyvours *n. pl.* deceits 3.1.12

declyne *v.* turn away 1.13.13; fall away 1.18.23; withdraw 1.20.10; turn aside 3.53.22; avoid 3.32.5. **declyneþ** *pr. 3 sg.* 1.13.13; **declyne** *pr. pl.* 1.18.23; *imp. sg.* 3.53.22

dedely *adj.* mortal 3.3.9

dedes *n. pl.* affairs 1.10.1

dedignacion *n. haue* ~ *to* disdain 3.63.44

defaute *n.* fault 1.16.13; **defautes** *pl.* failings 1.0.16; defects 1.22.11; sins 1.25.49

defendeþ *pr. pl.* keep 1.12.3

defoyle *v.* defile 1.21.8; **defoileþ** *pr. 3 sg.* 2.1.42; **defoyled** *pp.* 1.10.2

defouled, defowled *pp.* disfigured 1.7.7; defiled 3.53.7

deiecte *adj.* dejected 3.8.17

delectable *adj.* delightful 2.9.7

delectacion, delectacyoun *n.* pleasure 1.13.22; delight 1.24.34; **delectacions** *pl.* 3.13.10

delicate, delycate *adj.* fine 1.24.31; pampered 3.13.9

delyces *n. pl.* delights 1.24.24

delynge *pr. p.* giving 3.48.16

delite *v.* ~ *in refl.* enjoy 3.15.5; **deliteþ** *pr. 3 sg. impers.* pleases 3.54.11; **delite** *imp.*

sg. refl. ~ *in* rejoice in 3.13.18; delyted *pp. be delyted* have pleasure 1.24.39

demar *n.* judge 1.14.1

deme *v.* judge 1.2.4; *pr. 1 sg.* 3.48.16; demeþ *pr. 3 sg.* 1.3.9; deme *pr. pl.* 1.14.3; *pr. subj. sg.* 3.54.9; *imp. sg.* 2.5.17; demynge *pr. p.* 1.14.2; demed *pp.* 3.41.5

departe *v.* part 2.9.10; *refl.* separate 3.36.7; departe, departed *pp.* detached 2.1.41; separated 2.7.6

depresseth *pr. pl.* hold down 3.53.18

depreved, deprived *pp.* stripped 3.42.7; deprived of 3.45.15

derlynge *n.* darling 2.8.23

derogacion *n. doþe* ~ *to* disparages 3.63.20

deserve *v.* deserve comparison with 2.12.52; deserveþ *pr. 3 sg.* earns 1.25.15; is necessary 3.55.27

desiderable *adj.* desirable 2.12.26

desiderantly *adv.* eagerly *3.54.6

desirars *n. pl.* (those) who desire 2.11.2

desire *n. thou arte to me in* ~ you are my desire 3.64.7

desirouse *adj.* zealous 3.12.3

despecte *pp.* contemptible 3.6.33

despice *v.* despise 1.23.33; despiceth *pr. 3 sg.* 3.3.24; despice *imp. sg.* 3.55.28; despisinge *vbl. n. þine owne despisinge* 3.14.15 *see n.*

despisable *adj.* despised 3.24.16

despite *n.* despising 3.22.18; despites *pl.* 3.40.10; insults 3.35.34

despoyleþ *pr. 3 sg.* ~ *of* steals 3.45.14; despoyled *pp.* stripped 3.42.15

destruye *v.* destroy 3.58.15; destruyed *pa. t. pl.* 1.11.15

detraccions *n. pl.* slanders, sneers 3.5.2

dette *n.* debt 3.20.5

dewe *adj.* right 3.38.3

did *see* do

diffinicion *n.* definition 1.1.9

diffinite *adj.* determined 3.24.11

dignacyon *n.* favour 3.54.3

dignite *n.* honour 2.10.25

dilateþ *pr. 3 sg.* expands 3.10.12; dilate *imp. sg.* deepen 3.6.25; open 3.54.1; dilated *pp.* open 3.56.6

directe *pp.* ~ *to* aimed at 3.38.9

disciplines *n. pl.* teachings 3.6.7

disconuenient *adj.* inconvenient 3.54.26

discorde *pr. pl.* deviate 3.37.13

discourses *n. pl.* excursions 3.59.17

discovered *pa. t. sg.* betrayed 3.50.24

discrete *adj.* wise 3.8.10

discretely *adv.* with discretion 1.19.19; wisely 3.8.15

discusse *imp. sg.* consider 1.19.16; discussinge *pr. p.* 1.14.2

disdeigne *n. haþe* ~ is indignant 1.6.5 *see n.*

disparpled *pp.* distracted 1.3.15

dispercioun *n.* turmoil 1.20.34

displesance *n.* displeasure 3.5.8

dispose *v.* order 1.3.17; prepare 1.23.15; arrange 2.12.17, 3.44.1, 3.45.6. disposeþ, disposeth *pr. 3 sg.* 1.3.17, 1.23.15; dispose *imp. sg.* 2.12.17; disposinge *pr. p.* 3.45.6

disposicion *n.* purpose 3.24.16

dispreysed *pp.* blamed 2.6.18

disputacion *n.* discussion 3.63.2

dispute *v.* debate 1.1.7

dissolucion *n.* laxity 1.3.25

dissolute *adj.* lax 3.45.5

dissolued *pp.* released 1.12.8; destroyed 3.5.10

distance *n.* discernment 3.60.6

distente *pp.* racked 3.53.7

distraccion *n.* disquiet 3.12.9

distracte *pp.* distracted 2.1.39

distractely *adv.* distractedly 3.53.28

districcion *n.* strictness 3.10.9

diuerse, dyuerse *adj.* various 1.5.8; 3.45.8 *see* chaunged; dyverses *pl.* 3.38.4

diuersite *n.* variety 1.19.24

do *v.* do 1.14.6, 2.6.6; act 1.22.32, 3.36.22, 3.40.17; behave 1.25.33. doste *pr. 2 sg.* 1.22.32; doþe *pr. 3 sg.* 3.36.22; *doþe muche to* is a great cause of 1.10.11; done, doþe *pr. pl.* 1.14.6, 1.25.33; do *imp. sg.* let 3.26.4; *do so* work 2.2.1; did *pa. t. pl.* had 1.18.6; doinge *vbl. n.* action 1.22.23; do, done *pp.* 2.6.6; *done mercie with* had mercy on 3.11.7

doctoure *n.* teacher 3.48.16; doctours *pl.* scholars 3.64.14

doctrice *n.* teacher 3.60.25

doctryne *n.* teaching 1.0.3; doctrines *pl.* *3.20.10

doinge *see* do

dome *n.* judgement 1.3.26

done *see* do

donge *n.* dunge 1.3.35

doste *see* do

doute *n.* doubt 1.21.22; doutes *pl.* 3.43.3

doutefulle *adj.* anxious 1.25.10

doutelesse *adv.* doubtless 2.12.28

doutynge *pr. p.* wavering 1.25.7

dradde *see* dredest

draffe *n.* husks 3.15.5

drawe *v.* gain 1.5.10; turn 2.9.11; *refl.* turn 3.56.4; ~ *to refl.* advance towards 1.1.12; *pr. 1 sg.* tend 3.45.4; **drawest** *pr, 2 sg.* 3.5.10; **draweþ** *pr. 3 sg.* relates 1.3.10; attracts 1.14.5; turns 2.3.4; encourages 3.22.19; aims 3.28.6; draws away 3.59.3; tends 3.60.4; *draweþ fro* leads away from 3.45.14; *draweþ into* leads one to *3.47.12; **drawe, drawen** *pr. pl.* lead on 1.3.18; attract 3.43.1; put to use 3.43.1; *drawen to* encourage 1.20.34; draw us to 3.22.18; **drawe** *imp. sg.* ~ *not to thee* do not busy yourself with 1.21.11; **drawinge, drawynge** *pr. p.* leading 2.0.13; *drawinge to a man* involving oneself in 3.49.0; **drawen** *pp.* attracted 1.22.20; taken 1.23.36; taken for, pondered on 3.3.3; *as þinges ar drawen to him* as he draws things to himself 2.1.39; *drawen oute of* carried beyond 3.63.23

dredes *n. pl.* fears 3.41.11

dredest *pr. 2 sg.* ~ *of* are afraid of 3.41.9; **dradde** *pp.* feared 3.63.5

dredfulle *adj.* fearful 1.23.14

dresse *imp. sg.* address 1.23.47; direct 3.29.7; guide 3.62.24; **dressed** *pp.* directed 3.64.17

duely *adv.* as you ought 1.17.4

duete *n.* obligation 2.12.17

durable *adj.* lasting 3.35.5

duresse *n.* force 1.13.14

durynge *pr. p.* 3.54.34 *see* worldes

durre *n.* door 1.13.20; **durres** *pl.* 3.1.8

dwelle *v.* endure 3.11.28; **dwellynge** *ppl. adj.* abiding 2.1.18

eete *pa. t. pl.* ate 3.15.5

eya *interj.* oh *2.1.8

elacyon *n.* pride 1.0.7; **elacions** *pl.* pride 3.55.16

eligible *adj. more* ~ preferable 2.8.22

elles *adv.* else 1.15.1; *for* ~ otherwise 3.30.12

elleswhere *adv.* elsewhere 1.20.37

eloyned *pp.* far 3.26.1; separated 3.58.7

eminence *n.* excellence 3.0.30

eminent *adj.* outstanding 3.60.17

emprysoned *pp.* imprisoned 3.23.17

enclynethe *pr. 3 sg.* inclines 3.59.17

encombrance *n.* impediment 2.8.29

encombre *pr. subj. pl.* hinder 3.62.10; **encombred** *pp.* afflicted 1.25.7; hindered 3.5.9; absorbed 3.58.18

encrece *n.* improvement 1.10.11

encrece *v.* grow (spiritually) 1.11.7; **encreceþ** *pr. 3 sg.* causes to increase 1.23.11; **encrece** *imp. sg.* increase 3.25.12; **encrecinge** *vbl. n. þe encrecinge of* growth in 3.3.23

ende *pr. 3 sg.* ends 3.64.21

enforce *v. refl.* strive 1.11.11; **enforceþ** *pr. 3 sg.* 1.3.19; **enforce** *pr. pl.* 1.11.9; **enforce** *pr. subj. sg.* 1.17.8; *imp. sg.* 3.42.15; **enforcynge** *vbl. n.* 3.54.3

enfourme *v.* teach *imp. sg.* 3.6.7; **enfourmeþ** *pr. 3 sg.* 3.48.16; **enfourmynge** *pr. p.* 3.64.14; **enfourmed** *pp.* instructed 1.22.37; shaped 3.45.5

engendreþ, engendreth *pr. 3 sg.* produces 1.20.26; brings 3.22.15; **engendreþ** *pr. pl.* 3.28.10; **engendre** *pr. subj. sg.* cause 3.12.9; **engendred** *pp.* 2.10.6

enhance *v.* exalt 1.13.29; **enhaunced** *pp.* 3.61.14

enqueren *pr. pl.* ask 3.48.7; **enquered** *pp.* investigated 1.5.9; enquired 3.36.23

ensaumple *n.* example 1.18.17; **ensamples** *n. pl.* examples 1.0.18

enserche *v.* investigate 3.63.8; **enserchinge** *vbl. n.* investigation 1.3.3; **enserched** *pp.* 3.0.63

enserchoure *n.* examiner 3.48.16

enstreyted *pp.* afflicted 1.24.14

entencion *n.* object 1.14.4; aim 3.29.7

entendance *n.* attention, consideration 1.3.4

entendeþ *pr. 3 sg.* pays attention 1.2.8; **entende** *imp. sg.* aim 3.63.30

entise *pr. 3 sg.* inspires 3.6.11

entre *n.* entrance 1.13.20

entree *v.* enter 2.12.32

entrete *pr. 1 sg.* meditate on 3.53.21; *imp. sg.* 3.37.5

envyes *n. pl.* jealousies 3.63.7

envyouse *adj.* envious men 1.24.12

ere *n.* ear 1.1.19; **eres** *pl.* 3.1.3

erndes *n. pl.* business, affairs 3.0.44

erred *pa. t. sg.* strayed 3.11.4

esines *n.* ease 1.11.18

esynge *pr. p.* relieving 1.22.8

eslyoure *comp. adv.* more easily 3.21.8

estate *n.* position 3.45.7; 2.12.67 *see* pro-fite

estemed, estiemed *pp.* reputed 2.1.34; considered 2.11.26; reckoned 3.8.22

estimacion *n.* self-esteem 3.9.3; value 3.60.17

estraunger *n.* stranger 2.1.18

evagacions *n. pl.* wayward thoughts 3.27.2

euer *adj.* always 1.3.23

euery, eueri, every, eurie *pron.* every 1.2.1; each 1.10.5; all 2.7.11; every one 3.63.18

everlastinge *vbl. n.* eternity 3.53.13

everlastingnes *n.* eternity 3.29.13

evon *adj.* equal 3.11.27; straight 3.61.7; *one ~* one and the same 3.29.13

evon *n.* evening 1.20.35

evonly *adv.* equally 1.19.19; equably 2.8.34; rightly 3.60.4

evontyde *n.* evening 1.19.15

eurie *see* euery

exaudible *adj.* apt to be heard or granted 1.24.4

excede *v. ~ in worde* say too much 1.20.8

excellently *adv.* highly 3.63.1

excesse *n.* 3.7.14 *see* ravishe; ecstasy 3.36.5; excessez *pl.* 3.39.17 *see* iubil-ose; transgressions 3.51.7

exciteþ *pr. 3 sg.* inflames 3.54.2

excusacionz *n. pl.* excuses 1.24.1

execute *v.* attain 3.54.12

exempte *adj.* a free man 3.43.1

exercice *n.* spiritual exercise 1.19.10; exercices *pl.* *1.0.19

exercice *v.* exercise 1.20.23; practise 1.25.23; *~ himselfe in* meditate on 1.25.27. exerciceþ *pr. 3 sg.* 1.25.27; exercise *pr. pl.* 1.25.23; exercice *pr. subj. sg.* 1.20.23; exerciced, exercised *pp.* performed 1.19.20; experienced 3.8.11; tested 3.21.12; instructed 3.61.19

exercitacion *n.* trial 3.21.20; exercita-cions *pl.* toils 2.9.13

exercitate *pp.* exercised 2.9.30; put to the test 3.21.4

experte *pp.* experienced 2.9.17; *be ~ of* experience 1.11.8

exquisicion *n.* seeking 1.3.15; *propre ~* self-seeking 3.38.7

exute *pp.* removed 2.4.13

fables *n. pl.* gossip 3.50.25

faculte *n.* understanding 3.63.2

fader *n.* father 3.6.1; faders *pl.* 1.0.18

fail, fayle *v.* faint 3.6.28; give up 3.7.3; vanish 3.13.12; pass away 3.15.23; falter 3.24.4; be lacking 3.39.12; be deficient 3.51.19; be lacking to 3.63.36. failest *pr. 2 sg.* 3.7.3, 3.10.3; faileþ, fayleth, fayleþ *pr. 3 sg.* 3.6.22, 3.24.4, 3.51.19, 3.63.36; fayleþ *pr. pl.* 3.39.12; failinge *pr. p.* fickle 2.7.3; fayled *pp. fayled in her weye* fallen away 1.13.7

fayne *adv.* gladly 1.22.12

falle *v.* happen 1.14.7, 3.20.10; occur 2.11.7, 3.8.20; be downcast 3.35.31; be overcome 3.55.11; *~ fully to consente* give full consent 3.22.8; *~ into* turn to 3.35.23; *~ of* happen to 1.19.6; occur 3.6.35; *~ to him* falls to his lot *3.21.12; *~ vppon* fall back on 2.9.13; happen to 3.28.8. falleþ, falleth *pr. 3 sg.* 2.9.13, 2.11.7, 3.13.15, *3.21.12, 3.35.23; fallen *pr. pl.* 1.14.7; falle *pr. subj. sg.* 1.14.8, 3.22.8; fallen *pp.* 3.51.17

fame *n.* reputation 3.24.16

familyarez *n. pl.* familiar friends 3.24.13

familiarite *n.* friendship 3.28.9

fantasies *n. pl.* imaginings 3.7.12; phan-toms 3.53.23

farre *adj.* far from God 2.11.21; 2.11.18 *see n.*

farþermore *adv.* furthermore 3.23.3

fastynges *vbl. n. pl.* fasts 1.18.3

favtinge, fawtinge *vbl. n.* deficiency 3.52.13, 3.59.25

feble *adj.* weak 1.6.4

fecundite *n.* fertility 3.2.14

feders *n. pl.* feathers 3.8.9

feele, fele *v.* think 1.2.17, 1.12.2, 3.63.21; experience 1.11.16; perceive 1.15.14, 1.21.5; feel 3.25.11; find 3.44.2. feele *pr. 1 sg. refl.* 3.25.11; feele *pr. pl.* 1.11.16, 1.21.5, 3.63.21; *pr. subj. sg. þat eueri man ~ welle* that every man's opinion is good 1.9.12; *pr. subj. pl.* 1.12.2; fele *imp. sg. ~ not highe* do not be proud 1.2.13; felynge *vbl. n.* feelings 1.3.2; judgement, opinion 1.9.7; affec-tion 3.47.1; senses 3.59.28; felynges *pl.* opinions 1.9.9

feynynge *pr. p.* contriving 3.37.2; feyned *pp.* invented 3.51.11

feyre *adj.* good-looking 3.36.23

felawe *n.* companion 2.12.14; felawse *pl.* 2.11.3

fele *see* feele

felysheppe *n.* company 1.20.5

felyshipped *pp. ar* ~ have fellowship 1.10.12

fende *n.* devil 3.30.5; fendes *gen.* 1.19.17

fered *pp.* afraid 3.6.22

fereful *adj.* frightening 3.11.27

fereþ *pr. 3 sg.* frightens 3.35.13

ferme *adj.* safe 3.53.11; *adv.* firmly 3.40.4

ferme *v.* establish 1.12.5

feruent, fervente *adj.* earnest 1.0.25; keen 1.25.20

feste *n.* feast 1.19.28; festes *pl.* 1.19.27

fetred *pp.* fettered 3.23.17

fycched *pp.* ~ *in* fixed on 3.64.0

figures *n. pl.* symbols 3.5.20

filled *pp.* satisfied 1.20.40

final *adj.* ultimate 3.0.38

fynaly *adv.* at last 1.15.13

fixe *adv.* fixedly 3.40.4

flee *v.* ~ *to be* avoid being 1.20.32; fleest *pr. 2 sg. fleest to be* shrink from being 3.51.9; fleynge *vbl. n.* pursuit 2.12.54; *fleynge of* avoiding 1.14.0; fleeing from 1.13.11

fleysshe *n.* flesh 1.1.15

fleisshely, fleysly *adv.* carnal 1.6.4, 2.10.4

flyinge *ppl. adj.* fleeting 3.33.3

floure *n.* flower 2.7.11

floured *pa. t. sg.* flourished 1.18.19; *pp.* 1.22.19

floweth *pr. 3 sg.* ~ *oute to* seeps away to 3.49.7

fluctuacion *n.* wavering 1.25.10

fole *n.* fool 1.17.5

folye *n.* folly 3.45.21

folyly *adv.* foolishly 2.8.21

folyshe *adj.* foolish 3.18.8

folkes *n. pl.* nations 3.39.23

foloest *pr. 2 sg.* follow 1.24.9; folowinge, foloynge *vbl. n.* imitation 1.0.1, 1.1.0; *folowinge of* pursuing 1.18.19

folowar *n.* seeker 2.9.13

folowyngly *adv.* in consequence 1.20.47

for *prep.* because of 1.2.11; for the sake of 1.9.3; that 1.11.9; by 1.14.4; as 3.24.12; instead of 3.30.7; *conj.* because 1.21.24; ~ *I shulde* in order that I might 3.11.4; ~ *þou shuldest* in order that you might 3.14.9

forbedeþ *pr. 3 sg.* forbids 3.30.11; forbeden *pp.* 1.25.30

force *n. do* ~ *to* force 1.22.26

forgoinge *vbl. n.* loss 3.54.31

fornayce *n.* furnace 1.17.11

fortasteþ *pr. pl.* have a foretaste of 3.18.8

fortheryght *adj.* straight 3.38.9

foryete *v.* forget 1.23.25; *imp. sg.* 1.25.51; foryeton *pp.* 1.18.9

foryevenesse, foryivenesse *n.* forgiveness 1.24.5, 3.57.18

foryeveþ *pr. 3 sg.* forgives 1.24.5; foryive *imp. sg.* 3.51.28

fouchesave *pr. subj. sg.* vouchsafe 1.16.3; vouchesave *imp. sg. vouche þou save* 3.11.22; fouched save, vouched save *pp.* 3.6.1, 3.20.6

foule *adj.* disgraceful 1.25.36; shameful 2.10.5

frayle *adj.* weak 1.2.19

Fraunceis *proper n.* Francis 3.55.34

frely *adv.* for no reward 2.11.15

frende *n.* friend 1.20.27; frendes *pl.* 1.7.6

frenshippe *n.* friendship 2.0.8

freuyshe *see* fruyshe

friuoles *n. pl.* things of little value 3.27.9

fro, froo *prep.* from 1.1.2, 3.7.16

fructuouse *adj.* fruitful 1.15.4

fructuously *adv.* fruitfully 1.14.2

fruybly *adv.* joyfully 2.1.33

fruicion *n.* enjoyment 3.23.23; 3.42.12 *see* onhed

fruyshe *v.* enjoy 3.23.10; freuyshe 3.18.7

fruyshyngly *adv.* in joy 3.63.23

fulfille *v.* satisfy 1.2.9, 1.1.19; fill 1.24.14, 2.5.19, 3.4.6, 3.64.12; achieve 3.6.21; supply 3.11.22; have one's fill of 3.13.15. fulfilleþ *pr. 3 sg.* 3.6.21; fulfille, fulfylleþ *pr. pl.* 1.2.9, 3.13.15; fulfille *imp. sg.* 3.4.6; fulfilledest *pa. t. 2 sg.* 3.64.12; fulfillynge *pr. p.* 2.5.19; *vbl. n.* fulness 3.54.15; fulfilled *pp.* 1.1.19, 1.24.14

fulle *adv.* very 1.2.8; quite 3.59.1

fundement *n.* foundation 3.31.14

furste *adv.* first 1.3.17; *adj.* 1.11.17

Gabaonytes *proper n. pl.* Gibeonites 3.43.5

gapeþ *v. pr. 3 sg.* ~ *aftir* longs for 3.45.15

gate *see* gete

gedre *v. refl.* recollect 1.11.2; gather 1.19.15; acquire 1.23.42. gedreþ, gedrith *pr. 3 sg.* 1.11.2, 2.1.36; geder, gedre *imp. sg.* 1.23.42, 3.53.24; gederynge *pr. p.* 3.36.16

gentile *adj.* noble 2.10.6

geste *n.* stranger 1.23.45

gete *v.* obtain 1.9.3; geteste *pr. 2 sg.*
2.1.18; getinge, getynge *vbl. n.*
1.0.11; *for getinge* in order to obtain
3.45.9; gate *pa. t. pl.* 1.18.16; goten
pp. obtained 1.11.0; possessed 3.23.4;
acquired 3.31.11; *felycite to be goten*
obtaining happiness 3.64.15
gile *n.* guile 3.24.15
gilte, gylte *n.* guilt 2.10.16
gilty, giltie *adj.* guilty 3.51.4
glade *v.* gladden 1.24.29
gladnesse *n.* mirth 1.21.1
gloteny *n.* gluttony 1.19.17
glotenouse *adj.* gluttonous 1.24.11
gnare *n.* snare 3.44.8; gnares *pl.* 1.24.45
go, goo *v.* walk 1.1.1, 1.19.2, 3.63.46; pass
3.63.23; ~ *ayeyne* return 3.42.11; ~ *over*
walk on 3.14.12; ~ *oute of the weie* be
wrong 2.12.35. goeste *pr. 2 sg.* 2.12.35;
goith *pr. 3 sg.* 1.1.1; gone *pr. pl.*
3.42.11, 3.63.23; go, goo *pr. subj. pl.*
3.63.46; *go wee* let us go 3.61.27;
goinge, goynge *pr. p.* passing 3.6.26;
goynge bifore previous 3.63.18; *goinge
with* accompanying 3.64.20; *vbl. n.*
goynge oute departure 1.19.30; gone
pp. departed 3.25.11
gode *n.* blessing 1.13.10; good thing 3.6.9;
pleasure 3.30.4; 1.24.45 *see* stande;
godes *pl.* good 3.4.1; benefits 3.9.11;
good things 3.23.4
godly *adv.* divine 1.20.22
goinge, goynge, goith, gone *see* go
goodnesse *n.* good 1.25.12
gostely *adv.* spiritual 1.10.11
goten *see* gete
gouernaunce *n.* steering 1.13.17; control
3.0.43
greable *adj.* pleasing 3.25.2
gree *n. in* ~ graciously 2.10.26
gref *n.* sadness 3.29.10
grete adj. *not* ~ no great thing 2.3.13
grevance, grevaunce *n.* oppression
3.53.10; burden 3.54.28; hardship
3.59.25; grevaunces *pl.* difficulties
1.12.1
greve *v.* grieve 1.21.8; grevest *pr. 2 sg.*
trouble 2.12.27; greveþ *pr. 3 sg.*
oppresses 3.12.6; *pr. pl.* 3.30.3; grevynge *pr. p.* troubling 1.22.8; greved *pp.*
1.6.6
grevouse, greuouse *adj.* serious 1.2.18;
hard 1.11.19; troublesome 2.3.16

grevously *adv.* severely 1.1.15; seriously
1.13.11
grynnes *n. pl.* snares 3.7.19
ground *n. of alle þe* ~ *of* from the bottom
of 3.31.7
grounded *pp.* founded 2.10.21; rooted
3.8.22
groundelesse *adj.* unfathomable 3.15.16
groundely *adv.* from the root 1.11.15;
ultimately 3.59.27
groweth *pr. 3 sg.* ~ *of* 1.20.17 springs
from; growen *pp.* arisen 3.31.15
grucche *v.* complain 1.9.3, 1.20.34,
3.12.11, 3.41.15; ~ *ayein* complain
against you 3.13.23. gruccheþ *pr. pl.*
1.9.3; grucche *imp. sg.* 3.41.15; grucchynge *vbl. n.* 1.20.34
grucchingly *adv.* complainingly 3.20.1
gurde *imp. sg. refl.* prepare 1.19.17

habitacle *n.* dwelling 3.27.1
haboundante *adj.* rich 3.13.12
haboundantly *adv.* abundantly 1.25.27
haboundaunce *n.* abundance 1.22.9
had *see* haue
halyday *n. kepe* ~ keep yourself free 2.5.14
hangeþ *pr. 3 sg.* ~ *in* depends on 1.19.8
happeneþ *pr. 3 sg.* ~ *men to forsake*
happens that men forsake 1.19.7; happened *pa. t. sg.* *happened þee to dye*
happened that you died 1.24.40
happeth *pr. 3 sg.* happens 1.1.5
harde *adj.* hardened 3.3.5
harmes *n. pl.* hurts 1.21.5; injuries 2.12.43
hast *n. in* ~ quickly 1.19.29
haste, hath *see* haue
haunted *pp.* pursued 3.13.4
haue *v. refl.* comport 1.23.5; haste *pr. 2 sg.*
live 1.21.13; hath *pr. 3 sg.* bears 3.8.16;
haue *pr. pl.* behave 3.63.28; had *pa. t.*
pl. bore 3.40.15; hauynge *vbl. n.* com-
porting 1.11.22; *havynges and berynges*
behaviour 2.1.38; had *pp.* considered
1.7.9; directed 3.38.0
hede *see* heede
hedily *adv.* precipitately 3.44.8
hedlynge *adv.* headlong 3.52.13
heede, hiede, hede *n.* heed 2.6.20; *take* ~
to consider 1.1.17; pay attention to
3.1.4; *to take* ~ *to* for serving 1.18.9;
take ~ *þat* pay attention to the fact that
3.35.5
helde *see* holde

helefulle *adj.* ~ *ende* salvation at the end 3.5.5

helpeþ *pr. 3 sg.* ~ *noþinge to* does not at all help him to obtain 1.6.6; helpinge *ppl. adj.* helpful 1.19.14; holpen *pp.* helped 3.45.5

helthe *n.* salvation 1.2.8

hem *pron.* them 1.1.13; themselves 1.18.7; each other 3.63.21; 1.1.20 *see n.;* 1.14.7 *see* seme; her, hir their 1.1.21, 1.18.5

hemselfe *pron.* themselves 1.7.5

hengeþ *pr. 3 sg.* ~ *of* depends on 3.58.16

hennes *adv.* hence 3.7.22

her *see* hem

herby *adv.* by this 3.55.18

here *n.* hair 3.51.12

here *v* hear 1.1.5, 1.3.12, 1.4.5, 2.12.3; listen 1.5.11; hear of 1.25.20, 3.37.7; is listening 3.2.18. hereste *pr. 2 sg.* 3.37.7; hereþ, herethe *pr. 3 sg.* 1.4.5, 3.2.18; hereþ *pr. pl.* 2.12.3; here *pr. subj. sg.* 1.25.20; *imp. sg.* 1.5.11; heringe, herynge, hyringe *vbl. n.* 1.1.5; *herynge of* listening to 1.20.4; *the heringe* those who hear 3.2.15

hereto, herto *adv.* to this 3.1.8; ~ *hit longeþ* it is also part of this 1.4.5

hereþoroughe *adv.* hence 3.60.11

hertely *adv.* from the heart 1.20.24; earnestly 2.9.20

herþe 3.23.11 *see* yerthe

heuy, hevye *adj.* burdensome 1.13.5; sad 1.25.23

hevynesse, heuynesse *n.* affliction 1.13.31; anxiety 1.25.7; hevynesses *pl.* afflictions 3.40.14

hydels *n.* hiding place 3.15.18

hidde *pp.* hidden 1.1.4

hiderwarde *adv.* ~ *and thiderwarde* to and fro 1.13.17

hiede *see* heede

highe *adj.* deep 1.5.4; distinguished 1.22.7; *from* ~ from on high 1.23.37; *adv.* highly 1.2.17; 1.2.13 *see* fele

highest *adj. sup.* highest place 2.10.17; *to the highest* in full 3.54.33

highenes, highenesse, highnesse *n.* eloquence 1.5.3; high rank 3.45.21; height 3.64.16

him, hym *pron.* himself 1.6.5; someone 1.8.1; *refl.* 1.11.2; it 3.39.3; his *poss. adj.* its 1.1.9

himselfe *pron.* oneself 3.0.9, 3.0.37

hynderar *n.* hindrance 1.10.8

hindringe *vbl. n. doþe* ~ *to* disparages 3.63.20

hir *pron.* her 2.5.18; herself 3.59.3; *see* hem

hyringe *see* here

hirselfe *pron.* herself 3.36.8

his *see* him

hit *pron.* it 1.1.5; there 1.25.48

hitselfe *pron.* itself 1.3.1

holde *v.* consider 1.2.19; keep 1.3.13, 2.1.10, 2.3.17, 2.7.5; keep to 1.13.17; have 1.18.6; bear 3.58.8. holdeþ *pr. 3 sg.* 1.13.17; *pr. pl.* 2.3.17; holde *pr. subj. pl.* 1.3.13, 3.58.8; *imp. sg.* 2.1.10, 2.7.5; helde *pa. t. pl.* 1.18.6; holde, holden *pp.* considered 1.2.6; held 1.10.3; bound 2.6.27; restricted 3.6.15; possessed 3.6.26; ~ *vnder* subdued 3.59.32

hole, hoole *adj.* whole 1.11.9; entire 1.17.6; well 1.23.23; *adv.* altogether 3.63.23

holenesse *n.* health 3.60.6

holy *adv.* wholly 1.6.4

holpen *see* helpeþ

holsumly *adv.* beneficially 3.50.31

home *n. come* ~ return 1.10.4

honeste *adj.* honourable 2.10.6

honger *n.* hunger 1.24.11

hoole *see* hole

hope *v.* hope for 3.61.5

horroure *n.* dread 1.25.13; revulsion 3.7.17

houe *see* how

houndes *n. pl.* dogs 1.24.12

house *n. bere to my* ~ carry home 3.53.37

householde *n.* ~ *men* members of your household 3.24.13

howe, how, houe *interrog. adj.* what 1.18.4; how 1.18.19; *conj.* however 3.55.14

humiliacion *n.* humbling of yourself 3.23.22

ydel *adj.* free 1.3.15; useless 3.27.5; *in* ~ in vain 3.62.16

ydely *adv.* idly 1.10.9

ye, yee, yie, yghe *n.* eye 1.1.19, 1.25.22, 3.38.9, 3.43.1; yen, yenn *pl.* 1.3.5, 1.23.15

yerthe, herþe *n.* earth 1.13.2, 3.23.11

yerþely *adj.* worldly 1.3.35

ilyke *adv.* alike 3.19.9

illude *pr. subj. sg.* delude 3.35.18; illuded *pp.* 3.35.17

illuminacion, illumynacion *n.* enlightenment 3.0.27; light 3.7.25
illuminate *pp.* enlightened 1.14.11; created 3.39.15
illuminest *pr. 2 sg.* enlighten 3.2.13; illumyneþ *pr. pl.* 3.48.2; illumyne *pr. subj. sg.* 3.27.5; illumyned *pp.* 1.1.2
illuminoure *n.* enlightener 3.2.6
ymages *n. pl.* pictures 3.5.20
imagynacions *n. pl.* imaginings 3.35.17
ymagine *pr. 1 sg.* ~ *on* imagine 3.53.35; imagine *pr. pl. imagine in* imagine it to be with 3.63.28
immortalez *adj. pl.* immortal 1.23.42
imperfite *adj.* imperfect 3.6.6
imperturbable *adj.* that cannot be disturbed *3.53.11
implicamente *n.* entanglement 2.8.29
implyest *pr. 2 sg. refl.* meddle 3.28.5; implye *imp. sg.* 1.21.11; implyed *pp.* entangled 3.30.2
ympnes *n. pl.* hymns 2.9.26
importune *adj.* impatient 3.0.44; urgent 3.54.7
importunite *n.* impatience 1.13.14; over-eagerness 3.12.9
impugned *pp.* attacked 1.20.20
impute *imp. sg.* attribute 3.7.20
in *prep.* against 1.6.7; at 1.13.25; on 1.19.24; with 1.24.24; for 2.1.42; into 2.12.43; with regard to 3.0.16; within 3.1.1; to 3.24.1; by 3.35.28
incence *n.* incense 3.57.19
inclynacioun *n.* tendency 1.3.18
incline *pr. 1 sg. refl.* bow 3.55.22; inclyned *pp. is inclyned to* favours 1.9.6
incommutable *adj.* unchanging 3.3.14
incomodite *n.* bad fortune 3.6.13; incomoditees *pl.* discomforts 2.12.48
inconcussed *pp.* unshaken *3.38.4
increate *pp.* uncreated 3.39.15
indefferently *adv.* indiscriminately 3.50.28
indevoute *adj.* not devout 3.38.2
indignacion, indignacyon *n.* anger 1.7.13; *haue* ~ *of* be angry with 2.3.12; be angry about 3.35.31
indisciplinacion *n.* lack of restraint 3.12.9
indisciplynate *adj.* undisciplined 2.3.14
indulgence *n.* forgiveness 3.51.29
indurable *adj.* transient 3.27.8
inestimable *adj.* ineffable 3.3.14
infelicite *n.* unhappiness 3.23.9

infirmite *n.* weakness 1.4.2; infirmytees *pl.* 1.16.0
inflammate *pp.* burning 1.14.11
informacioun *n.* learning 3.0.13
infortunes *n. pl.* calamities 3.53.14
infounde *v.* pour down 3.23.2; *pr. subj. sg.* 3.55.7; infounded *pp.* 3.54.1
infused *pp.* poured 2.10.6
inordinate *adj.* disordered 3.13.16; without its proper place 3.43.1; rash 3.62.12
inordinatly *adv.* in a disorderly manner 1.25.23
inowe *adv.* sufficiently 1.2.12; enough 1.16.13
inquisicion *n.* searching 1.3.22; curiosity 3.63.33; ~ *of* enquiry into 3.0.28
institute *pp.* established 3.43.1
instructe *pp.* instructed 3.43.2
intencion *n.* aim 3.0.38; ~ *of* aiming at 3.30.1
intende *v.* ~ *to* aim at 3.36.6; indendeþ *pr. 3 sg.* aims at 2.4.3; intendinge *pr. p. intendinge to* set on 3.6.32
intente *adj.* ~ *to* intent upon 3.1.5
intentively *adv.* intently 1.25.27
interminable *adj.* eternal 3.61.6
into *prep.* to 2.6.8; on 3.19.5; in 3.41.15; *into one* 3.63.21 *see* one *pron.*
intrikeþ *pr. 3 sg.* entangles 2.1.42; intryked *pp.* 1.11.8
inwarde *n.* innermost part 1.11.5; ~ *of my secretes* my most hidden secretes 3.26.3; inwardes *pl.* heart 2.1.32; inner life 3.36.16; innermost parts 3.39.16; *alle myne inwardes* all that is within me 3.6.4; inwarde *adv.* inwardly 1.18.13
ipreysed *pp.* praised 3.45.17
yvel *adj.* bad 1.11.21; wicked 1.12.6; ill 1.25.45; evil 2.6.7; ~ *vse* bad habits 1.10.11; ~ *kepinge* poor guarding 1.10.11; *adv.* badly 1.12.2; *n.* evil 1.4.2; yvels *pl.* evils 1.24.2

iapes *n. pl.* trivial thoughts 3.7.14
iocunde *n.* pleasant, lovely 2.10.6
iocundite *n.* joy 3.52.13
ioye, ioy *v.* rejoice 1.15.12, 1.20.15, 3.8.22, 3.24.15, 3.63.46; ~ *of* rejoice in 1.24.32; ~ *to* rejoice in 1.25.36. ioyeth *pr. 3 sg.* 1.20.15; ioye *pr. subj. sg.* 3.8.22; *imp. pl.* 3.63.46; ioyed *pa. t. pl.* 3.24.15
ioyneþ *pr. 3 sg.* is joined *3.61.2
ioyngly *adv.* with joy 3.62.11

Iosue *proper n.* Joshua 3.43.5
iubilacion *n.* joy 2.1.43
iubilynge *pr. p.* rejoicing 3.6.28
iubilose *adj.* ~ *excessez* transports of joy 3.39.17
iuge *n.* judge 1.24.1
iugement *n.* judgement 1.0.14; iugemen-tez *pl.* 1.7.10
iustificacionz *n. pl.* statutes 3.55.16
iustifiest *pr. 2 sg.* acknowledge to be just 3.29.14

kepe *v.* guard 1.20.9; kepeþ *pr. pl. kepeþ hem in* remain submitted to 1.25.34; kepe *pr. subj. sg.* keep to 1.20.27; ~ *vnder* subdues 3.58.14; *imp. refl.* remain 1.21.1; kepte *pa. t. pl.* waged 1.18.6; desired 1.18.10; kepinge, kepynge *vbl. n.* guarding 1.10.11; guard 3.0.8; kepte *pp.* guarded 3.6.32; *yvel kepte* ill kept, i.e. little resorted to 1.20.26
kykeþ *pr. 3 sg.* ~ *ayein* kicks against him 3.14.2
kynde *adj.* grateful 2.10.23; ~ *to* thankful for 3.14.15
kynde *n.* nature 1.22.12
kyndenesse *n.* gratitude 2.0.10
knyghthode *n.* host 3.23.3; warfare 3.50.31
knowen *see* knoweþ
knower *n.* one who knows 3.24.16
knoweþ *pr. 3 sg.* knows how 2.11.25; knowen *pp. knowen men* acquaintances 1.20.30
knowleche *n.* knowledge 1.2.7; ~ *of* acquaintance with 1.8.6, acknowledging 3.0.22
knowleche *v.* acknowledge 3.22.1; ~ *him-selfe* acknowledge himself to be 2.10.15; knoweleche *imp. sg.* 1.2.13
kosse *n.* kiss 3.57.18
kunnynge, konnynge *n.* knowledge 1.2.1, 3.3.1; *adj.* knowledgeable 1.2.6
kutte *v.* cut 1.20.22; kuttynge *vbl. n.* cutting 3.13.19; kutte *pp.* 3.31.11

laborouse *adj.* laborious 1.24.15
laborously *adv.* earnestly 3.5.22; labori-ously 3.36.13
laboure *n.* toil 1.25.13; laboures *n. pl.* trouble 3.55.5
laboure *v.* work 3.17.1; 3.62.6 *see n.*

laddest *pa. t. 2 sg.* ~ *ayeine* brought back 3.11.4; ladde *pp.* led 1.10.2
lafte *pp.* left 1.15.1; omitted 1.19.10; not done 3.5.19
lakkeþ *pr. 3 sg.* is lacking 2.5.1; *him* ~ *impers.* he lacks 2.11.22; *pr. pl.* 3.22.12; lakke *pr. subj.* 3.18.14; lakkynge *vbl. n.* lack 2.0.9; lakked *pa. t. sg.* 3.62.18; *impers.* *3.20.2
langage *n.* language 1.5.3
languores *n. pl.* exhaustion 3.55.12
large *adj.* abundant 3.7.29; *more* ~ greater 3.51.28
largesse *n.* generosity 3.59.30
lasse *adj.* lesser 1.20.6; less 1.20.6
lasse *imp. sg.* lessen 3.41.15
late *adj.* a long time 1.14.11; after a long time 3.49.6
lawgheþ *pr. 3 sg.* ~ *vppon* is pleasing to 3.59.23
laxe *adj.* easy 1.25.32
Lazare *n.* Lazarus 3.38.8
leche *n.* healer 3.55.20
ledar *n.* leader 2.9.5; guide 3.61.25
leeffulle *see* lyefulle
leese *see* lese
leeve *see* leue
ley *pr. subj. sg.* ~ *oute* expose 3.64.11; leyde *pa. t. pl.* threw down 3.63.38; *pp.* laid it 3.61.24
leyne *v.* rely 2.7.11, 3.7.10; ~ *to* rely on 1.14.11, 3.51.21. leyne *pr. subj. sg.* 1.14.11, 3.12.7; *imp. sg.* 2.7.11
leyser *n. bi* ~ at length 1.4.1
lenger *comp. adv.* longer 1.12.8
lerned *pp.* instructed 1.2.14
lese, leese *v.* lose 1.20.25, 2.8.18; leseth *pr. 3 sg.* 1.21.3; *pr. pl.* 1.1.21; lese *pr. subj. sg.* 2.10.28; *imp. sg.* 1.22.21; lesinge *vbl. n.* 3.54.31
lesson 3.48.8 *see n.*
leste *adj.* smallest 2.10.24
lete *imp. sg.* ~ *meete hym* see that he is met 1.13.20
lette *n.* hindrance 3.36.15
lette *v.* hinder 1.3.16, 1.10.1, 1.21.7, 2.1.39, 2.4.4; ~ *but þat he sholde be* avoid being 3.41.6. letteþ *pr. 3 sg.* 1.3.16, *pr. pl.* 1.10.1; lettynge *ppl. adj.* 1.21.7; lette *pp.* 2.1.39
lettred *pp.* learned 3.36.12
lettur *n.* learning 1.5.5
leuke *see* lewke

leue, leeve, lyeve, *v.* believe 1.4.5, 2.3.3,
3.50.18; trust 2.5.1. leveþ *pr. 3 sg.* 2.3.3

leve *v.* leave alone 1.21.10; leveþ *pr. 3 sg.*
neglects 2.3.6

lever *adv.* rather 3.7.23

lewke, leuke *adj.* luke warm 1.11.7,
3.15.13

licence, lycence *n.* presumption 1.16.9;
leave 3.53.38

lyefulle, leeffulle *adj.* allowable 1.10.10,
1.20.33

lyfte *adj.* left 2.9.36

lyfte *v.* ~ *hymselfe on highe* exalt himself
1.1.14; lifte *imp. sg. lifte not vppe
thiselfe of* do not take pride in 1.7.7;
lyfte *pp.* ~ *vppe* elated 1.2.11; lifted
2.4.1

lyght, light *adj.* easy 1.11.20; little 1.19.7;
thoughtless 3.6.32; light-hearted 3.38.2;
lyghter *comp.* easier 1.20.8

lyghtenes *n.* levity 1.21.5

lyghter *see* lyght

lyghtly, lyȝtly *adv.* readily 1.4.3; easily
1.6.4; lightly 1.19.11; lightlyer *comp.*
more easily 3.22.9

lyghton *imp. sg.* ~ *oute thi shynynge* make
your lightning flash out 3.53.23

lyke, like, lyche *adv.* alike 1.19.19; likely
3.19.5; in common 3.36.5; similar
3.54.25; ~ *moche* the same amount
1.25.16

lyketh *pr. 3 sg. impers. hem* ~ they like
3.23.18

lykinge *vbl. n.* pleasure 3.35.27

litel, lytel *adj.* insignificant 3.14.12; ~ *and*
~ gradually 1.13.14; *in a* ~ in small
things 1.24.35

lyþe, lythe *pr. 3 sg.* lies 1.14.3; is sub-
merged 3.49.7

lyve, lyue, lyffe *v.* live 1.2.10, 1.3.24,
1.18.17, 1.23.18; exist 3.14.12; ~ *to*
serve 1.20.5. lyue *pr. subj. sg.* 1.2.10;
lyve *imp. sg.* 1.23.18; lyvinge *vbl. n.*
way of life 1.2.2; *lyvinge togydres* company 3.47.1

lyve *n.* life 1.0.25; lyves *gen.* 1.17.2; *pl.*
1.3.29

longanimite *n.* perseverance 1.13.14

longe *adj.* long-standing 3.29.14; ~ *hope*
patience 3.35.10

longe-abidynge *ppl. adj.* long-suffering
3.6.30

longeþ *pr. 3 sg.* belongs 2.2.6; *pr. pl.*

pertain 1.8.4; 1.4.5 see hereto; longynge *pr. p.* pertaining 3.30.8

lookynge *vbl. n.* look *1.24.2

lordeshipe *n.* mastery 3.22.11

lose *adj.* loosed 1.22.12

lothe *adj.* unpleasant 3.39.6

loþeþ *pr. 3 sg.* hates 3.59.12; loþinge *vbl.
n.* hatred 3.62.12

loved *n.* beloved 3.7.7

lovely *adj.* beloved 3.55.10

lover *n. the* ~ the one who loves 2.6.9

lowest *sup. adj. at the* ~ in the lowest place
2.10.17

lucre *n.* gain, advantage 2.7.13

made *pp. were* ~ became *1.13.7

mageste *n.* majesty 3.64.18

magre *prep.* ~ *me* in spite of myself
3.53.19

maie *v.* will be able to 1.2.18; is able to
1.3.10; can 1.10.1, 1.11.5, 3.4.7; can do
3.4.5, 3.41.12. maie *pr. 1 sg.* 3.4.7;
maiste, mayste *pr. 2 sg.* 1.2.18,
1.10.1, 3.4.5; may *pr. 3 sg.* 1.3.10,
3.41.12; myght *pa. t. pl.* 1.11.5

maister *n.* master 2.8.5; maistres *n. pl.*
masters 1.3.27

maistres *n.* mistress 3.60.25; *see also*
maister

malice *n.* evil 3.35.15

makeste *pr. 2 sg.* ~ *stronge* give strength
3.2.12; makeþ *pr. pl.* produce 3.50.29;
makynge *pr. p. makynge boste* those
who boast 3.41.7

man *n. a man* for a man 1.1.12; mannes
gen. 1.0.4; human 1.0.22; *mannes self*
oneself 1.0.2

maner *n.* degree 1.3.21; form 1.19.7; way
2.2.5; kind of 1.25.39; kind 2.12.37; *in* ~
to an extent 1.6.4; *as yn a* ~ *of* as 2.1.20;
maners *pl.* ways 1.1.2; behaviour 1.8.9;
ways 1.19.7; conduct 1.19.16; *alle* ~ see
alle; ~ *of wyse* see wyse

manyfolde *adv.* so ~ in so many different
ways 3.21.4

manly *adj.* strong 3.62.5; *adv.* manfully
1.21.9

mannes *see* man

margarite *n.* pearl 3.37.13

Marie *proper n.* Mary 3.38.8

marmayden *n.* siren 3.32.6

matier *n.* matter 1.9.12; ~ *of* cause for
1.21.18; *matier of brennynge* fuel for the

fire 1.24.9; **matiers** *n. pl.* works 1.20.3;
business 1.21.11; causes 1.21.21
Maudeleyne *proper n.* Magdalen 2.8.5
me *pron. refl.* 1.10.3; myself 3.25.11
me *impers. pron.* men 2.12.6
medeleþ *pr. 3 sg.* meddles 1.11.2; **medled**
pp. mixed 2.11.12; imparted 3.0.58;
medled with imparted to 3.58.0
mediocrite *n.* moderation 1.22.9
medled *see* medeleþ
meede, mede *n.* reward 1.25.3, 3.59.22
meete 1.13.20 *see* lete
meeue *see* meve
meke *v.* humble 1.13.29; **mekeþ** *pr. 3 sg.*
2.2.8; **meke** *pr. subj. sg.* 3.63.43; **meked**
pp. 1.13.5; **mekinge** *vbl. n.* 2.2.9 *see n.*
mene *pr. pl.* intend 3.36.16
mengled *pp.* mingled 3.58.1
mercie, merci *n.* 3.11.7 *see* do; *haue ~ on
me oute of* deliver me from 3.22.6
merite *n. tyme of ~* time to win merit
1.22.24; **merites** *pl.* deserving 3.55.3
meritory, merytory *n.* meritorious
3.0.30; *fulle ~* full of merit 3.20.5
merveyles *n. pl.* marvels 3.48.12
meselfe *pron.* myself 3.9.3
mesure *n.* extent 3.8.7; *in ~* in full measure 1.21.26
mesure *v.* govern 3.8.18
meve *v.* ask 1.3.25; trouble 2.5.11; move
3.23.11; stir up 3.39.21; suggest 3.54.36.
meveth *pr. 3 sg.* 3.39.21; **meeue** *pr.
subj. sg.* 3.54.36; **meve** *imp. sg. ~ thi
cause to* discuss your situation with
1.8.1; **meved** *pp.* disturbed 1.14.8;
troubled 2.3.5; moved with passion
2.5.4; moved 2.9.18; **meving,
mevinge, mevynge** *vbl. n.* impulse
1.13.22; moving 3.39.22; inclination
3.60.4; feeling 3.62.13; **mevinges** *pl.*
workings 3.0.59; passions 3.7.11
myght *n. ~ and power* powerful men
3.59.23; **myghttes** *n. pl.* powers 3.10.12
myght *v. see* maie
myghty, myghtty, myghtti *adj.* strong
1.7.6; able 1.25.17; powerful 3.27.2,
3.64.16; *~ to* able to do 2.8.32; **myght-
tier** *comp.* stronger 2.11.30
mightily *adv.* bravely 3.273
mylde *adj.* gentle 2.3.13
myldely *adv.* meekly 3.51.27
mynde *n.* recollection 3.7.16; *haue ~ of,
haue ~ on* remember 1.1.19, 1.25.25;

haue ~ remember 3.4.4; *haste ~ on* are
mindful of 3.45.1
myne *demons. adj. alle ~* all that is mine
3.55.24
minister *v.* supply 3.27.6
ministerie *n.* service 3.11.15
myre *n.* mud 3.14.12
mirye *adj.* pleasant 1.25.23
myrily *adv.* pleasantly 2.9.4
myrþe, myrthe *n.* joy 1.21.6; pleasure
3.39.11
mischieves, myschieves *n. pl.* misfor-
tunes 3.22.14; wickednesses 3.43.3
miseracions *n. pl.* mercies 3.4.6
myslyving *vbl. n.* living badly 3.9.9
mitigacion *n.* alleviation, rest 3.3.4
mo *see* moo
moche *adv.* 1.25.16 *see* lyke
modered *pp.* controlled 3.0.12
modulacion *n.* song 3.55.7
Moyses *proper n.* Moses 3.2.4
monchynes *n. pl.* nuns 1.25.35
moo, mo *adj.* more 1.2.12, 1.3.14
moorne *v.* mourn 3.64.7; *pr. 1 sg.* 3.23.9;
morneþ *pr. 3 sg.* 1.12.7; **moorneþ** *pr.
pl.* 3.62.19; **morne** *imp. sg.* 3.52.8;
moornynge *vbl. n.* 1.24.4; **moorninges** *pl.* 1.23.47
more *adj.* greater 1.22.15; *adv.* rather 1.1.9
morne, morneþ *see* moorne
morowetide *n.* dawn 3.55.12
mortifiynge *vbl. n.* mortification 2.12.15
moste *adj.* greatest 1.13.30
mote, motte *pr. subj. sg.* may 3.5.4, 3.6.29
mowe *v.* may 1.11.18, 3.64.14 *see n.; pr. 1
sg.* 3.18.1; *pr. 2 sg.* 1.24.36; *pr. 3 sg.*
1.20.29; *pr. pl.* 1.13.1; can 1.13.12; *pr.
subj. sg.* may 1.3.35; *pr. subj. pl.* 1.11.12
muche *adj. ~ þinge* many things 3.12.1
multitude *n.* abundance 1.6.2

naye *interj.* no 3.9.2
naked *pp.* detached 2.11.16
name *n.* reputation 3.28.9; *~ of* reputation
for 1.5.10
namely *adv.* especially 1.10.12
naturely *adv.* naturally 1.2.1
ne *conj.* or 3.28.1
necessaries *n. pl.* necessities 1.22.16
necessitez *n. pl.* needs 1.25.40
necglygence *n.* neglect 1.21.5; **necglygences** *pl.* sins of omission 1.20.42
nede *n.* poverty 1.21.25

neded *pa. t. subj. impers. hym* ~ he needed 1.12.5

nedefulle *adj.* necessary 1.9.7

nedes *adv.* of necessity 2.6.15

neyghe *v.* draw near 1.20.30; neyheþ *pr. 3 sg.* 3.47.6

ner, nere *conj.* nor 1.1.19; or 1.3.9; and not 1.19.19; ~ . . . *not* nor 1.15.12

nere *adv.* not 1.3.28

nere *comp. adj.* nearer 3.63.37

nerþelater *adv.* nevertheless 1.10.12

neþer *adv.* neither 1.22.3

newe *adv.* anew 3.56.4

nexte *adj.* nearest 3.35.21

nyce *adj.* strange 2.1.38

nyghe *adj.* near 1.7.4

nyghtes *adv.* at night 1.18.7

nys *pr. 3 sg.* ~ *not* is not 3.39.20

nobleyed *pp.* endowed 3.60.16

noblesse *n.* excellence 3.9.11

noght, nought, noȝt *n.* nothing 1.2.7, 1.3.4; *adv.* 1.15.3

noghty *v.* bring to nothing 3.47.9

noghttynesse *n.* nothingness 3.9.3

noye *v.* harm 1.7.12; noyeþ *pr. 3 sg.* 2.7.16; noyed *pp.* 3.50.30

noyce *n.* noise 1.20.24; sound 3.0.2

noyouse *adj.* harmful 1.19.11

none *n.* nothing 1.22.8; *adj.* no 1.1.16

noryshen *pr. pl.* encourage 3.63.7

noryshinges *n. pl.* sustenance 3.30.9

norþen *adj.* northern 3.27.4

not *pr. 1 sg.* do not know 3.36.16

noþer *see* nouþer

nought *see* noght

noumbre *n.* number 1.18.17

nouþer, noþer *adv.* neither 2.3.16, 2.6.16

nowyse *adv.* not at all 1.9.12

o *num.* one *1.23.29

obiectes *n. pl.* problems 3.62.8

oblocucions *n. pl.* insults 3.40.10

obserue *v.* watch for 3.28.11

obstacles *n. pl.* obstructions to progress 3.30.2

occasion, occacion *n.* occurrence 1.16.14; opportunity 3.31.15; occasions *pl.* opportunities 1.11.2; events 1.16.15

of *prep.* concerning 1.0.1; out of 1.0.15; because of 1.1.5; after 1.3.22; for 1.3.32; by 1.4.6; with 1.11.2; from 1.15.5; in 1.18.12; about 2.5.9; ~ *and þorowe* by means of 3.10.2

offendinge *vbl. n.* scandal 3.41.8

ofire *see* afire

ofte *adj.* frequent, repeated 1.1.5; *adv.* often 1.7.13; ofter *comp. adv.* more often 1.21.22

oftely *adv.* often *1.25.19

ofter *see* ofte

oftetymes, oftetyme *adv.* often 1.1.19, 1.14.2

oynement *n.* ointment 3.57.20

on *prep.* about 2.1.28; of 3.8.16

one *pron.* one thing 2.11.23; *many* ~ many 1.9.5; *alle* ~ all alike 3.63.21; *into* ~ as one 3.63.21; *indef. art.* an 3.52.5; a 3.52.9

one *v.* join 3.11.11; onethe *pr. 3 sg.* is united 3.61.2; oned *pp.* joined 2.8.31; *oned to* united with 1.3.14

onehede *see* onhed

ones *adv.* once 1.3.28

onhed, onehede *n.* single purpose 1.21.7; union 2.5.13; ~ *of fruicion* joyous union *3.42.12

open *adj.* in ~ *places* in public 3.59.18

openeste *pr. 2 sg.* reveal 3.2.9; openeþ *pr. 3 sg.* 1.13.19, 1.21.3

openly *adv.* plainly 2.6.25

opinate *adj.* imagined 3.51.29

oportune *adj.* 3.64.8 *see n.*

opteyne *pr. subj. sg.* obtain 1.6.6

or *conj.* before 1.14.11

ordeyne, ordeigne *imp. sg.* order 2.12.17; order things 3.13.2

ordynance *n.* ordering 3.44.2

ordinate *adj.* ordered 2.1.38; controlled 3.31.4

ordre *n.* ordering 3.32.4

oþer, other *pron.* others 1.8.9; anything else 2.12.35; other . . . oþer some . . . others 1.19.25

oþerweyes, oþerwyse *adv.* otherwise 1.14.10; oþerweyes . . . oþerwyse of one kind . . . of another kind 1.7.10

otherwhiles *adv.* sometimes 1.20.47

oureselfe *pron.* ourselves 1.11.8

oute *adv.* ~ *of the weye* absent 1.15.9; ~ *of trewe bileve* without true faith 1.22.17; ~ *of quiete* ill at ease 2.6.4; ~ *of the weie* wrong 2.12.35; ~ *of* without 3.9.8; apart from 3.29.7; *þat wolde* ~ that demanded expression 3.61.13

outetake *pr. 1 sg.* make an exception of 3.42.6

outwarde, outewarde *adv.* outwardly

1.3.17; outside his sphere 1.11.2; outside
1.20.11; *as* ~ outwardly 3.55.11
ouþer *adv.* either 1.19.18
ouþerwhiles *adv.* sometimes 2.12.19
over *prep.* beyond 3.11.15
oueralle *adv.* everywhere 2.12.23
over-casuely *adv.* too precariously 3.19.5
ouer-desperatly *adv.* with too great
despondency 3.8.16
overgo *v.* cover 3.42.14
ouer-grete *adj.* excessive 1.0.8
over-heped *adj.* overflowing 3.35.6
over-inordinatly *adv.* excessively 3.18.5
overpasse *v.* pass beyond 3.23.5
over-radde *pp.* read through 2.12.70
over-sory *adj.* too sad 2.8.20
over-sure *adj.* too self-confident 3.8.17
overthwarte *adj.* hostile 2.3.14; perverse
3.21.12
overthwartnes *n.* hostility 2.2.3
over-towghly *adv.* too firmly 3.8.2
owe *pr. 1 sg.* ought 3.10.1; owest *pr. 2 sg.*
1.2.18; oweþ *pr. 3 sg.* 1.5.2; *pr. pl.* 1.5.3;
owed *pa. t. sg.* 1.12.5; owedest *pa. t. 2
sg.* 3.29.14; owed *pa. t. pl.* 1.11.17

paynes *n. pl.* punishments 1.0.24
paleys *n.* palace 1.24.26
palle *n.* garment 3.54.34
parabolez *pl.* wise sayings, admonitions
1.5.11
paradice *n.* paradise 2.12.53
partie *n.* part 1.25.53
passe *v.* surpass 1.1.4, *2.10.4, 3.39.16;
avoid 2.12.29; pass through 3.6.22;
press on through 3.40.5. passeþ, passeth *pr. 3 sg.* 1.1.4, 3.6.22; passeþ *pr. pl.*
*2.10.4; passinge *pr. p.* 3.39.16
passingly *adv.* exceedingly 3.2.8
passionate *adj.* easily angered 2.3.3
passions *n. pl.* sufferings 3.56.7
pees *n.* peace 1.0.11
peynest *pr. 2 sg.* afflict 3.55.18; peynynge
pr. p. 3.35.33; peyned *pp.* 2.12.37
peyse *v.* consider 1.4.1, 3.8.1, 3.8.7,
3.54.28; weigh 1.13.27, 1.24.30,
3.29.13; pay attention to 1.15.5; judge
1.16.11; value 2.1.35; heed 3.33.3; ~ *litel*
consider as little 3.13.10. peiseþ,
peyseþ *pr. 3 sg.* 1.13.27, 1.15.5; peise,
peyse *pr. pl.* 1.16.11, 3.13.10; peyse
imp. sg. 3.54.28; peysinge *pr. p.* 3.8.7,
3.29.13; peysed *pp.* 1.4.1

penaly *adv.* as a punishment 3.30.3
peny *n.* penny 3.3.13
perauenture *adv.* perhaps 1.7.9
perceþ *pr. 3 sg.* penetrates 2.4.9; perseþ
pr. pl. enter into 3.1.6; persinge *pr. p.*
piercing 3.39.16
perdicion *n.* loss 3.7.15
perfite *adj.* perfect 1.4.3
perfitely *adv.* perfectly 1.6.3
perseverable *adj.* enduring 2.7.3
perseverante *adj.* persevering 3.50.10
perseuerantly *adv.* perseveringly 3.35.9
perseuere *v.* persevere in grace 1.25.7
persuasion *n. make* ~ *to* urge 3.37.10
pese *v.* bring peace to 2.2.8, 2.3.1; ~ *my
soule* let my soul find peace 3.17.6.
peseþ *pr. 3 sg.* 2.2.8; pesed *pp.* at
peace 3.24.16
pesible *adj.* peaceful 1.11.14
pesibly *adv.* peacefully 1.3.10
Petre *proper n.* Peter 3.58.8
pycche *n.* pitch 1.24.12
piere *n.* equal 3.21.12
pite, pitee *n.* piety 1.19.10; 3.43.5 *see n.*
plenarly *adv.* fully *1.1.6, 3.18.3; com-
pletely 3.58.18
plentuouse *adj.* abundant 3.13.19
plentuously *adv.* abundantly 3.24.9
plesance, plesaunce *n.* pleasure 2.1.6; *at
þi* ~ to your liking 1.16.6
plesant *adj.* acceptable 3.1.14; ~ *before me*
pleasing in my sight 3.5.7
plesaunce *see* plesance
pleseþ *pr. 3 sg.* is pleasing 1.19.24; plese
imp. sg. plese not þiself of do not take
pleasure in your 1.7.8
pleyneþ *pr. 3 sg.* complains, pleads 3.6.20
poerly *adv.* poorly 1.25.34
poynte *n.* moment 3.48.9
pondre *v.* consider 2.5.7; think 2.11.26
porte *n.* ~ *salutz* haven of salvation
3.62.22
possibilite *n. aftir þe* ~ *of* as far as possible
for 3.29.15
pouer *adj.* poor 1.7.2; poor men 3.63.46
Poule *proper n.* Paul 1.13.28
poureþ *pr. 3 sg.* devotes 2.1.36; poured *pp.*
poured one drenched 1.24.12
power *n. of power* able 2.9.16
prebende *n.* stipendiary ecclesiastical
appointment 3.3.12; prebendes *pl.*
1.3.28
preceptes *n.* commandments 3.24.1

preched *pp.* proclaimed 3.59.30

predestinate *pa. t. sg.* predestinated 3.63.12; *pp.* 3.63.18

prees *see* prese

preferre *v.* ~ *þiselfe bifore* believe yourself to be superior to 1.2.14

prelacye *n.* authority 1.9.2

prelate *n.* superior 1.9.1

prentes *n.* prints 2.1.25

prerogative *n.* privilege 3.30.1

prese, prees *n.* company 1.10.1; crowd 1.20.10

present *adj. ar* ~ exist 1.20.41

pressed *pp.* oppressed 3.27.7

pressure *n.* oppression 3.60.25

preste *n.* priest 2.9.7

presume *pr. 1 sg.* dare presume 3.15.4; presumeþ *pr. 3 sg. ner presumeþ noþinge* and is not at all presumptious 3.59.27; *pr. pl. presumeþ of hemselfe* are overconfident in their own ability 1.7.5; presume *imp. sg.* be presumptious 2.9.15; presumed *pa. t. sg.* expected 3.50.3; *pa. t. pl.* dared to aspire to 3.8.8; presumynge *pr. p. presumynge of hemselfe* who are over-confident in their own strength 3.7.31

pretende *v.* plead 3.45.3; pretendeste *pr. 2 sg.* intend 3.64.10; pretendeþ *pr. pl.* pretend to 3.59.2; pretendinge *pr. p.* putting forward 3.59.4

prevar *n.* vindicator 3.3.19

preve *v.* test 1.13.18, 2.9.24, 1.13.30, 1.17.11, 3.51.18; prove 1.24.36, 3.40.11; prove to be 2.11.14; approve 2.6.26, 3.16.3; declare 3.60.7. prevest *pr. 2 sg.* 2.9.24; preveth *pr. 3 sg.* 1.13.18; preven *pr. pl.* 3.40.11; preve *pr. subj.* 3.16.3; *imp. sg.* 1.24.36; previnge *pr. p.* 3.60.7; prevynge *vbl. n.* testing 1.16.2; previnges *pl.* 3.64.12; preved *pp.* 1.13.30, 1.17.11, 2.6.26, 2.11.14

prevented *pa. t. sg.* go before *3.63.11; prevente *p.p.* guided 2.8.31

previde *v.* provide 1.24.3; previded *pp.* 3.50.16

previnge, prevynge, previnges *see* preve

price, pryce *n.* value 1.6.3; worth 2.8.3; 2.9.1 *see* sette; 2.10.25 *see* vile

prykkes *n. pl.* goads 1.24.11

principal *n.* beginning 3.48.4

pryncipally *adv.* especially 1.13.20

private *adj.* ~ *fro* free from 3.58.7

pryve *adj.* private 1.20.24

pryve *v.* deprive of 3.31.6

prively, pryvely *adv.* secretly 1.14.6; quietly 1.20.9

privytees, privitez *n. pl.* hidden things 1.20.28; secrets, mysteries 3.1.6

probacion *n.* testing 3.18.14

proceden *pr. pl.* come 1.15.13

procutoure *n.* supplier 2.1.12

profitable *adj.* useful 2.1.14; *to noþinge* ~ useful for nothing 3.54.23

profite *v.* progress 1.25.17; *sumwhat* ~ *into better* make some improvement 1.3.20; profitynge, profytynge, prophitinge *vbl. n.* progress 1.10.11, 1.22.37; *zele of profytynge* zeal to make progress 1.0.11; *profitynge of* (desire for) progress in 1.18.24; *to profitynge* to make (spiritual) progress 1.25.3; *profitynge of oure estate* spiritual progress 2.12.67

profitablenes *n.* spiritual benefit 1.5.3

prolonge *imp. sg.* postpone 3.4.8

promesse *n.* promise 3.3.17

promission *n.* promise 3.23.2

promitte *pr. 1 sg.* promise 3.3.9; promittest *pr. 2 sg.* 3.23.4; promitteþ *pr. 3 sg.* 3.3.8; promitte *imp. sg.* 1.20.18; promitted *pp.* 2.9.31

promoter *n.* prompter 3.48.16

pronounce *v.* confess 2.11.26

propre *adj.* personal 1.15.11; appropriate 1.24.13; of oneself 2.0.5; own 2.7.8; one's own 3.0.22; distinctive 3.59.31; ~ *witte* his own desire 1.3.15; ~ *love* self-love 1.14.3; ~ *wille* self-will 1.15.9; ~ *truste* over-confidence in oneself 2.10.8; ~ *profite* desire for personal gain 2.11.12; ~ *resignacion* resignation of oneself 3.16.8; ~ *complacence* complacency with yourself 3.37.11; ~ *exquisicion* self-seeking 3.38.7; *her owne* ~ their own self-interest 3.42.11; ~ *exaltacion* self-exaltation 3.63.8

proprete *n.* selfish concern 3.42.2

proprietaries *n. pl.* lovers of property 3.37.2

providence *n.* 3.33.4 *see n.*

provideþ *pr. 3 sg.* looks forward 1.23.4

provisoure *n.* provider 2.1.12

prouoke *v.* stimulate 1.18.17; provoked *pp.* spurred on 3.37.7

prudence *n.* wisdom 1.0.4

prudente *adj.* wise 1.3.35
prudently *adv.* wisely 3.32.5
puple *n.* people 1.8.2
pure *adj.* clean 1.2.9; whole 3.42.0
purely *adv.* solely 1.17.7; wholly 3.37.8
purgacion *n.* purging 3.0.32
purged *pp.* purified 1.11.14
purpose *v.* intend 1.3.17, 3.22.3; resolve 1.19.6, 1.19.13, 1.22.32; propose 1.19.9, 1.19.16; make resolutions 1.19.28. purpose *pr. 1 sg.* 3.22.3; purposeste *pr. 2 sg.* 1.22.32; purposeþ, purposeth *pr. 3 sg.* 1.3.17, 1.19.6, 1.19.9; purpose *imp. sg.* 1.19.16; purposed *pp.* 1.19.13
put *v.* ~ *to* exert 1.11.18; stretch out 3.45.8; putteste *pr. 2 sg.* do 1.25.52; putteþ *pr. 3 sg. putteþ bihynde* sets aside 1.24.45; *putteþ inne* suggests 3.7.17; *putteþ thinges vppon me* accuses me of things 3.21.9; *pr. pl. putteþ aweye* take away 3.63.26; putte *pr. subj. sg.* put out 3.23.15; *putte aweye* throw away 2.12.28; *putte oute* remove 3.19.16; putte *imp. sg. putte þe to* prepare yourself for 2.10.2; set yourself for 2.12.47; *putte byhynde* put aside 3.37.11; *putte forthe* expose to danger 3.40.17; puttinge *pr. p. puttinge into* afflicting 3.55.19; *vbl. n. puttinge ayeine* constructing 3.37.2; put, putte *pp.* set 3.0.64; *putte vnder* subdued 3.58.17

queke *adj.* vivid 1.18.1; living 3.6.22
quemed *pp.* appeased 1.24.1
querelle *n.* quarrel 1.17.2
queres *n. pl.* choirs 3.53.38
quiete *n.* peace 1.9.4; rest 1.19.25; *oute of ~* uneasy 2.6.4
quiete *v.* give rest to 3.27.8
quyken *v.* enliven 3.39.17

radde *pa. t. pl.* read 1.3.31; *pp.* 1.5.2
rare *adv.* seldom founde 1.8.2
raþer, rather *adj.* earlier 1.18.23; *þe ~* the former 3.7.29
ravishe *v.* carry away 3.27.8; transport 3.36.8; ravished, ravyshed *pp.* enraptured 2.9.29; caught up 2.12.56; *ravyshed in an excesse* caught up in ecstasy 3.7.14
reaume, rewme *n.* kingdom 1.1.12, 1.22.16; kingdom of heaven 2.12.6
rebukes *n. pl.* reproaches 3.24.15

rebukeþ *pr. 3 sg.* beats back 3.22.7
recche *v.* care 2.6.20; ~ *of* care about 3.5.3; reccheþ *pr. pl.* 1.3.32; recching *pr. p.* 3.36.0
receyve *v.* accept 2.3.9; receyveþ *pr. 3 sg.* 1.24.1
rechesses *see* rychesses
recolleccion *n.* concentration 3.36.17
reconsiled *pp.* reconciled 3.57.18
recordacion *n.* recollection 3.24.0
recordynge *vbl. n.* remembering 3.0.24
recovered *pp.* resumed 1.19.10
recoveringe *vbl. n.* ~ *of* regaining 3.0.35
redemptoure *n.* redeemer 3.7.27
redy, redye *adj.* prone 1.4.3; at hand 1.15.9; easy 1.24.42; ~ *to* ready to do 1.19.21
reduce *v.* bring back 2.3.17; reduceþ *pr. 3 sg.* refers 3.59.27; reduced *pp.* returned 3.10.5
refeccion *n.* refreshment 1.18.9; refeccions *pl.* food 1.25.40
referreþ *pr. 3 sg.* ascribes 1.15.13; refere *pr. pl.* 3.39.14; referre *imp. sg.* 3.10.4; referred *pp.* 3.10.0
reflecteþ *pr. 3 sg.* turns 3.59.26
refounde *pr. pl.* return 2.10.10
refrayne *imp. sg.* curb 1.19.17; refreyned *pp.* disciplined 3.13.23
refreysshest *pr. 2 sg.* refresh *3.6.2; refreyssheþ *pr. 3 sg.* sets at rest 1.2.9; refreysshe *pr. subj. sg.* 3.23.17; refresshinge *vbl. n.* refreshment 1.22.25
refrenacion *n.* restraint 3.12.9
refute *n.* refuge 3.6.5
reherce *v.* repeat 3.39.5; reherced *pr. sg.* told 2.9.19
reynes *n. pl. þe hertes and þe ~* minds and hearts 3.51.24
reioyce, reioice *v. refl.* exult 3.0.45; ~ *hitselfe ayenis* boast against 3.15.20; reioyse *imp. sg.* 1.7.6; reioyced *pp.* pleased 3.35.16
rekkeþ *pr. 3 sg. impers. what ~ me* what do I care about 3.62.22
relesse *v.* let slacken 3.30.1
relevinge *vbl. n.* ~ *of* relief from 3.43.3
relicte *pp.* let alone 3.60.4
religion, relygion *n.* monasticism 1.18.18; *þe profitynge of ~* progress in the spiritual life 1.11.13; *man of ~* monk 1.20.32
religiouse, relygiouse *adj.* monastic 1.17.0; under vows 1.17.5; pious

2.9.28; *n.* monks 1.18.4; monk 1.25.30; monastic orders 1.25.35

religiously *adv.* piously, devoutly, reverently 1.3.26

remenante *n.* rest 3.35.27

remisse *adj.* free of restraint 1.25.32

renne *v.* run in 1.24.45; **renneþ, renneth** *pr. 3 sg.* runs 3.3.12, 3.6.15; **renne** *pr. subj. sg.* 2.12.24; *imp. sg.* *1.9.4; **rennynge** *vbl. n.* 3.59.17; **reonnen** *pp.* 2.5.12

repayred *pp.* restored 3.57.18

repente *pr. subj. impers. þee* ~ it cause you to repent 3.12.7

reprehensions *n. pl.* criticisms 3.20.3

reprevars *n. pl. þi* ~ those who find fault with you 3.14.14

repreve *n.* insult 2.1.32; shame 2.11.6; **repreves** *pl.* insults 1.18.3

repreve *v.* rebuke 3.57.13; *pr. pl.* 2.2.7; **repreving** *vbl. n.* 3.51.27; **reprevinges** *pl.* insults 2.2.11; **repreved** *pp.* corrupted 1.13.7; blamed 3.22.17

reputacion *n. had in* ~ held in high regard 3.45.12

require *v.* seek 3.55.17

rere *v.* lift 3.15.22; *pr. 1 sg.* raise 3.62.19; **rered** *pp.* 1.23.46

reserve *v.* keep 1.24.6; leave 2.2.5; **reserveste** *pr. 2 sg.* 1.24.9

resigneþ *pr. pl.* resign themselves 3.42.9; **resigne** *pr. subj. sg.* resign yourself 3.37.9; *imp. sg. resigne vppe* give up 3.42.13

resons *n. pl.* reasonings 3.48.9

resteful *adj.* at rest 3.36.4

resteþ *pr. 3 sg.* ~ *in* is content 3.7.8; remains 3.49.7; **reste** *pr. pl.* enjoy 3.13.13

restreyned *pp.* bound 1.16.10

resume *imp. sg.* take on 3.7.29

reteygne *imp. sg.* keep 2.11.24; **reteyned** *pp.* held back 3.6.12

revoke *v.* recall 1.24.44; keep 3.7.17

rewle *n.* rule 1.18.19

rewle *v.* govern 3.8.18

rewme *see* reaume

rychesses, rechesses *n. pl.* riches 1.1.13, 1.7.6

right, ryght *adj.* upright 3.6.32; true 3.31.14; *adv.* very much 1.9.1; very 1.13.5

rightwyse *adj.* righteous 1.1.8

rightwysly, ryghtwisely *adv.* righteously 1.3.9; justly 3.45.3

rightwysnes *n.* righteousness 3.51.29

rote *v.* ~ *oute* eradicate 1.3.25; ~ *vppe* uproot 3.58.15

rownynge *vbl. n.* whispering 3.1.3; **rownynges** *pl.* 3.1.3

rueþ *pr. 3 sg.* has pity 2.9.21

sadde *adj.* firm 3.7.16; secure 3.53.11

sadded *pp.* grounded 3.50.12

sadly *adv.* firmly 1.19.6

salace *n.* solace 3.18.9

salutz *see* porte

save *conj.* ~ *onely* with the sole exception of 1.1.11

savory *adj.* pleasing 1.19.24

savoure *n.* sweetness 3.35.28

savoure *v.* taste sweet to 1.25.41, 3.39.10; taste sweet 3.0.39; taste 1.11.8, 3.8.13, 3.8.16, 3.50.12; take pleasure in 3.0.58, 3.32.4; perceive 3.10.13; taste good to 3.52.15. **savourest** *pr. 2 sg.* 3.39.10; **savoureþ** *pr. 3 sg.* 3.0.39, 3.8.16; **savoureþ, savoureth** *pr. pl.* 3.0.58; *savoureþ but litel* have little savour 2.9.26; **savoure** *pr. subj.* 3.10.13; **savoured** *pa. t. sg.* 3.50.12; *pa. t. pl.* 3.52.15; *pp.* 2.1.32

scarsenesse *n.* fewness 2.0.11

science *n.* knowledge 2.11.21

sclaunder *n.* offence 3.12.9; **sclaunders** *pl.* 3.48.11

scoles *n. pl.* schools 1.3.27

secretari *n.* secret chamber 3.43.4

secrete *adj. in* ~ *wyse* secretly 1.19.20

see *v.* ~ *bifore see* bifore 1.1.17; **seene** *pp. to be seene* to seem 1.7.2

seeldon *adv.* seldom 1.15.9

seeke *adj.* foolish 1.22.6

seene *see* see

seie *v.* ~ *naye* deny it 3.9.2; **seye** *pr. 1 sg.* tell 1.19.32; **seide, seyne** *pp.* said to be 2.1.34; called *2.11.13; said 3.61.23; **seyinges** *vbl. n. pl.* words 1.11.1

seke *adj.* sick 3.5.11; weak 3.50.20

seke *imp. sg. refl.* seek 1.20.1; **sekeþ** *pr. pl. sekeþ hemselfe* are self-seeking 1.14.6; **soght** *pp.* sought 3.45.9

seme *v.* seem to 3.11.11; **semeþ** *pr. 3 sg.* 1.2.12; *hit semeþ hem also* to it also seems to them to 1.14.7; **semynge** *vbl. n.* view 2.12.17

sensible *adj.* tangible 1.6.4; 2.9.13 *see* swetenesses

sentence *n.* meaning 1.5.9; judgement 3.55.30; opinion 3.59.27; **sentences** *pl.* texts 1.5.4

sequestre *v.* cut off 3.36.7

serche *pr. pl.* seek for 1.5.9; **serched** *pp.* examined 1.19.14; studied 2.12.70

servage *n.* service 3.11.27

servandes *n. pl.* servants 1.16.4

sette, sete *v.* place 1.7.3, 1.19.32, 3.64.13; put 1.7.12, 1.11.14; make 3.8.9; store 3.59.14; ~ *at no price* consider as worth nothing 3.11.23; ~ *at noȝt* think nothing of 1.3.4; consider as worth nothing 1.3.34, consider as nothing 3.31.11; ~ *by* think of 1.12.4, 3.51.11, 3.59.21, set store by 2.5.15, 2.6.16; ~ *binethe* regard as inferior to 3.7.7; ~ *litel by* think little of 2.4.15, 3.5.11, 3.55.12; ~ *muche þerby* place much importance on 2.2.1; ~ *no cure of* not care about 2.6.14; ~ *no price bi* think nothing of 3.5.24; ~ *no pryce of* think nothing of 2.9.1; ~ *nought by* think nothing of 2.1.32; *noght to* ~ *by* consider as nothing 3.15.15; ~ *thiselfe to* prepare yourself for 3.40.8; ~ *with* let be dependent on 3.47.1. **sette** *pr. 1 sg.* 3.64.13; **setteste** *pr. 2 sg. whateuer þou setteste in* whatever trust you place in 2.7.10; **sette, setteþ** *pr. 3 sg.* 1.3.34, 2.4.15, 2.6.14, 2.6.16, 3.7.7, 3.59.14; **sette** *pr. subj. sg.* 1.7.12, 2.5.15, 3.47.1; **set, sette** *imp. sg.* 1.7.3, 2.2.1; **settynge** *pr. p. settynge at noȝt* thinking nothing of 1.3.4; **sette** *pp.* 1.12.4, 3.8.9, 3.15.15, 3.31.11, 3.55.12, 3.59.21; ~ *in Godde* placed in God's hands 3.0.19; ~ *in men* made dependent on men 3.0.47; ~ *for* synonymous with 3.60.4

shadoes *n. pl.* cover 3.51.7

shaken *pp.* disturbed 2.3.5

sharpe *adj.* hard 1.18.6; harsh 3.59.14

sharpely *adv.* sternly 1.13.5

shende *pp.* destroyed 3.53.23

shewar *n.* ~ *of* revealing 3.36.20

shewed *pp.* ~ *oute* revealed 3.51.17

shilde *n.* shield 3.40.3

shynynge *vbl. n. see* lyghton

shitte *imp. sg.* shut 1.20.44

shrewde *adj.* evil 1.13.22; sinful 3.58.19; ~ *spekars* slanderers, detractors 2.1.28

shrewdenes *n.* wickedness 3.15.3

shrewes *n. pl.* the wicked 1.20.17

shuffed *pp.* moved 3.44.5

side *n. on summe* ~ in some area 1.3.21; *on euerie* ~ entirely 3.22.5

signacle *n.* seal 3.59.31

signs *n. pl.* miracles 3.20.10

sihynge *vbl. n.* sighing 3.23.11

siker *adj.* sure 2.12.56; secure 3.52.10

symple, simple *adj.* innocent 1.10.1; single 3.36.4

singuler, singvler *adj.* personal 1.19.21; everything *3.55.25

singulerly, singlerly *adv.* specially 2.8.25, 2.8.27

Sistewx *n. pl.* Cistercians 1.25.35

sithe *conj.* since 1.2.14

sitteþ *pr. 3 sg. hit* ~ *me* I should 3.15.14; **sat** *pa. t. subj. sg.* would suit 1.21.13

Sixte *proper n.* Sixtus 2.9.7

skape *v.* escape 2.12.29; **skapinge** *vbl. n.* 2.12.49

sleeþ *pr. 3 sg.* kills 1.20.36

slyde *v.* fall 1.25.49; **slydest** *pr. 2 sg.* 3.5.10; **slydeþ** *pr. 3 sg.* 2.9.12; **slyde** *pr. pl.* 3.7.30; *pr. subj. sg.* 3.54.2; **slydinge** *ppl. adj.* fallible 1.4.3; **slydynge** *vbl. n.* lapse 3.0.50; **slyden** *pp.* fallen 3.60.4

slowe *adj.* slothful 1.21.24; ~ *to* lazy about 1.19.21; ~ *fro* slack in 3.8.4

slugged *adj.* (spiritually) slothful 1.18.17

sluggedly *adv.* lazily 3.21.8

sluggednes *n.* (spiritual) slothfulness 1.18.22

so *adv.* such 1.3.25; ~ *þat* provided that 3.3.18

socoure *n.* aid 3.45.8

sodeyne *adj.* sudden 3.62.7

softe *adj.* self-indulgent 3.6.32; easy 3.37.2; feeble 3.53.7

solace *n.* comfort 1.20.27; consolation 2.5.19; **solaces** *pl.* comforts 3.18.2

solaced *pp.* consoled 1.24.16

solaciouse *adj.* comforting 3.23.4

solempne *adj.* festal 3.39.7

solicite *v.* worry 3.50.13

somer *n.* summer 2.8.34

sone *adv.* soon 1.3.30

sonne *n.* sun 1.20.39

sonner *adv.* more readily *1.4.2; more quickly 1.23.25; **sonnest** *sup. adv.* most easily 1.13.20

soole *adj.* alone 2.11.28

sore *adv.* sorely 1.22.13; greatly 3.44.5

sory *adj.* sad 1.6.5

soriful *adj.* sad 1.20.35

soroed *pp.* lamented 3.49.6

sorowe *n.* pain 2.12.18

sorte *n.* inheritance 3.43.1

sote *adj.* sweet 3.57.19

soteltez *n. pl.* subtleties 3.48.13

sotylle, sotile *adj.* fine, elaborate 1.24.25; subtle 3.48.1

soule *n. gen.* ~ *helthe* soul's health 1.25.43, 3.5.16

souerayne *adj.* principal 1.1.3; the highest 1.1.12

soueraynly, soueranly, sovereynely *adv.* supremely 2.11.23; highly 3.24.9; above all 3.54.36

sauourly *adv.* with relish *1.1.6

soweþ *pr. 3 sg.* suggests 3.7.20

sowne *n.* sound 3.15.23

sowne *v.* speak 3.2.8; sowneth *pr. 3 sg.* sounds 3.50.20; sowne *pr. subj. sg.* 3.27.3; sownynge *vbl. n.* 3.1.4

spake *pa. t. sg.* spoke 3.48.12

sparkel *n.* scintilla *1.15.14; spark 3.60.5

special *n.* special friend 2.8.23; *in* ~ in particular 3.24.2

specially *adv.* particularly 1.5.18

speculacyon *n.* vision 1.3.21

spedde *pp.* helped 1.3.7; prepared 3.21.13; freed 3.36.6

spedefulle *adj.* expedient 3.56.4

spekynges *n. pl.* conversations 1.10.5

spotte *n.* stain 3.60.4

spotteþ *pr. 3 sg.* stain 1.1.21

springe *v.* rise up 3.25.10

stabilyshed, stabilysshed *pp.* established 3.10.7, made secure 3.46.8

stable *adj.* firm 3.6.8; constant 3.50.26

stande *v.* be 1.9.1, 1.9.2, 3.15.2; remain 1.17.8, 3.31.14; be found 2.12.15; stand firm *3.7.4; continue 3.31.14; exist 3.42.12; be placed in 3.47.3; ~ *at* be ready to do 2.8.34, 3.6.34; wait upon 3.31.9; ~ *ayeine* confront 3.9.2; ~ *ayenis* resist 3.57.10; ~ *in* result from 1.6.7; consist of 2.12.67, 3.29.11; rely on 3.43.2; ~ *in gode* continue in a good life 1.24.45; ~ *in her goode pees* make for a peaceful life for them 1.14.7; ~ *to* stand by 3.51.14; ~ *to see* stand and see 3.53.12; ~ *vppon* rely on 1.7.3, 2.9.12; ~ *welle* be in good standing 3.49.4; *howe hit is to* ~

how we are to behave 3.0.16. stande *pr. 1 sg.* 3.15.2; standest *pr. 2 sg.* 3.9.2, 3.43.2; standeþ, standeth, stondeþ *pr. 3 sg.* 1.6.7, 2.9.12, 2.12.67, 3.7.4, 3.29.11, 3.42.12; standeþ, standeth *pr. pl.* 2.12.15; *whereinne standeth* what constitutes 3.0.29; stande *pr. subj. sg.* 3.31.14, 3.49.4; stande *imp. sg.* 1.7.3, 2.8.34, 3.31.9

statutes *n. pl.* rules 1.16.10

stedefaste *adj.* made firm 2.7.4

stedefasteþ *pr. 3 sg.* establishes 3.15.22

steppe *n.* trace 1.22.36; steppes *n. pl.* footsteps 1.18.20; witness 3.20.5

styghe *v.* ~ *vppe* ascend 3.58.15; stieþ *pr. 3 sg.* 3.47.7

stylle *adj.* silent 1.20.8

styngynge *adj.* stinking 1.3.35

stired, styren *see* stirre

stirer *n.* agitator 3.28.7

stireþ, styrynge *see* stirre

stirre, styrre *v.* stir up 1.19.3, 1.25.51, 3.23.24; stir one up 3.6.11; drive 3.12.4; disturb 3.13.24. stireþ *pr. 3 sg.* 3.6.11; styren *pr. pl.* 3.12.4; stiredest *pa. t. 2 sg.* 3.23.24; stirre *imp. sg.* 1.25.51; styrynge *vbl. n.* suggestion 1.4.1; stired *pp.* tossed 1.13.17; troubled 2.12.19; incited 3.59.13

stokke *n.* stump 3.60.26

stondeþ *see* stande

stoppe *v.* shut 1.24.22; stopped *pp.* prevented 3.13.24

straunge *adj.* inappropriate 3.54.32; ~ *folkes* strangers 1.8.2; ~ *þinges* things alien to it 3.58.1

streccheþ *pr. pl.* ~ *hemselfe* reach out 3.58.18

streyned *pp.* afflicted 3.53.7

streyte *adj.* strict 1.18.6; disciplined 1.24.34; narrow 3.61.17

streyted *pp.* ~ *vnder* subject to 1.25.33

streytely *adv.* severely 1.16.8, closely 1.21.20

strenger *comp. adj.* harder 1.3.19; stronger 1.13.12

strengeþ, strenght *n.* strength 2.12.45, 3.51.26; strengthes *n. pl.* powers, strength 3.7.29

strengeþ *v.* strengthen 3.52.1; strengthe *imp.* 3.22.11; strengthinge *pr. p.* 3.60.13; strengthed *pp.* 2.12.39

strenght *see* strengeþ *n.*; strengthe,

strengthed, strengthinge *see* strengeþ
v.

stryves *n. pl.* arguments 3.63.7

stryveþ *pr. 3 sg.* disputes 3.59.27

stronge *adj.* hard 3.51.5

study *n.* ~ *of* zeal for 3.8.4; studies *pl.*
pursuits 1.25.38

study *v.* strive 1.1.6; studieþ *pr. 3 sg.*
3.19.2; *pr. pl.* 1.3.24; study *imp. sg.*
1.1.20; studyed *pa. t. pl.* 1.11.5

subdue *v.* submit 2.12.21; subdueþ *pr. 3
sg. refl.* 1.24.19; *pr. pl. refl.* 3.11.24;
subdue *pr. subj. pl. refl.* ~ *hemselfe for*
submit to 1.9.3

subieccion *n.* ~ *of* submission to 3.14.11

subiective *adj.* subduing 1.14.11

substance *n.* possessions 2.11.19

subtraccion *n.* withdrawal (of spiritual
consolation) 2.10.15

succeddinge *vbl. n.* success 3.35.28

succurre *v.* succour 3.53.25

sue *pr. pl.* follow 3.3.7

suete *v.* sweat 1.25.48

sufferaunce, suffrance *n.* bearing
*2.12.37; permission 3.51.17; endurance
3.51.28

suffice *v.* be adequate 3.11.19; ~ *to* be
adequate for 3.35.15

sufficiently *adv.* fully 1.25.28

suffragiez *n. pl.* intercessions 3.63.33

suffrance *see* sufferaunce

suffre, suffree *v.* allow 1.11.12, 1.13.20,
2.3.5; endure 1.13.28; leave 1.21.10;
suffer 1.21.23; allow oneself 3.8.12;
suffreþ *pr. 3 sg.* 1.11.12; *pr. pl.* 3.8.12;
suffred *pp.* 1.13.20

sugget *adj.* obedient 1.4.8

summe *n.* the height 2.12.9

sumtyme *adv.* once 1.3.27; sometimes
1.8.8

sumwhat *adv.* to some extent 1.3.20; *pron.*
something 1.13.10

superfluouse *adj.* needless 3.31.8

superfluite *n.* excess 1.0.10; superfluytes
pl. extravagances 3.30.11

supplante *v.* cause to stumble 3.30.5

supportacion *n.* bearing 1.0.16

sure *adv.* safe 1.9.2; secure 1.20.20

surely *adv.* safely 1.19.20

surete *n.* security 1.12.9

suspecion *n.* suspicion 2.3.5; suspecions
pl. 2.3.5

suspecte *adj.* mindful 1.23.30

suspende *imp.* lift 3.27.7

suspire *v.* aspire 3.37.7; *pr. 3 sg.* suspireþ
3.53.15

susteyne *v.* bear 2.9.33; *pr. subj.* 3.20.4;
susteyned *pp.* 3.20.3

swagest *pr. 2 sg.* calm 3.39.22; swage *imp.
sg.* 3.53.15

swerde *n.* sword 1.23.37

swete *adj.* pleasant 1.20.4; swetter *comp.*
sweeter 3.6.14

swettenesse *n.* sweetness 2.12.8; swetenesses *pl. sensible* ~ pleasant sensations
2.9.13

swetly *adv.* pleasantly 2.2.10

swetter *see* swete

swyftely *adv.* quickly 3.42.8

swoloed *pp.* swallowed 1.22.29

tabernacle *n.* tent 3.54.1; tabernacles *pl.*
1.23.44

taciturnite *n.* silence 3.41.8

taght *pp.* taught 1.4.6

take *v.* undertake 1.18.21; grasps 2.4.3;
receive 2.10.23, 3.1.2; understand
3.48.9; take hold of 3.53.17; ~ *vppon
the* assume, adopt 3.14.6. takeþ *pr. 3 sg.*
1.18.21, 2.4.3, 3.1.2; taken, take *pp.* felt
2.1.14; caught 2.1.22; received 3.55.3;
take ayein claimed back 3.42.3

talynge *vbl. n.* gossiping 1.24.32; talynges
pl. 3.57.6

tary *v.* delay 1.22.22; tarieþ, taryeth *pr. 3
sg.* 1.24.5; holds one back 3.0.31; tarieþ
pr. pl. hinders 3.30.3; taryed *pp.*
delayed 3.52.12

telle *v.* ~ *tales* talk idly, gossip 1.17.10; *pr.
pl.* ~ *oute* declare 3.2.11

temerary *adj.* rash 1.0.14

temerarily *adv.* rashly 3.29.8

temporalle *adj.* worldly 1.22.8

tendethe *pr. pl.* ~ *into* strive for 2.10.22;
tende *pr. subj. sg. tende to* lay for 3.7.19

þan *adv.* then 1.16.12

þankynges *vbl. n. pl.* thanks 2.9.14

þat *pron.* what 1.7.4; that which 2.12.29;
for 3.18.2; this 3.46.8; which 3.63.22; ~
more is what is more 3.37.6; *conj.* so that
1.16.3; when 3.54.6; *demons. adj.* ~ *þinge*
something 3.37.2

þe, þee *pron.* you 1.1.7, 1.3.14; *refl. pr.*
1.7.6; yourself 1.7.12

þees *demons. adj. sg.* this 3.63.1; þees, thes
pl. these 1.1.2, 1.19.16

þen *prep.* than 1.1.9

þenke *v.* think 1.3.28, 1.16.2, 1.21.19, 1.23.4, 2.11.14, 3.19.2, 3.27.7, 3.53.27; meditate 1.19.18; consider 1.19.26, 1.23.43, 3.8.19; intend 3.18.1. þenke *pr. 1 sg.* 3.53.27; þenkest, þenkeste *pr. 2 sg.* 3.19.2; *þenkeste to lyve* think that you will live 1.23.35; þenkeþ *pr. 3 sg.* 1.23.4; *pr. pl.* 2.11.14; þenke *pr. subj. sg.* 1.21.19, 3.8.19; *pr. subj. pl.* 1.3.28; thenke, þenke *imp. sg.* 1.16.2, 1.23.43; þenkynge *pr. p.* 1.19.18; *vbl. n.* thought 2.1.23; consideration 3.7.16

þens *adv.* thence 3.55.20

þerby *adv.* by 2.2.1

þerfore *adv.* for this reason 3.34.7; about it 3.41.15

þerfroo *adv.* from it 3.37.13

þerof *adv.* about it 3.35.31

þerþorowe *adv.* hence 3.35.5

þerto *adv.* with it 1.3.21; to the point 1.25.41; than that 3.31.15; for it 3.36.14; to the end 3.63.30

thes *see* þees

thider *adv.* thither 1.1.18

thiderwarde *see* hiderwarde

þiffes *n. pl.* thieves 1.23.37

þinge *n. the ~* something 3.35.23; þinges *pl.* qualities 1.7.11

þo *see* þoo

þoghe, þogh *conj.* though 1.13.5; even though 1.20.18; if 3.48.9; *so as ~* as if 3.35.24

þoght *n.* thought 3.53.30; þoghtes 3.35.28

þondrest *pr. 2 sg.* thunder 3.15.1

þoo, þo *demons. adj.* those 1.1.17, 1.19.13

þorowe, thorowgh *prep.* through 1.8.9; by 3.22.4

þousande *n. in ~ þousandes* a thousand thousand times 3.54.37

þraldame *n.* subjection 2.12.43; servitude 3.53.8

þridde *num.* third 2.12.56

þroweþ *pr. 3 sg.* casts 3.22.2; þrowe *pr. subj. sg. þrowe awey* reject 3.19.16; þrowinge *vbl. n. þrowinge downe* affliction 3.60.25; þrowen *pp.* given 3.42.3; *þrowen downe* dejected 2.8.34; discouraged 3.37.7

thurste, thruste *n.* thirst 1.18.3, 1.24.11

tyed *pp.* ensnared 3.53.7

tylle *conj.* until 1.9.3

tyme *n. þat ~* then 1.18.19

to *prep.* towards 1.2.9; with 1.8.5; for 1.11.22; of 1.15.11; until 1.17.2; in 1.25.42; on 2.1.23; as 3.11.11; by which to 3.20.10; into 3.61.9

to *adv.* too 1.20.20

to *num.* two 3.3.23

togydres, togydre, togedre *adv.* together 1.8.9, 1.10.4, 1.19.15

token *n.* sign 1.9.12

tonge *n.* tongue 3.50.26

toshakest *pr. 2 sg.* shake violently 3.15.1

towarde *prep.* within 3.55.5

translate *v.* turn 1.1.20 *see n.; pp.* brought 3.39.13

tremulynge *vbl. n.* trembling 3.15.1

trete *pr. subj. sg. ~ of* consider 3.63.30; *imp. sg.* 3.3.20; *~ of* discuss 1.8.4; tretynge *vbl. n.* discussion 1.10.1

tretes *n.* treatise 1.0.0

trewly *adv.* faithfully 3.52.7

tristesse *n.* distress 3.13.21

trone *n.* throne 2.7.8

trouest *pr. 2 sg.* think 3.13.8

trouþe *n.* truth 1.5.1

truste *n.* confidence 1.20.19

trustely *adv.* confidently 1.25.42

turbacion *n.* disquiet 1.20.47; turmoil 3.25.10

turne *pr. pl. refl.* turn 1.11.10; *imp. sg.* look 2.12.25; turnynge *pr. p. turnynge ayein* returning 3.62.13; turned *pp.* turned *aweie* diverted 3.37.7

twyes *adv.* twice 1.16.4

twylyght *n.* morning twilight 2.9.24

vnavysed *adv.* unexpectedly 1.23.19

vnccion *n.* anointing 3.30.7

vncovenable *adj.* unfitting 1.21.1

vndefouleable *adj.* inviolable 3.61.6

vndepartable *adj.* unbreakable 3.27.9

vnder *prep.* lower than 2.5.18; to 3.15.16; *adv.* subject 3.58.14

vndertaker *n.* upholder 3.18.3

vnderstander *n.* discerner 3.48.16

vndirstandeþ *pr. 3 sg. ~ God more necessary* understands that God is more necessary 1.12.6; vndirstandynge *ppl. adj.* knowledgeable 1.2.12; vndirstandinge *vbl. n.* meaning 3.2.10; vnderstonden *pp.* understood 3.31.12

vndiscretly *adv.* imprudently 3.8.7

vndoutably *adv.* without wavering 3.42.14

vnevon *adj.* unfair 3.6.9

vnexperte *adj.* inexperienced 3.8.10

vnferme *adj.* weak 3.64.13

vnfructuose *adj.* unfruitful 3.2.17

vngoodly *adj.* unseemly 1.8.9

vnkynde *adj.* ungrateful 2.10.10

vnlyke *adj.* different 3.39.15

vnmesurable *adj.* immeasurable 3.15.17

vnmyghty, vnmyghtye *adj.* weak 2.8.33; impotent 3.60.6

vnmortificate *pp.* unmortified 3.53.18

vnneþe *adv.* scarcely 1.18.11

vnpacience *n.* impatience 3.21.6

vnpaciente *adj.* impatient 3.8.5

unperfetly *adv.* wrongly 1.12.2

vnpesed *adj.* ill at ease 3.47.1

vnplesed *adj.* displeased 3.25.11

vnprovided *pp.* unforeseen 3.50.15

vnpure *adj.* impure 2.1.42

vnrelygiouse *adj.* ungodly 1.24.23

vnrested *pp.* made uneasy 1.6.1

vnrestfulnesse *n.* disquiet 3.33.10

vnrightwise *adj.* unrighteous 3.51.23

vnrightwisnesse *n.* unrighteousness 3.22.1

vnsavory *adj.* morally objectionable 1.24.2; dull 2.8.7

vnspekable *adj.* inexpressible 3.11.3

vnstable *adj.* insecure 1.22.33; inconstant 3.50.20

vnstablenes *n.* inconstancy 3.0.38

vnto *prep.* to 1.12.6; until 1.24.40; into 2.12.56; for 3.11.14; to the point of 3.21.3; ~ þis tyme so far 1.19.4

vntransnatable *adj.* uncrossable 3.15.17

vnware *adj.* indiscreet 3.44.8; vnwares *adv.* while he is unaware 3.22.13

vnwysdame *n.* foolishness 1.3.4

vppon *prep.* about 1.3.28; on 1.17.4; above 3.43.1

vs *refl. pron.* 1.11.10; ourselves 1.16.10

vse *n.* habit 3.21.8; 1.10.11 *see* yvel

vse *v.* enjoy 2.10.7, 3.60.6; exercise 3.59.6. vseþ *pr. 3 sg.* 3.60.6; vsed *pp.* 3.13.22 *see* custume

vtmast *adj.* furthest 2.11.18

vtter *adj.* outer 2.7.12

vtterly *adv.* entirely 1.18.24

vacacion *n.* ~ *to* time alone with 3.58.5

vacante, vacant *adj.* free 1.19.22; ~ *of* free from 3.31.14

vaylable *adj.* beneficial 3.16.4

valey *n.* valley 3.9.3

vailante *adj.* ~ *to* strong for 3.6.21

variant *adj.* various 3.38.9

veyne *adj.* empty 1.0.7; foolish 1.7.1

veyne *n.* vanity 1.20.43

venome *n.* poison 3.38.7

veri *adj.* true 1.2.16; very *adv.* truly 1.17.6

verily *adv.* truly 1.1.2

vertue *n.* power 1.14.11

vexed *pp.* harassed 1.18.6; afflicted 3.21.21

vice *n.* sin 1.11.7; vices *pl.* 1.3.25

viciate *pp.* corrupted 3.60.4

viciouse *adj.* immoral 1.3.18

viciously *adv.* sinfully 1.25.18

vile *adj.* mean 2.4.7; wicked 2.6.18; worthless 3.32.2; *of* ~ *pryce* of low value 2.10.25

vilete *n.* unworthiness 3.23.26

vilyfie *pr. subj. sg.* abase 3.9.3

violence *n.* *with* ~ forcibly 1.25.18

visage *n.* outwarde appearance 2.6.21; countenance 3.23.17

vituperable *adj.* reprehensible 1.19.11

voyde *adj.* empty 1.20.4; free 3.7.16

voyde *v. refl.* ~ *the* free yourself 2.7.9; voydeþ *pr. 3 sg.* ~ *from hym* renounces 1.21.8; voyded *pp.* dismissed 2.8.31

voluptes *n. pl.* pleasures 2.10.4, 3.30.2

vouchesave, vouched saue *see* fouchesave

wacchinge *vbl. n.* protection 3.15.10

wayle *v.* groan 3.56.3; bewail 3.57.16

wayte *v.* hope 3.59.21; waytest *pr. 2 sg.* expect 1.20.40

wake *v.* keep awake 1.10.9, 1.25.34, 3.6.22, 3.44.9; be watchful 1.13.3; be on one's guard 1.13.20; ~ *in preiers* stay awake and pray 3.28.12; ~ *vppon* watch 1.25.51. wakeþ *pr. 3 sg.* 3.6.22; *pr. pl.* 1.25.34; wake *imp. sg.* 1.25.51, 3.28.12; wakeþ *imp. pl.* 3.44.9; wakynge *pr. p.* awake 1.19.31; *ppl. adj.* watchful 1.25.1; *vbl. n.* wakynge over evon staying up late 1.20.35; wakynges *pl.* vigils 1.18.3

wantowne *adj.* be ~ *ayenis* rebel against 3.30.12

warde *n.* guard 3.8.0

wardeþ *pr. 3 sg.* guards 3.31.13

ware *adj.* careful 1.22.32

warely *adv.* carefully 1.4.1

warenesse *n.* caution 3.7.31; warning 3.8.20

waste *imp. sg.* rout 3.53.23

waxe *v.* become 2.4.14; waxest *pr. 2 sg.* 3.10.3; waxeth *pr. 3 sg.* 1.13.24; waxe *pr. pl.* 3.3.9; *pr. subj. sg.* 1.25.6; *imp. sg.* 3.35.6; waxed *pa. t. sg.* 1.23.37

wawes *n. pl.* waves 1.13.17

weel, weelle *see* welle *adv.*

weelle *n. comune* ~ common good 1.15.8; *see also* welle *adv.*

weie *n.* 2.12.35 *see* go

weyke *adj.* foolish 1.22.6; unable 3.22.7; weak 3.53.7

welle *v.* flow 3.47.9; welleþ *pr. 3 sg.* 3.36.13; *pr. pl.* 3.59.27; wellynge *pr. p.* 3.10.5

welle, weel, weelle *adv.* well 1.17.10, 1.18.17; *feele* ~ *of* feel positively about 3.7.9

welle-manerde *adj.* virtuous 1.8.4; self-controlled 1.25.17

welplesinge, welleplesinge *ppl. adj.* acceptable 1.25.11; *vbl. n.* good pleasure 2.9.24

welwillynge *vbl. n.* pleasure 2.9.8

wene *pr. 1 sg.* think 3.22.4; weneste *pr. 2 sg.* 1.23.25; weneþ *pr. 3 sg.* 3.24.8; *pr. pl.* 2.5.4; weene *pr. pl.* expect 1.23.19; *imp. sg. refl.* think 1.23.17; wende *pa. t. sg.* 3.50.2

wer *see* se

wery *adj.* tiresome 3.39.6

werke *n.* work 1.15.1; deed 1.19.16; werkes *pl.* actions 1.0.4; works 1.7.10

werkeman *n.* workman 3.43.1

what *conj.* why 1.22.2; ~ . . . þat whatever 3.16.8

whereas *conj.* whenever 1.20.5; where 2.12.26

whereof, wherof *conj.* the means by which 1.13.9; how 2.1.29; for this reason 2.9.18; by virtue of which 2.10.14; for what 3.45.12

whereto *conj.* why 1.2.14

wheþer *interrog. conj. introducing direct question* 2.8.8; *interrog. pron.* which 3.38.3

whiles *conj.* while 1.3.27; when 1.13.23; provided that 3.60.22

whither *conj.* ~ *I bicame* what I have become 3.9.4

whithereuer *conj.* whithersoever 1.22.1

who *pron.* ~ *þat* whoever 1.1.4

whom *rel. pron.* which 3.7.10

whommeever *pron.* whomever 3.55.14

whos *pron.* those whose 3.15.5

whoso *pron.* whoever 2.1.9

whowle *v.* howl 1.24.12

wyghtly *adv.* quickly 2.1.13

wilfully *adv.* willingly 2.12.17

wylynes *n.* cleverness 1.7.5

wille *v.* want (to) 1.1.2, 1.1.6, 1.2.14, 1.3.12, 1.22.2; wish 1.13.15; be willing to 1.14.10, 1.16.4; will 1.14.11; desire 1.20.32, 3.14.3, 3.31.6; ~ *of* desire 2.10.12. wille, wolle *pr. 1 sg.* 1.3.12, 2.10.12; wolte, willest *pr. 2 sg.* 1.2.14, 1.22.2; wol, wolle *pr. 3 sg.* 1.14.10, 1.14.11; *pr. pl.* 1.1.6; wolle, wille *pr. subj. sg.* 1.16.4, 3.14.3; wille *imp. sg.* 3.31.6; wolde *pa. t. sg.* would 1.3.25; was willing to 2.1.27; *wolde God þat* would that 1.3.31; woldeste *pa. t. 2 sg.* 1.11.22; would like 3.7.9; wolde *pa. t. pl.* 1.3.25; willinge *pr. p.* wanting 3.5.16; willing, willynge *vbl. n.* desiring 3.17.4; willed *pp. I have willed me* I wish 1.10.3

willes *n. pl.* wishes 3.14.11

wymmen *n. pl.* women 1.8.5

wyndy *adj.* wavering in the wind 2.7.11

wynne *v.* gain 3.42.2; wynnynges *vbl. n. pl.* gains 3.59.13

wise, wyse *n.* way 3.6.9; *maner of* ~ way 1.15.2; *in no* ~ not at all 1.16.10; *in secrete* ~ secretly 1.19.20; *in contrari* ~ in opposite directions 2.1.15; *in alle* ~ in every way 3.14.6; *in suche* ~ in such a way 3.45.8; wyses *pl.* ways 1.5.8

wyste *see* wote

with *prep.* by 1.13.17

withdrawen *pp.* dissuaded 3.8.11

withein *prep.* within 2.1.1

withholdeth *pr. 3 sg.* holds back 3.36.2

withinforthe, withinforþe *adv.* inwardly 1.3.17; inside 1.14.5

withoute *adv.* outside 1.20.25; *prep.* outside of 2.8.7

withouteforþe *adv.* from outside 1.14.5; outwardly 3.31.11

withouten *prep.* without *1.3.9

withstande *v.* resist 1.6.5, 1.11.21, 1.13.23, 3.13.22. withstandeþ *pr. 3 sg.* 1.6.5; withstande *imp. sg.* 1.11.21; withstandinge, withstandynge *vbl. n.* resisting 1.13.24; resistance 1.14.4; *withstandinge of* resistance to 1.0.13; resistance by 3.12.9; withstanden *pp.* 1.13.23

witnesseth *pr. 3 sg.* ~ *hymselfe to be herde* bears witness that he has been heard *2.9.21

witte, wytte *n.* intelligence 1.7.8; mind 1.9.6; opinion 1.14.4; understanding 2.5.1; meaning 3.2.9; *propre* ~ *see* propre; *wittes pl.* feelings 1.14.9; senses 1.21.1; mind 3.33.10

wo *n. wo me* woe is me 3.52.10

wode *adj.* mad *1.24.12

wol, wolde, woldeste, wolle *see* wille

wolde *adj.* old 3.22.11

wonder *n.* ~ *hit is* it is amazing 1.21.4

wonderful, wondirfulle *adj.* remarkable 2.1.38; admirable 3.59.30

wondringe, wondrynge *vbl. n.* admiration 3.59.28; *yive matier of* ~ provoke admiration 3.50.29

wonte *adj.* accustomed 2.9.31

worche *v.* perform 1.20.31; worcheþ *pr. 3 sg.* does 1.3.15; worche *pr. pl.* act 3.2.13; worchinge, worchynge *vbl. n.* working 1.25.5; action 3.36.20

worde *n.* saying 2.12.1

worde *n.* world 1.24.21, 2.6.10

wordly *adv.* worldly 3.39.12

worldes *n. pl. into* ~ *of* ~ for ever and ever 3.6.3; *by* ~ *infinite* 3.45.22; *durynge into* ~ 3.54.34; *bifore* ~ bifore the creation of the world 3.63.12

worshippe *n.* honour 1.3.15; worshippes *pl.* honours 1.1.14

worshippeþ *pr. 3 sg.* honours 3.63.19; worshippeth *pr. pl.* admire 2.11.6; worshyppinge *pr. p.* honouring 1.23.44; worshipped *pp.* 3.8.22

worþe *adj.* of any worth 3.47.4

worthi, worthy *adj.* worthy of 1.20.23; ~ *to* worthy of comparison with 3.56.7

worthily *adv.* properly 1.19.2

wote *pr. 1 sg.* know 1.3.28; woste *pr. 2 sg.* 1.2.18; wottest 1.23.29; wote *pr. pl.* 1.13.19; wyste *pa. t. subj. sg.* 1.25.7

wrappest *pr. 2 sg.* entangle 3.28.5; wrappeþ *pr. pl. wrappeþ inne* entangle 3.23.10; wrapped *pp.* entangled 1.21.21; *wrapped inne* entangled 3.6.13; *wrapped in* entangled by 3.30.8

wrastelest *pr. 2. sg.* ~ *ayein* fight against them 3.7.15

wrecche *n.* wretch 3.7.21; wrecches 1.22.18

wrecched *adj.* wretched 1.21.25

wryten *pp.* written 1.20.24

writinge *n.* scripture 1.5.2; wrytinges *pl.* scriptures 1.0.5

wronges *n. pl.* injuries 1.24.5

wrothe *adj.* angry 1.24.2

yate *n.* gate 3.20.5

yaue, yave *see* yive

yea *adv.* even 1.12.2

yeet, yeette *see* yette

yelde *v.* surrender 3.1.14; give 3.13.19, 3.20.6, 3.29.13; ~ *ayeine* repay 3.11.8. yelde *imp. sg.* 3.1.14; ~ *þe to thiselfe* follow your own inclination 1.19.22; yeldeþ *pr. 3 sg. yeldeþ the* assures you that you are 3.41.1; yeldynge *vbl. n.* 3.29.13; yeldon *pp.* 3.13.19

yette, yeet, yeette *adv.* still 1.2.12, 1.22.18

yeveþ, yif, yiffe *see* yive

yifte *n.* gift 2.9.14; yiftes *pl.* 1.24.1

yivar *n.* giver 2.10.25

yive, yiue, yiffe, yif *v.* give 1.2.9, 1.2.11, 1.3.4, 1.7.6, 1.21.2, 1.21.26, 2.1.10, 2.10.26, 2.11.11, 3.2.8, 3.2.14, 3.10.9, 3.29.1; devote 1.3.25, 1.6.8; provide 1.20.3; *hit is not to* ~ *credence* credence is not to be given 1.4.1; ~ *hem to* undertake 3.0.56; ~ *þe vnder* bring yourself to 3.14.11. yive *pr. 1 sg.* 3.29.1; yivest *pr. 2 sg.* 3.2.14; yeveþ, yiveþ *pr. 3 sg.* 1.2.9, 1.7.6; yiveþ, yiffe *pr. pl.* 1.20.3, 3.2.8; yive, yiffe *pr. subj. sg.* 1.21.26, 2.10.26; yive *pr. subj. pl.* 1.3.4; yive, yiffe *imp. sg.* 1.21.2, 2.1.10; yivinge *pr. p.* giving 2.10.9; returning 2.10.9; yaue *pa. t. sg.* 3.10.9; yave *pa. t. pl. refl. yave hem* devoted themselves 1.18.7; yiven *pp.* 1.2.11, 1.6.8

zelator *n.* striver after virtue *1.25.17

zeldeste *pa. t. 2 sg. þat þou* ~ *for the bettir* which you earnestly desired as though it were the better thing *3.12.7

zele *n. haue* ~ *to* be zealous for *2.3.8; *a* ~ religious zeal 2.5.4

INDEX OF BIBLICAL REFERENCES

As in the Notes, biblical references are to the Vulgate text, with the AV verse numbering, where different, shown in brackets; the standard English abbreviations for the books of the Bible are used. 'Vulg.' in brackets after a biblical reference implies that here it is only the Vulgate and not AV that provides a parallel with the *Imitation*.

INDEX OF MYSTICAL IMAGERY

This is an Index to the passages referred to in the Notes in connection with the use of mystical language and imagery in the *Imitation*.